An Intellectual History of China, Volume One

2014.5

Brill's Humanities in China Library

Edited by

ZHANG Longxi, *City University of Hong Kong*
Axel SCHNEIDER, *Universität Göttingen*

VOLUME 6

The titles published in this series are listed at *brill.com/bhcl*

An Intellectual History of China, Volume One

*Knowledge, Thought, and Belief before the
Seventh Century CE*

By

GE Zhaoguang

Translated by

Michael S. Duke and Josephine Chiu-Duke

BRILL

LEIDEN | BOSTON

This book is a result of the translation license agreement among Ge Zhaoguang of Fudan University, Fuda
University Press and Koninklijke Brill NV. This book is translated into English from an abbreviated version c
the original《中国思想史》(葛兆光著) (*Zhongguo sixiang shi, by Ge Zhaoguang*) with financial suppo
from the Chinese Fund for the Humanities and Social Sciences (中华社会科学基金), China Boo
International from the Information Office of the State Council of China, and Fudan University Press.

Library of Congress Cataloging-in-Publication Data

Ge, Zhaoguang, 1950–
[Zhongguo si xiang shi. English]
An intellectual history of China / by Ge Zhaoguang ; translated by Michael S. Duke and Josephine
Chiu-Duke.
    p. cm. — (Brill's humanities in China library ; v. 6)
    Translation of author's abbreviation of his own work.
    Includes bibliographical references and index.
    ISBN 978-90-04-17175-6 (hardback : alk. paper) — ISBN 978-90-47-42507-6 (e-book)
    1. Philosophy, Chinese—History. I. Title.

    B126.G43613 2014
    181′.11—dc23

                    2013045569

This publication has been typeset in the multilingual 'Brill' typeface. With over 5,100 characters covering
Latin, IPA, Greek, and Cyrillic, this typeface is especially suitable for use in the humanities.
For more information, please see brill.com/brill-typeface.

ISSN 1874-8023
ISBN 978-90-04-17175-6 (hardback)
ISBN 978-90-47-42507-6 (e-book)

This book is printed on acid-free paper.

Printed by Printforce, the Netherlands

Contents

    to the Early Tang Dynasty, I (ca. Mid-2nd to Mid-7th Centuries)   264
        Prologue: Foreign Influence Enters China   264
    1.   Evolution of Autochthonous Chinese Thought and Learning from
         Han to Jin   266
    2.   The Mysterious and Profound: A Turning Point of Intellectual History
         in the Third Century CE   277
    3.   Purification of Daoist Teachings: The Religionization of Daoist
         Thought, Knowledge and Techniques   293

6 Confucianism, Daoism and Buddhism from the Eastern Han to the Tang
    Dynasty, II   317
    1.   The Transmission of Buddhism to China and Its Significance in
         Intellectual History, I   317
    2.   The Transmission of Buddhism to China and Its Significance in
         Intellectual History, II   333
    3.   Buddhist Conquest of China?   350
    4.   Basic Outline of the Mainstream World of Knowledge and Thought in
         the Seventh Century   369

    Bibliography   379
    Index   395

Chronology of Chinese States and Dynasties

Xia 2000?–1600? BCE
Shang 1600?–1027? BCE
Zhou 1027?–256 BCE
   Western Zhou 1027?–771 BCE
   Eastern Zhou 771–256 BCE
Spring and Autumn Period 771–481 BCE
Warring States Period 481–221 BCE
Qin 221–206 BCE
Western Han 202 BCE–8 CE
Wang Mang 9–23 CE
Eastern Han 25–220 CE
Three Kingdoms 220–280
   Wei 220–265
   Shu 221–263
   Wu 222–280
Western Jin 265–316
Sixteen Kingdoms 301–439
North-South Dynasties 317–589
      South
   Eastern Jin 317–420
   Liu Song 420–479
   Southern Qi 479–520
   Liang 502–557
   Chen 557–589
      North
   Northern Wei (Tuoba Wei) Xianbei or Särbi 386–535
   Eastern Wei 534–550
   Western Wei 534–557
   Northern Qi 550–577
   Northern Zhou 557–581
Sui 581–618
Tang 618–907
Five Dynasties and Ten Kingdoms 907–960
Northern Song 960–1127
Southern Song 1127–1276

Liao Khitan 916–1125
Jin Jurchen 1125–1234
Xi Xia Tangut 1038–1227
Yuan Mongol 1271–1368
Ming 1368–1644
Qing Manchu 1636–1911

Abbreviations Used in Footnotes and Bibliography

CASS	中國社會科學院 Chinese Academy of Social Science
Chan, SB	*A Source Book in Chinese Philosophy.*
CHC	*Cambridge History of China.*
Commercial Press	商務印書館
CQFL	春秋繁露 *Chunqiu fanlu.*
CSJC	叢書集成 *Congshu jicheng.*
CTP	Chinese Text Project http://ctext.org/
ECT	Michael Loewe, ed., *Early Chinese Texts.*
ESEZ	二十二子 *Ershi-er zi.*
ESWS	二十五史 *Ershiwu shi,* Zhonghua punctuated edition.
HHS	後漢書 *Hou Hanshu.*
HS	漢書 *Hanshu.*
JTS	舊唐書 *Jiu Tangshu.*
LSCQ	呂氏春秋 *Lüshi chunqiu.*
MWD Explanations	老子乙本卷前古佚書釋文 *Mawangdui Laozi yiben*
SBBY	四部備要 Sibu beiyao.
SBCK	四部叢刊 Sibu congkan.
SKQS	四庫全書 Siku quanshu.
Soothill, Dictionary	*A Dictionary of Chinese Buddhist Terms,* online.
SSJZS	十三經注疏 *Shisan jing zhushu.*
SSXYJJ	世說新語校箋 *Shishuo xinyu jiaojian.*
SUNY	State University of New York
Tsukamoto, History	*A History of Early Chinese Buddhism.*
Watson, CT	*The Complete Works of Chuang Tzu.*
WSJC	緯書集成 *Weishu jicheng.*
XTS	新唐書 *Xin Tangshu.*
XZJJ	荀子集解 *Xunzi jijie.*
Zhonghua	中華書局 Zhonghua shuju.
ZZJC	諸子集成 *Zhuzi jicheng.*
ZZJS	莊子集釋 *Zhuangzi jishi.*
ZZTJ	資治通鑑 *Zizhi tongjian.*

Note on Translation

The work translated here was first published in two volumes as *Zhongguo sixiangshi, di yi juan: Qi shiji qian Zhongguo de zhishi, sixiang yu xinyang shijie* 中國思想史，第一卷，七世紀前的知識、思想與信仰世界 (1998) and *Zhongguo sixiangshi, di er juan: Qi shiji zhi shijiu shiji Zhongguo de zhishi, sixiang yu xinyang* 中國思想史，第二卷，七世紀至十九世紀中國的知識、思想與信仰 (2000). The original text ran to just over 1,400 pages. This translation represents Professor Ge Zhaoguang's abbreviation into a little over 660 pages of Chinese text. Volume One of this two-volume translation covers the first 371 pages of the Chinese text.

This extensive work was a considerable success in China. It has been printed ten times with more than seventy thousand sets sold after its first publication, quite unusual for such a scholarly book. There may be many reasons for this success. One is that it was published in an environment where education and scholarship were allowed to resume their proper place in society after decades of social and political turmoil during Chairman Mao's rule. A longing for knowledge and understanding of their own history has been widespread ever since the end of that rule. External causes can of course only explain part of the story. Without the great erudition and deep insights he employs in a reflective and open-minded manner, Professor Ge's work may not have appealed to so many Chinese readers in a manner that some earlier works of a similar nature have failed to do.

There have previously been valuable Chinese works on Chinese intellectual history both written and translated by prestigious scholars in the field. Fung Youlan's *History of Chinese Philosophy* was translated by Derk Bodde and published in 1952 and 1953 while part of Hsiao Kung-Quan's *A History of Chinese Political Thought* was translated by F. W. Mote and published in 1979. These texts have been regarded by many scholars as required classics and they have well served Chinese studies in the West. Fung's *History*, however, focuses on the exposition of Chinese thought as a branch of philosophical study, and Professor Mote's passing in 2005 meant that only half of Hsiao Kung-Quan's original work could be made available to the English speaking world. A translation of Ge Zhaoguang's most important recent study of Chinese intellectual history for the English speaking world would seem, then, to offer a rich supplement to the above texts as well as bringing in different perspectives and new understandings of a tradition that has more than two thousand years of history.

As Professor Ge's own "introduction" makes clear, his approach to Chinese intellectual history is very different from that of previous Chinese scholars in the field. Here, it is perhaps not out of place to state briefly that he discusses the importance of appropriating as wide a range of source materials as possible, especially those that only came to light recently and those that were neglected in the past. He also emphasizes the necessity of understanding ideas and thought in their proper historical contexts so that his Chinese readers can reduce their unavoidable preconceived modern assumptions and see the dialectical interaction between historical background and intellectual thought. Throughout, he stresses the complex dynamics involved in the interaction among the intellectual thought of elite Chinese scholars, their historical conditions, their canonical texts and what he calls the "worlds of general knowledge, thought and belief." In the process, some key issues, including the formation of the Chinese world order, its underlying value system, the origins of the Chinese cultural identity and the impact of foreign thought, emerged to underscore his narrative. Such discussions can no doubt help readers understand why this work was so well received in contemporary China and hopefully also help stimulate dialogue about these issues in the field since they are clearly relevant to our time.

As translators, we have been faced with the daunting task of trying to match our linguistic and intellectual abilities with Professor Ge's enormous scholarly range and coverage of Chinese textual and archeological source materials. The many excellent available translations of Chinese works and the various online Chinese texts have been most helpful to us. We have also greatly benefited from discussions of our questions with Professor Ge in Vancouver, Hong Kong and Taipei. Without his quick and careful answers through email exchanges to our questions on each chapter, it would have been impossible to complete this work within a reasonable time.

Some Technical Matters

All citations of the "twenty-five dynastic histories" (*Ershiwu shi* 二十五史) are from the Zhonghua shuju punctuated editions. In Chinese, Professor Ge's original work relies on very many Chinese translations of works originally in non-Chinese languages. Whenever possible, we have sought out the original texts that these translations are based on and reproduced them rather than re-translating from Chinese translations. We have noted any minor changes made to these published translations to match Professor Ge's overall format. To avoid unnecessary confusion, references to those Chinese translations are not included. In addition to using published translations of Chinese classic texts in many cases, all other translations of quoted Chinese materials are our own.

At the first appearance of a Chinese book, an italicized English translation is given with non-italicized Chinese Romanization in parentheses; subsequent appearances of the same text are given in English only. For example: The *Book of Songs* (Shijing) first, and *Book of Songs* from then on. Romanized Chinese titles are given in the notes. For traditional Chinese books we use j. for *juan* 卷 meaning chapter or volume. Page numbers for books and journals are given after the date of publication without p. or pp. Chinese characters are given for selected terms in hopes that readers will find them useful.

In dealing with the titles of Buddhist sources, we have done the same as with Chinese titles, giving an English translation with the Indian language titles in parentheses. For these English translations of titles, we have relied on Zenryû Tsukamoto, *A History of Early Chinese Buddhism* (Chûgoku Bukkyô tsûshi), as translated by Leon Hurvitz. In translating the titles of Daoist texts we have followed the same format and relied on Livia Kohn, ed., *Daoism Handbook*. If such standard translations of Buddhist and Daoist texts are unavailable, we have attempted our own.

Translating this volume has been a humbling experience, and any infelicities in our translation, in spite of Professor Ge's timely help, are unquestionably our own.

> Michael S. DUKE and Josephine CHIU-DUKE
> Vancouver, September 2013

Author and Translators

Ge Zhaoguang
is a Professor of History at Fudan University, Shanghai. He was the founder of
Fudan's National Institute for Advanced Humanistic Studies and served as its
Director for six years. He is well known for his studies of Chinese history and
the religious and intellectual history of ancient China. He has been a visiting
professor at Kyoto University in Japan, City University of Hong Kong,
Katholieke Universiteit Leuven in Belgium and National Taiwan University.
He was also appointed Princeton University Global Scholar for 2009-2010.
Among his many Chinese publications are *Zen Buddhism and Chinese Culture*
(1986), *Taoism and Chinese Culture* (1987), *Ten Chinese Classic Canons* (1993),
Chinese Intellectual History, 2 volumes (1998 and 2000), *Dwelling Here in China*
(2011).

Michael S. Duke
is Professor Emeritus of Chinese and Comparative Literature from the Asian
Studies Department of the University of British Columbia. He is the author of
several books including *Blooming and Contending* (1985). He has also translated many modern Chinese works of fiction such as *Raise the Red Lantern*
(1993), *The Fat Years* (2011) and most recently co-translated, with Timothy D.
Baker, Cho-yun Hsu, *China: A New Cultural History* (2012).

Josephine Chiu-Duke
is an Associate Professor of Chinese Intellectual History in the Asian Studies
Department of the University of British Columbia. She is the author of *To
Rebuild the Empire: Lu Chih's Confucian Pragmatist Approach to the Mid-T'ang
Predicament* (2000) and the editor of a Chinese work entitled *Liberalism and
the Humanistic Tradition—Essays in Honor of Professor Lin Yü-sheng* (2005).
She has also published many articles in both English and Chinese on tradi-
tional Chinese women and contemporary Chinese thought.

Series Editors' Foreword

The rise of China as an economic and political power is unquestionably one of the most striking phenomena of global significance as we enter the first decade of the twenty-first century. Ever since the end of the "Cultural Revolution" and the death of Mao Zedong in 1976, tremendous changes have transformed China from an isolated and relatively weak country into a rapidly developing and dynamic society. The scale and speed of such transformations have taken the world—even the Chinese themselves—by surprise; China today is drastically different from, and in a remarkably better condition than, China thirty years ago despite the many economic, social, and political difficulties and problems that yet remain to be dealt with. China scholars in Europe and North America are called upon to provide information and explanation of the rise of China, a country with history and tradition reaching back to antiquity and yet showing amazing strength and cultural virility in the world today. Interest in China is not limited to the traditional field of Sinology or China studies, nor is it confined to the academic world of universities, for more and more people outside of academia are curious about China, about its history and culture, as well as the changes taking place in the contemporary world. The Western news media brings images from China to every household; Sinologists or China scholars publish numerous articles and books to satisfy the general need for understanding: China is receiving a high-level of attention in the West today whether we turn to the scholarly community or look at popular imagination.

In understanding China, however, very little is available in the West that allows the average reader to have a glance at how China and its culture and history are understood by the Chinese themselves. This seems a rather strange omission, but in much of the twentieth century, the neglect of native Chinese scholarship was justified on the grounds of a perception of political control in China, where scholarship, particularly in the humanities and social sciences, was dominated by party ideology and strictly followed a prescribed party line. Such politically controlled scholarship was thought to be more propaganda than real scholarship, and consequently Western scholars rarely referred to contemporary Chinese scholarship in their works.

In the last thirty years, however, Chinese scholarship and public opinion, like everything else in China, have undergone such tremendous changes that the old stereotype of a politically controlled scholarship no longer holds. New and important archaeological findings in China have changed our knowledge of ancient texts and our understanding of Chinese history in significant ways, and detailed studies of such new materials are available in native Chinese scholarship. Since the 1980s, many Chinese scholars have critically reflected on the nature of scholarship and questioned the old dogma of political and ideological orthodoxy, while many important books have been published that present a new outlook on Chinese history and culture. The time has come for Western scholars and other interested readers to engage academic perspectives originating in China, and making important academic works from China available in English is an important step in this engagement. Translation of influential academic works from China will greatly contribute to our better understanding of China from different perspectives and in different ways, beyond the dichotomies of the inside and the outside, a native Chinese view and a Western observer's vantage point.

Brill's Humanities in China Library is a newly established book series that has been commissioned by Brill in response to that need. The series aims to introduce important and representative works of native Chinese scholarship in English translation, in which each volume is carefully selected and expertly translated for the benefit of Western scholars as well as general readers who have an interest in China and its culture but may not read the Chinese language in the original. It is our hope that this series of representative books in translation will be useful to both specialists and general readers for understanding China from a different point of view, and that it will be an important step towards a fruitful dialogue and an exchange of ideas between Chinese and Western scholars.

ZHANG Longxi
Axel SCHNEIDER

Chinese Intellectual History Writing

Prologue: The History of Chinese Intellectual History Itself

In his 1946 classic *The Idea of History*, R. G. Collingwood asserted that "all history is the history of thought."[1] If we say that history is the people, objects and affairs of the past, then they have all disappeared; they are only preserved in monuments, artifacts and memories, and have been narrated in various ancient documents and modern materials for the teaching of history. Several thousand years of deliberations about issues, reflections on tradition, understandings of history and all of the various accumulated concepts, however, that have been passed down to this day and that still influence the present—these should all be considered as "ideas and thoughts." These ideas and thoughts persist from generation to generation, and just because they persist, present day people can revisit and reexamine the deliberations of the ancients, and those deliberations can enlighten and inspire them. People's reflections on problems, methods of thought, interpretive discourse and ways of realizing them have been repeated, transformed, circulated and renewed generation after generation since ancient times. This process constitutes the history of thought or intellectual history.

This is also why the writing of intellectual history is important. Nevertheless, if we review Chinese academic history, we find that the term "intellectual history" (*sixiangshi*) is not as highly valued as "the history of philosophy" (*zhexueshi*). Why is this? First, because the Western history of philosophy paradigm made it very convenient for the Chinese academic world to re-organize Chinese history and thought during a period of transition. Second, the term philosophy in the Western sense, just like science, was rather appealing and challenging to Chinese scholars in the first half of the twentieth century. Third, modern Chinese universities divide their curriculum according to Western subjects and are thus in need of corresponding teaching materials.

Some Chinese scholars have tried to employ the ready made terms and logic of Western history of philosophy to sum up the development of Chinese scholarship and thought; other Chinese scholars have tried to find something akin to Western philosophy in Chinese scholarship in order to prove that ancient China also had the same sort of knowledge; still other scholars have written

---

1 R. G. Collingwood, *The Idea of History*, 1956 [1946], 317, 215, 115, 117, 120–121.

university teaching materials for the history of philosophy. As a result of all this, in twentieth-century Chinese academic bibliographies, there are fewer works entitled "intellectual history" than those entitled "history of philosophy," and these works of intellectual history have not had the benefit of such a complete process of development, nor have they accumulated such a body of mature experience as works in the history of philosophy category.

Let us briefly review the process of the writing of histories of Chinese philosophy. In 1916, Xie Wuliang (1884–1964) wrote a *History of Chinese Philosophy* (Zhongguo zhexueshi). This work only had a modern-sounding title and a good deal of roughly assembled materials, but the narrative was not able to establish a new paradigm.[2] In 1919 Hu Shi (1891–1962)'s *Outline History of Chinese Philosophy* (Zhongguo zhexueshi dagang) quickly replaced it. Cai Yuanpei (1868–1940) said that Hu Shi's book had four important strong points: "a method of proof," "concise presentation," "evenhanded judgment," and "systematic research,"[3] Nevertheless, Hu's book was incomplete, having only Part One but no Part Two, and when Feng Youlan (1895–1990) published his complete *History of Chinese Philosophy* (Zhongguo zhexueshi) in 1930 and 1933, it replaced Hu's *Outline*, though not completely. Hu's research still has heuristic significance today, but this significance does not primarily concern the narration of the history of philosophy per se; rather, it established a new model of academic history that had greater demonstrative than explanatory significance.[4] Still, Feng's work was systematic and complete and its content was suitable for general readers. This was especially so because he combined China's "orthodox" scheme and "standard" narrative practice—China's "tradition of Confucian moral principles" (*daotong* 道統) and Western "history of philosophy" narrative—into a mixed narrative form that was particularly suited to Chinese tastes. When his Tsinghua University lecture notes were published, they received very positive reviews.[5]

---

2   Xie Wuliang, *Zhongguo zhexueshi, xu yan,* 1916, 1.

3   Cai's Preface is contained in the front matter of Hu Shi, *Zhongguo zhexueshi dagang,* 1919.

4   Yu Yingshi has pointed out that the significance of Hu Shi's *Zhongguo zhexueshi dagang* lay in the establishment of a new "paradigm" and that Feng Youlan did not go beyond this "paradigm." This so-called "paradigm" was simply that the content was Chinese but the form and concepts were taken from the West. See Yu Yingshi, "Xueshu sixiangshi de chuangjian ji liubian" in *Gujin lunheng* 3 (1999), 68–69.

5   See the "Report" by Chen Yinque and Jin Yuelin, published as an Appendix to Feng Youlan, *Zhongguo zhexueshi,* 1930 (1984). See also Hu Shih's review of Feng Yu-lan, *A History of Chinese Philosophy. Volume I, The Period of The Philosophers (From the Beginnings to Circa 100 BC)* and *Volume II, The Period of Classical Learning (From the Second Century BC to the Twentieth Century AD),* translated by Derk Bodde, in *American Historical Review,* 60/4 (July

Following changes in the political situation, however, Feng Youlan's history was replaced by Ren Jiyu (1916–2009)'s *History of Chinese Philosophy* (Zhongguo zhexueshi), a text that was written in easier to understand language and followed a simpler and clearer thread of logic more in accord with the political ideological manner of interpretation of that time.[6] Feng's work was republished in the 1980s by Zhonghua Book Company, and then later on the People's Publishing Company brought out a seven-volume edition entitled *A New History of Chinese Philosophy* (Zhongguo zhexueshi xinbian). The history of philosophy now seems to have come full circle and returned to its original starting point. After eighty years, however, we have accumulated a rich store of experiences and lessons that may serve as reference materials for "re-writing" the history of philosophy in China.

We have considerable narrative experience in writing the history of philosophy, and right from the beginning we received from the West and Japan clear and ready made models, including cosmology, life philosophy and epistemology. As Feng Youlan wrote at the start of his *History of Chinese Philosophy*: "Philosophy was originally a Western term. If we now want to discuss the history of Chinese philosophy, one of our principal tasks is simply to select and discuss those various forms of knowledge or learning in Chinese history that can be called philosophy in the Western sense."[7] For a long time, however, I have harbored the stubborn idea that, as much as the great Western tide of thought poured into Chinese "philosophy" and "history of philosophy" by way of Japan and provided us with very good conceptual tools and narrative frameworks to deal anew with ancient Chinese thought, still completely to employ an unmodified Western philosophy to discuss and interpret Chinese learning will probably lead to distortions and mistaken interpretations. In short, I think

---

1955), 898–900. Hu's important criticism of Feng's work was that it should "be read as a history of Chinese philosophy written from the 'orthodox' Chinese standpoint." And, Hu asks, "what is the standpoint of Chinese 'orthodoxy' which our author so frankly and proudly admits to be the main standpoint of his history? Broadly stated, the traditional 'orthodox' standpoint was (1) that Truth (*tao*) began to unfold with Confucius, the great inheritor and teacher of the sacred tradition of the sage-rulers of antiquity; (2) that this Truth was obscured and actually swept aside by the deluge of heterodox and depraved doctrines such as those of Mo Ti and Yang Chu of ancient times and Buddhism and Taoism of medieval China; and (3) that this Truth which for long centuries had remained dormant in the sacred scriptures, was revived by its latter-day saints, the leaders of the Neo-Confucian movements from the eleventh century on." (899).

6 Ren Jiyu, *Zhongguo zhexueshi*, 4 vols. 1966.
7 Feng Youlan, *Zhongguo zhexueshi*, 1930 (1984), vol. 1, 1.

that it is highly problematic whether ancient Chinese learning and thought can be described as the "history of philosophy."

Others had long ago become aware of this problem. For example, Fu Sinian (1896–1950) pointed out in a 1918 letter to Cai Yuanpei that history is the foundation of Chinese philosophy and that Chinese "philosophy" simply cannot be considered philosophy in the Western sense. Ten years later, he wrote even more directly that ancient China "originally did not have so-called philosophy."[8] In 1924, when Cai Yuanpei, who had translated *The Essentials of Philosophy* (Zhexue yaoling), wrote his *Brief Outline of Philosophy* (Jianyi zhexue gangyao), he would seem to have recalled Fu Sinian's words. On the one hand he compared philosophy to the Learning of the Way (*daoxue* 道學) while on the other hand emphasizing that "our nation's philosophy is not based on scientific premises." And so he wrote with great regret that "if we want to speak of the outline of philosophy now, we have no choice but completely to adopt European theories."[9] Further on, under the influence of Fu Sinian, in 1929 Hu Shi also stated quite explicitly that he intended to change the title of his soon to be completed *Outline History of Chinese Philosophy* to *History of Chinese Thought* (Zhongguo sixiangshi) and that he had "already decided not to use *Outline* in the title."[10]

Indeed ancient China did not even have a term similar to "philosophy." Ancient China also did not have any knowledge, thought or learning the meaning of which conformed to the Western concept of philosophy. By comparison, to use the "History of Thought" or "Intellectual History" to describe the various types of learning in Chinese history seems much more appropriate. This is so because the modern word "thought" (*sixiang*) is much richer and more inclusive than "philosophy."

Some Chinese scholars employed the concept of "intellectual history" quite early on. By 1935 Rong Zhaozu (1897–1994) had already edited a volume of *Resource Materials for Chinese Intellectual History* (Zhongguo sixiangshi cankao ziliao), and in 1936 Chen Zhongfan (1888–1982) was also planning with Cai Shangsi (1905–2008) to write *A History of Chinese Thought* (Zhongguo sixiangshi). He wrote quite clearly that "to narrate the systems and schools of thought

---

8   Fu Sinian, "Yu Gu Jiegang lun gushi shu," No. 3, "Zai Zhou Han fangshujia de shijie zhong jige quxiang," in *Fu Sinian xuanji*, 1967, vol. 3, 423.

9   In 1903 Cai published his translation, from a Japanese translation, of a book by Raphael von Koeber that Cai gave the title *Zhexue yaoling*; it is in Gao Pingshu, ed., *Cai Yuanpei quanji*, 1989 (1929), chapter 1, 176–228; Cai quote is from chapter 3, 395.

10   In "Xiandai xueshu yu geren shouhuo," chapter 12 of *Hu Shi koushu zizhuan*, 1989, he also said that after 1929 he was happy that he changed "History of Chinese Philosophy" to "History of Chinese Thought." See *Hu Shi wenji*, 1998, vol. 1, 415.

of various ages and the processes of their development is the History of Thought."[11] In 1939, Cai Shangsi published his *Research Methods for Chinese Intellectual History* (Zhongguo sixiangshi yanjiufa), while Chang Naide (1898–1947) published his *Short History of Chinese Thought* (Zhongguo sixiang xiaoshi) a bit earlier.

But how should Chinese intellectual history be written? That was still a problem without a clear solution. If we say that intellectual history—the history of thought—is richer and more inclusive than the history of philosophy, this entails a rather troublesome dilemma—namely that, due to the very inclusiveness of intellectual history, "thought" itself may be rendered limitless. At that, "intellectual history" will then take on an overly heavy responsibility, so much that it cannot even clearly understand its own scope and contents.[12] Therefore in the eighty years that histories of philosophy have been repeatedly written, there have been only a small number of general histories with the title "Intellectual History."[13] Even if we add in all of the histories of "Political Thought," "Religious Thought," "Schools of Thought" and histories of thought limited to single dynasties, they still cannot compare with histories of "Philosophy."[14] What is even more disheartening is that these works labeled "intellectual history" are often just extra large "histories of philosophy" that borrow the general format for writing the "history of philosophy" but incorporate many things that should never be included in "philosophy" in the first place.

Among the few intellectual histories, Hou Wailu (1903–1987)'s *General History of Chinese Thought* (Zhongguo sixiang tongshi) was dominant for nearly half a century. I do not intend to offer a critique of this work here because that would take up too much space. In any case it is a work of

---

11 Originally published in Cai Shangsi, *Zhongguo sixiangshi yanjiufa*, 1939; then in *Chen Zhongfan lunwenji*, 1993, 8.

12 In the past there were few essays on the style and subject of writing the history of Chinese thought. The most important ones were in Cai Shangsi's *Zhongguo sixiangshi yanjiufa* and Chen Zhongfan's preface.

13 According to statistics given in the *Bashi nian lai shixue shumu, 1900–1980* (1984), except for Hou Wailu's *Zhongguo sixiang tongshi* (discussed in this text), there were Chang Naide, *Zhongguo sixiang* xiaoshi, 1930; Qian Mu, *Zhongguo sixiangshi*, 1952; Yang Rongguo, *Jianming Zhongguo sixiangshi*, 1962; Wei Zhengtong, *Zhongguo sixiangshi*, 1979; Hou Wailu, *Zhongguo sixiang shigang*, 1980 & 1981); He Zhaowu, *Zhongguo sixiang fanzhan shi*, 1980; Chu Bosi, *Zhongguo sixiang shihua* (1980) and so on.

14 Works like Chen Zhongfan, *Liang Song sixiang shuping*, 1938; Rong Zhaozu, *Ming dai sixiangshi*, 1962; Ji Wenfu, *Wan Ming sixiangshi lun*, 1944, etc.; works on periodization. Also, Lo Genze's "Preface" to volume 4 of *Gushi bian*, states that his "ultimate goal was to write a detailed and systematic academic intellectual history," but he never did so.

great scope, rich content, complex sources and complete and accurate documentation. Even though it bares many traces of its contemporary political milieu, to analyze it would require one to be very conscientious and serious. Here I just want to share some of my feelings and reflections on reading Hou's work in preparation for writing my own *Intellectual History of China*.

In 1947, when the first volume of his *General History of Chinese Thought* came out, Hou Wailu wrote a preface representing the Chinese academic institutes. In this preface full of high-flown rhetoric, he said that the subjects included in the history of thought are "logical methods," "academic approaches," "social consciousness," and "world views." In 1957, however, when a revised version of this *General History* came out, Hou wrote a brief preface in which he said that it integrates philosophic, logical and social thought and also includes the base, the superstructure and ideology. It is just here in these concepts, the implications and connotations of which are not very clear, that we would seem to see the difficulty of writing intellectual history. In addition to the understandable influence of the political environment, the unclear boundaries of the histories of thought, philosophy, ideology, theories of logic and so on is one of the important reasons for this difficulty. We have to ask, then: is intellectual history a species of "super history" that is capable of including philosophy, ideology, theories of logic and even politics, law and science? If it is, then Collingwood's idea that "all history is the history of thought" would be confirmed. But who would be capable of writing such an all-embracing intellectual history?

The makeup of Chinese "intellectual history" is still unclear and some problems remain to this day. First, does the significance of intellectual history lie in its establishment of a "tradition of Confucian moral principles" (*daotong*) in history that deserves to be praised, establishing a "genealogy" of thought, or in narrating the historical process of thought? Posing this question is actually asking whether intellectual history belongs in the final analysis to thought or to history? Second, if it is the latter, then should intellectual history re-establish *de novo* the subjects of its narrative? In intellectual history, there are not only elites and classics; there are also worlds of common and ordinary knowledge, thought and belief. There are not only ages when intellectual talents abound, but also ages of mediocre thought. Should the latter, then, also be subsumed and considered in intellectual history? Third, if we want to describe worlds of knowledge, thought and belief involving an even broader scope, then how is intellectual history going to handle properly its relationships with cultural, social and political history? In other words, is it necessary for the history of thought to draw a clear boundary around itself in order to avoid overlapping with the domains of social history, cultural history and the history of scholarship?

How then should intellectual history be written? I still have many questions about this, and, to tell the truth, even after I finished this intellectual history, I was still not completely clear. What follows are just some ideas that I have about how to write intellectual history; they are not intended to be a comprehensive discussion of how to do it.

1. The History of General Knowledge, Thought and Belief

1.1

In general most "history of Chinese thought" or "history of Chinese philosophy" works in circulation today present a series of great thinkers, from Confucius (551–479 BCE) to Kang Youwei (1858–1927), and the classics, from the *Book of Songs* (Shijing) to *The Book of Great Unity* (Datong shu). The history of thought is laid out in chronological order in chapters and sections, with the great thinkers given a full chapter and lesser lights given a full section while some not so qualified *dramatis personae* are lumped together in a single section. In this way the history of thought becomes little more than a museum of thinkers surrounded by a library of the great books of China. The origin of this way of writing is perhaps related to the genre of Chinese historical biography and the Chinese bibliographical tradition. Putting the thinkers together with the classic texts creates works similar to the biographies of wise men in the scholarly cases genre (*xue-an*) with the classics added. This kind of traditional arrangement overlapping with the structure of the modern Western history of thought and history of philosophy came to constitute the regular manner of writing and explicating the history of Chinese thought.

This narrative method is not only easy to use, but also has theoretical support. In the first place, most people are accustomed to the idea that intellectual history is composed by the elite and constitutes the thought of the elite and the classics. This is the essence of intellectual history and it dominates both politics and everyday life. To describe the elite and the classics is to describe the world of thought and also to describe the world of everyday life. Secondly, intellectual history is comprised of a sequence of thinkers who continually develop thought and ideas. To describe this sequence of thinkers then amounts to describing intellectual history. Finally, there is a perhaps not fully conscious hypothesis behind this way of writing—that the materials about the elite and their classic texts that we have today are complete and true to their times, and that history has not filtered them by elimination and selection. Even if it has, it has done so accurately and impartially, and we should accept the authenticity and the integrity of the existing historical records and their assertions.

I have some reservations about all of this. First of all, in intellectual history, there are some geniuses whose influence lasts for several generations, but there are also some people whose influence is only fleeting. Some ideas are quite fruitful in their own time while some ideas are only discovered anew and disseminated many generations later. Sometimes the thought of those "geniuses" or "elites" transcends the boundaries of the world of common knowledge and creates historical "ruptures" and intellectual "leaps." I believe that an intellectual history constructed solely from the ideas of the intellectual elites and classic texts will not necessarily offer a clearly contextualized path of transmission. The general knowledge residing in the world of common everyday life, however, in its gradual evolution, may indeed allow us to see quite distinctly the continuity of intellectual history.

Secondly, precisely because the thought of the elite and the ideas in the classics transcend general knowledge, they do not necessarily play a genuine role in the life of contemporary society. Because the general population's knowledge and thought usually does not derive its support from the highest elite or the best classic texts of the time, their thought and their writings tend to be separated by some distance from the general knowledge and everyday life of their society. The world of so-called thought and learning is a space in which sometimes only a small number of the elite operate. This world is above the world of society and everyday life. Not everything that influences the general knowledge of people in life and society really comes from this small elite and the classics.

Thirdly, the reason that certain elite thinkers or classic texts are discussed in intellectual histories tends to be due to "a need to trace the origins," or "later affirmation of their worth," or "to emphasize the significance" of a thinker or work—all due to the later recognition and endorsement accorded by the intellectual historians themselves. It is actually highly questionable whether some of the elite thinkers and classic texts written up in intellectual histories were really so great and profoundly influential in their own times and actually deserve to occupy such a lofty place in the historical sequence. For example, the status and significance attributed to Wang Fuzhi (1619–1692) in late Ming and early Qing intellectual history is a result of such later affirmation. On the other hand, there are some scholars and works that are not at all mentioned in intellectual histories, but that may have had a very profound and lasting influence on the contemporary history of thought. Works like Timothy Richard's translation of *The Nineteenth Century: A History* (Taixi xinshi lanyao) and John

Fryer's *On Methods of Curing Mental Illness and Avoiding Disease* (Zhixin mian-bing fa, 1896) are nowhere to be found in intellectual histories due to their lack of recognition by later historians. In their time, however, their influence was extremely great. The inspiration they offered, as found in the diaries, letters and essays of many first rate scholars of the late Qing, would seem to go beyond their content and quality. Not only did Song Shu (1862–1910) include them as school textbooks, but they even had a rather deep influence on Tan Sitong (1865–1898)'s *Exposition of Humanity* (Ren xue, 1896/1897).

A narrow concentration on a small number of elite thinkers and classic texts and a disregard for the larger life and general knowledge of the past has meant that some thoughts have been overly-obscured while others have been given exaggerated prominence. What then appears to be a contextualized path of transmission turns out to be merely the personally conceived "tradition of the Way" of the compilers or a "genealogy" created according to later appreciation.

I am certainly not saying that I don't intend to write an intellectual history of elite thinkers and classic texts. I am only saying that we should pay attention to the background of their knowledge, thought and belief. To put it quite frankly, past intellectual histories were only the intellectual histories of think-ers and classic texts, but we should take notice that in the real historical world, there was another form of general knowledge, thought and belief that served as the background and the cornerstone of the thought of the elite and the classics.

This general knowledge, thought and belief genuinely functioned in peo-ple's decisions, interpretations and dealings with the world around them. For this reason it seems that there should be an intermediate "world of general knowledge, thought and belief" between the thought of the elite and the clas-sics and the world of ordinary social life. The continuity of this intermediate "world of general knowledge, thought and belief" would then constitute a con-tinuously expanding process of intellectual history, and certainly belongs within its purview.

1.2

I really started to think about this problem a few years ago when I considered the following scenario. Suppose, in the past, an intellectual genius had sud-denly appeared and just as suddenly disappeared. Some profound thoughts had been developed but they received no response, and some of his works long lay hidden away in a well or a mountain retreat. Then many years later, these works were suddenly discovered. How, then, do we go about assessing their status in intellectual history? This is not an impossible chain of events. I have been wondering, then, whether or not the real continuity of intellectual history is perhaps hidden in the slow incremental development of ordinary or general knowledge, thought and belief.

What I mean by "general knowledge, thought and belief" is not at all what the anthropologists call the "little tradition." I particularly do not want my readers to use "little tradition" or "the thought of the masses" to interpret what I call "general knowledge, thought and belief." My "general knowledge, thought and belief" refers to the world of common sense knowledge. It is neither the wisdom of talented intellectuals nor the result of mature and deliberate reflection, and certainly not the lowest level of the so-called "collective unconscious." It is rather a form of "thought that is used every day without thinking."

By means of the most basic education, this kind of common sense and general thought come to constitute authentic cultural features of a people or ethnic group (*minzu* 民族). Unlike the ideas in the classic texts, this general knowledge, thought and belief is really not disseminated through the elite reading of the classics, mutual correspondence and literary interaction, or even wholly by means of narrative transmission or higher-level education. This knowledge is rather disseminated through the most common channels, such as public entertainments (religious ceremonial assemblies, dramatic performances on commercial market days); general education (in private schools, elementary schools, and guidance in their popularizing interpretations of the classics by parents and relatives); popular readings and oral performances (fiction, literary anthologies, collections of moral teachings, and oral storytelling) and so on. The scope of its dissemination goes far beyond that of the classics.

Nevertheless, all members of the elite classes also lived within these worlds of common sense knowledge, and so that knowledge could become the direct background to the thought of the elite and the classic texts. The strange thing, however, is that our works of intellectual history very rarely try to retrieve, describe or speculate on this fertile intellectual soil as a background. They rather regard big national political events and economic changes that only remotely influenced the average person as the "panoramic backdrop" to their narratives of intellectual history.

I am certainly not saying that my research on intellectual history is not concerned with elites and classic texts. In fact, elite thought and the ideas of the classics still occupy by far the greatest amount of my narrative. I merely want to point out, however, that geniuses are, after all, quite rare. From the point of view of intellectual history, the thinking of such talented people is perhaps wondrously ahead of its time and deviates greatly from ordinary intellectual history. Of course I intend to write about these elites and classic texts because that is the only way to tell the fascinating story of the high and low points of

Chinese thought as well as the only way to offer us material for reflection today. And besides, "the worlds of general knowledge, thought and belief" may perhaps not exhibit much change for rather long periods of time and do not provide any new edification for the present, but they are still the background of intellectual history.

For example, I summarize the various ideals and desires that dominated the everyday world of the ancient Chinese people from materials for the fifth to the third centuries BCE. I found that these ideals and desires did not exhibit any particularly large changes all the way through the Qin and Han dynasties. Even after Buddhism entered China in the second to sixth centuries CE, they continued to dominate the world of Chinese people's everyday life—only some new ideas were added concerning life and death, suffering and happiness, reincarnation, good, evil and retribution. We need, then, to use the French Annals School concept of the so-called *longue duré* or long time scale to measure and describe this general knowledge, thought and belief in our research on intellectual history. Despite the fact that it evolved slowly it was still a continuous change and it formed the true foundation and baseline of intellectual history.

I have had this idea for a long time, but I know there are still some problems, and people will ask the following question: Since history has already disappeared, and these worlds of general knowledge, thought and belief rarely left behind written records, how are you going to reconstruct them from the extant documents and other materials?

1.3

This is undoubtedly a valid question. And so we need a genuinely workable new method of writing. If intellectual history is to pay attention to the worlds of general knowledge, thought and belief, then we have to examine critically the range of the documents and materials relied upon in traditional intellectual history writing.

Traditional intellectual history generally relies on various history books and other works that have been handed down from ancient times. These document have percolated down through history and also derive from the elites. They do not necessarily reflect the worlds of general knowledge, thought and belief. We know that all archives or history books may have gone through the organized recording of history, the affirmation of certain texts as more valuable, and certain ideological filtering, omission and simplification. Thinkers and their discourse have been subjected to repeated discussion and validation in these records. Someone has been affirmed as the exemplum of intellectual history in some era; someone has been said to have put forth significant ideas or concepts in some era; someone has been said to have carried on someone else's thought . . . and in this way intellectual history has been presented as a well-ordered narrative. However, the ideas that were truly continuous and had direct effects on social life were often common universal knowledge and thought instead of brilliant elite thought. But where then, are we to seek materials for these ideas?

Let us imagine for a moment that a hundred years from now historians writing the intellectual history of the 1990s rely solely on the public pronouncements of political leaders, works of celebrated writers, editorials in official newspapers, material from government approved archives and news statements prepared ahead of the facts by political spokespersons. The world they described would be a completely different world from our lived experience of the 1990s. If, however, the materials they relied upon also included today's popular news stand reading materials, popular songs sung in karaoke and disco halls and the topics of conversation in restaurants and tea houses, then perhaps their account of 1990s thought would be closer to the world we experienced then. For this reason, once people cast their attention on the worlds of general knowledge, thought and belief, then, just as Jacques Le Goff wrote in his *La Nouvelle Histoire*, they will expand the range of historical documents, free historiography from the limitation of written documents from the past, and replace it with a foundation of multivariate historical materials.[15]

Let me give a couple of examples. In discussing Han dynasty thought, besides using the works of people who are "clearly recorded in history" like Jia Yi (200–168 BCE), Dong Zhongshu (ca. 179–ca. 104 BCE) and Wang Chong (27–ca. 97?), we might do well to pay attention to some sources that are not individually mentioned in the histories and that were not intentionally prepared for historians. Things like the silk manuscripts from Mawangdui and their implied meanings, the inscriptions on the back of bronze mirrors from Han archeological sites, and the inadvertently expressed thoughts written out on various bamboo and wooden slips. These articles will not necessarily only yield superficial material knowledge. From them we can actually discover the common hopes of the age, the strategies suggested for realizing those hopes and the conceptual world underlining both the hopes and the strategies.

Also for Buddhism in the North-South dynasties period, intellectual histories generally mention Dao-an (312–385), Huiyuan (334–416), Kumârajîva (334–413), Sengzhao (384–414) and other brilliant Buddhist monks. But in the ordinary life of that time, how many people really immersed themselves in discussions of the "Buddha nature," "*Shûnyatâ*" (emptiness), the "Way of Eight

15   Jacques Le Goff, *La Nouvelle Histoire*, 1978, 16.

Proscriptions" (*babu zhongdao* 八不中道) and similar theories? When we examine the historical materials unconsciously passed down from that time, we will sense the true influence of Buddhist thought in everyday life. Among these materials, the first are the engraved stone inscriptions concerning Buddhism from the North-South dynasties period and the second are the epigraphs and inscriptions in various documents unearthed at Dunhuang and Turfan. Since they have not been subject to either conscious arrangement or too much mediated exposition and interpretation, these stone inscriptions and documents place the contemporary people's general thought right before our eyes. In them, we see that the great majority of Buddhist disciples were not really preoccupied with the discussion of arcane theories. More commonly they exhibited their religious beliefs in the expression of their earthly desires.

Since what I call "general knowledge, thought and belief" does not refer to the popular consciousness of the lowest levels of society, I do not mean to say that we should concentrate all our attention on these marginal materials. Family instructions (*jiaxun*), lineage regulations (*zugui*), manuals of morality (*quanshanshu*), primers (*tongmeng keben*), precious scrolls (*baojuan*) and so on are also undoubtedly excellent resources.

These historical materials do not actually tell stories, they only display them. Telling carries the consciousness of the teller, but showing is direct presentation. It is most unfortunate that in the past, a great many of these unconscious historical resources were excluded from intellectual histories with the result that those histories do not come as close as they could to the actually existing worlds of thought covered.

I know the writing of intellectual history receives influence from generation to generation and the materials used in past intellectual histories will also influence the works of later historians. Consequently, through this influence from past to present the range of what constitutes a historical resource becomes limited by conventional usage. And for this reason a great deal of material unfortunately cannot come within the purview of intellectual history.

Let me give two examples, the first being encyclopedias (*leishu*) I believe that the extant *leishu* encyclopedias are excellent texts for intellectual history because the knowledge formation that emerges from the classifications in these texts is exactly what may make it possible for us to recover and understand the level of general knowledge, thought and belief. Buddhist and Daoist *leishu* may also make it possible for us to speculate about the common Buddhist and Daoist knowledge widespread in society. My second example is *Zhu Xi's Family Rituals* (Zhuzi jiali). Zhu Xi (1130–1200) will always be mentioned in any intellectual history's discussion of Song dynasty thought. Relatively few scholars study his *Family Rituals* even though Qiu Jun (1418/1421–1495)'s *Family Rituals and Etiquette* (Jiali yijie) dominated Ming life for a very long time. During the Republican era, the general society still relied on *Zhu Xi's Family Rituals* for their ceremonial activities. What we see expressed in these sorts of ceremonial regulations is precisely the worlds of general knowledge, thought and belief.

But when have these materials been taken seriously and analyzed by intellectual historians?[16]

1.4

From the 1980s on, many Chinese scholars, including myself, wanted to re-write Chinese intellectual history. As I wrote in some articles in the early 1990s, there was a need for "a different form of intellectual history," a need to re-write Chinese intellectual history. I have to admit, though, that this "'re-writing' remained a popular but difficult topic throughout the 1980s." Due to the lack of theoretical or documentary preparation, this so-called "re-writing" was just an emotional expression of a reassessment of values; to this day no successful example of it has been published.[17]

In writing this intellectual history, I have been conscious of many insufficiencies of both theory and methodology. Although I received much heuristic support from Anthropology, Sociology, Religious Studies and Historical Linguistics, their theories and practices could not really be directly applied to a narrative of intellectual history, especially not in the history of general knowledge, thought and belief in China. I have tried very hard in my regular narration of intellectual history to work in some sections regarding general knowledge, thought and belief. In Chapter Three, I employ the overall content of the Mawangdui silk manuscripts and paintings to discuss how archeology has rediscovered the general background thought of the Qin and Han dynasties. I also use the silk paintings and paintings on funerary bricks to analyze the people of the Qin and Han's beliefs about the three worlds of Heaven, Earth and the Human while employing the various concepts in bronze mirror

16   For research on *Zhuzi jiali*, see Shu Jingnan, "Zhu Xi 'Jiali' zhenwei bian" in *Zhuzi xuekan* 5 (1993), 112–120; Chen Lai, "Zhuzi 'Jiali' zhenwei kaoyi," *Beijing daxue xuebao* 3 (1989), 115–122; Yang Zhigang, "Zhuzi jiali: minjian tongyong li," *Chuantong wenhua yu xiandaihua* 4 (1994), 40–46. Also see Patricia B. Ebrey, *Confucianism and Family Rituals in Imperial China*, 1991 and *Chu Hsi's Family Rituals*, 1991, translated with annotation and introduction. There is still little Chinese language research on *Zhu Xi's Family Rituals*.

17   See Ge Zhaoguang, "Sixiang de ling yizhong xingshi de lishi," "Zhiyu sixiangshi de shiye zhong," and "Gudai Zhongguo haiyou duoshao aomi?," in *Dushu* 9 (1992), 10 (1994), and 11 (1995) respectively.

inscriptions to discuss contemporary ideas concerning life, happiness, off-spring, and the state. In Chapter Four, I specifically include a section discussing the influence of Buddhism on general thought during the early period of its entrance into China—the religious consciousness found in Buddhist manu-scripts, portraits and confessionals (*chanfa* 懺法, methods of repentance)—and their changes in Chinese society. I also employ several Buddhist inscriptions on stone tablets or handwritten manuscripts (*shiyu* 識語) from the mid-third to the mid-sixth centuries to analyze and summarize the content of people's Buddhist beliefs. All of this is still obviously not enough.

In order to describe general knowledge, thought and belief, I think we need to pay attention to three other sorts of source materials. The first is the content of beginning instructions for the young. Every person experiences this sort of education and it remains part of their thought development process. Therefore it is very important to analyze the knowledge and thought embodied in mate-rials for the education of the young and primary texts, such as the texts used by family and private school instructors and primers issued by the government. The second kind of source material constitutes the origin of basic knowledge. This is simply the experience and knowledge supplied to every ordinary per-son. To describe it requires various inadvertently transmitted but widespread materials, such as graphic images (pictures on stone, copper mirrors, religious images, sculptures, buildings) and widely circulated articles of print (answers to talismanic questions asked in temples, *qianwen jieshu* 簽文解書, village compacts, lineage regulations, family instructions and popular almanacs). The third source is the channel of thought dissemination. Elite thought cannot be directly transformed into popular thought. We need to locate the mediums of dissemination that served to popularize it, especially the literary materials that some intellectual historians pay little attention to, such as early Buddhist lec-tures on the sûtras, transformation texts (*bianwen*), later manuals of morality, song lyrics prepared for performers, story-telling texts from fixed locales, fam-ily sacrifices or performances during village gatherings, and so on.

I've been thinking about it for several years, and I believe that if a stratum of general knowledge, thought and belief had been added between the "back-ground" and "focus" of former intellectual histories, perhaps those histories would have been somewhat more lucid and true to life. I know of course that adding this stratum would be very difficult. To describe "general knowledge, thought and belief" would require following too many possible approaches, employing too many comprehensive source materials, and even more interpretive background sources. That is why in this work I have only provided a not too fully developed train of thought and some summarized and orga-nized materials for future intellectual historians to use.

2.   Between the History of Knowledge and the History of Thought

In the 1990s while I was writing this intellectual history, the Chinese academic world was rather hotly engaged in a debate concerning scholarship (*xueshu* 學術) versus thought (*sixiang* 思想). I should say that this was both an old and a new topic. It was old because it could be traced back to the Qing dynasty debate between Han and Song learning, to the Song dynasty debate between the schools of Zhu Xi and Lu Xiangshan (Lu Jiuyuan, 1139–1193), and even to the two ancient scholarly traditions of either valuing inquiry into knowledge (*dao wenxue* 道問學) or valuing the cultivation of moral virtue (*zun dexing* 尊德性) from the "Doctrine of the Mean" (Zhongyong) in the *Book of Rites*.

It was new because it manifested the orientational differences present in the contemporary academic world with regard to their views on continuing tradition and walking toward the world, seeking knowledge or expressing concepts, and appreciating history or worrying about the present. Against this background, I thought of another related topic while writing this book. That is, how should the history of thought be connected to the history of knowledge? How should intellectual history treat the relationship between knowledge (*zhishi*) and thought or ideas (*sixiang*)? In other words, in the course of ancient intellectual history, how did the knowledge background support and give birth to ideas, thoughts and concepts? And how did these ideas and concepts express and explain their contemporary intellectual world?

2.1

If we believe that intellectual history is continuous, then we must discuss the problem of knowledge and thought from the origins of Chinese intellectual history on. Knowledge of the cosmos and knowledge of history are the two great foundations of ancient Chinese intellectual history.

Observations and conceptions of astronomical phenomena provided the ancient Chinese with various kinds of knowledge about the cosmos. They knew or believed the following: Heaven is round and Earth is square;[18] Heaven is like a hemisphere covering the earth, it has north and south celestial poles (*tianji* 天極) and an ecliptic plane of the solar system (*huangdao* 黃道) while Earth has five directions (including the center); *qi* 氣, the life force or energy of the universe, is divided into *yin* (dark, female, moon etc.) and *yang* (bright, male, sun) forces, the polar axis (*jizhou* 極軸) occupies the center of the dome of Heaven; the state (*guo* 國) occupies the center of the cosmos; the capital

---

18   *Tian* 天 is also the Chinese word for sky. It is sometimes the numinous concept Heaven;
      di 地 earth is also sometimes the numinous concept Earth.—translators.

occupies the center of the state, and the royal palace occupies the center of the capital—everything else develops out from the two sides of the palace in the center in two symmetrical and corresponding halves. By means of symbolism, suggestion and various related ceremonies, all of this knowledge of a putatively correct conception of space was transmitted to the populace and enabled them to establish a foundation for rational thought. It also enabled them to unify all sorts of concepts and ideas on the basis of this foundation and to maintain their unity, continuity and harmony.[19]

Their imagination, memory and investigation of history provided the ancient Chinese with their constitutive knowledge about time. This knowledge then provided the intellectual world with a form of sacred proof derived from ancient times that made them believe from the very beginning that the words and activities of the ancient sages were both reasonable and legitimate. Thinkers frequently sought out historical evidence for their ideas, and in ancient China these historical ideas were not just ornamental memories; they carried great weight. The Way of the Sage Kings and the affairs of the earliest dynasties were the foundations that authenticated meaning and significance. This was already so in the pre-Qin period. As the *Discourses of the States* (Guoyu) put it, "when undertaking tasks and applying punishments, one must consult the earlier instructions and the previous practices."[20]

Through transmission and application, this accumulated knowledge came to permeate all kinds of learning and technology. It was also sacralized and rationalized in the formation of many different classic texts.

The most important forms of knowledge in early China were studies of the astronomic calendar, sacrificial offerings to the gods and ancestors and mantic and medical arts. Astronomical measurement and calendar-making comprised knowledge for managing the cosmos; sacrifices and ceremonies represented knowledge for rectifying the human order; medical and mantic knowledge served to examine the mysteries of the human body itself. Through these forms of knowledge was discovered numerology (*shushu*), rites and music (*liyue*) mantic and medical arts (*fangji* 方技) along with Yin-Yang thought, Huang-Lao Daoism, Confucianism and Legalism, etc. that would have great influence on later Chinese thought. The "classics" were also formed and they would be repeatedly cited.

---

19 See Joseph Needham, *Science and Civilization in China*, volume 2, *History of Scientific Thought*, 1962, and Mircea Eliade, *A History of Religious Ideas 2: from Gautama Buddha to the Triumph of Christianity*, II, 1982.

20 *Guo yu*, "Zhou yu shang," 23.

We can see a rather complex background behind these classic texts, and also note that these classics contained all kinds of knowledge. Prior to the Han dynasty, the concept of using the Six Classics—*Book of Songs*, *Book of Documents* or *Book of History* (Shangshu), *Book of Rites* (Liji), *Classic of Music* (Yuejing), *Book of Changes* (Yijing), and the *Spring and Autumn Annals* (Chunqiu)—as the repository of knowledge and the foundation of truth had already been developed. This was because these classics were not only the "Canon of the Sage Kings" with a glorious origin and a long history, but their contents were extremely rich, and yet they left behind rather broad explanatory leeway. In his Preface to *Records of the Grand Historian* (Shiji), Sima Qian (145/135–ca. 86 BCE) wrote that the content of the Five Classics (no Classic of Music) included Heaven and Earth, Yin-Yang, Four Seasons, Five Phases (*wuxing*), regulating human relationships, mountains, rivers, streams and valleys as well as grasses, trees, fish and animals . . . they did not stop at spirit and personality, but also touched upon every aspect of the cosmos, politics, nature and society.

Our intellectual history research has, however, tended to overlook the knowledge contained in numerology, rites and music, mantic and medical arts and the study of the classics. This makes concrete knowledge and abstract thought into two isolated specialized subjects. While the history of philosophy and intellectual history are widely discussing thinkers or philosophers, things like numerology, rites and music, mantic and medical arts and the history of the classics become "abandoned learning." By separating itself from numerology, rites and music, mantic and medical arts and other knowledge, intellectual history departs farther and farther away from its background. How, then, can it clearly explicate the history of Chinese thought?

2.2

In intellectual history, the gradual accumulation of knowledge can give rise to changes in thought, and changes in thought can then give rise to changes in knowledge. To give one example, when discussing the Mysterious Learning (or Neo-Daoism, *xuanxue* 玄學) of the Wei-Jin period, one can see that there was a rather complex and profound background knowledge behind its superficially mysterious philosophical theories. Precisely because the scholastic tendency of the Eastern Han erudite Confucians (*ru* 儒) led contemporary knowledge to take a path of enormous expansion, the result of this sort of expansion of knowledge was the collapse of the unique monopoly position of the Confucian classics as the only valid knowledge.[21] "Nature and the Way of

---

21   In recent scholarship, *Ru* has been defined by Michael Nylan either as "classicist" or "committed followers of Confucius." For convenience sake, we will, nevertheless, translate *ru*

Heaven" (*xing* 性 and *tiandao* 天道), topics that Confucians had not given much thought to, suddenly opened up a space for the invasion of various kinds of ideas. It was precisely against this background, that the ideas of Laozi and Zhuangzi so naturally became an intellectual resource, and that Mahayana Buddhism's discourse on "emptiness" and the "Buddha nature" came to be studied by so many people.

Another example is the rather significant phenomenon of the revival of Buddhist studies in late Qing thought. Why did it revive? One important reason was that the traditional knowledge used to interpret the cosmos and society suddenly lost its effectiveness, and people were anxious to find intellectual resources that could both bolster their self-confidence by matching Western thought and also effectively interpret the world. Buddhist studies, especially the refined and profoundly abstruse Consciousness Only School, served temporarily as such a new explanatory resource. The result of this revival of Buddhist studies, contrary to expectations, was the introduction of Western learning, and in a sense it led to a sweeping transformation of the intellectual history of the late Qing to the early Republican periods.

The history of knowledge usually changes very slowly. There are, of course, some events that have great influence, but in the final analysis it relies on the gradual accumulation of experience, practical experimentation and production before its influence can be noticed in the public's perception. For this reason, compared to intellectual history with its constant appearance of talented individuals, fluctuations and anomalies are much less common, and you may not observe any particularly exciting event throughout a rather long period of history. Nevertheless, it is just this sort of knowledge background that supports the sudden changes in intellectual history and makes the background of its various ideas understandable. If intellectual history is separated from the history of knowledge, it loses part of its context and some phenomena cannot be reasonably explained.

2.3

What I mean here by "knowledge" is not limited to operational knowledge, like numerology and mantic and medical arts, or written knowledge, like commentaries and notes to the classic texts. It also includes mastery of ceremonial activities, understanding ways of living, transmitting the techniques of production and manufacturing, the categorization of terms used to name things and so on. In an entry on "Intellectual History" in the *International*

---

and *ruzhe* as Confucian scholar or Confucian and *Rujia* as the Confucian School. See Michael Nylan, *The Five "Confucian" Classics*, 2001, 364–365.

Encyclopedia of Social Science, historian Crane Brinton wrote that intellectual history is like a "retrospective sociology of knowledge."[22] I believe this is because the intellectual content of very many ideas about the cosmos, society and human life has been extracted from the content of background knowledge.

Intellectual history can expand its own horizons by tracing the course of development of this concrete background knowledge. This proposition does not require further demonstration and explanation. All that is needed is for intellectual historians to pay a modicum of attention to the historical production of this knowledge, and they will obtain much of heuristic value. From discussions about medical prescriptions (*yifang*), pharmacology, techniques for maintaining life, channels of *qi* or vital energy, acupuncture and moxibustion, they can analyze ancient Chinese concepts of "the human;" from various "formulas" (*shi*), sundials and gambling games like *liubo* 六博, they can explain ancient Chinese concepts of "Heaven" or the sky; from geomancy (*fengshui*), they can understand the ancient Chinese concept of "Earth." If we continue to expand the field, we will discover that some unnoticed materials for the history of knowledge still remain and that they also harbor some very rich contents of ancient Chinese intellectual history.

Knowledge from different eras, different methods of disseminating knowledge and the intellectual interests of different social strata can all bring forth different ideas or serve as background support for different forms of thought. All these different forms of knowledge produce exceptionally rich intellectual worlds. When we take the history of knowledge as the explanatory background for intellectual history, then, we will have to attend to many more historical materials. If we pay attention to the systems of production and dissemination and the levels and channels of development of knowledge, intellectual history will become more lively and authentic.

Let me offer two examples. First, can issues in the history of education become part of our interpretations of intellectual history? What teaching materials were used in ancient private schools? What were the content and grading standards for their examinations? These schools and their examinations might well become the background of intellectual history. Because even the most brilliant thinker grew up absorbing this common general knowledge, such knowledge constituted the most direct background of his thought. If such knowledge is brought within the scope of intellectual history, then the education of the young, the environment of their growing up and their regional culture will all become objects of historical investigation. Second, can issues in

---

22   *International Encyclopedia of Social Science*, 1972, 463.

the history of technology become part of our interpretations of intellectual history? The use of printing technology and paper production methods that people early on paid widespread attention to might well become a crucial background to intellectual history. The earliest wood block printed materials were calendars and Buddhist images, and from this we can imagine and infer the center of gravity and orientation of general knowledge and thought at that time.

It goes without saying that these topics concerning knowledge and thought have also received heuristic inspiration from some chance opportunities. Especially among the archeological discoveries of recent years there have been a rather large quantity of materials relating to numerology and mantic and medical arts. This has created the conditions for a renewed understanding of the relationships between knowledge and thought. Lifting the heavy curtain between the worlds of ancient knowledge and thought has greatly benefited from the clues provided by various discoveries from Yinqueshan, Fangmatan, Shuihudi, Mawangdui and Zhangjiashan. Knowledge and techniques of numerology, and mantic and medical arts actually make up quite a large proportion of the information contained on a large number of bamboo and wooden slips. This has caused us to reconsider what the real picture of the world of ancient Chinese thought was. I believe that once issues in the fields of the history of education, technology, architecture, archival studies and so on become resources for the interpretation of intellectual history, we will have indeed begun to re-write that history.

2.4

These ideas of mine began gradually to take clear shape in the beginning of the 1990s when I re-read Joseph Needham's *History of Scientific Thought* and Alfred Forke's *The World-Conception of the Chinese*.[23] As I read, I began to think that there must be some sort of relationship between the thought that values practical experience, knowledge and techniques and the thought that emphasizes meaning and values. For example, taking the North Pole as an astronomical phenomenon not only grew into the knowledge ancient Chinese used to interpret astronomy, develop calendrical science and calculate calendars, but also, through suggestion and association, was turned into the thought they used to interpret and explain the cosmos. Through imagination and symbolism, it was also transformed into a set of myths that supported their beliefs.

How, though, should intellectual history precisely formulate this relationship and then explain it? In the long process of history, thought may have

---

23   Alfred Forke, *The World Conception of the Chinese*, 1925, 223.

already separated from the knowledge that produced it and become a seemingly self-sufficient system. Will we, then, still be able to discover and recover the mutual relationships between thought and knowledge?

3.   The Foundational Presupposition of Chinese Thought: "Dao" or the "Way of Heaven"

3.1

A now famous silk painting was unearthed in 1970 from the Mawangdui tomb in Changsha, Hunan. On the T-shaped painting there is a depiction of the three connected worlds of heaven above, earth below, and the human realm in between. At the bottom is a strange figure holding up these three worlds with his head and hands. When I saw it, I remembered a passage in R. G. Collingwood's *Autobiography* where he writes about a philosopher who offers a theory of scientific method without offering a theory of historical method. Collingwood writes that this philosopher is "defrauding his public by supporting his world on an elephant and hoping that nobody would ask what kept the elephant up."[24]

To trace any type of culture, knowledge or thought, then, we need to ask this important question: just what is the essential foundation of this culture, knowledge or thought? People give this foundation different names, including "cornerstone," "consensus," and "presupposition." In the historian Oswald Spengler's analysis of various cultures in his *The Decline of the West*, he discovered that the root or foundation of each type of culture is always a concept and symbol of the world that is specific to that culture. This concept and symbol supplies the people of that culture with their foundational understanding of the world and it also sets that culture apart from other cultures. Every form of expression in that culture is determined by that foundation.

The ancient Chinese called this foundation the "Dao" or the "Way of Heaven" (*tiandao*).

3.2

People gradually form their own basic concepts and subjective consciousness throughout their history. What I mean by "form" here is something like continually applying layers of paint until a basic background is formed in the deepest layers of consciousness. This foundation generates a people's own characteristic system of knowledge and thought and is like the roots of a tree

---

24   R. G. Collingwood, *An Autobiography*, 1939, 87.

that support the trunk, the branches and the leaves and provide moisture and nutrition to the tree. This foundation also serves as the background for all this people's knowledge and thought. It actually conditions or supports all of their decision-making and interpretive explanations as well as bestowing rationality on those explanations and decisions.

Since knowledge and thought become continually richer and more complex with the passage of time, eventually their background or foundation is lost to memory. Then, even though the various forms of knowledge and thought grew up out of those roots, as time goes by they come to occupy different spheres, have diverse perspectives and employ divergent lines of reasoning. Just as the *Zhuangzi* has it: "How sad!—the hundred schools going on and on instead of turning back, fated never to join again. The scholars of later ages have unfortunately never perceived the purity of Heaven and Earth, the great body of the ancients, and 'the art of the Way' in time came to be rent and torn apart by the world (*daoshu jiang wei tianxia lie* 道術將爲天下裂)."[25] "To be rent and torn apart by the world", however, really did not mean to separate from the ultimate Way, but only that each school found its own position.

When we reach the Warring States period (475–221 BCE) with its hundred schools of thought contending, there were different Confucian (*Ru*), Mohist (*Mo*) and Daoist (*Dao*) ways of thought, diverse knowledge of various types of numerology and masters of mantic and medical techniques as well as many divergent tactics and strategies concerning the use of law (*fa* 法), special methods (*shu* 術) and power or circumstances (*shi* 勢). Nevertheless, no matter what, the ancient Chinese people were still vaguely aware of the importance of those earlier "foundations." When they wanted to express the authoritative and self-evident nature of their knowledge and thought, they would have to give the reasons for their positions. This so-called "Way" and "Reason or Principle" (*dao* 道 & *li* 理) were no less than that original and ultimate foundation.

Discussing ancient Chinese thought in his *History of Religious Ideas*, Mircea Eliade mentions the concepts of primal chaos (*huntun* 混沌), the Way and the Yin-Yang thought that the various schools of pre-Qin thought used concerning the origin and formation of the world. He writes that belief in the Way must have been a universal idea in ancient China.[26] Indeed, a common system of knowledge did serve as the foundational background of the thought of ancient

---

25 Burton Watson, CT, 364. "Comes" has been changed to "came" to fit this context and earth has been capitalized. ZZJS, 10B, 1069.

26 Mircea Eliade, *A History of Religious Ideas 2*; Chinese translation is from the French version: *Histoire des croyances et des idées religieuses*, II, 1982, 25.

Chinese schools of thought like the Confucian, Mohist, Logician, Daoist, Legalist, Yin-Yang specialists, etc. This self-evident foundation was implicit in every thinker's use of the key term "Dao" without needing any argument to prove its existence. In their book *Thinking Through Confucius*, David L. Hall and Roger T. Ames quite correctly point out that behind Confucius' thought there was an assumption that dominated the Chinese tradition. They believe that the idea of "an immanental cosmos," a "conceptual polarity" and the use of "tradition as interpretive background" were self-evident "presuppositions" in ancient Chinese thought.[27] They say these "presuppositions" render ancient Chinese thought different from Western thought with its habit of employing an external cosmic ontology and dualism and interpreting everything based upon reason. In *The World of Thought in Ancient China*, Benjamin I. Schwartz also wrote that the presuppositions of the various schools of thought in ancient China had three common points: (1) a central concept that kingship dominates everything, (2) a concept of universal order embracing both Man and Heaven, and (3) an holistic concept of immanent order.[28]

They are quite right in what they say, but we still need to ask some further questions: How did these key words in ancient Chinese thought, like the Dao and so on, originate? Why could they be used by different schools of thought? How were the habits of mind or lines of thought like a theory of the cosmos as immanent, a conceptual polarity and the use of history as the background of interpretation established? How did they come to serve as axiomatic "presuppositions" or common self-evident "understandings?" In other words, we need to ask what was it in the mind of the ancient Chinese that led to the acceptance of the inherent reasonableness of these concepts? There are many things that appear to be naturally reasonable, but when we examine them more closely, they turn out not to be inherently correct. It is only that over a long period of time many people have come to accept them. If we get to the bottom of them, though, they too have their historical origins and antecedents.

This is the case with the much mentioned "Way" and "Way of Heaven" in ancient China. There are two important ancient Chinese passages about this Way. One is from the first chapter of the *Laozi*: "The Way (Dao) that can be spoken (*dao*, also means to speak) is not the constant Way." It is ineffable and "cannot be spoken" because, hidden in the deepest layers of thought, it transcends language and form and it influences from afar all types of knowledge. The second is in the *Commentary on the Appended Phrases* (Xici zhuan) section of the *Book of Changes*: "The reciprocal process of Yin and Yang is called the

---

27   David L. Hall and Roger T. Ames, *Thinking Through Confucius*, 1987, 11–25.
28   Benjamin I. Schwartz, *The World of Thought in Ancient China*, 1985, chapter 1.

Way (Dao). . . . It functions for the common folk on a daily basis, yet they are unaware of it." Why are they "unaware of it?" Because they have been accustomed to it for too long.[29]

The two things that the people of ancient China were most aware of, ideas that dominated everything in their lives and that later Chinese most easily became accustomed to and never departed from, were probably Heaven and Earth, the markers of space and time.

3.3

I want to repeat an ancient Chinese saying: "Heaven is constant and unchanging, and the Dao is also constant and unchanging" (*Tian bu bian, Dao ye bubian* 天不變, 道亦不變)."[30]

This Dao (Way) has very ancient origins, and is certainly related to Heaven. At the beginning of this book, I discuss the heuristic significance for Chinese intellectual history of archeological discoveries such as the jade tubes (*yucong* 玉琮) from Liangzhu (near Hangzhou, Zhejiang), the dragon and tiger cosmograms (*longhu tu*) from Puyang (Henan) and the jade blocks (*yuban*) from Lingjiatan (Anhui). I hope to offer the following speculation: it is very possible that the controlling concepts behind much knowledge and many ideas in the world of ancient Chinese thought were derived from and established on the basis of originally groundbreaking astronomical and geographical observations like "Heaven is round and the Earth is square," the "transformations of Yin and Yang," and "the earth has five directions (including the center)."

The earliest ancient Chinese knowledge and culture was controlled by shamans (*wuxi* 巫覡) whose profession was related to astronomy and topography. From astronomy and topography, a framework of space and time was formed in people's minds, and this framework was used to explain and interpret all the phenomena in the universe. The images of ancient Chinese ideas, like Heaven is round and the Earth square, the apparent leftward movement of the heavenly path (*tiandao*), the center and four cardinal directions, the changes of Yin and Yang and the passage of the four seasons, were transformed through suggestive symbols and ceremonial sacralization until, reasoning by analogy, they became the starting point for an increasing amount of accepted knowledge and thought. Eternal and unchanging "Heaven" became the background for an eternal and unchanging "Dao," and that eternal and unchanging Dao supported very many principles (*li*) that upheld the reasonableness or rationality

---

29   *Laozi* or *Dao De Jing*, chapter 1 in any edition. *Yijing* translation is from *The Classic of Changes*, translated by Richard John 1994, 53. Original of *Yijing* is in SSJZS, 78.

30   HS, "Dong Zhongshu zhuan."

of many different arts or techniques (*shu*). In people's minds, the Dao was the Way *and* Heaven *and* Unity (*yi* 一 The One), and it could even be the god or spiritual being (*shen* 神) known as the "Great Unity" (*taiyi* 太一). According to documents from the third century BCE, Taiyi gave birth to water, water in turn assisted Taiyi to give form to Heaven, and Heaven and Taiyi then worked together to give form to Earth.[31] In the world of ancient Chinese life, this Heaven, however, became the Dao and gave form to the "order" (*zhixu*) of knowledge and thought.

Over a long period of history, by means of ceremonies, signs and symbols this Dao gave form to an entire conceptual system. On the basis of analogical reasoning and inferential imaginativeness, this system permeated all forms of knowledge and thought, including the following: (1) places like the Hall of Brightness (*mingtang* 明堂) and the Circular Mound Alter (*huanqiu* 圜丘) and ceremonies like the imperial Fengshan sacrifices (*fengshan* 封禪) and the suburban sacrifices to Heaven, Earth, Sun and Moon (*jiaoji* 郊祭); (2) imitation of astronomical phenomena to give the imperial palaces and the imperial cities a spatial order based on that of the heavens; (3) explanation of the physiology of the human body by correspondence to the four seasons, twelve months and three hundred and sixty days.[32]

It may perhaps be hard to imagine today the extreme importance the Way of Heaven had for ancient China. Due to the regular repetition of these ceremonies, symbols and signs, people were reminded of their feelings, concepts and practical experience of Heaven until, in a certain sense, Heaven came to constitute the foundation of all truth—the most secret and irresistible background of all knowledge.[33]

---

31   "Taiyi sheng shui shiwen," in *Bamboo Manuscripts from the Guodian Chu Tombs* (Guodian Chumu zhujian), 1998, 125.

32   See Ge Zhaoguang, "Zhongmiao zhi men—Beiji, Taiyi, Dao, Taiji," *Zhongguo wenhua* 3 (1990), 46–65.

33   Certainly "man or human being" (*ren* 人) was also one of the important foundations of the world of ancient Chinese knowledge and thought. A great deal of knowledge and thought received support for its reasonableness from human nature, human emotions and human existence, especially in Confucian theory. In ancient China, however, before the Tang and Song (618–907 & 960–1127) dynasties to be precise, "man" did not really completely serve as the ultimate foundation for the rationality of knowledge and thought. "Man" remained under "Heaven." At most, "man" was only the foundation of social order, but not yet the absolute presupposition for all knowledge, thought and belief in the cosmos. The real change in the order of importance between "Heaven" and "Man" probably took place with the appearance of Song dynasty Neo-Confucian School of Principle (*lixue* 理學). At that time, people were concerned more with the spirit of the humanities, human affairs and the social order.

In the world of ancient Chinese knowledge, thought and belief, the idea that "Heaven is constant and unchanging, and the Dao is also constant and unchanging" acted as a naturally rational order and standard. It supplied the underpinning for almost everything, including astronomy and calendar-making, interpretation and explanation of natural phenomena, people's experience of and treatment for human physiology and psychology, the creation of kingly or imperial power and hierarchical societies, legitimation of political ideologies, symbolic meaning of sacrificial and ceremonial procedures, the style and basic patterns of cities, royal palaces and the dwellings of ordinary people; it further supported the rules of popular games and the appreciation and explanation of aesthetic beauty in art and literature.[34]

The so-called theory of "the Unity of Heaven and the Human" (*tianren heyi* 天人合一) really means that the entire rationality of Heaven (the cosmos) and the Human realm is basically built upon the same foundation, and this foundation is, in reality, the supporting background of all ancient Chinese knowledge and thought. When a system of culture, knowledge and thought is established on the basis of such a background foundation, for a certain period of time it will present the appearance of absolute stability and express its uniqueness as a civilization among different civilizations. This is because knowledge and thought in a civilization during a certain period of time always require, and in fact possess, a unified order. But once this basic foundation is shaken and this order is disturbed, and the culture's knowledge and thought loses its effective capacity to explain the world, that civilization will face a crisis.

There was at first no real resistance in the Ming (1368–1644) and Qing (1636–1911) dynasties when Western missionaries brought in their new knowledge of astronomy, calendrical science and geography. This was because such knowledge was regarded as being merely a "tool" for practical use on technological problems. When this new knowledge shook and then basically even destroyed the ancient Chinese Dao, however, this led to a great intellectual upheaval and transformation. That is why a few sensitive or stubborn scholar officials finally began passionately to resist Western astronomical studies. The chapter in this book that discusses the Christian missionary dissemination of Western astronomy and geography in the Ming and Qing is entitled "Heaven Crumbles and Earth Splits Asunder" (*tianbeng dilie* 天崩地裂) . I believe that

---

34   For example, the spatial arrangement of palaces of the ancient Son of Heaven and the sacrificial ceremonies, games of chance like *liubo* and *weiqi* (better known today as *go*). See, Lao Gan, "Liubo ji boju de yanbian," *Lishi yuyan yanjiu jikan* 35 (1964), 15–30, especially 25. See also Li Ling, *Zhongguo fangshu kao*, 1993.

only this phrase can express the deep anxiety felt by those scholar officials at that time as well as the shock of this attack on the Dao that was brought on by a transformation of Heaven.

3.4

As mentioned above, knowledge and thought are closely related. After the ultimate foundational Dao of thought and knowledge was established, its existence generally went unnoticed—"it function[ed] for the common folk on a daily basis, yet they [were] unaware of it." It served as the self-evident background that supported the rationality or reasonableness of various kinds of knowledge and thought. History is constantly changing, however, and when that knowledge and thought together with their background support is violently altered or destroyed, the old knowledge and thought is like a boat set adrift from its moorings. It is quickly sunk by the new knowledge and thought, and then to preserve themselves people search for a new foundation to anchor their knowledge and thought. After this transformation has passed, though, time again erects a memory block, and the former foundation of thought they earlier possessed and relied upon becomes unfamiliar to later generations. This is why intellectual history needs "archeology" to search for the roots of thought and to understand how ancient people so confidently constructed their world of knowledge, thought and belief upon that former foundation.

The ancient Chinese spoke of "laws of Heaven and principles of Earth" (*tianjing diyi* 天經地義), and this perfectly describes the absolute and ultimate foundation of knowledge and thought at that time. It is not that no one was ever really aware of it. Occasionally someone would ask: why does it not need to be verified? Or what special privilege does it have to receive immunity from the questioning of intellectual history? The *Classified Dialogues of Master Zhu* (Zhuzi yulei) is an extraordinary and interesting book. Zhu Xi discussed matters related to the workings of Heaven, Earth and the cosmos many times with his students. The burden of much of what he said was to inform his students that many of what they considered to be minor principles were dependent upon that Great Principle (*da daoli*) revealed at the primal beginning of Heaven and Earth. He said: "The Supreme Ultimate (*taiji* 太極) is simply the Principle of Heaven and Earth and the myriad things; speaking of Heaven and Earth, the Supreme Ultimate is within Heaven and Earth; speaking of the myriad things, the Supreme Ultimate is in every one of the myriad things. Before the existence of Heaven and Earth, this Principle already existed."[35] Later, the editors of the *Classified Dialogues of Master Zhu* put this passage at the begin-

---

35   *Zhuzi yulei*, j. 1, 1.

ning of the text because they considered these ideas as the basic foundation of all rational principles. In the same fashion, the various *leishu* encyclopedias from the Sui-Tang era on that were intended to contain and present all of the existent knowledge and thought titled their first volumes "Heaven and Earth." Behind this practice most probably lies the unconscious mind set of the ancient Chinese people.

4.   The Continuity of Intellectual History Emerges

4.1

The writing of intellectual history seems to produce "guided tour books." If we say that the course of intellectual history is genuine "intellectual history," then we should label with italics as *intellectual history* only those works that describe just this development of ideas in history.[36] Once this intellectual history has been filtered through later people's imaginations, understanding and interpretations, recorded and written up as *intellectual histories*, then these books have already become "guided tour books of a constructed course of thought." Because the actual course of thought has already gone by, the authors of *intellectual histories* are only guiding their readers on the basis of the path that they themselves understand. Just like present day tour guides, they take away our freedom and replace it with their own conception of the course of thought in order to guide us on our tour through Chinese thought.

It is nearly impossible for descriptions of history to avoid the "brilliance of hindsight" in any of three possible forms used to write intellectual histories.

The first is the "establish-the-fact" form. On the surface, the writers of these long compilations of resource materials are trying to restore the original state of intellectual history according to the historical documents. They tell us, for example, who wrote what, who came up with what ideas, when these works and these ideas were produced and so on. They bring together the most accurate historical materials in chronological order, making it possible for readers to stroll through a museum or exhibition room where they seem able to experience personally the trajectory of thought. What exhibits are in this museum and how they are displayed is, however, an expression of the museum keeper's own ideas. It is just that those ideas are hidden behind a seemingly objective presentation.

36   We italicize *intellectual history* when the author uses the standard Chinese punctuation [《》] for book titles; he means it to indicate published Chinese intellectual histories.—trs.

Second is the "value-assessment" form. In this form, besides narrating the facts, the writer is even more concerned with an evaluation of intellectual history. What is good, what is bad, what advanced human intelligence, what was an impediment to the advancement of human intelligence and so on. In this mode of writing, the author's intentions, likes and dislikes are openly expressed, and, written this way, history is viewed as an "upside down" map. For the readers, such a map leaves them with no other choice but to "follow along reading" history as a guide book.

The third and final form I'll discuss is the "trace-a-journey" form. Some idealistic intellectual historians are confident that they can reconstruct the context of ancient intellectual history. They try as much as possible to gain an empathetic understanding of the feelings of the ancients and to understand the contexts and patterns of their thought. They narrate the trajectory of thought according to the passage of time. They view intellectual history by "following along" and attempting to travel its path.

I must admit that I hope to write this third type of intellectual history, but I also confess that this still does not actually amount to an escape from authorial subjectivity.

4.2

Intellectual history is, then, different from intellectual history. *Intellectual history* has continuity, unity and consistent contextualization. As soon as *intellectual history* contextualizes the history of ideas, then it has already altered the original nature of intellectual history. Thought and ideas that actually existed in history, did not have any particular arrangement or prior design in their own time; although they all had their own backgrounds, there was no sequential order. Intellectual historians cannot, however, allow intellectual history to remain in this "primary condition" because they would then be unable to serve it up as a completely prepared dish. What historiography can least tolerate is for history to remain chaotic and without order.

Continuity, unity and consistent contextualization are what intellectual historians traditionally look for. In recent years, however, new theories have emphasized that history should not be continuously progressive, characterized by ever increasing rationality and full of "regularity" or "continuity." On the contrary, "chance" and "rupture" continually intervene, and, therefore, historians ought to pay attention to the "non-sequential" or "disconnected" in history.

At first glance, this theoretical position seems to call into question the very foundations of historiography. Just think, if historiography no longer searches for continuities and order, but only regards history as a series of scattered and fragmented episodes, then historians would be reduced to mere collators of documents. What scope would be left for the display of historiographical skill? I do not think that the new theories are actually intended to remove context and rationality from history. Rather they are opposed to the excessive subjective intervention of historians. This excessive subjective intervention lends to history a consistently contextualized narrative form and makes people accustomed to tracing genealogies. It also projects teleology into history and misleads readers into accepting history-book history as the genuine original face of history. Therefore, the practitioners of new historical theory hope to avoid any accommodation to excessive "continuity" and "contextualization" in history. By doing so, they hope to sort out anew the historical documents and material objects, especially those that have been ignored in the past, and to reconstruct a history that is closer to the true historical situation as it emerges from those documents and material objects.

In light of this, the following two metaphors are both reasonable. The first metaphor is that history is a mirror shattered into thousands of pieces, and every little piece shines a part of the sky into the face of anyone who picks it up. No one can possibly unify this sky shining out from the thousands of broken pieces of mirror. The second metaphor is that the historian's responsibility is to put these shattered pieces back together to make a new mirror—to "imagine," generation by generation, what past history was like; to restore, at its points of rupture, the continuity of history from the evidence in fragmentary and sporadic archives and other records and silent relics, and to fill in history in its otherwise blank spaces. From the reality faced by historians, they cannot help admitting the truth of the first metaphor, but in terms of the significance of their quest, historians cannot avoid choosing to work in the manner of the second metaphor. How are we to handle these two metaphors? I think that intellectual historians can only try as much as possible to understand, speculate and imagine history based on a wide range of documents, historical relics, pictures and writings. In this way they can reconstruct the continuity of *intellectual history*.

Of course we could employ several different methods and styles to reconstruct the continuity of *intellectual history*. We could use the dialectic "law of the negation of the negation" from Marxist theory. Against the background of evolutionary theory, we could regard all changes from one era to the next as a criticism and rejection past thought. We could also follow Benjamin Schwartz's reasoning that "[intellectual history involves] men's conscious responses to their situations" and place our emphasis on the analysis of extrinsic social, political, economic and life circumstances. We could also use Qian Mu (1895–1990)'s idea of "advancing with every (historical) turn" (*meizhuan yijin* 每轉益進) or Yu Yingshi's theory of "inner logic" (*neizai lilu* 內在理路) emphasizing internal changes in knowledge, thought and belief.[37] No matter which method we choose, they can all review the course of intellectual history and reconstruct the continuity of *intellectual history*.

4.3

I want to point out here that when various past *intellectual histories* presented the continuity of thought, it was quite important how they arranged their division into chapters and sections (*zhangjie* 章節). Just as I mentioned above, the habitual method of writing *intellectual history* was according to chronological order, arranging thinkers into chapters and sections—an entire chapter (*zhang*) for major thinkers, a full section (*jie*) for important lesser thinkers, lumping several not so important thinkers into a single section and allowing many of the least important people only a single paragraph (*duan* 段). Linking all of these thinkers together in chronological order was then intellectual history, and the great majority of *intellectual histories*, especially college textbooks, were written this way. This way of writing was influenced both by the old textual tradition of writing history and the modern consideration of history as an academic discipline.

The traditional scholarly cases genre is said to be the embryonic form of today's intellectual history. It employed the "biographical sketch" and the "selected works" method to write the history of thought or scholarship. Today's histories of philosophy and intellectual histories, under the influence of Western and Japanese models, also employ this method—taking a single thinker's "life / background / thought / impact to construct sections and then combining several chronologically sequential sections to construct chapters— as their basic narrative framework.

There is no doubt that this style of writing can do many things. It can arrange the divisions of intellectual history on the basis of individuals or their works; it can work out rather clearly the essentials of each section and chapter; it can briefly summarize all the commonly accepted knowledge in intellectual history; and it can provide readers and students with the materials needed for memorization and recitation. Nevertheless, once the original process of intel-

---

37   Benjamin Schwartz, "The Intellectual History of China: Preliminary Reflections," in John K. Fairbank, ed., *Chinese Thought and Institutions*, 1957, 16 & 17. The Qian Mu quote is in his *Qing ruxue an xu*, in *Zhongguo xueshu sixiangshi luncong*, vol. 8, 1980, 366; for "inner logic," see Yu Yingshi, "Qingdai sixiangshi de yige xin jieshi," in his *Lishi yu sixiang*, 1976, 124–125.

lectual history is written up as this sort of *intellectual history* arranged on the basis of several sections and chapters, then the earlier "intellectual history" is submerged and replaced by the later *intellectual history*. The real process of "intellectual history" disappears in these divisions into periods and the continuity constructed later is privileged by these divisions. In this way, intellectual historians slice Chinese thought up into pieces, package it and then display their wares for readers to purchase and consume.

This is the textbook model. From the beginning of the twentieth century on, the dissemination of knowledge in the Chinese humanities has been steadily transformed from the traditional format to that of modern academic subjects. The style of humanities writing learned from the West and Japan has a very strong textbook flavor. To this day, when scholars think about writing history, they most easily think of this trick of the history-writing trade.

I originally wanted to write a set of lectures on Chinese intellectual history, and as a teacher I was well aware of the positive significance of this sort of textbook—generation after generation of students first enter the world of intellectual history by means of such textbooks. As a research scholar, however, I was becoming increasingly cognizant of the negative influences of such textbooks. For convenience in teaching, memorization and testing, they simply reduce intellectual history to the status of biographical dictionaries and crib sheets for the essentials of the great works. It is especially bad when these textbooks employ a particular political ideology, are written in a seemingly authoritative language, presented in an inflexibly periodized manner and turn their historical narratives into official documents. Then they will cultivate a large number of people who box themselves in with textbook knowledge. That so many mediocre essays are produced in China's present day academia is very likely a symptom brought about by such textbooks.[38]

With this mode of writing you can only write one kind of intellectual history, or you can only write many completely identical *intellectual histories*.

---

38   Once, before beginning an elective course in the history of the Jin through Tang dynasties, Professor Chen Yinque introduced some reference books to his students. He made many critical remarks about those textbooks that "were plagiarized through many hands and whose scope of topics was also very limited;" he only praised Xia Zengyou's *Zhongxue lishi jiaokeshu*. He did not give many reasons, but only said that "the author comments on history from the point of view of the Gongyang New Text scholars and expresses unique views." Today such "unique opinions" would, I'm afraid, not meet the approval of the reviewers and would not be qualified to be in a textbook, especially not a middle school history textbook. See *Chen Yinque xiansheng biannian shiji*, revised and enlarged edition, 1997, 94.

So long as you stick to this textbook model, you can only write that way because it is practical, reasonable and it has official legitimacy.

While I was writing this book, I taught intellectual history for two academic years at Tsinghua University. As soon as I started, I wanted to break through this textbook lecture framework by not lecturing according to "individual thinkers" and "works" and the background, life and thought model, but rather explain intellectual history in accordance with its continuous context. But as I lectured I began to realize the difficulties involved in this lecture model. Not only was it extremely hard work for me as the instructor, but it was also very difficult for the students to understand. This was because by explaining the continuity of intellectual history according to my understanding of its continuous context, I was not giving them a clear framework and even less was I giving them chapter divisions that were easy to memorize and repeat. Some students even criticized me for this, and for a while I nearly decided to abandon this difficult yet thankless method of teaching. If I abandoned my method it would mean that I would also be giving up my pursuit of a continuous line of reasoning in intellectual history.

After thinking about it for some time, I still decided to stick to my new method of lecturing and writing. I abandoned the textbook model. I believe that there is perhaps only one form of continuity of intellectual history as it actually developed, but when later people come to write *intellectual histories* on the basis of their understanding and vision, this continuity may take many forms. As long as the writing of intellectual history makes room for individual reflection and the pursuit of alternative ways of writing, then newly written *intellectual histories* should not be completely without significance. Perhaps intellectual historians will actually come up with a new form demonstrating a continuous line of reasoning in intellectual history.

There are several reasons to search for the continuity of intellectual history. First, what needs to be organized and discussed in what I understand as intellectual history does not only include elite thought and the ideas of the classic texts. Also included is the history of the world of general knowledge, thought and belief. There is no way to deal with this world by dividing "individual thinkers" and "texts" or any particular short time period into chapter divisions. Second, the elite thought that I want to discuss in my intellectual history is also not limited to either the genius or the sudden enlightenment of elite thinkers. In the background both before and after their thought and in the spirit of the age, Chinese thought generally followed a line of cause and effect. Thoughts and ideas and thoughts and knowledge mutually intersected and combined just as thought and politics also mutually influenced each other. Those thinkers simply articulated and recorded these ideas, providing a marker for them or giving them a name. But intellectual history is not merely a matter of providing a rank order evaluation of their accomplishments because intellectual history is not a simple "roll call of the deceased." Third, the ideas of the classic texts that I want to discuss in my intellectual history are also not limited to single-volume works with named authors and an official imprimatur. Various forms of thought tend to intersect in ancient classical texts, and this was especially true in ancient China. Ancient Chinese texts were repeatedly quoted, excerpted, rearranged and reassembled; later people's new exegeses were then incorporated into the earlier original texts, and hand copied texts even incorporated new and later vocabulary. All of these things were common occurrences, and so the former intellectual history writing style that insisted on assigning "rights of origination" to certain ideas on the basis of the authors of certain texts and on arranging these authors in chronologically ordered chapter divisions customarily attributed to a single person ideas that were built up through a long process of accumulation.

When Sima Qian wrote his *Records of the Grand Historian*, he deliberately "cross-referenced" his various biographies by discussing the same events in different places, and after Sima Guang (1019–1086) composed his annalistic *Comprehensive Mirror to Aid in Government* (Zizhi tongjian), someone still had to invent the topically arranged history style (*jishi benmo ti*) to make up for its deficiencies. In essence these styles were all developed to avoid the rupture that was created by writing history using the biographies of individual persons or the annals of individual years. Should contemporary writers of intellectual history not give serious thought to the fact that the continuity of intellectual history is a lengthy process that cannot be captured in the thought of one thinker or in a single text? This is especially the case with ideas from the world of general knowledge, thought and belief that require a very long duration of time before their changes become apparent. How can they be properly represented in those intellectual histories arranged on the basis of individual persons or texts?

4.4

How, then, can continuity be embodied in *intellectual history*? Besides the continuous and uninterrupted general knowledge, thought and belief developed over a "*longue duré*" that can serve as the foundation of continuity in *intellectual history*, the continuous lines of thought of the elites and the classic texts are also capable of precise representation. Let me use some examples to explain three types of continuity in *intellectual history*.

One type of continuity of *intellectual history* emerges out of the continuous interpretation of traditional intellectual topics.[39] For example, Confucius once told his disciples "You do not understand life. How can you understand death" and "You do not know how to serve the living. How can you serve the dead (or the spirits)?" His students are also reputed to have said of him that "we have been unable to hear the Master discuss the Way of Heaven together with Man's nature."[40] These brief passages express both Confucius' rejection of such unknown things as ghosts and spirits, the Way of Heaven in relation to human nature and his affirmation of the real world of family, lineage and society. Later on, however, these passages came to be understood as deliberate coded messages that Confucius left behind to posterity.

By the age of Mencius (ca. 372–289 BCE or 385–303/302 BCE) and Xunzi (ca. 312–230 BCE), they already gave explanations of the Way of Heaven and human nature that went well beyond what Confucius is recorded to have said. By the third century CE, individuals who wanted to change the direction of thought also made use of this lacuna in Confucian thought to bring the Daoist ideas of Laozi and Zhuangzi in as new resources and open up new roads for the expansion of thought. Xun Can (209?–238?) quoted these passages and sought to marginalize Confucian thought about society and ethics. He Yan (?–249)'s comment on the "human nature and Way of Heaven" passage in his *Collected Commentaries on the Lunyu* (Lunyu jijie) places them at the center of thought. Wang Bi (226–249) went even so far as to find support for Daoist thought in the Confucian classics; in his comments on the *Book of Changes*, he found materials for the elaboration of Daoist thought.

In the same manner in the fourth century CE when Buddhism entered China, the Buddhists even more extensively employed explications of these passages for their own ends. *Master Mou's Treatise on the Removal of Doubt* (Mouzi lihuo lun) tactfully explained that Confucius had the ability to discuss the world of life after death, but he just did not want to discuss it with his disciple Zilu.[41] This ploy gave Buddhism room to lecture on the three worlds of the past, present and future (Buddhas, or the unborn, the born, and the dead) as well as ghosts and spirits (*guishen*). In his fifth-century *Essays Explaining Buddhism* (Ming Fo lun) discussion of the limitations of Confucianism, Huiyuan's disciple Zong Bing (375–443) brought up these passages and filled

---

39   Arthur O. Lovejoy, *The Great Chain of Being: A Study of the History of an Idea*, 1964 [1933]. Also see Li Hongqi, "Shilun sixiangshi de lishi yanjiu," in *Zhongguo sixiangshi fangfa lunwen xuanji*, 1981, 252.

40   From *Lunyu*, "Xianjin," 11.11 & "Gong Ye Chang," 5.12.

41   *Hongming ji*, SBBY, j. 1, 9. For a sample Mouzi's text, see Theodore De Bary and Irene Bloom, eds., *Sources of the Chinese Tradition*, 2nd Edition, vol. 1, 1999, 421–426.

this gap in Confucian thought with a Buddhist emphasis on life after death, karmic retribution (*yinguo baoying*), human nature and Buddha nature.[42]

A second type of continuity of *intellectual history* is manifest precisely in those areas of seeming rupture such as, for example, the origins of Confucian thought. In the past the origins of Confucian thought were sought by looking for ideas about certain terms, such as "Heaven," "Humanity" (*ren* 仁, sometimes translated "benevolence"), "virtue" or "power" (*de* 德) and so on. This then became a form of retroactive affirmation: first confirming that these ideas and terms are Confucian, then searching for their beginnings and finally sorting out their ancestral origins. The ancient customs of daily life, sacrifices and ceremonies were rarely, however, mined to see if they might have given rise to some of these concepts. For example, could the order and sequence of ancient ceremonies have led to ideas regarding rites and music, love of humanity (*ren-ai* 仁愛) or social position and status (*mingfen* 名份)? Can the search for the origins of Confucianism derive heuristic support from Confucian sartorial regulations concerning clothing styles and colors or from the Confucian emphasis on symbolic meanings? After thought has become pure thought, its knowledge content is soon stripped away and becomes pure knowledge. Then a curtain is drawn between thought and knowledge and rupture takes the place of continuity.

In the same fashion, the formation of the Daoist religion or religious Daoism (*daojiao*) was related to the stripping away of its "shamanistic traditions." During its formative period, the early Daojiao's quasi-military organization, rather arduous secret ceremonies, complex and chaotic genealogy of worship, various religious practices that violated mainstream ancient Chinese norms and so on were all discarded like the molting of a snake. After the formation of Daojiao, those shamanistic practices receded and Daojiao became a "religion" (*zongjiao*) and also entered the intellectual hierarchy. A "rupture" would seem to have been created here between the original and the later Daojiao, but this rupture is in reality an even deeper continuity.

The third type of continuity in *intellectual history* occurred when Chinese thought came under attack by knowledge and thought from abroad. In order to deal with changing conditions, the Chinese, being accustomed to relying on knowledge from their own history, regularly looked for pre-existing knowledge and intellectual resources to supply new understandings and new interpretations of new knowledge and new ideas. Through these understandings and interpretations, foreign knowledge and thought was incorporated into the

---

42   *Hongming ji*, SBBY, j. 2, 23.

Chinese tradition and in turn changed that tradition so that, through such seeming transformations, knowledge and thought was actually continuing.

This was the situation when Buddhism entered China. As Chen Yinque (or Yinke, 1890–1969) pointed out, the ancient Chinese employed resources from their own knowledge and thought to make various new interpretations of Buddhism; this was known as using the methods of *geyi* 格義, "matching the meaning" and *heben zizhu* 合本子注, "explanation through collating and comparing texts."[43] This served to bring Buddhism into the world of Chinese thought while at the same time incorporating Chinese thought into Buddhism. Likewise, during the great changes in the Late Qing, the reason there was a revival of Buddhist studies at that time was also because modern Chinese needed to use traditional resources to understand the new Western knowledge and thought. New Western ideas like germs, celestial bodies, logic and psychology could be explained by means of Buddhist learning. Therefore Buddhist studies flourished anew in the Late Qing and changed the Chinese understanding of Western learning (*xixue*) while at the same time changing their understanding of Buddhism.[44]

Intellectual history simply continues in this way. Reactions to reality revive historical memory, and historical memory in turn awakens long sleeping knowledge and intellectual resources, and these resources become source materials for understanding and interpreting new knowledge and thought. Under these conditions, history connects traditional resources together with newly arrived resources and in the course of time the two fuse into one continuous intellectual history.

4.5

As I wrote this *Intellectual History of China*, I searched for the consistent contextualization of intellectual history according to my own understanding. I do not arrange the book on the basis of individual thinkers; my narrative time frame is rather broad and I hope to describe the process of intellectual history over a comparatively long time span. On this account I may, perhaps, omit some intellectual phenomena formerly regarded as important while at the same time giving excessive space to phenomena once considered of lesser significance. I may not be concerned with some thinker's life, works, and historical status, but may discuss at greater length intellectual history that does not completely belong to any individual thinker. For example, I discuss topics like

---

43   Chen Yinque, "Zhi Mindu xueshuo kao," *Chen Yinque xiansheng lunwen ji, xia*, 1977, 1229–1254.

44   See Ge Zhaoguang, "Lun wan Qing foxue fuxing," *Xueren* 10 (1996), 89–120.

how the symbolic significance of ancient ceremonies gave rise to systematic thinking, how the cultural level of the knowledge and thought behind mantic and medical arts was raised and broke into the classical text tradition, how the coming of Buddhism stimulated and changed Chinese ideas about the "four barbarians" (*siyi*, Eastern Yi, Western Rong, Southern Man, Northern Di), how the seemingly shamanistic knowledge and arts and the quasi-militaristic religious organization of early Daoist Religion were transformed under political power pressure and became part of the mainstream tradition . . . In my understanding, these things are more important because intellectual history is not just a rank order list of ancient people or a chronological chart of ideas. What readers really need are not only those easily memorizable lists of names and chronologies or information to be used only for writing examinations. What they need is answers to the following sorts of questions: How was the knowledge, thought and belief of modern China actually passed down from ancient China? What sort of train of reasoning was responsible for the continuation of the knowledge, thought and belief of ancient China? What resources exist in the continuous reasoning of ancient Chinese knowledge, thought and belief that can be re-interpreted by contemporary thought?

Chinese academic circles have discussed many different topics since the 1980s, and "to re-write" was an important one of them—how to re-write literary history, cultural history, history of philosophy, and of course, intellectual history. Re-writing is a very serious undertaking. After a certain period of time has passed, history always looks back to consider the road it has traveled. Continually understanding and interpreting anew is the process by which knowledge and thought are renewed, and the course of this process constitutes intellectual history. I, too, have been reflecting anew on intellectual history, but I'm not saying that this history of mine is necessarily a completely accurate description of the true course of Chinese thought. On the contrary, I want to state clearly that my *Intellectual History* represents only my own personal understanding, and I am only offering one way of understanding intellectual history.

5.   Historical Memory, Intellectual Resources and Reinterpretation

In past historical research, especially research on intellectual history, there are a number of frequently used terms. One of these terms used in discussing the continuity of intellectual history is "influence." The impression that this term "influence" gives one is that if a particular form of thought once flourished, then it would have always influenced later ages. The habitual use of this term indicates that intellectual historians value "dissemination" but overlook "reception." For this reason, in discussing the "influence" of the forerunners, they generally overlook the "selection" and "interpretation" of the successors.

I am not denying the importance of "influence," but whether or not "influence" is able to reappear and become a new intellectual resource is directly related to the situation of the recipients. The contemporary life situation of the recipients acts as a kind of accelerant. It can awaken some historical memory and certainly it can also repress some; through this awakening and repressing, and through the process of selective historical memory, the world of ancient Chinese knowledge, thought and belief becomes a resource for new knowledge and thought. Through this process of excavation and interpretation, the world of knowledge, thought and belief is both transmitted and transformed. In light of this process, intellectual history may be understood as follows: pre-existing intellectual resources are continuously awakened by historical memory; they are then given new interpretations under new life conditions, and as these new interpretations are being arrived at, they reproduce a similar process.

I employ this process involving historical memory, intellectual resources and re-interpretation partially to replace "influence" as my terminology for describing continuity in intellectual history.

5.1

In the absence of any impetus from a foreign civilization, people usually can only rely on their historical memory to reinterpret their classical past in response to generational changes. For this reason, "using restoration to seek renewal" is very commonly seen. Even when under attack from foreign knowledge, thought and belief, however, traditional intellectual resources do not just disappear. Rather, they serve the functions of making analogies and translations to facilitate comprehension of incoming ideas. Traditional knowledge, thought and belief undergo transformation through this process of analogy, translation and comprehension, and, at the same time *mutatis mutandis* the foreign knowledge, thought and belief are also transformed. This is the way intellectual history proceeds. Which intellectual resources are awakened and which are repressed is, of course, mainly due to whether or not the selection made in the actual background context required the support of history and tradition. This is also determined by the concrete situation. In China, due to the Chinese propensity to rely on history for support, new changes often appear in the guise of old history. The Chinese employ old terminology to explicate new knowledge, pouring new wine into old bottles. They seem to be forever performing in an age old drama entitled "restoration." In reality, though, their "historical memory" is just leading China's intellectual world to the expression of hitherto unknown orientations and attitudes through its connection to new intellectual resources.

In general, historical memory exhibits two different types of orientation.

The first orientation is the "tracing-the-origins" (*huisu benyuan* 回溯本原) type—looking backward to create a cultural identity, confirming that one belongs to an ethnic culture with a long and powerful history having traditional resources that are fully capable of adequately responding to changes. Feeling oneself a part of this cultural tradition and ethnic memory, one can rely on it to achieve the self-confidence and cohesiveness one needs. This type of historical memory is generally labeled "searching for one's roots"—by gathering all of the innumerable scattered branches of one's culture together into one commonly shared root (origin), one not only obtains a foundation for mutual recognition but also finds a source of great strength.

In the process of "looking back to one's origins," people are not necessarily accurately tracing back the path their culture has actually traveled, looking for their ancestors and genuinely returning to their origins and recuperating their beginnings. Sometimes when people are consciously or unconsciously rummaging through their "historical memory," it has already experienced many deletions, alterations and changes of appearance. Sometimes they will deliberately knock on the wrong door and mistakenly claim the wrong family as their forebears. It is the same with intellectual history. Writing a genealogy to praise glorious ancestors and affirming an intellectual line of descent are two methods that are always fraught with problems. Many ideas and scholarly views in history can borrow from each other and be mutually interchangeable, especially if they involve everyday "common sense." The difference between them is not really as great as might be assumed, and so they may easily serve as "resources" for each other. Tracing one's historical roots, then, is not necessarily accurate. Nevertheless, this type of not altogether accurate searching for historical roots is still a very common method of uncovering intellectual resources.

The other type of orientation of historical memory is the "root-and-branch-destruction" (*zhancao chugen* 斬草除根) method. When faced with a new culture and new thoughts, people dredge up their historical memory to engage in introspective soul-searching about the origins of their traditions. Then they cut off those roots of their culture that they believe are dragging them down. In reality, this is also a form of continuity in intellectual history. It is just that in this type of remembering and interpreting, people take an attitude opposite to the "looking-back-to-origins" orientation. Although they are working hard to remember their history, they regard this history as a process of continual change; they do their best to weaken the constraints of that history, transcend the boundaries of traditional culture and join up with the new knowledge and experience. In this instance, they search for their roots in order to "eradicate" them more thoroughly. Just as was the case with the constant occurrences of "revolutions" from the May Fourth era (1915–1937) to the period of Cultural Revolution (1966–1976), this historical memory was expressed through constant criticism and resolute rejection of past traditions.

This process was especially obvious in the Late Qing. Faced with the violent tsunami of Western knowledge, people were shocked and at a loss as to what to do. Once they were forced by the West's military power to accept the new universal value that "wealth" and "power" are the only measures of civilization, they began to use the West as their frame of reference. Comparing the differences, the gap, between the East and the West, they began to ponder the origins of that gap. At that point, historical memory was called upon, and in the face of criticism and interrogation, the period from the Late Qing to the May Fourth era was seemingly the beginning of a radical critique of Chinese history. History was made responsible for the present situation, and once people lost hope in their entire history and tradition, the intellectual theories that had supported that history and tradition came to be seen as a "historical tail" that had to be cut off. Their criticism of history was actually intended to magnify the legitimacy and reasonableness of the new knowledge and new thought and to enable them as rapidly as psychologically possible to enter into the world of the new knowledge, thought and belief.

If we say that nationalism and cultural conservatism are implicit in the "looking-back-to-origins" orientation to historical memory, then internationalism and cultural radicalism are implicit in the orientation of "root-and-branch-destruction." In recent Chinese history, however, these two orientations have been intertwined in that they both exhibited a high level of tension. "Searching for" or "breaking away" from China's traditional roots, these two opposite yet comparable orientations to historical memory clearly demonstrated a high level of apprehension and anxiety for their ethnic group and their state (*guojia* 國家). Both orientations raised many questions about China's past and cast a pall over the future development of Chinese history.

5.2

I want to employ the method of historical memory, intellectual resources and reinterpretation to replace some of intellectual history's habitual use of "influence." I also hope that I can mitigate the conflict between these two types of research orientation and reasoning.

For a very long time, research on the history of nineteenth- and twentieth-century China was carried out using the "impact-response" framework.

According to Paul A. Cohen, "the impact-response framework, by focusing on China's response to the 'Western challenge,' . . . prompts historians to define aspects of recent Chinese history that had no obvious connections with the Western presence as unimportant . . ."[45] The "impact" or the "influence" of the West on Chinese history was the main focal point of research. In his *Discovering History in China: American Historical Writing on the Recent Chinese Past*, Cohen called into question the validity of this long-time "impact-response" paradigm in American academic research on Chinese history. Cohen wanted to use a different research rationale—an internal approach to under-standing recent Chinese history. Although to a certain extent, this historical reasoning that he called "a China-centered history of China" (title of his Chapter 4) represented a refutation of the "impact-response" model and was very well received in Chinese intellectual history circles, it is, however, possible that it went from one extreme to another.

That is, two orientations have appeared in the analysis of Chinese history. One is the extrinsic approach that believes in "influence" from outside China. In modern intellectual history, for example, this approach holds that modern China only experienced change due to the impact or stimulus of Western knowledge, thought and belief. The other is the intrinsic approach that empha-sizes "selection" and holds that if it were not for China's own intellectual evolu-tion, if it were not for the transformation of China's internal intellectual resources, outside influences would not necessarily have been able to push Chinese tradition toward modernization. To put it another way, due to the evo-lution of Chinese knowledge and thought, China had already acquired the same modernity characteristic of the West.

There are always drawbacks to any theory. In essence emphasizing external or internal cause and effect, emphasizing external influence or the internal logic of thought, both employ a one-sided argument to express an important insight. Might there not be a more appropriate and even-handed way of writing modern Chinese history? I believe that employing the method of exca-vation of historical memory, intellectual resources and re-interpretation of meaning and significance may be able to integrate the mutual functions of "influence" and "selection."

For example, the influence of new Western knowledge has been said to be a variable in the changes in Late Qing intellectual history. If we only pay atten-tion to external influence, though, we will only be concerned with the active stimulus from the West and the passive response by China. However, if we only pay attention to China's internal changes, then we may well have some difficulty

45   Paul A. Cohen, *Discovering History in China*, 1984, 3.

appreciating the significance of Western influence. On this account, there is a very complex series of changes here that have rarely been subject to meticulous analysis and narrative. To wit, how did the new Western knowledge enter into Chinese knowledge, thought and belief? How did the Chinese attempt to understand and explicate this new knowledge on the basis of their original intellectual resources? How did this traditional knowledge, in the midst of great change, enter into the system of new knowledge and thought, and go on from there to change the new Western knowledge while at the same time transforming China's traditional learning? And, finally, how did the world of knowledge, thought and belief continue to develop?

In this book, then, I attempt to employ the trilogy of historical memory, intellectual resources and re-interpretation to describe China at the time it faced the new Western culture. I discuss the excavation of Chinese history, the re-interpretation of its intellectual resources, and the intellectual changes that followed this re-interpretation, including those in the traditional study of the classics, the study of the different schools of ancient thought and Buddhist studies. With this, I want to make it clear that when this traditional classical learning was regarded as a resource for writing history, the apprehension and anxiety of facing new knowledge came to the fore, and when people re-interpreted this traditional knowledge and used it to decode the new knowledge, it simply caused the tradition to merge into the new knowledge and the new knowledge to merge into the tradition. In other words, the world of modern Chinese knowledge, thought and belief is neither completely new nor completely old. It would appear that some seemingly Western discourse was already permeated with Chinese elements. It would also appear that some seemingly traditional ways of thinking were not necessarily so traditional either.

This is actually how the continuation of tradition takes place.

5.3

The short story "The General's Monument" is very interesting in this light. In it, a former general in the Nationalist army spending his last years in Taiwan lives within the half-true half-false memories of his past. As the author Zhang Dachun puts it, the general frequently "revises his interpretations of history, fabricates some new memories, and glosses over some old memories."[46] Since, Zhang says, everyone acts just like the general in this regard, history has long since ceased to be authentic history.

---

46   "Jiangjun bei," is in *Zhang Dachun ji*, 1993; citations are from 132, 136, 152.

The history of a people or a nation, including intellectual history, is just like the general's ceaseless remembering. Past history is recorded on the basis of resources such as books and documents, cultural relics and historical remains. Under the stimulation of immediate circumstances and emotions, some things, some persons, some periods of time and some ideas so recorded are taken up from that historical memory and examined. By that time, though, these memories have already undergone revision, fabrication and glossing over. History book writers have always been engaged in such recollection. It is precisely due to the re-interpretation of this sort of historical memory and use of it to serve as historical resources that history continues ceaselessly to move forward. Because of this, what sort of memories people seek from history determines what sort of "roots" are used to reconstruct a tradition; what sort of memories are repressed will cut off some "roots" and transform the orientation of tradition. From the point of view of intellectual history, historical memory is not merely the process of remembering those past events that are about to be forgotten or of forgetting those past events that may sometimes reappear. Through its interpretations, it is quietly controlling the construction of history while changing the present in order to control future historical resources. Various different cultural, religions and ethnic communities are all tracing their history and searching for their roots. That is, through the reorganization of their histories, they are defining and delimiting their traditions and determining their own identity and their relationships with their neighbors.

For these reasons, intellectual history is not only a matter of predecessors influencing their successors, but of successors also interpreting their predecessors. "Remembrance of things past" from different positions, standpoints and times generally leads to different understandings. Understanding traditional resources anew on the basis of different feelings, practical realities and circumstances generally leads to different interpretations of those resources. Such phenomena are not limited to individual memory, but also occur in the collective historical memory of a national community (*minzu gongtongti* 民族共同體). Intellectual history continues on by means of these types of historical memory, intellectual resources and reinterpretation.

6.   **Pictures Where There Are No Pictures: How to Deal with Empty Spaces in Intellectual History**

Intellectual historians generally do not want to discuss mediocre periods of history. In terms of the form and style of works of intellectual history, a period without any talented thinkers makes intellectual historians who are used to

arranging their chapters and sections according to individual thinkers feel like
they have no way to write about it. Therefore, intellectual history cannot avoid
the presence of "empty spaces." In terms of their conception of intellectual history research, perhaps the optimism of evolutionary theory leads some intellectual historians to believe that they can safely omit such periods of history
since their responsibility is only to write intellectual histories of uninterrupted
progress. In terms of the feelings of some of those who write intellectual history, perhaps it is difficult for them to be inspired by these so-called "mediocre"
thoughts.

This existence of "empty spaces" in intellectual history is, however, on the
one hand due to present day people's reliance on their contemporary system of
values to decide that some period is an "empty space." This is also due, on the
other hand, to the aforementioned practice of "chapter division according to
individual thinkers." Since there are not enough individual thinkers who qualify for a chapter or a section, these historians simply disregard all of what they
believe are third- and fourth-rank ideas of the period. In this way, ruptures and
"empty spaces" appear in intellectual history.

If we think about it in another way, however, perhaps "empty spaces" are
simply full of some other interesting contents, and "ruptures" are just another
significant form of continuation. In Chinese discussions of calligraphy and
painting, there is a very Chinese idea that where there are "empty spaces,"
there are also pictures and where the brush strokes end, one can see the spirit
of the picture. The place where no ink or color has touched the paper is the
empty space that conceals the most imaginative content of the painting. Of
course intellectual history is not painting and calligraphy, and we cannot
expect readers to fill in the blank spaces in intellectual history. So intellectual
history cannot just discuss those periods replete with changes; it also has to
deal with those mediocre periods of continuation. The greatest difference
between readers of history and admirers of art is that they cannot imagine history's empty spaces just any way they please.

Nevertheless, because some researchers do not appreciate those mediocre
periods, intellectual history is left with some empty spaces. This phenomenon
may not actually be so normal. Since intellectual history tends to alternate
between continuity and change, there is always a tension between a so-called
stable order and change. Every age is overshadowed by these two tendencies.
Sometimes seeking a conservative and fixed cultural order, intellectual history
expresses mediocre stability. Sometimes striving mightily to locate those circumstances that lead to the creation of new cultural forms, intellectual history
expresses what seem to be extraordinary leaps. Between "change" and "continuity," the "obvious" and the "hidden," intellectual historiography has always

been writing its own history. During those periods of apparent stagnation, intellectual history was actually moving forward; behind those "empty spaces" are a great many narratives that have yet to be published.

6.1

The traditional way of writing intellectual history is heavily influenced by the concept that "intellectual history is the intellectual history of thinkers," and that way of thinking is itself the product of a certain value orientation. That is, in the minds of many intellectual historians, intellectual history is not just a narrative of history, but also an evaluation of history. For them, history is like a roll of honor; not just anyone can easily be included on that list, and the standard for inclusion cannot be lowered.[47]

Although this is a respectable way of writing, on the one hand it turns intellectual history into a progress report—if one does not represent progress one is not eligible for inclusion on the list; and on the other hand, it brings the traditional Chinese praise and blame (*baobian*) principle in through the back door. If honors are handed out incorrectly, it would send intellectual history in the wrong direction. The problem is that no one ever asked the question: did intellectual history originally have such first, second and third class rankings, or are they the product of differentiation by successive intellectual historians? Is the purpose of writing intellectual history really to commend and repeat the thoughts of the elite thinkers? Why are other intellectual phenomena unworthy of becoming chapters in intellectual histories? Why must those recognized as elite thinkers take up all the chapters?

For example, in many works of Chinese intellectual history, especially Confucian-centered histories, the seventh- and eighth-centuries are almost completely empty. If we examine several relatively representative works—Xie Wuliang, *History of Chinese Philosophy* (1916), Zhong Tai (1888–1979), *History of Chinese Philosophy* (Zhongguo zhexueshi, 1929), Feng Youlan, *History of Chinese Philosophy* (1930)—besides discussing Sui and Tang Buddhist thought, all of them jump from Wang Tong (584–617) of the Sui dynasty to Han Yu (768–824) of the mid-Tang era. In 1937, in the section on Sui-Tang philosophy, Fan Shoukang (1896–1983)'s *General History of Chinese Philosophy* (Zhongguo

---

47   This situation may also reflects influence from the history of philosophy. Arthur F. Wright once suggested that intellectual history replace the history of philosophy because, as George Boas said, the history of philosophy is only concerned with linking "core ideas" and "recording their substance," but often does not touch upon the overall intellectual life and neglects the social background of how a concept comes into being, becomes outdated and is abandoned. See Zhang Duansui's abbreviated translation of Wright's article on how to study Chinese thought in *Zhonghua wenhua fuxing yuekan* 15/5 (1982), 17.

zhexueshi tonglun) still states that "there were only Han Yu and Li Ao" as Confucian thinkers.[48]

Perhaps this was just a chance agreement in the way of writing in the 1920s and 1930s. Or perhaps they were also influenced by Japanese historians, since Endô Ryûkichi's *History of the Development of Chinese Thought* (Shina shisô hattatsushi), Takase Takejirô's *History of Chinese Philosophy* (Shina tetsug-akushi), Watanabe Hidekata's *Outline History of Chinese Philosophy* (Chûgoku tetsugakushi gairon) and so on nearly all jumped from Wang Tong all the way to Han Yu, adding only a section on Sui-Tang Buddhism in between them. This style of writing did not undergo many changes for several decades after that. Even the largest section in volume four of Hou Wailu's *General History of Chinese Thought* (1957), only added Lü Cai (fl. 7th century) and Liu Zhiji (661–721) while Ren Jiyu's somewhat later *History of Chinese Philosophy* (1966) added chapters on the materialist and atheistic ideas of Fu Yi (555–639), Liu Zhiji's progressive conception of history and Li Quan (fl. 8th century)'s materialism and dialectic military. As with the previously mentioned books, there is noth-ing, however, on the ideology that had the most real influence on daily life in society at the time nor on general knowledge, thought and belief—on these, the period from the Sui to the mid-Tang is also a complete blank.

All this reminds me of the Confucian scholars' narrative on "Confucian orthodoxy" after the Song dynasty. From the legendary sage kings Yao, Shun, Yu, and Tang (founder of the Shang) to Wen Wang and Wu Wang (founders of the Zhou), from Confucius to Zisi (ca. 483–402 BCE), from Zisi to Mencius, then from Han Yu and the Cheng brothers (Cheng Hao, 1032–1085 and Cheng Yi, 1033–1107) to Zhu Xi, Confucian scholars seemed to be rewriting intellec-tual history. They asserted that Confucius and the *Analects* (Lunyu), Zengzi and the "Great Learning" (Daxue), Zisi and the "Doctrine of the Mean" (Zhongyong) and Mencius and the *Mengzi* were no less than the continuous thinkers and texts that rendered this one continuous intellectual history. Four great thinkers and four classical texts constituted a continuous genealogy of truth, but this genealogy was, however, cut off after Mencius, and it was not until the mid-Tang that Han Yu inherited it and carried forward the truth. As a result, this intellectual history contains more than a thousand years of blank spaces.[49] Even though, from history and documentation, some people long since questioned this orthodox transmission, from the point of view of the

---

48   See Xie Wuliang, *Zhongguo zhexueshi*, second edition, 45–55; Zhong Tai, *Zhongguo zhexueshi*, 1929, vol. 1, 170–182; Feng Youlan, *Zhongguo zhexueshi*, 1930 (1984) vol. 2, 800–01; Fan Shoukang, *Zhongguo zhexueshi tonglun*, 1937, 1941, 252.

49   Zhu Xi once said that after Yao and Shun, if it were not for Confucius, later generations could not have known the truth; and after Confucius, if it were not for Mencius, it would

Confucian scholars the continuity of the Confucian orthodox succession was much more important that the continuity of "history." Although the continuity of this sort of leap-frogging intellectual history is quite dubious, for Confucian scholars the continuity of this genealogy of truth was sacrosanct and inviolable.

We know that the model for writing Chinese intellectual history, history of philosophy and history of learning today was partially influenced by the West. It can also be traced back, though, to Huang Zongxi (1610–1695)'s *Scholarly Cases of Song and Yuan Classical Scholars* (Song Yuan xue-an) and *Scholarly Cases of Ming Classical Scholars* (Mingru xue-an), and they can be traced back to Zhu Xi's *Record of the Virtuous Conduct of Thinkers from Yi and Luo* (Yi Luo yuanyuan lu, the thinkers concerned are Zhou Dunyi (1017–1073), Zhang Zai (1020–1077) and the Cheng brothers). In the final analysis, Confucian histories of learning and thought were written in just this manner.

But it is just at this point that we see the difference in the standpoints of history and of thought. From the standpoint of thought, how can an era with no "thought" be the subject of intellectual history? What intellectual history wants to bring to the fore is a "tradition of the Way" or a genealogy of truth that needs to be honored. From the standpoint of history, however, there is no period of time that is without thought; as in art, there are pictures where there are no pictures, and history does not have to think about constructing any particular tradition of the Way. Because of this, tensions begin to appear between stubborn attachment to the continuity of an intellectual genealogy and stubborn attachment to the continuity of a process of history.

Perhaps the next question we need to ask is, then: should intellectual history be considered as thought or history?

6.2

Putting this question aside for now, let us first discuss whether or not those mediocre periods of time should be the subject of intellectual history.

It is said that when no stirring events occur and no extraordinary personages appear in a particular time period, then that era has neither time nor history. A rigid and mediocre era goes by smoothly and uneventfully, and when people come to remember its history, they seem to loose the very concept of time. They forget what happened and when it happened and they forget what events influenced people's lives. Everything seems to dissolve into a series of grey images in which time is truncated or even disappears. Therefore, in the

---

have been the same; after Mencius, it was not until the Cheng brothers that "this Principle (*li*) was discovered." See *Zhuzi yulei*, j. 93, 2350.

historical memory of such an era, it is as though nothing happened; they forget that an entire century or even two centuries passed that contained the history of several generations of human beings. Do those eras that the memory of and reflection on have been so deeply buried really deserve such neglect from intellectual historians?

I believe that brilliant ideas should all be honored in writing intellectual history, but I believe that the history of all so-called mediocre eras should also be narrated. Many periods of time having no great intellectual brilliance, may still actually contain many points of interest worthy of exploration and description by intellectual historians. Take China's "Cultural Revolution" era for example. That era had perhaps only one type of thought and it seems to have been as mediocre and as oppressive as humanly possible. But is this era not just the sort of period that intellectual historians should especially do research on? If the "Cultural Revolution" is omitted from twentieth-century Chinese intellectual history, how can it even be called "Chinese intellectual history?"

Every person is always thinking, and no matter whether those thoughts are great or insignificant, or whether they can be remembered or are forgotten, all of those thoughts, great or small, once also existed in history. So we need to abandon the honor roll style of writing and the idea of linear social evolution. If, while they are tracing back history, intellectual historians do not intend to make intellectual history into a glorious genealogy of great thinkers or imagine it as a process of linear social evolution, then they should examine all thought and ideas equally and re-assess the significance of those thoughts and ideas in their own time. Sometimes there may actually be some very important elements behind those mediocre ideas.

In my discussion of High Tang thought in volume two, I particularly include a section entitled "mediocrity in a flourishing age." My goal is to point out how this era without any particularly brilliant thought may still have significance for intellectual history. In general, after knowledge, thought and belief have been completely rationalized and systematized into a grand summary, an era characterized by the "establishment of one fixed standard" (*ding yu yi* 定於一) will probably emerge; all knowledge, thought and belief will be unable to escape from this "one." This leads to the disappearance of insight and critical thinking. Should this disappearance of insight and critical thinking not be an important historical phenomenon in the study of intellectual history?

We can see that in Chinese intellectual history when these mediocre, vacuous and repetitive elements overshadow all thought, such an era witnesses the elimination of alternative modes of thought, collapse of criticism and suppression of great depth of knowledge or thought. We should also notice, however, that just such mediocrity is precisely the thing that can stir up new changes in intellectual history. If we do not clearly explain the mediocrity of the High Tang, then, how will we be able to explain the profundity of the mid-Tang, not to mention the even more profound thought of the Northern Song?

6.3

Historical narrative is said to be of two types. The first type is written according to a precise scale. Regardless of whether or not any events occur to attract people's attention during a period of time, time passes as usual and history is recorded as usual, just as in writing annals history or chronicles (*biannianshi*). The second type is the combined annals and biography style of history writing (*jizhuanti*) according to the historical memory of events. If no important figures appear to attract people's attention during a period of time, then no time seems to pass. Even though sometimes our histories are written in the former style, our impressions of history tend to follow the latter style. Therefore a period of time in which no stirring events occur and no admirable persons appear may be filtered out and relegated to oblivion in a forgotten corner of our memory.

Indeed, ever since the establishment of official historiographers, Chinese history has undergone filtering, selecting, recording and ignoring. Remembering and forgetting always accompany each other because there are too many events and persons, and historians cannot possibly record them all. Various value judgments as to what is "important," "of secondary importance," "insignificant" and so on always dominate the writing of history. Intellectual history only records periods that "excite popular feelings" because such a period "excites the popular feelings" of some later period and these later people feel that it should go on "exciting the popular feelings" of posterity.

What, after all, are the events, personages and ideas that "excite popular feelings?" The understanding of every era is certainly not the same. An example is the way contemporary Chinese intellectual historians emphasize the role of Fan Zhen (ca. 450–515) and Wang Fuzhi while ignoring the significance of Huangfu Mi (215–282) and Qiu Jun. Every time intellectual history is written, then, the writers have to establish a new set of value judgments. I always feel that intellectual history should not ignore those periods that have been regarded as "empty spaces" because they may contain important elements that were neglected by earlier observers. This is not, of course, to say that we do not need to be selective when writing intellectual history. Rather, we should as far as possible set out to clarify the context of history and be on guard that those habitual value judgments do not monopolize our reading of the literary remains. We must also be careful that the author's likes and dislikes do not dominate the evaluation of thought and ideas, and be especially vigilant that any particular political ambition with overly practical concerns does not monopolize the historical narrative. Finally, we must prevent past conceptions of intellectual history from obscuring those so-called periods of empty spaces and allowing them to remain as empty spaces. To re-write intellectual history means, then, to return to the practice before the presently popular narrative conventions took shape—to observe and ponder history afresh.

6.4

"There are pictures where there are no pictures," but the key is how the narrators understand and interpret intellectual history. "Understanding" and "interpretation" belong to each subsequent generation, but this certainly does not imply that we can interpret history simply according to our whims. What I mean by narrating the history where there are so-called "empty spaces" only refers to the following three activities: First, we should regard those ideas previously seen as "mediocre" and "backward" as legitimate phenomena of intellectual history and discuss them in the usual manner. This is because intellectual history is not merely a process of monumentalizing and glorifying the ideas of elite thinkers and classic texts, but one of narrating all intellectual history. Second, we should treat those ideas that were not greatly noticed in their own time as potential historical resources and discuss them when they come to prominence and exert their influence later. These ideas may not have been so glorious in their own time, but when they are revived in another age, they may indeed have great force and stimulate new thought and new culture. And third, we should bring to the fore those ideas previously regarded as background thoughts and make them the focus of our inquiry. The standpoint, perspective and focus of concern of everyone who writes intellectual history in each generation are different, and some of these differences cause some brilliant intellectual phenomena to be relegated to oblivion. But if we look at it from a different angle, perhaps it is right there before our eyes. We need to carry out with great care and patience a meticulous and painstaking salvage operation on those areas and literary remains rarely touched upon by previous intellectual history. And we need even more to adopt a different standpoint and perspective for observing history. In this way perhaps we can accomplish the task set out by the Annals School historian Jacques Le Goff when he writes that "At the same time, it is necessary to define and explain the gaps and silences of history and establish it as much on its empty spaces [where it was lived but not inscribed] as on its surviving areas of full inscription [where it was both lived and inscribed]."[50]

---

50   "En même temps, il faut cerner, expliquer les lacunes, les silences de l'histoire et asseoir l'histoire aussi bien sur ces vides que sur les pleins qui ont survécu." Jacques Le Goff,

7. Addition and Subtraction Methods in Intellectual History Research

In class one day, a student said that many past intellectual histories or histories of philosophy were called "the history of the development of..." Then he asked: was there really so much "new" thought? Is intellectual history really a history of the "development" of new thought? His question was very interesting because previous histories of philosophy and *intellectual histories* really were generally concerned only with new ideas and new thinkers. This reverence for "the new" became an axiom of history writing—they felt that history was simply the narration of these new things that were constantly being added. Therefore the compilers always hoped that they could discover new ideas and new knowledge, and since in the past they believed that both thought and knowledge followed a law of evolution, the later the ideas occurred the more progressive they were believed to be. That is how "the history of philosophy" could be called "the history of the development of philosophy" and "intellectual history" could be called "the history of the development of thought." If they displayed these new phenomena stacked up like toy building blocks, they thought they were illustrating the "progress," "development" and "evolution" of thought. I call this narrative method based on discovering new ideas the "addition method."

We can also see, however, a "subtraction method" at work in intellectual history. What I call the "subtraction method" refers to the practice of gradually subtracting and deleting some ideas and concepts during the writing of intellectual history. Past intellectual histories employed both "addition" and "subtraction" methods because they seldom discussed those disappearing elements of knowledge, thought and belief that they censured as barbarian, backward, absurd and lascivious and that were later marginalized and esotericized. It is just at this point, however, that we can observe how ancient China's imperial power and ideology obfuscated history by forcing all other heresies to "submit" to them. At that time writing history was like sifting grain, and many events could not get past the history writers' censorship because their grains were too big—the more history was sifted this way, the less history was left to write about.

"L'histoire nouvelle," in *La Nouvelle Histoire*, 1978, 238 of 210–241. I think this is just a change in the perspective on and evaluation of the literary sources for intellectual history; if this sort of change took place, we would find "blank spaces" in the commonly used sources like the thirteen classics, the various philosophers, the twenty-five dynastic histories, various literary collections and so on. With this change of perspective, of course, we would even more easily discover the traces of intellectual history in hitherto neglected sources like official documents (*gongwen* 公文), *leishu* encyclopedias, pictures and paintings, popular gossip, folk songs and so on.

Can intellectual historians actually "discover history" using this method? If we are able to bring these "subtracted and deleted" elements back into history again, can we possibly find a new way of interpretation?

7.1

We usually look at history from our modern subjective point of view, and follow our contemporary value system. Values, like "civilization," "reason," "equality," "democracy," "life" and "liberty," have legitimacy for us today. On this account, when modern scholars write intellectual history, they often employ their later conception of values to choose what ideas and thoughts to write about. They especially privilege those ideas deemed to be "reasonable" and "civilized." Ancient writings tell us, however, that some "uncivilized" and "irrational" ideas and practices of the past were once regarded as reasonable or even sacred.

Take for example something the French Sinologue Marcel Granet noticed some time ago. Our classical scholars and historians deliberately avoid or block from memory an incident from the *Guliang Commentary* to the *Spring and Autumn Annals* (Guliangzhuan)—the Jiagu Conference in the tenth year of the reign of Duke Ding of Lu (r. 509–495 BCE). At this conference, it is reported that Confucius killed one You Shi who had been ordered by the state of Qi to dance before the Duke of Lu. Confucius is even said to have dismembered You Shi's corpse and "scattered the pieces all around." This incident is also recorded in Sima Qian's *Records of the Grand Historian*. Granet asks, then, if Confucius was such a great humanist, why would he order You Shi so cruelly beheaded and dismembered and have his body parts scattered about?[51]

This incident itself is very strange, and so are the records, or lack of records, about it. Not only do the *Zuo Commentary* to the *Spring and Autumn Annals* (Zuozhuan) and the *Gongyang Commentary* (Gongyangzhuan) not mention it, neither the interpretive commentaries on the *Guliangzhuan* by Fan Ning (339–401) nor Yang Shixun (fl. 7th century) say anything to clear up this issue. In the Song dynasty, this incident actually gave rise to a polemic. On the one side, those who accepted the incident as genuine offered a special interpretation based on the Confucian concept of justice (*zhengyi*) to justify the legitimacy of Confucius' actions. On the other side, those who rejected the reality of this incident and wished to protect the image of the Sage, angrily criticized it

---

51   *Guliangzhuan*, Dinggong, year 10, in SSJZS, 2445. *Shiji*, j. 33 "Lu Zhougong shijia," 1544 and
      j. 47 "Kongzi shijia," 1915. For Granet's views, see *Danses et légendes de la Chine ancienne* as
      quoted in the translator Li Huang's "Granet yu shehuixue fangfa," *Faguo Hanxue lunji*,
      1975, 98.

as quite unbelievable. Even the Qing scholars who particularly emphasized evidence simply rejected the ancient evidence for this incident. If we accept the opinion of the Qing scholars, then the Jiagu Conference would simply be deleted from history, and might well be forgotten.

Our past intellectual histories have no trace of the "Jiagu Conference." Granet, however, started from there and made a detailed investigation of the history of what was included in the dances and sacrifices of ancient China that had already been expunged by rationalistic history writing. Actually, the historical custom of "killing to establish one's power" was carried on for a very long time in ancient China, and behind this custom was a concept that supported its legitimacy and reasonableness. This concept has not, however, been brought up and discussed in intellectual history; it has simply disappeared from it.[52]

In similar fashion, from the history of Six Dynasties religious Daoism, we have discovered that some ceremonies have also been forgotten by history— things like the purification ritual known as the Mud and Soot Levee (*tutanzhai* 涂炭齋) mortification of the flesh to obtain the remission of sins, or rites of passage involving sexual behavior. These things disappeared from orthodox historical narratives. What sorts of ideas, then, are behind their existence in and disappearance from history? Should these ideas not be the subject of discussion in intellectual histories?[53]

This is an issue worth discussing. This sort of "subtraction method" in history writing is not due only to the passage of time causing people to forget. Sometimes it comes about because later people rely on their own way of thinking to delete a great deal of material from history. This causes history to become fragmented, but then they paste the fragments together just as in the process of editing a film. But can we gather up and collate all of the film on the cutting room floor to search for the complete record of times past?

7.2

Archeology has been very popular in recent years because it has often helped us discover forgotten history and cultural relics. Previously preserved literary remains no longer serve this purpose, and so now we speak of "archeological discovery." Nevertheless, there are still very many abandoned and marginalized resources among those literary remains. They have been abandoned because, according to contemporary ideas of history, they cannot be fitted into

---

52 This Jiagu Conference is discussed in Michael Nylan and Thomas Wilson, *Lives of Confucius*, 2010, 15–16.

53 See Ge Zhaoguang, *Qufushi ji qita—liuchao daojiao sixiangshi yanjiu.*

place in a certain historical narrative. Our idea of history has already subjectively determined what is and what is not worthy of inclusion in any historical narrative. If ideas of history change, however, the value of these "marginalized scraps" might suddenly increase. After all, what is "peripheral" and what is "central" in history, is determined by the position and view point of the historian.

Of course there is a great deal of history that is impossible to retrieve; the disappearance of history has carried away many previously existing ideas. We will never be able to know the historical context of some ancient knowledge and thought that was regarded as fair and reasonable or even sacred in its time. If we carefully recover those abandoned and marginalized materials, though, we may still be able to discover some "deleted" history. Through excavation and retrieval, we can at least recover the historical images of some things like the portraits of twelve gods on Chu silk manuscripts from Zidanku in Changsha, some ancient ideas about divination by the stars (*xingzhan*), clouds and weather phenomena (*yunqizhan*), the military style organization of early religious Daoism, and so on.

We might well speculate a bit from these recovered images of history. We might ask how much difference there is between today and the time when this knowledge and thought was considered reasonable? This difference is simply intellectual history. We might continue to imagine what might happen if the knowledge of traditional Chinese medicine gradually disappears under the onslaught of Western ideas. Will Chinese people living several generations from now even be able to know that the techniques of the Yin and Yang and Five Phases system of knowledge were believed in for so many centuries and that they really could cure illnesses? Perhaps the people of that future age will only be able to understand anew the context of those things that have been deleted from history—breathing exercises manipulating one's vital essence or *qi*, Yin-Yang, Five Phases, etc. that were the dominant concepts for so many generations of people—by rediscovering those ancient concepts from the source materials, re-assembling the understanding and knowledge of medical treatments, the human body, the universe and people's trust and dependence on Chinese medicine due to their conceptual world.

All of the knowledge, thought and belief regarded as "uncivilized" does not really disappear without trace from history, and all subtracted customs were not "barbarian." What we call "civilized" today is sometimes the result of evaluating the past with contemporary consciousness. A celebrated example of this process is the rise and fall of cremation. After Buddhism entered China, its believers began to practice cremation. In the Sui and Tang dynasties, not only were Buddhist monks cremated and pagodas built for them, but many lay

Buddhists were also cremated. In the Song dynasty, however, due to opposition based on traditional Chinese funerary practices from Confucian scholars, especially those from the School of Principle, earthen burial was promoted from "barbarian" to "civilized" and cremation was demoted from "civilized" to "barbarian." Cremation gradually disappeared from the lives of the upper levels of society.[54] Before they entered China, however, members of the Manchu royal family practiced cremation. As far as they were concerned there was nothing uncivilized about it, but after they entered China, the Manchu imperial family began strictly to avoid their former cremation practices. Does the process of continual change in the legitimacy of "cremation" not actually demonstrate changes in the history of ideas?

Every age has its own ideas. Much knowledge and many ideas and beliefs of ancient times have been hidden from view by "reason," "civilization," "morality" and other such modern concepts, or they have been pushed to the margins of life by urbanization and the intellectual strata of society to be forgotten by history. Should intellectual history not consider why these things were so widely accepted in their own times? In the ages when these things were still regarded as common sense, was the world of thought different from what it is today? Should intellectual history not describe the processes leading to those differences? Why does intellectual history not pay appropriate attention to this aspect of history? If we examine these elements of thought that have been banished to the forgotten corners of memory or to secret places in the life of society, perhaps we can salvage some lost history in the same way that archeologists dig up fragments of ancient artifacts. When these artifacts are put back together, perhaps we will be able to discover history in them.

It may be that past narratives have already constructed a context that we are all too familiar with, and this context has made us lose any sense of curiosity or unfamiliarity. If today we want to work our way free from this format so replete with ideology, academic systematization and traditional concepts, should we not engage in some "defamiliarization" to provide a different contextualization for our intellectual history?[55]

---

54 See Liu Yizheng, "Huozang kao," in *Shixue zazhi* 1/3 (1929), 1–5. (Jacques Gernet's book *Daily Life in China on the Eve of the Mongol Invasion, 1250–1276*, 1959, 173–176, discusses the "widespread" use of cremation in the Southern Song, and believes that it began with upper class Buddhist. The point here is that it was not accepted by Song dynasty Confucian scholars.—tr.)

55 See Wang Fansen, "Zhongguo jindai sixiang wenhuashi yanjiu de ruogan sikao," in *Xin shixue* 14/4 (2003), 177–191.

7.3

The "addition method "in history refers to those new elements that are constantly being added to history while the "subtraction method" refers to those
old elements that are constantly being lost from history. These two "methods"
are not at all antithetical; much of the time, the two of them are one and the
same process. Once "the civilized" becomes legitimate in various areas of life
by means of "the new," then "the uncivilized" or "the barbarian" can only
become "the old" and quietly withdraw from those areas of life. In the conclusion to his *Modern European Thought: Continuity and Change in Ideas, 1600–
1950*, Franklin L. Baumer wrote that, in the interests of truth, intellectual
history should expound those concepts that have "not merely survived but
helped to build what men have adjudged to be great civilizations," and that it
can and should also clearly expound those "other ideas [that] have lived only
briefly or been associated with decadence."[56] Here I just feel somewhat regret-
ful that our intellectual history over-emphasizes continually emerging "new"
intellectual phenomena while somewhat neglecting the "old" ones that are
daily disappearing.

8.   What Can Be a Resource Material for Intellectual History?

What the scope of historical research materials are, and what methodologies
are used in historiography are not just a question of "the study of historical
materials." Even a global change in historiography can be brought about by
what historical resources are used and how such materials are treated. In a
1997 article entitled "What Can Become Evidence for History?," Professor Wang
Fansen showed how scholars of the 1920s—Fu Sinian, Gu Jiegang (1893–1980),
Hu Shi, Li Ji (1896–1979)—worked hard to expand the scope of historical
research materials. He also discussed the influence on Chinese historiography
of the Ming and Qing archives and the materials dug up at the Yinxu ruins of
the ancient Shang dynasty near Anyang in Henan province.[57]

Chinese historiography certainly did experience monumental changes in
the 1920s and 30s.[58] If we compare the differences between the Qing dynasty

---

56   Franklin L. Baumer, *Modern European Thought: Continuity and Change in Ideas, 1600–
      1950*, 1977, 518.

57   Wang Fansen, "Shenme keyi chengwei lishi de zhengju?," *Xin shixue* 8/2 (1997), 93–131.

58   Ge Zhaoguang, "'Xin shixue' zhi hou—1929 nian de Zhongguo lishi xuejie," *Lishi yanjiu* 1
      (2003), 82–97.

evidential school scholars (*kaoju xuejia* 考據學家) and historians of the 1920s and 1930s in fields of research, methods of argument and scope of resources, we will find that by the later time the conception of what materials could be employed as resources for writing history had already undergone a great change. Besides the so-called "four great discoveries of the twentieth century"—oracle bone divination script, Dunhuang manuscripts, Ming and Qing archives, Qin and Han bamboo and wooden slips—popular opera librettos, fiction, drama and so on had all become historical research materials. In Liang Qichao (1873–1929)'s *Methodology of Chinese History Research* (Zhongguo lishi yanjiufa), he mentions not only archives and other official documents but also the significance for social history of common people's daily account books as well as the Tongrentang Chinese medical shop, and other shopkeepers' ledgers.[59] This is obviously quite different from the Qing scholars' dependence on the Confucian classics, various schools of classical thought, official histories, *Comprehensive Mirror to Aid in Government*, and important literary collections (*wenji*) with the occasional random jottings (*biji*) and unofficial histories thrown in. Because the concept of "what is history" changed, the field of historical research was greatly expanded.

We may also note, however, that these changes in the fields of intellectual history and history of philosophy have not been very obvious. Throughout the entire twentieth century, the scope of resource materials for the history of philosophy and intellectual history did not undergo any fundamental change. How then, can we draw support from new research concepts and methodologies to bring about some changes in the scope of resource materials for intellectual history?

8.1

That resource materials for intellectual history became, in recent years, a problematic subject of discussion for researchers was probably related to archeology. A continual series of archeological discoveries from the 1970s on astonished many scholars of Chinese intellectual history. At first, everyone's thinking was quite similar. They believed that archeology had provided them with a great deal of new material, and, due to the large number of newly excavated records, they came to a new recognition of many texts formerly labeled "apocrypha" (*weishu* 偽書), and early Chinese intellectual history had even more material

---

59   Liang Qichao, "Shuo shiliao," chapter 4 of his *Zhongguo lishi yanjiufa*, 1922, 66.

for discussion.[60] In time, however, people began to feel that these new resource materials were insufficient because there was still no way to use many more archeological materials in intellectual history studies. Many archeological finds included texts on numerology, mantic and medical arts and military affairs as well as implements and pictures with no texts. In the traditional view of intellectual history and the history of philosophy, these things did not qualify as "thought" or "philosophy," and so for a long time, intellectual history and the history of philosophy continued to deal primarily with the elite and the classics. They simply did not have an explanatory method for dealing with those archeological materials, and so they did not include them in intellectual history.

Chinese scholars have been pondering since the 1990s how to change the original intellectual history model so as to bring these new discoveries into the field.

Naturally intellectual history primarily depends on the elite and the classics as resource materials. Things like the Confucian classics and the various schools of thought with their commentaries and annotations, large numbers of literary collections, selected sayings (yulu), official histories and biographies as well as Buddhist and Daoist scriptures are the most natural materials for intellectual history.

Many people feel that they have not even exhausted these materials, so there is no need to broaden the scope of research materials. But if we want to discuss more than elite thought and the classic texts; if we want to discuss general knowledge, thought and belief, then researchers have to pay attention to many more historical resources. If intellectual history continues to be written according to the traditional model, these "obscure," "anonymous" and "nontextual" materials will never qualify for inclusion in the field of vision of intellectual historians. Let me offer a few examples of the kinds of materials I mean.

---

60   Besides the discovery of lost texts like the Mawangdui silk manuscripts (boshu 帛書) of the Yellow Emperor's Four Classics (Huangdi sijing), the Laozi, the Yijing, the Five Phases (Wuxing); the Yinqueshan text of the Sun Bin (military strategy text), the Ding County text of the Book of Master Wen (Wenzi, supposed disciple of Laozi), archeological discoveries also brought new knowledge about various other ancient texts such as the Six Secret Strategic Teachings (Liu Tao), the Book of Wei Liaozi (Wei Liaozi, a military classic), the Yanzi, the Pheasant Cap Master (He Guanzi, Daoist and military classic), the Gui Repository (Guizang, said to be the Shang dynasty text of the Yijing), and also new ideas and discussions about texts like the "Black Robes" (Zi yi, chapter from the Liji), the "Robber Zhi" (Dao Zhi, chapter from the Zhuangzi), and the "Big Talk Rhapsody" (Dayan fu, of Song Yu). For information on all of this, see Li Xueqin, Jianbo yiji yu xueshushi, 1994 & 1995.

First, calendars and almanacs under various names, such as *lishu, tongshu, huangli* and *shixianshu*. In ancient China, the regulation of time was one of the most important tasks for officials. Almanacs for everyday use, or "Day Books" (*rishu* 日書) are also among the most common archeological finds. The earliest extant officially printed items are also calendars or almanacs, and such almanacs have been printed in the greatest quantities among Chinese printed materials from ancient times to this day. According to the traditional mode of writing intellectual history, though, these things were regarded as unimportant. They did not represent any thought, and certainly not "new" thought.

Could we not look at these materials from a different angle and deal with them differently? For example, we could employ these Day Books to reconstruct ancient Chinese people's views of life and death and their daily lifestyles. Most aspects of daily life in ancient China—travel, agriculture, marriages and taboos—were regulated according to these almanacs.[61] Furthermore, for ancient China, "time" was definitely not simply a matter of importance for the common people; even the legitimacy of the government (dynasty) depended on "correcting (amending) the first day of the lunar month" (*gai zhengshuo* 改正朔) and periodically "changing the name of the reign period" (*gai nianhao*). This is why the Northern Song scholar Shao Yong (1011–1077) edited the *Imperial Book for Administering Affairs* (Huangji jingshi), and the Southern Song scholar Zhang Shi (1133–118) edited his *Chronological Record of Administrative Affairs* (Jingshi jinian). During the Ming and Qing dynasties, the significance of the regulation of time and calendar making was even more profound because it involved the conflict and the intermingling of Western and Chinese knowledge, thought and culture. In an age when old and new knowledge were changing places, calendrical knowledge was also changing, and those changes led to changes of knowledge used in the lives of ordinary people.

Second, writings like the *Treatise on Architectural Methods* or *State Building Standards* (Yingzao fashi, Northern Song dynasty) and the *Qing Dynasty Rules of Craft* (Jianzuo zeli) contain much of great importance for intellectual history. Things like records of imperial honor guards and ceremonial tours contain many rules for making distinctions between the imperial family and the common people. Ancient China's ceremonial systems were actually symbols of order; they delimited and implied social distinctions such as higher and lower, inner and outer, self and other, and the implements used in these ceremonies are also rich in similar implications.

---

61   Pu Muzhou, "Shuihudi Qinjian 'rishu' de shijie," *Lishi yuyan yanjiusuo jikan* 62/4 (1993), 623–675.

In the past, very few intellectual histories discussed these sorts of things. Our intellectual history research is not much like Western history of ideas studies.[62] A history of ideas carries out historical study taking one or a few ideas as its central theme. By doing so, it may discover many resources that express this idea or set of ideas, and it may involve very marginal and common images, ceremonies, scenarios and customs, etc. However, intellectual histories, especially those written taking individual thinkers as a unit, will rarely pay any attention to these materials because they neither belong to any particular thinker nor do they directly express any particular idea.

Third are various kinds of archives. In the 1920s and 30s, many scholars said that historiography should pay attention to the extant Ming and Qing archives. From then on, these archives have been used in many areas of history, but vary rarely in intellectual history. Some of the information on daily life recorded in these archives could, indeed, be used for comparison with the ideas of the upper elite strata of society. For example, to see whether or not Confucian ideas and principles, such as "benevolent father, filial son" (*fuci zixiao*), "faithful unto death" (*congyi er zhong*, discouraging widow remarriage), family and lineage status ranks, etc., were effectively practiced among the general population. If we analyze these archives, we may find that many elements of real life and popular thought in ancient Chinese society were quite at variance from the principles recorded in the classics. Studying these archives can provide a rich store of details about social life, and it is just these sorts of details that manifest people's real thoughts.

Fourth, *leishu* encyclopedias, primary education texts (*mengshu*), handbooks, instructional readers and so on are another large category. *Leishu* (literally "classified books") are not exactly like our present day encyclopedias that one consults occasionally to look up information. Many of them were widely popular handbooks of knowledge like the *Portable Treasure* (Suishenbao), *Questions and Answers on the Classics and History* (Jingshi wenda) and *Confucius Answers Questions* (Kongzi beiwen shu) used in Dunhuang during the Tang dynasty. Everyone could carry one of these texts as an aid to memory, and such texts then became the repository of basic knowledge and a place to go for answers to many questions. Primary texts, like *Children's Jade Forest* (Youxue qionglin) and *Dragon Essays to Encourage Study* (Longwen bianying), were also very important. Such elementary texts once served as every cultured

---

62   The differences between intellectual history or history of thought and the history of ideas is a question that Western academics discussed a long time ago. Most people believe that the paradigm for history of ideas works is Arthur O. Lovejoy's *The Great Chain of Being*, and that he explained his standard methodology in "The Historiography of Ideas" in his *Essays in the History of Ideas*, 1965 [1948], 1–13.

person's childhood primers, and they also provided the foundational knowledge for every form of advanced thought. From these texts we may discern what sort of general knowledge the ordinary people needed most. These texts gave them their common sense ideas about what is right or wrong, what comes first or last, what is good or evil, what Heaven and Earth are, why human beings are born and why they die, what happens after death and so on. This sort of most common knowledge constituted the foundation for their future thought and ideas.

Fifth are popularly circulating fiction (*xiaoshuo*), vernacular short stories (*huaben*) and song lyrics (*changci*). These can be very effective channels for discussing some important topics in intellectual history, especially the popularization of ideas. We can use Song dynasty intellectual history as an example. From the Song on, many kinds of stories began to circulate, like the stories about the Yang family (the Yang Saga, *Yangjia jiang*), about the incorruptible "Judge Bao" (Bao Gong), about the Three Kingdoms . . . and all of these works can be used to study changes in the Chinese concepts of state or country (*guojia*), "order" and "history." Of course, from the theme of a single story or drama, we can perhaps only see one aspect of intellectual history. However, if we analyze the combined themes of many popular stories and the ideas involved in them—ideas concerning such topics as boundaries between different peoples or ethnic groups (*minzu*) and between different states (*guojia*), control by the legal system and the actual customs of social life, and the political legitimacy of the dynasty—we may actually be able to see the moods, feelings, anxieties and tensions in Song society. These moods, feelings, anxieties and tensions represent the world of general thought and become the background for elite thought and the classic texts as well as evidence for the reasonableness and urgency of their reflections.

8.2

But has our intellectual history or history of ideas actually discussed these resource materials?

Some Chinese historians, did in fact long ago take notice of such materials. According to his biographer, Professor William Hung (Hong Ye, 1893–1980)'s "best tool for training future historians was his historical methods course. Every day he had a library clerk go out to the market and buy some scrap paper; among these scraps of paper were calendar pages, medical prescriptions, pornographic reading materials, written charms and so forth . . ."[63] I believe that Hong Ye was using this insignificant waste paper to train his students to have

---

63   Chen Yuxian, *Hong Ye zhuan*, 1992, 176.

the historical sensitivity to find and the skill to recognize resources where there seemed to be none.

There are actually many other things passed down from ancient China that could be used as resource materials, but that have rarely been used in intellectual history. Things like local gazetteers (*difang zhi*), lineage and family genealogies (*zupu* and *jiapu*), individual diaries (*riji*) and the spatial designs of mausoleums and houses, the latter being previously explained only in terms of theories of geomancy. Medical case records (*yi-an*) in Chinese medicine contain considerable information on the body and human biological life, but they have not been attended to.

Why, after all, have these sources been ignored? It is simply because the intellectual history of our past intellectual historians has been, one, the intellectual history of elite thinkers and the classics, two, divided into chapters and sections on the basis of individual thinkers, and three, an intellectual history based on a theory of evolution. There was naturally no place for these materials in such an intellectual history.

This is not to say that just anything can be included in intellectual history, but we should make clear that intellectual history is first of all history. The historical situation, discursive context and moods form an important background for understanding thought and ideas. Just as Benjamin Schwartz wrote, "the focus of intellectual history [is] men's conscious responses to the situations in which they find themselves," and as Isaiah Berlin put it, "the history of ideas is the history of what we believe that people thought and felt."[64] What is meant by the "situation" and what people "felt" here is not something that can be described by relying exclusively on elite writings and the classics. Elite writings and the classics may be able to describe thought in history, but they cannot necessarily describe the history behind that thought. They may be able to express "ideas," but they would be hard put to express what people "felt." This is really a question of our conception of intellectual history research. Is the "thought" that intellectual history wants to research limited only to that of "some major scholarly cases" and the elite and classics in the "table of contents of the official dynastic histories?" What, essentially, is the "background" of society and social life that is linked to intellectual history? Does the core "content" of intellectual history have to come from written words expressed in "texts."

---

64   Schwartz, "The Intellectual History of China: Preliminary Reflections," in *Chinese Thought and Institutions*, 1957, 16. Berlin quote from Ramin Jahanbegloo, *Conversations with Isaiah Berlin*, 1991, 28.

To put it simply, this is a question of what should intellectual history write about and how should intellectual history be written.

What *should* intellectual history write about? How *should* intellectual history really be written? The answer to these questions in Chinese academic circles changed after the 1990s. This change was influenced by the French Annals School and by the stimuli received from thinkers like Michel Foucault. After the 1990s, then, intellectual history experienced a rather important change of direction (though not as great as sometimes assumed). Even more importantly, of course, were the background changes in political history that were behind the post-1990s changes in the Chinese academic world. In intellectual history research, there was the question of resisting a single unified political ideology and rejecting old intellectual history textbooks as well as the question of how to re-establish a system of intellectual history and re-evaluate modern thought in the educational system.

The following are some ideas that directly affect the way intellectual history is written and the scope of its resource materials.

8.3

First off, if intellectual history emphasizes understanding the *longue duré* and pays attention to general knowledge, thought and belief, then many marginal and scattered materials can be considered in intellectual history writing. I want to clarify here again that I am not talking about any "little tradition," but rather "general knowledge of average quality" and "the background or soil of elite thought." This is a part of social history because the relationship between thought and society is very close. If we pay attention to this background, then *leishu* encyclopedias, textbooks, almanacs, dramas, fiction, mediocre things and common-sense knowledge should all be discussed.

Secondly, links have to be re-established between the history of knowledge and intellectual history. There really isn't such a great divide between so-called Dao (Way/the metaphysical) and "Qi" (器 tools/the material), but, under the overwhelming influence of the history of philosophy, the writing of intellectual history is generally only concerned with metaphysical phenomena and pays little attention to physical or material things. Our recent archeological discoveries are, however, generally material, concrete objects embodying practical, usable knowledge. In this area those conducting research on the history of technology, medicine, life sciences, numerology, and the mantic and medical arts have made great contributions. They recognized that these things are closely related to advanced thought and even constitute the direct knowledge background supporting the reasonableness or perceived rationality of such thought in social life. Thus numerology mantic and medical arts and the arts of war (*bingfa*)—the last three categories in the "Monograph of Arts and Letters" (Yiwenzhi) section of the *History of the Former Han Dynasty* (Hanshu)—have become resource materials for intellectual history.[65]

Thirdly, equal stress should be placed on growth and diminution. Traditional intellectual history paid attention to the successively emerging elite thinkers, classic texts and advanced thought because it was animated by a concept of "rise" and "progressive evolution." The inspiration behind these ideas was a "rationalist" and "axiomatic" historical teleology, as though reason was constantly pushing forward the new, history was always moving forward toward "the modern," and thought was always tending toward "the civilized." However, intellectual history should re-discover those things that were filtered out by "the modern," "the rational" and "the civilized." Intellectual history should consider why things like human sacrifice to the dead ancestors, religious masochism and public sexual behavior were marginalized, driven underground or even expelled outright from civilized history. Such a recovery of memory in intellectual history will serve to make it more well-rounded, and not only allow us to reveal even more abandoned resource materials, but also to reach a new understanding of formerly erased intellectual "history" through an examination of these neglected and forgotten materials.

8.4

Conceptual changes in intellectual history research have already made it possible for many elements, including those things that were previously not used or could not be used, to become resource materials for intellectual history. As advantageous a change as this is, it has undoubtedly entailed some problems. Now even I feel that one perplexing problem is how intellectual history can establish its own boundaries so as not to encroach upon other areas of history and, at the same time, defend well its own territory. Intellectual history has always had unclear boundaries. How great a scope should it have after all? Should it follow R. G. Collingwood's idea that "all history is the history of thought?"[66] Or should it follow Arthur O. Lovejoy and only regard ideas and concepts as the object of historical research? Some people are bound to criticize this kind of intellectual history as an enormous jumble that does not resemble real intellectual history, but I do not agree. Who stipulated what

---

65   See Li Xueqin, *Jianbo yiji yu xueshushi*, 1994 & 1995, and his *Zouchu yigu shidai*, 1998; Li Ling, *Zhongguo fangshu kao* (revised), 2000 and *Zhongguo fangshu xukao*, 2000.

66   R. G. Collingwood, *The Idea of History*, 215, 317, 304.

intellectual history should be and how great a scope it should have? Still others may say that intellectual history can push its way around expanding any way it wants to. This, too, would be very problematic because of the simple fact that the unlimited expansion of intellectual history would lead to its own self-destruction. Now let us turn to this intellectual history of China.

Tracing the Origins of Chinese Intellectual History in the Three Dynasties (Ancient Times to ca. 6th Century BCE)

Brief Prologue: Remote Antiquity

What is "intellectual history" and what is "Chinese intellectual history?" This is a very complicated question that I can only briefly discuss here. The Chinese characters for "thought" (*si* 思) and "to think" (*xiang* 想) both have the radical meaning heart and mind (*xin* 心), and so intellectual history (*sixiangshi*) concerns what the Chinese have thought about and how they have thought about it since ancient times. The Chinese character for "history" (*shi* 史) is said to mean both "fair" or "just" and "to write down" or "to record." That is to say history is a branch of learning that traces back the past to discover its traditions and origins. "Chinese" intellectual history, then, discusses why, since ancient times, the Chinese thought this way and not that way. Since history is the basic thread of the discipline called "intellectual history," to trace Chinese intellectual history, I have to begin the discussion with remote antiquity.

I say "remote antiquity" because, when we want to write intellectual history, we tend to feel that ancient times are very far away from us. Chinese history has already gone through several thousand years, and that history has become a stack of books, a few oracle bone fragments, a few bronzes and scattered historical ruins. These historical resource materials originally embodied the thought, feelings and frames of mind of ancient people, and we find it very difficult to understand them today. What ancient people thought, said and did has already disappeared into the past, and so when we want to engage them in an intellectual dialogue, we feel them to be both remote and unfamiliar. This remoteness separates ancient times from the present while unfamiliarity makes it impossible for us to understand ancient people clearly.

As an example, in the 1970s in a Han dynasty tomb in Mawangdui, a silk manuscript text called *The Ten Great Canons* (Shi da jing 十大經) was discovered. One chapter entitled "Correcting Chaos" (Zhengluan 正亂) tells a story about the legendary Huangdi or Yellow Emperor, previously recorded to be the "progenitor of human culture" (*renwen shizu* 人文始祖). Traditional accounts of the Yellow Emperor portray him as a paragon of civilization and benevolence, but this document, dating at least to the first century BCE, relates how the Yellow Emperor captured his rival Chi You, flayed off his skin to make a target, used his hair to make a pennant, made his stomach into a ball and cut his flesh up into mincemeat.

This story involves extreme cruelty and is very different from our general conception, but perhaps it is true to life because quite a few examples of "killing people to bury them with the deceased" (*sharen yi xun* 殺人以殉) have been found in ancient tombs, and oracle bone inscriptions also record many "human sacrifices" (*sharen yi ji* 殺人以祭). Not only were commoners and prisoners of war killed and sacrificed to the spirits or ancestors, but in ancient times when there was a severe drought, they would immolate shamans or witches to please the spirits (*shenling*) and pray for rain.[1]

This kind of what we today would regard as barbaric behavior actually continued into eras that are considered quite civilized. Even the paragons of virtue, King Wen (cultured) and King Wu (martial) of the Zhou dynasty, acted in a similar manner. When we read the *Remaining Zhou Documents* (Yi Zhoushu), we learn that they both acted in a cruel and deceitful fashion. When King Wu defeated the last Shang king, Zhou 紂, he acted just like a blood-thirsty barbarian, and the blood of the slain flowed like a river. When he reached the Shang capital, he shot his enemies' corpses full of arrows; he hacked off their heads with a sword and slaughtered a large number of prisoners of war as a sacrifice. He also took back to his own territory the Nine Cauldrons (*jiu ding*) that symbolized the power to rule granted by Heaven together with the priests (*wu*) and invocators (*zhu*) who transmitted the will of the spirits.

It would seem that an unfamiliar, mysterious, stately and treacherous atmosphere pervaded that time, but we find it hard to imagine today. Being difficult to imagine makes it feel remote. We might well ask: are these stories of barbaric acts true? If these records are true, then is what the people of remote antiquity thought, their *mentalité*, impossible for us to comprehend today? Why, also, did the ancient people love to discuss these stories as records of the great deeds of heroes? Was their understanding of the terms barbaric and uncivilized completely different from our modern understanding?

History is remote and unfamiliar, then, especially when we want to discuss intellectual history because we have to try to experience remote antiquity by means of the extant historical resource materials. Perhaps we can reconstruct what really happened in history by reference to these materials, but the *mentalité*, the feelings, of ancient people are deeply concealed behind these materials, and this makes it impossible to grasp them clearly. This task is rendered

---

1   The Chinese character *shen* 神 can mean both god or spirit; we will use one or the other or both to suit the context.

even more difficult because these resource materials are also bound up with their compilers' imaginations, ideas, concealments, packaging and understandings of the thoughts and feelings of the ancients. This always renders the beginning of intellectual history obscure and hard to perceive.

Should intellectual history just abandon the search for the thought of the most ancient period of history? Should we emulate Hu Shi by simply ignoring Yao (Tang Yao) and Shun (Yu Shun) and the Xia and Shang dynasties and starting our discussion with the later *Book of Songs*?[2] I think this is unacceptable because thought is, after all, one long river and intellectual history has to search up stream for the beginnings of thought among the ancient Chinese.

There are at least three criteria for discussing the origins of Chinese intellectual history. First, ancient people must actually have "thought." Everything in the consciousness of ancient people cannot be considered thought. It is only when the activities of ancient people's consciousness embodies something non-utilitarian that transcends practical everyday life activities and is without concrete implications for production that this activity can be considered "thought." Second, this thought has to be formed into some sort of consensus, some commonly acknowledged ideas or concepts. That is to say the activities of thought have to reach a certain level of universality. No individual's wild fantasy can simply be regarded as thought. Thought has to be commonly acknowledged by at least a certain community of people, and this thought, idea or concept must be able to explain more than one fact before it can be regarded as thought. Third, "thought" must be recorded in symbolic fashion such as writing or images because if it is not symbolically displayed in this way it cannot be communicated or transmitted and would be impossible to study. Only when ancient people began to transmit their thoughts and feelings to others and later generations through written words, pictorial representations and material objects did they truly enter into history.

This is simply to say that for us today, it is only when written materials, cultural anthropological knowledge and archeological discoveries are sufficient to recover some ideas and concepts of the ancients that genuine intellectual history is possible.

Let us now begin the search for the fountainhead of Chinese intellectual history on the basis of written materials, cultural anthropological knowledge and archeological discoveries.

---

2 According to Gu Jiegang (*Gushibian zixu*, 1982 reprint, 52–53), when Hu Shi taught the history of Chinese philosophy at Peking University, he did not lecture on Yao, Shun, Yu, Tang, and kings Wen and Wu, but rather "eliminated the earlier traditions" and began with the *Shijing*.

1. Reconstructing the World of Ancient Thought: Traditional Written Documents, Modern Theory, and Archeological Discoveries

1.1

The written materials that we now have concerning earliest antiquity in China represent for the most part the imaginings and reflections of cultured people living after the fifth century BCE; they are not the records of the most ancient people themselves. Written so many years after the events depicted, these materials often evince strong feelings of nostalgia—time has filtered out those things that the writers did not want to remember and left behind impressions worthy of fond recollection. These somewhat fanciful recollections of past events from antiquity are always quite beautiful, especially when the writer is dissatisfied with his contemporary status quo. At that point, these imaginative remembrances of things past turn into a mirror opposite of the present to remonstrate against it. Reflected in this mirror is always a warm historical memory.

Among the most representative writings about ancient times are the *Book of Rites*, the *Laozi*, the *Hanfeizi*, the *Pheasant Cap Master* (He Guanzi), and so on. From these works, we can see that when ancient people imagined the most archaic times, they admitted the harsh nature of life at the time. They say that people in those early times were like animals living in caves in the winter and in nests in the summer, lacking fire, hence drinking blood and eating uncooked meat, wearing animal skins and being attacked by snakes and other ferocious beasts. From the legends of "Suiren-shi" (inventor of fire), "Youchao-shi" (inventor of houses and buildings), and "Shennong tasting all the herbs" (discovering agriculture) to "Great Yu taming the waters" these stories reveal the perilous environment of most ancient times. Life then was especially miserable during times of great floods.

With the exception of a few extreme realists like Han Fei, the majority of later cultured people, due to dissatisfaction with their own times, idealized remote antiquity in fanciful depictions that serve as a repository of their ideals. In their writings, the most ancient times are often beautiful and serene, just like Tao Yuanming's famous "Peach Blossom Spring" (a Chinese Shangri-La). The first section of the "Ceremonial Usages" (Li yun) chapter of the *Book of Rites* describes ancient times as a Society of Great Unity (Datong shehui). At that time, according to this classic, "all under Heaven was public (*tianxia wei gong*); men of virtue and ability were chosen; their words were truthful and they cultivated harmony … the aged were provided for until death; the able-bodied were given employment; the young were nurtured; kindness was shown to widows, orphans, the childless and the ill so that everyone was well provided for."[3] The first section of chapter 13, "Necessary Knowledge" (Beizhi), of *Pheasant Cap Master* states that at that time "there were no roads through the mountains; there were no bridges over the lakes; people did not communicate with each other, as boats and carriages did not come through. Why was this? Because the common people were childlike, educated people did not trick each other into laboring for each other, and strong people did not mutually divide into lords and subjects."[4] Even though they were aware of the difficulties of life in ancient times, they still believed that people then were tranquil of mind, that their life was peaceful and stable, that everyone was of equal status and that their thoughts were simple and uncomplicated. They believed, just as Book 11, "Equalizing Customs" (Qi su) of the *Huainanzi* put it, that antiquity was a peaceful time in an innocent and unsophisticated world.[5] In summary, the extant writings on the most ancient periods of Chinese antiquity present them more or less as follows:

(1)   Various fixed villages were the people's basic unit of life. They "went out to work at sunrise and came home to rest at sunset," and their lives were quite stable. Although they had very few possessions, they were neither greedy nor ambitious. Living plain and simple lives, they maintained plain and simple hearts and minds, and this simplicity of living and thinking was the prerequisite for the stability of their society.

(2)   People lived in many natural villages (*cunluo* 村落), some of them that surrounded comparatively larger and stronger "towns" (*cheng* 城) formed into communities called "states" (*bang* 邦). These communities of natural villages also belonged to one enormous alliance within which they lived in peaceful coexistence. These people really lived in a single unified entity that was known as "all under Heaven" (*tianxia* 天下, the whole world). On this account, they very early on had a consciousness that this *tianxia* was self-evidently unified.

(3)   This *tianxia* was naturally a unified world entity. The leader of the alliance was elected and came to symbolize a great and just personage. He had no selfish motives, just like the great legendary Sage Kings Yao, Shun and Yu. He appointed men of worth and talent, upheld justice, held authority on the basis of moral example and brought stability and order to the world. He relied on his personal charisma to make virtue the

---

3   Translation is a modified version of James Legge's translation in CTP.

4   *He Guanzi*, 13.1, CTP.

5   For the view of antiquity in *Huainanzi*, see Roger Ames, *The Art of Rulership: a Study of Ancient Chinese Political Thought*, 1994, 16–17.

self-evident ruling principle. People believed that his authority came from his moral character and that power was not something privately-owned. When someone better suited to undertake the responsibility of leadership came along, then power would be happily transferred to him.

We know, of course, that this was not the actual situation in the ancient world. It is the imaginary image of people who lived in the several hundred years after the fifth century BCE, during the Spring and Autumn, Warring States, and Qin through Han dynasty eras. Before the Qin unified China, in the first place, due to the collapse of the power of the "kings" (wang), the Regional Rulers (zhouhou 諸侯) were constantly fighting for hegemony. They wanted a common leader and a unified "all under Heaven." Secondly, due to the collapse of ethics and morality and great social disorder, they also hoped to establish a state (guojia) with a system of rites and normative standards. And finally, due to the ever growing desires and the deceitfulness of the people of that age, they wanted to return to the simple thought and unadorned lifestyle of ancient times. In their imaginations, they created a picture of a well-ordered ancient era and bequeathed to us the image of ancient people's simple and uncomplicated thought.

The life and intellectual world of highest antiquity may have really been comparatively simple and unadorned. But simplicity and plainness was not the entire content of that ancient intellectual world, and even less was life. Much of it reflected the imagination and hopes of later people. Through these images painted over with the ideals and hopes of later people, and with the support of some occasionally appearing fragmentary records, we can ask an important question: did those early people really respect and look forward to this primitive order that much? Did they really possess such self-aware moral consciousness and wisdom? Was the intellectual world of that time really so simple and serene?

Everything is still questionable.

1.2

How, then, do we understand and interpret ancient Chinese thought on the basis of contemporary theory, especially anthropological theory?

Early anthropologists mainly investigated some tribes or people who had not yet entered so-called "civilization" and then used the information to speculate about the history of peoples already considered part of "civilization." If we say that ancient Chinese educated people's "recollections" of the more ancient past were only a product of their imaginations, then we can say that the speculations about ancient peoples made by more recent anthropological theorists are assumptions and analyses based on external observation. Once they had transformed the "remote" time difference between modern and ancient times into a spatial difference between "civilized peoples" and "pre-civilized peoples," they then treated those "uncivilized" tribal peoples as historical specimens from wild landscapes and exotic atmospheres. For them, the lives of "uncivilized" tribal peoples offered the finest resource materials for tracing past history. Lewis Henry Morgan (1818–1881) could not return to the long disappeared past; he could only observe different tribal peoples from his own era, but the subtitle of his famous study, *Ancient Society*, is "Researches in the Lines of Human Progress from Savagery, through Barbarism to Civilization."[6]

When early anthropologists studied these so-called "pre-civilized" or "semi-civilized" peoples, they used their family or lineage systems, religious beliefs, ceremonies, social customs, stories, legends and myths that had not been influenced by so-called modernization as resource materials for the history of the development of human civilization. They also used this material to speculate about and reconstruct ancient history. They came in for some rather serious criticism from later scholars for both of these practices.[7] In that age, though, every researcher in the West believed in optimism and universalism, and they generally believed that "humanity shares a common origin" and "history follows regular patters of development." They did not believe that spatial differences led to cultural differences. Rather, they believed that cultural differences were due to differences in historical position on a single historical path. Today we can see that a "self-evident" Euro-centrism lay behind their great self-confidence. On the basis of their studies of these so-called backward peoples, they believed that in civilization's ancient times people lived and thought the same way as these "pre-civilized" peoples. They should be the same both in social organization and intellectual culture. Morgan's *Ancient Society*, Sir James George Frazer (1854–1941)'s *The Golden Bough: A Study in Magic and Religion* (1890–1915) and Lucien Lévy-Bruhl (1857–1939)'s *La mentalité primitive* are nearly the same in this regard.[8]

---

6 See the title page of *Ancient Society*, 2000, with a new introduction by Robin Fox.
7 For these criticisms, see John and Jean Comaroff, *Ethnography and the Historical Imagination*, 1992.
8 See *The Golden Bough: A Study in Magic and Religion*, Chapter LXIX, "Farewell to Nemi," 711–714 of abridged 1987 edition and the introduction to Lucien Lévy-Bruhl, *La mentalité primitive*, 1922. In 1865, E. B. Tylor published a book with the title *Researches into the Early History of Mankind and the Development of Civilization*.

This style of research was the dominant form of anthropological thinking throughout the nineteenth century and into the twentieth; from Sir E. B. Tylor (1832–1917) to Bronislaw Malinowski (1884–1942), it remained the way anthropologists tried to understand the life and intellectual world of ancient society. This thinking also influenced historical research, including the study of Chinese history. From Jiang Shaoyuan (1898–1983)'s *On Superstitions Regarding Hair, Beards and Fingernails* (Fa, xu, zhao—guanyu tamen de mixin, 1928) and Zheng Zhenduo (1893–1958)'s *The Prayers of Shang Tang* (Shang Tang dao, 1933) to some contemporary academic works on ancient Chinese history, especially mythology, Chinese historians have also continued this research tradition. With the passing of time, Euro-centrism has, of course, been replaced by cultural relativism and intellectual pluralism. Belief in historical regularities based on theories of social evolution have also disappeared in favor of more complex historical models. Although anthropologists warn us to be on guard against such ideas, in many contemporary anthropological works, we still see the equation of the extant cultures of pre-civilized peoples with the early civilization of mature peoples and of anthropological research on early civilization with historiographical records. As Claude Levi-Strauss put it in a book first published in 1958, "owing to the archaic nature of their techniques and institutions, these peoples recall what we have been able to reconstruct about the social organization of peoples that lived ten or twenty thousand years ago."[9]

We should not, of course, be too demanding, but should rather thank these anthropologists. We who study Chinese intellectual history should remember that they were the first ones to raise the question of the thought of ancient times. According to their theories, ancient humanity, without exception, had a very different mode of thinking from modern people.

First, ancient people believed that "mysterious powers" dwelled in ordinary objects and events. If they could master the rules or the secret codes of these mysterious powers, they could take positive (magic) or negative (taboo) actions to use or avoid them. These rules or codes in general relied on cognitive association to produce their effects and they were quite effective. They were believed in because of humanity's own thought association. That is to say, they were the product of thought. As James Frazer put it, there are two "principles of thought on which magic is based . . . that like produces like, or that an effect resembles its cause" and "that things which have once been in contact with

---

9 Claude Levi-Strauss, *Structural Anthropology*, 1958, Chapter 6, "The Concept of Archaism in Anthropology," 103.

each other continue to act on each other at a distance . . ." through what the Chinese called resonance (*ganying* 感應).[10]

Second, ancient people's classification of things was different from our modern systems. Like modern people, they also sought an intellectual order that was identical to the external world—that is, a well-regulated system of thought for understanding the external world order. But they believed that between all mutually connected things and events there was a mutually influencing, even determining, relation of cause and effect.[11] In other words, they classified and understood all objects and events in terms of their own imagination. They did not classify phenomena as we do into abstract concepts like phylum, class, order, family, genus and species according to the principles modern physics, chemistry and biology, and then make inferences and determinations on that basis. Rather, they relied on their feelings and experience and employed analogies to express them.[12]

Third, when this mode of thinking and expression is transferred from the majority of the population to an elite minority, then intellectual history begins. A few of the most able individuals gain a monopoly of explaining natural phenomena and the mysterious powers of the world. They convert their explanations into various types of secret knowledge and arcane arts that are universally applicable, such as praying for rain, sacrificing to avoid calamity, curing illness, escaping danger and communicating with the gods and spirits. When these powers are further concentrated, they develop into cultural "charisma"—that is the power and authority of thought.

There is no doubt that these ideas represent great insight. But is the ancient society constructed by these anthropologists on the basis of their investigations of so-called "pre-civilized" peoples in our modern era really a representation of historical ancient times? We have to ask a few questions about this. One, did these European anthropologists really think about and understand conditions in the world of ancient China? Two, can the passage of time in

---

10   *The Golden Bough*, Chapter III, "Sympathetic Magic," 11 of abridged 1987 edition.

11   Claude Levi-Strauss, *The Savage Mind*, 1962, Chapter 1, "The Science of the Concrete" offers many examples of analogies and categorizations.

12   Lévy-Bruhl called this way of thinking the "primitive mentality" and Levi-Strauss called it the "savage mind." This originally referred to the mode of thinking of the "primitive" or "pre-civilized" people in history. However, Lévy-Bruhl often cited J. J. de Groot's six-volume *Religious System of China* (1892–1910), and also said that his ideas about the primitive mode of thinking were inspired by reading the French translation of Sima Qian's *Records of the Grand Historian* by Édouard Chavannes (*Les Mémoires historiques de Se-ma Ts'ien*, 5 volumes, 1895–1905). This seems to have made him feel that the idea of "primitive mentality" was applicable to the entire intellectual world of ancient China.

intellectual history really be converted into differences in ethnic, territorial and cultural space? Three, does human history, especially intellectual history, really develop along the same evolutionary path? We cannot answer all these questions and resolve our doubts now, but at least we believe that the intellectual world of ancient China was really not a replica of the thought of any other place in the world. It had its own origins, its own background and its own knowledge and technical code.

In the end, we can not completely believe the "recollections" of ancient Chinese literati, nor can we completely agree with the reasoning by analogy of Western anthropologists. We must still use the archeological materials discovered in China to reconstruct the landscape of the ancient Chinese intellectual world.

1.3

The remains of China's most ancient Three Dynasties—Xia, Shang, Zhou—that have been discovered so far can be divided into to three classes.[13] First and most numerous are articles of everyday use. These of course reflect material production and daily life in the Three Dynasties, but from them we can also sense something of the general social situation and standards of ordinary knowledge of those ages. Second, and also quite numerous, are ancient grave goods buried with the dead or goods put on display by those conducting the burials. The former are articles used or particularly liked by the deceased in life, and the latter are things that the living believed would be of use to the deceased in the afterlife. Some of these articles obviously embody traces of these ancient people's ideas. In the third category are things that we can be quite certain were used by ancient people in their sacrificial ceremonies or in their symbolic activities. Although we cannot yet call them "ritual vessels," they do figuratively demonstrate some of the ancient people's most deeply held secret ideas.[14]

---

13   Very much has been written about Chinese archeological discoveries, and I cannot discuss them all here. I can only introduce a few typical examples that embody the ancient intellectual world.

14   Articles found in Paleolithic cultural sites are almost all things used in material production and daily use; things like stone and bone tools are basically without interest for intellectual history. Neolithic sites contain other articles in daily use, such as pottery, bone implements and jades whose designs, decorative motifs, shapes and applications unrelated to practical use make them reflect the contents of human thought. They are resource materials for the study of "pre-intellectual history," but their analysis is quite difficult and mostly depends on the interpretations of modern intellectual historians.

Those ancient Chinese archeological finds that have attracted the interest of intellectual history scholars include at least the following four phenomena. (1) Corpses of the deceased being painted red, and other people being buried with the deceased. This would seem to be a clear indication that these ancient people already had the ideas of an "afterworld" and an "undying soul." Especially notable is a pottery urn burial found at Banpo (near Xi-an) that has a small hole on the bottom; whether or not it was intended as an escape route for the soul is a most interesting problem. (2) Ancient people already had very delicate and even abstract design patterns and motifs in their pottery, jade pieces and bone implements. The human face and fish design of Yangshao Culture pottery unearthed at Banpo, the weird decorative motifs and sun design from Dahekou, the blackish green jade dragons from the Sanxingtala Township of the of Wengniute Banner of Inner Mongolia, and the ivory carved double bird totem of the Hemudu Culture...all clearly demonstrate that ancient people had an esthetic consciousness and regarded symmetry, order, exaggeration and strangeness as beautiful. (3) Archeology has also discovered that ancient people had a sense of respect and awe toward the mysteries of male and female. The Hongshan Culture "goddess temple" at Dongshanzui and Niuheliang in Liaoning, the prominent breasts and buttocks on the altar statue of a goddess or the female group sculpture at Dongshanzui, the clay phallus (*taozu* 陶祖) of the Longshan Culture in Hua county, Shaanxi province, the pottery jars with designs of naked men from Liuwan, Ledu in Qinghai...all demonstrate that ancient people had imaginative ideas and a sense of awe concerning the life processes. These feelings also gave them a powerful desire to search out the origins of all things. (4) Archeology has discovered some symbols, like those carved on the hundred or more pots from Banpo and other pots from Liuwan with engraved signs. Especially significant are the recently discovered engraved characters from the Longshan Culture site in Dinggongcun of Zouping county in Shandong province that show just how early Chinese writing began. Does this indicate that approximately five to six thousand years ago ancient Chinese people already had the ability to express, record and communicate their thoughts through the use of symbols?

Of course things like being curious about the origins of life, having reverence and awe about life after death, pursuing esthetic beauty and possessing symbolic thought are not just characteristic of Chinese thought. They cannot be considered the starting point or foundation of Chinese knowledge and thought.

I have always believed that several archeological discoveries offer more important heuristic value for scholars of Chinese intellectual history. These are the jade tubes (*yucong*) from the Liangzhu Culture, the dragon and tiger cosmograms from Puyang, and the jade blocks (*yuban*) from Lingjiatan.

It was first believed that the jade *cong* were from the Zhou and Han dynasties, meaning that they appeared very late, but in 1976, fourteen jade *cong* were found in the Shang dynasty tomb of Lady Fu Hao. In recent years, both stone and jade *cong* have been found in Neolithic sites, especially in the Liangzhu Culture site where a large jade *cong* was discovered and authenticated. Jade *cong* can now be dated back to three thousand years BCE. *Yucong* are jade tubes that are square on the outside and round and hollow on the inside, and they are decorated with animal designs like the face of a wild beast or bird patterns. In the *Rites of Zhou* (Zhouli), it is recorded that ancient people "used dark green jade disks (*cang bi* 蒼璧) to sacrifice to Heaven, and used yellow tubes (*huang cong* 黃琮) to sacrifice to Earth."[15] In ancient times, these jade *cong* may have been extremely important ritual objects for sacrificial ceremonies. According to Zhang Guangzhi (1931–2001)'s *Bronze Age China* (Zhongguo qingtong shidai), "*Cong* symbolized the connection between Heaven and Earth, and they were also a method or ritual tool (*faqi*) for connecting Heaven and Earth together."[16] Because its shape symbolized Heaven and Earth, it was inscribed with designs of various animals who could assist the mystic powers, it was made of jade, a pure and sacred material said to be able to "contact the spirits," it was carved square on the outside to correspond to the ancient idea of the great Earth and round on the inside to correspond to the ancient idea of the dome of Heaven; it could be used to symbolize the interconnection of Heaven and Earth. It could be used in sacrifices consecrated to both Heaven and Earth and it had the mystic power to communicate with Heaven and Earth and to receive the spirits and ghosts (*shengui*).[17]

If Zhang Guangzhi's speculation is correct, then the ancient Chinese very early on had the spatial concepts of "Heaven is round and Earth is square," above and below and of four directions. Very conveniently for this idea, in the Warring States period tomb of Marquis Yi of Zeng in Leigudun in Sui county, Hubei province, archeologists discovered a Big Dipper dragon and tiger cosmogram and an astronomical diagram of the twenty-eight constellations on the lid of a lacquer trunk. A similar Big Dipper dragon and tiger design was

---

15 *Zhouli*, "Da zong bo," SSJZS, 762.

16 Zhang Guangzhi, *Zhongguo qingtong shidai*, erji, 1990, 71.

17 I have introduced only one interpretation of the role and significance of these ancient jade *cong*, still a disputed topic. The Japanese scholar Hayashi Minao believes that jade *cong* were the "bodies" (*zhu*) that the spirits relied upon, and their round holes provided a place for the returning dead to rest on (see his *Chugoku kogyo no kenkyu*, 1991, 119–120); the Chinese scholar Yang Jianfang, however, believes that the relief sculptures on the jade *cong* represent a combination of ancient deities and mythological animals (see his "Yu cong zhi yanjiu," *Kaogu yu wenwu* 2 (1990), 56–57.

also discovered in a tomb at the Yangshao Culture site of Xishuipo in Puyang, Henan, but this time the design was formed by an arrangement of clam shells and human bones. We know that in ancient times the four cardinal directions and the four seasons were intimately connected, especially in that the dragon and the tiger symbolized east and west respectively, and extended to the two seasons of spring and autumn that ancient people were most concerned about. From these archeological discoveries, it is obvious that the spatial and temporal concepts of the ancient Chinese implicit in the four directions and four spirits (*sifang sishen*) go back to a rather early time. Even more opportune, in 1987 a set of jade tortoise blocks (*yugui yuban* 玉龜玉版) was unearthed from the approximately 4,500 year-old tomb number four at Lingjiatan in Anhui. The piece was square outside with a circle on the inside within which was carved around a smaller circle a design pointing in the four cardinal directions and the eight points of the compass. The jade tortoise block was found in the very center on the bottom of the tomb, and many scholars believe that it is similar to later models (*shi* 式) and mirrors used to symbolize the four poles (*siji* 四極) and eight points of the compass (*bafang*) that comprise ancient Chinese ideas of space and time. Some scholars believe that this represents the spirit tortoise (*linggui* 靈龜) beliefs mentioned by Sima Qian in the "Biography of Tortoise Shell and Yarrow Stalk Divination" (Guice liezhuan) chapter of the *Records of the Grand Historian*.[18] Other scholars believe that it is a tool the ancient Chinese used to indicate "position" (*fangwei* 方位) and "mathematics" (*shuli* 數理) before they had a writing script.[19] Some other scholars even take it to be "a primitive depiction of the eight trigrams that were used in the Xia dynasty or even earlier as a calendrical chart to indicate the four seasons."[20]

No matter what, we must agree that this find is full of mysterious significance. It may very possibly be connected to the ancient shamanistic arts (*wushu*). The character *wu* for shaman has two "workers" *gong*, 工, standing side by side, and *gong* is the ancient character for a carpenter's square (*ju*, 矩 or 榘, also meant rule, regulation, pattern). The earliest *wu* shamans were just people who used this carpenter's square to measure Heaven and Earth. And so managing Heaven, Earth, the cosmos, the four poles (*siji* 四極) and the eight

---

18 Yu Weichao, "Hanshan Lingjiatan yuqi he kaoguxue zhong yanjiu jingshen lingyu de wenti," *Wenwu yanjiu* 5 (1989), 57–63.

19 Rao Zongyi, "Weiyou wenzi yiqian biaoshi fangwei yu shuli guanxi de yuban," *Wenwu yanjiu* 6 (1990), 48–52.

20 Chen Shengyong, "Dongnan diqu Xia wenhua de mengsheng yu jueqi," *Dongnan wenhua* 1 (1991), 14.

points of the compass could have early on been the core of the "knowledge of the *wu* and *shi* diviners."[21]

These finds lead us to believe even more firmly that long before previously known the ancient Chinese already had the ideas that Heaven is round and Earth is square, that the Great Earth has four poles and eight compass directions and that there are four deities corresponding to the four cardinal directions and all these served as their symbolic concepts of space. These spatial ideas have tremendous significance for intellectual history. If the above exposition is tenable, then this evidence illustrates that:

One, Chinese intellectual history was connected to "Heaven and Earth" from the very beginning. The idea that the universe and Heaven and Earth have centers and peripheries was produced from their observations, experience and awareness of celestial bodies and terrestrial topography. Implicit in this was the ancient Chinese notion that they were dwelling in the center of Heaven and Earth. This notion was certainly related to the name *zhongguo* (中國, modern term for China, originally meaning "central states" and translated as the "Middle Kingdom"). These feelings and notions about Heaven and Earth would be related to many kinds of abstract concepts held by later Chinese.

Two, these feelings and conceptions about Heaven, Earth and the four cardinal directions were perhaps also the original starting point of ancient Chinese thought. In other words, they were the self-evident foundations of ancient Chinese thought. In this line of thought and with the aid of a system of connected metaphors inferring this from that, the following ideas were produced: in spatial relations, the center governs the four cardinal directions; in temporal sequence, the center is earlier than four cardinal directions; in rank and value, the center is superior to the four cardinal directions; the revolution of the heavens and the apparent leftward movement of the heavenly path led people to the idea that Heaven and Earth were created in a spiraling movement from the center; the feeling that the poles did not move and that Heaven was like a canopy led people to the ideas that Heaven and Earth both had a center and four cardinal directions. Once this idea was embodied in mythology, in human consciousness and ceremonies it would take shape as an orderly genealogy of the central god (*diwang* 帝王) and deities of the four directions; and when this idea was extended into the social realm, it became the foundation for the political legitimacy of a system in which a central ruler reigned over subjects of the four regions (*fanchen* 藩臣).

---

21   See Li Xueqin, "Lun Lingjiatan yugui yuban," *Zhongguo wenhua* 6 (1992), 144–149.

Three, the implements that symbolized Heaven and the knowledge to interpret the cosmos possessed mysterious powers because the former had "the same nature" as Heaven and Earth and the latter had interpretive "authority;" they became a kind of sacred knowledge. These implements did not belong to everyone in society, nor did everyone possess this kind of knowledge. Only the shamans who could communicate with the spirits and the diviners (or scribes) who observed and measured Heaven and Earth possessed them. The practice of these arts and techniques became, then, the exclusive right of a minority, and thought also became the profession of thinkers.

Although the rise of *wu* shamans and *shi* diviners/scribes and their merging with the power of the greatest *wu-shi* of all—the king (*wang*) destroyed the peaceful, tranquil atmosphere and simple, uncomplicated mentality of ancient times, it did, nevertheless, serve to separate "thought" from the practical, individual, concrete and general activities of consciousness. On the one hand, thought was raised to the level of universal and directing "concepts," and on the other hand, it was concretized into systematic and operative "knowledge."

2.   The Shang Conceptual System as Recorded in the Oracle Bone Inscriptions

In various legends about the ancient Three Dynasties, after the Five Di (or legendary emperors) came the Xia, Shang and Zhou dynasties. Xia dynasty history is vague and uncertain, combining myths and legends with history. Archeologists cannot verify it, and there are not enough written sources to prove it's history, so it is best to lay it aside for the time being. For the Shang (or Yin) dynasty, we not only have the "Basic Annals of Yin" (Yin benji) in the *Records of the Grand Historian*, but we also have some 100,000 or more oracle bone inscriptions. And even more, we have the astonishing archeological finds from Anyang in Henan, Dayangzhou in Jiangxi and Sanxingdui in Sichuan that transmit down to us the history of that era, and this makes it possible for us to discuss in a general way the knowledge and thought of the Shang. Of course, most of that knowledge and thought comes to us from *wu* priests, *zhu* invocators, *shi* diviners/scribes and *zong* 宗 temple masters. They can be said to be the earliest group of knowledge workers and thinkers in China after the invention of the written script.

2.1
The first thing that my attention was drawn to was the gradual systemization of the Shang people's ideas about mystical powers.

Early human beings all had experiences and impressions of a mystical nature, described these mystical experiences as mystical powers and even imagined these mystical powers to demonstrate the existence of a multitude of gods and spirits. This is a universal phenomenon of the early human world, but once people systematized a genealogy of the multitude of gods and spirits, this not altogether similar order revealed the different understandings of the world present in different regions and different civilizations. When we read the ancient and terse oracle bone inscriptions, we find that the Shang people had already apotheosized these mystical powers and generally arranged them into an orderly genealogy. The highest rank in this genealogy belonged to the highest ranking entity in the Shang spirit world—the Di 帝 (Supreme Lord). According to the interpretation of some paleographers, the etymological meaning of the Chinese character *di* is to give birth to the ten thousand things, that is, to all the world. In very early China, it is quite likely that the word Di was used to represent "Heaven" as the progenitor of the whole world.

In Shang oracle bone inscriptions, Di eventually came to mean the god or spirit with the highest authority among the multitude of gods and spirits. According to Chen Mengjia's research, we know that the Shang people believed that Di could order the wind and rain, send down calamities, protect the harvest, control floods and droughts, protect their towns and cities and so on. Di dwelled on high, did not enjoy sacrifices of animals and slaves, rarely received sacrifices from people, and had no blood relationship with former and deceased Shang kings and ancestors. As Chen wrote, during the Shang dynasty the will and power of Shang Di 上帝 (Lord on High or the High God) showed both benevolence and malice. Shang Di supervised the annual harvests, warfare, building of towns and the movements of the Shang kings.[22]

Besides Di, the Shang people also revered many other spirits. The structure of their hierarchy was closely connected to the ancient ideas of Heaven and Earth and the four directions discussed above.

First, there were descriptions of concrete celestial bodies and meteorological phenomena such as the sun, moon, wind, clouds, rain and rainbows. Because these were directly observed and experienced heavenly phenomena, the Shang people considered them to be deities and bringers of good or bad fortune. This is not surprising, but what is worth noting is that among the objects of Shang sacrifices there were "the Mother of the East" (*dongmu* 東母) and "the Mother of the West (*ximu* 西母)." Some people say they refer to

---

22   Chen Mengjia, *Yinxu buci zongshu*, 1956, 1981, 580. For Di, also see Sarah Allen, *The Shape of the Turtle: Myth, Art, and Cosmos in Early China*, 1991, 59 and David N. Keightley in *The Cambridge History of Ancient China*, 1999, 252–53.

the goddesses (*shen*) of the sun and the moon. As evidence they cite section 17 of the "Meaning of the Sacrifices" (Jiyi) chapter in the *Book of Rites*: "They sacrificed to the sun in the eastern suburb; they sacrificed to the moon in the western suburb." Also noteworthy is that the oracle bone inscriptions record sacrifices to the winds of the four directions and give them special names that match the names of gods. Hu Houxuan and Yang Shuda compared the four direction wind names in the oracle bone inscriptions with those in "The Canon of Yao" (Yaodian) chapter in the *Book of Documents* and the *Classic of Mountains and Seas* (Shanhai jing) and demonstrated that the provenance of this idea of a mutual correspondence between the four directions, the four winds and four gods or spirits was very early.[23]

Corresponding to the celestial bodies were many earthly phenomena. Shang oracle bone inscriptions have a great deal to say about gods and spirits of the Great Earth, but the most noteworthy are the mention in sacrifices of the concept of "four directions" or the "five directions." From ancient times, people used sunrise and sunset to determine east and west. The Chinese character *dong* 東 for east pictures the sun coming up behind a tree, and *xi* 西 for west is the sun setting in a tree. Later people used the stars to determine the compass positions of north and south. They discovered that everything in the sky moved to the left with the exception of the eternally motionless North Pole, that is the northern Polestar or Polaris. Fixing the correct direction was a very important matter in ancient times, not only for its relation to calendar-making but also for the constructions of towns and settlements. The oracle bone inscriptions already give the names of the "four directions" as Xi, Yin, Yi and Fu (析, 因, 彝, 伏). There are very many references to the "four directions," and with the addition of the center where the Shang lived, there were "five directions (or regions)." The oracle bone inscriptions sometime combined central Shang and the four directions and conducted harvest divination for the five directions. Not only did the Shang people clearly recognize the four directions, they also made regular sacrifices to the spirits associated with them, and the four directions had a definite sequence of east, south, west, north. The *Pheasant Cap Master, Huainanzi* and the Han dynasty apocrypha all record the east, south, west, north movement of the Big Dipper corresponding to the spring, summer, autumn, winter order of the four seasons; this demonstrates how very far back the origin of these ideas goes.

The second part of the "Summary of the Rules of Propriety" (Quli) chapter of the *Book of Rites* states that "the Son of Heaven sacrifices to Heaven and

---

23 Hu Houxuan, "Jiaguwen sifang fengming kaozheng" in *Jiaguxue Shangshi luncong chuji*, 1944. Yang Shuda, *Jiaguwen zhong sifang fengming yu shenming*, in *Jiweiju jiawen shuo*, 1954.

Earth and to the four directions."[24] This was, of course, written by later people, but from the oracle bone inscriptions we already know that, carrying on an older tradition, there was already a rather complete idea of spatial order during the Shang era. The Great City (or Settlement) Shang (*Da Yi Shang* 大邑商) was in the center of "all under Heaven" and the four non-Shang tribes (*siyi* 四夷, later rendered barbarians) were on the four sides, in the four regions. Besides "Di" in the center of Heaven serving as the symbol of their first progenitor, the Shang also had a center of the Earth— the god of the soil and his altar (*sheshen* 社神) in the Great City Shang—while the four regions each had their own deities. The Shang believed that they were dwelling in the center and the four non-Shang tribes were in the four regions. Directly above their heads was Heaven, and the four regions continuously rotated around this central Heaven. Everything up and down and in the four directions—later to be called the "six conjunctions" (*liuhe* 六合) of north, south, east, west, up and down— the whole world—was full of mysterious powers, and, just like the human realm, these mysterious powers had an orderly structure.

2.2

The second thing worthy of our attention in the oracle bone inscriptions is the unfolding of Shang ancestor worship and its conceptual systematization when combined with the power of the Shang kings.

As discussed above, ancient Chinese people had a kind of natural worship of biological life, and this worship gave rise to curiosity about all origins. This was first manifest in their curiosity about the origins of humanity. At first they believed that humanity originated from the female sex,[25] but, after the male sex became the dominant force in society, the character for ancestor (*zu* 祖) representing the progenitor of humanity through birth and reproduction, actually referred to the male sex. They then believed that the power of these male ancestors made it possible for human beings to populate the world. Because of this they also believed that the spirits of their male ancestors could also protect the prosperity and safety of their offspring, and for this reason they instituted sacrifices to these spirits of their deceased ancestors.

This attention to ancestors and posterity became one of the most important ideas in traditional China; it could even be said to be the source of all value orientations in Chinese intellectual history. When traditional Chinese considered

---

24   *Liji*, "Quli xia" in SSJZS, 1268.
25   Examples like the pottery figure of a pregnant woman from the Hongshan Culture of Dongshanzui, Kazuo County, Liaoning and the pottery pots with nude female images from the Majiayao Culture of Sanpingtai, Liuwan, Qinghai would all seem to corroborate this idea.

their ancestors, themselves, and their sons and grandsons, they would feel that their life stream flowed on without end. And when they thought that they were a part of this stream of life, that they had a family and were not alone, they would feel that the meaning of their lives was expanding so much that it filled the whole universe. Grave and tomb burials, ancestral shrines and memorial halls and sacrifices were the stately occasions and places that confirmed and strengthened the meaning of their lives. They brought the continuation of kinship lines and the transmission of culture together as one unit; only when family and lineage bloodlines and cultural traditions were so united could they form the foundation of an ethnic "identity." Grave and tomb burials, ancestral shrines, memorial halls and sacrificial activities supported communication with relatives of the same lineage, solidarity of bloodlines and cultural identity through the commemoration of the deceased ancestors, family members and relatives.

There are many elements of significance for Chinese intellectual history in the importance attached to burial styles, articles placed in graves, sacrificial structures and the reverence and awe involved in the offering of sacrifices since Shang times. First, they contained the germs of people's belief in the duality of body and soul and the idea that the living and the dead travel different paths. They realized that they would die and believed that after death people inhabited a different world. Second, they express the increasing significance of blood relationships and the affections of kinship. Ceremonies were the temporary embodiment of these feelings of kinship. The ritual etiquette, offerings and grave articles present in such ceremonies reflected people's consciousness of the value of blood relationships. Third, sacrificial ceremonies confirmed the closeness or distance of personal relationships within secular society, and then developed into conventions established by popular usage. These conventions further reinforced people's consciousness of distinctions of kinship closeness or distance. When, through the power of the Shang kings, these ceremonies based on kinship relationships came to be frequently used for the former lords and kings of the Shang, the oracle bone inscriptions begin to contain very many reports on the sacrifices to these former lords and kings. They believed that the spirits of the former lords and kings were definitely in Heaven above, and so for the sake of these ancestors, they conducted "burnt offerings" (*liaoji* 燎祭) by burning wood and causing great plumes smoke to rise into Heaven. When this smoke rose into Heaven, they believed that it could transmit their prayers and blessings from their descendents on earth up to the ancestral spirits.

Shang oracle bone inscriptions show that from the reign of King Zu Jia on (approximately 1187 BCE), the Shang people carried out a long and magnificent sacrificial ritual for their former lords and kings. The ritual known as the "*yi* 衣 sacrifice" or the "*zhou* 周 sacrifice,"[26] involved a series of ceremonies performed one after another. These sacrificial ceremonies were extremely complex and required a full year to complete a cycle. They reflected the Shang people's, especially the Shang royal family's, worship of the spirits of their ancestral former lords and kings. They sacrificed to the collective ancestors in rank order, combining various ceremonies that included calling down the spirits (*jiangshen*), offering blood sacrifices (*xianxing*), serving food (*kuishi*), including millet, reading aloud appointment orders (*zhuce*), drum beating and feather dancing (*wuyu*). It was all extremely solemn and detailed.[27]

Besides those male ancestors directly related to the former lords and kings, the oracle bone inscriptions from the Shang ruin Yinxu also record sacrifices to female ancestors and various elder brothers of the former lords and kings. This hierarchical system of sacrifices demonstrates that in the Shang era a definite idea about lineages, society and the *tianxia* (world) had already formed. To wit, in the formation of the order and structure of lineages, society and the whole *tianxia*, kinship relationships were most important. This was so in life and continued to be so after death; it was so inside lineages and in society as a whole. As the warp and woof of Shang social structure, the significance of blood relationships was equally important for the Shang royal lineages and the social strata below them. Although quite a few ancient tribal traditions were preserved during the Shang era, and various elder brothers (including the elder and younger brothers of great-grandfathers, the cousins of paternal grandfathers and second cousins of the fathers' generation) could all receive sacrifices in the Shang ancestral temples, yet an axis of lineages and society was eventually established.[28] At the same time, the vertical inheritance system with the primary line through the directly related male line (grandfathers, fathers, sons) with their spouses forming an auxiliary line also came into being in the Shang era.

We can at least say that in the Shang era, their idea of social organization was very orderly and systematic.

---

26 Equivalent to the *yin* 殷 sacrifice in the Zhou dynasty; *yi* should be read as "*yin*" meaning magnificent or majestic.

27 See Guo Baojun, *Zhongguo qingtongqi shidai*, 1978, 228.

28 See Chen Mengjia, *Yinxu buci zongshu*, 1956, 1981, 404–05. Wu Ding sacrificed to all of his father's elder and younger brothers (from *jia* to *gui*, that is the first to the tenth *gan* stems by which Shang kings were named); after Wu Ding, in the time of Zu Geng and Zu Jia, only the six ancestors *jia, bing, wu, geng, xin* and *yi* remained; in the time of Zu Xin and Kang Ding only four former kings, Yang Jia, Pan Geng, Xiao Xin, and Xia Yi were left to receive sacrifices.

2.3

The third thing worthy of our notice is the regularization of the Shang knowledge system as expressed in sacrificial and divination ceremonies.

The *Rites of Zhou* divides sacrificial music and dance into six categories according to the object of the sacrifice: gods of Heaven and Earth (*tianshen* and *dishi* 地示), spirits of the four directions, mountains and rivers, female ancestors (*xianbi*) and male ancestors (*xianzu*). Sacrifices are also divided according to size into major, medium and minor. The major sacrifices are for Heaven and Earth, the medium for the ancestral spirits, and the small are the five state sacrifices (*wusi* 五祀). There are also three categories according to the sacrificial offerings: offerings of jade, silk, domestic animals, including perfect oxen of a single color are major sacrifices; offerings of domestic animals and money are medium sacrifices; and offerings of domestic animals only are minor sacrifices.

If these sources from a later time are reliable, then the Zhou dynasty sacrifices can be divided into an orderly sequence of ranks: the objects of the first rank sacrifices were Heaven and Earth and the ancestors—sacrifices to the cosmos and the spirits of the ancestors; the object of the second rank sacrifices were the sun, moon and stars or the gods of earth and grain (*sheji*) and the five sacred mountains (*wuyue*)—sacrificing to the great gods or spirits of Heaven and Earth; the objects of the third rank sacrifices were wind, rain, thunder, lightning or all things in the mountains and rivers—sacrificing to the lesser gods or spirits of Heaven and Earth.

What, then, was the situation in the Shang era before the Zhou dynasty?

From the oracle bone inscriptions we see that the Shang sacrifices included burnt offerings, sending up smoke to demonstrate their sincerity to the spirits of Heaven. There were also drowning and burying sacrifices involving drowning domestic animals and sinking jade disks or burying sacrificial animals in the ground; most of these sacrifices were to the river gods. The oracle bone inscriptions also show that the Shang sacrifices had a definite classification into different ranks with definite sacrifices leading to ideas of divisions and connections. The gods of the universe and the spirits of ancestors, the lords of Heaven and Earth and the ancestors of Shang kings, and the gods of the mountains and rivers were all sacrificed to in different groups, and each rank of gods and spirits received the sacrifice of the number of animals and so on suitable to their rank. Among the contents of the very many sacrifices recorded in the oracle bone inscriptions, the following three phenomena are worth noting:

First is the gradual joining of the gods of Heaven, Earth and nature with the spirits of the male and female ancestors. For example, allowing the earlier ancestors and former lords and kings to go up and visit Heaven (*bin yu tian* 賓與天) was known as "Bin Di" (賓帝 visiting Di)—that is, the former kings are on the left and right of the supreme deity or Lord on High (Shang Di), and Di can protect, assist and reprimand the kings, and the former kings also protect and assist the living kings. Another example is the phenomenon of sacrificing jointly to the twenty-eight constellations and the former lords and kings when sacrificing to Heaven. This could be the beginning of the idea of "receiving the Mandate of Heaven" (*tianming* 天命). And there is also the practice of matching sacrifices to the sun with those to the former kings. Some scholars have pointed out that an oracle bone inscription from the time of kings Wu Yi and Wen Ding records that at the time of the *churi* (sunrise) and *ruri* (sunset) sacrifices they connected them by analogy with King Shang Jia. This is very much like what later people said: "Sacrifice to Heaven ... and respect your original ancestor as a match for the gods of Heaven."[29]

Second is the gradual regularization of sacrificial procedures. After the time of Zu Jia, the sacrifices of the Shang royal house generally followed the sacrificial list or schedule (*sipu*) in carrying out a formalized cycle of sacrifices in which various ceremonies of drum beating, feather dancing, offering meat, wine and millet, and sacrificing animals were formally regularized. The inner significance of these sacrifices was crystallized into a few symbols through this process of formalization, and these symbols in turn always suggested some sorts of ideas to the Shang people.

Third is that relationships with the heavenly rulers became concentrated in the person of "the king alone" (*wang yi ren* 王一人). Some scholars have pointed out that according to the oracle bone inscriptions the reign of Zu Jia was a period of great religious and political change. Zu Jia not only established the order of the above mentioned *zhou* (or *yi*) sacrifices but also obtained religious confirmation for his authority by personally calling down the spirits of the ancestors and communicating with the Heavenly Di by practicing the so-called "Bin" ritual.[30]

2.4

Being able to "communicate with Heaven" gave the Shang kings mysterious powers, but the kings alone did not complete the sacrificial rituals. Sacrifices

---

29 Song Zhenhao, "Jiaguwen churi ruri kao," *Chutu wenxian yanjiu*, 1985, 34–5. *Churi* and *ruri* were sacrificial ceremonies dedicated to the sun. Yao Xiaosui and Xiao Ding say that these ceremonies are mentioned in the *Shangshu* "Yaodian" and belong to spring and autumn, but in the Shang era, however, "both *churi* and *ruri* were performed on the same day." See their *Xiaotun nandi jiagu kaoshi*, 1985, 77. Final quote is from *Guyangzhuan zhushu*, text at http://gj.zdic.net/archive.php?aid-2884.html.

30 Itô Michiharu, "Ôken to Saishi," *Huaxia wenming yu chuanshi cangshu—Zhongguo guoji Hanxuejia yantaohui lunwen*, 1995, 327–332. Also see Hu Houxuan, "Chonglun 'Yu yi ren' de wenti," *Gu wenzi yanjiu* 6 (1981), 15–33.

required the services of *zhu* invocators and *wu* priests. In the "Discourses of Chu" (Chuyu) chapter of the *Discourses of the States*, Guan Shefu tells King Zhao of Chu that priests and invocators had to understand the names of mountains and rivers, the situation of the ancestors, the temple ceremonies and the sacrificial rules. They concentrated their minds and spirits in a solemn and serene manner and not only possessed a wealth of knowledge and technical skill but also mysterious mental powers and wisdom. This is to say that those who managed the sacrifices represented the most cultured people of the age. They made up a group of mystics surrounding the kings who helped the kings to receive orders and decrees from the Di in Heaven and were responsible for communication between the spirit world and the human realm. They were professional mind and spirit workers, possessed knowledge and technical skills and exercised spiritual powers as agents of the kings to bring together the spirit world and the world of men. The records they left behind became the resource materials of our intellectual history.

According to legend, in the time of the Shang founder Shang Tang there was Yi Yin; in Tai Wu's time there was Wu Xian; in Zu Yi's time there was Wu Xian (different character)—all of whom were probably very important priests. We have more than 120 names of "diviners" listed on the oracle bone inscriptions from the Shang ruins. They must be considered ancient China's first learned men. Their role was two-fold: on the one hand, they employed sacrificial rites to communicate with the spirit world and divination to pass on the words of the gods and spirits—this was "divination" or *wu* 巫; on the other hand, they recorded the people's (mainly the kings) wishes and actions, verified the decrees of the gods and passed them on to later generations—this was "writing down the divination" or *shi* 史. Because they undertook these responsibilities, they became professional thinkers and educators. To do so, they had to understand the structure, changes and omens of the cosmos; the birth, propagation, health and death of humanity; and the rules and language of the ceremonies for communicating with the gods and spirits. Their intellectual system included the following:

One, mastery of astrological divination by the stars and calendrical calculation of the external world. The oracle bone inscriptions demonstrate the contemporary development and popularity of such knowledge. Divination by means of turtle shell plastrons indicates their mastery of the cosmos. Prayers and sacrifices to wind, rain, thunder and lightning shows their understanding of natural meteorological phenomena. The use of the heavenly stems and earthly branches (*tiangan dizhi*, sets of 10 and 12 units used to record time), the four seasons, the twelve months and the placement of intercalary days or months demonstrates their familiarity with calendar-making. All of these things constitute the origins of later numerological techniques as well as illustrating the Shang people's knowledge of the external world.

Two, knowledge of the course of sacrificial ceremonies to rectify the order of the human world. The various operational regulations of sacrificial rites, such as the names of the gods, the sequence of the sacrifices, the rank of those receiving the sacrifice, the quantity of the offerings, the contents of prayers and the methods of divination all contained extremely specialized techniques for contacting the gods as well as knowledge of intensely solemn lineage laws. These were the origins of later religious rites and ceremonies and also the contemporary way of distinguishing degrees of kinship relationships and the ethical order of society.

Three, knowledge of the human body and medical skills. Legend has it that ten *wu* priests, including Wu Xian and Wu Peng could communicate directly with the gods and spirits. These ancient priests not only knew the arts of communicating with the spirits, but many of them also had medical skills. We often see records of "wind sickness" (*fengji*), "painful afflictions" (*tongji*) and even information about twins in the Shang oracle bone inscriptions. From this, we can see that Shang priests were experts both at bringing down the gods and in curative medical practices. This was the beginning of later mantic and medical arts, and it also represents the Shang people's knowledge of biological life and their own bodies.

These were the most important contents of the knowledge, thought and belief worlds of Shang times.

3.   Evolution of Thought as Recorded in the Written Documents and Bronze Inscriptions of the Western Zhou

In 1027 BCE, the Zhou people from the western margin of the Shang defeated the Shang of the Central Plains, replacing them as rulers of the *tianxia* and establishing the Zhou dynasty.[31]

We have many more surviving resources for the Western Zhou than we do for the Shang. Among these written documents, the *Book of Documents* contains

---

31   The exact date of the Western Zhou conquest of the Shang has long been a contested question in Chinese history; there are said to be over thirty theories about it. I have chosen the date of 1027 BCE because Pei Yin's "Collected Interpretations" (*jijie*) on the "Zhou benji" (Basic Annals of Zhou) in the *Shiji* quotes the *Bamboo Annals* (Zhushu jinian) that there were 257 years from the time the Western Zhou King Wu established the dynasty until it ended under Zhou King You, and King You's reign ended in 770 BCE.

some believable records and the *Remaining Zhou Documents* also has several credible chapters.[32] Then we have the comparatively detailed account in the *Records of the Grand Historian* "Basic Annals of Zhou," (Zhou benji) and the *Shiben* can also serve as a reference. Recent archeological discoveries include truly remarkable repeated caches of oracle bone inscriptions at the Zhouyuan capital of the Western Zhou near Mount Qi in Fufeng county, Shaanxi province. As sources of intellectual history, though, several problems render these materials insufficient. They are scattered and unsystematic. They are very indirect and do not directly express thought. They are very complicated to use, with the authentic and the false (forgeries) hard to distinguish. Nevertheless, since the Zhou materials are more numerous than those for the Shang, we can still rely on them to explore the following questions.

Did the Western Zhou inherit the Shang traditions or did they change them?

Did the basic structure of the Western Zhou intellectual system differ in any essential qualities from that of the Shang?

Are there any fundamental differences between the basic foundations of the Western Zhou intellectual world and those of the Shang?

3.1

For a long time, intellectual historians believed that a fundamental change took place between the Shang and the Zhou. For example, in his "Essay on the Yin (Shang) and Zhou Systems" Wang Guowei wrote that "There has been no greater political and cultural change in Chinese history than that between the Shang and the Zhou."[33] Many scholars and many published works have asserted that, at least in their attitude toward the spirits and ghosts (of the ancestors), the Zhou differed greatly from the Shang. This became virtually a dead certainty in Chinese intellectual history. The Shang was an age that "oppressed the people and served the spirits" (*canmin shishen* 殘民事神), and the Zhou was an age that "venerated Heaven and protected the people" (*jingtian baomin* 敬天保民). Some scholars went on to conjecture that the people of the Western Zhou both doubted and worshiped Heaven at the same time. Their discourse on worshipping Heaven was, then, intended for the people of the Shang, but their discourse on doubting Heaven was intended for the Zhou people. Their continuation of the Shang idea of worshipping Heaven was, then, "only a political perpetuation—they used religious thought as a policy

---

32   It is generally accepted that the "Shi fu," "Ke Yin," the "Shang shi," "Du yi," "Zuo luo," "Huang men," "Zhai gong," and "Chang mai" sections of the *Yi Zhoushu* are genuine historical sources.

33   Wang Guowei, "Yin Zhou zhidu lun," in *Guantang jilin*, 1959 & 1994, 453–54.

to keep the people ignorant." As the "Record of Examples" (Biaoji), chapter of the *Book of Rites* puts it, "the Zhou people served the ancestral spirits (*gui*) and respected the gods (*shen*), but kept their distance from them."[34]

This was not necessarily the case. The quite numerous records of Zhou dynasty sacrifices and divinations certainly do not prove that their "worshipping Heaven" was only a political tactic. Besides, the Zhou was a non-Shang state (*fangguo* 方國) that had received investiture from the Shang, and the thought and culture of the Zhou people was not very different from that of the Shang. Among the oracle bone inscriptions discovered at Zhouyuan, the early capital of the Zhou, there is a record of the Shang kings Di Yi and Di Xin (King Zhou of the Shang) sacrificing to the former King Da Jia in the ancestral temple of the Zhou. I have always believed, then, that the Shang represented the mainstream of Chinese knowledge, thought and belief, and that the Zhou, a small political community (*bang* 邦) on its western border, and its later development and prosperity were really due to its inheritance of Shang culture.

We can look at several essays in the *Remaining Zhou Documents*—the "Conquest of the Yin" (Ke Yin), the "Great Capture" (Shi fu) and the "Declaration to the Shang" (Shang shi)—for information on Zhou sacrifices to the gods and spirits. The "Conquest of Yin" is a record of the Shang to Zhou transfer of power and the "Declaration to the Shang" is a speech made by Zhou King Wu to the former Shang aristocracy, and we can see the following points from them. First, in general the various Zhou sacrifices continued the Shang tradition. As quoted above, the "Summary of the Rules of Propriety" chapter of the *Book of Rites* states that "in one year, the Son of Heaven sacrifices to Heaven and Earth and to the four directions and performs the five state sacrifices." This was the Zhou system, but, according to Zheng Xuan's annotations, it was also the Shang system.[35] The Zhou ceremonies generally followed the Shang. The major Shang burnt offering ritual involved human sacrifice and so did that of the Western Zhou. The "Great capture" records that when Zhou King Wu conquered the Shang, on the *guichou* 癸丑 day, he killed more than a hundred Shang prisoners of war. From this we can see that before and after the change of dynasties this kind of sacrificial tradition did not really disappear for a rather long time.

Second, the Zhou people equally believed in and revered symbolic curses (*yansheng*) and taboo rituals (*jinjiyishi*), including some that we would consider absurd today. For example, the *Records of the Grand Historian* "Basic Annals of Zhou" records that when King Wu attacked the last Shang king,

---

34   For the above discussion, see Guo Baojun, *Zhongguo qingtongqi shidai*, 1978, 226 and Guo Moruo, *Qingtong shidai*, 1957, 20.

35   *Liji*, "Quli xia" in SSJZS, 1268.

Zhou, he sacrificed to the war-controlling star Reticulum (*bisu* 畢宿 the Net) and also paid close attention to any unusual omens in the natural world. All of this demonstrates that the Zhou people felt just as strongly about protection and assistance from the gods and the intimations of omens, and were really not as civilized and rational as later generations have believed them to be.

Third, the Zhou continued to worship "Di" (High God or Lord on High) or "Tian" (Heaven) as much as the Shang had. In his "Declaration to the Shang," Zhou King Wu mentions the Lord on High (Shang Di) eleven times. From the references to "Tian" in the bronze inscriptions on the "Cauldron of Da Yu" (Da Yu ding) and the *Book of Songs*, Zhou Eulogy (Zhou Song) "Wo jiang" ("We bring our offerings"), we can see that the awe-inspiring nature of "Tian" remained in the heart's of the Zhou people.[36] In sum, the intellectual worlds of the Western Zhou and of the Shang were much more similar than different. The people of the Western Zhou believed as much as the Shang did that the "Di" was in Heaven, and, just like the human world, there was a world composed of deities who ruled over everything under Di's rule.

3.2
Equally similar to the Shang, the Zhou people still attached great importance to the protection they received from their ancestral spirits. There was one important difference, however: besides the will of Heaven being the ultimate foundation of ethical values, human feelings were also considered a reasonable foundation for them. Familial affection and its extension outward was regarded as the foundation of harmonious human relationships. The closeness or distance of blood relationships was the origin of social order, and the rites became the symbolic rules for the maintenance of that social order. By relying on this set of rules, the world would become civilized.

The Duke of Zhou is said to have initiated the ancient Chinese system of rites, but it is difficult to say how much truth there is to the tradition that "the Duke of Zhou established the rites and music." The Western Zhou should have been an era with a highly developed ritual system. Their ritual ceremonies and rules could not have been devised by a few talented people like the Duke of Zhou; they must have been inherited from the earlier Shang tradition. A truly mature ritual system, however, was indeed only established during the time of King Cheng and the Duke of Zhou.[37] The heart of the Zhou ritual system

---

36   *Maoshi* 272 is translated in Arthur Waley, *The Book of Songs*, 1960, 229.

37   For the tradition that "the Duke of Zhou established the rites and music," see *Zuozhuan*, Ji Wenzi of Lu in "Wengong shiba nian," and the Han Xuanzi (minister of Jin) in "Shaogong, er nian."

was designed to institute a unified order of kinship relations and social status and to create a social order based on this unity of kinship and status. In other words, it combined the father to eldest son relationship as the vertical axis, the husband to wife relationship as the horizontal axis, and the older to younger brother relationship as the auxiliary line to demarcate the sequence of near and far blood relationships and establish a "family" order. Then, it combined the ruler to minister relationship as the principal vertical axis, the ruler to affined Regional Rulers relationship as another horizontal axis, and the ruler and subordinate high ranking ministers and officials relationship (*qingdafu*) as the auxiliary line to confirm high and low social status in a hierarchy of regional "states." And, finally, the family order was superimposed on the states' order as overlapping systems.

This system embodied some rather profound and complex moral and ethical connotations. During the Western Zhou, the *jia* "family" was a small version of the *guo* "regional state" and the "regional state" was the "family" writ large. As the *Book of Rites* put it, "Honor parents as parents, seniors as seniors, elders as elders, and maintain the proper distinction between male and female— that is the highest development of the Way of Mankind (*rendao*)."[38] To extend these principles of a small family to a lineage, then to extend the principles of the lineage to the general community, then to extend the principles of the general community to the state was simply "the highest development of the Kingly Way (*wangdao*). The "Great Treatise" (Da zhuan) chapter of the *Book of Rites* says that the political system can be changed, but the ethics (*lunli*) of the family and lineage cannot be changed because they establish the complete foundation of this tradition.

Within this system of family to lineage to lineage-controlled settlement (*bang*) to regional state (*guo*), to confirm bloodlines was to establish the legitimacy or not of identity, position and power. That made the sacrifices to the ancestors and the arrangement of one's closeness or distance from the ancestors extremely important, and the grandiose solemnity of the Western Zhou ancestral temple sacrifices is a prime example of this importance.[39]

---

38   *Liji*, "Sangfu xiaoji" (On mourning garments), section 11, ssjz, 1496.

39   In the lineage laws at the beginning of the Zhou, the difference between the eldest son of the wife and the sons of concubines—that is, the system of primogeniture—was not necessarily as clear as in later times. When sacrificing to the ancestors, they continued to use the Shang method of calculating the title of deceased's spirits on the basis of the order of their deaths. However, after the establishment of primogeniture, the Shang customs eventually disappeared.

3.3

The Zhou sacrificed to Heaven on the suburban altar, to Earth on the alter to the gods of earth and grain (*sheji*), and to their ancestors in their ancestral temple. "The Meaning of the Sacrifices" (Jiyi) chapter of the *Book of Rites* states that "they built the sites for the altars to the gods of earth and grain on the right, and for the ancestral temple on the left." According to Zheng Xuan's annotations, "the Zhou favored the left," and therefore we can see that the protection they received from the ancestral spirits was more important to the Zhou than abundant agricultural harvests.

The ruins of a Zhou dynasty ancestral temple was discovered in 1976 in Fengchu village, Qishan county, Shaanxi province. Research shows it to have been a very large-scale structure. Inside, it had a Grand Temple in the center where the spirit tablets (*shenzhu* 神主) were displayed, "courts" (*ting* 庭) for the many officials to worship and offer sacrifices, "chambers" (*qin* 寢) containing the ancestors' attire, and small "side rooms" (*wu* 廡) where secondary spirits could receive sacrifices. From the outside in, there were three gates—the *gaomen* (皋門 high gate, main gate), the *yingmen* (應門 reception gate) and the *qinmen* (寢門 inner gate); on the two sides of the main gate, there were also "rest and repose" rooms (*shu* 塾).[40]

In the four seasons of every year, the Western Zhou royal family had to sacrifice to their ancestors in the ancestral temple, and in the summer they also had to carry out a major combined sacrifice. Whenever something important happened, like the king appointing an official, they also had to report to the ancestors in the temple, carry out a sacrificial ceremony and cast and inscribe a bronze cauldron (*ding*) to commemorate the event. At each seasonal sacrifice, they had to offer up seasonally fresh agricultural products and animals.[41] There were many different formalities of protocol in these sacrifices. Someone had to lie down to symbolize the deceased ancestors (*lishi* 立尸); then followed offerings of wine, the ritual of nine offerings, and further bowing to pay respects to the ancestors. On the second day, wine was again offered in the "continuation sacrifice" (*yiji* 繹祭), and of course there was no lack of music and dancing to entertain the ancestral spirits. The *Book of Songs*, Lesser Elegantia (Xiaoya) ode, "Thick Caltrop" (*Chu ci*, Maoshi 209, Waley 199) is a song for Zhou sacrifices. It says that their wine-millet and cooking-millet harvest is abundant and their granaries are full. Then it goes on to describe the sacrificial offerings of food and wine, slaughter of bullocks and goats, the invocator arranging the

---

40   See *Wenwu* 10 (1979), 29.

41   The rules of major sacrifices are quite complex. For further details, see Ma Heng, *Fanjiangzhai jinshi conggao*, 1977, 4 and Yu Weichao and Gao Ming, "Zhoudai yongding zhidu yanjiu (yi)," *Beijing daxue xuebao* 1 (1978), 84–98.

sacrifice and the ancestral spirits, "Protectors" (*shenbao* 神保), descending to enjoy the sacrificial offerings. Then it describes how the food is cooked and presented, how "our lord's lady" serves the dishes to the ancestral spirits and every action is performed with great solemnity and reverence.

Arthur Waley's translation can serve to describe the closing of such ceremonies:

> The rites have all been accomplished,
> The bells and drums are ready.
> The pious son goes to his seat,
> And the skillful recitant conveys the message:
> "The Spirits are all drunk."
> The august Dead One (the *shi* impersonating the ancestors) then rises
> And is seen off with drums and bells;
> The Spirits and Protectors have gone home.
> Then the stewards and our lord's lady
> Clear away the dishes with all speed,
> While the uncles and brothers
> All go off to the lay feast.[42]

After the ancestral spirits have enjoyed the feast, the people themselves feast on the sacrificial bounty in the belief that it will bring them great good fortune.

The court appointment ceremonies (*ceming* 册命) carried out in the Great Temple in front of the spirit tablets of the high ancestors was an even more stately and solemn affair. First, the king who was making the appointment would stand on the north side of the hall facing south while the person receiving the appointment was ushered into the center of the courtyard to stand facing north. Then the king would give the document of appointment to the royal scribe who would stand on the right hand side of the king and read it aloud, after which the new appointee would bow to express his gratitude. Still later, the new appointee was expected to perform a libation in his own ancestral temple and have a ritual vessel like a goblet (*zhong* 鐘) or a tripod (*ding*) cast in bronze to commemorate the occasion. It would be placed in the temple for future generations to treasure, revere and pass down as an heirloom reflecting the glory of the family.[43] Such appointment ceremonies were

---

42   Waley, *Book of Songs*, 211.

43   Most of the inscriptions on these commemorative bronzes conclude with the admonition for "sons and grandsons to treasure and use them forever." For the court appointment (*ceming*) system, see Chen Hanping, *Xi Zhou ceming zhidu yanjiu*, 1986, chapter 3, 101–130 and conclusion, 318–19.

extremely grand affairs as we can see from music and song in the *Book of Songs*, Greater Elegentia (Daya), "King Wen" (Maoshi, 235; Waley, 241).

3.4

It should be pointed that although there were no fundamental changes between the Shang and Zhou sacrifices to Heaven and the ancestors, still there were some signs of change in the knowledge system and intellectual concepts of the invocators, diviners (*bu* 卜), scribes and priests who carried out the Zhou ceremonies. Some subtle distinctions seem to be appearing in the knowledge and thought of the Zhou invocators, temple masters and priests.

First, during the Shang, these invocators, diviners, scribes and priests were originally in charge of sacrifices and divination, but various written materials indicate that during the Western Zhou their responsibilities became differentiated. The royal scribes, for example, no longer only participated in major state ceremonies, but were also charged with making written records of these sacrifices to Heaven and the ancestors, drafting, reading aloud and preserving official appointment documents, reading the archives of royal commands and so on. They were not only responsible for distinguishing generational ranks and making sure that the rank order both in and out of the lineage did not become confused, but they also had to be proficient in astronomy, calendar-making and astrological predictions of good and evil.[44] Their consciousness of time and space grew along with these activities. In the conduct of sacrificial ceremonies for the ancestors, they may well have come to have an understanding of the origin and development of the cosmos, society and humanity. That is, they observed the will of the spirits, the heavenly movements, the great changes in the external world and in human history. Because they were involved very early on in observing the cosmos and heavenly phenomena, explaining the human order and recording historical events, their knowledge system and ways of thinking changed.

Second, these invocators, scribes, temple masters and priests were extremely familiar with the sacrificial ceremonies and the hierarchy of the lineage laws. The *Rites of Zhou* states that the *zhu* invocators not only were in charge of using the proper rhetoric to speak to the gods and spirits, they also had to know how to summon them so as to pray for well-being. They had to know the names of all the paraphernalia used in the sacrificial rituals and to distinguish the different uses of the various sacrifices. They had to be expert in the various techniques and methods for dealing with Heaven, Earth and the gods and spirits.

---

44   See the *Zhouli*, "Dashi" (Grand Scribe) chapter in SSJZS, 817–18.

In this way, when something significant happened, they would be able to offer prayers for the avoidance of calamity.

According to the *Rites of Zhou*, their techniques and methods included things such as divination by yarrow stalks or turtle plastrons (*shi* 筮 or *bu*), examining the oracles (*zhanyan* 占驗), interpreting dreams and praying for rain, the Chief Priest would "lead the priests in dance."[45] They were extremely familiar with Heaven, Earth, and the gods and spirits and they had a great store of knowledge and techniques for "reaching the gods." They also had the most ample understanding of rituals and lineage law, and they could very easily convert the names of the gods and spirits into symbolic form and, using the ceremonies as intermediaries, connect the human and spirits worlds, and from this develop an integrated system of knowledge concerning the sacred lineage laws and the sacrifices to the gods and spirits.

Once ritual ceremonies and the system of lineage laws became accepted by the political authorities and the general population, the techniques embodied in them could then be generally applied in very practical life strategies. The cluster of ideas implicit in these practices also came to seem correct and unquestionable. People obtained stability and a feeling of order in their lives from these sacrifices and ceremonies. Through their repeated ritual performances, these invocators, scribes, invocators and priests with their ritual expertise were later to be known as shamans or wizards and adepts (*shushi* 術士). As they continued to explain the world, they began to be regarded as intellectuals and thinkers. The generally accepted ideational content of the ceremonial system also became widely accepted as general "truth," and the various interpretations of things on the basis of this truth gave rise to many ideas that could become resource materials for our study of intellectual history.

4.   Chinese Script and Chinese Intellectual History

Thought or ideas and writing (*wenzi*) are very closely related. No one can think without language, nor can anyone pass thought on through time without the use of writing. Thinking in a different language is likely to lead to different ideas, and using a different written language to transmit thought or ideas is likely to lead to a different kind of intellectual transmission. On this account, the nature of the Chinese written script—*hanzi* or Chinese characters—is a topic that must be considered in Chinese intellectual history; this is especially so since the Chinese script is one of the oldest in the world and is also still

---

45   SSJZS, 802, 816, 811–12.

in use today. I believe that there is some connection between the continuity
of the Chinese script and the continuity of Chinese intellectual history. Some
scholars assert that in different writing systems we can see the deep structure
of different people's modes of thinking and consciousness. If this is so, then
what distinctive features of ancient Chinese thought can we discern from the
structure of ancient Chinese characters and the syntax of the ancient Chinese
language?

4.1

The first thing that should be pointed out is the pictographic nature of ancient
Chinese characters and its influence on the Chinese people's habitual tradition
of concrete thinking.

The Chinese script is the world's only script still in use that is based on pictographic foundations. Its pictographic script was created by abstracting and
standardizing concrete images. The people of the Three Ancient Dynasties
could not have produced all of a sudden the highly generalized concept of "categories" of things and events. Their cognition of the external world began with
concrete, individual, images of things—that have since evolved into today's
hanzi. Characters like dog (*quan* 犬), person (*ren* 人), sun (*ri* 日) and moon
(*yue* 月) were all concrete pictographic representations. We know that the earlier the script, the more concrete and specific it was. The Chinese use of their
script as written symbols of their language was the same. Early Chinese script
clearly shows that the ancient Chinese were used to the concrete rather than
the abstract. The pictographically-based Chinese script further strengthened
this characteristic of Chinese thought.

We can discuss this fact using the comparatively mature oracle bone script
as an example. The oracle bone inscriptions demonstrate that the contemporary people were used to direct observation and pictorial expression of the
concrete external world. The ancient graph for "ox" (*niu*), for example, was
always a front view of an ox head with two horns on the side. Again for foods,
there are rice (*mi*), paddy rice (*dao*), standing grain (he 禾), broomcorn millet
(*shu* 黍), common millet (*zi* 粢), barley and wheat (*mai*) and so on, but there is
no general category term like the modern words agricultural crops (*zhuangjia*)
or cereal foods (*liangshi*).

The question should not be limited to the pictographic nature of the ancient
Chinese script. We need to pay attention to the influence that the continuous use of this sort of pictographic script had on the ancient Chinese intellectual world. A written language or script is a set of symbols that allows the
external world to appear before our eyes, and every kind of script employs a
particular method to describe and categorize all things and events. When the

people who live within any language area learn their written language they naturally accept the world view it presents to them.

Compared to other systems of writing in the world, the Chinese script is the only one that did not experience fundamental changes over time. If we admit that thought is carried on with language, that knowledge relies on language and writing for its transmission, and that civilization is, to a considerable extent, a kind of language system, then we have to agree that the continuous use over a very long period of time of a pictographic script prevented the Chinese intellectual world from ever separating from the concrete images of the external world. The (mathematical) operations, inferential reasoning and decision-making of Chinese thought was never a set of purely abstract symbols, but rather pictographic symbols and metaphors of the actual world.

For several thousand years, the Chinese seem to have had a kind of attitude of mystery and reverence toward the written word. From the philological interpretation of pictographic characters to associational explanations of the meaning of these pictographs,[46] or from the constructions of mystical diagrams (*tufu* 圖符) by borrowing from pictographic characters[47] to making predictions of good and evil based on the shape of the characters,[48] whether in the so-called "great tradition" or the "little tradition," the influence of the Chinese script on Chinese thought is apparent everywhere.

4.2

In the second place, the growth and classification of Chinese characters reveals the ancient Chinese people's ways of understanding the world.

The creation and multiplication of Chinese characters was like the growth of a tree. Many people believe that the *wen* or "single-bodied characters" (*dutizi*) were independently produced during the creation of *zi* or "joint-bodied characters" (*hetizi*). These are what Zhang Taiyan (1869–1936) called the "first *wen*" (*chuwen*). These "first *wen*" frequently became "graphic classifiers" (literally, section headers, *bushou*) that served as the radicals (literally, roots, *gen*)

---

46   Telling the meaning of characters from their shapes was a very useful principle in ancient Chinese philology, but sometime various associations would be added. For example the phrase "one vertical line connecting three horizontal lines" becomes the character for king (*wang* 王). Sometimes this became a general way of thinking.

47   Like the magic figures to ward off evil (*huafu* 畫符) of religious Daoism after the Eastern Han. See the pottery jars with auspicious cinnabar writing from the Han dynasty Cao family tomb in Hu County, Shaanxi, and from the western suburb of Luoyang, Henan. Written up in "Shaanxi huxian de liangzuo Hanmu," *Kaogu yu wenwu* 1 (1980), 44–48, and "1954 nian chun Luoyang xijiao fajue baogao," *Kaogu xuebao* 2 (1956), 1–33 respectively.

48   Like the glyphomantic technique (*cezishu*) and so on from time immemorial.

by which other characters (*zi*) were arranged. The six methods of forming characters—combined ideograms, joint ideogram or associative compounds (*huiyi* 会意), self-explanatory characters or character that indicate an idea (*zhishi* 指事), phonograms, phonetic compounds or picto-phonetic characters (*xingsheng* 形声), and so on—grew out of these radicals to produce the "joint-bodied" *zi* characters.[49] The original meaning of *zi* is to give birth (*sheng* 生), and groups of associated *zi* tend to come from a single radical (*gen* or *bushou*). The ancient Chinese believed that the phenomena or objects represented by the characters (*zi*) associated with a certain radical formed a "category" (*lei*) in the real world. In the oracle bone script, there are already quite a few self-explanatory (*zhishi*) and associative compounds (*huiyi*) characters while phonetic compounds (*xingsheng*) already made up twenty percent of the whole. Later on, the percentage of "joint-bodied characters" was much greater.

Guo Baojun (1893–1971) once made a statistical analysis of the three radicals for clothing (*yi* 衣), food (*shi* 食) and roof (*mian* 宀) in Rong Geng's *Dictionary of Bronze Inscriptions* (Jinwen bian). In the Yin-Shang oracle bone inscriptions, he found only the *yi* character for clothing, but in the Zhou bronze inscriptions, there are already twelve characters listed under the *yi* (clothing) radical, and in Xu Shen's *Explaining Wen and Analyzing Zi* (Shuowen jiezi) dictionary of 121 CE, the number has increased to 116. For the *shi* (food) radical, the oracle bone inscriptions have only that character, the Zhou bronzes have ten characters under it, and the *Explaining Wen and Analyzing Zi* has 62 characters. For the *mian* (roof) radical, the oracle bone inscriptions have only the twelve characters family (*jia*), house (*zhai*), room (*shi*), to announce (*xuan*), to face towards (*xiang*), quiet (*an*), precious (*bao*), constellation (*su*), to lie down (*qin*), guest (*ke*), reside (*yu*) and ancestor/temple (*zong*); the Zhou bronzes have thirty-six characters and the *Explaining Wen and Analyzing Zi* has seventy.[50] From this we can see that more and more Chinese characters were developed out of the self-explanatory (*zhishi*), associative (*huiyi*) and phonetic compound (*xingsheng*) methods, and this ever greater number of words represented the ancient Chinese people's increasing knowledge of the world around them.

Even more importantly, we can see that, from the process of increasing the number of Chinese characters and their classification in terms of radicals,

---

49   The *wen* [文] are "characters consisting of only a single graphic element . . . not suscepti-ble of analysis into constituent parts smaller than the graphs themselves." The *zi* [字] "are characters that are made up of more than one identifiable graphic component, and are thus capable of analysis into those individual parts." William G. Boltz, in Michael Loewe, ed., ECT, 431.

50   Guo Baojun, *Zhongguo qingtongqi shidai*, 1978, 245–46.

the myriad phenomena and objects in the world came to be given a regular order in Chinese thought.

From the characters that were placed under the same radical, we can see that the ancient Chinese classification system is somewhat different from the Western or modern classification of things. The Chinese paid particular attention to some distinctive feature of an object or phenomenon and made that feature the basis for their classification. For example, the pictorial compound method originally gave prominence to the characteristic image of the new character, while self-explanatory characters contain a particular clue to their meaning. Phonetic compound characters, no matter what radical they belong to, always have some connection to the original form of the character so that one can easily see what general category it belongs to.

What we need to notice is that because this method of classification is based on the perception of some particular distinctive feature, the categories created may lack the scientific basis of modern taxonomy. They rather start from a particular feature and create a connection by association and metaphor. Take the "wood" or "tree" (*mu* 木) radical as an example of a "category name." It was originally an abstract character for tree, and so things under this radical should all be trees, like plum (*mei* 梅 and *li* 李), peach (*tao* 桃), cassia or laurel (*gui* 桂) and so on, but in fact the scope of this "category name" goes far beyond trees per se. It can cover some trees, something made out of wood, some kinds of tools, some things that have characteristics similar to wood, or even things that have no direct connection to wood, but extend by analogy from wood, like the character *dong* 東 for east. *Dong* is a pictogram of "the sun rising behind the trees" that symbolized the direction of the sunrise; *mu* was only the background, but *dong*/east was classified under the wood radical by a process of association. Perhaps it was due to this association that in the later Five Phases thought, the east (*dongfang*) was associated with wood. Another similar example is the fire (*huo* 火) radical. Among the characters placed under the fire radical are situations involving "fire," usages of "fire," and products, effects and feelings related to "fire." Hot (*re* 熱), bright (*ming* 明), dry (*gan* 乾) and even the color black (burnt black, *hei* 黑 with fire radical on the bottom) were all linked together to make up an ancient Chinese idea of a "category."

The formation of these "categories" was a very long process that probably took place during the one thousand or more years of the Shang and the Zhou dynasties, or even longer. This kind of classification of the written word (the Chinese script) had quite a close connection with the world of thought. It at least had an influence on the thought of the people who used the Chinese written language. In other words, classifying, in their thought, the diverse, confused and complex phenomenal world, the ancient Chinese used association and metaphor to join together a series of characters. By extending the connotations of a single character to form a series of characters, they could also link together a chain of meanings, and make it seem as though they had some sort of mysterious connection.

Let us take two more examples of characters that would later develop into extremely important ideas in Chinese intellectual history. The first is the character *you*, "to have" (有). Scholars have pointed out that in the Shang oracle bone script the character *you* (又), originally meaning "right hand" (*youshou* 右手), was used to express *you* "to have." There was an extension of the meaning of this character from the convenience of using the right hand, to *youzhu* (佑助), "to assist, help, or protect," to *lingyou* (領有), "to possess, to own," and to *you* (有), "to have." However, the Shang "right hand" *you* 又 character signified temporary possession, at most protection or assistance (*huyou*, 护佑) from the gods. In the Western Zhou bronze inscriptions "to have" *you* was made up of "right hand" *you* 又 and "meat" *rou*, 肉. Holding a piece of meat was a concrete representation of the concept of possession or having and it was "something that clearly could be controlled by human will." All of these characters and the extensions of their meanings continued to maintain a connection with the "category" of "right hand" *you* 又, a pictogram for the right hand.[51]

The second example is the character *li* (理) that developed extremely rich and significant connotations. The character is said to have obtained its meaning of "to cut jade according to its veins" from jade (*yu* 玉), and its meaning was something close to *pouxi* 剖析, "to cut open." Later, however, *li* was extended to mean "to mark out divisions of fields."[52] We might say that this meaning is not too far from the original carving or cutting, but later usages certainly go beyond those earlier meanings. *Li* comes later to mean the "Principle of Heaven" (*tianli* 天理) and, by association, the "Principle" inherent in all the "ten thousand things" of the world. In time the character *li* indeed came to encompass very many fields and became an extremely important concept.

4.3

Thirdly, the syntax of the ancient Chinese language illustrates the ancient Chinese people's habitual mode of thought.

As difficult as it is to read the oracle bone script as inscribed on bones and plastrons with its relatively simple syntax, we can still see in general some

---

51 On all this, see Liu Xiang, "Guanyu 'you' and 'wu' de quanshi," *Zhongguo wenhua yu Zhongguo zhexue* (1989, 1991), 67–86.

52 The quoted translations are from Bernard Karlgren, *Grammata Serica Recensa*, 1964, where *li* is number 978d.

of the logic of these ancient people's thinking. Usually syntax that is rather more rational, complete, and amply formulated should be standardized and structurally sound. Researchers have found, however, that the oracle bone inscriptions contain much syntax that is quite different from today's Chinese language. Here are a couple of examples: (1) subject and object can be reversed (*shou nian Shang* is given for *Shang shou nian*, "the Shang received the annual harvest;" (2) causative sentences have no obvious markers (*gui zai Chuan ren*, "return in Chuan people" is given for *shi zai Chuan zhi ren gui lai*, "cause/make the people in Chuan return," and (3) an object can be divided with the subject in between: "The Shang King Dayi received as a (human) sacrifice thirty Xi people" *Dayi zhi Xizhi*, but it is written as *Zhi Xi Dayi zhi*; Xizhi is the object, but it is divided and has Dayi in between.

We need to ask three questions about this. First, ancient Chinese language, especially the written language, seems to be less rigorous and meticulous than modern, especially Western, languages. Parts of sentences are often omitted or reversed. Why, then, were ancient Chinese readers able to "grasp the meaning on the basis of their own ideas" (*yi yi ni zhi*) and not make mistakes? Was that a reflection of an impressionistic tendency in ancient Chinese thinking? Second, was it because of the pictographic nature of the ancient Chinese script that the characters could express meaning independently and it became possible to express the correct meaning in any context without a rigorous syntax? Third, was it that the rules of ancient Chinese syntax were rather loose, and this possibly led ancient Chinese thought to pay less attention to logic and order, while attaching more importance to symbols and metaphors?

If we say that from the origin, growth and usage of ancient Chinese, we can generally understand "how they thought," then, from their usage of Chinese characters, we can also understand "what they thought." That is, we can search out the origin of some idea or system from the graphic shape of a character, and we can understand the fundamentals of ancient Chinese life and their interests from their classification of characters. To give an example, the most important activity in ancient Chinese life and thought was their ritual sacrifice to the ancestors, and the character most closely associated with these sacrifices was *shi* 示, meaning to manifest or reveal, to show, to inform and so on. According to Tang Lan's research, the character *shi* 示 and the characters *zong* 宗 and *zhu* 主 were all extracted from one character.[53] Chen Mengjia further asserted that "the character '*shi* 示' in the oracle bone inscriptions should be considered a symbol for the stone spirit tablets (*shizhu*, 石主)."[54] We know

---

53   Tang Lan, "Shi shi, zong ji zhu," *Kaogu shekan* 6 (1937), 328–332.
54   Chen Mengjia, *Yinxu buci zongshu*, 1956, reprint 1981.

that when ancient Chinese sacrificed to their ancestors in their ancestral temples or on their altars, they set up stone spirit tablets (later, they also set up spirit tablets or had someone lie down to symbolize the deceased ancestors—*lishi*). We also know of many other character combinations using shi 示 as their classifier (modern radical): the early character *dian* 电 for lightning combined with *shi* 示 to make *shen* 神, god or spirit; the character *tu* 土 for earth combined with *shi* 示 to make *she* 社, god of the soil (later means society); the character 𠬞, the right hand holding a piece of meat combined with *shi* 示 to make *ji* 祭, sacrifice; the *zu* 且, ancestor, of the memorial spirit tablets combined with *shi* 示 to make another character *zu* 祖 for ancestor (still in use today); and the character 豐, for a vessel offering jade combined with *shi* 示 to form *li* 禮, ceremonial rite. From the growth and development of these characters, we can understand the contents and meaning of the ancient Chinese sacrifices. The great number of characters (words, ideas) with the character *shi* 示 as their classifier, demonstrated the feelings of reverence and awe that the ancient Chinese had for the world of the unknown, mysterious experiences and the gods and spirits. Only with this reverence and awe could they have produced so many characters related to the gods, sacrificial ceremonies, and methods of communicating with the spirits of their dead ancestors.

Behind the written characters and the language based on them, there are, of course, deeply hidden backgrounds and significances. Once we include ancient Chinese script within our historical purview, we are able to investigate their significance for Chinese intellectual history.[55]

5.   Ceremonies, Symbols and a Numerological World Order as the Background of Later Intellectual History

5.1
The Western Zhou worship of Heaven and Earth and the ancestors does not seem to have been much different from that of the Shang. This does not mean, though, that the Western Zhou and the Shang were completely identical or that the Zhou worlds of knowledge, thought and belief did not change. In terms of the later development of intellectual history, what is most notable about the Western Zhou is the process of rationalization and systematization of knowledge, thought and belief.

---

55   Besides the written characters, ancient Chinese design patterns and decorative motifs can also serve as resources for intellectual history. Some of them are mentioned in the text above.

Scholars often cite a passage, mentioned above, from the "Discourses of Chu" chapter of the *Discourses of the States* in which the official Guan Shefu tells the Chu King Zhao (reigned 515–489 BCE) that in ancient times the people (*min*) and the gods or spirits were not mixed up together, and there were people who naturally possessed the mysterious ability to communicate with the spirit world. The males were called *xi* and the females *wu*. Those of them who possessed many different kinds of knowledge were called invocators (*zhu*) while those who understood the ceremonial ritual rules were called temple masters (*zong*). There arose out of these people of culture a cadre of officials who "each had his proper duty." They were responsible for calling down the gods and spirits, and the mass of people grew accustomed to obeying the decrees of the gods and spirits that these experts passed down. In this way, the gods and spirits were able to be effective and to enforce moral conduct, and the mass of people no longer participated in the spirit world. They just gave their trust and loyalty to the gods and spirits. With this new situation, the entire world order became firmly stabilized.[56]

This account is, of course, somewhat fanciful, but still in Shang and Zhou times, except for the "political" activity of military campaigns, the greatest source of power and authority came from the "culture" of sacrifices and communication with the spirits. The order, rules and protocol of the sacrificial ceremonies constituted the most important "knowledge" of that time, and those priests, invocators and temple masters who possessed and employed this knowledge were the most important contemporary "thinkers." They were a small minority who made up an elite that monopolized culture. Because the sacrifices to communicate with the spirits, the so-called "rites" (*li* 禮), were the center of the Shang and Western Zhou intellectual world, they encompassed almost the entire corpus of contemporary thought, observation and belief. Just as Xu Bingchang (1888–1976) wrote in his *Age of Legend in Ancient Chinese History* (Zhongguo gushi de chuanshuo shidai), in earliest times, because everyone could be a *wu* or a *xi* and could communicate with the spirits, no one could establish their authority or order; in this way, the world of the gods and spirits was meaningless. It was not until the Sages appeared "to break the communication between Earth and Heaven" (*jue di tian tong* 絕地天通) that the chaos of the people and the gods and spirits willfully communicating was

---

56   "Chu yu xia," *Guyou*, 559–560.

brought to an end.[57] Xu concludes that "restricting the religious profession to a minority was also a progressive change."[58]

This change should have been achieved during the Western Zhou, and the completion of the sacrificial ceremonies was probably accomplished somewhat later. This systematization divided the application of the ritual articles into several categories, divided the participants into several ranks and located the sacrificial ceremonies in symbolic places that faced in symbolic directions, all in order "to rectify relations between rulers and ministers, make sincere the relations between fathers and sons, make harmonious the relations between older and younger brothers, adjust the relations between the high and the low, give husbands and wives their proper station—all this may be called receiving the blessings of Heaven."[59] Embodied in this consummation of the sacrificial rituals is the Zhou people's search for order, confirmation of values and reflections on the connections between symbolic ceremonies and real life in society.

What kind of intellectual world was implied by this ceremonial system? Moving forward from such a distinct intellectual background, what kind of unique way of thinking was going to emerge as Chinese intellectual history unfolded?

5.2

It is reported that once when his disciple Yan Yan asked Confucius about the importance of the rites or *li*, he answered that "these rituals certainly originate from Heaven and are effective on earth. They are applicable to the gods and spirits, and they include rituals for funerals, sacrifices, ceremonial archery, charioteering, capping ceremonies for young men reaching maturity, marriages, court levés, and friendly ambassadorial missions." [60] The "Ritual Vessels" (Liqi) chapter of the *Book of Rites* also states that "when the first kings instituted the rites... in their great undertakings, they definitely followed the heavenly seasons; in their morning and evening activities, they imitated the sun and the moon; in what required height, they went up into the hills and

---

57   The translation of *jue di tian tong* is that of Bernard Karlgren in *The Book of Documents*, 1950 reprint, 74. The passage from the *Shangshu*, "Lüxing" (Marquis of Lü on Punishments) reads in full: "The charge was given to Chung and Li to break the communication between earth and heaven so that there was no descending or ascending (i.e., no Spirits coming down, no men rising to divine powers the spells worked by Miao failing.)"

58   See Xu Bingchang, *Zhongguo gushi de chuanshuo shidai*, 1960, 76–84; and Zhang Guangzhi, *Zhongguo qingtong shidai*, 1990, 47.

59   *Liji*, "Liyun," section 7. See James Legge in CTP.

60   *Liji*, "Liyun," section 3, in SSJZS, 1440. See James Legge in CTP.

mountains; in what required low ground, they went to the banks of the rivers and lakes."[61] These two passages remind us to be aware that these ritual ceremonies symbolizing order in both the known and unknown worlds had a background of deep knowledge supporting them. As their self-evident foundation, this background was no less than the ancient Chinese understanding of the heavens and earth and the entire cosmos.

As noted above, in Shang and Zhou times, the universe as a spatial area was believed to be regulated and orderly. Heaven and Earth were complementary and they were both made up of a symmetrical and harmonious center and four cardinal directions. The center was ranked above the four directions that surrounded it. The four directions also had the aspects of celestial bodies and were connected to the four seasons with their own cyclic natural phenomena. The Shang people called the spirits of the four directions Xi, Yin, Yi and Fu; their phenological nature is said to be the foundation of the saying "to plant in spring, grow in summer, harvest in autumn, store in winter." The person who wrote the Lesser Elegentia poem "The Great East" in the *Book of Songs* first looked up to the heavens and sighed, then mentioned the Milky Way, the Weaving Girl (Vega), the Cowherd (Altair) and went on as follows:

> In the east is the Opener of Brightness,
> In the west, the Long Path. . . .
> In the south there is a Winnowing Fan;
> But it cannot sift, or raise the chaff.
> In the north there is a Ladle,
> But it cannot scoop wine or sauce.[62]

From this we can see how familiar they were with celestial phenomena and how they had already systematized them. We only have to read the "Canon of Yao" (Yaodian) in the *Book of Documents* to see how the ancient Chinese gradually systematized their observations of celestial phenomena as a structure of rational knowledge: the apparent leftward rotation of the heavenly path, the fixed location of the stars, year following year, the year divided into four seasons, the four seasons paired with the four directions—spring/east, summer/south, autumn/west, winter/north—not only the direction of the handle of the Big Dipper, but also the divisions that people made of the heavens above

---

61   *Liji*, "Liqi," ssjzs, 1414–1415. Translation a modified version of Legge's translation from
      CTP.

62   ssjzs, 461–462. *Maoshi* 203, Waley, 284, *Book of Songs*, 319–320.

their heads.[63] The earth was divided into five zones (*wufu* 五服)—the central *dian* (甸) zone (the royal domain), the lord's *hou* (侯) zone, the guests' *bin* 賓 zone (states pacified by the Chinese), the Chinese-controlled *yao* (要) zone, and the wild uncontrolled *huang* (荒) zone—moving out from the center in ever wider rings. There were also five directions radiating out from the center and most important direction, and the earth was also said to contain nine continents radiating out in the eight compass directions from the center (the ninth direction). All of this was, of course, an imaginary territorial scheme, but it probably did represent an ideal spatial order in the intellectual world of the Western Zhou—their idealized systematization of "all under Heaven."[64]

Precisely because there is such order in Heaven and Earth, the ceremonies that deal with the human world should have a corresponding order. From materials that were somewhat idealized in a later period, we see that the Western Zhou came to rely on a series of ideas and an intellectual system that had developed over time. "The Son of Heaven sacrifices to Heaven and Earth," they wrote, and for those sacrifices there were the Circular Mound Altar (*huanqiu* 圜丘), the Square Mound Altar (*fangqiu* 方丘), the Hall of Brightness (*mingtang*) and so on, all of them constructed to symbolize Heaven and Earth.[65] They also wrote that the Son of Heaven "sacrificed to the four directions." These sacrifices were carried out in the four suburbs (*sijiao* 四郊) of the capital city and had to be arranged according to the sequence of the four seasons: spring, summer, autumn and winter. Even the Son of Heaven's ceremonial weaponry had to copy celestial phenomena: "The placement of (banners) should be: the Vermilion Bird of the South (*zhuniao* 朱鳥) in front, the Black Tortoise (Warrior) of the North (*xuanwu* 玄武) in back, the Azure Dragon of the East (*qinglong* 青龍) on the left, and the White Tiger of the West (*baihu* 白虎) on the right … (thus) there are positions on the left and right and each one manages his own office."[66] When the Son of Heaven received the Regional Rulers, he had to build palaces modeled upon Heaven and Earth

---

63   The "Yaodian" is translated in Bernard Karlgren, *The Book of Documents*, 1950, 1–8.

64   SSJZS, 153; also see the words of Jigong Moufu in the *Guoyu*, "Zhouyu shang." For the five zones and nine continents theories, see Yü Ying-shih, "Han foreign relations," in *CHC, Volume 1, The Ch'in and Han Empires*, 1986, 379–381. We have used Professor Yu's translations of these zones.

65   *Liji*, "Quli xia," SSJZS, 1268.

66   *Liji*, "Quli shang," SSJZS, 1250. See Legge in CTP. Legge takes the passage to refer to a military march, but does not translate the full name of these four important Chinese constellations of the four directions.

to demonstrate that his relation to the Regional Rulers was one of self-evident reasonableness and authority just like those of Heaven, Earth and the cosmos.

This "spatial concept" of Heaven, Earth and the cosmos reflected the ancient Chinese people's deep-rooted consciousness of a natural "hierarchical order of Heaven and Earth" with the center as its core and the myriad stars saluting the North Star as the four directions ringed the central state (*zhongguo*). This natural order supplied them with the idea that everything that originated later, including social organization and humanity itself, must also have an order identical (or at least corresponding to) that of Heaven, Earth and the cosmos. This correlative idea also provided a basis for their behavior, that is, that humanity should understand, analyze, decide about and deal with the phenomenal world in accord with this relationship between the cosmos, human society and humanity itself. At the same time, because the phenomenal world contained different things having the same origin, structure and properties, they all had correlative connections. In this way, the idea of a highly systematized and comprehensive order was developed out of their experience and imaginative conception of the relations between Heaven, Earth and the Human. Within this order, the ancient Chinese established the foundation of their value system, their conceptual style and the basis for their behavior.

5.3

This cosmic order was embodied and realized throughout the rites. As noted above, the reasonableness of this order was derived from human experiences, observations and conceptions of Heaven, Earth and the cosmos, and the rites, especially the ranks and forms of the sacrifices, were used to confirm and express it. The reasonableness of the rites was originally based on human feelings and reason. The hierarchical organization of both society and the ceremonies were derived from the blood relationships and familial feelings of fathers, sons, brothers, and spouses. Therefore the original thinking about these matters must have also been derived from human feelings and rationality. The whole order of family, lineage, society and state was founded on human feelings and knowledge, and these feelings and knowledge were spontaneously produced rather than the result of compulsion. Therefore they came from familial affection and led to harmony and order among older and younger, close and distant relations within families and lineages. In the same manner, the different depths of feeling of sons for fathers and grandfathers, younger for elder brothers and later for earlier generations led to different grades of memorial and mourning ceremonies. Despite the fact that later generations expanded them from kinship relations and familial feelings to politeness and manners between different social strata, those feelings of respect, worship, obedience, love and protection originally derived from people's inner feelings and rationality.

After a system of ritualistic regulations was established and acquired an unquestionable authority, however, it departed from human feelings and knowledge. People then regarded the rites as inherently reasonable rules and no longer asked what they were based upon. Their experiences, observations and conceptions of Heaven, Earth and the cosmos caused them to believe in an unquestionable "Way of Heaven." When that happened, these ceremonies known collectively as the rites, had to find their rational foundations in this "Way of Heaven." The *Book of Rites* quotes Confucius to the effect that the "rites" are a "Way" (*dao*) that Heaven bequeathed to the ancient kings to regulate human "feelings."[67] The Way of Heaven and human feelings were actually quite different. The Way of Heaven derived from the rules of cosmic order, but human feelings arose out of a consciousness of kinship and familial relationships. They were originally unrelated, but the ancient Chinese mixed them together, and, in the earlier ages, had a tendency to privilege the Way of Heaven and neglect human feelings. This is just what the "Ritual Vessels" chapter in the *Book of Rites* means by stating that "... 'the rites that come closest to human feelings are not the superior rites...' "[68]

In time, the status differences between rulers and ministers and fathers and sons ceased to be automatic emotional differences based on nearness or distance of kinship relations. Rather, they were regarded as being received from the "Way of Heaven" and, thus, unquestionable class differences. The hierarchy of Heaven and Earth and the four directions was projected on to the human world, and relations of closeness, distance, higher and lower grew into ideas of a fixed status hierarchy. Even the ceremonies and the symbolic objects used in them further confirmed and strengthened the reasonableness of these distinctions. There were different sacrifices for different ranks. The Son of Heaven sacrificed to Heaven and Earth, the four directions, and performed the five state sacrifices.[69] Local rulers sacrificed to mountains and rivers and performed the five state sacrifices; senior officials (*dafu* 大夫) performed the five state sacrifices; scholar-officials (*shi* 士) only sacrificed to their ancestors. Dress for sacrifices and ceremonies was also ranked so that the Son of Heaven, dukes,

---

67   In *Liji*, "Liyun," section 3, Confucius is quoted as saying "As for the rites, the ancient kings carried on the Way of Heaven to regulate human feelings."

68   *Liji*, "Liqi," Zheng Xuan annotation: "What is close to human feelings is disrespectful, but what is far from them is respectful." SSJZS, 1439.

69   The five state sacrifices are listed in the *Guoyu*, "Luyu," section 9 as *di* 禘, *jiao* 郊, *zu* 祖, *zong* 宗, and *bao* 报.

Regional Rulers and senior officials all wore different costumes for these occasions. The content of sacrificial ceremonies were also different, and even the participant's deportment, appearance, and state of mind and the overall atmosphere seemed to have natural status differences.

The structure of the universe, kinship feelings and social status all overlapped in these ceremonies. Heaven and Earth, the cosmos, the center and the four directions provided a foundation derived from the Way of Heaven, and bloodlines and kinship affections provided a way of thought derived from the heart. In the past, many people firmly believed that the rites embodied the meaning of ancient Chinese ethics and morality and that the three bonds and five constant virtues (*sangang wuchang* 三綱五常) were derived from human feelings and accorded with basic human nature (*benxing* 本性); on this account, the significance of the rites was undeniable.[70] But others have criticized the rites for being a part of the so-called "feudal" system (*fengjian zhixu*) that restricted human nature and feelings.[71] They believed that the rites violated both human nature and human feelings and should be abandoned.

Neither of these groups went any further to analyze how the rites came to be seen as reasonable. As symbols of order, the reasonableness of the rites had at least two origins. On the one hand, they were a reasonable extension of human nature and temperament, while on the other hand, they were seen to derive their rational foundation from the order of the cosmos. The rites brought the Way of Heaven and the "human heart/mind" (*renxin*) together by means of a system of formalistic rituals and ceremonies that both affirmed and expressed the connection. By bridging the gap between the gods and spirits and human beings, the ritual ceremonies not only established their own authority, but also affirmed the reasonableness of the order they symbolized. This was the overall implication of the rites—in a certain sense, the rites simply constituted the civilization of early China.

---

70 The three bonds are that sons are subordinate to fathers, officials are subordinate to rulers and wives are subordinate to husbands; the five constant virtues are *ren* 仁, humanity, often translated "benevolence"; *yi* 義, rightness, justice, duty; *li* 禮, propriety (same character as "rites"); *zhi* 智, wisdom; and *xin* 信, trust or trustworthiness.

71 Much has been written about the Chinese *fengjian zhidu* and its supposed comparison to Western European feudalism. The best recent revisionist studies of this issue are Li Feng's "'Feudalism' and Western Zhou China: A Criticism," *Harvard Journal of Asiatic Studies*, vol. 63, No. 1 (Jun., 2003), pp. 115–144; also see his *Bureaucracy and the State in Early China: Governing the Western Zhou*, 2008 and *Landscape and Power in Early China: The Crisis and Fall of the Western Zhou, 1045–771 BC, 2006.*

5.4

As ceremonials, though, the rites were only a system of symbols. Some anthropologists believe that the meaning of symbols is so important that they can be compared to the emergence of human life itself. Once human beings could use symbols, then all sorts of phenomena could be expressed and information could be passed on by means of a small number of symbols. Once mankind became accustomed to the use of symbols, they could function to bring the world from a state of (untrammeled) disorder into a state of (intellectual) order.

Ceremonies are dependent on a system of symbols for their performance and completion. Although a symbol is a type of sign, metaphor, clue or indicator, it is not the thing itself. In the ancient Chinese intellectual world, however, symbols were extremely important, and sometime actually replaced real-world phenomena as the repository of meaning. During the several thousand years of ancient Chinese history, a complex and orderly system of symbols was created. Owing to people's genuine belief in this symbolic system it actually took on the functions of maintaining the order of both the cosmos and human society and supporting the Chinese system of knowledge and their psychological equilibrium. That is, of course, why the collapse of the symbolic system often brought on the collapse of social order.

The ancient Chinese people believed that there was some kind of mysterious connection between their symbols (the significs) and the things symbolized (the signified) and that this caused them to have a certain mutual correspondence. By means of this correspondence, symbols could function to regulate the social order. Ancient Chinese believed, for example, that dress could regulate as well as suggest social order. They said that upper *yi* 衣 jackets and lower *shang* 裳 skirts symbolized the traditional ethics that men are superior to women (*nan zun nü bei* 男尊女卑) because the difference between upper and lower garments made it publicly clear that *yang* (the male symbol) was superior to *yin* (the female symbol). Distinctions in the dress of the Son of Heaven, regional rulers, superior officials, lower aristocrats and the common people all symbolized their status differences. The psychological process of symbols being confirmed in the Chinese people's minds was at the same time the process of their acceptance of the natural and reasonable nature of reality.

The rites were just such a system of symbols. Not only were the use of sacrificial animals (like oxen, sheep and hogs, or fish), differences in dances (like eight rows of dancers (*bayi* 八佾) for the Son of Heaven and six rows (*liuyi* 六佾) for the Regional Rulers, dress distinctions (like the Son of Heaven's jeweled crown and royal robes), objects of sacrifice (like Heaven and Earth, the ancestors, or mountains and rivers), and so on symbols of order in human society, even the exhibits used, behavior practiced and locations of the sacrifices were all replete with symbols.

It was precisely in the midst of these symbol-laden rites that their significance became apparent—they suggested that order existed in people's minds and they imparted an aura of sacredness to that order. Even though this order was originally a product of human history, people came to accept these ceremonies and symbols that they had created and took them to be evidence of the rationality of the cosmos; people were then conditioned and regulated by their own constructions. As symbols of civilization and refined cultivation, the status of the rites became increasingly exalted and the formalities of their performance became increasingly magnificent.

The *wu* priests, *zhu* invocators, *shi* diviners/scribes and *zong* temple masters who officiated at these ceremonies possessed the power to bring together men and the gods, men and the ghosts of their ancestors, and men and Heaven, and their "thought" simply became the process of using symbols to explain and interpret reality.

As some of these symbols were used repeatedly in ancient China, they grew increasingly abstract until they formed sets of fixed and mystical concepts that were expressed with numbers. These numbers emerged as a result of ancient people's repeated classification of various phenomena. As the *Zhuangzi* says, "much of the intelligence of the men of old that was embodied in numbers and regulations (*shudu*) is still reflected in the old laws and records that have been handed down from of old."[72] This tradition of numerical classification was handed down by the *shi* diviners/scribes and *wu* priests. This categorization or classification (*lei*) by means of numbers (*shu*) was only in a rudimentary stage during the Shang and Zhou dynasties, but it already possessed great mystery and authority. Because these numeralized concepts that originally had no particularly obvious connection were granted the support of people's ideas of the order of Heaven and Earth and the cosmos, they possessed a natural reasonableness. Therefore, they were unquestionable in the contemporary people's minds. Later generations called them "fixed numbers" (*dingshu*), like "I, the one man," the five punishments, the twelve continents, and so on.[73]

There were also such numerological schools of philosophy elsewhere in the world, like that of Pythagoras and his school in ancient Greece, but numbers

---

72   *Zhuangzi*, "Tian xia," see Watson, CT, 362 with some changes.

73   For discussions of this numeralization of ideas, number-mysticism or numerology and numbers of the universe, see Joseph Needham, *Science and Civilization in China*, volume 2, *History of Scientific Thought*, 1962, 312, and Yang Ximei, "Zhongguo gudai shenmi shuzi lungao," *Zhongyang yanjiuyuan minzu yanjiusuo jikan* 33 (1972), 89–118.

and categories were soon separated. In China, however, numbers were always connected to concrete things and events and never became purely abstract. An example is the Five Phases of metal, wood, water, fire and earth; sour, sweet, bitter, spicy, and salty; east, west, south, north, and center; green (blue), red, white, black, yellow, and so on. Even one, two and three had their other connotations. For example, "one" (*yi*): the "one" in "*Yu yi ren*" ("I, the one man") naturally gave prominence to the king, the one person in the world with unique and unmatched authority and power.

If the *Old Text Book of Documents* (Guwen Shangshu), has any believable records of ancient life, then, at the beginning of the Shang, the phrase "*Yu yi ren*" ("I, the one man") already existed. "I (*Yu*)" here is contrasted with "every other region" (*wanfang* 萬方), and "the one man (*yi ren*)" is contrasted with "the masses of people" (*youzhong* 有眾)—they are both highlighting the "center" (*zhongxin*). The phrase "*Yu yi ren*" appears in the oracle bone inscriptions as well and proves that the Shang certainly had the idea of the king as the "One." This idea was carried on at the beginning of the Zhou dynasty. The "Great Declaration" (Taishi) of the *Book of Documents* has the phrases ". . . The people blame me, the one man, . . ." and ". . . You must diligently support me the one man and reverently carry out Heaven's punishment."[74] This illustrates the stability and continuation of the consciousness of central authority and power in the Shang and Zhou dynasties.

This concept was not only applied to the power of the kings; it was extended to every sphere that could be divided into center and periphery. The so-called "royal perfection" (*huangji* 皇極) in the "Great Plan" (Hongfan) of the *Book of Documents*, is simply "to revere the center" (*shangzhong* 尚中) because in spatial terms only "the center" has no contrasting counterpart; it is unique. In people's minds, then, "one" became a symbol of authority and order. The center of the heavens, the one unmoving fixed point in the firmament—the North Star—and the highest-ranking deity in Heaven—"Heavenly Di" (*tiandi*)—were also associated with "the One" (*yi*) or the "Great Unity" (*taiyi* 太一). The Chu state bamboo slips unearthed at Guodian also have the phrase "Taiyi generated water," but making "one" the origin of the cosmos was, of course, a later idea.[75]

A mystical belief in the number "five" (*wu*) had also begun in the Shang dynasty where it was used to arrange many diverse things and events into categories of five. The Shang people regarded "five" as an easily handled number. Guo Moruo noticed that when the Shang "divined how many oxen to

---

74   *Taishi, zhong*, section 2 and *Taishi, xia*, section 3 respectively. Translations are revisions of those of Legge in CTP.

75   See "Taiyi shengshui shi wen," in *Guodian Chumu zhujian*, 1998, 125.

sacrifice ... after one, two and three divinations, they jumped right to five."[76] After that, it was probably very easy to regard "five" as a fixed number and to continue the practice in later times. In the *Book of Documents*, for example, there are "five canons," (*wudian* 五典) "five celestial bodies," (*wuchen* 五辰) "five rites," (*wuli* 五禮), "five jades" (*wuyu* 五玉), "five punishments" (*wuxing* 五刑), "five levels of dress" (*wuzhang* 五章), "five constant virtues" (*wuchang* 五常), "Five Phases," "five regions" (*wufu*), "five instructions" (*wujiao* 五教) "five things a ruler must do" (*wushi* 五事), "five ranks" (*wupin* 五品), "five divisions of time" (*wuji* 五紀), "five kinds of good fortune" (*wufu* 五福), "five virtuous words" (*wuyan* 五言), "five musical notes" (*wusheng* 五聲), "five colors" (*wuse* 五色 or *wucai* 五彩), "five misdemeanors that can be granted leniency" (*wuguo* 五過), and so on. In the Spring and Autumn era "five" had become a generally accepted magic number. Astronomical and calendrical elements— year, month (moon), day (sun), stars, divisions of the day—were called the "five positions" (*wuwei* 五位); the sacrificial ceremonies were divided into the "the five state sacrifices" (*wusi*); the gods associated with the Five Phases were named the "five upright ones" (*wuzheng* 五正); even weaponry could be called the "five weapons" (*wubing* 五兵) and food seasonings were dubbed the "five flavors" (*wuwei* 五味). A document called "Rong Cheng shi" (name of an ancient ruler) in the recently discovered Warring States era bamboo slips from the state of Chu has the following sentence: "The eastern banner is the Sun, the western banner is the Moon, the southern banner is the Serpent, the central banner is the Bear, and the northern banner is the Bird."[77] I believe that by this time the Five Phases idea had become fully mature.[78]

Twelve was also a magic number. The ancient people observed the sky and used the orbit of Jupiter (*muxing* 木星 "wood star" or *suixing* 歲星 "year star") to mark the passage of time, with one complete cycle being twelve years; they used the waxing and waning of the moon in the same way, with twelve cycles

---

76 Guo Moruo, *Yinqi cuibian*, 1965, 65.

77 "Rong Cheng shi," in *Shanghai bowuguan cang zhanguo Chu zhu shu* (2), 2002, 265–266.

78 The *Shiji* chapter on calendars, "Lishu," states that "the Yellow Emperor investigated the stars, fixed the calendar and set up the Five Phases." This is of course a legend that cannot be given credence. Nevertheless, modern writers have had a general tendency to fix the date of Five Phases thinking very late, even as late as the Warring States period, but some of them, like Liang Qichao's "Yin-yang wuxingshuo zhi laili," *Dongfang zazhi* 20/10 (1923), 70–79; Hu Shi's "Qixue de zhengtong," in his *Zhongguo zhonggu sixiangshi changbian*, in *Hu Shi quanji*, vol. 6, 8–21; and Gu Jiegang's "Wuxing zhongshishuo xia de zhengzhi he lishi," *Qinghua xuebao* 3 (1984), 71–268), left a bit of leeway for change. From the more recently discovered archeological materials, we can see that Five Phases thinking was probably much earlier than we had ever imagined.

making one full year; on this account the number "twelve" was regarded as having a definite magical nature. The Shang people already had a complete system of heavenly stems and earthly branches to mark various times and other things. There were ten heavenly stems and twelve earthly branches. When the *Rites of Zhou* says "In charge of twelve years, twelve months, and twelve double hours," it is connecting time to the number "twelve."[79] It was as though time should naturally be divided into twelve equal divisions, and in the ancient people's minds the rules of the calendar had to be associated with the number twelve in order to obtain legitimacy. In the same manner, many spatial things, like the "twelve continents" (*shi-er zhou*) had "twelve" as their fixed number. The idea of twelve as an important category is carried forward into both the *Rites of Zhou* and the *Erya*.

It is as though using this "number twelve" received its rationality from Heaven itself, and so the great earth was divided into twelve continents, sacrifices were offered to twelve famous mountains, twelve officers were appointed to administer the earth and twelve military units were set up in the twelve continents. And many other things, the shapes of which were modeled on Heaven and earth, also had to match the number twelve. For example, in upper and lower garments, there were "twelve different pieces of cloth to conform to the twelve months," and there had to be "twelve tassels symbolizing the brightness of the sun and moon on the Son of Heaven's "jade cap" and "dragon banner."[80]

Among these "fixed numbers" with their natural legitimacy there were two categories of "numbers" that included everything and were mutually opposed to each other—that is the categories of odd and even numbers. The ancient people believed that these odd and even numbers symbolized the phenomena of the natural world such as Heaven and Earth, sun and moon, male and female, white and black and so on. In their extremely broad and generalized inductive way of thought, odd and even were the most abstract and the most accessible symbols of these cosmic binary phenomena. From those people's reasons for believing in the symbolism of odd and even numbers, we can

---

79   *Zhouli*, "Chunguan zongbo, Fengxiangshi" section 146 in CTP.

80   Later generations went on to develop many things associated with the number "twelve," such as the "twelve animals" (*shi-er shou*) and the "twelve gods" (*shi-er shen*), etc. Guo Moruo believed that the "twelve constellations" (*shi-er gong* 十二宮) and the "twelve animals" came from the Western Regions (*xiyu* 西域). Recent archeological discoveries, however, indicate that the ideas of the "twelve animals" is definitely not any later than the Warring States period, and that it is completely autochthonous; see Li Xueqin, "Ganzhi jinian he shi-er shengxiao qiyuan xinzheng," *Wenwu tiandi* 3 (1984), 41–43. The "twelve gods" in the Chu silk manuscripts from Zidanku in Changsha are also Chinese symbols of the twelve months; see Li Ling, *Changsha Zidanku Chu boshu yanjiu*, 1983.

glimpse the connection of this belief with the somewhat later Yin-Yang think-ing. We can grasp the following three points: One, that odd and even numbers were taken to correspond with such binary opposites as Heaven and Earth, sun and moon, male and female, white and black, cold and hot and so on demon-strates that in the minds of the ancient Chinese people these binary phenom-ena were believed to have certain mystical connections. Two, in the ancient Chinese people's thought, the myriad phenomena of the universe could be abstracted into highly generalized numerical symbols. And three, as symbols these numbers not only possessed a sacred symbolic nature and natural legiti-macy, but they also had the ability to take the place of things and events in the real phenomenal world. It was precisely from this practical knowledge and its related techniques that the doctrine of Yin and Yang, one of the most impor-tant ideas in Chinese intellectual history, was gradually emerging.

5.5

Let us summarize the exposition offered in this chapter.

First, order in the human realm came from the Shang and Zhou people's understanding of Heaven and Earth and the cosmos, and then it was stabilized through ceremonial rites. Through these ceremonies, the order of the universe and human nature and feelings were converted into an overlapping system. The ceremonies employed a number of symbols that confirmed and strength-ened the natural legitimacy and irrefutable nature of these two orders; they also provided people with a foundation for their values. The repeated use of these symbols created in people's minds a consciousness that the sym-bolic order was identical with the world order and that the collapse of the symbolic order would entail the collapse of the world order.

Second, over time, there emerged from within this forest of symbols a series of numerically expressed concepts that possessed mystic power and author-ity. Owing to their irrefutable foundation and their long use over time, these numeralized concepts became symbols of a most coherent order in the human world.

Third, the *wu* priests, *zhu* invocators, *shi* diviners/scribes and *zong* temple masters working at the royal courts of the Shang and Western Zhou after the "break in communication between Earth and Heaven," came to monopolize the right to perform and interpret these ceremonies and their attendant sym-bols. They also came to monopolize Chinese thought.

In what direction, then, was Chinese thought going to develop after the Shang and Western Zhou dynasties? That is, where was this long and unbro-ken Chinese intellectual history headed on the basis of the distinct intellectual background discussed in this chapter?

CHAPTER 2

The Hundred Schools of the Spring and Autumn and Warring States Period, I (ca. 6th to 3rd Century BCE)

Brief Prologue: China's "Axial Age"

From the 9th to the 8th century BCE, the Western Zhou dynasty's peaceful order was greatly disturbed. The dynasty was destroyed in 771 BCE, and the Eastern Zhou dynasty began.[1] After the establishment of the Eastern Zhou, the power of the Regional Rulers (*zhuhou*) gradually increased while the area actually controlled by the Son of Heaven was reduced to a region around today's Luoyang in Henan province. The Son of Heaven had to depend on the support and contributions of the Regional Rulers even to maintain this much territory. The harmonious and integrated order of the *tianxia* world of all under Heaven had finally collapsed.

With the political world in chaos, the intellectual world was also in turmoil. There were at least three reasons for changes in the Eastern Zhou intellectual world. First, the change in the political order caused the once self-evident "knowledge" and "thought" to lose it authoritative nature. A re-establishment of the worlds of thought and knowledge was inevitable. Second, with the decline and weakness of the Zhou royal house, its monopoly of culture, thought and knowledge passed into the territories of the Regional Rulers. At the same time, the long-term stability and prosperity of Regional States (*zhuhouguo* 諸侯國) led to the gradual emergence and nurturing of a new group of educated men of culture. The ups and downs of these men of culture at the courts of the Regional Rulers meant that their intellectual positions were in a state of flux. Third, different emphases were placed on knowledge and thought within different professions. This differentiation among educated men of culture caused similar divisions in knowledge and thought and resulted in the emergence of various disparate schools of thought. Just as the "Tianxia" (The World) chapter of the *Zhuangzi* has it: "'the art of the Way (*daoshu* 道術)' in time came to be rent and torn apart by the world."[2]

---

1 See *Shiji*, "Zhou benji," 140–149 for this period of history.

2 Burton Watson, CT, 364. "Comes" has been changed to "came" to fit this context.

That "the art of the Way" was "torn apart" was not really a sad ending, but rather a splendid beginning. After the collapse of former truths, people were forced to ponder things for themselves. After the disappearance of their self-evident beliefs, people were forced to re-establish their confidence. After the downfall of their ideas of the order of Heaven and Earth, people were forced to restore the order of the cosmos through their own observations. In this age of intellectual division, people finally began to use their own reason without completely relying on facile truths and conceptions of their gods. From the late years of the Spring and Autumn period to the Warring States era, from the 6th to the 3rd centuries BCE, Chinese intellectual history began to take its own path. This was perhaps, to use Karl Jaspers' term, China's "axial age."[3]

1. General Knowledge and Thought in the Spring and Autumn Period

The thought of cultured individuals is often conditioned by the general level of knowledge in a given period of time. What I mean by "the general level of knowledge" is the average quality of knowledge in a certain era. It is supported by a number of received ideas and concepts and expressed as common sense that corresponds to external changes. While these forms of knowledge are manifest in repeated practice, they are also being passed on from generation to generation through the general education of the time. Although it is not the highest form of knowledge, it is the starting point of thought. Intellectual history grew out of the soil planted with this general knowledge.

1.1
In the life of the Regional Rulers, high ranking officials and the common people in the Spring and Autumn and Warring States periods, there was said to be something called the "six arts" (liuyi 六藝). That is knowledge or ability in rites (li), music (yue), archery (she), charioteering (yu), mathematics (shu), and calligraphy (shu). Aside from the political, economic and military skills that were of great practical use, the most important spiritual knowledge embodied in the "six arts" remained, astronomical studies primarily involving calculating the calendar and astrological divination (by the stars), ritual studies primarily involving the sacrificial ceremonies and divination and prognostication using

---

3 In *The Origin and Goal of History*, 1953 (1949) Karl Jaspers theorized that the time from around 800 to 200 BCE was an "Axial Age" of human civilization, a time that saw the emergence of Confucius, Laozi, the Upanishads, the Buddha, Elijah, Isaiah, Jeremiah, and many other men of wisdom.

tortoise plastrons and yarrow stalks. All of these practices were continued on from Shang and Zhou dynasty performances. In the ancestral temples and courts of the aristocracy, these practices influenced the ideas of the Regional Rulers and the aristocrats; in the life of the common people, they dominated their behavior. For these reasons, any educated person having a certain amount of status in society would generally have some understanding of the following three forms of knowledge.

1.1.1   The Arts of Astrological Divination and Calendar Calculation
These are the arts, skills and knowledge of the "diviners" (*rizhe* 日者) who used them to examine celestial phenomena and predict calamities, auspicious times and good and evil fortune. According to the *Zuo Commentary* (to the *Spring and Autumn Annals*), "Huangong, year 17," "The Son of Heaven had an official in charge of days (*riguan* 日官), and the Regional Rulers had officers to keep track of days (*riyu* 日御)." The Zhou court and the various Regional Rulers all had such educated men working for them. Their first task was to calculate and promulgate the calendar because it was the symbol of order. They had to publish the calendar for the following year because it was important for both the wealthy and the common people. Secondly, they were responsible for conducting the four seasonal sacrifices in the third, sixth, tenth and twelfth months. If these ceremonies were not carried out at the proper times, the diviners would criticize the process. Thirdly, besides understanding calendar-making and seasonal sacrifices, they had to observe celestial phenomena and record heavenly conditions in order to predict auspicious or calamitous times to come. Lastly, because their celestial observations and their analyses of human affairs were frequently linked, they had to observe the stars and verify predictions of good and bad fortune. In their knowledge system, the Way of Heaven symbolically apprised the human world of potential good and evil fortune. This was an extremely old and deep-rooted idea. For example, in 564 BCE, in discussing a fire in the state of Song, an official named Shi Ruo remarked that the people of Song predicted fires from the positions of the celestial bodies "Quail Fire" (Jupiter, *chunhuo* 鶉火) and "Great Fire" (Antares, *dahuo* 大火) and they sacrificed in advance to those stars.[4] This kind of knowledge came down from the Shang dynasty and was widespread in the states of the Regional Rulers.

---

4   *Zuozhuan*, "Xianggong jiunian," SSJZS, 1941.

1.1.2   The Art of Divination and Prognostication by Means of Tortoise
Plastrons and Yarrow Stalks

During this time, major events, like possible victory or defeat in war or the
advantages or disadvantages of moving the capital, and minor events, like
someone's living or dying or the advisability of taking a wife, were all subjected
to the forecasts of divination. Divination by tortoise plastrons (*bu*) or by casting yarrow stalks (*shi*) was done by these professional men who possessed the
requisite knowledge. Although the Regional Rulers could ignore their advice
and persist in following their own judgment, the opinions of the diviners were
in most situations efficacious, and this explains why their type of knowledge
was so widely believed. In the words of Han Jian, an attendant at the court of
Duke Hui of Jin, tortoise plastrons were used to observe the images (*xiang*) and
bamboo or yarrow stalks (*zhushi* 竹 筮) were used to investigate the numbers.
The ten thousand phenomena all have their characteristic images and their
fixed rules (or numbers, *shu*).[5] They thought that this was the structure of the
cosmos, and tortoise-plastron or yarrow-stalk divination was the way to understand the cosmos by means of the "images" and the "numbers" that naturally
had to be believed. In the Qin dynasty bamboo slip *Book of Days* unearthed at
Shuihudi in 1970, there are many examples of such divinations. This means
that in the Qin and Han eras people were still calling on diviners to help
them "settle their doubts and determine what is right or wrong" (*ding xian yi,
jue shi fei*) because they themselves could not employ reason and knowledge to
predict their future fates.

1.1.3   Conducting and Interpreting Ritual Ceremonies

As the Zhou ruling house lost its position of authority in thought and culture,
the Regional Rulers began to act any way they wanted to, and wrongly to carry
out the ritual ceremonies. Some of the Regional Rulers' officials in charge of
culture simply used their own ideas to interpret and criticize the sacrificial
ceremonies, half to preserve the traditions and half to establish a new order.
From the beginning of the Spring and Autumn era, however, people no longer
resolutely defended the old conventions; they added and subtracted ceremonial elements at will. For example, the state of Lu was descended from the
Duke of Zhou and so they were permitted to perform the suburban sacrifice to
Heaven (*jiaotian* 郊天), but they first conducted a divination and received a
bad answer. Then, on their own initiative, they exempted themselves from the
sacrificial offering of oxen and refused to carry out the sacrifice.[6] There was a

---

5 *Zuozhuan*, "Xigong shiwu nian," ssjzs, 1807.
6 *Zuozhuan*, "Xigong shiwu nian," ssjzs, 1831.

solar eclipse visible from the state of Lu in the sixth month of 612 BCE, and, according to tradition, they should not beat the drums and slaughter animals in the Great Temple to the God of Grain. Rather, the Son of Heaven should carry out a sacrifice for avoiding calamity. Nevertheless, the state of Lu went ahead and carried out a Great Temple sacrifice that only the Son of Heaven was entitled to perform.[7] From this, we can see that knowledge of the system of ritual ceremonies was changing as the system of world order changed. It was just at that juncture that the symbolic meaning and ranking system of the sacrificial ceremonies needed to be revised and reinterpreted by the above mentioned ritual experts.

1.2
The contemporary background of intellectual history was precisely the above mentioned calculation of the calendar, astrological-, tortoise plastron- and yarrow stalk-divination and the management of the ceremonies. These practices deriving from the monopolistic knowledge and techniques of a small minority of educated individuals, were widespread in society and were accorded great validity. Within this seemingly complex body of knowledge, there was actually a highly well-organized and elaborate system of ideas. The ancient Chinese may not have been fully conscious of the existence of this system, but just such a "system of ideas that functioned for the common folk on a daily basis, yet they were unaware of it" was extremely powerful and deeply embedded in the people's minds, and it served as the foundational support for their thought.[8]

As I have repeatedly emphasized above, the ancient Chinese believed that the cosmos was an interrelated holistic entity. For them, "Heaven, Earth and the Human," had a profoundly mysterious mutual interconnection or correspondence. They believed that not only did Heaven in astronomical terms, Earth in geographical terms, "human beings" in physiological terms and even "the state" (guo) in political terms mutually influence each other, but that "Heaven, Earth and the Human" were also mutually connected spiritually, mutually manifest in phenomenal appearances, and interactive in the sphere of concrete reality. These ideas continued into the Spring and Autumn and Warring States eras. In the minds of contemporary people, astronomical knowledge, ceremonial practice, prognosticatory techniques and even people's daily life styles all seemed to be bound up together. The mysterious interactive and matching connections between these things were, to their minds, self-evident and presumptive premises.

---

7 Zuozhuan, "Wengong shiwu nian," SSJZS, 1855.
8 Yijing translation is from Lynn, Changes, 53.

At this point, I want to discuss "Yin-Yang" and Five Phases thought.

The concepts of Yin and Yang were in existence very early on. They may originally have been related to geography, referring to the shady or sunny side of hills and the northern or southern sides of rivers. For example, in the *Book of Songs*, Lesser Elegantia, "Duke Liu" (Gong Liu), when the Duke was looking for a place to live, he noted "which parts were in the shade, which in the sun, as well as view[ing] the streams and the springs."[9] At least in the Shang or Western Zhou, this concept was already linked to the sun, moon and such celestial phenomena. This concrete Yin-Yang idea gradually grew into an enormously complex conception of binary elements that were both opposite and complementary. Yin and Yang also became connected to odd and even numbers. In the *Book of Changes*, the two significs Yin and Yang are generated by numbers and abstracted into two fundamental concepts. This illustrates that the Chinese already had very early on the concept of two opposite yet complementary binaries. The phrase "deliberating on the principles and methods for governing the state, and harmonizing the principles of Yin and Yang (nature) (*lun dao jing bang, xie li yin yang* 論道經邦, 燮理陰陽)" demonstrates that as early as the Western Zhou, Yin and Yang no longer referred only to the south and north of hills and streams. It had come to include celestial phenomena in which "we see the clouds but not the sun and then the clouds disperse and we see the sun," odd and even numbers, and even the antithetical existence of every thing in the world.[10] By the Spring and Autumn era, the Yin-Yang concept was even more widespread and seems to have already become a kind of Truth that derived from rational explications and conscious inductions about the cosmos and society.

Section 3 of the "Discourses of Zhou, 1" (Zhouyu shang) in the *Discourses of the States*, records that there were earthquakes near the Jing, Wei and Luo rivers in the Western Zhou. At the time, the Grand Scribe (*taishi*) Boyangfu said that the vital energies (*qi*) of Heaven and Earth had lost their proper order. These vital energies of Heaven and Earth were considered to be the two fundamental elements of the universe. Boyangfu attributed the earthquakes to a blockage of the source of the rivers, linked this blockage to an imbalance of Yin and Yang, and further connected this imbalance of Yin and Yang to the rise and fall of the state. At that time, Yin and Yang were no longer concrete nouns,

---

9   ssjzs, 543. Maoshi number 250, Waley number 239, Waley, *Book of Songs*, 1960 (1937), 246 with one change.

10   *Shangshu*, "Zhou guan," section 3.

and so he averred that Yin and Yang were the vital energies of Heaven and Earth and they must not lose their proper order.[11]

Of course, at that time Yin-Yang thought did not really have any clear theoretical explanation; Yin and Yang were often regarded as something between concrete nouns and general ideas, but these ideas about Yin and Yang in Chinese intellectual history could certainly not remain at the level of phenomena like hot and cold, clear and rainy and so on. The ancient Chinese mode of thinking very easily linked this idea up to other phenomena and objects of a similar nature. People at that time believed that "things are produced in twos . . ." two by two in pairs; "the body has the left [side] and the right, and every one has his mate or double." Everything in the universe had "clear and thick, small and large, short and long, fast and slow, solemn and joyful, hard and soft, lingering and rapid, high and low, the commencement and close, the close and the diffuse, by which the parts are all blended together."[12] And because of this there then arose the idea, stated in the "Discourses of Yue" (Yueyu) chapter in the *Discourses of the States*, of "following the constancy of the Yin and Yang, and submitting to the regularity of Heaven and Earth."[13] This, then, raised the Yin and Yang to the status of the two fundamental elements of the cosmos.

Now let's look at the Five Phases.

As mentioned in chapter one, the custom of employing numbers began very early on, but some scholars believed that Five Phases thought began rather late and they attributed it to Zou Yan (ca. 305–ca. 240 BCE) of the Warring States period. Written materials would indicate, however, that although the content and finalization of the Five Phases idea was somewhat later, Five Phases thought was pervasive throughout the Spring and Autumn and Warring States eras. It followed the belief in some fixed numbers and developed into a widely accepted concept. It is said that the Five Phases were also first connected to geography and derived from Shang dynasty spatial concepts.[14] The Five Phases concept very quickly went beyond the scope of the "five directions" (*wufang*, east, south, west, north and central) and became a commonly used category name (*leiming*) in many different areas.

To take some examples from the Spring and Autumn period, from the *Zuo Commentary*, it would appear that the people then already had the ideas of the

11 *Guoyu*, 1988, 26–27.

12 *Zuozhuan*, "Zhaogong sanshi-er nian, ershi nian, SSJZS, 2128, 2093. James Legge translation from http://www.google.ca/books?id=_KhxPnWF6moC.

13 *Guoyu*, 1988, "Yueyu," 646.

14 See Pang Pu, "Wuxing manshuo," *Wenshi* 39 (1994), 30.

Five Phases mutually engendering and subduing each other, of the Five Phases and the four directions, and of the five colors corresponding to the Five Phases. A passage in the *Zuo Commentary* quotes Zi Chan discussing the "rites." He says ". . . Heaven and Earth have their regular ways, and men take these for their pattern, imitating the brilliant Heavenly bodies, and according with the natural diversities of the Earth. (Heaven and Earth) produce the six atmospheric conditions (*qi*), and make use of the Five Phases (*wuxing*). Those conditions (and Phases) become the five flavors, are manifested in the five colors, and displayed in the five notes."[15] From this we know that at some time before this was recorded, Five Phases thinking already existed and it was believed that "in Heaven there are three *chen* (辰 sun, moon, and stars); on Earth there are the Five Phases; the body has the left [side] and the right, and every one has his mate or double."[16] At least as early as the reign of Duke Zhao of the state of Lu (r. 542–510 BCE), this thinking was already widely accepted.

1.3

A consciousness that the cosmos, society and humanity form one holistic entity along with Yin-Yang and Five Phases thought led the ancient Chinese to conceive one very general belief. That is, that between Heaven, Earth and Humanity, all of the symmetrical and corresponding elements had some sort of mysterious connection. On the basis of their experience, they generalized this balanced symmetry and correspondence into the concepts of Yin-Yang and the Five Phases. Through the relationships between Yin, Yang, the Five Phases and a few less important elements, the universe became a harmonious and unified whole. The various interrelated parts mutually interacted and these interactions were manifest in various signs or omens. There were several different methods of evoking the spirits and getting rid of calamity, such as ethics, morality, good and evil and the prayers of *wu* priests, *zhu* invocators, *shi* scribes and *zong* temple masters. Any one of these could be the key force to accomplish one's purpose. Perhaps in the minds of those people the interactions and connections between the cosmos and human beings were even larger in scope than we now know. From their perspective, the universe was a holistic entity replete with mysterious connections.

There is no need for modern people to criticize the structure of knowledge of that age, nor should intellectual historians ignore the level of the thought they inherited from the cultural traditions of the Shang and Zhou dynasties. As

---

15   *Zuozhuan*, "Zhaogong ershi-wu nian," SSJZS, 2107. Legge translation from http://www
     .google.ca/books?id=_KhxPnWF6moC.

16   *Zuozhuan*, "Zhaogong sanshi-er nian," SSJZS, 2093. See note 12 above.

long as the system of ceremonies symbolizing order in the cosmos and society and its associated thought had not completely collapsed, they simply went on thinking that way.

There may be some leaps in intellectual history, but they are usually in the thought of elite and very talented thinkers. The intellectual world of general knowledge does not experience such sudden transformations, but only slow incremental change, and this is especially true for ancient Chinese thought. Breakthroughs in the history of Chinese civilization are gradual and moderate. Even in the "axial age" when "the collapse of music and rites" (*libeng yuehuai* 禮崩樂壞) was a major change of the Spring and Autumn and Warring States periods, it was not sudden, but rather a gradual decline. Traditional remnants and historical symbols can be very strong and difficult to get rid of.

Nevertheless, the Way of Heaven having already changed, thought was bound to change along with it. Even if the change was slow and quite gentle, it was still change. In the following generations, we will see the signs and the direction of intellectual change.

1.4

It was during this Spring and Autumn and Warring States era, that Chinese culture experienced one of its most significant changes: the emergence and rise of the *shi* 士, the class occupying the bottom rung of the aristocratic hierarchy.

As discussed above, the earliest Chinese intellectual world was dominated by the *wu* priests, *zhu* invocators, *shi* scribes and *zong* temple masters who had the power to communicate with Heaven. With the decline of the Zhou royal house and the rise to power and affluence of the Regional Rulers, the former monopoly of knowledge and thought was dispersed as the educated men moved away from the Zhou court. Then a group of men of culture analogous to the royal court officials (the king's officials, *wangguan*) appeared in the various Regional States. In the *Zuo Commentary*, "Duke of Shao, 17th year" (Shao gong 17), it is recorded that Confucius (ca. 551–479 BCE) once lamented the fact that "the Son of Heaven has lost his officials, and learning is dispersed to the small states in the four regions" (*tianzi shi guan, xue zai si yi* 天子失官, 學在四夷).[17] The former "king's officials"—that is, the knowledge and culture that the king once monopolized—was carried to the various Regional States by these educated men of culture.

The growing power of the Regional Rulers and the decline of the Zhou King was not, however, the only reason that "the Son of Heaven lost his officials, and

---

17   ssjzs, 2084.

learning dispersed to the small states in the four regions." Looking at the background of those who explain and apply culture, a more important reason was perhaps the rise of the *shi* "scholars" themselves. From the Spring and Autumn to the Warring States, the most remarkable change in ancient Chinese culture was the vitality of the *shi* class, that is, a group of men ranked between the lower aristocracy and the commoners who engaged in the production of knowledge.[18]

In general the rise of the *shi* took place in two ways. In the early stage, during the Spring and Autumn period, most of them were educated men and royal officials and who migrated to the Regional States, while some of them were cultured aristocrats whose status declined to that of *shi*. It was essentially their social status that declined and the downward mobility of this social stratum brought with it a downward shift of thought and knowledge in the Spring and Autumn period. In the later period, from the late Spring and Autumn into the early Warring States period, most of the *shi* were highly educated commoners who entered into the official service of the Regional States, or formed an independent intellectual stratum with cultural authority in society. If we say that in the early and middle part of the Spring and Autumn era, this group of men possessing culture and knowledge could for the most part only serve as counselors for high ranking official ministers in the Regional States, like Confucius and his disciples, we can say, then, that in the Warring States period, quite a few of these *shi* were very well-regarded.[19] If we say that in the early period, these expounders of knowledge still had to attach themselves to some political power-holders, we can say, then, that in the later period, based upon their intellectual expertise, men of knowledge frequently claimed to be equal to the political power-holders (*fenting kangli* 分庭抗禮). That is to say, there was then a space for the independent development of thought, and this demonstrates the rise and decline of educated men as well as a difference in the two eras. This change was also related, of course, to the increasing popularization of education. Besides philosophers like Confucius and Mozi (ca. 468–ca. 376 BCE) who had their own private place to lecture to their disciples, the contemporary official schools were also different from before. Quite a large number of men who understood politics and produced much critical discourse taught and studied in those schools. What sort of people were they, then? They are

---

18   There has been a great deal of generally acceptable research on the rise of the *shi* 士. See Yu Yingshi, *Shi yu Zhongguo wenhua*, 1987.

19   In his *Zhanguo shi*, 1957, 194, Yang Kuan mentions in this regard Zixia (disciple of Confucius), Li Kui (disciple of Zixia), Wu Qi (disciple of Zengzi), Zisi (Confucius' grandson) and so on.

described as follows in the "Discourses of Lu" (Luyu) chapter, section 13, in the *Discourses of the States*:

> In the morning the *shi* scholars received teaching, during the day they studied and discussed, in the evening they reviewed what they learned, at night they reflected on their errors and having no regrets, they could then feel at ease.[20]

Besides practicing the "six arts" mentioned above, it seem that their duties also included keeping track of public opinion and freely discussing their views—such men were *shi* indeed.

It is noteworthy that these changes led to a separation between thought and both politics and practical application. When thinkers examined politics, they tended to feel that it did not accord with humanistic values and moral standards, and so it deserved to be criticized. Political power-holders sometimes wanted the support of thinkers, and so they would on occasion heed their advice, but if it became completely impractical to them, they would soon discard it.

When thought separated itself from practical application, it did not seem to need to rely on knowledge to prove its reasonableness. At that, thought was able to transcend the limitations placed on it by both politics and knowledge and establish itself as an independent discourse with multifarious contents. The vitality of thought in this era led to a rapid proliferation of various different schools and sub-schools.

At this time, the estrangement of "thought" and the "authorities" provided the perfect training ground for contemporary thinkers. Two things followed closely the king's loss of his officials and the downward shift of learning: the number of those responsible for thought and culture increased greatly at the same time that they lost their authority; and the intellectual stratum of society became separated from the holders of indisputable power. Scholarly thought also became separated from self-evident truth.

The *shi* class was on the rise and becoming independent and so was their thought, and only this change could bring about a splendid age of "a hundred schools of thought contending" (*baijia zhengming* 百家爭鳴) from the Spring and Autumn to the Warring States period.

---

20   *Guoyu*, 205.

1.5

Chinese intellectual history was quietly changing. An age of unrest generally causes people to begin to doubt their established values just as a constantly changing situation causes them to question their fixed structure of beliefs. They were regarded as "correct and unalterable," but a major social and political upheaval at this time caused those self-evident principles to lose their supporting foundations. Compared to the stable and peaceful situation of the past, the people of this Spring and Autumn and Warring States era had much more freedom, but they also experienced much more suffering. When those truths that were once accepted without justification lost their authoritative nature, then those who explained reality had to start all over on the interpretation of any and all phenomena. They had to establish a new self-justifying system of principles. Scholars were compelled to question and reassess the knowledge and the ceremonies and symbols that embodied order and meaning in the cosmos and society. What, they asked, is the ultimate foundation of that knowledge and those symbols? Are they "correct and unalterable" or not? Those contemporary reflections were generally concentrated in three areas and led to three different directions of change in Chinese thought.

First, the symbolic system of rites itself and the ethical values that it symbolized were separated. Mere ceremonies no longer possessed meaningful authority, and this suggests that people began to examine closely the foundation supporting the reasonableness of the ceremonies themselves. That is, people asked at least three related questions: One, why should this ceremonial system employing animal sacrifice, formal dress, music, dance and so on have unquestionable symbolic significance? Two, if the practitioners of this ceremonial system themselves act in unreasonable ways, then can their sort of consciousness still gain the support of the Will of Heaven? And three, should not the Way of Heaven and Earth accord with wisdom and morality and not necessarily depend on the ceremonies?

Second, the rational foundations and the values of their system of order were originally bestowed by Heaven and originated from the feelings and inborn nature (*tianxing*) of "human beings." After this order had become the order of the human world and normative for human society and its behavioral standards, it came to possess its own "power" both as a "Mandate of Heaven" and as "human reason" (*renli* 人理). It seemed to be both natural and rational, and following this logic Heaven and "the Human" became its absolute foundations. But then thought was faced with two choices between Heaven and Humanity. Should thought comply with the orders of Heaven and obey the Way of Heaven in everything, or should thought value human reason and give rational recognition to the system of order?

Third, contemporary questioning of the reasonableness of the human order involved looking back in history, and this developed into the custom of going back to history in search of meaning. The Way of the Ancient Kings and the acts of the former dynasties were both the epitome and the foundation of meaning.[21] Contemporary thinkers believed that the distinctions between right and wrong and good and evil were completely clear from antiquity on. The meanings and values embodied in ethics and morality had been passed straight down to the present from ancient times. History was, therefore, a repository of useful experience, and a sort of perfectly correct symbol that could be applied to the correction of contemporary errors. Furthermore, the perfection of ancient times served as a mirror for examining the imperfections of the present. Without a foundation in history, human actions would lack any convincingly correct justification.[22]

Rites and "rightness," Heaven and "human beings," "ancient" (gu 古) and "modern" (jin 今)—all of these elements of Chinese thought split apart. With this background of intellectual schism, the world of thought at the end of the Spring and Autumn and the beginning of Warring States periods was the scene of continual change and confrontation.

2.   Continuation and Renewal of the Intellectual Tradition, I: Ru or the Confucians

2.1

Many scholars have pointed out that the ru arose from the ranks of those educated and cultured wu priests, zhu invocators, shi scribes and zong temple masters who supervised and managed the ceremonial rituals of the Shang and Zhou dynasties.[23] From ancient literary sources we can see that the ru seem to have been very fastidious about their dress. To pay particular attention to the symbolic meaning of certain attire was a custom that derived from the management of the early ritual ceremonies. In the early mysterious ceremonies the wu priests and zhu invocators who stood for the gods and spirits regarded the symbolic implications of ceremonial dress as especially important. From

---

21   For example, Shang and Zhou bronzes contain phrases like "for sons and grandsons to treasure forever." These sorts of inscriptions demonstrate both that those people wanted to pass on their glory from generation to generation and that they were beginning to have a rudimentary historical consciousness.

22   Zuozhuan, "Zhaogong, shiwu nian," SSJZS, 2078.

23   For "scholar," "litteratus," and "weak and timid" as early meanings of ru, see Karlgren, Gramata Serica Recensa, 1964, #134c.

literary sources, we see that the dress these *ru* emphasized had a rather traditional or restorationist flavor. In the *Analects* (Lunyu), one of the disciples of Confucius, Gongxi Hua, is reported to have told the Master that he would like to wear "the Straight Gown and the Emblematic Cap (*zhangfu* 章甫)" and join in the ancestral temple ceremonies.[24] The attire mentioned was from Shang times and probably only worn while participating in ritual ceremonies, but it is here given as emblematic of Confucian scholars.

From the *Analects* and the *Book of Rites*, we can see that *ru shi*, such as Confucius and his disciples, indeed paid particular attention to the symbolic significance of various types of clothing. The clothing for every occasion, like propitious days, funerals, major sacrifices and everyday situations, had its own style. The *ru* or Confucians paid particular attention to the symbolic implications of clothing colors and what colors were to be worn on what occasions. In ancient China, colors themselves were symbolic: "the Xia favored black," "the Shang favored white" and "the Zhou favored red." The Confucians strictly followed a set of rules that were said to "accord with the rites."

This tradition was fiercely attacked by Daoist scholars. It is said that Zhuangzi encouraged Duke Ai of Lu to forbid the wearing of this sort of clothing by men who had no real learning. The Duke issued the order, and "within five days, there was no one in the state of Lu who dared wear Confucian garb." We can see that Confucian garb (*rufu* 儒服) was distinctive and carried symbolic implications.[25] This anecdote is not necessarily credible, but the idea that the Confucians emphasized the symbolic nature of clothing is certainly true. Up until much later times, the attire of the *rusheng* 儒生, or Confucian scholars, was still quite unusual—in the period between the Qin and the Han dynasties, the high Confucian cap (*ruguan* 儒冠) was emblematic of the Confucians. The *Records of the Grand Historian* reports that when Li Sheng (Li Yiji, 268?–ca. 204) had an audience with Liu Bang, the future first emperor of the Han, an envoy told Liu Bang that Li had the appearance of a "major Confucian scholar" (*da ru*) because he was "dressed in Confucian garb and wore a high hat that made people turn their heads to look at him" (*yi ru yi, guan ce zhu*).[26]

Of course the Confucian scholars paid attention to the symbolic and commemorative value of many other things, including the symbolic meaning of the positioning of the sacrificial ceremonies, their rules of time and place, the

---

24 SSJZS, 2500. *Lunyu*, "Xianjin," 11.25 or 26. Waley, *The Analects of Confucius*, 1938, 160. Legge's translation from CTP is ". . . dressed in the dark square-made robe and the black linen cap . . ."

25 *Zhuangzi*, "Tian Zifang," Guo Qingfan, ZZJS, 718. Watson, CT, 227.

26 *Shiji*, j. 97, 2692, 2704.

various behaviors and attitudes required and so on. These things were not simply a few concrete details; they constituted an entire cultural education that was passed down from aristocratic society. Confucius had an obvious nostalgia for the traditional order, and so he described himself as one who understood not only the ceremonial rules of the three ancient dynasties, but also comprehended the civilization behind these rituals. For him and his followers, the ceremonial order symbolized an entire civilization that had already been lost or was about to disappear. In the past that ceremonial order was regulated by the *wu* priests and *zhu* invocators. As their descendents, the Confucian scholars inherited the customs of the rites and ceremonies, carried forward the ceremonial and symbolic tradition and mastered the symbolic knowledge behind the rites. Through their efforts the ceremonies, symbols and knowledge embodied in those practices of the Xia, Shang, and Zhou dynasties were passed on from generation to generation.

2.2

This does not mean that there were no changes. By the time of Confucius and his disciples (about the middle of the fifth century BCE—the beginning of the Warring States period), changes in the ideas behind the ceremonies were quite obvious. Three of these changes were most important: from the rules of the rites and ceremonies down to the human social order, they emphasized the significance of *li* as propriety; from the symbolic implications of the ceremonies, they developed ideas about "names" (*ming* 名); and from investigating the value foundations of the rites and ceremonies, they went on to discover "humanity" (*ren* 仁)—that is, they highly regarded the psychological foundations of order and rules.

Let us examine rites first. In all aspects of the sacrificial rites and ceremonies including their object, time, place, sequence, ritual implements and protocol ever since the Shang and Zhou dynasties, they were intended to establish a hierarchical structure of sequential ranks. The rules of the rites and ceremonies were so expressed in order to regulate and rectify the human order. All of the formal differences taken together—*tailao* (sacrifice of oxen, goats, and hogs) versus *shaolao* (sacrifice of hogs and sheep only), eight rows of dancers (*bayi*) for the king or Son of Heaven versus six rows (*liuyi*) for the Regional Rulers, nine versus seven cauldrons for funerals, the rules of the suburban sacrifices versus those of ancestral temple sacrifices—were called "rites and ceremonies." For the Confucian interpretation, however, the meaning of these rites and ceremonies was not merely ceremonial and not even merely the ethical system implicit in the ceremonies. For them, the rites and ceremonies represented a set of meanings and values—that is, an entire civilization.

In the age of Confucius, the Confucians not only emphasized the various external forms and rules of the rites and ceremonies, but were even more interested in the thought and ideas expressed and the significance of these ideas for social order. When his disciple Yan Yuan (Yan Hui) asked him how to achieve *ren* (humanity), Confucius once said "look at nothing that is contrary to propriety (*li*), listen to nothing that is contrary to propriety, say nothing that is contrary to propriety, and do nothing that is contrary to propriety."[27] All of this was intended to nurture a habit of conscientious compliance with social propriety and to bring about a society with a well-ordered hierarchical structure. This was not just a matter of performing certain actions with certain attitudes and following certain rules, nor was it simply a system of sacrifices with music and dance. According to Confucius, then, what sort of a man could be accepted by society and be a well-rounded man? In both cases, he answered that to be such a man he must understand propriety and proper behavior (*li*).

It is said that Confucius himself was very well-versed in every kind of ritual and ceremony, not only those of the Zhou but also of the Xia and the Shang dynasties. In his life activities, he also exhibited excellent manners, maintained a proper bearing and held fast to duty and right. In short, he possessed the proper cultivation for a member of the lower aristocracy. He believed that if every contemporary social stratum and every individual could be regulated according to propriety and good moral standards, then their society could maintain good order. For that reason, Confucius greatly despised those who overstepped the bounds of established norms of propriety. He twice said that "if you do not learn propriety, you cannot establish yourself" (*bu xue li, wu yi li*).[28] This was because, as noted above, Confucius clearly understood that the rites and ceremonies were not just a group of systematized actions and attitudes, nor just a system. Rather, they were symbols of order. It was precisely people's respect for the propriety derived from the rites and ceremonies that guaranteed the stability of this order. And people's respect for these rites and ceremonies was dependent on their conscientious practice of ethics and morality. Without the rites and ceremonies, individual morality would have no forum to express itself and there would be no way to maintain order in society.

---

27 *Lunyu*, "Yan Yuan," 16.1. Translation based on Legge and Waley. However, Legge renders *ren* as "perfect virtue" and Waley as "Goodness."

28 *Lunyu*, "Ji shi," 16.13 and "Yao yue," 20.3. ssjzs, 2522, 2536. "Establish yourself" (*li*, literally, stand up) may mean to establish one's moral character or to establish one's place in society.

Let us now examine "names" (*ming*). A celebrated passage in the *Analects* says that "If names are not correct, then words will not mean what they say; if words do not mean what they say, then affairs cannot be carried out properly; if affairs are not carried out properly, then rites and music will not flourish; if rites and music do not flourish, corporal punishments and fines will not be appropriate to the crimes; if corporal punishments and fines are not appropriate to the crimes, then the common people will not know how to act correctly (literally, will not know where to put their hands and feet)."[29] Attaching such importance to "names" was related to attaching great importance to the symbolism of the rites and ceremonies.

As discussed above, the symbolic meanings of those sacrificial ceremonies were extremely powerful. The orderly regulation of those symbols encouraged the orderly regulation and of the human social order, and the collapse of those symbols ushered in the collapse of that same human social order. As people came increasingly to believe in the function of "names" to limit, regulate and rectify "reality" (*shi* 實), they then hoped to employ clarification and confirmation of such significs to clarify and confirm reality.

For example, the rulers of the state of Chu were originally entitled to be called Prince (*zi* 子, literally, son of an aristocrat) but they called themselves King (*wang*), and they actually were very powerful.[30] Nevertheless, the official historians (*shichen* or *shiguan*) still called them "the princes of Chu" (Chu *zi*) as though they could rely on the correct "name" to express their just attitude. That is, they hoped to "rectify reality" (*zhengshi*) by means of the "rectification of names" (*zhengming*). In other words, they wanted to use the stipulation of names to compel society to accept the reasonableness of proper order, and for this reason the Confucians wanted very much to practice the "rectification of names."

By relying on the systemization and symbolization of rites and names, Confucius hoped to arrive at a harmonious and peaceful hierarchical society in which everyone, high and low, played their proper roles. Nevertheless, he discovered some deep-seated problems. Where did the general reasonableness of the ceremonies expressing propriety and social norms come from? What was the original basis for distinguishing names? What could be relied upon to guarantee people's willing acceptance of social norms and names? What

---

29 SSJZS, 2506. *Lunyu*, "Zi Lu," 13.3. Translation based on Legge and Waley.

30 Except for *Zuozhuan* citations, we do not render the "five ranks" *gong, hou, bo, zi, nan* using the European feudal ranks of duke, marquis, count or earl, viscount, and baron. For the reasons why, see Li Feng, " 'Feudalism' and Western Zhou China: A Criticism," *Harvard Journal of Asiatic Studies* 63/1 (2003), 115–144.

could be relied upon to guarantee that this social order would not be over-turned? To answer these questions, Confucius put forth the concept of *ren* or "humanity." Rules of propriety or rites (*li*) had to be complied with because they conformed to *ren*, and names should be respected because only in that way could one attain to *ren*.

What, then, is *ren*? What does *ren* mean? According to the most direct state-ment in the "Yan Yuan" chapter of the *Analects*, Confucius said that *ren* means simply "to love all men" (*ai ren*).[31] This feeling of "love for other people" comes from the heart and is a common, natural feeling of empathy. When Zhong Gong asked Confucius about *ren*, he answered in part with the celebrated neg-ative Golden Rule: "do not treat others in a manner that you would not want to be treated yourself."[32] For Confucius, this was the only way one could gain other people's respect. This rule expresses a deep feeling of equality and close-ness with other human beings. This feeling that "all human beings" (*ren*) and "oneself" (*ji* 己) form a single body could easily lead to the idea that an indi-vidual "person" should respect other "persons."

The "Discourses of Jin, Four" (Jinyu si) chapter of the *Discourses of the States* quotes the following passage from the "Essay on Rites" (Lizhi): "If you want to ask a favor from someone, you must first do something for them; if you want others to love you, you must first love others; if you want others to get along with you, you must first get along with others."[33] From this we can see that quite a few people at that time already had this sort of idea. They already considered this notion of transcending "the individual" and moving on toward "society" to constitute a reasonable general principle. They could use this feeling of moving from self to other people to establish a foundation for social ethics.

How was this kind of "love" and "respect" to be produced, though? Confucius traced this human tendency to "love other people" back to kinship and family feelings. He said that "By nature men are similar, but by practice they grow far apart."[34] By "nature" he meant basic human nature. Confucius believed that of all the human feelings the love and affection fostered by kinship relationships were beyond question. That sons love their fathers and younger brothers love their elder brothers was a natural expression of their true nature, and their true nature brought out genuine feelings of "filial piety" (*xiao*) and "brotherly love" (*ti*). As You Ruo said in the *Analects*, "the gentleman (superior man, *junzi*)

---

31   In *Lunyu*, "Yan Yuan," 12.22, "Fan Chi asked about *ren*. The Master said "Love all men."
32   *Lunyu*, "Yan Yuan," 12.2.
33   *Guoyu*, 1988, 358.
34   *Lunyu*, "Yang Huo," 17.2.

devotes his efforts to the roots (*wu ben*); for once the roots are established, the Way will grow therefrom. Are not filial piety and brotherly affection the roots of humanity?"[35] Confucians believed that this sort of kinship and family affection unquestionably conformed to morality and reason and was the foundation of goodness and justice—it was "the root of humanity."

When people had these genuine feelings and conducted their relationships with other people on the basis of them, then they would be disposed to "love other people." These feelings, and kinship itself, could be expanded outward from loving one's father and elder brother to loving other people. This extension could produce a stable and peaceful society because, as You Ruo said in the same passage, "very few men who treat their parents and elder brothers with filial piety (*xiao*) and brotherly affection (*ti*) are inclined to oppose their superiors, and there has never been an instance of one being disposed to foment rebellion, but not wanting to oppose his superiors."[36] In this emphasis on the foundation of human behavior, Confucius already differed from his predecessors with their simple reliance on ceremonies and symbols to rectify human social order. Confucius said that the root of rites and music was *ren*— "humanity," but rites and music were already regarded as outward forms of human behavior.

By this time, Chinese intellectual history had already delved deeply into man's inner world. Just as the self-evident authoritative rules of social order moved from outer rites and music to inner human feelings, the mysterious intimations of the ancient Chinese intellectual world began to fade and the spirit of morality began to come into prominence. Chinese intellectual history had now completed a process of shedding its old skin, and what emerged from this transformation was a self-consciousness that relied on feelings and human nature to actualize a theory of human socio-political order.

2.3

According to the *History of the Former Han Dynasty* "Biography of Scholars" (Rulin zhuan), after Confucius passed away his disciples dispersed to various places. Some of them became retainers of Regional Rulers, some became friends of aristocrats, and some even became hermits.[37] A few of them— Zizhang (503–? BCE), Zi Yu (Tantai Mieming, 512–? BCE), Zixia (507–? BCE), Zigong (520–446? BCE), Zengzi (505–435 BCE), Zisi (483–402 BCE), the grandson of Confucius—had considerable influence. They carried on the tradition

---

35   *Lunyu*, "Xue er," 2.2. SSJZS, 2457. Modified from Lau, *Analects*, 59.

36   *Lunyu*, SSJZS, 2457.

37   HS, j. 88, 3591.

of private teaching inaugurated by Confucius and soon made the Confucians a noted school of thought. At the same time, due to differences in their styles of study, academic preferences, and understanding, they also caused the Confucian School to split up into a number of different branches.[38]

The disciples of Confucius may have had some differences among them; for example Zigong, Ziyou (Yan Yan) and Zixia were not very much alike. We can still point out, however, some common tendencies that they shared. First, they all insisted on the efficacy of the ceremonies of rites and music and their symbols. They continued to pass down knowledge about the system of music and ritual and to expound upon their cultural significance. Second, they relied comparatively more on the ancient classics as textual support for their understanding and interpretation of ideas. Third, they emphasized more using historical knowledge to support their position. They had their own system of historical legends from sage kings Yao, Shun, Yu and Tang to kings Wen and Wu. Whenever necessary, they would reach back into ancient history to locate indisputable support for their views. From the historical materials on them, we can see that the Confucians of this age, like Zengzi, Zisi and the rest, also developed two intellectual tendencies that differed from what had gone before.

The first tendency involved a further development toward using intrinsic human nature as the ultimate foundation of thought. If the "Great Learning" and the "Doctrine of the Mean" were really written by this branch of Confucian scholars, and regardless of their later influence, we have to admit that they introduced certain new ideas into Confucian teaching. That is, by particularly foregrounding the deep structure of human nature, they advanced a step forward both the emotional and the rational foundations of Confucius' emphasis on rites and music. In the age of Confucius, the heart/mind that loves other people or the natural goodness of man's basic nature were still based on the natural expression and outward extension of kinship feelings. The Confucians of this later generation, however, regarded the human heart/mind—universal human nature—as the foundation of the moral and ethical order. They regarded the sincere tendency toward goodness of the human heart/mind as the foundation of a naturally endowed innate knowledge (*liangzhi* 良知). They regarded the highest good behavior that human beings could cultivate as the ultimate goal of human life. Therefore, the "Great Learning" and the "Doctrine of the Mean" proposed starting from self-conscious spiritual beginnings/self-awakenings, like the "investigation of things" (*gewu*), the

---

38   "After Confucius and Mozi, the Confucians split into eight (branches)." *Hanfeizi*, "Xianxue," ESEZ, 1185.

"extension of knowledge" (*zhizhi*), "sincerity of thought" (*chengyi*), "rectification of heart/mind" (*zhengxin*) and so on, and then following a path of "cultivating one's self" (*xiushen*), "ordering one's family" (*qijia*), and "regulating the
state" (*zhiguo*) in order to "bring peace to all under Heaven" (*ping tianxia*)—
that is, they sought to establish a train of reasoning leading to the establishment of a rational order in the world. They also proposed methods to enable
people to acquire pristine, sincere and honest temperaments and characters,
starting from "Heavenly endowed life" (*tianming*), "human nature" (*xing*), "the
Way" (Dao) and "instruction" (*jiao*), that is, to accord with the natural expression of their heavenly bequeathed nature, and continuously to nurture these
reasonable feelings. On the one hand, this would allow humanity's sincere and
good basic nature to embody Heaven's mandate, and on the other hand, it
would lead people carefully to concentrate their efforts on nurturing this basic
nature. Mencius's theories of human nature and morality later emerged from
this milieu.[39]

The second tendency developed toward communication with the Way of
Heaven and seeking for an ultimate rationality in the cosmos. This tendency
was simply to employ explanations of the cosmic Yin-Yang and Five Phases to
explain Confucian thought. Materials on this tendency are, however, lacking,
and we only have a passage in the *Xunzi*, "Contra Twelve Philosophers" chapter.
In it Xunzi (ca. 313–238 BCE) criticizes the later followers of Confucius as follows: "Some men follow the model of the Ancient Kings in a fragmentary way,
but they do not understand its guiding principles. Still their abilities are manifold, their memory great, and their experience and knowledge both varied and
broad. They have initiated a theory for which they claim great antiquity, calling
it the Five Phases theory."[40]

The archeological discoveries of the twentieth-century, however, offer us
some further clues to the intellectual history of two thousand years ago: two
separate works both entitled "The Five Conducts" (Wuxing), one silk manuscript from the Mawangdui Han tombs in Changsha and one bamboo slip
manuscript from the Chu tombs of the Warring States period in Guodian. They
are believed to be works in the tradition of Zisi and Mengzi. They "discuss the
Confucian 'Five Conducts theory of 'humanity, rightness, rites, wisdom and
sageliness' (*ren, yi, li, zhi, sheng*). Their genre style is that of the "Great Learning"

---

39   See *Daxue*, section 2 for the eight steps of cultivation. Mencius is said to have "learned
     from a disciple of Zisi." *Shiji*, j. 74, "Biography of Mencius and Xunzi," 2343.

40   *Xunzi*, "Fei shi er zi," 6.7. Translation is by John Knoblock, *Xunzi: A Translation and Study
     of the Complete Works*, vol. 1, 1988, 224. Knoblock's "Five Processes" is here changed to
     "Five Phases."

and their rhetoric follows the discourse of Mencius."[41] It is very possible that this represents the mature thought of the Zisi and Mengzi tradition. They combined the Five Phases that are the foundation of the cosmos with five character traits advocated by the Confucians in order to bring Heaven and human beings together. These new materials demonstrate that the later Confucian scholars believed that human character traits and human nature are connected to the Five Phases. Metal, wood, water, fire and earth are the outward display of the Mandate of Heaven, and humanity, right, rites, wisdom and sageliness are its inner manifestation. The reason that the Sages on high could communicate with the Way of Heaven above was because they embody the Five Phases/ Conducts, but ordinary people have to develop their "inner heart/mind" because they lack the element of "sageliness" (*sheng* 聖) and only have four of the Five Phases/Conducts. Therefore the Sages have "virtue or moral power" (*de*), while the ordinary people must strive for "goodness" (*shan* 善).

3.   **Continuation and Renewal of the Intellectual Tradition, II:**
        ***Mo* or the Moists**

It is said that the rise of the Mohist tradition was also related to the study of rites and ceremonies. Mozi lived one or two generations after Confucius, about the same time as the second generation of Confucius' students. Like Confucius, Mozi lived in the culturally rich states of Zou and Lu. Their intellectual backgrounds should also be quite similar. According to one record, Mozi once studied the suburban temple sacrifices with a descendent of the Eastern Zhou official Shi Jiao. The "Ruler's Techniques" (Zhushuxun) chapter of the *Huainanzi* says that "Confucius and Mo Di cultivated the techniques of the former sages and had a penetrating understanding of the theories of the six arts."[42] Mozi, however, was quite dissatisfied with the followers of Confucius and their endeavors to preserve the cultural traditions of the aristocracy. He launched a fierce attack on them. Based on the "Gongmeng" and other chapters of the *Mozi*, these criticisms were in four areas.[43]

---

41   See Han Zhongmin, "Changsha Mawangdui Hanmu boshu gaishu," *Wenwu* 9 (1974), 41.

42   *Huainan honglie jijie*, 1989, 302–303. John S. Major, et al., trans. and eds., *The Huainanzi: A Guide to the Theory and Practice of Government in Early China*, 2010, 326.

43   Gongmeng is said to have been a follower of Zengzi. See, ECT, 336–341 for an introduction to the *Mozi*.

3.1

First, the Moists criticized Confucius and the later Confucians for emphasizing sacrifices even when they did not believe in ghosts and spirits. By this, they could easily fall into a hypocritical theism or a genuine atheism, and so the Moists strongly condemned this contradiction in Confucian practice. In the "Heaven's Intention/Purpose" and "Percipient Ghosts" chapters, Mozi pointed out, against the Confucians, that Heaven is the arbiter of everything, and Heaven has a will to good or evil that it manifests through granting life and death, wealth and poverty, good government or chaos and so on. Therefore, political figures should follow the example of the sage kings of the Three Ancient Dynasties and "comply with the intentions of Heaven."[44] Mozi also believed that ghosts and spirits could foresee things several hundred years in the future. He felt that ghosts and spirits could "reward the worthy and punish the wicked" without any omissions.[45] He further argued that the contemporary chaotic situation in the world was due to the fact that people doubted the existence of ghosts and spirits and did not "clearly understand that ghosts and spirits are able to reward the worthy and punish the wicked." Bereft of the scrutiny and restraint of ghosts and spirits, rulers and ministers, superiors and inferiors, lack kindness and loyalty, and fathers, sons and brothers lack compassion, filial piety and brotherly respect. Many ancient texts are marshaled to demonstrate that ghosts and spirits are everywhere, and that if people want to make all under Heaven stable and peaceful and create a well-ordered society, they should follow the example of the ancient Sages and "in [one's] conduct honor Heaven in the upper realm, serve the ghosts and spirits in the middle realm, and love the people in the lower realm." People should certainly not follow Confucius by "respecting the ghosts and spirits, but keeping them at a distance."[46]

Second, the Moists criticized the Confucians for their elaborate ceremonial funerals. "Moderation in Funerals III," criticizes the Confucians for their excessive emphasis on formalistic rites and ceremonies, and points out that this is really not the way to express the feelings of a filial son.[47] The *Mozi* says that "the benevolent man (*renzhe*) plans (*du* 度) for the whole world, and his planning fulfills the "three responsibilities" (*sanwu* 三務): to make everyone in the

44   *Mozi xiangu* (*jiangu*), j. 7, 177. Ian Johnston, *The Mozi: A Complete Translation*, 2010, 26.4, 236.

45   *Mozi*, "Ming gui xia" (Percipient Ghosts, III), Johnston, *Mozi*, 31.1, 279.

46   *Ibid.*, j. 7, "Tian zhi shang," (Heaven's Intention I), 177. Johnston, *Mozi*, 26.5, 237–238 with slight changes. *Lunyu*, 6.22.

47   *Mozi*, j. 6, "Jie sang xia," (Moderation in Funerals, III), 154. Johnston, *Mozi*, 210–231.

world rich, to make the population numerous, and to bring order and stability to society.[48] Lavish funerals and long mourning periods do not accomplish any of these things.

The *Mozi* bitingly points out that lavish funerals and prolonged mourning periods waste a great deal of wealth, prevent the normal pursuits of life and the normal production of the masses. They also harm people's health, are detrimental to procreation and lead to illness and death. Lavish funerals and prolonged mourning periods cannot make the people prosperous, more numerous or bring them stability and peace because, if people are preoccupied with funerals and mourning, they will not have enough money, and this will lead to resentment; they will not be able to find suitable mates, and this will lead to disputes—all this will lead to great social unrest. Therefore, the Moists advocated moderation and simplicity in funerals rather than simply abolishing them.[49] In this way, people can cultivate a humanity and rightness that would accord with the Way of the Sages and the interests of the common people.

Third, the Moists criticized the Confucians for their excessive emphasis on rites and music, important elements of various kinds of ceremonies that Confucians paid particular attention to.[50] According to Confucius, music had the power to "stimulate the emotions" (*xing*), aid in the practice of "self-observation" (*guan*) and "conviviality" (*qun*) and teach one how to properly "express grievances" (*yuan*).[51] The Confucians also believed that music was a symbol of social class differences. It was not that Mozi did not enjoy listening to fine music or looking at beautiful colors, but, he argued, they could not solve the people's "three hardships" (*sanhuan* 三患): "to be hungry and not find food; to be cold and not find clothing; to be weary and not find rest." The external symbolism of music could not eliminate social injustice, but

---

48 *Mozi*, "Jiesang xia" (Moderation in Funerals, III), 25.1, Johnston, *Mozi*, 211. Johnston's complete translation is: "A benevolent man's planning for the world is in no way different from a filial son's planning for his parents. Now what will a filial son's planning for his parents consist of? I say that, if his parents are poor, he works to make them rich. If the people [of his family] are few, he works to make them numerous. If they are numerous, but in disorder, he works to bring them to order . . . . [his] making provision for the world is just [the same]."

49 Johnston, *Mozi*, 165.

50 On the Confucian emphasis on music, see *Liji*, "Yueji."

51 See *Lunyu*, "Yang Huo," 17.9 for *xing, guan, qun, yuan* in relation to studying the *Book of Songs*.

would lead rather to the abandonment of production, and therefore music is not necessary.[52]

Fourth, the Moists criticized the Confucians for believing in Fate (*ming* 命). They said that the Confucians believed in "fatalism"—that poverty or wealth, long life or early death, well governed or chaotic times, safety or danger were all depended on Fate. Even though Confucius urged people on conscientiously to work hard, in the final analysis this hard work was subordinate to the workings of Fate. By contrast, Mozi criticized this "fatalism" on the basis of the actions of the ancient sage kings, using the advantages and disadvantages to the common people as his standard and referring to the gains and losses due to punishments and government decrees as evidence. He pointed out that good government and chaos, flourishing and decline, and disasters or happiness really have nothing to do with Fate. First, they depend on whether or not the state or the ruler practices "universal love and exchange of mutual benefit" so that "Heaven and the ghosts [will] enrich him, the regional rulers [will] join him, [and] the ordinary people [will] love him."[53] Second, it depends on whether or not there are reasonable decrees, rewards, and punishments so as to make the people strive to "exalt the worthy/worthiness" (*shangxian* 尚賢) and preserve the way of filial piety and fraternal love. If you followed the logic of fatalism, the Moists said, then nothing would depend on good or evil, right or wrong, and people would lack the proper sense of reverence and awe and would not work hard. The result would be that everything would be thrown into complete chaos. "Therefore, with regard to Fate, it is of no benefit to Heaven above; it is of no benefit to the spirits in the middle realm; it is of no benefit to the people below."[54]

3.2

From Mozi's critique of Confucian thought, we can see that it represented a sort of aristocratic humanism. The Confucians believed in an ultimate ideal world based on an a priori moral foundation. The "past" that they recalled was too idealized and full of imagination. They hoped to use the ceremonial and symbolic rites to preserve the ideal order they believed in. On this account, they did not very much want to discuss the practical problems of actual society. In their thinking, the significance of the idealized and formalized rites

---

52   *Mozi*, "Fei yue shang," (Condemning Music I), *Mozi xiangu* (*jiangu*), j. 8, 1986, 228, 229. Johnston, *Mozi*, 32.4, 309.

53   *Mozi*, "Jian ai zhong" (Universal Love II), 15.3, Johnston, *Mozi*, 139 *Mozi*, "Fei ming shang" (Against Fate I), Johnston, *Mozi*, 35.6, 323–324.

54   *Mozi*, "Fei ming shang" (Against Fate I), Johnston, *Mozi*, 36.1, 331.

was overly inflated. Once the shamanistic laws and regulations of the past were transformed through their moralization and internalization, the rites no longer had much power to restrain human behavior. Nevertheless, the Confucians still hoped that rites, music and the individual's moral conscious-ness and ethical creed could save the world and bring about an ideal social order. Therefore, they continued to lodge their hopes in education, culture and thought, and to believe that ceremonies and symbols could regulate and restrain humanity.

On the contrary, Mozi and the Moists were firm this-worldly pragmatists who followed a very practical way of thinking. In order to make the world rich, to make the population numerous, and to bring order and stability to society, all that convoluted and overly-elaborate ritualistic formalism should be abol-ished. At the same time, it was necessary to think deeply about all of society's practical problems. If we say that the Confucians represented a form of ideal-istic humanism, then the Moists were quite different in that the foundation of their reflections was the reasonableness of the real world. They believed that their ideas should be realized in this world. First, people should obey Heaven and the ghosts because they are the external forces that control and restrain human behavior, and they can help to make the world stable and peaceful and give a proper order to human morality. Secondly, funerals and prolonged mourning are detrimental to the accumulation of wealth and the increase of population, and music is not relevant to producing wealth but only squanders it. From this point of view, a system that depends on external forms to express internal feelings has no practical efficacy and should be abolished. Thirdly, fatalist ideas cause the common people to lose their sense of reverence and awe, to lack confidence, and not to do their work while at the same time lead-ing the ruler to neglect the practice of good governance; they should be done away with.

Quite obviously, Mozi's extremely practical thought had nothing but con-tempt for ritual ceremonies and symbols. The only standard for the rationality of his thinking was whether or not something was useful or beneficial for con-temporary society. Mozi's standard for judging any theory was his famous "three criteria" (*san biao fa* 三表法) that were basically methods by which he attempted to bring together historical foundation, value rationality and instru-mental rationality, or, as the *Mozi* puts it "that there be a basis (*ben zhi* 本之)," "that there be an origin (*yuan zhi* 原之) and that there be a use (*yong zhi* 用之)."[55] Any correct theory must have a historical foundation, logical think-ing and practical utility. On this account, Mozi established "religion" (*zongjiao*), strengthened "punishments and government decrees" (*xingzheng*) and

---

55 *Mozi*, "Fei ming shang" (Against Fate I), Johnston, Mozi, 36.1, 331.

promoted "operative thought" (*caozuo sixiang*). If something could not be put into operation in the real world, then it was worthless. Perhaps these philosophical differences between Confucius and Mozi were related to their different social origins, Confucius being from the lower aristocracy and Mozi from a lower strata of society.

The polemic between Confucians and Moists also reflected changes in contemporary social mores. From the Spring and Autumn to the Warring States period, an old era came to and end. Those intellectuals who had experienced the earlier culture, were familiar with the rules of that culture and who enjoyed a historical sense of cultural superiority, now began to experience feelings of anxiety and consternation. The old aristocracy who had lived in the cultural atmosphere of the Shang and Zhou dynasties were estranged from the new environment that witnessed the collapse of the old system of rites and music. They had lost all sense of security, and were naturally prone to be nostalgic, to construct an ideal image of the historical past, to rely on tradition to criticize the present reality and to ridicule secular society on the basis of their cultural spirit. Their habit of never having to worry about their livelihood impelled them all the more to think about ultimate and abstract spiritual questions and to reveal their idealistic humanism with everything they said. The consciousness of their past status and discursive power naturally made them nostalgic for the culture and political system of the past. Confucius and his school of thought were exactly of that type.

After their era had gone past, however, a practical tide of thought certainly had to come along to fill the vacuum in the intellectual world during a later age of social change and turmoil. A group of thinkers who had not experienced the old culture and had no feelings of cultural superiority then came along. They very perceptively addressed the needs of contemporary life in the real world. They transformed the former excessively idealized discourse of the Confucians into practically applicable strategies while attacking the older generation's cultural experience. Mozi and his school of thought were of this type. The Moists were unconcerned about any cultural and intellectual rupture; they just wanted to establish a system and rules and regulations suitable to their age. One can say that they employed an intellectual system full of practical rationality to criticize the thought that defended value rationality.

On this account, the *Xunzi*, "Dispelling Blindness," says that "Mo Di was blinded by utility (*yong* 用) and was insensible to the value of good form (*wen* 文)."[56] *Yong*, "utility," is simply practical efficacy, and this kind of thought is focused on the real, practical world, but *wen*, "good form," is a formalistic and

56   *Xunzi jijie*, j. 15, "Jiebi," zzjc, 261, Knoblock, *Xunzi*, vol. 3, 1994, "Dispelling Blindness," 21.4, 102.

symbolic harmony and ornate beauty, and that kind of thought is usually focused on tradition.

3.3

During the Warring States period, the Moists were once mentioned together with the Confucians as famous schools (*xianxue* 顯學). Although the literary remains pertaining to the Moists have mostly been scattered and lost, from a few fragmentary records we can still glimpse the flourishing situation of Mozi's disciples at that time. According to Hu Shi, the later Moists split into two tendencies: one evolved into a religious organization with the Leader (*juzi* 钜子) as its center; the other was the "different Moists" (*bie Mo*) that went from social life as its center toward technology and logic as its center. These are the "Cannons A and B" (Jing, shang, xia), "Explanations A and B" (Jingshuo shang, xia), "Choosing the Greater" (Daqu), "Choosing the Lesser" (Xiaoqu) that contain discussions of logic or dialectic theories while the "Gongshu Ban," "Preparing the Wall and Gates" and so on discuss technological and military defense matters.[57]

All of this is generally true, but there are a few things more that need to be said. First, unlike the Confucian emphasis on intellectual transmission and basic education in culture, the later Moist continuation was more involved with personal attachment and organizational exclusiveness. This imperceptibly weakened their intellectual unity and led to different factional rules (*zongfa* 宗法). When the halo of "sageliness" disappeared from their Leader, their organization would fall to pieces and their intellectual unity would also collapse. Second, the Moists made extraordinarily difficult demands on the individual by insisting on an almost draconian simplicity to restrain human desires. This regime was very difficult for their scholarly followers to bear. The gradual disappearance of the Moist school was due precisely to this sort of self-destruction. Third, for the later Moists, intellectual theories were eventually transformed into pure action, and the need for such action led them to search for the right technology. This led them to transform their doctrines into internal reasons for action. Moist thought began with a very strong sense of the practical, and when such practicality became too dominant, it weakened altogether the Moist interest in thought itself. Was this just what the movement of Moist thought toward technology and logic implied? Was it the inner reason why Moist thought finally vanished from the scene?

---

57   Hu Shi, *Xian Qin mingxue shi*; also Hu Shi, *Zhongguo zhexue shi*, in *Hu Shi xueshu wenji*, 1991, vol. 2, 819. Chapter titles are those in Johnston's *Mozi*.

4.   Continuation and Renewal of the Intellectual Tradition, III:
        Dao or the Daoists

In the early years of the Warring States era, the Confucians and the Moists were
already well-known schools of thought, but the Daoists differed from them in
that they were not a school of thought with any obvious genealogy. Their
thought was not even clear-cut or unified. This was probably because the
Daoists at that time represented only a general way of thought—a group of
like-minded individuals with a similar approach to thought and similar interests. The Confucians, on the other hand, emphasized master-disciple relations
in teaching, and the Moists advocated hierarchical relations in groups, so that
both schools were able to transmit their systems of thought in an organized
manner.

In recent decades, a number of bamboo and silk manuscripts containing
the thoughts of ancient Daoists have come to light. These materials have made
it possible for us to understand the relationship between the Daoists and the
astrological and calendrical knowledge controlled by ancient court scribes.
From them, we have also come to understand the ancient knowledge of the
Yin-Yang and Five Phases theories that formed the intellectual background of
the entire system of Chinese thought and their embroilment with Daoist
thought. The court scribes of ancient China were in charge of recording historical events and verification of the astronomic calendar and divination so
they had a great deal of experience with the natural and human worlds of time
and space. They understood the changes and the unchangeable of the Way
in the cosmos, and then they extended this Way to all of human society. This
was the commonly practiced way of thinking of all Daoists. In other words, all
of their thought began with the Way of Heaven.

Around the fifth to the fourth centuries BCE, thought about the Way and the
knowledge and techniques that were produced by ruminations about it had
already generated several similar but somewhat distinct lines of thought. Fan
Li's thought in of the "Discourses of Yue" (Yueyu) chapter of the *Discourses of
the States* and the "Jiran" chapter in *Yue's Destruction of Wu* (Yuejueshu) repre-
sent one trend. Several chapters in the *Huang-Lao Silk Manuscripts* (Huang-
Lao boshu: the *Jing Fa*, Normative Standards; the *Shiliu jing*, Sixteen Canons;
Cheng, Collected Sayings; and *Daoyuan*, The Source that is the Way) from
Mawangdui and several chapters from the *Guanzi* represent another trend.
The *Laozi* and the *Zhuangzi* represent a third trend. The first of these lines of
thought should perhaps be called "Ancient Daoism," the second line is then
"Yellow Emperor or Huang-Lao Daoism" and the third is close to what was later
called "Lao-Zhuang Daoism." Besides these three trends of thought, there were,

of course, many other Daoists. Perhaps they did not necessarily have any direct connections in thought or doctrinal transmission, and they differed in many areas, but they all shared a comparatively similar vocabulary and way of thinking, and so the general characterization of Daoist School (*daojia*) was later applied to all of them.

4.1

I believe that Fan Li (ca. 571–? BCE) and Jiran (said to have been Fan Li's teacher) of the ancient state of Yue and the later "Daoist School" share similar origins, but materials on them are few and fragmentary. We can only know that during the Spring and Autumn and Warring States eras some philosophical theories based on astronomy, calendar-making and Ying-Yang thought gradually took shape.

4.1.1   Yellow Emperor or Huang-Lao Daoism

From the extant materials so far uncovered, we can say Yellow Emperor (or Huang-Lao) Daoism began very early; it was at least already developing during the early Warring States period (around 400 BCE).[58] First off, its scholarly tradition was much different from the Confucian and Moist traditions. If we say that the Confucians and Moists from the areas of Zou and Lu followed the line of Yao, Shun, Yu, Tang, Kings Wen and Wu, and Zhou Gong (Duke of Zhou) as their historical progenitors, then Yellow Emperor Daoism followed (or put forward) the much earlier Huang Di (the Yellow Emperor). All their words, thoughts and knowledge were attributed to the Yellow Emperor. Secondly, the Confucians and Moists appealed to man's basic nature and human needs as the foundation of their thought, but Yellow Emperor Daoists regarded the Way of Heaven or "the natural way" as the mainstream of their thought.[59] For them, every thing and every event in the world was based upon cosmic nature (*ziran*). Secondly, unlike the relatively greater concern for morality, ethics and government of the Confucians and Moists, Yellow Emperor Daoist ideas were more extensive. Behind their metaphysical background, they had a rather rich store of knowledge of astronomical, calendrical, geographic, physical and legal matters, star divination, almanac preparation, prognostication by observing the

---

58   The words of the Yellow Emperor are found in the *Guanzi*, the *Shenzi* 慎子, the *Wei Liao-zi*, the *He Guanzi*, the *Zhuangzi*, the *Shenzi* 申子, the *Shirzi* 尸子, the *Xunzi*, the *Zhanguoce* and other early books.

59   "The natural way" is R. P. Peerenboom's translation of *tiandao*. Peerenboom argues that for Huang-Lao Daoism *tian* refers to "an impersonal nature." See *Law and Morality in Ancient China: the Silk Manuscripts of Huang-Lao*, 1993, 42.

cloud vapors, power, geomancy and phrenology. They also put forth various ways to govern the world and get along in it.[60]

It must be pointed out, however, that Yellow Emperor Daoism was a body of knowledge and thought that started from Heaven and was all deduced by inferences based on Heaven. The "Postface" (Xuyi) of the *Annals of Lü Buwei* (Lüshi chunqiu), the last great compendium of Warring States knowledge, quotes the Yellow Emperor's charge to his grandson Zhuan Xu as the foundation for its own teaching: "There is a great circle [Heaven] above and a great square [Earth] below. If you are able to make them your model, you will be as father and mother to the people."[61]

From an examination of the words of the Yellow Emperor quoted in the Mawangdui *Huang-Lao Silk Manuscripts* and various other Warring States texts, we can see that Yellow Emperor Daoists were extremely interested in questions about the cosmos. They discussed Heaven and Earth and the rotation of the heavens, and they extended cosmic principles to three aspects having to do with "Heaven," "Earth" and "the Human." Their basic line of thought was that every thing in the world should emulate Heaven and Earth. For them, astronomy, calendar-making, miscellaneous divination, medical prescriptions, military strategy and the art of ruling all had a common "principle"—"The four seasons have their standards, and this is the principle of Heaven and Earth (*sishi you du, tian di zhi li (li) ye*)"[62]—and this "principle" was derived from an understanding of the cosmic world. The "Discourses of Yue" chapter in the *Discourses of the States*, the "Circumstances" chapter in the *Book of Master Guan* (Guanzi) and the Mawangdui "Collected Sayings" (*Cheng*) all mention the "Heavenly Ultimate" (*tianji* 天極). The so-called "Heavenly Ultimate" is in

---

60   The bibliography of books on military, mantic, medical and numerological arts in the HS, "Yiwen zhi" contains quite a few books with "Huang Di" in the title. *The Yellow Emperor Defeats the Red Emperor* (Huang Di fa Chi Di) and the "Didian" 地典 recently unearthed at Yinqueshan, along with the bamboo slip manuscript *Ten Questions* (Shiwen) and the silk manuscript *The Ten Great Canons* (Shi da jing) from Mawangdui also belong to the Yellow Emperor school. I believe that such books already existed before the Qin to Han period, and that mantic, medical and numerological arts since the Qin and Han pretended to rely on the "Yellow Emperor" because their intellectual genealogy was very close.

61   John Knoblock and Jeffrey Riegel, *The Annals of Lü Buwei*, 2000, 272. This sentence is perhaps the core idea in Yellow Emperor Daoism; that is, they regarded the great circle and the great square, meaning Heaven and Earth, as the self-evident foundation for creating a system of practical techniques and theoretical ideas. LSCQ, j. 12, ESEZ, 665.

62   "*Jing fa*" (Normative Standards), "Lun yue" (On Restraint), in *Laozi yiben juanqian gu yi shu shiwen*, 1974, 16A.

reality a cosmic astronomical or celestial principle related to the waxing and waning of the sun and moon and to the four seasons.[63] The concrete manifestation of this sort of "principle" is simply a series of regular "numbers" (*shu*). According to their ideas, in their behavior, people should consult the rules of these "numbers." This is the "standard" (*du* 度) that "The Source that is the Way (*Dao yuan* 道原)" is referring to when it says "hold on to the Way and follow the regularity (*bao dao zhi du*)."

It may be that through their observations and associative thinking regarding celestial phenomena and calendar science, the transmitters of Yellow Emperor Daoism summarized a number of principles based on natural laws. Then they employed the good or evil fortunes derived from celestial phenomena and almanac lore to confirm or verify the accuracy of those principles.[64] There are many passages in the *Huang-Lao Silk Manuscripts* that link Heaven, Earth and the Human and emphasize that people should consult the three areas of astronomical, geographical and human affairs in all their actions.[65] They believed that the Dao was the basic law of the entire universe and that it also connected all of Heaven, Earth and the Human. Every rational thing had to be supported by this basic law of Heaven, Earth and the Human.

In general, Yellow Emperor Daoism had the following intellectual background and content:

One, the vault of Heaven theory (*gaitian shuo*) that Heaven is a round cap above the square Earth. This was a kind of knowledge of the cosmos that derived from the observation of the apparent movement of the celestial bodies

---

63   According to R. P. Peerenboom, the term *tianji* is used "to delimit the natural order" and "refers to the limits or extremities of heaven-nature-the natural order" that are regarded as "non-negotiable standards." *Law and Morality in Ancient China*, 1993, 49–51.

64   Punishments and rewards (*xingde* 刑德) made up a popular way of thinking and technique from the Warring States through Qin and Han. In general, the sun was yang and the moon was yin, yang was rewards (*de*) and yin was punishments (*xing*). Rewards were born in the spring and reached their peak in the summer; punishments began in the autumn and reached their peak in the winter. If punishments and rewards were not out of order, the four seasons would be in order; otherwise there would be disorder. Following *xing* and *de* was originally a way of predicting good and evil from Yin-Yang and almanacs, but when applied to the art of war (*bingfa*), it became the basis for the idea of a hundred battles with a hundred victories; applied to government, it was proof of correct governance.

65   For example, "Observe Heaven above, look at Earth below, and link them to male and female." See "Guo Tong" in *Laozi yiben juanqian gu yi shu shiwen*, 1974, 24A. The *Huang-Lao Hanmu boshu* from Mawangdui were so important that they ranked as a classic or canon (*jing*) in Yellow Emperor Daoism. See Li Xueqin, *Jianbo yiji yu xueshushi*, 1994 & 1995, 323.

around the North Pole as the center. This eternally unmoving high point in the universe led them to conceive of entities like "the One" (*yi*) or the "Great Unity" (*taiyi* 太一) or the "Supreme Ultimate" (*taiji* 太極). The overall spatial symmetry of Heaven and Earth and their regular rotation was understood as a most elegant natural order.

Two, the idea that Yin and Yang, the Four Seasons and the Five Phases constituted the common rules of Heaven, Earth and the Human. Due to their partaking in the "same category" (*tonglei*) and having the "same voice" (*tongsheng*) and the "same vital energy" (*tongqi*), this "vital energy" passed between them and created a mutual interaction or complementary reaction.[66]

Three, since the rules of calendar science and the orbits of the celestial bodies could be represented by numbers, they had very many basic concepts that were expressed in numerical form. When these ideas were extended to social categories, a rather large number of specialized numeric terms were created. These included "the One" (*yi*, Dao), "the Two" (*er*, Sun and Moon, or Yin and Yang), "the Three" (*san*, Sun, Moon, Stars), "the four seasons" (*sishi*), "the five rulers" (planets, *wuzheng* 五政), "the six handles" (*liubing* 六柄, controls over life and death and so on held by rulers), "the seven rules (or laws) of nature" (*qifa*), "the eight breezes" (*bazheng* 八正) and so on—these are the so-called "numbers" (*shu*), "standards" (*du*) and "locations/positions" (*wei* 位).[67]

Four, these ideas of the material universe and the correspondence thinking that Heaven, Earth and the Human are mutually interconnected, combined with some seemingly concise yet mysterious numerical concepts, led people to believe that the affairs of human life and society could be conducted on the basis of the rules (or laws) of the natural order. On the one hand, they invented various "formulas" (*shi* 式), and on the other hand, they came up with "standards" (*du*) that extended this system of thought into human society. This is the idea that "Dao gives birth to laws" (*dao sheng fa*). It is only because they

---

66 This way of thought appeared very early. See LSCQ, j. 13, "Ying tong," (Resonating with the Identical). Later on, it was taken up by other schools of thought. Lu Jia's *Xinyu* (New Talk), j. *shang*, "Shushi di-er" has "affairs follow according to their categories, and sounds follow according to their tones." In *Xinyu jiaozhu*, 47; HS, j. 58, p. 2616, "Gongsun Hong zhuan," records Gongsun Hong as saying "if the *qi* are the same, they follow each other, and if the sounds are equal, then they echo each other"; Dong Zhongshu, *Chunqiu fanlu*, "Tong lei xian dong, di-wu-shi-qi" states that "if the *qi* are the same, they come together, and if the sounds are equal, then they echo each other; this can be clearly verified." ESEZ, 798. These ideas were therefor Confucianized.

67 See "Taihong" in *He Guanzi* and "*Jingfa, lun*," in *Laozi yiben juanqian gu yi shu shiwen*, 1974, 12B.

derive from the Way of Heaven, that laws are able to be self-evidently reasonable.[68]

4.2

4.2.1   Some other Daoists of Around the Fourth Century BCE

Song Xing (ca. 370–291 BCE) and Yin Wen (ca. 360–280 BCE) were scholars at the Jixia Academy in the state of Qi around the time of kings Wei, Xuan and Min. There is very little material on their thought, but according to pre-Qin texts, they probably maintained a gentle and harmonious attitude. They tried to curtail social strife and avoid contradictions and to settle all of the world's problems by achieving a "pure heart" (*baixin* 白心). That is, by purifying their heart and spirit, suppressing their desires and eliminating any obstinacy. Theirs was probably an attitude toward life that they derived from the Way of Heaven or the quietude and non-action (*wuwei* 無爲) of the cosmos. The *Zhuangzi* says that "they hoped to bring men together in the joy of harmony" (*yi er he huan* 以聏合歡),[69] but the *Xunzi* criticizes them saying that "Song Xing was blinded by desire and was insensible to satisfaction."[70]

It is said that Song Xing took his disciples around everywhere disputing and teaching in a effort to make people understand that human desires were really very few in number and only mistakenly believed to be many. If people could only understand this, they could control and restrain their feelings. In social morality, he advocated the elimination of strife, and in human life, he advocated that everything should be seen as natural (*ziran*). Much of this sounds somewhat similar to the Moist doctrines of opposition to war, universal love (*jian-ai*) and frugality. No wonder the *Xunzi* considers Song Xing and Mozi under the same category in "Contra Twelve Philosophers."[71]

The thought of Peng Meng (fl. 4th century BCE), Tian Pian (fl. 4th century BCE), and Shen Dao (ca. 395–315 BCE) was rather tilted toward anti-intellectualism. According to "The World" chapter of the *Zhuangzi*, they advocated throwing off all external restraints, discarding human knowledge, eliminating intransigence, destroying rational authority, practicing a kind of self-indulgent

---

68   "*Jingfa, Daofa*," in *Laozi yiben juanqian gu yi shu shiwen*, 1974, 2A. I discuss the Huang-Lao Daoism transformation of Dao toward "law" in a later section.

69   ZZJS, j. 10, 1082. Watson, CT, 368 with slight changes.

70   Knoblock, *Xunzi*, vol. 3, 1994, "Dispelling Blindness," 21.4, 102. *Xunzi jijie*, j. 15, "Jie bi," ZZJC edition, 262.

71   According to Guo Moruo, *Qingtong shidai*, 1957, 264, the "The Art of the Heart" (*Xinshu*), "The Inner Life" (*Neiye*), "Pure Heart" (*Baixin*), and "Pivotal Words" (*Shuyan*) chapters in the *Guanzi* are their writings. For the *Xunzi* quote, see Knoblock, *Xunzi*, vol. 1, 1988, 213, section 6.4, 223. Allyn W. Rickett, tr. *Guanzi*, 1998, is a complete translation.

naturalism in life and relativism toward all differences between everything
in the world. "The Way, they believed, lay in making the ten thousand
things equal."[72]

They believed that human reason was limited and the sages only had a partial understanding of things. In terms of their understanding of the Dao, they
were aware that it was unobtainable, and they knew that "material things"
(*wu*) were too rich in their manifold diversity. They hoped, then, to transcend
everything by practicing a sort of relativism or simply to accept everything
with an attitude of naturalism.[73] They also believed that Heaven and Earth had
their own laws and the cosmos had its own rules, and so they thought it unnecessary to be intransigent about anything. All they had to do was follow nature's
laws in order to achieve the natural (*ziran*, the Dao). The *Xunzi* says that "Shen
Dao was blinded by law and was insensible to worth" and was ignorant of the
importance of human freedom and effort.[74] Because they denied the significance of individual thought and removed any need for reform, this kind of
thought could easily become the intellectual foundation of despotism. This is
a key to why Daoism was later transformed into Legalism.[75] An ironic thing
about all this, however, is that because these ideas were a starting point for
doubt, they could also undermine obstinate or even despotic forms of thought.
They could lead people to look at everything equitably and fairly, to escape
from all concrete considerations of gain and loss, advantage and disadvantage,
and to seek out their own natural and transcendent realm—their ideal Dao.

The later philosopher Yang Zhu (fl. 4th century BCE), said to be unwilling to
pluck out one hair from his body to benefit the whole world, is especially worth
discussing.[76] He represented a contemporary trend of thought that valued the
individual or egoism. In the early Warring States period, Yang Zhu was quite
popular among the general public. According to the *Mencius*, "Teng Wengong
B," "the teachings current in the world are those of either the school of Yang or

---

72   Watson, CT, 369.

73   *Zhuangzi*, "Tianxia," ZZJS, j. 10, 1086. Watson, CT, 369–371.

74   Knoblock, *Xunzi*, vol. 3, 1994, *Xunzi*, "Dispelling Blindness," 21.4, 102.

75   The later connection between theories of legalism and various other forms of thought
      began here. As will be discussed later, Shen Dao, Shen Buhai and Hanfeizi all took ideas
      from the Huang-Lao, but turned to valuing the method of "performance and title" (*xing-
      ming*, matching rewards and punishments with the title of one's office or position).
      "Performance and title" is Herrlee G. Creel's translation. It is similar to today's idea of
      "accountability" for office holders. For his reasons, see his *Shen Pu-hai: A Chinese Political
      Philosopher of the Fourth Century B.C.*, 1974, 119–124.

76   For Yang Zhu, see *Mengzi*, Book VIIA, "Jinxin shang," section 26; also see D. C. Lau,
      Mencius, 187.

the school of Mo."⁷⁷ That Yang Zhu and Mozi are considered together indicates that at the time the Yang Zhu school was on a par with the other famous schools. There were two reasons for this popularity. First, because their thought was in accord with the general attitude of self-interest and pragmatism in an age of turmoil. Second, because egoism was the foundation of their thought, it hit squarely the desire for survival in the depth of everyone's consciousness.

Unlike the Confucians and Moists, Yang Zhu did not ask how humanity could benefit society or how society could benefit humanity. The question he asked was what is really beneficial and useful to the individual? For this reason, he put forth the slogans to "be for myself" (*weiwo* 爲我) and "treasure myself" (*guiji* 貴己). According to the scattered references in the *Zhuangzi, Hanfeizi, Annals of Lü Buwei* and *Huainanzi*, the reason that he was "for myself" was because he gave prominence to the values of human survival and freedom— "exhaust your nature to obtain authenticity, and do not allow material things to tire you out."⁷⁸ His thought was, on the one hand, a kind survivalist naturalism—that is, human life also belongs to "the nature of the Way of Heaven." On the other hand, he had a principle of value that placed the value of human life and freedom ahead of any benefit for society or the group. He advocated never serving in the army and never placing oneself in danger. He had absolute contempt for empty fame and profit and he encouraged both escapism and hedonism.⁷⁹

There were many differences between the various ideas that were later lumped together under the name of Daoism or Daoists, but they had in common the preservation of human life, anti-intellectualism and a search for transcendence. From their experience and understanding of Heaven, Earth and the cosmos, they came away with wisdom rather than practical operational knowledge, with an ineffable meaning of individual life rather than quantifiable laws and standards of nature. They tried to transcend the rational framework of human history while living within that framework and to break away and free themselves from human society while living within that society. Yang Zhu probably represented the extreme form of their thought. Despite the fact that this form of thought was never the Chinese mainstream, it nevertheless provided potential resources to stir up those scholars who advocated resistance to the mainstream ideology.

---

77   Lau, *Mencius*, 114 with minor changes.

78   *Huainanzi*, chapter 13, "Fan lun xun, section 12, in CTP.

79   *Liezi jishi*, 1979, 1985, j. 7, 220.

4.3

4.3.1 The Daoism of the *Laozi*

The most conspicuous and most influential of early thought concerning the Dao was that of Laozi or the *Laozi*.

We do not know the exact origin of the Daoist school of Laozi, and the dating of the *Laozi* has always been the subject of scholarly debate that remains without a definitive solution. In light of the many documents that have been unearthed in recent decades, however, we can now speculate that the final textual compilation of the *Laozi* was at least in the middle Warring States period. What it represents is probably early Warring States Daoist thought and it was more or less contemporaneous with the *Mozi*.[80]

The thought of the *Laozi*, in terms of its system of knowledge, has in general three origins: one, the understanding of the changes in the Way of Heaven by the ancient *zhu* invocators and *shi* scribes; two, the reflections of cultural aristocrats on the collapse of contemporary "social morality;" and three, the people of the state of Chu's everlasting pursuit of "the proper way of human behavior."

As noted above, calculating the astronomic calendar facilitated the formation of the concept of Yin and Yang, and then this sort of knowledge gave rise to techniques of cosmic observation and the prediction of human affairs which in turn provided an experiential foundation for those ideas. Among those who were proficient in this knowledge, *zhu* invocators and *shi* scribes were extremely important, and there is a story that the man Laozi was a Zhou dynasty scribe or court recorder. If so, he would have been proficient in the study of the astronomic calendar and divination. Such men had a profound experience and strong conception of Heaven or cosmology.

The ancient Chinese were very interested in the Way of Heaven in the first place, but the *Laozi* emphasizes even more prominently the significance of the Dao that existed before Heaven and Earth. It turns the Way of Heaven and Yin and Yang, concepts that were originally connected to the concrete natural phenomena of Heaven and Earth, into a form of thought with rich philosophical implications. There are quite a few passages in the *Laozi* that discuss "Heaven and Earth." They probe the origin of Heaven and Earth, regard the Dao as the origin of the cosmos and "the gateway to the multitude of mysteries" (*zhong miao zhi men* 眾妙之門). Dao is also "the One"—the foundation of everything. Heaven, Earth and the entire cosmos come forth from the Dao so that,

---

80　In 1992, a bamboo slip manuscript version of the *Laozi* was discovered in a Chu tomb from the middle period of the Warring States in Guodian, Jingmen, Hubei, and thus the idea that the *Laozi* was finalized in the late Warring States period can no longer stand.

Dao produced the One.
The One produced the two.
The two produced the three.
And the three produced the ten thousand things.[81]

Yin and Yang are produced from "the two," and from there on are produced Heaven, Earth, the Human and everything in the universe (the "ten thousand things"). The multifarious universe is thus subsumed under the rules of the Dao and the Yin and Yang. This is precisely the knowledge of the *zhu* invocators and *shi* scribes with which

One may know the world without going out of doors.
One may see the Way of Heaven without looking through the windows.

As a form of thought, Laozi's ideas are no longer constrained by observations of astronomic calendrical phenomena and predictions of good and bad fortune as was the case with calendrical calculations and divination. These ideas took the Way of Heaven as their ultimate foundation and then extended it into the realms of "social morality" and "the proper way of human behavior." He said that since Heaven and Earth began when the "Dao produced the One," then governing the world should also begin with Dao or "the One." This Dao or "One" is the ultimate foundational principle of everything. As the *Laozi* 39, says:

Heaven obtained the One and became clear.
Earth obtained the One and became tranquil.
The spiritual beings obtained the One and became divine.
The valley obtained the One and became full.
The myriad things obtained the one and lived and grew.
Kings and barons obtained the One and became rulers of the empire.[82]

When Laozi felt dejected about the collapse of the contemporary socio-political order, he then relied on the tranquility of the Way of Heaven to criticize it harshly. He said (*Laozi* 73) that

---

81   Professor Ge's citations from the *Laozi* are all made with reference to Chen Guying, "Laozi jiaoding wen," the appendix to his *Laozi zhushi ji pingjie*, 1985, 442–473. The translation is from *Laozi* number 42 and the next one is *Laozi* numbers 47 from Chan, SB, 160 and 162 respectively.

82   Chan, SB, 159.

The Way of Heaven does not compete (*buzheng*) and yet it skillfully achieves victory.
It does not speak (*buyan*), and yet it skillfully responds to things.
It does not beckon (*buzhao*), but things come to it of themselves.[83]

Following the Way of Heaven, the proper way to govern society (*Laozi* 37) should be to "always do nothing and everything will be done."[84]

The people of his contemporary world, however, misused their knowledge and intelligence and even engaged in plots and conspiracies such that society was easily sent into disorder and the masses were difficult to govern. As *Laozi* 65 says, "people are difficult to govern because they have too much knowledge."[85]

Compared to the Confucians who looked back to Yao and Shun and the Moists who looked back to the Xia dynasty, Daoist of the Laozi school looked back even further for their historical foundations. In order to provide legitimacy for their theories, they created an imaginative world that was an even more ancient, plain and simple Golden Age of humanity. In that age, the masses lived in "a small country with few people" with neither weapons nor warfare, and "though neighboring communities overlook one another and the crowing of cocks and barking of dogs can be heard, yet the people there may grow old and die without ever visiting one another."[86]

Laozi believed that only this sort of life conformed to the Way of Heaven. Therefore, in terms of knowledge and reason, these Daoists were not only different from the Confucians, but they went even further than the Moists. In everything, Confucius appealed to the establishment of a value rationality, and in everything Mozi appealed to the implementation of practical reason. Laozi, however, advocated a radical denial of both reason and civilization and aspired to go back to a time before the appearance of civilization. He launched an all out attack on the Confucian rites or propriety, arguing that the rites do not establish social order, but rather bring about chaos. In *Laozi* 38, an argument from history demonstrates his point:

Therefore, only when Dao is lost does the doctrine of virtue arise.
When virtue is lost, only then does the doctrine of humanity arise.

---

83   Chan, sʙ, 173 for the first two lines; Arthur Waley, *The Way and Its Power*, 1948 & 1958, 233 for the third line. Translated this way in order to preserve Professor Ge's emphasis on three things the Dao does not do.

84   *Wuwei* has been variously translated as "non-action," "inaction," "action-less action," or as "taking no action contrary to nature." Here the translation aims to fit the context.

85   Chan, sʙ, 170.

86   Chan, sʙ, 175.

When humanity is lost, only then does the doctrine rightness arise.
When justice is lost, only then does the doctrine of propriety arise
Now, propriety is a superficial expression of loyalty and faithfulness, and
the beginning of disorder.[87]

When the Dao is lost and virtue, humanity, and justice (rightness, duty) can
no longer restrain human behavior, then the rites or propriety that control
people's minds and actions must be resorted to. These rites or propriety are
very far removed from the original Dao. In this way Laozi presents a serious
challenge to the value rationality of the Confucians and the practical reason of
the Moists.

Besides the Way of Heaven and social life, Laozi was also concerned with
the correct way of human behavior, referring to how an individual human
being as a person should follow the Dao in order to reach eternity. From his
experience of the silent and everlasting Way of Heaven, Laozi created techniques for preserving life and overcoming alienation. He expanded the concept of nature or spontaneity (*ziran*) behind China's ancient techniques for
nurturing life to an entire life and came up with a theory that encompassed the
Way of Heaven, social morality and the correct way of individual human
behavior. He believed that "Heaven is eternal and Earth everlasting" because
they are a Void or Nonbeing (*wu*) that dwell in a free and unrestrained realm,
in a state of non-action transcending both time and space. If one wants to preserve life for ever, then s/he must follow this Way of Heaven, have no desires
and no ideas, be just "like an infant," spurn fame and profit, and practice the
methods of withdrawal, self-restraint, the appearance of weakness and soft-
ness—all in order to maintain in oneself a tranquil and undisturbed mental
attitude. Because all of the enjoyable stimulations of the vulgar world "cause
one's mind to go mad," Laozi warned humanity that if they want to preserve
their lives for ever, they simply must follow nature (*ziran*). As *Laozi* 25 says:

Man models himself after Earth.
Earth models itself after Heaven.
Heaven models itself after Dao.
And Dao models itself after Nature.[88]

---

87   Chan, sb, 158; Tao changed to Dao and righteousness to rightness.
88   Quotations in this paragraph are from *Laozi* numbers 7, 10, 20, 12 and 25, and translation
       from Chan, sb, 142, 144, 150, 145, and 153 respectively with some changes.

Perhaps the *Laozi* was written by a man named Laozi ("the old one") or perhaps it was a work of the Warring States period that edited and compiled the words of ancient Daoists. In any case, we should have no problem if we examine it as part of early Warring States intellectual history. In this time of rapid social and intellectual change, we can see that Laozi was also searching for some sort of order.[89] It is only that the foundation of the order he was seeking came from the order of the cosmos that was so familiar to the official scribes— that is, the Way of Heaven—and from the most easily idealized "archaic or even primordial times."

Due to his disappointment and fear concerning society, reason and civilization, he paid more attention to the value of individual human life. He hoped that humanity could return to an earlier simplicity and tranquility, remain in a state of harmony with the cosmos and other human beings and preserve forever the sustainability of human life. For this reason, he developed a train of thought in the traditional intellectual world that was completely different from that of the Confucians and the Moists, a train of thought that contained within it many resources for its continuation. One was an anti-societal tendency centered on the individual person. This trend of thought would give rise to different results from a search for individual freedom or for the preservation of individual life. A second was an anti-intellectual tendency centered on internal experience and understanding. This trend of thought would lead to ideas of transcending the concrete forms of the material world to explore directly the realms of ultimate mystery. The resources of these two thought trends were taken up and expanded upon in the somewhat later text of the *Zhuangzi*.

5.   Elite Thought and General Knowledge: Implications of Mantic and Medical Arts in Intellectual History

Without question the Spring and Autumn and Warring States period was an age of flourishing intellect. The Confucians, Moists and Daoists illustrated three main intellectual tendencies. The moral idealism of the Confucians

---

89   In his *The Book of Lieh-tzu*, 1960 (1973), A. C. Graham argues that all of the pre-Qin schools of thought represented the ruling strata of ancient society and that from its inception the Daoist school was a life philosophy for the private individual. This is a mistaken view. The early Daoists actually had a very strong sense of practical engagement with the real world. To understand this point, one only has to look at the Daoist understanding of and emphasis on laws and rules and their passionate ideas about conspiracies , warfare, and governing the masses.

sought the cultivation of moral character and urged people to maintain their inner dignity and sense of human worth. The pragmatism of the Moists sought to achieve practical benefits and urged people to maintain order, individual survival and a populous and affluent society. The goal of the Daoist was to seek the perpetuation of life and spiritual transcendence. Their ideas were based on anti-intellectual tendencies. Under various social pressures, they tried to protect individual survival and spiritual freedom. For the intellectual upper strata of society the seemingly absurd mystical ideas and techniques weakened until they ended up as simple ceremonies, allegories or symbols. Many higher status cultured individuals treated these mystical thoughts, knowledge and techniques with respect while keeping them at a distance—as Confucius advised—and so mysticism lost its influence among the intellectual upper levels of society.

This was only the situation, however, among the intellectual elite. The situation among the masses was rather different. As much as the elite world produced rational ideas and theories, the masses, and even the aristocracy, did not generally believe in or depended upon them. They relied more often on a system of common sense and mystical techniques or arts (*jishu*) rather than philosophy. This system included (1) the interpretations of the cosmos and society handed down from the Shang and Zhou dynasties, (2) techniques for communication between humans and the gods and spirits, and (3) ritual customs and ceremonies for maintaining social order.

5.1

Intellectual history cannot ignore this part of Chinese knowledge and thought. Its efficacy supported the life of the general population, and it is precisely its standards that provide a baseline for estimating the value of intellectual activity in that age. Previous Chinese intellectual histories concentrated too much on the intellectual elite and the classic texts. The question we should ask, however, is where did this "advanced thinking," "higher culture" and "scholarly tradition" come from? Culture is not really always transmitted from the top to the bottom of a society. As I argued earlier, there was a background of general knowledge and ideas and experiences that were transmitted and cultivated through education, and they were the foundations that produced elite knowledge and high culture. Cultural influence was really not always "from top to bottom."

The Spring and Autumn and Warring States era was an extremely vibrant one, and the medical and mantic arts and numerological knowledge from the

Shang and Zhou periods still permeated the general life of society. It included at least the following three areas.

One, the mantic arts related to Heaven, such as the astronomic calendar, star and cloud divination, choice of divination methods, tortoise shell and yarrow stalk divination and divination by the four winds and the five musical tones. With the ancient Chinese knowledge of celestial phenomena as their foundation, these practices speculated on cosmic changes and expanded this knowledge to produce various methods for avoiding evil and achieving good fortune. There were many ways to determine the prospects for the questioner's activities, including, for example observations of the movements, positions and changes in the color and luster of the stars, or the shapes and colors of the clouds, or correspondences between the twelve constellations and the earth, the arrangement of activities involving the seasons, the sun and the moon, minute signs (taken as omens) from the various sounds in nature and so on. The green dragon and white tiger design and astronomical diagram of the twenty-eight constellations on the lacquer trunk of the Marquis of Zeng's coffin, the Chu silk manuscripts from Zidanku in Changsha, the two Qin bamboo "Book of Days" (*rishu*) from Fangmatan and Shuihudi and the Mawangdui silk manuscript "Planetary (Five-Planets) Divination" (*Wuxing zhan* 五星占) may all reflect the content of these mantic arts.

Two, mantic arts related to the Earth, such as geomancy. Research has shown that this type of geographical knowledge has more than geographic implications. It also includes meteria medica (*bencao*), natural science (*bowu*) and records of strange wonders (*zhiguai*). I believe these arts also have significance for avoiding calamities and obtaining good fortune. The ancient ideas of "widening one's knowledge of the names of plants, trees, fish and animals" and "distinguishing local products, topography and the principles of things"[90] all certainly involve practical knowledge, but knowledge of gods, demons and evildoers in order to avoid calamities was also one of the main sources that helped to maintain people's faith in the natural world. Everyone in ancient China lived on a vast and unknown earth. They could only feel safe and at ease in their lives if they knew it well. The descriptions of the earth in the "Tribute of Great Yu" (Yu Gong) chapter in the *Book of Documents*, the imaginings about the world in the *Classic of Mountains and Seas* (Shan hai jing) and the legend of Great King Yu casting a tripod with the images of various material objects very likely reflect the significance of such mantic techniques.

---

90   *Lunyu*, Yang Huo 17.9; SSJZS, 2525.

Three, mantic arts relating to the Human. They include oneiromancy (*zhan-meng*), summoning souls (*zhaohun*), warding off calamities (*yanhe*), ingesting elixirs (*fushi*), arts of the bedchamber (*fangzhong shu*), breathing exercises (*daoyin*) and so on. These techniques concerned with human psychology and physiology well express people's understanding of their own bodies during the Warring States period. Two of their conscious ideals were to preserve their individual lives for ever and to seek a perfect mode of existence, but they also knew that these ideals could not necessarily be achieved. They believed that there were ghosts and demons in the external world and that they themselves had two souls, a *hun* (cloud soul) and a *po* (new moon soul) in their internal makeup. Their physiological lives and the life of the cosmos beyond were equally supported by *qi*, vital essence or energy. The preservation of this *qi* within one's body was the foundation of everything. According to this way of thinking, they believed that people should rely on the mantic arts of communication with the ghosts and spirits to ward off calamities and summon their souls back from the dead. They also believed that they should draw support from external things to strengthen their bodies or emulate the cosmos by expelling stale air and breathing in fresh air, using breathing exercises to exchange the breath of life with the universe. Textual references to just these sorts of mantic arts are found in the "Summoning the Soul" (Zhaohun) and the "Traveling Afar" (Yuanyou) poems in the *Songs of Chu* (Chu ci); in the "Jade Pendant Inscription on Breath Control" (Xingqi yupei ming); in the picture of a "winged man" (*yuren*) in the Marquis of Zeng's Warring States tomb, in the *Zhuangzi* passages on breathing techniques for directing the *qi* as well as ancient bamboo slip medical texts unearthed from Warring States archeological sites.

All of the above forms of knowledge were derived from the ancient Chinese experiences with and observations of Heaven, Earth, and the Human. From these experiences and observations, they not only came up with set after set of medical, mantic and numerological arts to handle time (predicting good and evil to come), space (imagining the world of the unknown) and their own bodies (feeling their living being). At the same time, they used their imagination, to create a pantheon of gods and demons to deal with the worlds of "Heaven above," "Earth below" and the "human realm." The "Nine Songs" (Jiu ge) in the *Songs of Chu* and the silk manuscripts from Mount Bao and Mount Wang in Hubei all demonstrate that in the minds of the people of that time there was an orderly genealogy of gods, spirits and ghosts.

The spirit of the average member of Warring States society roamed around in the worlds of these "Heavenly gods," "Earthly spirits" and "human ghosts."

Under the guidance of learned shamans, they prayed for protection and assistance and to avoid calamities. They also relied on set after set of ceremonies, medical, mantic and numerological arts to bring Heaven, Earth and the Human together, to master knowledge and life techniques and inquire into the mysteries of the cosmos, society and humanity. At the same time, they employed a series of symbols to describe in writing their understanding and experiences of Heaven, Earth and the Human and to pass them down as the object of thought and an accumulation of knowledge.

5.2

What sort of intellectual situation do we see, then, when we examine all this general knowledge concerning Heaven, Earth, the Human and Ghosts?

First, we see that in the mind of the average person, the world they faced was still an integrated whole made up of an orderly and symmetrical space that extended limitlessly out from the center toward the four (sometimes six) directions.[91] The sun, moon, stars, winds, rain, thunder and lightning each had its own role and their own trajectory. Heaven, Earth and the Human were intimately connected. Any peculiar change in one of them would become a special omen. Any unusual phenomena in one of them would trigger a response in the other symmetrical elements. When the ancient Chinese reflected on questions concerning Heaven, Earth, the Human and Ghosts, they always regarded the cosmos as an undivided and integrated unity that enveloped everything in existence, and, from that, they derived a deeply-rooted sense of order.

Second, the essential factors that combined Heaven, Earth, the Human and Ghosts together into an integrated whole were the ideas of Yin and Yang, the Five Phases, the Eight Directions, and so on from ancient China's long distant past. They run through everything and make it possible for Heaven, Earth, the Human and Ghosts to become a vast mutually connected system.

Take the concept of "punishment and reward" (or blessing, *xingde*) for example. *Xing* originally referred to the laws of punishment (*xingfa*), and *De* originally referred to morality, virtue and its power. They were also adapted to refer to the cyclical changes in the natural world and to indicate good and evil prognostications. Not only could they be used for celestial phenomena, but could also be used to interpret politics. They were both methods for man-

---

91 In the contemporary Chinese concept of space, the world was shaped like the character *jing* 井 or *ya* 亞 with the place of human habitation in the center; this conception went back to the Shang dynasty. See Zhang Guangzhi, "Shuo Yindai de yaxing," in *Zhongguo qingtong shidai, erji*, 1990, 82–94, and Sarah Allan, *The Shape of the Turtle*, 1991, chapter 4, "The Shape of the Cosmos."

aging officials and subjects as well as tactics for Heaven to check and balance the power of the rulers. They could even be used to interpret changes in human feelings. In the system of general knowledge, "punishment and reward" could also be used in conjunction with the heavenly stems and earthly branches to examine and verify predictions of good and evil and all the changes in the ten thousand things. This is why the status of "punishment and reward" and someone's rise and fall had to be measured completely on the basis of celestial phenomena and calendrical calculations. *Xing* and *De* actually ran through almost every realm and connected everything.

Another example is the art of divination by the four winds and the five tones (*fengjiao wuyin*) that was very widespread in ancient times. The record of this practice in the "Duke of Xiang, year 18" chapter of the *Zuo Commentary* indicates how early on Chinese people believed that celestial phenomena and the sound of the winds contained important information for the human world. Some scholars have pointed out that the Shang oracle bone inscriptions use the direction and sound of the four winds to divine and predict good and evil outcomes.[92] In later times, the four directions were subsequently matched up with the concepts of Yin and Yang, the Five Phases and the eight directions, and then the direction and sound of the winds were assigned their corresponding places in this system of ideas. The directions of the winds corresponded to the five directions of east, south, west, north and center; the sounds of the winds corresponded to the ancient Chinese pentatonic scale (*gong, shang, jue, zhi, yu,* 宮商角徵羽, roughly do, re, mi, sol, la) and the Five Phases metal, wood, water, fire and earth. Within this mode of thinking, everything in the universe was brought together to form an integrated whole.[93]

Third, since their cosmos was a mutually connected and harmonious whole, and since Heaven, Earth, the Human and Ghosts were bound together like a continuous thread by the basic elements of the cosmos—Qi, Yin and Yang, the Five Phases, the eight directions and so on, and since there were common forms of existence within this Heaven, Earth, the Human and Ghosts continuum, then mysterious yet necessary connections and resonances could well occur between the realms of Heaven, Earth, the Human and Ghosts. The medical, mantic and numerological arts basically constituted the beliefs and the "scientific" phenomena that were produced on the basis of this sort of thinking. Through associational thinking and practical experience a variety of techniques for avoiding calamity and obtaining good fortune were created.

---

92   See Li Xueqin, "Shangdai de sifeng yu sishi," in *Li Xueqin ji*, 1989.

93   See Wu Jiulong's "Tian di bafeng wuxing kezhu wuyin zhi ju" in *Yinqueshan Hanjian shiwen*, 1985.

At this point we can imagine that even though the thinkers of the Warring States period had initiated rational thought, this was, after all, only the work of a small minority. The great majority of the population still needed knowledge and techniques that were more accessible and effective and that could at least comfort their minds and strengthen their self-confidence. This is why there were so many mystical ideas and strange mantic arts during the Warring States era. They believed that they faced a cosmos that was a harmonious whole made up of a combination of the realms of Heaven, Earth, the Human and Ghosts. It had a clear center and vague boundaries, each part of it was mutually balanced (symmetrical) and orderly and everything was put together by a combination of the essential elements of Yin and Yang, the four seasons, the Five Phases, the eight directions, the twelve double hours of the day (*shi-er shi* 十二時) and so on. The realms of Heaven, Earth, the Human and Ghosts had a sort of mystical and necessary relationship of correspondence. If you mastered this relationship of correspondence, you would be able to understand and interpret the entire universe, and then you could achieve a much better life.

5.3

What, then, was the relationship between this "general knowledge and its related techniques" and the "thought of the elite and the classics?" There can be no doubt that the former was once the background of the latter, but did those who believed in that "general knowledge and its related techniques" just passively accept the "thought of the elite and the classics?"

Many scholars believe that the "axial age" in China was not the same as that in Europe. In its axial age, Chinese culture did not experience a rupture that denied the value of the past and tradition. The Chinese relationship to its cultural past and tradition was rather one of inheritance, reinterpretation and affirmative continuation. Even the ever-changing thought of the cultural elite and the classics served to elevate the pre-existing general knowledge and its related techniques rather than abandon it. Given that this general knowledge and its related techniques had such a wide social presence and dominated the lives of the great majority, with the exception of a small minority of elite thinkers, how could it fail to have any influence on Chinese intellectual history? It obviously could not. General knowledge and its related techniques seem to have formed the background for all thought and they blended into the thought of the elite and the classics and backed it up just the way a chorus backs up a solo performance.

Let me give three examples.

First, Yin and Yang. In the life of the general population, Yin and Yang represented a few concrete things, appearances and sense perceptions. In the mantic and numerological arts, Yin and Yang were two hexagrams (*Qian* and *Kun*, the first two in the *Book of Changes*) as well as the punishment and reward of Heaven. In the mantic and medical arts, Yin and Yang represented the correspondence between the inner workings of the human body and cold and hot in Nature (*tian*). These ideas of Yin and Yang were all related to various forms of knowledge and techniques, but not to any disputations concerning philosophical concepts.

We can see, then, that for a very long time, Yin and Yang remained a summation of concrete knowledge and general every day life experiences. Although these concepts had already been elevated to a high level of regularity, they were still somewhere between the abstract and the concrete, and they had not been separated from their relationship with ordinary experiential knowledge and technical practices. The Way of Heaven was definitely not a completely abstract Way, and Yin and Yang were certainly not merely two abstract concepts as essential elements of the cosmos.

In the writings of thinkers after the *Laozi*, "the Dao that can be spoken, is not the constant Dao." That is, the Dao seems no longer to have been the Way of Heaven in the natural world, and Yin and Yang were no longer the concrete manifestation of Heaven and Earth, punishments and rewards or cold and hot. Through philosophical disputation, these concepts in intellectual history were being transformed in the direction of metaphysics.

Second, is the even more obvious *Commentaries on the Book of Changes* (Yizhuan). The *Book of Changes* was originally a record of the arts of divination. The reason that its statements could be regarded as reliable was because it was believed to emulate the cosmos and to reduce its fundamental structure to two categories of odd and even numbers. It also went a step further in abstracting the Yin and Yang as two signifiers that simplified the complicated changes between Heaven, Earth and the Human into changes in the position of the six lines (*liu yao* 六爻) of the trigrams that made up sixty-four hexagrams. Although the thought behind it and its practical usage contained many rich elements of ancient Chinese knowledge and thought, the *Book of Changes* still belonged to the shamanistic arts.

From the contents of the *Commentaries on the Book of Changes*, generally agreed to be a product of the middle of the Warring States period, we can see that once its latent ideas were discovered and used to interpret philosophy, it became a classic text of elite thought. From then on, "the reciprocal process of Yin and Yang is called the Dao" became the general guiding principle of ancient Chinese cosmology, and the symmetrical and consecutive sequence of the hexagrams was philosophically regarded as brilliant reasoning and logic.[94] The random numbers of the six lines of the trigrams were explained as rational metaphors for the Yin and Yang inherent in the "three ultimates or powers" of Heaven, Earth and the Human.[95] In the silk manuscript "Yao" essay (Yaopian) from Mawangdui, Confucius says that he is not satisfied with the practical nature of the *Book of Changes* and that he wants to transcend divination practices and elevate "virtue and rightness" (*deyi*)—that is, ideas and thought. He said that the *Book of Changes* should start from "understanding the numbers to reach an understanding of moral virtue." This was because to communicate with the underworld and gods and demons makes you merely a shaman or diviner. We can see that the numbers used to predict fate are only those of the shamans and scribes, but a genuine and morally upright person (a superior man, *junzi* 君子) should understand morality, the principles of human nature (*xingli* 性理) and even the Mandate of Heaven. It is clear that by that time the *Book of Changes* no longer represented only the art of divination; it had become a classic of elite intellectual thought.

Third, let's look again at knowledge about Heaven and Earth. Originally, celestial phenomena and changes in the course of time were often correlated with actual movements of the stars and the progression of the four seasons. From at least the Warring States period, however, the concreteness of Heaven and Earth began to recede and they were given more prominence as conceptual abstractions. At that time, Heaven and Earth represented, on the one hand, the actual multifarious world full of rich abundance that people could know on the basis of their experience and feelings , and on the other hand, they also represented a conceptual world that had been systematically arranged and summarized by human intellect. As such, they possessed an orderly likeness. For example, Yin and Yang, the four seasons, the five and six directions, the twelve months and so on were already recognized and described

---

94   Quotation is from the *Xici zhuan*, shang, #5, Lynn, *Changes*, 53.

95   The *Yizhuan* contains the following texts: "Commentary on the Appended Phrases" or "Great Commentary" (*Xici*), "Explanations of the Hexagram Statements" or "Images of the Judgments" (*Xiangci*), "Judgments" (*Tuanci*), "Explaining the Trigrams" (*Shuo gua*, philosophical account of hexagrams and special attributes of trigrams), "Providing the Sequence of the Hexagrams" (*Xu gua*, moralistic explanation of the hexagram's order), "Commentary of the Words of the Text" (*Wenyan*, complete commentaries on the first two hexagrams, *Qian* [Pure Yang] and *Kun* [Pure Yin]), and "Hexagrams in Irregular Order" (*Zaguo*, one word or phrase characterizations). There is also a silk manuscript of the *Xici* and other related texts from Mawangdui. We follow Edward L. Shaughnessy and Richard John Lynn's translations and characterizations of the sections of the *Yijing* commentaries found in ECT, 220, 216–228 and Lynn, *Changes*, 1–23 respectively.

as a series of numbers and concepts. In short, the rich feelings and experiences of the people of that time had already been integrated through the ratiocination of elite intellectuals. They believed that the sages could rely on rule derived from reason to establish and expand a cosmic order to understand and interpret the unknown world. From this belief emerged the concept of principle (*li* 理), a concept that came into being after reason or intellect (*lixing* 理性) was used to organize and summarize every manifestation of nature. Then the concept of the order of the world was no longer the order of the real world; it was a standard or rule (*guiju* 規矩) created by the human mind, that is, it became a form of conceptual knowledge and thought. This kind of conceptual knowledge and thought would be very powerful and would exert its influence on people's feelings and experiences while at the same time being transformed into the "thought of the elite and the classics" and distancing itself from "general knowledge and its related techniques."

CHAPTER 3

The Hundred Schools of the Spring and Autumn and Warring States Period, II (ca. 6th to 3rd Century BCE)

1.   Warring States Hundred Schools Contend, I: Cosmic Space and Time

The *Book of Master Shi* (Shizi) text says that "Heaven and Earth and the four squares are called *yu* (宇); from ancient time to today is called *zhou* (宙)."[1] The ancient Chinese concept of the "cosmos" (*yuzhou*, from *yu* + *zhou*) includes both time and space. We can certainly believe that the thinkers of the Warring States period intensely pondered the following questions: What is the nature of Heaven (or "the sky") above our heads? What is the shape of the Earth we walk on? Where is the origin of time? How were Heaven, Earth and the Human formed in that distant beginning?

1.1
In the Warring States period, it was a view of the cosmos similar to the later "vault of Heaven" (*gaitian shuo*) theory that was most likely absolutely domi-nant. The ancient Chinese noticed the visible movement of celestial bodies very early on. Living in the northern hemisphere, they could very easily see from the rotation of the earth that the dome of the sky (*tianqiong*) moved from east to west. Owing to the earth's rotation around the central axes of the north and south poles, exact north seemed to be a motionless place like an axle on a wheel. All of the stars and the sun and moon appeared to rotate around this stationary point, the north pole. When the *Analects* ("Wei zheng" 2.1) says that "the Pole Star remains in its place while all the myriad stars do homage around it," this is what it means. In the minds of the ancient Chinese, Heaven was round like a conical bamboo hat covering the earth below. Because the north pole never moved, its spatial position occupied the axis between Heaven and Earth and had no point of symmetry, and it also transcended the temporal position that was marked by sunrise and sunset; for this reason, it was viewed as the center of Heaven and it occupied the highest position as the "One." Furthermore, the handle of the Big Dipper (*beidou*) rotated following the sea-sons and was believed to announce the "Will of Heaven" that controlled the

---

1   *Shizi*, j. *xia*, ESEZ, 373.

changes of seasons and organized time in the human world. During a single year, the handle of the Big Dipper pointed in the four directions of east, south, west and north, and each of them had their own sacred symbolic spirit—the Azure Dragon (East), Vermilion Bird (South), White Tiger (West) and Black Tortoise (or Warrior, North)—their symbolic colors of azure, vermilion, white, black and later yellow, to accord with the Five Phases, and their corresponding seasons of spring, summer, autumn and winter. The ancient Chinese used the regular movements of the celestial bodies and the stellar or planetary orbits to divide the years, season, months, solar periods (*jieqi* 節氣), days and hours, and this transformed spatial movements into temporal changes.

Through continuous association, migration and warfare, the ancient Chinese gradually understood the earth they lived on. They imagined it to be formed in the shape of a large character *jing* 井 for "well." This very early on probably led them to the idea that there were "nine continents" (*jiuzhou* 九州) since the character for "well" has nine spaces. Although this division into nine continents was derived from creative imagination, it nevertheless reflected the ancient Chinese understanding of "all under Heaven." The clockwise north-east-south-west rotation of earth particularly corresponded to the apparent leftward rotation of the heavenly path (*tiandao zuoxuan*, 天道左旋), and this further demonstrated the ancient Chinese understanding of the Earth and observations of Heaven. In both, they sought mutual correspondence. Although the various contemporary Regional States might have had slightly different understandings of all under Heaven, they all had the same understanding and conception of the Earth. They all took Earth and Heaven to be mutually corresponding, and imagined an outwardly expanding space with a precise order and both a center and borders. The "five zones" (*wufu* 五服) and the "nine zones" (*jiufu* 九服) mentioned in the "Tribute of Yu" (Yu Gong) chapter in the *Book of Documents*, the "Discourses of Zhou, I" (Zhouyu shang) chapter of the *Discourses of the States* and the "Summer Officials: Map and Tribute Official" (Xiaguan, Zhifang shi) in the *Rites of Zhou*, are all basically representations of the picture of the world held in the minds of the people of that age. These assumptions about all under Heaven led the people of the Warring States period to continue the general Shang and Zhou dynasty traditional idea of the Earth—that it had a center and four or eight directions in the shape of the character *hui* 回 for "return." The great square of the earth was composed of four or eight directions, and these four or eight directions each had its own associated symbolic spirit, season and color. In this way, Earth and Heaven had identical structures, interconnected symbols and relationships of correspondence.

The meaning of Heaven and Earth was always one of the central issues in ancient Chinese thought. The next question is, then, what sort of concepts or ideas in Chinese intellectual history did these ideas about Heaven and Earth that derived from experience, understanding and even imagination actually give rise to? And, how did these concepts and ideas support the contemplation of other issues?

1.2

First, the discussion of space and time in the cosmos was raised to the level of philosophy. The universe had a center, and this center of time and space was regarded as the mysterious Dao. It was the One and the Supreme Ultimate and it possessed an absolute nature that nothing else in the phenomenal world possessed. Even in the socio-political sphere, it seems that only by occupying the center between Heaven and Earth could the ruler obtain self-evident legitimacy. As the *Mencius* says, "to stand in the center of the Empire (the world, *tianxia*) and bring peace to the people within the Four Seas is what a gentleman delights in . . ."[2] Just as the "Taihong" chapter of the *Pheasant Cap Master* says, "the center is the position of the Great Unity, and the spirits look up to it and regulate the world from it." This center of Heaven and Earth was conceived to be the absolute Dao, the Ultimate (ji 極) of the Supreme Ultimate and the Supreme Unity (One, yi). Everything in the universe originated from this center; Heaven and Earth encompassed everything, and the center was the foundation of everything. Although the idea of such a center of the cosmos was originally derived from observations of the celestial bodies and earthly geography, through speculative inferences and creative imaginings, it had by now been elevated to the highest point of philosophical abstraction.

Cosmic time was also a starting point. Although the *Laozi*'s saying that the "Dao produced the One; The One produced the two; The two produced the three; And the three produced the ten thousand things" is only an abstract assertion, still very many ancient Chinese believed that everything in the universe came into being from one or the simple to many or the complex. No matter how multifarious and complex the "ten thousand things" were, they were all believed to have a single common origin, and this One was both the spatial center of the cosmos and the beginning of time. It remained outside of all Being (you 有) as a form of Nonbeing or Nothingness (wu 無) that was, nevertheless, the origin of all Being. In other words, it was the One among the many, the origin (root, *ben* 本) of the ten thousand things (*wanwu*) and the beginning

---

2 *Mengzi*, "Jinxin shang" #21, SSJZS, 2766, D. C. Lau, *Mencius*, 185.

of the ten thousand affairs (*wanshi*), but it always remained outside of time and space. Everything was born from it, and everything returned to it again.

Once the absolute nature of this Dao, One, or Great Unity was accepted, people then began to regard it as the certain and self-evident foundation of both experience and reason. They then put the various phenomena that they had previously measured, experienced or felt under the control of this Dao and maintained that the harmonious and perfect natural order was simply the result of silent transformation by the Dao. Accordingly, the movements of heavenly bodies, progression of the four seasons, rising and setting of the sun, waxing and waning of the moon, transformations of the Yin and Yang, the arrangement of both earthly and heavenly phenomena, and even the social order and human morality were all believed to be the ineffable manifestations of the Dao. The Dao represented the correct and unalterable laws of nature as well as the will of the spirits and gods from the non-human world.

This way of thinking almost became the common consensus among a variety of thinkers from the Warring States period on. For example, the *Commentaries on the Book of Changes*, generally believed to represent Confucian ideas, was influenced by this concept of the cosmos.[3] The most important expression of this is the idea that the evolution of the cosmos is a process in which "in change there is the Great Ultimate" and it "generates the two modes (Yin and Yang)" that then "generate the four basic images" that "generate the eight trigrams." This process confirms the truth that "the reciprocal process of Yin and Yang is called the Dao".[4]

In another example from a Daoist text, the "Nine Observances" (Jiushou) chapter of the *Book of Master Wen* regards the evolution of the cosmos as a process of the unfolding of the Dao. The Dao is the One, and the transformation

---

3 Whether the *Yizhuan* (Commentaries on the Classic of Changes) was a Confucian or a Daoist text is still being debated among modern scholars in China, but I think it is questionable to believe that there were such self-awareness of schools and disciples in that early time. It is more reasonable to regard *Yizhuan* thought as a general background for all thinkers of that age. This also makes it easier to understand and explain the various complex and overlapping ideas of the time.

4 The complete translation of this passage from the *Xici zhuan*, Part One, #11: "Therefore, in change there is the great ultimate (*Yi you taiji*). This is what generates the two modes [the yin and yang] (*shi sheng liang yi*). The two basic modes [— and --] generate the four basic images (*liang yi sheng si xiang*)...and the four basic images generate the eight trigrams (*si xiang sheng ba gua*) [by adding first one unbroken (yang) line – to each, then one broken (yin) line --]." Lynn, *Changes*, 65–66; original in SSJZS, 77, 82, 78.

of the One into the many is simply the evolution of the cosmos.[5] The "Normative Standards" (Jingfa) text in the *Huang-Lao Silk Manuscripts* states that "Heaven grasps the one, illuminates the three, establishes the two, creates the eight breezes, and puts into effect the seven laws (of nature)." The "one" here is simply the Dao of infinite possibilities; the "two" are then the "One dark, one bright" of Yin and Yang transformations; the "three" are "standards" (*du* 度), "numbers" (*shu* 數), and "honesty/fidelity" (*xin* 信), one of the five constant virtues. This entire regulated order of the cosmos is simply the Way of Heaven.[6] This order was originally arrived at by observation and rational inference, but for thinkers from the Warring States on it was believed to be the result of laws of nature manifested by the Dao. This conception of the Dao was widely employed at that time. On the one hand, it quite naturally followed Yin-Yang and Five Phases thought, extending it to the structural analysis of Heaven, Earth and the Human to form an important background of ancient Chinese cosmology. On the other hand, it was used to support the reasonableness of basic human nature and interpersonal ethics. By involvement in polemics about proper social order, it came to form an important background of ancient Chinese social thought.

1.3

Second, with this background, there was a tendency toward greater systematization of the temporal and spatial structure of the cosmos. In the Warring States world of thought, since it was a rapidly expanding and changing age, they had a great need for a theory that could interpret and explain the phenomenal world better than concrete verification and operational knowledge.

The *Records of the Grand Historian* "Biography of Mencius and Xunzi," says that Zou Yan "first examined small things and then went on to big things." That is, he used speculative reasoning from experiential foundations to describe the world. "First examining small things" was his experiential foundation. On the one hand, he enlarged his spatial experience. For example, when imagining the world, he first enumerated China's "famous mountains and great rivers, went on to birds and animals, plants cultivated in water and soil, and all sorts of valuable material objects." After that, he "went on to discuss those things that people outside of China were unable to see." On the other hand, he

---

5 For the complete text of the *Wenzi*, see http://lib.jmu.edu.cn/departments2/magazine/philosophyol/chh59.htm and CTP http://ctext.org/wenzi/jiu-shou. This work is also known as the *Authentic Scripture of Pervading Mystery* (Tongxuan zhenjing 通玄真經); see Cleary, Thomas, tr. *Wen-tzu: Understanding the Mysteries, Further Teachings of Lao-tzu*, 1991.

6 According to Li Xueqin, the "Jing fa" was compiled in the middle period of the Warring States. See *Jianbo yiji yu xueshushi*, 1994 & 1995, 98.

enlarged his temporal experience through theoretical speculation. For example, he searched for "traces of Yin and Yang" and tried to track down the time "before Heaven and Earth were born" on the basis of the popular Ying-Yang theory of his day. At the same time, he used the Yin-Yang and Five Phases theory of nature, Heaven and Earth to speculate on issues in other fields.[7]

According to Zou Yan's speculations, the great earth was not made up of only "nine continents." He expanded these nine continents to nine regions each of which contained nine continents. China was only one area out of eighty-one which he called the Spiritual Continent of the Red Region (*chixian shenzhou* 赤縣神州); he said that this Continent of the Red Region contained nine continents where Yu the Great tamed the waters.[8] We can see from this that Zou Yan did not actually reject the early concept of "nine continents," but that his thinking followed the ancient cosmological theory that the earth was shaped like the character *jing* 井 or *ya* 亞. Zou simply "extended this theory to a boundless extent."[9] In intellectual history, we can say that Zou Yan's importance lies in his theoretical expansion of the ancient Chinese consciousness of space, but this further illustrates how the thought of people at the time endeavored to expand space in order to interpret the daily increasing world of knowledge.[10]

---

7   This line of thought is inseparable from knowledge about calendrical calculation, heavenly bodies and geography, and so he was later called "Zou who talks about the development of Heaven." The "Zhuzi" (Various Scholars) chapter 17 of Liu Xie's *Wenxin diaolong* also says that "Zou Yan discussed governance on the basis of knowledge of Heaven." This book has been translated and annotated by Vincent Yu-chung Shih as the *Literary Mind and the Carving Of Dragons*, 1959.

8   *Shiji*, j. 74, 2344. Also see, Yu Yingshi (Ying-shih), "Han foreign relations," in CHC, vol. 1, 1986, 377–462.

9   Zhou Yan's speculations had, of course, their own experiential foundations. According to the "Discourse on Heaven" (Tan Tian) chapter of Wang Chong's *Balanced Inquiries* (Lunheng, a 1st century CE text), we know that Zou Yan once said that "today's world (*tianxia*) is situated in the southeast of the earth." Zou Yan's ideas must have been based on contemporary astronomical and geographic observations. Chapter 8 of the *Commentary on the Waterways Classic* (Shuijing zhu, a 5th to 6th century CE text) also records that Zou Yan once "slowly climbed up the walls of Min and gazed out on the capital of Song state." This makes it clear that he made on the spot observations of many geographic conditions.

10 There is a note in Joseph Needham, *Science and Civilization in China*, vol. 2, 1962, page 236 where he writes that the final sentence in the *Shiji* about Zou Yan's thought—". . . around their outer edge is a vast ocean which encompasses them and stretches to the bounds where the heavens and the earth meet"—refers to "the contact of the peripheral sky with the rim-ocean, characteristic of the *Gai Tian* [gaitian] cosmology."

The idea that had the greatest influence on later political ideology was the "cycle of the Five Powers" theory. This was an ancient Chinese concept of historical change. As noted above, at least before the Warring States period, the Five Phases theory was very popular, but most of the time it was used for correlative analysis of space. For example, taking metal, wood, water, fire and earth as the basic elements in the structure of the cosmos and linking them together with the five colors, five notes, five flavors, five viscera (*wuzang*: heart, liver, spleen, lungs and kidneys) and five sense organs (*wuguan*: nose, eyes, lips, tongue and ears). This was already Warring States knowledge, but from the later period of the Spring and Autumn era on, a cyclical and temporal idea involving the order of the Five Phases began gradually to emerge.[11] The "Strategic Advantage" (Shi pian) chapter of *Sunzi: the Art of Warfare* (Sunzi bingfa) and the "Origins of the Way" (Dao Yuan) chapter of the *Book of Master Wen* contain nearly identical passages explaining how, according to ideas current during the Warring States, the multifarious and complex world of phenomena was not only structurally assembled on the basis of the Five Phases, but in its sequential changes it was also a product of the alternation of the Five Phases. Perhaps this sort of thought was very popular in the region of the state of Qi. The *Book of Master Guan* frequently mentions this sequential revolution of the Five Phases, their control of seasonal changes and their linkages with the five notes and five colors and so on. This is just what we discussed above: the method of using "numbers" (or rules, *shu*) to control all knowledge and mentally integrate all cosmic phenomena.

Zou Yan probably carried on this line of thought and used the Five Phases theory in the arena of temporal or historical change as cycles of endings and beginnings. It is said that after him, then, came the so-called "cycle (beginnings and endings) of the Five Powers" (*wude zhongshi* 五德終始) theory. This theory regarded human history, especially political history, as an unending process of cyclical change. The power-holders of every period of history all had to possess a mutual relationship with a certain "virtue" or "power" (*de*)—a special quality corresponding to one of the Five Phases of metal, wood, water, fire or earth—in order to obtain political legitimacy and authority. Once a ruler received the approval of one of the Five Phases, then he not only possessed the distinctive characteristics of this Phase, but also had to abide scrupulously by it or he would be acting contrary to the Way of Heaven. Every historical era (or dynasty) also vanquished the period before it and would be vanquished by the next historical era as if this sort of historical change was necessarily both

---

11   For examples, see Cai Mo's words recorded in *Zuozhuan*, "Zhaogong, ershi-jiu nian," SSJZS, 2123–2124.

inevitable and reasonable. These changes were analogous to the manner in which the Five Phases/Powers vanquish one another: wood vanquishes earth; earth vanquishes water; water vanquishes fire; fire vanquishes metal; metal vanquishes wood, and thus nothing remains unvanquished." The *Records of the Grand Historian* "Treatise on Calendars" (Lishu) records that there was great turmoil during the Warring States period, and people's minds were focused on "strengthening the state and capturing their enemies, relieving suffering and resolving conflicts." Nobody had time to make observations of the heavens and draw up calendar regulations. Only Zou Yan used this sort of Five Phases and Yin-Yang idea to persuade the Regional Rulers.[12] This concept of history, with its seemingly cosmological support, became extremely popular in China. According to the *Records of the Grand Historian* "Treatise on the Feng and Shan Sacrifices" (Feng shan shu), the First Emperor of the Qin was the earliest ruler to adopt this idea by declaring that his own dynasty was under the "power/virtue of water" (*shuide* 水德) in order to inherit and vanquish the "power/virtue of fire" (*huode*) of the Zhou dynasty.

In intellectual history, aside from their practical value, both the "eighty-one continents" or the "cycle of the Five Powers" theories can be regarded as Warring States concepts of cosmic space. Their contemplation of space had already gone beyond concrete measurements and calculations in the area of one state, but their technical level was insufficient to carry out overall, practical measurements and observations. They had already reached the stage of inquiring into the origins of human history, but they still could not give any fair-minded and dispassionate account of it. They would usually rely on their experience to subsume all phenomena under some basic "numbers" or "rules" from which they would derive general knowledge through speculation and imagination. Using this knowledge as their foundations, they would then proceed to speculate and imagine the much larger world and much more ancient history. This, then, was simply their method of "expanding to big things." The *Commentaries on the Book of Changes* is a typical example of this sort of thinking. It first subsumes everything in Heaven and Earth under the essential elements of Yin and Yang. Next it reduces every event and thing in the universe to eight categories engendered by Yin and Yang. Then it matches these eight categories with the eight trigrams, and from there it goes on to deduce a whole series of phenomena.

According to Han dynasty scholar officials, this kind of speculation and imagination concerning cosmic time and space was used by Zou Yan and others of like mind to criticize the intellectual limitation of the Confucians and the Moists and to provide cosmic support for human thought.

---

12   *Shiji*, j. 26, 1259.

1.4

Using cosmic time and space as the foundation of values became, for a segment of Warring States thinkers, the starting point for the examination of everything, but using the Way of Heaven to weigh the value of everything, came into conflict with another way of thinking. As previously discussed, two different foundations of value were latent even in the early ceremonies. Did one rely on the order of Heaven, or on Human feelings? As much as the ancient Chinese regarded Heaven and the Human as harmonious and undivided, in reality they were not completely integrated. If one's thought relied on the Way of Heaven as its foundation, then human beings would have a passive role in society and cosmos. The order of nature would have an authority of its own because it comes from the Way of Heaven. People can only obey the Way of Heaven, and this holds true for rulers and masses alike.[13] However, if one's thought relied on the Human as its foundation, things would be completely different. Although the *Commentaries on the Appended Phrases* (Xici) to the *Book of Changes* say that "the reciprocal process of Yin and Yang is called the Dao," this Dao did not really inspect or function in the human realm; it was made manifest through the Human. Therefore, the origin of its reasonableness was transferred to the Human, and it was not the Way of Heaven, but rather the Way of the Human. The discourse had taken a very big turn. The legitimacy that the Dao had hitherto derived from Heaven was now transferred to the Human. As the "Doctrine of the Mean" (article 1) says: "What Heaven imparts to man is called human nature (*Tian ming zhi wei xing*). To follow our nature is called the Way (*Shuai xing zhi wei Dao*). Cultivating the Way is called education (*Xiu Dao zhi wei jiao*)."[14] The most important element was no longer an external Heaven, but an internal Human. According to the "Doctrine of the Mean," in order to be as everlasting as Heaven and Earth, human beings must be able to realize their basic nature. Human nature had become the foundation and the precondition of everything. It is also the same in the "Five Conducts" silk manuscript from Mawangdui. Although it states many times that "the Way is the Way of Heaven," from first to last it connects the Way of Heaven and the Way of the Human together and even makes the Way of the Human the prerequisite for the Way of Heaven.

The *Commentaries on the Book of Changes*, "Doctrine of the Mean" and "Five Conducts," all seem to be somewhat connected to Zisi and Mengzi. Their common tendency was to shift the focus of the Human and Heaven to the Human,

---

13 This is very strongly expressed in the *Mozi*. In "Heaven's Intention, I," (chapter 26) Mozi makes Heaven the ultimate foundation of all judgments of right and wrong. *Mozi jiangu* (or xiangu), j. 7, 179. See Johnston, *Mozi*, 232–243.

14 Chan, SB, 98.

but they did not completely separate them. Xunzi, however, pushed this issue to the extreme. The *Xunzi*, book 17, "Discourse on Nature" (Tianlun) introduces a different way of thinking in which Heaven is only the Heaven of Nature, or rather, Heaven equals Nature.[15] It is no longer a Heaven that has a conscious will or a Heaven that is the foundation of social and cosmic order. Xunzi wanted to separate Heaven and the Human.[16] His conception of Heaven and Earth was simply one of Nature without any conscious will. All one needed to fathom completely the meaning of Nature was to grasp the phenomena and the seasonal changes of the heavens, to understand the geographic and physical elements of the earth and to modulate the workings of the Yin and Yang. There was nothing particularly mysterious between Heaven and Earth, and they did not possess the power to bring chaos or order to the human world. Therefore human beings were the ultimate foundation of everything. For Xunzi, Heaven belonged to Nature and human beings could change Nature. As he said, "if you cast aside the concerns proper to Man in order to speculate about what belongs to Heaven, you will miss the essential nature of the myriad things."[17] These ideas were very different from those of other thinkers. Xunzi criticized Zhuangzi, saying that "Zhuang Zhou was blinded by Nature and was insensible to man,"[18] because Zhuangzi regarded Heaven as the ultimate foundation of all thought and did not understand that human beings were the source of all fundamental values.

Xunzi and his followers' thinking on the Dao shifted from Heaven to the Human, and on that account theirs was no longer a discussion of cosmic space and time, but a reflection focused on the order of human society.

2.   Warring States Hundred Schools Contend, II: Social Order

Just before and after the beginning of the fourth century BCE, China seemed to be even more chaotic. Right at this time of strife between states and even individuals, the space of activity for the intellectual strata of society was nevertheless relatively increasing, and each of the large states brought together quite a few *shi* scholars. Following the collapse of the old order, the question of how to

---

15   John Knoblock's translation of *Xunzi*, book 17 makes this point very clear. In his introduction to the chapter, he states that "the primary meaning of the word *tian* in this book and in Xunzi's thinking more generally is 'Nature.'" Knoblock, *Xunzi*, vol. 3, 3 of 3–22.

16   *Xunzi*, j. 21, ESEZ, 327.

17   *Xunzi*, "Discourse on Nature," 17.10, Knoblock, *Xunzi*, vol. 3, 21.

18   *Xunzi*, "Dispelling Blindness," 21.4, Knoblock, *Xunzi*, vol. 3, 102.

establish a new social order was one that everyone was concerned with. What force, thinkers asked, could be relied upon to turn this generally chaotic society into a well-ordered one?

From the point of view of traditional historians, there should be three reasons for the great chaos everywhere under Heaven of the Warring States. First, blame should be placed squarely on the increasing desires of the Regional Rulers. Second, one should consider contemporary improvements in transportation that had led to increased interaction and conflict. And third, one should look to the collapse of the old social order—the royal house of Zhou's loss of authority. For the Confucians, however, with their emphasis on ordered social hierarchy, the main cause of chaos was simply the breakdown of the kingly system of rule and the degeneration of the rites. If there was no one to enforce the commonly respected order of "all under Heaven," then great disturbance would ensue. To restore order or to establish it anew was thus not only something that demanded immediate action, but it was also the central problem that most deeply concerned the thinkers since the middle Warring States period.

The problem was that contemporary thinking about how to restore the old order or to establish a new order was not at all uniform. The first problem encountered when attempting to restore order was: what was the legitimacy of this order to be based on?

To the Confucians who upheld traditional values, the ceremonies and symbols and the regulated hierarchical system passed down from the Zhou dynasty was the indisputable foundation of social order. The Daoists who saw clearly the changes in history put the blame on the development of society in which the expansion of wealth led to excessive greed and political "wisdom" created an extortionate legal system. The tension between the individual and society and between restraint and freedom, then, led to the collapse of the old order. The Daoists then asked three questions. Was the old order naturally reasonable? Did it exist from the beginning of history? On what basis does it demand our respect?

Different ways of thinking naturally led to different answers to the question of social order.

2.1

A society is constructed by people and they need a common social order, value system and rules and regulations for their life in society. For the social order, value system and rules and regulations to seem reasonable to the people in society, they need first of all a feeling of respect for social order, acceptance of the value system and a will to abide by the rules and regulations. This will is simply the goodness to restrain individual desires and respect other people's rights or privileges.[19] According to Mencius, "goodness" (*shan*) is inherent in basic human nature. The *Mencius* says in two places that all human beings have "the heart of compassion (*ce yin zhi xin*), the heart of shame (*xiu e zhi xin*), the heart of respect (*ci rang zhi xin*), and the heart of right and wrong (*shi fei zhi xin*)." Mencius said that these feelings were innate and not acquired through practice (or education), and that they caused people naturally to have feelings of sympathy (and empathy), a sense of justice, consciousness of shame and an attitude of respect or polite deference toward others. If, according to Mencius, a ruler rationally and correctly guides and expands his basic nature, "treat[s] the aged of [his] own family in a manner befitting their venerable age and extend[s] this treatment to the aged of other families; treat[s] [his] own young in a manner befitting their tender age and extend[s] this to the young of other families, [then he could] roll the Empire on [his] palm."[20] That is, if he could extend this good nature to the entire society, he could restore the kingly order the loss of which brought on the contemporary chaos.

As Feng Youlan pointed out, Mencius' statement that human nature is innately good is quite similar to Aristotle's ethics.[21] Mencius not only affirms the idea that human beings possess the origins of "goodness," but also guarantees that human beings have "good" rationality. Mencius sees this good rationality as the basic difference between human beings and the beasts. He says that the difference between man and the beasts is slight, and that slight difference resides in the fact that animals act on the basis of natural instinct but human beings behave on the basis of their good basic nature.[22]

In ancient Chinese characters, the original character for "nature" (*xing* 性) was the modern character for "to give birth" or "to be born" (*sheng* 生). The original meaning of *sheng* was vegetation sprouting out of the earth, then it was extended to mean to give birth (*shengyu*) and later to mean life itself

---

19   Confucians before Mencius had already discussed this question. According to the "Basic Nature" (Benxing) chapter of the *Lunheng*, 13.2, "Shi Shuo of the Zhou believed that human nature contains both good and evil . . . thus Master Shi wrote his "On Cultivating One's Nature" (*Yang* [*xing*] *shu*), and "People like Fu Zijian, Qi Diaokai and Gongsun Nizi also discoursed on human nature and emotions (*xingqing*) and more or less agreed with Master Shi that our nature contains both good and evil." See *Lunheng jiaoshi*, 132–133.

20   For Mencius' discussion, see *Mengzi*, "Gongsun Chou I," 2A, "Gaozi I" 6A and "Liang Huiwang, I," 1A in ssjzs, 2691, 2749 & 2670. Also see Lau, *Mencius*, 82, 163 & 56.

21   Feng Youlan, *Zhongguo zhexueshi*, 1930, 1984, 156.

22   *Mengzi*, "Li Lou, I," 4B.19, ssjzs, 2727; Lau, *Mencius*, 131.

(*shengming*).[23] In Confucian discourse, *sheng* belongs to the natural world and *xing* belongs to the spiritual realm; they are no longer one character with a single meaning. When Mencius refutes Gaozi's idea that "what is inborn (*sheng*) is what we call nature (*xing*),"[24] it is obvious that for him *sheng* (existence) was not equivalent to the ethical *xing* (nature). For Mencius, human nature was not only our basic existence, but a combination of our natural being and rationality. Heaven is the Creator of natural life, and if one extends and exhausts one's Heaven-given innate knowledge (moral sense) and innate goodness (*liangzhi, liangneng*), then one will be able perfectly to realize the meaning of the life that Heaven has bestowed upon one.[25]

Of course discussions about individual ethics and morality would have to be implemented through a reorganization (or restoration) of the social order. Mencius saw society as being made up of "great men" (*daren*) and "small men" (*xiaoren*), "those who use their minds" and "those who use their muscles" and gentlemen (men of noble character, *junzi*) and common people (peasants, uncultured people, *yeren*). He tried to explain the necessity of the social division of labor because "each individual" cannot make "the products of all the hundred crafts." Mencius used this concept of the division of labor to expound his ideas on social status distinctions by equating occupational differences with social status distinctions. In this way, the reasonableness of occupational differences was also the reasonableness of social status distinctions, and these hierarchical differences were also regarded as differences in levels of culture or civilization. Mencius then further said that cultured gentlemen and ordinary peasants were different in morality and knowledge due to their different natural endowments, but in society they were nevertheless interdependent.[26] He believed that the distinctions of noble rank, status position, grants of land and corvée labor of the ancient system were reasonable.

---

23   *Sheng* and its related ancient Chinese characters is Karlgren, *Gramata Serica Recensa*, 1964, #812.

24   *Mengzi*, "Gaozi, I," 6A.3, Chan, SB, 52.

25   *Mengzi*, "Jin xin, I," 7A.1, SSJZS, 2764, Lau, *Mencius*, 182.

26   For Mencius on these issues, see Lau, *Mencius*, 99, 101, 168. The most important passage, from *Mengzi*, "Teng Wengong, I," 3A.4 is rendered as follows by Lau: "Now, is ruling the Empire such an exception that it can be combined with the work of tilling the land? There are affairs of great men, and there are affairs of small men. Moreover, it is necessary for each man to use the products of all the hundred crafts. If everyone must make everything he uses, the Empire will be led along the path of incessant toil. Hence it is said, 'There are those who use their minds and there are those who use their muscles. The former rule; the latter are ruled. Those who rule are supported by those who are ruled.' This is a principle accepted by the whole Empire." See SSJZS, 2705 and 2702.

The problem for all of this was that this sort of order and structure could only be re-established on the basis of two conditions: strong royal power and individual self-awareness. In the Warring States period when the Zhou royal power had disintegrated, Mencius could only lodge his hopes for the restoration of order in the innate moral sense and goodness that he believed resided in everyone's heart/mind and that they could use to practice forbearance and respect for others and have a proper dread of evil.[27]

2.2

There was another way of thinking about how to reestablish social order, however, and it was quite the opposite of that of Mencius. It would re-establish order on the basis of a belief that human nature is "evil" (e 惡).[28]

In this chaotic era when order had broken down, morality virtually collapsed under the pressure of conflicting interests. In response to a society in disarray, people usually measured things by the calculus of personal interest. Judging from the practical conditions of contemporary society, it was very easy for people to believe that human nature was "evil." Most realistic thinkers also tended to uphold the view that "human nature is evil" (renxing e), because it was useful for the establishment of a practical political system. In the early Warring States period, the Mozi already contained some elements of this thinking, but the basic prescription in the Mozi was the idealistic "universal love" and "condemnation of offensive warfare." This sort of "universal love" and "condemnation of offensive warfare" was about as useful against the general "evil" in society as trying to stop water from boiling by scooping it up and pouring it back in the pot. Such illusory "goodness" and "love" could hardly solve society's problems.

In the middle of the Warring States period, some men had already begun to adumbrate ideas on the basis of the observation that human nature is evil, and these ideas would later be called Legalism or Legalist thought. Shen Buhai (died 337 BCE) advocated "relying on law and not on wisdom, and on rules but not on talk." Shen Dao also proposed that people "follow the law and rely on rules and regulations." Li Kui (455–395 BCE) even more emphatically said that one should not hope to rely on human nature to maintain social order, but rather one should rely on laws to maintain order and eliminate the lure of luxurious living.

---

27   See *Mengzi*, "Teng Wengong, II," SSJZS, 2715. Lau, *Mencius*, 106–116.

28   As Knoblock, *Xunzi*, vol. 3, 139 points out this word *e* or "'evil' does not carry the sinister or baleful overtones of the English word.... [nor] does it suggest that [human beings are] inherently depraved and incapable of good [if given the proper education]."

The most extreme of these thinkers was Shang Yang (Lord Shang, ca. 390–338 BC). His *Book of Lord Shang* (Shangjun shu) says that in earliest times people's "way was to love their relatives and to be fond of what was their own."[29] These feelings of love for their kin and selfish personal desires gave rise to social disorder. The requirements of existence and ever increasing desires pushed people even more toward utilitarian ideas. It was quite ineffectual to rely on the Confucian beliefs in ancestors, gods, ghosts and ceremonies to control humanity. Living in that age of chaos, people had already developed a most callous and thoroughgoing practical reason. Ceremonies, symbols, conscience and morality seemed little more than tattered men of straw. The only way to restore social order was to employ the punishments of law. Therefore, Shang Yang believed that a "Sage" was needed to establish "distinctions" (*fen* 分) in land allocation, wealth and property, and between male and female. Then "powers" and "authorities" must employ "laws" of rewards and punishments to establish and control social order. On the one hand, one must ban all those impractical idealisms and bring everything within the scope of the legal system. On the other hand, one must rigorously supervise and discipline the thoughts and actions of the officials and the masses.[30] He hoped to establish a strict and effective bureaucratic control system and form a highly regulated social order that would replace ethical norms based on bloodlines and family feelings, and moral consciousness based on individual self-discipline. He believed that if human thoughts and actions could all be regulated by law, then there would be no need for any spiritual freedom and transcendence or any social morality based on an innate goodness (sense of right and wrong) to establish social order.

Xunzi, who was somewhat later than Mencius and Shang Yang, took some ideas from each of them, but rejected both of their extremes. For Xunzi, excessive stress on the idea that human nature is good inevitably led Mencius into cultural idealism, while excessive reliance on the constraints of the legal system inevitably led Shang Yang into a narrow utilitarianism that easily neglected human feelings. As a Confucian, Xunzi insisted on the significance of rites and music and reason to regulate humanity. He also valued the practical utility of laws in the government and administration of this world. As much as Xunzi agreed with Zisi and Mencius that society is made up of human beings and that each individual must exist within society, he still did not completely agree

---

29   *Shangjun shu,* "Opening and Debarrring" (Kai Sai), J. J. L. Duyvendak translation, *The Book of Lord Shang,* 1928, 225. ESEZ, 1106.

30   *Shangjun shu,* 25, "Attention to Law," (Shen fa) Duyvendak, *Lord Shang,* 322–327, ESEZ, 1114.

with them. Because "even the able find it impossible to be universally skilled, and it is impossible for an individual to hold every office,"[31] human beings have to form a "collectivity" (*qun* 群), that is, a society. How, though, can they better form such a "collectivity?" Xunzi put forth a very interesting idea about this. He said that avoiding turmoil and bringing order to a collectivity depended precisely on how to "make distinctions" (*fen*). His *fen* can be explained both as to differentiate (*qufen*) and to play one's assigned role (*benfen*). If there are hierarchical distinctions in society and everyone plays his proper social role within the hierarchy, then society will be well-ordered. The principle of *fen*, for Xunzi, was propriety (*li*). Propriety and etiquette served both to make human relationships harmonious and to make distinctions between different classes of people. The basis of this kind of thought was an evaluation of human nature, and its goal was to find a practical method to rectify social order.

In "Man's Nature is Evil" the *Xunzi* has this to say about the question of what human nature is: "Human nature is evil; any good in humans is acquired by conscious exertion."[32]

It goes on in "On the Correct Use of Names:"

> What characterizes a man from birth is called his 'nature.' What is produced out of the harmony of inborn nature, out of the sensibilities of the organ tallying as the senses respond to stimuli, and what from birth is effortless and spontaneous are called 'nature.' The feelings of liking and disliking, of delight and anger, and of sorrow and joy that are inborn in our nature are called 'emotions (*qing*).' The emotions being so paired, the mind's choosing between them is called 'thinking (*lü*).' The mind's thinking something and the natural abilities' acting on it is called 'conscious exertion' (*wei*).[33]

On the one hand, he acknowledges that human beings have reason/rationality (*lixing*), but he believes that learning is even more important. People must rely on knowledge acquired through education to teach them the habits of abiding by rules and regulations and complying with social order to become refined and civilized. On the other hand, he paid particular attention to the moderating influences of an external system of rites and ceremonies on human nature.[34] Although he admitted that nature is inborn, he emphasized the need

---

31   *Xunzi jijie*, j. 6, "Fu guo," ZZJC, 113. Knoblock, *Xunzi*, "On Enriching the State," 10.1, 121.
32   Knoblock, *Xunzi*, vol. 3, 23.1a, 150. ZZJC, j. 17, ZZJC, 289.
33   Knoblock, *Xunzi*, vol. 3, 22.1b, 127. ZZJC, j. 16, "Zhen ming," ZZJC, 274.
34   ZZJC, j. 15, 263.

to balance the emotions to make people understand where "disaster and happiness" actually reside. Besides their inner rationality, human beings need systems of propriety and laws to balance their emotions.[35] Good and kind people should be treated with propriety, while malicious people should be treated with punishments. In other words, gentlemen should be treated with propriety while small men should be treated with laws. This is the only way to warn people to be vigilant and have a proper sense of fear.[36]

2.3

The thinking of both Xunzi and Mencius each had their influence on the later Confucian schools of thought. In their own age of general chaos and practical concern with profit, Xunzi's thought was, however, clearly more influential than that of Mencius. Although Mencius ranked much higher in the later Chinese intellectual world, Xunzi was of more consequence and his thought occupied a very important position in the ideology of Qin and Han China. There were at least three reasons for this. First, Xunzi influenced a large number of disciples through his teachings on the classic texts, and his disciples then relied on their interpretation and exegesis of these classics to gain control of the cultural discourse. Xunzi held a pivotal position in the system of transmission of the *Book of Songs*, the *Book of Documents*, the *Book of Changes*, the *Spring and Autumn Annals* and the *Book of Rites*.[37] Second, Xunzi's way of thinking was no longer only the humanistic idealism of the Confucians; it contained many very practical elements that could be employed in moral self-discipline and be extended to have ideological significance for a system of legal control that could be put into practice by the government. Third, Xunzi's thought was already very open-minded. It was no longer restricted to the narrow confines of Confucian idealism and inner cultivation, but it widely absorbed various other practical trends of thought, and vigorously concentrated its interest on pragmatic this-worldly thought. For Xunzi, the so-called Dao was no longer an abstract and mystical object of thought, but rather a concrete and profound method of action. Precisely because he sought such practical efficacy, his thinking moved from the Dao towards "arts" or "techniques" (*shu*) of government; his position moved from propriety or

---

35   ZZJC, j. 16, 286.

36   ZZJC, j. 13, 231 and j. 14, ZZJC, 252.

37   The transmission of such Confucian texts as the *Shijing, Zuozhuan, Guliangzhuan, Liji* and *Yijing* was closely connected to Xunzi. As Pi Xirui in the second chapter of his *Jingxue lishi*, 1981, writes that "Xunzi could transmit the *Yi, Shi, Li, Yue* and *Chunqiu*; his followers were extremely flourishing in the early Han."

rites towards law; and the focus of his thought moved from the people (*min*) towards the ruler (*jun*).[38] One may say that his thought moved gradually toward becoming an ideology.

Originally Confucian and Legalist thought both emphasized order, and there were no insurmountable differences between them. To move from propriety to laws was a natural development for contemporary thought about the restoration of social order.[39] Self-consciously complying with social propriety was not enough to discipline people's heart/minds and rectify society; this would naturally require the use of coercive laws. On the surface, most Confucians believed in ritualism, a system of regulation through propriety or rites, while most Legalists who engaged in the practical governance of society believed in a system of control through laws. On many occasions their reasoning was actually very similar. They were both concerned with restoring social order and they were both founded on an evaluation of human nature. When social order was so chaotic that it was impossible to rectify the situation though personal reflection; when morality had collapsed to the extent that it was impossible to maintain on the basis of ceremonial symbolism; and when those Confucians who liked to sit and discuss the Way joined the ranks of the practitioners of practical administration, then they very easily changed their positions. Consequently the transmission of thought from Xunzi to Hanfeizi (ca. 280–233 BCE) and Li Si (ca. 280–208 BCE) was a natural continuation in intellectual history.

Following the increasing importance of military might in the late Warring States period, along with expansion of the territory of the various states and the need for more governance, thought about laws became progressively more vocal and powerful. At that time Hanfeizi and other thinkers later known as Legalists appeared. For Hanfeizi, to employ the suggestions of relaxed and leisurely symbolic rites and music to urge people on and to rely on individual reflections based on their not-necessarily-good human nature to save society was impossible. The two elements behind his thought were the idea that human nature is evil and the widespread social chaos. His thinking was different from most Confucians; his ideal was that everyone should obey the laws rather than do good works. His thought represented a form of practical utilitarianism rather than a perennial idealism. He hoped to strengthen the

---

38   "On Strengthening the State" (Qiang guo), Knoblock, *Xunzi*, vol. 2, 235–249.

39   In the *Zuozhuan*, "Zhaogong, ershi-wu nian," when Master Dashu quotes Shuxiang, he had already gone from rites to "laws," and also linked both rites and "laws" to Heaven and Earth, Nature and human nature, and accorded them both the same reasonableness and value.

external constraints of laws and regulations and the government's supervision of state officials. This was the only way, he believed, to achieve practical results in the governance of society. He ridiculed the stupidity and inflexibility of idealists. When the *Hanfeizi* says, in "Eminence in Learning" (Xian xue), "he who claims to be sure of something for which there is no evidence is a fool, and he who acts on the basis of what cannot be proved is an imposter," it is really not an abstract philosophical enquiry into truth, as various intellectual histories have speculated, but an expression of contempt and ridicule aimed at useless and ineffectual idealists.[40]

Of course the various Legalist thinkers did not all have the same ideas regarding social order. Some valued the individual ruler's control of power; some insisted on the ruler's manipulation of power within the bureaucratic structure; and some emphasized the absolute and pragmatic nature of the legal institutions themselves. However, they all had in common a lack of concern with people's ultimate ideals and spiritual transcendence and a lack of interest in the foundations and value of history and rationality. They were much more interested in how ideas or a doctrine could be operationally implemented and become institutionalized as a system that could solve the increasingly urgent problem of social order.[41]

2.4

Not everyone was so practical and utilitarian. If they searched for it in history or "historical memory," many people would conceive of an ideal ancient world. The "Ceremonial Usages" (Liyun) chapter of the *Book of Rites*, regarded as a Confucian classic, is one example of this. The ancient world it describes is an ideal one, and it calls for a return to the simple and honest popular customs of that world where one never needed to lock one's doors at night and no one would pick up and take away anything one might lose in the street. It regards that utopian World of Great Unity (*Datong shijie*), or universal commonwealth, as the ideal form of social order. This was of course a criticism of the unbearable contemporary world, and it also provided material for utopian thought.

---

40   *Hanfeizi*, j. 19, "Xian xue," 50.1. ESEZ, 185. Burton Watson, *Han Fei Tzu: Basic Writings*, 1964, 119. Almost every history of Chinese philosophy quotes this passage, but they always interpret it as a statement of abstract thought.

41   The flourishing of "laws" near the end of the Warring States period was quite likely also related to the fact that many *shi* ceased to be "wandering scholars" and became professional officers in state bureaucracies, entering the ranks of government administrators, especially after the state of Qin prohibited such "wandering scholars." These new government administrators were particularly interested in the practical efficacy of the laws.

Amid this general practice of tracing back history and using the past to disparage the present, however, on the subject of social order, there was one most discordant voice that emanated from Zhuangzi and others of his ilk. Their questioning of "history" led them to some more extreme ideas.

First, when they examined history, they discovered that the so-called "social order" was nothing but a man-made and artificial product of history that was produced after a much earlier order of nature had been destroyed. Their habit of requiring a historical foundation for thought led them to maintain firmly that the contemporary social order was not reasonable. Rather, for them, it was actually the muddled yet simple and unadorned primal order way back at the beginning of history that possessed genuine reasonableness. They believed that the world was in turmoil because of an increase in knowledge or wisdom and an inflation of desires that led to disorder and hypocrisy. With this disorder and hypocrisy came laws to control the disorder and humanity and justice to correct the hypocrisy. Because the so-called "social order" that was compulsorily created through the enforcement of these laws and humanity and justice was not upheld by simple and tranquil feelings, it only served to further incite people to crime and all sorts of evil and create even more disorder. As the "Rifling Trunks" (Qu qie) chapter of the *Zhuangzi* puts it, ". . . when the sage is born, the great thief appears" . . . And if the sage is dead and gone, then no more great thieves will arise." So one must "cut off sageliness, cast away wisdom, and the great thieves will cease."[42]

Second, in their belief that their contemporary disorder was certainly derived from the confusion of human nature, their thinking was in accord with that of the Confucians. The Confucians, however, held that human nature is absolute and innate. Their doctrine that "human nature is good" takes this good original nature as *the* everlasting human nature. The doctrine that "human nature is evil" maintained that desires are also an innate part of the human disposition. Zhuangzi's ideas on this were different. He believed that human nature was constantly changing. At the beginning of history, human nature was tranquil and unsophisticated, but as history changed, human knowledge began, human desires were activated and human nature began to engender evil. Later on, people obeyed the norms of the social order, but the evil desires of their hearts were not pacified. When people relied only on governance or administration and valued rationality, then they lost the "unrestrained" (*ziwei* 自爲) natural condition of their simple and sincere original nature and entered into an "artificial" (*renwei* 人爲) age of restraint by reason and knowledge. In that age their honest and unsophisticated human nature was overwhelmed by outward shows of intellect, humanity's natural

42   ZZJS, j. 4, 359, 350, 353. Watson, CT, chapter 10, 109, 110.

Heaven-bequeathed nature was obscured by desire for personal interest, and, because of this, the originally harmonious social order degenerated so much that "order" could only be maintained by governmental control and coercive force. On this point, Daoist and Legalist thought were mutually connected.

Third, following this line of thought, realist thinkers who relied on laws and power to establish social order found historical support for the legal system in contemporary use. Zhuangzi, with his persistent idealism, was, however, hard put to find a strategy for putting his ideas into practice in the real world. He could only race ahead and give free range to his unbridled imagination. He felt that since human nature was in the midst of historical changes, and society was steadily deteriorating, the only thing for humanity to do was to abandon all the cares of this life, forget all the enticements of the world and return to its original primal-age tranquility and unsophisticated simplicity. From Zhuangzi's point of view it was futile to explore the moral nature of one's heart/mind or to try to train one's moral consciousness. To illustrate this, he related the following anecdote about a supposed meeting between Confucius and Laozi in which Laozi ridiculed Confucius for his belief in cultivating the heart/mind:

> Confucius said [to Lao Dan/Laozi], "Your virtue, Sir, is the very counterpart of Heaven and earth, and yet even you must employ these perfect teachings in order to cultivate your mind. Who, then, even among the fine gentlemen of the past, could have avoided such labors?"
>
> "Not so!" said Lao Dan.... "Without cultivating it [virtue], [the Perfect Man] possesses it to such an extent that things cannot draw away from him. It is as natural as the height of heaven, the depth of the earth, the brightness of sun and moon. What is there to be cultivated?"[43]

In a time when human desires were overflowing and both rites and laws were needed to maintain social order, disappointment with and criticism of society was hard to avoid, and when people felt dejected, their critiques took on a somewhat idealistic tone. Such criticisms often received sympathetic responses, especially from those thinkers who would later be lumped together as members of the Daoist school. The *Book of Master Wen* and the *Pheasant Cap Master* both contain many such critical discussions.

2.5

Among these dejected and hopeless voices, then, there was quite a bit of socially engaged thinking. It was very easy for ideas about rectifying the social order through legalistic control and power manipulation to arise from such

---

43   *Zhuangzi*, "Tian Zifang" (chapter 21) ZZJS, j. 7, 716. Watson, CT, 226.

pessimistic feelings. This was especially true near the end of the Warring States period with the appearance of the so-called "convergence of Daoism and Legalism" in intellectual history.[44]

First, their extreme attacks on the depravity of human nature and contemporary social disorder served as a perfect basis for the idea of using laws to regulate society. Their idea of going back in history was originally an expression of their feelings, but it provided legalist thinking with just the support it needed. The "Reform the Law" (Gengfa) chapter in the *Book of Lord Shang* and "The Five Vermin" (Wudu) chapter of the *Hanfeizi* both assert that the Golden Age can never be recovered, and humanity's harmony and tranquility are things of the historical past. In an age where human nature has degenerated so far, rule by a legalist system was, thus, unavoidable.[45]

Second, their understanding of the Dao as both transcendent and universal served exactly to provide cosmic support for the absolute and universal power of the ruler. According to the *Book of Master Wen* and the *Pheasant Cap Master*, the Dao comes forth out of the "One." It is not within the sphere of legal rules and regulations and yet it has jurisdiction over everything. It is in itself a self-evident "force" (*shi*) and "principle" (*li*). This "force" is a form of political power, and this "principle" is a form of power over truth. The power of the Dao transcends that of Heaven—it is the unique "One." Once these absolute intellectual concepts of Dao and the One were brought together with the absolute worldly power of ruler and king, they formed a strong support for rule by law and authoritarianism.[46]

Although the *Zhuangzi* is rather disdainful of human social order, in "Heaven and Earth" (Tian Di) it says that "the sovereign finds his source in Virtue (*de*), his completion in Heaven." In "Wielding Power" (Yangquan), the *Hanfeizi* advocates concentration of power in the ruler. He says that "government reaches to the four quarters, but its source is in the center. The sage holds to the source and the four quarters come to serve him."[47] The foundation for these

---

44 Li Zehou, *Zhongguo gudai sixiangshi lun*, 1985, 97–103, discusses the relationship between *Laozi* and *Hanfeizi*.

45 "Reform of the Law" is in Duyvendak, *Lord Shang*, 167–175; "The Five Vermin" is in Watson, *Han Fei Tzu*, 96–117.

46 *Wenzi*, "Daode," "A ruler must hold on to the One before he can hold on to the multitude." In *Wenzi yaoquan*, 1988, 107. *Shizi*, j. *shang*, "Fen," also says "Heaven and Earth gave birth to the myriad things and the sages divided them in order to regulate divisions (shares, *fen*) and establish offices for each task. So rulers, ministers, fathers, sons, high and low, old and young, noble and base, close and distant can all obtain their proper status (*fen*)." ESEZ, 369.

47 Watson, CT, "Heaven and Earth," 126 and "Knowledge Wandered North," 235 on *wuwei*; Watson, *Han Fei Zi*, section 8, 35.

assertions is the everlasting "One." It is the symbol of order, and, because the human world mirrors the cosmos, it naturally also possesses an everlasting "One"—the ruler—and on this account the ruler becomes the embodiment of cosmic and social order.

Third, from the *Laozi* on, the state of primal simplicity that Daoists held up as a model for the world was always imbued with a sort of anti-intellectualism. As much as they hoped to return to a state of pure uncultivated simplicity, they also hoped to keep the popular masses totally ignorant and unaware in an age of knowledge expansion and the rise of reason.[48] In contrast to this, they made rulers the center of society. Superficially emulating the ancient sages and the Way of Heaven while also advocating non-action (*wuwei*), they actually put the masses under the control of the rulers, keeping the masses in a state of ignorance while enthusiastically promoting the ruler's control over everything. In this way, they felt that social order could be effortlessly maintained. The Daoists said that in an age of incessant depravity when the Great Way did not prevail, morality had collapsed and humanity and justice were lost, the only way definitely to uphold right and wrong was to rely on clearly delimited rewards and punishments (*shangfa*) and to ensure that each person "kept to his own role" (*fenshou* 分守). That way, brilliant and enlightened rulers would not have to worry, they could do nothing (practice *wuwei*) and yet there would be nothing that was not accomplished. As the *Zhuangzi* says, "this was called the Great Peace, the Highest Government."[49]

Social order was a central topic in Warring States intellectual history because of the felt necessity of establishing a unified political ideology. It was precisely during discussions of this topic that not only did Confucian thought begin to harbor elements of legalism that led the Confucians to go from rites to laws and from the people to the ruler, but some Daoists began to move toward the convergence of Daoism and Legalism. At that time, Shen Dao and Shen Buhai combined Daoism and Legalism, the *Zhuangzi* integrated discussions of names, laws and the Dao, and the "Jielao" and "Yulao" chapters of the Legalist *Hanfeizi* along with the *Book of Master Wen* and the *Pheasant Cap Master* contain many arguments very similar to Legalism.[50] From this we can see that the blending of Daoism and Legalism and the tendency to move from the abstract Dao toward the practical arts (techniques, *shu*) of governance began very early on.

---

48   *Laozi*, chapter 19. Chan, SB, 149.

49   ZZJS, j. 5, 465 & 471. Watson, CT, 146–147.

50   For *Wenzi*, "*Daode*" and "*Xiade*," see *Wenzi yaoquan*, 109; also see SBCK *Pheasant Cap Master*, j. *shang*, "Huanliu."

3.   Warring States Hundred Schools Contend, III: Life of the Individual

The two topics of debate in the Warring States intellectual world that we discussed above concerned cosmic time and space and social order and morality.
Both of these topics were concerned with the natural environment and the
social background of human existence, and "the individual" was not a salient
part of the debates. The vast cosmos and complex society in which the individual resides was the center of discussion, but the individual was neglected.
In another topic of individual existence, the Human, however, finally became
the real central focus.

3.1

Warring States thought concerning the Human began with the search for everlasting individual life. The focus of Confucian thinkers was not, however, on
this; they were more concerned with the noble meaning of human life in society. For example, we have the *Analects* statement of Confucius that "you do not
know how to serve the living. How can you serve the dead (or the spirits)?"[51]
There was no need to worry about human life before birth and after death
because human beings live in the real world, and so the Confucian concern
with the Human was with the relationships between individuals and society.

The desire for life to last forever is an ancient and widespread one, and it
was also one of the core ideas of Daoist thought. The background of the intellectual trend concerning individual existence was ongoing long before the
middle of the Warring States era. It derived from the suffering of humanity
since the beginning of human life on earth; it relied on contemporary ideas
about nourishing one's vital essence (*yangqi*) and so-called refining one's body
(*lianxing*) through breathing exercises; it may even have been supported by
the thought of the Chu area in the south (present day Hunan and Hubei). We
do not know the exact date of the *Songs of Chu* poem "The Far-off Journey"
(Yuanyou), but I believe that it expresses a consciousness of life that goes back
to the distant past, and the attitude toward life as well as the methods of nurturing life (*yangsheng*) it manifested were common to much Warring States
thinking.[52]

There were two trends of this sort of thought. One was the Daoist concept
of life, and it belonged to cosmology and attitudes toward human life. In this

51   *Lunyu*, "Gong Ye Chang," 5.12 and *Shiji*, j., 47, "Kongzi shijia."
52   Hong Xingzu, *Chuci buzhu*, 1983, 164–166. See David Hawkes, *Ch'u Tzu The Songs of the
      South*, 1962, 81–87 for "The Far-off Journey." Hawkes writes that the poem describes
      "a celestial journey which ends … in triumphant fulfillment."

conceptual world, human beings were born out of the transformation of Yin and Yang, and they must "follow Heaven and obey Earth."[53] The other trend was one of concrete experience and practical techniques. The idea was that if one practiced the correct techniques for maintaining and refining one's individual life, one could obtain the state of everlasting life enjoyed by the Daoist immortals. This trend led to later techniques of nurturing life and refining one's body in order to seek immortality.

3.2

In general, Chinese thinkers interested in social order paid more attention to human social existence and social cooperation and not so much to individual freedom. This goes without saying for thinkers who were strongly in favor of legalism and government control, but even Confucians like Mencius and Xunzi used moral character and social achievement as their standards for judging a person's individual value. If a person was not praised by society, given political recognition, or esteemed by his family and lineage, that person would hardly be judged to have realized his value as a human being. Although Confucian doctrines embraced the ideals of spiritual self-perfection and moral self-improvement, the final appraisal of a person still depended upon his significance, value, morality and behavior in society. The significance of a person's existence also depended upon his nature and feelings, differences in nature and feelings depended upon cultivation, and differences in cultivation depended upon social rank; from the very beginning, social status determined a person's moral character and value. Section three of the "Duke Ai Asks About the Five Virtues" (Ai gong wen wuyi) chapter of the *Da Dai Book of Rites* also has Confucius saying that "mediocre people" (*yongren*) have no ultimate ideals or moral position and absolutely no self-awareness about their own thought and behavior.[54] In contrast, *shi* scholars (*shiren*) make their own value judgments, have their own intellectual positions; that is, they possess the wisdom to judge right and wrong. Gentlemen or superior men make even more correct moral judgments and have even higher standards of behavior. The great worthies (*xianren*) could serve as models for the world, while the ancient sages were able to employ their own nature and feelings to understand clearly the nature of all the people and things under Heaven. This is why the "Great Learning" starts from a tranquil state of mind, rational thought, accumulating knowledge and an upright and earnest nature. Only from such a beginning would it be possible to "rectify one's heart/mind," "cultivate one's self," "order

---

53   All these ideas are found in the "Nine Rules" (Jiushou) chapter of the *Wenzi*.

54   *Dadai Liji jiegu*, 1983.

one's family," "regulate the state," and "bring peace to all under Heaven." All this is not about the individual's existence in the cosmos, but rather the realization of the individual's value within society. Apart from existence within society, the individual had no place.

Why, though, would the individual's thought and behavior not have self-evident significance if they were not in society? Why must the value of the individual be realized only within society? Can the individual's solitary existence have its own meaning or significance? All of these questions may have served as contemporary topics of discussion. In view of these considerations, thinkers who were more concerned with the naturalness (spontaneity, *ziran*) and freedom (*ziyou*) of individual life introduced another way of thinking about the Human in their critiques of the contemporary world. The most profound among them was Zhuangzi.

3.3

3.3.1 Zhuangzi on the Individual

Although Zhuangzi and his followers from the middle of the Warring States on had inherited the ideas from earlier discussions of the Dao, his way of thinking was not quite the same. His thought was just like the title of one chapter of the *Zhuangzi*—"Mastering Life" (Dasheng)." For him "mastering life" did not mean working hard to seek the continuation of life itself, but rather seeking to complete your life and to reach a stage of spiritual transcendence. There is no doubt that Zhuangzi imagined that there was everlasting life, but he was more concerned with whether or not people's understanding of life and death would be able to lead them to transcend life and death themselves. In "The Great and Venerable Teacher" (Da Zongshi), it is said that anyone who can regard life and death as empty or nothing (*xuwu*) can transcend them and banish their mind's longing for life and fear of death. In "The Way of Heaven" (Tiandao), he calls this attitude "Heavenly joy" (*tianle*) because this is the kind of philosophical equanimity one has only after coming to understand the natural (heavenly) processes of life. Conceptually, reducing the boundary between life and death does not, however, mean passively adjusting to one's life; it means rather to follow nature to complete one's proper life. Because life is bestowed upon human beings by Heaven, human beings should make their lives embody nature (*ziran*)—this is what Zhuangzi meant by "mastering life." Any behavior that harms life is contrary to nature. Zhuangzi held up the example of what he called "the True Man (*zhenren*) of ancient times" and said that he did not use knowledge to engage in worldly disputes, did not violate ordinary customs due to his own individuality and did not have lust in his heart. He submitted to

Heaven, Earth and the four seasons, and in this manner reached the state of the unity of Heaven and the Human.[55]

The central issue of Zhuangzi's thinking about the Human was the significance of human existence in the cosmos; he was not really very concerned with the value of human life in society. "Fit for Emperors and Kings" (Ying Diwang) asserts that the "fame, schemes, projects and wisdom" (*ming, mou, shi, zhi*) considered to be very important as social values, are in reality injurious to human life.[56] The "Perfect Man" (*zhiren*) should not, as the Confucians said, have a mind full of moral ethics such as rights and wrongs, pros and cons, hoping for the approval and praise of "others." Rather, "the Perfect Man uses his mind like a mirror." The mirror reflects the form of everything, but does not preserve them; "going after nothing, welcoming nothing..."[57] What human beings receive from Heaven is nothing less than a natural and free individual life, and the real meaning of life resides precisely in spiritual freedom. In "Free and Easy Wandering" (Xiaoyaoyou), a chapter we are all familiar with, what Zhuangzi wanted to say was that to enter the realm of absolute spiritual freedom, human beings cannot rely on any external values, including empty fame, meritorious deeds, and self regard. This is the only way to lead the human spirit to transcend the vulgar world and the human ego. Only by getting rid of all that, maintaining a mindset of "no self," "no merit" and "no fame" and entering the realm of unbounded freedom would it be possible for one to be just like the "Way of Heaven," dwell in a state of "Nothingness" (Nonbeing, *wu*) and embrace the "Unlimited" (*wuxian*).[58] Only by dwelling in Nothingness or Nonbeing can a human being have absolute freedom and experience the true meaning of existence.

3.4

There are three elements of the thought of Zhuangzi and his followers that we should understand.

---

55   "To harmonize with men is called human joy; to harmonize with Heaven is called Heavenly joy." Watson, CT, 143 and 78.

56   ZZJS, j. 3, 307. "Do not be an embodier of fame (*ming*); do not be a storehouse of schemes (*mou*); do not be an undertaker of projects (*shi*); do not be a proprietor of wisdom (*zhi*)." Watson, CT, 97.

57   Watson, CT, 97.

58   For "no self," "no merit" and "no fame," see *Zhuangzi*: "Therefore I say, the Perfect Man has no self (*wuji*); the Holy Man (*shenren*) has no merit (*wugong*); the Sage has no fame (*wuming*)." Watson, CT, 32.

First, their concept of human life had cosmic support. Zhuangzi saw Heaven as giving birth to human beings, and so they should conform to Nature and in everything follow the natural disposition bestowed upon them by "Heaven." This was different from Mencius and Xunzi because the Confucians regarded the basic foundations of the Human as the innate nature of either good moral reason or evil feelings and the norms of human behavior that should necessarily derive from them. Zhuangzi, however, regarded the Heaven-sent, natural, free individual life existence as the basic foundation of the Human. Therefore he constantly employed the free and unrestrained realm of Heaven to demonstrate the correct state of human existence. He opposed the principles of artificial ethics and morality that he believed were injurious to this state of being. In his view, so-called humanity and rightness represented a kind of moral restraint that was unfortunately created after human society became far removed from its plain and simple state of primal chaos and innocence. They were not suitable for humanity's natural feelings.

Humanity and rightness are very noble, but people should not demand them of others because they make people live in a state of constant anxiety and loss of spontaneity and freedom. The celebrated story of "Drilling seven openings in Hundun (Chaos)" illustrates how when reason arose human spontaneity was lost and when desires began human beings lost their basic nature.[59] What for the Confucians was basic human nature, for Zhuangzi was exactly the ruination of humanity's original inborn nature.

Second, their concept of human life also had historical support. For Confucians, the norms of good and evil and right and wrong were inborn, but for Zhuangzi, this set of value standards was an artificial human construct. People only believed them to be inborn, and as a result some unverified yet authoritative values were impressed on people's minds. Confucians equated these values with humanity's inner rationality—truth, goodness and beauty accorded with these values while fraud, evil and ugliness violated them. When Zhuangzi traced these value norms to their origins at the beginning of thought, he discovered that they were simply created by human beings after the loss of natural spontaneity and harmony. He believed that there were no absolute values in the world. Except for eternity and nothingness, there was no absolute right or wrong in anything. He wanted to employ his belief in "making all things equal and regarding life and death as one" (*qi wanwu yi sisheng*) to

---

59   For the Hundun story, see *Zhuangzi*, " 'All men [said Hu (Sudden) and Shu (Brief)], have seven openings so they can see, hear, eat, and breath. But Hundun alone doesn't have any. Let's try boring him some!' Every day they bored another hole, and on the seventh day Hundun died." "Fit for Emperors and Kings," Watson, CT, 97, with slight modifications.

eliminate all rationality and values and allow humanity to transcend the everyday world and achieve absolute spontaneity and freedom.

Third, their concept of human life had its practical significance as well. According to Zhuangzi, humanity's innate nature longs for spontaneity and freedom in the same way that birds naturally seek the deep forests and fish live in the rivers and lakes.[60] The reason human beings face so many different dangers and difficulties in life is because they had fallen into a frightening and complex society full of anxiety and struggle that they should never be in. Humanity's innate nature had been injured and obscured. If they could return to their original state and the consciousness of being one with Nature, they could then "preserve their inborn nature" (*quan qi tian*). On the contrary, if they possessed knowledge and rationality, they would most probably "harm their bodies and enslave their spirits." As Zhuangzi lamented, "yet how many gentlemen of the vulgar world today endanger themselves and throw away their lives in the pursuit of mere things! How can you help pitying them?"[61]

In the Warring States period, such ideas of spiritual transcendence and a life of freedom could not avoid being rather too impractical. It was not easy to protect human freedom in the midst of violent change. When the whole of society was conscious of the practical importance of the struggle for existence and obtaining personal advantages, even imagination and fancy could undergo transformation. As it turned out, these Daoists fell from Heaven to earth and entered the most practical intellectual world.

4.   Language and Reality: The Warring States Period Disputations
        on Names

Thought depends on language for its expression. People use language to transmit their thought, and the thought that is so transmitted by language in turn influences people's knowledge, even to the extent of transforming the world of reality. Confucius' answer to Zilu's question about the first measure he would apply in administering a country—"it would certainly be to rectify their names/ language" (*bi ye zheng ming hu*)—makes it clear that thinkers of that age already had an appreciation of the significance of language in the world.[62] People were quite naturally asking the following questions: Can, or how can language really explain the world/reality? Can, or how can human beings

---

60   *zzjs*, j. 6, "Zhi le," 621 and "Da sheng," 665–666.

61   "Giving Away a Throne" (Rang Wang) in *zzjs*, j. 9, 971. Watson, CT, 313.

62   *Lunyu*, "Zilu," 13.3.

adjust the conditions of the world/reality through language? Can, or how can human beings transcend language and directly touch the world/reality itself? The study of disputations on names that gradually developed during the Warring States period was both the product of concrete arguments and the result of metaphysical explorations in the philosophy of language. As much as I doubt that any thinkers were in their own time referred to as coming from the School of Names (mingjia 名家), nevertheless "disputing about names" (*mingbian* 名辯) was one of the techniques that thinkers of that age had to pay attention to. The study of disputations on names (*mingbian zhi xue* 名辯之學) simply referred to the questions contemporary thinkers asked about the relation between language (names/words) and the world/reality.

4.1

From the Spring and Autumn on, thinkers had differing attitudes toward language. Confucius and his followers firmly believed that language could explain the world of reality. Society was at the center of their concerns; they scrupulously abided by the traditional usage of language and hoped that social order could be maintained using traditional language. They stubbornly maintained that when "the ruler acts like a ruler, the minister like a minister, the father like a father and the son like a son" (*Analects*, "Yan Yuan," 12.11), this relationship between "names" (*ming*) and "reality" (*shi* 實) would be unalterably correct and naturally reasonable. A name confirmed a reasonable reality; any change in reality should not change the orderly sequence of names.

Legend has it that in the Spring and Autumn period Deng Xi (ca. 545–501 BCE) "took wrong for right, and right for wrong," not abiding by the traditional rules of names and caused the state of Zheng to be thrown into great disorder.[63]

Thus when Confucius said "rectify their names/language" (*zhengming*), he hoped to harmonize the relationship between names and reality in order to correct the social order and maintain a consistency between the status positions (*mingfen*) of the old order and the reality (*shishi*) of the new era. In his mind, names/words had eternally stable contents; no matter how time galloped ahead and the affairs of the world constantly changed, the proper names of things absolutely could not vary. The Confucians hoped to use "names" to maintain the social stability, while the changing world should also adjust itself so as to fit the order created by existing names. The *Zuo Commentary* has an old saying that was attributed to Confucius: "It is only proper functions and their names that cannot be given to others [who do not deserve them]." *Qi* 器,

---

63   See LSCQ, j. 18, "Li Wei," 104.3 for an example of this. ESEZ, 694.

proper functions, here is a symbol for the chariots and ceremonial clothing
(*ju fu* 車服) that represented social status and order, while *ming*, their names,
certified the hierarchical status and order of noble ranks.[64] For Confucius, as
much as names might only be vocabulary items of language, nevertheless they
symbolized an immemorial and immutable sacred order. Even though it was
often out of sync with reality, it was still the fundamental framework for regulating reality and putting social order in place.[65]

Mozi's view of names differed from that of Confucius. Mozi did not rely on
either an already fixed order or ancient traditions; he particularly emphasized
practical reality and often relied heavily upon experience to ascertain knowledge. He believed that names did not have eternal meanings, but they depended
upon the content of reality for their determination. Language, for Mozi, was
not immemorial and immutable; it had to be revised on the basis of historical
facts. As the *Mozi* says, "theories must have three criteria" (*yen bi you san biao*)
of "foundation" (*ben*), "source (*yuan*), and "application" (*yong*). First, one must
examine "the actions of the ancient sage kings above" to obtain historical support (the "foundation"); then one must experience "the truth of the evidence of
the eyes and ears of the common people below" (the "source") to obtain the
support of the living; finally one must verify government policies to make certain that it "is seen in the benefit to the ordinary people of the state" (the
"application").[66] Mozi obviously tended toward empiricism when it came to
the relations between names/words and things/reality. He believed that language depended on the testimony of history and lived experience to verify its
effectiveness and reliability.

Laozi's views on language were even more extreme; he had a fundamental
disbelief in language. The focus of his interest was on a Dao that transcended
both experience and language; language could neither explain nor describe
this Dao. The "material things" (*wu*) that language was able to explain were also
constantly in flux. For that reason, he firmly maintained that names were neither eternal nor absolute in nature. To cling stubbornly to language could actually obstruct human wisdom and understanding.

Laozi warned people that they must be aware of the limitations of language
because, on the one hand, the ten thousand things were constantly in flux and,
on the other hand, "the Dao has no constant name." The Dao is ineffable and

---

64   *Zuozhuan*, "Chenggong, ernian," CTP, http://ctext.org/chun-qiu-zuo-zhuan/cheng-gong-
      er-nian.

65   Chad Hansen, in his *Language and Logic in Ancient China*, 1983, argues that in ancient
      Chinese philosophy the functions of language were both "regulative" and "descriptive."

66   Johnston, *Mozi*, "Against Fate I," 35.3, 320–321. *Mozi jiangu*, j. 9, 240–241.

indescribable, and we should always be distrustful of language and vigilant about experience. He felt that language certainly did not have the power to regulate order, but only to impede people's experience of the Heavenly Way. If we say that Confucius insisted on the regulative nature of language and Mozi insisted on the reliability of experience, then Laozi insisted only on the transcendent nature of intuition and was skeptical of both language and experience.

What was the situation in the middle of the Warring States period? We should say that the attitude toward language of the thinkers at the end of the Spring and Autumn and the beginning of Warring States mostly derived from their feelings and their need to use language; they really did not particularly study language per se. This was because they did not regard language as a means for recreating or regulating the world (the Confucian view) or as an instrument for describing the world of experience (the Moist view), or even as "an obstacle" to understanding the ultimate mysteries of the universe (the Daoist view). Human social order, experiential knowledge and the Heavenly Way of the cosmos were the focal points of their concerns, and the question of language was outside of these concerns. The Confucians and the Daoists were both quite antipathetic to merely "disputing about names (words)." It was not until the middle of the Warring States period that the later Moists emerged with their interest in thinking about the relationship between names/words and reality. At that time, Moists like Hui Shi and Gongsun Long made names and techniques of disputation the object of their enquiries. With them, thought and disputation about language or the techniques of debate were finally raised to the genuine level of metaphysical study.[67]

4.2

Let us first look at Hui Shi (ca. 380–ca. 305 BCE), Gongsun Long (ca. 325–ca. 250 BCE) and so on who were widely known as scholars interested in debates specifically focused on names/words.

"The World" (Tianxia) chapter of the *Zhuangzi* records that Hui Shi attracted many "rhetoricians" (*bianzhe*) and that Gongsun Long was also famous for his "disputing about names." From this, we can see that for Hui Shi and Gongsun Long "names" (language) became an object of discussion and disputation

---

67 The HS "Yiwen zhi" says that the *Mingjia* practitioners emerged from the ritual officials (*liguan*): "Official ranks (*mingwei*) were different in ancient times, and the rites accorded them also had their distinctions." This means that the original study of names only discussed concrete discriminations of social status; Confucius carried on this tradition, but those who later practiced the study of names/words per se were actually heretics from the point of view of this tradition.

became the central concern of their discourse. This interest in "names" eventually declined, but skill in disputation became a prominent object of thought. That led to a change in intellectual history that was to have far-reaching implications. First, language and reality became separated, and language became a set of mere symbols for the exercise of one's mind. Furthermore rhetoricians began to manipulate these symbols arbitrarily and deliberately violate common sense and the long established language usage. In the end, they made altering and distorting language itself the content of their philosophical disputations.

Most of Hui Shi's argumentation has been lost, and we now have only the few materials presented in the *Zhuangzi*. Below are a few examples of Hui Shi's use of contradictory language to undermine ordinary common sense.

(1) Normally the ideas that "Heaven is high and noble and Earth is low and humble," "the mountain is high and the lake is low," the sun rises and sets and the ten thousand things are born and die are were all regarded as self-evident general knowledge.[68] Hui Shi said, however, if we start from the point of view that "the largest thing has nothing beyond it" and "the smallest thing has nothing within it," then there can simply be no distinction between high and noble, low and humble, above and below, rising and setting and birth and death—all of these changes are simply the result of human feelings and cognition. If we eliminate humanity's stubborn anthropocentric standpoint, how could there be any spatial difference between Heaven, Earth, mountains, lakes, far, near, high and low? How could there be such changes as the sun rising, the moon going down, birth and life and decline and death?

(2) Hui Shi said that everything in the universe has a name, and different names imply differences in shape, color and nature, but these differences are only relative because, looked at from the largest scope, all things are still similar. Goats, horses and bulls are all animals (*dongwu*, "things that move"), but, looked at from the standpoint of the tiniest things, goats, horses and bulls are also all "material things" (*wu*) and all such things are also different. Following this logic, Hui Shi then said that "the ten thousand things are all similar and are all different."[69]

(3) He also stated that "south and north" are only directions determined from one particular position and "present and past" are only times deter-

---

68   The first quotation is from the *Yijing*, "*Xici zhuan, shang*," #1, Lynn, *Changes*, 47; the second is a reference to *Yijing*, Hexagram (*gua*) 41: Diminution (Sun 損), Lynn, *Changes*, 387–396, "Below the Mountain, there is the Lake: Diminution," 388. Other scholars, like Watson in next quotation, have "marshes" rather than "lake."

69   Watson, CT, 374.

mined from one particular set time. If we consider them from a point of view that transcends both time and space, then there would be no such concepts as south or north or the present or the past.

(4) Linked rings cannot be separated, but the "matter" (*wu*) of a linked ring is always created in some time and some space, and also has to be destroyed in some time and space. From the point of view of transcendent people, the destruction of the ring's matter is the separation of the linked ring. Hence, "linked rings can be separated."[70]

(5) The center of "all under Heaven" is only a man-made central point and it has no particular significance. When humanity dwells in the world, every observer can map out a cosmos with himself at its center. When we realize, however, the unboundedness of "the largest thing has nothing beyond it" and that the immeasurably vast cosmos really has no center, then we can overcome humanity's stubborn and narrow-minded view of center and periphery and undermine all absolute human positions and perspectives. We can say with Hui Shi that "I know the center of the world: it is north of Yan and south of Yue."[71] Yan refers to the farthest northern region and Yue to the farthest southern region in China at that time. Apparently Hui Shi is asserting the contradictory proposition that the center is north of the northernmost north and south of the southernmost south.

The significance of these propositions was to undermine the certainty people obtained from common sense knowledge and the stubbornness they derived from language. Hui Shi wanted people to start from "the One of largeness" (*da* yi, derived from "the largest thing has nothing beyond it") and "the One of smallness" (*xiao yi*, derived from "the smallest thing has nothing within it") in order to understand that the myriad things and affairs "are all similar and are all different." This would undermine humanity's fixed and narrow-minded perspective and help people to obtain an open-minded attitude toward everything in the world. The purport of Hui Shi's thought was that it would eliminate people's anxieties and perplexities about concrete knowledge and value judgments, allow people to obtain relaxation, liberation and freedom, and lead them to understand how to "let love embrace the ten thousand things; [because] Heaven and earth are a single body."[72] In as much as the myriad things and affairs have no absolute distinctions, mountains and lakes, and Heaven and earth are neither high and low or far and near, Yan in the north and Yue in the south are both in the center of Heaven and earth, and goats,

---

70   *Ibid.*
71   *Ibid.*, 375.
72   *Ibid.*

horses, bulls and dogs are all of the same category, then everything returns to the One (Unity) and people have no reasons to maintain different feelings toward any phenomenon in the world.

We should say that Hui Shi's views of knowledge and language were quite close to those of Zhuangzi.[73] They both hoped to transcend the distinctions created by language and the limitations created by knowledge and to reach the realm of freedom by "making all things equal and regarding life and death as one." They had their difference, however. Zhuangzi employed an attitude of "fasting of the mind" (*xinzhai*), "sitting down and forgetting everything" (*zuowang*) and "mindless[ness]" (*wuxin*) to achieve spiritual transcendence.[74] Hui Shi, though, wanted to employ names/words—disputations about language—to destroy language, undermine humanity's customary stubbornness about language and common sense in order to seek a realm of freedom and transcendence.

4.3

If we say that Hui Shi's views were similar to those of the so-called Daoists in that his way of thinking still employed "making all things equal" to undermine differences of language and in his partiality for "harmonizing sameness and difference," then Gongsun Long seems to have emphasized "separateness of hardness and whiteness" (*li jian bai* 離堅白).

Two of Gongsun Long's propositions are in his essays "On the White Horse" and "On Hardness and Whiteness."

In "On the White Horse," he asserted that "a white horse is not a horse" (*bai ma fei ma* 白馬非馬) The relevant passage is:

A. "Is it correct to say that a white horse is not a horse?"
B. "It is."
A. "Why?"

---

73   The *Zhuangzi* also has such passages as ". . . where there is birth there must be death; . . . There is nothing in the world bigger than the tip of an autumn hair, and Mount T'ai is tiny. . . . Heaven and earth were born at the same time I was, and the ten thousand things are one with me." All from "Discussion on Making All Things Equal," Watson, CT, 39 & 43. One phrase in "The Sign of Virtue Complete," particularly demonstrates Zhuangzi's position: "If you look at them from the point of view of their differences, then there is liver and gall, Ch'u and Yüeh. But if you look at them from the point of view of their sameness, then the ten thousand things are all one." Watson, CT, 69. This shows that Zhuangzi and Huizi both agreed that "the ten thousand things are all one."

74   Watson, CT, 57–58; 90–91; 237.

B. "Because 'horse' denotes the form (*xing* 形) and 'white' denotes the color (*se* 色). What denotes the color does not denote the form. Therefore we say that a white horse is not a horse."

For Gongsun Longzi, "horse" is a linguistic term (word) that denotes "form" while "white" is a linguistic term (word) that denotes "color." One could also call for a yellow horse, a brown horse or a black horse, but when you call for a "white horse" the others cannot answer. According to his logic:

Now the yellow and the black horse remain the same. And yet they answer to a horse but not to a white horse. Obviously a horse is not a horse.[75]

This proposition seems to be a purely linguistic game in which language and the concrete entities of the phenomenal world have been separated. "On Hardness and Whiteness" is similar too but also somewhat different from "On the White Horse." In "On Hardness and Whiteness," Gongsun Longzi argues as follows:

A. "Is it correct that hardness, whiteness, and stone are three?"
B. "No."
A. "Is it correct that they are two?"
B. "Yes."[76]

Why is it not all right for them to be divided into "three," but all right for them to be divided into "two?" Because Gongsun Long believed that hardness, whiteness and stone were one concrete thing, if we split them into the three parts— hard, white and stone—it will not work. Why? Because without stone, the "hardness" and "whiteness" do not exist. It is all right, however, if we separate them into a hard stone and a white stone. Why is this all right?

Let's examine Gongsun Long's strategy here. First, he transforms hardness, whiteness and stone into one term. Second, he transforms the content (connotations) of this term into human perceptions. Finally, he separates these human perceptions, according to the sense organ involved, into the senses of sight and touch. According to Gongsun Long's view, "hardness" from the sense of touch and "whiteness" from the sense of sight can stand alone and be

75   Wang Guan, *Gongsun Long xuanjie*, 1992, 34–35. *Gongsun Longzi*, chapter 2, Chan, SB, 235–236.

76   Wang Guan, *Gongsun Long xuanjie*, 77. *Gongsun Longzi*, Chapter 5, Chan, SB, 240–241.

separated from the concrete world and exist in the world of language, and so "hardness" and "whiteness" can be separated.

In the phenomenal world, however, hard, white stone is one integral whole, and form, color and nature also form one integral whole. In this regard, the later Moists, who emphasized the experiential world, did not at all agree with Gongsun Longzi on this. The *Mozi*, states clearly that "Hard and white do not exclude each other."[77] They are only separated in the realms of perception and language. If the function of language is to describe and illustrate the world, then the proposition that "hardness and whiteness are separate" is meaningless. If the function of language is divorced from the world, the proposition that "hardness and whiteness are separate" would be all right, but what significance would a language have if it was divorced from the world of reality?

In the time of Hui Shi and Gongsun Long, disputations about language were said to be quite fashionable; these disputations came up with various outlandish propositions. The following are but a few:

An egg has feathers.
A chicken has three legs.
Ying contains the whole world.
A dog can be considered a sheep.
Horses lay eggs.
Toads have tails. Fire is not hot.[78]

These disputations on names (language) were originally intended to undermine common sense and spread enlightened thinking. When these disputations became nothing more than pure argument for argument's sake, however, their significance for intellectual history began to change. They were no longer closely related to the phenomenal world; their Dao was brought down to the level of a few artful techniques; their intellectual explorations were reduced to mere cleverness. For all these reasons, many thinkers did not much favor this sort of disputational concept of language.

4.4

On the surface, the ideas of the later Moists—emphasis on experience, knowledge and logic—would seem to have some definite similarities with these rhetoricians' concept of language. The *Mozi*, "Canon A," says that what is used to refer to or indicate something is a name (*ming*); what is being referred to or

---

77   *Mozi jiangu*, 1986, j. 10, 284. Johnston, *Mozi*, "Canons A," A67, 431.
78   *Zhuangzi*, "Tianxia," *zzjs*, 1105–1106; Watson, CT, 375.

indicated is an entity (*shi*, reality); name and entity/reality are really not the same thing. This line of thought seems to be similar to that of the rhetoricians or disputers.[79]

The later Moists differed form the rhetoricians, though, in that they did not really separate language from reality; they rather emphasized much more the relationship between names and reality (entities). They believed that language (names) should be employed to symbolize real things (entities). Furthermore, they believed that it was not enough to have individual, "particularizing" (*si*) words (names); there must also be classification (*lei*) and generalization (*da*) before one can bring clear order to the phenomenal world. They pointed out that "thing" (*wu*) is a general term, but one must employ the "particular name" (*siming* 私名) before one can clearly distinguish each and every thing. Only through "classificatory names" (*leiming*) can one carry out the systematization of the phenomenal world. Because language (names) can transmit knowledge and point to the world of reality, it should be correct and succinct. Obviously the later Moists did not regard language as a mere collection of symbols for the exercise of one's mind; they regarded it as a cognitive tool for understanding the experiential world. They maintained that names and reality (entities) should match and that the recognition and knowledge of reality should be accomplished through the use of the most suitable and well matched names.

Since language has such significance, the next question, then, was how to make names and reality match. The trend of thought of the later Moists was as follows: First, one must affirm the powers of cognition of human experience and rational intellect. Second, one must believe that these powers of cognition are able to use names/words/language to describe and transmit information about the world. Third, they separated names into the three categories of "generalising," "classifying," and "particularising," that is, large, medium and small. Fourth and finally, they used the different methods of "transferring" (*yi*)

---

79   The *Mozi*, "Canon A," has the following passage:
      C: *Ming* (a name) [may be] "generalising" (*da*), "classifying" (*lei*) or "particularising" (*si*).
      E: *Ming* (a name): "thing" (*wu*) is generalising [*da*]. If there is an entity (*shi*), it necessarily gets this name. Naming it "horse" is classifying [*lei*]. If it is an entity like this, it is necessarily named by this. Naming someone Zang is particularising [*si*]. This name stops at (is limited to) this entity. The words issuing from the mouth all are names—like the pairing of surname and style. Johnston, *Mozi*, "Canons A," A79, 443. Johnston's "Comment" to A31, on page 398, explains the translation of *shi* (reality) as "entity." Brackets [ ] indicate additions.

"raising/picking out" (*ju*), and "applying/adding" (*jia*) to account for the linguistic functions of generalization, description and indication.[80]

They believed, then, that human beings could interpret and master the phenomenal world by means of language. They held that disputation should be used to distinguish right from wrong, point out the differences between good governance and chaos, illuminate similarities and differences, investigate the relationship between names and reality, manage advantage and disadvantage (gain and loss) and confirm or deny suspicions. Therefore the first important thing was to have good reasons for believing something; second, one must make reasonable analogies; and third, the meaning and boundary conditions of linguistic formulations must be clear. The implications of these ideas are that the later Moists believed that the crucial relationship between names and reality was that names coincide with reality and that human knowledge can make names and reality mutually coincide. In this way, they did not strip language away from the world. They believed that human beings were able to know and master the world and that language could point to that world. People must rationally distinguish the differences between language and the world, confidently determine the significance of linguistic analyses, inductions and descriptions of the world, and optimistically believe in the functions of language. They also believed that human beings could at least systematize and bring order to the phenomenal world by means of language. We should say that this is a rationalist concept of language and it also represents their conclusions about language and the world.[81]

4.5

There was still another opposing view of language—the suspicion of language put forth by Zhuangzi and his followers.

This suspicion of language came first from their misgivings about linguistic determinacy. Every name for any phenomenon lends that phenomenon a certain determinacy. History, though, is constantly changing and depriving everything of any eternal determinacy. Changes between names and reality regularly cause the connotations and distinctions of words to loose their significance. This situation is exactly the same as what we read in the *Zhuangzi*: "The life of

---

80   Johnston, *Mozi*, Chapter 40, "Canons A," A 80, 442–443. Johnston's comment on page 442 reads: "Thus 'transferring' refers to the transfer of the same name from one entity to another, i.e. a pup may be called a dog; 'referring' or 'raising' is picking out separate entities, i.e. a pup or a dog; whilst 'applying' or 'adding' is the application of an additional word-meaning…"

81   See Hu Shi, *Zhongguo zhexueshi da gang* (1919) in *Hu Shi xueshu wenji* (*Zhongguo zhexueshi*), 1991, 154.

things is a gallop, a headlong dash—with every movement they alter, with every moment they shift."[82]

Zhuangzi and his followers seem to have been dissatisfied with the contemporary ideas both of names as reality and of names as names. The former could easily fall into a stubborn and limiting attachment to names. Take "left" and "right" for example. Originally there was no left or right, but when a person is in a fixed position and chooses a fixed direction, then prominence is given to left and right. As soon as left and right are firmly established, people can no longer freely change their position and direction. It is the same with right and wrong and this and that. In fact, Zhuangzi would ask rhetorically, if one transcends specific coordinates and looks at these differences from a vast spatial and a very long temporal vantage point, what is the difference between any of them? And so, the *Zhuangzi* says ". . . those who divide fail to divide; those who discriminate fail to discriminate."[83] The latter idea of taking names as names, separating names and reality and exercising the mind exclusively on names was not part of the quest of Zhuangzi and his followers.

The *Zhuangzi* criticizes Hui Shi for getting mired down in various terms and concepts, such that ". . . he went on tirelessly separating and analyzing the ten thousand things, and in the end was known only for his skill in exposition. What a pity[!] . . ." A similar critique was leveled at Gongsun Long and other rhetoricians. According to Zhuangzi, "they could outdo others in talking, but could not make them submit in their minds . . ." and they did not, "really plumb the depths of the true Dao."[84] Zhuangzi and his followers were clearly opposed to disputes about right and wrong because they were bogged down with various names/words and did not understand when "you look at them from the point of view of their difference, it is like that of liver versus gall, and Ch'u versus Yueh. But if you look at them from the point of view of their sameness, then the ten thousand things are all one.' "[85] This "one" was of course the everlasting and transcendent Dao.

In "Autumn Floods" (Qiushui), the *Zhuangzi* argues that language can be used to discuss concrete and individual things, but intuition and ideas can be used to understand the abstract notions of ordinary thought and philosophy. There is something else, however, that even language and consciousness cannot reach, and that is the ultimately mysterious Dao—"the Dao that can be spoken, is not the constant Dao" (*Laozi*, 1). The *Zhuangzi* ranks writing (*wenzi*,

---

82   ZZJS, j. 6, "Qiushui," 585. Watson, CT, 182.

83   ZZJS, j. 1, "Qiwulun," 83. Watson, CT, 44.

84   ZZJS, j. 10, "Tianxia," 1111–1112. Quotes from Watson, CT, 377 and 376.

85   ZZJS, j. 2, "Dechongfu," 190. Modified from Watson, CT, 69.

characters, script), language and meaning in that order. It argues that the vulgar world prized accounts written down in words, but accounts written down in words are nothing more than language. True value, however, resides in the Dao that cannot be transmitted by the use of language. Zhuangzi lamented the fact that human beings only understand forms, colors, names and sounds, but these things really have no true value. Therefore "those who know do not speak; those who speak do not know."[86]

For Zhuangzi, language was only a tool and not an object of study. He believed that people should understand that "The fish trap exists because of the fish; once you've gotten the fish, you can forget the trap.... Words exist because of meaning; once you've gotten the meaning, you can forget the words."[87] People should employ a pure, unpolluted and tranquil mind to understand the Dao. They have to forget rational language, forget organs of feeling, and forget all of their accumulated experience and knowledge. In this way, for the Daoists, the art of disputation about names also had no intellectual standing.

4.6

Unlike Zhuangzi and his followers, the later followers of Confucius continued to be quite enthusiastic about the regulative powers of language. They still believed that language not only could discuss all phenomena and express all thought, but that it also had the normative power to regulate and adjust to changing phenomena. They also believed that once the relationship between names and reality was established through common usage, then names or words became reality (things). In their view, the proper usage of language was an extremely serious affair because the improper use of language could result in social chaos. Social order, for them, was to be regulated and maintained by the correct use of names. Confusion in the use of names and reality could lead to a situation in which "what is noble and base is unclear, and things that are alike and things that are different are not distinguished." There must be distinctions in names, and reality must be comprehended by means of names. The *Xunzi* calls this "institut[ing] names to refer to objects [*shi*, reality]."[88] That is, deciding on a name for something and then using the name to confirm, regulate and adjust objects and events in the real world.

---

86   zzjs, j. 5, 488. Watson, ct, 235. Also in *Laozi*, 56: "He who knows does not speak. He who speaks does not know." Chan, sb, 166.

87   zzjs, j. 9, "Waiwu" (External Things), 944. Watson, ct, 302.

88   Knoblock, *Xunzi*, "On the Correct Use of Names," 22.2b, 128–129.

According to Xunzi's ideas, language has to be regularized. One has to clearly distinguish terms of "the greatest generality" (*da gongming* 大共名) like *wu*, "thing," "names of the largest divisions of things" (*da bieming* 大別名) like "bird" and "animal" and names that "draw distinctions" (*bieming*) like "turtle dove" (*jiu* 鳩).[89] Organizing names this way, the taxonomy of the phenomenal world and the cosmic order of the conceptual world will not become disordered. In the same manner, by employing this type of terminology, in which different levels and ranks are clearly demarcated, to regulate society, one can bring order to a disorderly society.

Xunzi sternly criticized the fashion of carrying on disputations about names for "caus[ing] the people to be suspicious [and] multiplying arguments and litigation among them."[90] Nevertheless, he supported the Confucian "rectification of names (language)" because he believed it to be an effective method for straightening out social order. The reasoning of the later Legalists "demanding that names and reality match" (*xunming yi zeshi* 循名以則實) can be seen to have developed out of these ideas about language.

It should be noted that the idea of "demanding that names and reality match" represented an extremely rational and clear-headed realism. In an age that was no longer very romantic or idealistic, people started to pay more attention to practical problems and were no longer so interested in purely linguistic ideas and empty disputations about names. Ideas similar to Xunzi's came to capture the mainstream, and the Warring States rhetoricians—later to be known as the School of Names—disappeared. Their sort of purely linguistic thought and analysis also exited the stage of intellectual history; it was not until the writings of the Consciousness Only School of Buddhism (Yogâcâra, *weishi zong*) and the sharp-witted *gong-an* sayings (*koan* in Japanese) of Chan Buddhism emerged during the Tang dynasty that such thinking briefly reappeared. The Chinese people who were most concerned with practical issues seemed no longer to welcome these purely linguistic disputations, while those who were seeking spiritual transcendence did not want to become indulge in linguistic games. It is most interesting, however, that in later times the School of Names eventually developed into a study of how to evaluate people's moral conduct and social status. Arising out the Confucian idea of "rectification of names," the Warring States School of Names developed through Hui Shi, Gongsun Long, the later Moists, Zhuangzi and his followers and then returned again to the "rectification of names (language)" of the Confucian school. This was certainly a most thought-provoking historical development.

---

89   *Ibid.*, 22.2f, 130.

90   *Ibid.*, 22.1c, 128. *Xunzi jijie*, j. 3, 59, 62.

CHAPTER 4

Intellectual Convergence in the Qin and Han Dynasties, from ca. the 3rd Century BCE to ca. the Mid-2nd Century CE

Prologue: Coda to the Hundred Schools of Thought Contending

The Spring and Autumn and Warring States period was a glorious age in Chinese intellectual history during which China formed its own characteristic systems of knowledge, thought and belief, and these systems dominated the following two thousand years of Chinese intellectual history.

However, if we pay closer attention to the intellectual tendencies of later generations, we cannot but attend more closely to the phenomenon of intellectual convergence that took place during the period from the late Warring States to the early Western Han. There are a number of reasons why we should do so. First, it was during this period of time that the ancient Chinese knowledge of the cosmos, society and humanity genuinely coalesced into one grand system. Second, the Chinese intellectual world after the unification of the Qin and Han was built upon the foundation of this large, complex, organized system of knowledge. It constituted the background of Chinese culture, combining humanistic and social thought as well as various sorts of knowledge for practical application. Third, the "breakthrough" that took place during China's "axial age" was different from that in other civilizations. It was not a rejection of or a rupture with past thought and culture; it was rather an inclusion and a continuation of compatible elements—a continuation that included reorganization and new interpretations. Scholars early on summed up the intellectual characteristics of this period as having a tendency towards eclecticism. Indeed, whether it was the Huang-Lao in the early Han or the Confucian doctrines, they both embraced, in their different ways, mutually related phenomena like the Legalist methods of matching names with results (*xingming fashu*), magic arts, preservation of life, immortals, arts of war, Yin and Yang and medical, mantic and numerological arts. All this represented a tendency toward the gradual convergence of systems of knowledge and thought between the end of the Warring States and the Qin-Han era.

Recent archeological discoveries have also provided us with more new materials with which to outline the intellectual trajectory of this period. If we regard the ever increasing store of Qin and Han archeological discoveries as

© KONINKLIJKE BRILL NV, LEIDEN, 2014 | DOI 10.1163/9789047425076_006

materials that embody ordinary people's knowledge and thought, then things like silk paintings, wall frescoes, portraits in stone, terra cotta figures and bronze and jade funerary objects can also tell us a great deal about the mentality of the people of that era. If we collect and examine the extant literary remains, regard the large trove of recently unearthed silk manuscripts as background materials for the interpretation and understanding of contemporary intellectual phenomena, and have reference to the various types of archeological discoveries, it should not be difficult to discern that the main intellectual trend of the time was to continue moving forward on the intellectual path laid down in the past. First, various forms of past knowledge of the cosmos, society and human life (Heaven, Earth and the Human in ancient Chinese terms) was gradually systematized and blended together. Second, these same forms of knowledge were given identical metaphysical foundations and came to be regarded as self-evident in nature. Third, the metaphysical foundations and material operations of knowledge and thought—the ancient Chinese "Way/Dao" and techniques (or arts, *shu*)—were then connected and formed a set of norms and models.

Although the First Emperor of the Qin dynasty (r. 247–210 BCE) is said to have "burned books and buried scholars," people continued to think, and their thinking was still quite vigorous even under much political pressure during the chaotic time before the Qin-Han unification.[1] In the Han dynasty, however, due to the establishment of a unified dynasty and the tendency toward a unified consciousness, intellectual history moved from the *Zhuangzi's* "the art of the Way in time came to be rent and torn apart by the world" to the *Huainanzi's* "the hundred schools have different specializations, yet they all strive to rule (govern *zhi*)."[2] For the sake of ruling or governing, thought had to be re-integrated into one unified and all-inclusive system that would set out a model encompassing both theoretical explanations and interpretations and a practical system of government. This process was known as "returning to unity" and "the integration of the Way and the arts of government." From the end of the Warring States period, as political unification was about to be established,

---

1 For the history of the "burning of the books" and the related "burying of the scholars," see Derk Bodde's "The State and Empire of the Qin," in the CHC, vol. 1, 1986, 69–72 (a general account) and 94–96 (discussion of "interpolations in the *Shiji*").

2 Burton Watson, CT, 364. "Comes" has been changed to "came" to fit this context. Translation slightly modified from John S. Major, Sarah A. Queen, Andrew Seth Meyer, and Harold D. Roth, trans. and eds., *The Huainanzi: A Guide to the Theory and Practice of Government in Early Han China*, 2010, "Boundless Discourses" (Fanlun), 13.5: "The hundred lineages [of learning] have different specializations, yet all strive for [good] governance."

various thinkers were already at work constructing this grand ideological system. From the *Annals of Lü Buwei* to the *Huainanzi*, they all manifested their intention to create one unified system of their own. This vast tendency toward eclecticism, amalgamation and re-integration constituted the mainstream of the intellectual world during those hundred years and more.

The "Hundred Schools of Thought Contending" came to an end not just because the First Emperor of the Qin "burned the books and buried the scholars" or Emperor Wudi (the Marshal Emperor, r. 140–87 BCE) of the Han "banned the hundred schools of thought."[3] It was also because eclecticism and amalgamation had already made the various schools so compatible that the boundaries between them were increasingly blurred. The price for unification of thought is often the loss of independent characteristics, but this was something about which nothing could be done. History generally proceeds by means of such unavoidable changes about which nothing can be done.

1. General Knowledge Background and Intellectual Achievement in the Qin and Han Dynasties

The archeological finds discovered in the Han tombs at Mawangdui in Changsha in the 1970s have given us unprecedented materials for a new understanding of the Qin and Han intellectual world. Prior to these discoveries, historians had only relied on the *Records of the Grand Historian*, the *History of the Former Han Dynasty* and a few other ancient records to understand the intellectual world of these two early dynasties, but the silk manuscripts and paintings from Mawangdui have unfolded to us a rather different world from that previously described in our intellectual histories.[4] Because the reading materials placed in these tombs consist of the books that were read and enjoyed by the occupant of the tomb, they show us the scope of his reading and they represent a contemporary reading community. From these books and this reading community, we can survey the general scope of reading at the time, and that in turn reveals to us the level of intellectual achievement and the interests of the age.

A great deal of knowledge about many subjects is included in the Mawangdui silk manuscripts and paintings. In general they include classic texts, Confucian texts on the *Book of Changes* and Five Phases theory, texts on the Yellow Emperor and Laozi, records of recent history, and mantic, medical and numerological arts, including punishment and reward, medicine and medical prescriptions,

---

3   As recorded in HS, "Wudi ji." For Han Wudi's reign see Michael Loewe, "The Former Han Dynasty," in the CHC, vol. 1, 1986, 152–179.

4   See He Jiejun and Zhang Weiming, eds., *Mawangdui Hanmu*, 1982, 71–75.

divination and breathing exercises. There were also records of contemporary techniques related to sacrifice, burial and funeral practices. When we further examine other recent archeological finds—the Qin tombs at Shuihudi; the Han tombs from Shuanggudui, Fuyang county, Anhui and Bajiaolang in Ding county, Hebei; Yinqueshan in Linyi county, Shandong; and Zhangjiashan in Jiangling county, Hubei, etc.—we see that this knowledge corresponds very nicely to the summary found in the "Monograph of Arts and Letters" section of the *History of the Former Han Dynasty*: the six arts, various philosophers, poetry, military texts, mantic and numerological arts and medical techniques. This bibliographical classification represents precisely the condition of the intellectual world during the Qin and Han eras. At that time, people were not only concerned with the philosophy of the Way of Heaven, how to govern the world, and the ethics of human society, they were also interested in various forms of practical knowledge and techniques. In their intellectual world and mode of thinking, all of this thought, knowledge, and their related techniques were part of a vast intellectual system. Intellectual history cannot and should not ignore the existence and significance of this background of general knowledge and its intellectual level of achievement.

1.1

From the existing literary remains, we can see that the Qin-Han people had other thoughts and beliefs aside from Huang-Lao and Confucian ideas. According to the *Records of the Grand Historian* "Treatise on the Feng and Shan Sacrifices" (Feng shan shu) and the *History of the Former Han Dynasty* "Treatise on the Suburban Sacrifices" (Jiaosi zhi), various areas practiced different sacrifices. For example, the Qi state region (modern Shandong) sacrificed to the Eight Spirits (*bashenjiang* 八神將)—the Lord of Heaven, Lord of the Land/ Earth, Lord of Arms, Lord of the Yin, Lord of the Yang, Lord of the Moon, Lord of the Sun, Lord of the Four Seasons;[5] the Qin state region (modern Shaanxi) sacrificed to famous mountains, big rivers, great burial mounds and the spirits of the stars, but as the *Records of the Grand Historian* says "... the Lords on High [who were] worshiped at the four Altars of Yung were regarded as the most honorable of the gods."[6] From the "Nine Songs" and the Chu bamboo slip manuscripts from Wangshan and Baoshan, we know that the Chu region (modern Hunan and Hubei) had a set of well-organized sacrifices with the Great One, Lord of the Eastern World (*Donghuang Taiyi* 東皇太一) as their

5   *Shiji*, 28, translated in Watson, *Records of the Grand Historian*, 1996 (1961), vol. 2, 13–69; sacrifices to the Eight Spirits are discussed on 24–25. HS, j. 25, 1202–1203.
6   HS, j., 25 1207–1209; Watson, *Grand Historian*, vol. 2, 29.

chief recipient.[7] In the Han dynasty, the government still followed these sacrificial customs and had an eclectic and syncretic attitude toward the beliefs of the various regions. Again according to the *History of the Former Han Dynasty* "Treatise on the Suburban Sacrifices" (Jiaosi zhi), the sacrificial traditions of the Liang (Henan), Jin (Shanxi), Qi and Qin regions were all officially permitted. The only change made was in the Qin court's most important sacrifices to the Lords on High of the four Altars of Yung. Han Gaozu (the founder of the Han, Liu Bang, r. 202–195 BCE) created the Altar of the North for sacrifices to the Black Lord of the North so as to have Five Heavenly Lords or Gods (*Di*) corresponding to the Five Phases, five colors and five directions.[8]

To maintain any belief requires a store of knowledge and a set of techniques; divination by the four winds and the five tones, geomancy, astrological divination by the stars and choosing auspicious days were all widespread techniques that were believed in by both the general population and the nobility at that time. The "Punishments and Rewards" (Xingde) silk manuscript from Mawangdui is a record of techniques used by Five Phases adepts, while the Han dynasty bamboo slip *Book of Changes* from Shuanggudui is a practical guide to divination.[9] Divination plates in the shape of Heaven and Earth with astrological diagrams unearthed from various locations demonstrate contemporary people's interests in the positional correspondences in the orbits of earth and the heavenly constellations and their firm belief in their astrological predictions of good and evil fortune. This general knowledge both supported the beliefs of the common people and influenced the psychology of the nobility and the rulers.

1.2

From predominately pictorial archeological materials, we can also understand the background knowledge and intellectual situation of Qin and Han dynasty people. Based on their experiences, the people of the Qin and Han believed that there was definitely some kind of mysterious relationship between symbols and the phenomena they represented. These pictorial objects were not necessarily just simple works of art; they might have some kind of practical and mystical implications. It is said, for example, that during Han Wudi's reign, the adept (magician, *fangshi*) Shao Weng could use painted portraits to call down the spirits. He is said to have painted chariots in the shape of clouds and

7   The "Nine Songs" are in Hawkes, *Songs of the South*, 1962, 36–44.
8   HS, j. 25, 1210. Watson, *Grand Historian*, vol. 2, 31.
9   See Marc Kalinowski, "The *Xingde* 刑德 Texts from Mawangdui," *Early China*, 23–24 (1998–99), 125–202.

then rode the chariots on the five auspicious days (corresponding to the Five Phases) in order to avoid evil spirits, and to have painted various deities such as the Great Unity, Heaven and Earth to invite down the spirits of Heaven.[10] Such experiences probably occurred quite early on, and so we believe that these symbolic images with their mystical and practical applications embodied some genuine contemporary ideas. From the rather large number of Qin and Han silk paintings, portraits on stone and wall frescoes we can discern a number of themes, but the ones that occur most are people's imaginings about the unknown and the world after death.

On the four sides of the Chu silk manuscripts from Zidanku in Changsha there are portraits of twelve gods or spirits whose names we do not know. They have monstrous shapes that seem to reveal people's imagination of another "non-human" world. Another silk painting, the so-called "rising dragon" (*shenglong tu* 升龍圖)—a man brandishing a sword and riding a dragon and a phoenix—seems to demonstrate even more the contemporary people's longings for another world. In Han times this world still occupied much of the general knowledge and thought system. It was embodied in particularly captivating form in silk paintings, portraits on stone and wall frescoes, especially those silk paintings from tomb number nine at Jinqueshan in Linyi county, Shandong. The top level has the three-legged Golden Crow (*jinwu* 金烏) that lives in the sun and the toad that lives in the moon; the middle level depicts the ordinary world of humanity; and the bottom level has two back to back dragons.[11] The Han tomb at Mawangdui has a similar silk painting. On the top are the chief deities of Heaven as well as the Golden Crow, Fusang (an ancient mythical island), the toad and a dragon; in the middle are the occupants of the tomb and their servants; and on the bottom are two large fish and a giant holding up the great earth. All of these images express the Han people's picture of the difference between their world of the living and the other world of the spirits and the dead. People lived in this world, but they longed for the mystical other world and revered the after-death world to come.

Most of the Han dynasty wall frescoes discovered so far date from the late Western Han (202 BCE–8 CE) to the Eastern Han (25–220 CE), but the general knowledge, thought and intellectual level was unlikely to have undergone any great changes in a short period of time. For this reason, we can still rely on this material for an understanding of a more extensive range of Qin and Han knowledge and thought, and we can see many other similar images. Although

---

10   HS, j. 25, 1219.

11   See "Fajue jianbao," *Wenwu* 11 (1977), 24–26, and Sahara Yasuo, "Kandai shidô kasho ko, *Tôhô gakuhô* 63 (1991), 26.

there are fewer frescoes depicting the occupant of the tomb ascending to become an immortal (*shenxian*) and more that depict his life before he died, this does not mean that past understandings and concepts of the non-human world did not remain an important part of social life. Actually the conception of a mysterious world, belief in mysterious powers and worship of Heaven and Earth in general knowledge, thought and belief always dominated people's understanding of life. We can still see these conceptions at work everywhere in the Eastern Han portraits in stone. On the portraits in stone from late Western and early Eastern Han tombs, we frequently encounter subject matter depicting ideas about ascending to become an immortal, praying to avoid epidemics and warding off evil spirits. The structure and themes of the portraits in stone in an Eastern Han tomb from Zhoucheng, Gaoli village in Shandong describe scenes similar to the wall frescoes previously discussed. The first portrait in stone has the three-legged Golden Crow that lives in the sun and a figure with the face of a man and the body of a dragon holding up the earth; the second one shows an immortal feeding a mythological dragon and phoenix; two sides of the third stone depict dancing immortals.[12]

1.3

Bronze mirrors offer another type of archeological material that can also reflect people's ideas about life. There are inscriptions on the backs of most of these mirrors. Of course the inscriptions are usually full of much used auspicious clichés, but they do in general reveal contemporary thoughts; they can be divided into at least three categories. The first category expresses a desire for everlasting life; they hope to extend life in this world and envy the eternal freedom of the immortals: "a thousand autumns and ten thousand years," "as everlasting as Heaven and Earth," "extend life and ward off evil" and so on.

The second category expresses the desire for happiness in this world. The mark of this desired "happiness" was usually wealth and high status: "happy with nothing to do, pleased with oneself, meeting a beautiful woman, being entertained by pipe and harp" and including also "a regulated market with fair goods, health and strength in old age as well as a smooth and peaceful rebirth." Both business and pleasure had to be successful, and so they hoped for "great happiness, wealth, high status, and obtaining all things desirable" plus "long life with good food and drink." Another aspect of "happiness" was a harmonious and united family life, and so the mirror inscriptions included things like "I feel sad thinking of you, and hope you are faithful to me;..." "when you are unhappy, I hope you will always think on me; when you joined the army, my heart ached; not seeing you for a long time, I have been unable to serve you."

---

12   "Shandong Zhoucheng Gaolicun Han Huaxiang shimu," *Wenwu* 6 (1994), 25–27.

Of course the most realistic way to gain everlasting life was to do so genera-tionally—to produce an unbroken line of descendents. There are quite a few inscriptions expressing this sentiment, like "seven sons and eight grandsons residing at home; husband and wife accompanying each other time without end; let them have good fortune and their descendants prosper" and so on.

The third category expresses an early stage of contemporary people's con-cept of living in a unified state. At that time the great vigilance against the barbarians of the four directions (the *yi, rong, man*, and *di* of east, west, south and north) and the ever increasing knowledge of the border regions magnified people's consciousness of the "Chinese state." The mirror inscriptions include many that demonstrate that the concept of "state" (*guojia*) was widespread in the Han dynasty. To give one example:

> The X lineage produced this mirror celebrating the submission of the four barbarians and greatly congratulating the state and the people on the achievement of peace. With the destruction of the barbarians, the *tianxia* has been restored, and the right rains and winds produce a rich harvest of the five grains.

An inscription from the end of the Western Han also reads

> Banish all bad fortune, and China will experience great peace, sons and grandsons will increase and prosper, and the Yellow Emperor's great good fortune will remain our guiding principle.

An inscription on a bronze mirror unearthed at Yiyang in Hunan contains almost all of the ideals and hopes of the contemporary people:

> The Li lineage produced this mirror celebrating the submission of the four barbarians and greatly congratulating the state and the people on the achievement of peace. With the destruction of the barbarians, the *tianxia* has been restored, and the right rains and winds produce a rich harvest of the five grains. May we receive Heaven's power forever to pre-serve our parents and transmit good fortune forever to their descendants. From time immemorial there have been immortals above who did not know old age. When thirsty, they drink from the Jade Spring; when hun-gry, they eat dates. Husbands and wives (here below) love each other like dignified mandarin ducks, and their descendants prosper forever.[13]

---

13   All items quoted above without citation are from Zhou Shirong, "Hunan chutu Handai tongjing wenzi yanjiu," *Gu wenzi yanjiu* 14 (1986), 69–185.

1.4

At this point we can summarize the general knowledge, thought and belief of the Qin and Han eras.

First, the external "cosmos" or "Heaven and Earth" were still the fundamental bases of understanding and decision making. People of that time believed not only that human beings existed in the time and space created by Heaven, but also that Heaven was the fundamental basis of all their understanding of and decision making about everything. Imitating the structure and movements of Heaven and obeying the rules (laws, regulations) of Heaven was the way that thought and behavior became rational. Not only the general masses believed this; power holders like the Son of Heaven and the nobility also believed that everything was derived from Heaven. The architecture of Qin and Han imperial palaces had to be modeled on the arrangement of the heavens; the ceilings of Han tombs had to be decorated with paintings of the celestial bodies in Heaven on high; the Han imperial family had to offer sacrifices to all of the gods and spirits of Heaven on high; the sacrificial locations had even more to be identical with the arrangement of the celestial bodies. This reverence for and emulation of Heaven was the origin of legitimacy and rationality in everything. In the general knowledge, thought and belief of the age, Heaven continued to occupy a position of incomparable sublimity.

Second, following the ancient Chinese intellectual tradition, the natural rules revealed by "Heaven" were increasingly expressed by a series of numerological concepts, and these concepts were in turn concretized in a number of operational techniques that also linked together Heaven and the Human. The first number was of course one, a concept that could be understood as the center, the absolute, the sacred, or the unique. In the Qin and Han eras, the "one" was the center of the cosmos, the unity of all under Heaven, the power of the ruler, the laws of reason and the cornerstone of knowledge; in other words it was the ultimate foundation of everything. Next came "two" which of course referred to Yin and Yang, but could also symbolize the sun and moon, Heaven and Earth, ruler and officials and up and down (higher and lower). Yin and Yang could be extended further to represent cold and warm, wet and dry, seniors and juniors, noble and base as well as pointing to an entire system of regulatory techniques.[14] Next in importance was "five." People generally believed that

---

14   Take "*yin*" for example. It can be extended to include "moon" (the character for yin has the character for moon on its right side—trs.); some animals are born in "water" and for that reason belong to "*yin*"; they are in the same category as "moon" while at the same time "moon" is related to "water." Changes in these animals could, then, be explained on the basis of the waxing and waning of the moon. As the *Huainanzi* put it:

the Five Phases had the power systematically to arrange everything in the universe and make it both regular and well-ordered, in perfect accord with human reason. If the Five Phases were to become disordered, people would have to employ certain techniques to restore them to order; otherwise, they would suffer from sickness, society would be in disarray and the whole universe would fall into chaos.

Third, the power to connect Heaven, Earth, the Human and the gods and spirits remained in the hands of a small minority of adepts. Most people believed that owing to their unusual natural endowments and training they had the power to communicate with the mysterious world beyond. They were considered both the channels of communication between humanity and Heaven, humanity and ghosts (the dead) and humanity and gods and spirits, and also a screen of obstruction between humanity and Heaven, humanity and ghosts (the dead) and humanity and gods and spirits. People needed to rely on them as intermediaries to communicate with Heaven, the gods and the ancestors. On the one hand, these experts in the occult relied on systematic natural laws to "distinguish the Way of Heaven and Earth, the movement of the Sun and Moon, and the principles of Yin-Yang and Good and Evil."[15] On the other hand, they relied on their secretly transmitted technical arcana to monopolize the techniques, such as ceremonies and other methods, for communication with Heaven, Earth, the Human and the gods. They could use sacrifices and other ceremonies to transmit the wishes of the living to the gods and ghosts, and they could use written charms and curses to confer the power of the gods and ghosts on the living. Even though they lost their position in the intellectual world of the Han dynasty elite, however, their influence on the general public remained steadfast.

Fourth, the issues that people of that age were particularly concerned about included the following three areas. (1) Human life itself. It would seem that the people of the Qin and Han eras believed that human beings could avoid death, but they also believed that achieving immortality was extremely difficult. (2) Happiness. It is obvious that in the general intellectual world of the Qin and Han, freedom and transcendence as the content of human happiness

---

"As the moon waxes and wanes above, snails and clams respond below. Those of the same *qi* bestir each other (*tong qi xiang dong*); they cannot get very far apart." Major, et al., *Huainanzi*, 635, *Huainanzi* 16.33. All at once "moon," "water" and "living creatures" were associated with "*yin*." Once people understood these correspondences, they could employ various techniques to regulate and manage everything, including bodily ailments, social difficulties, military strategy and changes in physical matter.

15   *Shiji*, j. 127, "Rizhe liezhuan," 127.3 in CTP; 3216.

gradually receded to a second order position. The longing for spiritual freedom and transcendence became concretized and vulgarized due to a widespread belief in immortals, and such a longing consequently turned into one for physical freedom and transcendence, that is, into a pursuit of bodily immortality. At the same time, wealth and high status and a greater number of sons and grandsons became an even more practical form of happiness in life. (3) The state (*guojia*). As the Regional States were weakening or being annihilated day by day and the various culture regions were intermingling to form one single cultural community, the people of the Qin and Han began to identify with one another. The term "all under Heaven" was in general a more purely political concept at that time. As people began to have greater geographical knowledge, they came to realize that the area in which they lived and were familiar with was only one part of "all under Heaven." Then they began to use the term "within the seas" (*hainei*). "Within the seas" became a term for Chinese cultural territory. Everyone who lived "within the seas" and shared a common language, common customs, ideas and costume could, in this cultural sense, be considered Chinese. The first Qin Emperor's unification of China was one sign post and Sima Qian's record of Chinese history and validation of the Han dynasty's territory in the *Records of the Grand Historian* was another. Due precisely to this historical work, the term "Han" 漢 became the name of both a people (*minzu*) and a state. We turn our attention now to the intellectual history of the educated class.

2.   Toward a Synthesis of Knowledge and Philosophy: From the
        Luxuriant Dew of the Spring and Autumn Annals to the *Huainanzi*

With the unification of the Qin and Han, thought developed from division toward convergence and synthesis. The struggles between the different Regional Rulers stimulated a different sort of intellectual communication in which various forms of local thought began to converge into one. As travel and communication became more convenient, the pace of this coalescence of thought quickened greatly.

This tendency toward intermingling and coalescence was not actually spurred on only by external causes; the first signs of it in the knowledge and intellectual world had appeared much earlier. The criticisms of various schools of thought in the *Zhuangzi, Xunzi* and *Hanfeizi* were already a kind of general summation. Each of these critics naturally made a certain amount of sense, but they each also had their own biases. Zhuangzi hoped to undermine the foundations of the various schools of thought, but he was still partial to the many

Daoist thinkers outside of the mainstream, and he did not particularly touch upon the social, political and ethical ideas of Confucianism and other schools. Xunzi only presented a general summing up of the common social thought and discourse of the Confucians and the Legalists and so on, but he still could not find a common foundation to link the various schools of thought together. Hanfeizi merely criticized other thinkers on the basis of practical benefits and effectiveness; he only dealt with surface phenomena and never touched upon the intellectual foundations of thought.

Be that as it may, criticism is also a form of dialogue, and as they carried on their critiques these critics came to connect with one another. To carry out a critique, one had to arrive first at a practical understanding and interpretation, and regardless of whether these understandings and interpretations were correct or mistaken, they nevertheless constituted the beginnings of an inter-penetration and intercommunication between different thinkers. At the end of the Warring States period, an intellectual coalescence was already apparent in their works. The most important of these works was the *Annals of Lü Buwei* (Lüshi chunqiu).[16]

2.1

Ying Zheng, the future First Emperor of the Qin dynasty, ascended the throne as King of Qin in 247 BCE.

At that time China was already moving toward political and military unification under the Qin. Lü Buwei (ca. 291–235 BCE), a former merchant turned regent during Ying Zheng's minority, gathered together a group of retainers to compile his encyclopedic *Annals of Lü Buwei*. Lü wanted to present a unified attitude in knowledge and thought, and the tendency toward a comprehensive and encyclopedic summation of thought is readily apparent in this work. Scholars have done a statistic analysis of the classic texts and scholars quoted in the work and concluded that it represents "a great summation of the pre-Qin classics, the various scholars and the hundred schools of thought."[17] Indeed, the *Annals of Lü Buwei* brings together the thought of the major thinkers and schools, including Confucian doctrines, ancient Daoists sayings reputed to

---

16   At the beginning of the twentieth-century Liang Qichao already valued this work greatly, and Hu Shi did some very detailed research on it in 1930. See "Du *Lüshi chunqiu*" in *Hu Shi wencun sanji*, later included in his *Zhongguo zhonggu sixiangshi changbian*, in volume one of *Hushi xueshu wenji*, 1991. The complete English translation of the LSCQ is by John Knoblock and Jeffrey Riegal and entitled *The Annals of Lü Buwei*, 2000.

17   Xu Fuguan, *Lüshi chunqiu ji qi dui Handai xueshu ji zhengzhi de yingxiang*, vol. 2 of *Liang Han sixiangshi*, j. 5 of *Xu Fuguan wenji*, 2002.

belong to the Yellow Emperor, pragmatic ideas of Mozi and the later Moists, and Laozi and Zhuangzi's philosophy of the Way of Heaven and the Way of Humanity. The text quotes and adopts an enormously complex number of earlier ancient texts as well as a comparatively rich store of contemporary texts.[18] It is little wonder that Lü proudly asserted that no one would be able to either enlarge upon or delete from and revise his great work. As he claimed in the "Postface" (Xuyi) of this work: "When this has been accomplished, people will not be ignorant of right and wrong nor of the permissible and impermissible."[19]

Such a claim pretty clearly sums up Lü's ambition to encompass the thought and knowledge of all under Heaven.

Ambition naturally implies confidence, but mere confidence is not enough to establish a vast system of knowledge and thought. The *Annals of Lü Buwei* could not really "encompass the totality of the affairs of Heaven and Earth, of the myriad things, and of the past and present," but it was planned to encompass every manifestation of nature and discuss all the knowledge up to that time within its framework.[20] The "twelve almanacs" of the *Annals* were intended to establish a framework for the inclusions of "the totality of the affairs of Heaven and Earth, of the myriad things, and of the past and present."[21] They follow the rotation of the earth and the changes of the four seasons and the twelve months—to plant in spring, grow in summer, harvest in autumn, store in winter—and bring together into one connected whole the celestial bodies, the natural phenomena of the seasons, agricultural work, political activities and other human affairs. It compiles information on all the known ideas, knowledge and techniques in these fields and lays out an order of general thought and action that can be used in any and all situations.

In the twelve Almanacs we can see that the foundations of this intellectual framework are the three frequently discussed Warring States concepts of the Way of Heaven, social morality and the proper way of human behavior. This derived from the very popular Yellow Emperor Daoism. Following the sequence

---

18   Liu Rulin has already separated and analyzed the various Confucian, Daoist, Moist, Legalist, Names, Yin Yang, Diplomacy, Agriculturalist, Small Talk and Military schools in his "Lüshi chunqiu zhi fenxi," in *Gushi bian*, vol. 6, 340 ff.

19   LSCQ, "Xuyi," ESEZ, 726; Knoblock and Riegel, *Annals*, 272–273.

20   *Shiji*, "Lü Buwei liezhuan," 85.9, Knoblock and Riegel, *Annals*, 14.

21   LSCQ is divided into twelve almanacs (*ji* 紀), eight examinations (*lan* 覽) and six discourses (*lun* 論). According to Machida Saburo's research, and I believe it is correct, the twelve almanacs, eight examinations and six discourses of the LSCQ were not compiled at the same time. See his "Kaisetsu," in *Ryoshi Shunshyu* (LSCQ), 1987, 556. I believe that the twelve almanacs are the main part of the LSCQ and that they constitute a well ordered system or a complete structure.

of the twelve months, the Almanacs record changes in the heavenly bodies and seasonal natural phenomena, agricultural activities and the order of sacrificial ceremonies. The origins of this format are very ancient. The extant old texts of "Xia xiaozheng" (Lesser Annuary According to the Xia Calendar, Book 47 of the *Da Dai Book of Rites*), the "Months of Zhou" (Zhouyue) and the "Regulations of the Season" (Shize) chapters of the *Remaining Zhou Documents*, and the Chu silk manuscripts from Zidanku in Changsha are all written in this form. The Day Books widely used among the masses represent the popularization of the genre. The "Xia xiaozheng" and the two chapters from the *Remaining Zhou Documents*, however, were simply almanacs, while the Chu silk manuscripts and Day Books from the Qin bamboo slips concentrated mainly on taboos and medical contraindications and belonged much more to divination and the mantic arts.

The *Annals of Lü Buwei* is quite different from these works. At the beginning of each month, it describes the astronomical phenomena (the visible position of the sun and the stars), the spirits, animals, musical notes, numbers, smells, sacrificial offerings and the seasonal natural phenomena. It then goes on to specify the Son of Heaven's proper residence, chariot, color of clothing and correct ornaments, suitable food and serving vessels, and then lays out rules for government, ceremonials and the taboos involved in military affairs and agricultural ceremonies that pertain to that month. After that, it extends the implications of the affairs of Heaven and Earth into the realm of social morality and proper human behavior according to the seasonal changes encountered in the various natural phenomena. In the *Annals* the changes in Heaven and Earth clearly became the self-evident foundation of discourses on various principles of human society.

This system of exposition was obviously based upon the contemporary intellectual world's understanding of Heaven and followed the customary ideas of the day. For example, spring is the season for *sheng* or 生 "planting," "engendering life," "giving birth." The first month of spring is when the myriad things begin to grow, and so discussions of human life (the same *sheng*) are put in this section. *Sheng* conforms to the order of nature; it is a product of the quiet transformation of Heaven, and thus human life also must "keep intact the endowment Heaven gave" it.[22] An excessive search for comfort, power and pleasures would run counter to Heaven or Nature. Yet on the other hand,

---

22   LSCQ, 1/2.4: "Thus, in regulating the myriad material things the sages used them to keep intact the endowment Heaven gave them (*quan qi tian ye*)." Knoblock and Riegel, *Annals*, 66.

excessively to repress comfort, power and pleasures would also be contrary to Nature.

This system of thought was also extended to the sage rulers and labeled as "the power (*de*) of the Three August Ones and the Five Sovereigns" (*sanhuang wudi*). This means that the thought of the *Annals of Lü Buwei* also enlisted the historical support of the ancient legendary sage rulers.

As it says:

> Heaven and Earth are so great that while they give life they do not raise anything as their own, and while they bring things to completion they do not possess them. The myriad things all receive their blessings and obtain their benefits but no one knows whence they first arose. So it is with the power (*de*) of the Three August Ones and the Five Sovereigns (*sanhuang wudi*).[23]

As such, the thought of the *Annals of Lü Buwei* represents a great compendium that links together natural celestial phenomena, the abstract concept of the Way of Heaven, individual human existence, social norms and ideals while at the same time very ingeniously incorporating the frugality of Moism, the spontaneity of Daoism, Yang Zhu's elevation of one's own life, the personal ethics and social idealism of Confucianism and even the Yin and Yang ideas incorporated in the mantic and medical arts.

2.2

Yellow Emperor Daoism took Yin and Yang, the four seasons and the Way of Heaven as its main ideas, and this sort of thinking pervades the twelve Almanacs. The "Great Music" (Da yue) section of the *Annals of Lü Buwei* "Almanac for the Second Month of Summer" (Zhongxia ji) has the following programatic statement:

> Great Unity brought forth the Dyadic Couple (Heaven and Earth);
> The Dyadic Couple brought forth Yin and Yang.
> Yin and Yang metamorphize and transform,
> The one rising, the other falling,
> Joined together in a perfect pattern.[24]

---

23   LSCQ, 1/4.2 D, Knoblock and Riegel, *Annals*, 71. Romanized terms added.

24   LSCQ, 5/2.1, Knoblock and Riegel, *Annals*, 136. "Grand One" changed to "Great Unity" and some Romanized terms added.

This is the foundation of *Annals of Lü Buwei* thought. Following this line of thought, the Way of Heaven was projected into the human world so that the sun, moon, stars, four seasons, hot and cold, or astronomical phenomenon and calendrical science all appear to be rules of the natural movements of Heaven, and the proper way of human behavior in the world should be a natural extension of these rules.[25] Throughout the "spring life" section, from the "Almanac for the First Month of Spring" through the "Almanac for the Third Month of Spring," there are many discussions of the meaning of human existence. In these discussions, the *Annals* strikingly expresses the idea that the individual should have priority over society. It says that although the world of all under Heaven is extremely important, it should not be used to endanger individual human existence. Individual existence is a complete "world" for human beings. Human life is bestowed by Heaven, and the way that human beings can best respond to Heaven is to continue to exist and to live out their allotted years in the best way possible. According to this idea, the individual takes priority over the collective and over society because here the foundation of the human is Heaven. The rationality of the existence of Heaven grants rationality to the existence of the human, and only the rationality of the existence of the human determines the rationality of social existence. In order to rule or govern the world of all under Heaven, the first important requirement of the ruler is to let people live out their life spans and "keep intact their Heavenly endowed lives." Only then, can the ruler extend this spirit into social life.[26] This is really the meaning of the "Placing the Self First" (Xian ji) chapter. This sort of thought appears to be similar to that of Yang Zhu's extreme egoism, but in the *Annals* it is no longer just an individualist attitude; rather it connects the ideas of greatly valuing individual life, living in a natural and peaceful manner and the Way of nurturing life as though they all emanated from a single cosmic principle. It even extends this cosmic principle from individual human life into the socio-political realm.

Moving on to the summer "growing season," it is as if human society had moved from the age of primitive chaos into an age of mature civilization. According to Yellow Emperor Daoist thought, the age of civilization is a time when individual life and humanity's pure and simple spirits disappeared and people could only restrain themselves through reason and acquired knowledge while striving to coexist in society through mutual harmony. Only in such an age were Confucian doctrines deemed reasonable. On this account, in the

---

25 In the *Laozi jiaben ji juanhou guyishu*, 1974, from Mawangdui there is a similar record. See, 17–18. The annotators say that this is the lost "Yi Yin" (伊尹) Daoist text.

26 ESEZ, 636. Knoblock and Riegel, *Annals*, 102–106.

Annals of Lü Buwei thought of the "Almanac" of Summer, the discussion turns to acquired education, study and social restraint, ethics and morality.

In discussing social ethics, that is loyalty and filial piety, the *Annals of Lü Buwei* agrees that through knowledge acquired in study people can not only stimulate their inner feelings toward goodness, but they can also rationally understand the proper order between rulers and officials, fathers and sons and teachers and students. It especially stresses that for a person to develop naturally and in good health he must both follow his inborn nature and moderate his desires. This is in accord with the myriad things of the natural world, and is not merely a question of natural growth and development, but also depends on avoiding inclement weather. The entire process of growth and development is one closely linked chain of many causes and effects. Although human beings receive their natural endowment from Heaven, if they lack the summer-like education, study, control and restraint, they will be unable to mature properly. Then, if "the Yin and Yang will lose their order, and the four seasons will exchange their positions [and]..., one is certain to lose one's natural endowment."[27]

This train of thought was carried on into the seasons of "autumn harvest" and "winter storage." In the "Almanac" of Autumn, the *Annals of Lü Buwei* discusses military affairs and punishments that are correlated with the austere and desolate weather of autumn by bringing in ideas from the Legalists and the Military School (*bingjia*). According to the Five Phases order, autumn belongs to metal, and metal rules over the military and punishments. Since human society had moved from primitive chaos on to civilization and people's mental states had also changed from plain and simple to much more complicated, society had to have some sort of order. Besides education, study, self-restraint and supervision, this social order also had to rely on a military establishment and legal punishments to guarantee it. This was regarded as analogous to the way the seasons changed from spring to summer and from summer to autumn. At this point, the *Annals* first discusses the rationale for using an army. The army has to be imposing, awe-inspiring, full of vitality, and the officers should care for the soldiers as if they were the same as themselves. Political leaders should also follow the people's hearts, be good at finding and employing the best *shi* scholars and be capable of self-reflection—that was the only way they would be able to establish an effective government.[28]

---

27   LSCQ, 6/5 "Ming li," ESEZ, 647. "Elucidating Patterns" 6/5.2, Knoblock and Riegel, *Annals*, 167 of 167–170 and "Extravagant Music," 5/3.3, Knoblock and Riegel, 141–142.

28   See LSCQ, "Shunmin," "Zhishi," "Shenji," and so on in the "Jiqiu ji." ESEZ, 654–655.

In the "Almanacs" for winter, the *Annals of Lü Buwei* discusses the subject of death and dying in association with the freezing cold, dark and confined nature of winter. First comes funerals and burials. Because people have kinship feelings, they naturally have funerals for their dead relatives, and this is analogous to the necessary "storage" of food in the winter. The *Annals of Lü Buwei*, however, introduces Moist thought by arguing that the custom of lavish funeral is meaningless, and actually leads to grave robbing that prevents the dead relatives from resting in peace.[29] Second is the significance of the death of *shi* scholars. Loyal advice could be unwelcome, and *shi* scholars could be executed by ignorant and foolish rulers. The *shi* scholars could not capitulate to power, and so if they suffered humiliation, their sense of justice prohibited them from living on in ignominy. This is what is meant by "accepting death in order to live up to humanity" (*sha shen cheng ren* 殺身成仁, *Analects*, 15.9). Only by doing this could a *shi* fulfill the meaning of his life as well as complete his dream of being a true gentleman (*junzi*).

As the *Annals of Lü Buwei* passed through the four seasons, building a system of thought through such symbolic associations, the ideas of the School of Agriculture (*nongjia*), Military School, Confucianism, Moism, Daoism and Yin Yang were all included. It is clear that in the minds of the compilers of the *Annals* Heaven and Earth and the fours seasons included everything, and everything in Heaven and Earth could be recorded. Using Heaven and Earth as a framework and following the logic of the Dao, Yin Yang and the Five Phases, various forms of thought were regarded as compatible and were thus syncretized, as were also the self-evident Way of Heaven and Way of Earth and the strategies and principles that could be developed in accord with Heaven and Earth. We can see, then, that the *Annals* constructed a vast network of thought based on the Great Unity, the Dyadic Couple of Heaven and Earth, Yin Yang, four seasons, Five Phases and twelve months as the framework of time and space.

It is especially interesting that in principle the *Annals of Lü Buwei* finally brought all of the nexuses between Heaven and the Human completely together so that human nature and the Way of Heaven were seen to have the same fundamentally self-evident significance. Confucian ideas about ethics, morality, rites and music and government, Moist ideas about moderation in funerals, exaltation of worthiness, condemnation of offensive warfare and universal love, Yang Zhu's attitude of egoistic love of one's own life, Laozi's philosophy of natural tranquility, Zhuangzi's concern for spiritual freedom and transcendence, the Warring States disputation techniques of the rhetoricians,

---

29   LSCQ, "Jie zang," ESEZ, 657. Knoblock and Riegel, *Annals*, 227–230.

and even the ideas about the authority of rulers put forth by those entrusted with law enforcement and administration—all of these various schools of thought were subsumed into one great system. This system of thought provided some extremely valuable heuristic ideas for the intellectual world of later times. One, that there was still a space for the continued development of the philosophy and knowledge found in Yellow Emperor Daoism. Two, that Heaven and the Human, the two ultimate foundations of thought, could be mutually connected. Three, that it was also possible to make a comprehensive and integrated synthesis (that is, a syncretic system) of the ideas in the various schools of thought. The intellectual world of the Western Han continued to develop in precisely this manner.

2.3

During the dynastic change between the Qin and Han, the school of thought called Yellow Emperor Daoism was very pervasive. Besides the *Annals of Lü Buwei*, from the *Book of Master Shi*, the *Pheasant Cap Master*, the *Book of Master Wen* and parts of the *Book of Master Guan* (Guanzi) of the later Warring States period all the way down to such Western Han figures as Chen Ping (?–178 BCE), Zhang Liang (?–185 BCE), Le Jugong, Tian Shu, Gaigong and Cao Shen (?–190 BCE), who directly applied Yellow Emperor Daoist thought, and Huang Sheng and Sima Tan (?–110 BCE) who studied Daoist theories, to Sima Jizhu and Taicang Gong (Chunyu Yi, 205–150? BCE) who practiced medical arts at the beginning of the Han . . . All of these men can be said to have shared in this current of thought. Even Lu Jia (240–170 BCE), author of the *New Talk* (Xinyu) and Jia Yi, author of the *New Writings* (Xinshu), both of whom were basically in the Confucian camp, were also inevitably influenced by this intellectual trend. According to scholarly research, however, the early Han trend of thought that was later broadly termed Daoist was actually a mixture of many different schools of thought.[30] Nevertheless, what the *Annals of Lü Buwei* represented was a trend of thought that comprehensively amalgamated the various schools following the logic of Yellow Emperor Daoism and paying balanced attention to nature, society and individual life. In the final analysis, it was becoming an intellectual consensus. With the support of Cao Shen, Grand Empress Dowager Dou and others, it subsequently became a major intellectual trend. In his treatise entitled "Central Themes of the Six Schools" (Lun liujia yaozhi), Sima Tan subsumed this trend under the name of Daoism.

---

30   Jin Guzhi, "Han chu daojia de paibie," *Riben xuezhe yanjiu Zhongguoshi lunzhu xuanze* 7 (1993), 34.

The book that continued to link up Heaven, Earth and the Human in the grand spirit of the *Annals of Lü Buwei* was the *Huainanzi* (The Master of Huainan), collectively compiled by Liu An, King of Huainan (179–122 BCE) and his assembled disciples and retainers.

As with the *Annals of Lü Buwei*, the *Huainanzi* was also a syncretic compendium that attempted to present the intellectual world with a framework that included all knowledge up to that time. The early Han *Huainanzi* was, however, different from the Qin dynasty *Annals of Lü Buwei*, and the difference was not just, as Hu Shi wrote, that it was "more accurately and carefully compiled, and the writing was more forceful."[31] It was in fact intellectually very different. There were at least five important differences, as follows:

One, the *Huainanzi* emphasized the absolute priority of "the most exalted Way" (*taishang zhi dao* 太上之道) and placed it above the natural laws and original principles of Heaven, Earth and the Human as the starting point of its thought and the foundation of its values.[32] In the *Huainanzi* the Way is not only the origin and foundation of everything, it is also the dominant force in the universe; it is even regarded as a god with a personality and a will. It runs through and connects nature, society and humanity and makes clear the laws that should be respected in both the underworld of ghosts and spirits and the human world. The three laws of the Way are weakness and tranquility (*rouruo qingjing*), spontaneity and non-action (*ziran wuwei*), and return to the roots (or original truth, *fanben fuchu*). This means that people should have no thoughts or anxiety and be in accord with nature just like the Way; their minds should be just like still water or a mirror: although they do not consciously observe things, still there is nothing that escapes them. Their original nature should be just like Heaven: "That which is tranquil from our birth is our heavenly nature" (*ren sheng er jing, tian zhi xing ye*).[33] People who truly understand the Way do not allow either excessive desires or rationality to suppress or obstruct their innate nature. Society should also behave just like the Way. The ruler should practice government by non-action. There is always a limitation to any administration by means of a human legal system, however perfect, but the Way, on the contrary, is everywhere, and if society follows nature everything will be governed without governing at all. In the *Huainanzi* the Way is both Heaven and Nature, and the sages "do not allow the human to obscure the heavenly

31   Hu Shi, *Zhonggu sixiangshi changbian*, chapter 5, in his *Hu Shi xueshu wenji*, vol. 1, 1991, 362.

32   *Huainanzi*, "Yuan dao," Major, et al., "Originating in the Way," *Huainanzi*, 1.3, 51.

33   *Ibid.*, Major, et al., "Originating in the Way," *Huainanzi*, 1.5, 53.

and do not let desire corrupt their genuine responses."[34] This is somewhat different from the *Annals of Lü Buwei* relying on both Heaven and the Human.

Two, on the appearance of the Dao in Nature, society and humanity, the *Huainanzi* revises and enriches the simplistic thinking of the *Annals of Lü Buwei* that only uses time as the chief strand of its theories (the celestial phenomena and calendrical rules of the twelve months and the popular ideas of planting in spring, growing in summer, harvesting in autumn and storing in winter, and so on). The *Huainanzi* contains detailed discussions of the origin of the universe, cosmic space (astronomical phenomena, earth topography) and time (seasons, calendrical science), the various subtle correspondences between the cosmos and human life, the interactive relationships between the worlds of the living and the dead and the origin and survival of humanity itself. The *Huainanzi* also combines all of these elements into a thoroughly complete and integrated intellectual framework.

Chapter two, "Activating the Genuine" (Chuzhen), is an extended discussion of cosmogony, chapters three, four and five, "Celestial Patterns" (Tianwen), "Terrestrial Form" (Dixing), and "Seasonal Rules" (Shize), describe the mutual interactions upward and downward between Heaven, Earth and the Human in accord with time and space. Chapter six, "Surveying Obscurities" (Lanming), further discusses the all important concept of resonance (*ganying*) or stimulus and response. Because the "most exalted Way" that transcends everything is the ultimate foundation of the *Huainanzi*'s discussions of Heaven, Earth, the Human and ghosts (spirits), the *Huainanzi* comprises an even larger and more abstruse system of thought than the *Annals of Lü Buwei* in its expositions on the relationships between cosmic space and time and Heaven, Earth and the Human.

Three, starting from the relations between Heaven, Earth and the Human and spirits, the vision of the *Huainanzi* expands further into the realm of social issues. From chapter eight, "The Basic Warp" (Benjing), through chapter thirteen, "Boundless Discourses" (Fanlun), the *Huainanzi* continues to center on the Way in discussing government and morality. The text repeatedly emphasizes that a society in accord with the Way should be primitive and unsophisticated, and people who live in accord with the Way should be without thought or anxiety. "They are not sorrowful or joyful; are not happy or angry. They sit without disturbing thoughts, and sleep without dreams."[35]

The compilers of the *Huainanzi* were well aware, however, that those primitive times could not come again, and so they turned their attention squarely

---

34   *Huainanzi*, "Yuan dao," 1.8, Major, et al., *Huainanzi*, 58.

35   *Huainanzi*, "Mou cheng." Major, et al., "Profound Precepts," 10.1 *Huainanzi*, 349.

on practical problems of social governance and administration. In "The Basic Warp" and "The Ruler's Techniques" (Zhushu) they put forth the methods of ruling a hierarchical society. The best way for them of course was to practice rule by non-action, the second best was to employ ritual, music and education, and the third best would be for the ruler to control the officialdom and his subjects in the manner advocated by Shen Buhai and his followers.

In chapter ten, "Profound Precepts" (Mou cheng) they discuss the distinctions between morally superior men and small men. Seeing that in the practical world humanity and rightness (*renyi*) had become the last line of defense, they agreed that people had to guard the boundary of "the human" (*ren*) as "the human" with much trepidation and rely on humanity and rightness to become a morally superior man. In order to distinguish clearly between morally superior men and small men, the ruler should match the name with the reality. A superior man emphasized humanity and rightness while a small man emphasized greed and lust—this was their greatest difference. After clearly distinguishing the boundary between the morally superior man and the small man, the ruler should employ the ways of the morally superior man to reform society. Thus chapter eleven, "Integrating Customs" (Qisu), expounds on how to bring about a situation in which all of the common people have the virtue or moral power (*de*) of the superior man. The compilers also recognized that they were living in the final days of an era and that the ancient customs had already disappeared; basic human nature was the same as that of the ancients, but the environment had already caused humanity's spirit and mentality to differ greatly. They wanted to rely on study and education to transform the people's minds and thought, and also to "modify habits and change customs" and bring excellent social customs back into being.[36]

Four, besides the twelve Almanacs, the *Annals of Lü Buwei* also contains eight Examinations and six Discourses, while the *Huainanzi* also supplements the most important fundamental chapters mentioned above with several less focused but still important ones. Unlike the eight Examinations and six Discourses, however, these chapters do not stand alone but are supplementary explanations of matters within the foundational framework already established and so they embrace the various Spring and Autumn and Warring States schools of thought to form one vast system. From chapter fourteen, "Sayings Explained" (Quanyan), through chapter nineteen, "Cultivating Effort" (Xiuwu), the text eclectically chooses ideas on human affairs from various schools and separately discourses on questions of government, the military, social relations, individual moral cultivation and so on. Among them, "Sayings Explained," that

---

36   *Huainanzi*, "Zhu shu." Major, et al., "The Ruler's Techniques," 9.7 *Huainanzi*, 301.

focuses on the Way, "An Overview of the Military" (Binglüe), that concerns military affairs, and "A Mountain of Persuasions" (Shuoshan) and "A Forest of Persuasions" (Shuolin) use the method of linking subjects through similes and metaphors to gather together different philosophic theories about human life and society. "Among Others" (Renjian) considers the origin of omens about good fortune and calamity and methods of bringing on good fortune and avoiding evil calamities, while "Cultivating Effort" discusses how, following the decline of society, a sage, the ideal ruler, should set out to govern, administer and reconstruct the social order based on what we might call society's post-lapsarian circumstances.

Five, the *Huainanzi* was obviously written from a more careful and ingeniously integrated design than the *Annals of Lü Buwei*. After discoursing on the various aspects of Nature, society and humanity, it returns back to its overall themes. The final chapter, "The Exalted Lineage" (Taizu), and the first chapter, "Originating the Way" (Yuandao), echo each other from afar. "The Exalted Lineage" elucidates the internal structure of this vast system, a structure that is based on "reason" or "principle" (*li*). What exactly is this *li* then? In the *Huainanzi* it is precisely the relations of resonance (*ganying*) between Heaven, Earth and the Human, and that is simply what, we recall, is said in the *Laozi*:

> Man models himself after Earth.
> Earth models itself after Heaven.
> Heaven models itself after Dao.
> And Dao models itself after Nature.[37]

If we say that the first chapter, "Originating the Way," is a vertical discussion of the beginning and the end of the cosmos, then the last chapter, "The Exalted Lineage," is a horizontal layout of the mutual relations between Nature, society, humanity and ghosts and spirits. It uses their mutual resonance and emulation to combine these different fields, phenomena, material things, events and principles into one vast structure that represents the establishment of a distinct form of cosmology.

2.4

The compilers of the *Annals of Lü Buwei* made Heaven the basic foundation of their intellectual system and also connected the Human with Heaven. Because of this, nothing was of higher importance for them than individual human existence and the laws of the universe. This would undoubtedly imply some

---

37   *Laozi* 25, Chan, SB, 153.

dissolution of secular political power; it would especially influence the foundations of the authority of rulers, the sanctity of laws, standards of the political institutions and social ethics and morality. The world of all under Heaven belonged to all who live under Heaven; the laws of government had to conform to Heaven, that is to the laws of nature. Rulers should practice non-action and tranquility, live simply and have few desires—following the Way of Heaven—and the value of individual existence should be higher than that of the collective. In this way, the *Annals of Lü Buwei* placed the Way of Heaven and the Way of the Human above the political power of rulers and the norms of society in their value hierarchy.

Since this Way of Heaven was verified by the intellectual class and not monopolized by the nobility, it gave prominence to certain demands—that power should defer to truth, politics to culture and rulers should defer to educated men of culture. All this symbolized the idea that the intellectual class should "be the teachers of rulers" (*wei dizhe shi* 為帝者師). This idea not only represented the contemporary intellectual strata's own search for value and position, it also paved the way for the idea of later generations that the "tradition of Confucian moral principles" (*daotong*, loyalty to the Way) took precedence over the "tradition of political power" (*zhengtong*, loyalty to the ruler). In that time of incessant warfare urgently in need of unification, this sort of lofty idealism was obviously not enough to make the holders of power sit up and listen. Sometime after 237 BCE, Lü Buwei was banished from the Qin court and died; records say that he either committed suicide by drinking poison or died during his banishment to Shu (Sichuan).[38] His death seems to have symbolized that the resistance of the intellectual class had failed. With his death, their dreams of becoming "the teachers of rulers" also dissipated like smoke. Nevertheless, their spirit of freely expressing their views and carrying the tradition of the Way was manifested again and again in the thinking of later generations of educated men and became a symbol of unyielding spirit in Chinese culture.

If the *Annals of Lü Buwei* symbolized in some sense a struggle between the "tradition of the Way" upheld by the scholar class and the "tradition of the political power" of rulers, then the *Huainanzi* symbolized to some extent a conflict in the early Western Han between peripheral regional thought and that of the centralized state. Yellow Emperor Daoism was in the center or mainstream for some time at the beginning of the Han, chiefly due to the background of contemporary society or the preferences of Cao Shen, Emperor

---

38 For the life and death of Lü Buwei and discussion of the various sources, see Knoblock and Riegel, *Annals*, 1–26.

Wen and Grand Empress Dowager Dou. When Han Wudi came to the throne, everything quickly changed.

We can say that the compilers of the *Huainanzi* also had a very strong tendency toward criticism of the present. Since they made Heaven the ultimate determinant of the rationality of the social order, took the ultimate realm of the Dao as the goal of their life search, promoted ancient times as their ideal society and regarded nonpurposive action as a rational strategy for dealing with reality, they would undoubtedly have harsh criticisms for their actually existing, very flawed social order, tactics and lifestyle. According to "Activating the Genuine" (Chu zhen), the learning of the Sages and the wise men (*daren*) both sought for a superior ideal realm, while rulers who commanded the discursive power of ideology, the legal system, and ethics and morality were of secondary importance and were only installed as administrators when nothing else could be done. Above the rulers were the mysterious and everlasting Dao and the not to be questioned Heaven. Below the rulers were the wise men who sought to perfect their individual lives and those who wandered beyond the world and could not be controlled by political power.

The thought of the *Huainanzi* was probably derived from Laozi and Zhuangzi and was thus not quite the same as the ideas of the *Annals of Lü Buwei* that derived more from Yellow Emperor Daoism. It has long been pointed out that the *Huainanzi* was probably the first text to combine the thought of Laozi and Zhuangzi into Lao-Zhuang thought. As we have seen, the *Zhuangzi* has a very pronounced anti-establishment and anti-mainstream tendency as part of its quest for freedom and spiritual transcendence, and all of this gave the *Huainanzi* a very obvious flavor of opposition to the center (the mainstream) and to the monopoly of power by one person as well as a quest for freedom. The *Huainanzi* holds that there are no definite customs, no unchanging rites and ceremonies, no fixed laws, and there can never be any everlasting political system.

If this is so, then how could *Huainanzi* thought also raise the state, society, rulers and the ethics and morality that maintained their order to the prominent position of self-evident truths and serve as the mainstream ideology and the intellectual theory of the government?

Things changed very rapidly. In 135 BCE, the sixth year after Han Wudi established his first reign period, Grand Empress Dowager Dou passed away, and very rapidly after that a group of Confucian scholars (*wenxue zhi shi*) became the central actors on the political stage. They were all experts on Confucian classics like the *Book of Songs, Book of Documents*, and the *Spring and Autumn Annals*; Confucian ethical theory was their basic form of thought, and they regarded the ceremonial system as the foundation of social order. In 122 BCE, the King of Huainan, Liu An died in disgrace (committing suicide), the kingdom of

Huainan was abolished and its name changed to Jiujiang prefecture. Many of his subordinates were implicated in his coup plot and executed. Following the change in the political situation and the Han dynasty's centralization of imperial power and active expansionism, Yellow Emperor Daoism moved from the center of the national consciousness to a position of marginal inconsequence. This change marked the end of an era and the beginning of a new age.

3.   Establishment of a State Ideology: From the *Luxuriant Dew of the Spring and Autumn Annals* to the *Discourses in the White Tiger Hall*

Quite a few scholars who held Confucian ideas as their basic thought used the Qin to Han transition as an example to discuss the reasonableness of adopting Confucian learning as the political ideology of the state.[39] Although they used practical values to induce the ruler to adopt their Confucian ideas, they still tried to maintain their idealism, making equal claims for knowledge and power and even hoping to transcend political power. Their world had changed, though, and in this disorderly and fluid situation most Confucian scholars could not avoid abandoning their insistence on idealism and their past dignity as teachers of rulers. In an age in which the establishment of state authority was greatly needed, they had no choice but to allow their thoughts and ideas to depart from pure humanism and idealism. For the survival of their ideas and the implementation of their teachings, both had to incorporate a thoroughly practical and worldly orientation.

Some contemporary Confucian scholars did indeed put forth various practical schemes; especially notable among them was Shusun Tong (?–ca. 194 BCE). This learned scholar who set up the ritual system for the founding emperor Han Gaozu was an extremely able, clever and flexible person. Because he and other Confucian scholars around him were able to change with the times, Confucian idealism finally began to draw close to pragmatism and Confucian thought began to incline toward becoming a state political ideology.[40] During Han Wudi's reign, another Confucian scholar, Gongsun Hong (200–121 BCE), also employed similar extremely practical strategies to preserve his political position, and his life on the political stage symbolized the transformation of the Confucian learning into an ideological practice (*rushu*, literally, Confucian methods). In that age when the power of the emperor was increasingly domineering, the fate of any doctrine did not merely depend on the quality of its

39   See Jia Yi's memorial to the throne in HS, j. 48, "Jia Yi zhuan," 2230–2258, and quotation of Jia Shan's memorial "Zhiyan" in j. 51, "Jia Shan zhuan," 2327–2336.
40   *Shiji*, j. 99, "Liu Jing, Shusun Tong liezhuan," 2722–2723, 2726.

thought; it was also dependent on its propaganda tactics and its strategies for
adapting to the world. That is, it depended on whether this doctrine could be
transformed into a state or national ideology, and it also depended on the preferences and inclinations of some random figures who nevertheless were the
key to making final decisions.

In the Western Han process of transformation from the ideas of Yellow
Emperor Daoism to Confucian thought, then, several important events were
especially critical. First, Shusun Tong formulated the Han ritual and ceremonial system. This clarified the hierarchical order of seniors and juniors
in the Han court from top to bottom and affirmed imperial power. Second,
during Han Wudi's reign imperial academicians or erudites (*boshi*) were commissioned to compose the "Royal Regulations" (Wangzhi), now a chapter in the
Book of Rites. This document conceived and inscribed an ideal political order
in which the status of the center and the peripheries was fixed, the power of
the emperor was made more prominent and the responsibilities and powers
of various individuals were made extremely clear. This ideal order strengthened the idea of the state. Third, Zhang Cang (ca. 256–152 BCE) established a
new calendrical system on the basis of the sequence of the Five Powers (*wude*
五德, another name for the Five Phases) and celestial calendrical techniques
that made the Han dynasty orthodox and the Qin heterodox. This gave the
succession of the Han imperial house cosmic legitimacy. Fourth, during Han
Wudi's reign, court officials Zhao Wan and Wang Zang (?–139 BCE), relying
on support from the influential officials Dou Ying (?–131 BCE) and Tian Fen
(?–131 BCE), invited their teacher Master Shen Pei (ca. 219–135 BCE) to court
and presented him to the emperor. They advised the emperor to construct a
Hall of Brightness on ancient models to symbolize the power and authority of
the emperor. They also proposed a series of projects such as imperial tours
of inspection, reviving the *feng* and *shan* sacrifices to Heaven and Earth,
changing the calendar (that is, changing the month on which the year
began), changing the color of court vestments (to yellow, representing earth,
the symbol of Han power over the water symbol of Qin) and so on, all designed
to ensure the power, authority and legitimacy of the emperor. Even though
all of these projects were not completely carried out, still they had the support
of Confucian ideas and were also in accord with the practical needs of the
time; they obviously influenced the general orientation of the emperor and his
government.

After the death of Grand Empress Dowager Dou in 135 BCE, the official ideology of the Han state experienced fundamental changes.[41]

41   *Shiji*, j. 121, "Rulin liezhuan," 3118.

3.1

As a school of thought, Confucian scholars were able to maintain their tradition and the distinction between their school and others in large part because they relied on their teacher-student relationships and the teaching and transmission of their classic texts. These Confucian scholars used the five classics as their basic texts. Doing so gave them a definite foundation for their knowledge and a basis for their mutual recognition; whoever took his knowledge from the five classics and engaged in the interpretation and exposition of these texts was considered a *ru* or a Confucian. The various erudites in these classics during the early Han reigns of emperors Wen (r. 180–157 BCE) and Jing (r. 157–141 BCE), their teaching and transmission of the classic texts and the state's approval of that transmission all guaranteed the continuation of this intellectual system. In order for this intellectual doctrine to become the state ideology during this age of rapid social change and to occupy the position of sole orthodoxy, it had to establish a system of knowledge and a political strategy that would be suitable for practical socio-political reality, employ that knowledge and strategy for state norms, regulate the world order and determine the direction of historical development.

As the ideology of an ethnic state, the cosmology of early Confucian thought was not particularly developed. On this account, the reasonableness of Confucian theories about individual and social morality and their system of rites and music lacked the support of the laws of nature. For the same reason, Confucian thought was unable to connect with the practical knowledge and procedures that the masses venerated and needed in their daily lives. Confucian thought seemed to be able only to deal with questions about morality, but was unable to enter deeply into people's lives. As a result, in the early Han at least, some thinkers like Lu Jia accepted the foundational ideas held in common by Yellow Emperor Daoism, and the theories of Yin and Yang, the Five Phases and even mantic and medical arts. They wanted to use these ideas to establish a metaphysical foundation for Confucian learning.

From the existing literary materials, however, the thinker who took Heaven as the rational background for the human social order and who had the most to say about using these cosmic laws to interpret nature and history was Dong Zhongshu (179–104 BCE). It was said that there were some intellectual connections between Dong and Lu Jia, but Dong's importance in the Western Han and his influence on later generations was much more far-reaching than that of Lu Jia.[42] It was Dong Zhongshu who reconstructed and established a vast

---

42 Wang Chong wrote in his *Lunheng*, "Anshu," that "*New Talk* (Xinyu) was written by Lu Jia, and when Dong Zhongshu was in office he relied on it; it is all about rulers, ministers, and political gains and losses." See Huang Hui, *Lunheng xiaoshi*, j. 19, 1169.

theoretical framework for Confucianism and transformed it into a state ideology. Dong was not really successful as an official in the political arena, but as a thinker his influence was extremely profound and far surpassed that of any other contemporary Confucian scholar. In the third of Dong's famous answers to Han Wudi's questions on imperial policy, he asserted that the cosmos or Heaven's importance for the human world could be summarized under the following three aspects.[43]

One, the center and the beginning of Heaven is the Origin (*yuan* 元) and the Origin is simply the One. It (Heaven) is the original basis for social and political legitimacy as well as the foundation of human beings becoming human beings. Human beings are like a projection of Heaven, and even the physical body is a product of emulating Heaven. The head is round like Heaven, the ears and eyes are like the sun and moon, the nose and mouth are like the wind and the air, the bones and joints correspond to the number of the heavenly bodies, big bones and joints correspond to the number of months (moons), the five viscera correspond to the Five Phases, the four limbs are like the four seasons, and even the blinking of the eyes are like day and night.[44]

Two, Heaven "divides Yin and Yang, makes up the four season, and arranges the Five Phases."[45] Yang comes out from the south and Ying comes out from the north; they follow the seasons and the directions of the compass and come and go in cycles. Yin and Yang are also matched with good (*yang*) and evil (*yin*) as well as punishments (*yin*) and rewards (*de*, also power: *yang*); people possess both good and evil, and for that reason the government implements both punishments and rewards. Yin and Yang are further related to the four seasons, and the four seasons are correlated with the Five Phases. In keeping with the ideas of planting in spring, growing in summer, harvesting in autumn and storing in winter, Yin and Yang and Five Phases ideas were extended to attitudes toward and strategies for governing society, to behavior and norms for ethics and morality and to virtually all things, events and phenomena.

Three, Heaven was not only the shape of cosmic space, it was also the guarantor of cosmic time. Besides the laws of nature, historical experiences were also rational foundations for the human social order. As discussed above, from the Spring and Autumn and Warring States periods on, the Chinese were always seeking in history for a rational foundation for their social order; as a scholar of the *Spring and Autumn Annals*, Dong Zhongshu naturally inherited this tradition. He wrote in the opening of the first chapter of his *Luxuriant Dew of the*

43   HS, j. 56, "Dong Zhongshu zhuan," 2495–2526.
44   CQFL, j. 13, "Ren fu tianshu di wushiliu," ESEZ, 797.
45   CQFL, j. 58.1, "Wuxing xiangsheng."

Spring and Autumn Annals (Chunqiu fanlu), "Chu Zhuangwang" (King Zhuang of Chu, d. 591) that "the Way of the *Spring and Autumn* is to revere Heaven and imitate the ancients."[46] To "revere Heaven" naturally meant to regard the cosmos as the support system for human knowledge, while to "imitate the ancients" meant to regard history as the rational foundation for the human social order. In this way, then, not only did the classic texts monopolized by the Confucian scholars become textbooks for practical governance, but education in and the study of these texts became an important source of knowledge.[47] Legends about the morality of the ancient rulers—the Three Ancient Dynasties changing the calendar (the month on which the year begins) and the color of court vestments—recent experiences of regicides destroying kingdoms, combined with ideas about the traditional (if imagined) government systems, laws, ritual ceremonies and social norms all provided profound minatory examples from history. At this point historical knowledge was transformed into a philosophy of history, but the Confucian position could be undermined if it only developed to this point.

3.2

Continuing logically to follow this trend of thought, if human beings were born having inherited the rationality of Heaven, and the human body was modeled on the structure of Heaven, then the existence of "the Human" would undoubtedly possess a natural rationality and value priority. If Heaven really moved naturally in an orderly manner and through silent non-action, then human beings should also practice such nonpurposive action and transform themselves in tranquility.[48] Following this logic, Confucianism would be transformed into the doctrines of the Yellow Emperor, Laozi and even Yang Zhu.

However, on the question of "the Human" Dong Zhongshu made an extremely critical revision of the idea that human beings were born with an inheritance from Nature (Heaven). In the first section of chapter 41, "Heaven Makes Man" (Wei ren zhe tian), of his *Luxuriant Dew of the Spring and Autumn Annals*, Dong denies that humanity's inborn nature can serve as the foundation

---

46   CQFL j. 1.5, "Chu Zhuangwang."

47   CQFL, j. 3, "Jing hua di wu,": "Ancient people had a saying: we do not know the future and so we examine the past. Today, the *Chunqiu* as an object of study talks about the past and illuminates the future." ESEZ, 775.

48   This is just what Wang Chong later questioned: "Human beings are born between Heaven and Earth. Heaven and Earth do not act (*wuwei*). Human beings receive their nature from Heaven, they should also practice non-action (*wuwei*). What, then, would be the purpose of their action?." See *Lunheng xiaoshi*, 781.

for a human being as a human being. He cleverly adds "nature" (*xing*) between Heaven and the Human, and makes distinctions between "life" (*sheng*), "nature" (*xing*) and feelings or emotions (*qing*). Dong argues that human life is *sheng* and it comes from Heaven; *qing* (feelings, emotions) are human desires and they come from "the Human." The "nature" that establishes a human being as a human being does not merely include a person's innate original nature; it must also incorporate acquired (not innate) cultivation. In chapter 35, Dong writes that the term nature is not what is inborn (*sheng*) because the Human and Heaven are the same; that is, Heaven has Yin and Yang, and human beings have humanity (*ren*) and greed (*tan*). It is only in this sense that the Way of Heaven and the Way of the Human are uniformly the same.[49]

Dong employs a very clever simile to make his point. Human nature (*renxing*) is like rice stalks (*he*) and goodness (*shan*) is like rice (*mi*). Rice grows out of the rice stalk, but not all of the rice stalks become rice. Human nature, too, does not all become good. Goodness is just like rice: although it exists among the stalks, not all the stalks become rice. In this way, the ultimate goal for a human being is not simply involuntary existence, and existence does not automatically possess rationality. The logic of Dong's thought naturally moves on to the significance of regulations, education, and administration, and "the production (of this acquired goodness requires) training and cultivation."

Based upon the so-called Seven Moral Lessons (*qijiao*) from the "Royal Regulations" mentioned above, Dong correlated them with the theory of Yin-Yang and the Five Phases, and advocated matching the Three Bonds (*sangang*) with the Yin and Yang and correlating the Five Phases with the Five Constant Virtues (*wuchang*) of Confucian doctrine.[50] This is what he meant by "the standards of humanity and rightness and the socio-political system are all derived from Heaven."[51]

These values and norms were the pivotal foundation of Confucian doctrine and also the area in which Confucian scholars were most proficient. That is, ethics and morality, education on ethics and morality and establishing the

---

49   CQFL, j. 10, ESEZ, 791.
50   The *sangang* are the relationships in which "husbands bind wives, fathers bind sons, and rulers bind ministers." *Wuchang*: the sequence of the mutual production of the Five Phases represents the relationship between fathers and sons; earth residing in the center and metal, wood, water and fire taking charge of the four directions and the four seasons represents the relationship between rulers and ministers; the Five Phases correlation with humanity (*ren*), wisdom (*zhi* 智), honesty (*xin* 信), rightness (*yi*) and propriety (*li*) represent the quality of human morality in correspondence to Heaven.
51   CQFL, j. 12, "Ji yi," ESEZ, 797.

study of the five classics and the six arts. At this time the ceremonial system set up on the basis of the five classics and the six arts demonstrated its most important significance. More importantly this ceremonial system was the logical starting point for the establishment of the content of an entire set of institutions. This ceremonial system was also the key which transformed Confucian teachings into an official state ideology.

Nearly all of the most important contents of Confucian teachings in this regard can be briefly set out here. (1) In as much as human beings cannot rely only on their innate nature to become truly human, the highest realm of human life is really not simply living on in non-action. In this regard, the necessity of administration and education—a legal system and educational measures—comes to the fore.

(2) In as much as Heaven does not directly cause human beings to become truly human, the Will of Heaven has to be communicated and implemented through an earthly authority. A ruler who communicates with Heaven above and the people below is extremely important. The king (*wang* 王, three horizontal lines connected by one vertical line) combines the three realms in one, communicating with Heaven above, occupying the earth below and regulating the people in the middle.[52] He carries out the Way on behalf of Heaven, brings peace to the world and morally transforms the people, overseeing both the moral teaching and transformation (*jiaohua*) of society and the political system; in short, he is the key to "modeling (one's actions) on Heaven and implementing the Way."

In the Qin dynasty, people tried to establish a state that was governed entirely by an impersonal system and laws. Because of this, they tried to have "officials serve as the only teachers" (*yi li wei shi* 以吏爲師).[53] What really succeeded in the Han dynasty, though, was moral education based on the Confucian classics plus external control based on a legal system—the so called method of mixed government through "a combination of the ways of the overlords [hegemons] and the sage kings" (*wang ba dao za zhi* 王霸道雜之).[54] Having "officials serve as the only teachers" became "appointing teachers as officials" (*yi shi wei li* 以師爲吏), an extremely important change. This change caused China's political ideology and its methods of government operation to include rites and music, law, emotions and reason. It also caused the Chinese intellectual stratum to

---

52   CQFL, j. 11, "Wang dao tong san, 44," ESEZ, 794.

53   This phrase is from the "Five Vermin" (Wudu) chapter of the *Han Fei Zi*, see Burton Watson, *Han Fei Tzu*, 1964, 111.

54   HS, j. 9, 277, in De Bary and Bloom, *Sources*, 313. For *wangdao*, kingly and *badao*, hegemonic rule, see *Mengzi*, "Gongsun Chou shang," & Lau, *Mencius*, 1970, 80.

become a part of the dynastic government regime, and this changed forever the fate of the Chinese intellectual elite.

As discussed above, it was people like the *wu* priests, *zhu* invocators, *shi* scribes and *zong* temple masters who were responsible for communication between Heaven, Earth and the Human in ancient times. They relied on their knowledge and technical arts to control the power to interpret meaning, value and rationality in the age after the "breaking off of communication between Earth and Heaven" (see Chapter One). At that time there was a certain mutual restraint between "cultural power" and "political power." After the Spring and Autumn and Warring States periods, the emergent *shi* scholar class employed all sorts of methods to disseminate their opinions about meaning, value and rationality. There was a certain amount of balance between cultural power and political power as well as a certain amount of freedom in society at that time. After the Qin-Han period this balance was destroyed. In times when a genuinely unified state was in need of authority, unity and stability, the position of the ruler was greatly enhanced. That is why we see Dong Zhongshu ranking human beings (or the people), ruler and Heaven in that order from lowest to highest and declared the great importance of the king or ruler. Then he argued that names (appellations) and titles (*ming* and *hao* 號) are all the Will of Heaven. The title of ruler possesses natural (Heaven-given) legitimacy and authority; to occupy the position of ruler is to be indisputably sacred.

In terms of actual rule, Dong Zhongshu pointed out that the ruler has unquestionable power, but he also has manifest responsibilities. These responsibilities fall into two categories; first, to "establish government through power and prestige"—to draw up penal laws and legal rules—and second, he "must implement moral education"—that is, value education based on moral virtue.[55] In this way not only would the ruler's system-building strategies achieve legitimacy, but the civil scholars whose métier was thinking freely would also have to acknowledge the political correctness of the bureaucratic administrative system.

In the ancient Chinese intellectual world, spring and autumn originally symbolized *de*, virtue, power, rewards, blessings, and *xing*, harm, punishments. *De* as "virtue" represented moral teaching and transformation, while *xing* as

---

55   HS, j. 60, "Du Zhou zhuan," quotes Du Zhou as follows: "The things that the former rulers considered to be right were written down as rules; what the later rulers considered to be right were promulgated as orders. Both the former and the later rulers were correct in their time. How did they follow the ancients? (i.e., they did not.)," 2659. CQFL, j. 11, "Wei renzhe tian," Chapter 41.3, ESEZ, 793.

"punishments" represented rule by laws. In the past, moral teaching depended upon civil scholars while the legal system depended upon officialdom; the former set up an Imperial University, studied the five classics, attached great importance to selecting the best officials and respected morality and virtue, while the latter appointed talented people, attached great importance to achievements in office, were experts in laws and commands and clearly understood merits and demerits. These were two very different professions and lifestyles, and they required very different value systems.[56] The former can be classified as following the "tradition of the moral principle" (*daotong*), while the latter can be classified as following the "tradition of political power" (*zhengtong*).

Under the absolute power of the state and the ruler, however, there appeared in Dong Zhongshu's thinking a tendency to equate the *daotong* and the *zhengtong*. To his way of thinking, since the intellectuals had entered the bureaucratic system, moral education and technical education, the cultivation of moral character and the selection of officials, were being united. This process also eventually eliminated the independent position of their knowledge and spirit. Secondly, because education and administration were understood as moral virtue and punishments and both were part of the ruler's actions to implement the Way on behalf of Heaven or to provide for the people's lives, they were complementary rather than contradictory. Morality then was the foundation of the legal system, the laws were the guarantor of morality, and this constituted the idea of "the unity of rites and laws" (*li fa he yi* 禮法合一) or "regarding rites as laws" (*yi li wei fa* 以禮爲法) in the Chinese political ideology. At this point a distinction began to emerge in the intellectual sector between so-called "reasonable officials" (*xunli* 循吏) and "harsh officials" (*kuli* 酷吏). The former stressed education and the latter stressed punishments, but they were actually very similar.[57]

The blending of these two ways of thinking led to the formation of a Chinese ideological system that was full of both flexibility and tension. This system also richly influenced the formation of the character and spirit of the Chinese intellectual strata. By that time the Confucian intellectual system had finally established as a state ideology that was intellectually coherent, embraced both

---

56   In 124 BCE Han Wudi accepted Gongsun Hong's suggestion to establish fifty students under the erudites and to allow them to be promoted to become state officials. This was an extremely important event in Chinese history. See HS, j. 88, "Rulin zhuan," 3594.

57   Watson, *Grand Historian*, vol. 2, 413–418 and 419–451 are respectively "The Biography of Reasonable Officials," and "The Biographies of Harsh Officials."

material and metaphysical aspects and functioned in society; this completed its transition from idealism to pragmatism.[58]

3.4

Here I want to discuss the question of the "resonance between Heaven and the Human" (*tian ren ganying* 天人感應). Many Chinese intellectual histories and histories of Chinese philosophy have all noticed the tendency in the thought of Dong Zhongshu and later Confucian scholars to connect calamities and strange occurrences in nature with human political affairs. We should not, however, regard this sort of "resonance" or "correspondence" theory as some kind of theological idealism because there was always in ancient China a very old and strong traditional idea that the affairs of the cosmos, society and humanity necessarily constituted a mutually interconnected and mutually interacting whole. As previously mentioned, this was the background of almost all ideas, knowledge, thought and techniques in Chinese intellectual history.

The idea of the Unity of Heaven and the Human (*tianren heyi* 天人合一) provided cosmological support for Confucian approaches to the social system and legal strategies. Just as the Confucian Literati (*wenxue*) group of critics said in their critique of the Imperial Secretary (*dafu*) group supporting the government in *The Discourses on Salt and Iron* (Yantielun) in 81 BCE: the Confucians obtained political support from the laws of the universe and then derived ideas about legal institutions from them. "Things are born and grow in spring and summer, die and hide in autumn and winter" and thus there is both moral teaching and penal law, but all of this must be "authorized from above." That is to say, all legitimacy must come from the emperor, and so "sages" and "rulers" became one, the rulers gained Heaven's support, and this could provide a rationale for autocracy.[59] The connection between the classic texts of the humanities and worldly laws and commands also provided ethical and moral justification for harsh penal laws, and on such a foundation official Confucianism steadily developed toward Legalism.

58　In his *Zhongguo zhonggu sixiangshi changbian*, Hu Shi correctly pointed out that Dong Zhongshu and others "not only established the basic model for the Han empire, but also influenced Chinese political thought and institutions for two thousand years." See *Hu Shi xueshu wenji*, 439. Also see Yu Yingshi, "Handai xunli yu wenhua chuanbo" in his *Zhongguo sixiang chuantong de xiandai quanshi*, 1987, 182.

59　*Yantielun*, j. 10, 58.7, CTP; *Yantielun jiaozhu*, 1992, 595. For a translation of chapters 1–19, see Esson M. Gale, *Discourses on Salt and Iron*, 1931. Gale translates the debaters as the "Literati" and the "Lord Grand Secretary."

I need to emphasize here, however, that there was another trend of elite thinking behind the "resonance between Heaven and the Human." On the one hand, from pre-Qin times on Confucian tradition emphasized slogans like "rulers should act like rulers, ministers like ministers, fathers like fathers, and sons like sons," "great unification" (*da yitong* 大一統), and "honor the king (royal house) and repel the barbarians" (*zunwang rangyi* 尊王攘夷) that provided a textual basis for the formation of a state ideology for the Han dynasty. On the other hand, they also employed ideas like "humane government" (*renzheng* 仁政) and "rule by virtue" (*dezhi* 德治) that provided a scholarly foundation for criticism by the intellectual elite. Originally the idea that the Way of Heaven and human nature are of primary importance could hold the autocratic power of rulers within certain limits, but the urgent need for symbolic authority during the process of Han dynasty state ideology formation brought the absolute position of the ruler to the fore and established a relation of equality between Heaven and the ruler. After the power and authority of the ruler had become so inflated, what force was left that could restrict or supervise this "Heaven-granted kingly power?"

From the Qin and Han on, the power and prestige of the ruler was raised to the extreme and the ruler had become the projection of Heaven or the incarnation of the gods. The title "Son of Heaven" had in reality once more cut off the natural relationship of the unity of Heaven and the Human. To explain this another way, the ancient "breaking off of communication between Earth and Heaven" (mentioned above) gave rise to the first generation of cultured or educated people (the *wu* priests, *zhu* invocators, *shi* scribes and *zong* temple masters) who were in charge of communication between Heaven and human beings. This Qin-Han "breaking off of communication between Earth and Heaven," then, strengthened the position of the Son of Heaven between Heaven and the human world and gave the Son of Heaven a monopoly on the power to communicate the Will of Heaven and the people's feelings. In this way, political power and cultural power were both concentrated in the person of the Son of Heaven. He was at once the political leader, the moral leader and the religious leader of the state.

Although the intellectual class could not but give prominence to the symbolic role of the ruler, they were still deeply worried about the possible limitless expansion of the ruler's power such that he might become the final arbiter of everything. For this reason, Dong Zhongshu repeatedly reminded the ruler that justice (*zhengyi* 正義) was a higher value than his interests, that conscience was more important than mere force and that Heaven's judgment was higher than his power. The reason Dong repeatedly mentioned calamities and strange occurrences in nature was simply in hopes that the ruler would exercise some restraint because Heaven could send down such calamities. In this way, the intellectual class could be able to speak out again on Heaven's behalf and have some power to contend against the government and restrain the power of the ruler. This was another meaning of the "resonance between Heaven and the Human" that should be seriously considered.

In 140 BCE, Han Wudi brought together many able, virtuous, honest and forthright scholars to the imperial court to answer his questions on government. At this time, Dong Zhongshu offered his opinions to the emperor on three occasions in his celebrated "three answers on Heaven and the Human." He confirmed the principles of the theory of "the Unity of Heaven and the Human" and the power of the ruler being granted by Heaven, drew up his ideas concerning Yin-Yang theory and its relation to punishments and rewards, laid out clear approaches to the political system and education, sought cosmological and historical foundations for these views, and emphasized the necessity for the state to unify thought and culture.

As much as Dong Zhongshu's "three answers" established the change of direction for Han Confucianism, and even laid the foundations for the Chinese state ideology for two thousand years to come, he did not personally experience a rapid rise in his official rank. In the end he retired and went home where he continued to write until he died. Nevertheless the influence of his thought paradigm was enormous, and it gradually took its place in the political life of the Han dynasty and was accepted throughout the intellectual interpretations and reasoning of generation after generation. The *History of the Former Han Dynasty* repeatedly says that Dong Zhongshu was the model for later scholars and the leader of Confucianism.[60] Such is the significance of his thought for Chinese intellectual history.

3.5

Under Han Wudi after 135 BCE, Confucianism became the center of the intellectual world and seeped into the general consciousness and daily life. From this point on, Confucianism also began to move away from its pre-Qin humanistic nature and orientation. The "discussions on salt and iron" called by Han Emperor Zhaodi in 81 BCE and the "Pavilion of the Stone Canal discussions" (*Shiquge yi*) called by Emperor Xuan (r. 74–49 BCE) in 51 BCE were two important events in this process of transforming Confucianism into the Han state ideology.[61] In the salt and iron debates, Confucian scholars and state officials carried on intense debates on the subjects of rule by moral teaching or by

---

60   HS, j. 27, "Wuxingzhi shang," 1317.

61   See HS, j. 7, "Zhaodi ji," and j. 8, "Xuandi ji," 223 and 272.

coercive laws, valuing agriculture or commerce, putting virtue or power first and other issues pitting idealism against pragmatism.[62] In the Stone Canal Pavilion debates between the Gongyang and Guliang schools of *Spring and Autumn Annals* interpretation, we see the inevitable situation in which different Confucian factions struggled for survival after Confucianism came to serve as the state ideology and the emperors became both political and spiritual leaders of the state.

Confucian doctrines receiving official approval would appear on the surface to have been a great victory for Confucianism, but it actually caused them to lose their freedom of independent criticism. When Confucian scholars became state officials under imperial power, they could not help being controlled and restricted by that power. Due precisely to this mutual interaction between political power and intellectual authority, Confucianism was gradually changed. A very important element in this transformation was the changes of the Confucian scholars themselves. They became state officials through the government selection system, with the result that the core values and behavioral norms contained in Confucian teachings were disseminated to the common people through education and administration while at the same time being embodied in the laws by means of the political system and textual practices.[63] Confucian doctrines became the inner core of the system of criminal laws, and Confucian scholars became government administrators—Han Confucianism had step by step risen to the position of a state ideology.

We should emphasize that this was a long process. Han Wudi's policies only took a step forward in raising the status of Confucius, but did not mean that state promotion of Confucian teachings had been firmly established. In his advice to his heir apparent, Emperor Xuan said "the House of Han has its own institutions and laws based on a combination of the ways of the overlords (hegemons) and the sage kings. How could we rely solely upon moral instruction and the governmental system of the Zhou?"[64] This shows that at that time the implications of Confucian teachings serving as a state ideology was not fully recognized, and the ceremonial worship of Confucius was only carried out by his decedents. The emperor and some officials occasionally paid their respects, but that did not mean the Confucian teachings had already become the "state teaching" (*guojiao*). It was not until the time of the emperors

---

62   On the discussions of salt and iron, see *Yantielun jiaozhu*, 1992, and Tang Zhijun et al., *The Classics and Politics in the Western Han* (Xi Han jingxue yu zhengzhi), 1994, chapter 5.

63   On the question of Confucian scholars becoming state officials, see Yan Buke, *Shidafu zhengzhi yansheng shigao*, 1996, 420–421.

64   HS, j. 9, 277, in De Bary and Bloom, *Sources*, 313.

Guangwu, Ming and Zhang of the Eastern Han—that is almost two hundred years after Dong Zhongshu—that Confucian thought or Confucianism finally completed its fundamental change.

According to the *History of the Later Han Dynasty* (Hou Hanshu), "Biographies of Confucian Scholars" (Rulin zhuan), Emperor Guangwu (r. 5 BC–57 CE) rebuilt the Liu family dynasty (Liu being the surname of the Han imperial family) after the Wang Mang usurpation (9–25 CE). He gathered together Confucian scholars from all over the empire, set up fourteen erudites of the five classics in government schools (*xueguan*), set up the Imperial University (*taixue*) and carried out ceremonies based on the precepts of the Confucian classic texts. Emperor Ming (r. 58–75) went on to insure the legitimacy and authority of succession to the throne by means of the ceremonial and symbolic system revered by the Confucians.[65] He called many Confucian scholars together and personally discussed the implications of the Confucian classics with them; he was even said to have made "being proficient in every part of the *Classic of Filial Piety* (Xiaojing)" the minimum educational and cultural standard for office holders.[66] Later on, in 78 CE, during Emperor Zhang's reign, a great conference was held in the White Tiger Hall in which political power was used to create a general and detailed outline of Confucian doctrine.[67]

3.6

The *Discourses in the White Tiger Hall* (Bohu tong), compiled from materials contained in the "Memorials on the White Tiger Hall" (Bohu yizou), was not just a report of the individual ideas of Confucian scholars, but it rather records the theoretical formulation of a state ideology that was already endorsed by the emperor.[68]

---

65   HHS, j. 79, 2545–2546.
66   According to HHS, j. 2, 95 "Mingdi ji," when Emperor Ming was "ten years old he could understand the *Spring and Autumn Annals* ... he studied with the academician Huan Rong and also learned to understand the *Book of Documents*." Also see ZZTJ, j. 44, 1434–1435.
67   HHS, j. 3, "Zhangdi ji," 138.
68   As for whether or not our extant *Bohu tong* is the same book as the Bohu tong delun mentioned in the HHS, j. 33, "Banbiao liezhuan, xia," see the "Bohu tong yi kao" in Wu Zehu's edition of the Qing scholar Chen Li's *Commentaries on the Discourses in the White Tiger Hall* (Bohu tong shuzheng) and Liu Shipei's "Bohu tong yi yuanliu kao." I agree with their view that the "Bohu yizou" is the original record and the *Bohu tong* is a later overall summary of the discussions. For a translation and the most complete introduction to the *Bohu tong*, see Tjan Tjoe Som, *Po-hu t'ung: The Comprehensive Discussions in the White Tiger Hall*, 1952.

The ideas in the *Discourses in the White Tiger Hall* were similar to those of Dong Zhongshu in that they also were supported by supposed knowledge of the natural laws of the cosmos. They inherited Dong's thinking about the relationship between Heaven and the Human, adopted ideas about astronomy (astrology), geography, Yin and Yang, Five Phases, and mantic and medical arts found in the very popular contemporary apocryphal texts (*weishu* 緯書), and imitated the overall structure of the *Huainanzi* to create a very well ordered and harmonious framework. The chapters entitled "Heaven and Earth," "Sun and Moon," and "The Four Seasons" describe how Heaven and Earth were born out of the "Great Origin" (*Taichu* 太初) leading to the "Great Beginning" (*Taishi* 太始) and the birth of "Primal Matter" (*Taisu* 太素).

The *Discourses in the White Tiger Hall* asserts that the cosmic Heaven above and Earth below symbolize the reasonable nature of a hierarchy of higher and lower status groups. Heaven and Earth were produced first and then in turn produced Yin and Yang; the movements of Heaven, Earth, sun and moon symbolize the relations between rulers and ministers and men and women; that the cosmos has day and night and winter and summer, and a year has four seasons are all suggestions to human beings of the significance of order and rules and regulations. The "Five Phases" chapter goes on to pair the Five Phases with the four seasons and the four directions, and to employ the increase and decrease of Yin and Yang to explain the sequence of changes in the four seasons and the four directions. It also expands upon these relationships in terms of the resonance between metal, wood, water, fire and earth and human beings. Then it goes on to link up the rise and fall of dynasties in history one by one with the Five Phases, the five flavors, the five notes, the calendar and the heavenly stems and earthly branches system. In this way the mysterious, sacred, silent and orderly actions of the natural laws of the cosmos became the ultimate origin of the rationality of everything.

Delineations of these natural cosmic laws were focused on order in the human world. First, all reasonable order in human society was derived from the natural order of the universe: since Heaven and Earth have Yin and Yang, then human society has higher and lower status groups; since the cosmos has a center and four directions, then human society has a central ruler and various regional rulers; since "Heaven has a myriad stars" (*tian you zhongxing* 天有眾星) symbolizes "the ruler has a myriad subjects" (*jun you zhongmin* 君有眾民), then it is rational for human society to have a hierarchical system of status ranks. Second, having established that, with cosmic support, these human norms go without saying, the *Discourses in the White Tiger Hall* goes on to discuss status ranks, forms of address, posthumous names and titles, sacrifices and so on from the emperor down to the common people. Relying on the symbolic nature of cosmic laws, it established a human social order centered on the ruler and also affirmed a state structure with a hierarchical *fengjian* system centered on the Son of Heaven.[69] In "The Three Bonds and Six Ties" (sangang liuji 三綱六紀) chapter, *Bohu tong* further explicates the ordered relations between human beings, Heaven and Earth, the sun and moon and the four seasons as well as the unquestionable nature of a socially stratified order.[70] Third, Confucian teaching as the state orthodoxy is confirmed in the "Biyong" (辟雍 Central Academy) chapter. The Confucian scholars acknowledged imperial power through their institutional ceremonies of rites and music, and the emperor reciprocated by granting them pedagogical power. In the realm of education, the way or principles of being a teacher (*shidao* 師道) maintained to some extent the dignity of culture and values and allowed the educated strata at least some power to "carry on the Way for Heaven" (*dai tian xing dao* 代天行道). Since these moral ideals also received support from Heaven, Earth and the Human, value, meaning, truth and knowledge could still maintain, with difficulty, their powers of judgment, and everything was not completely forced to submit to imperial power and be controlled by the cruel political rationale of raison d'état.

Up to this point, it all seems very concise and clearly understood. Those mystical numbers that the ancient Chinese believed in so much made all of these ideas seem naturally reasonable, and the picture of the universe composed by this set of numbers seemed to be exquisitely designed by the Creator (*zaohua*). All of the principles of the human world that this set of numbers summarized also seemed to have been meticulously arranged by the ancient Sages. The five Sages (Shennong, Yao, Shun, Yu, Tang) and the five feelings (*qing*)—humanity, rightness, propriety (rites), wisdom and trust, or joy, anger, grief, happiness, love and hate—not only represent human nature (*xing*) and disposition (same *qing*) but are also in tune with the cosmos. As the "The Three Bonds and Six Ties" has it, "the ruler is the mainstay of the minister, the father is the mainstay of the son, the husband is the mainstay of the wife," and this not only corresponds to the idea that "the alternation of Yin and Yang constitutes the Way," but also has cosmic support. That is because "The Three Mainstays model themselves on [the triad] of Heaven, Earth, and the Human. The Six

---

69   On *fengjian* as not equivalent to the European feudal system, see Chapter One. Also see Li Feng, " 'Feudalism' and Western Zhou China: A Criticism," *Harvard Journal of Asiatic Studies*, vol. 63, No. 1 (2003), 115–144.

70   See De Bary and Bloom, *Sources*, 345–346, where the "Three Bonds" are translated as "The Three Mainstays."

Ties model themselves on the six directions [the four quarters of east, west, north, and south and above and below]."[71]

All this was an attempt both to cover everything with one system of ideas or doctrine and to transform that doctrine into the political ideology of the state. From the *Discourses in the White Tiger Hall*, we can see that in the process of establishing this state ideology Confucian scholars both preserved their own cultural position and made some unavoidable political compromises. These compromises were apparent in their inclusion and syncretization of the cosmology of Huang-Lao, Yin and Yang, Five Phases and medical and mantic arts, and in their concessions to Legalism and the bureaucratic state system in the administration of society. This was the only way that Confucianism could become a political ideology that actually controlled the world of daily life. After this ideology was ultimately established in the Eastern Han, Confucianism, or rather state Confucianism, quickly developed into China's most powerful and inclusive intellectual doctrine. Once everyone became accustomed to accepting this doctrine, however, they had already unconsciously abandoned their ability to question. At that, an age of uniformity of thought had unexpectedly arrived.

4.   Classics and Apocrypha—The Consequences of Mutual Interaction between General Knowledge and Elite Thought

Qin and Han intellectual history continually revolved around the study of prophetic omens and apocryphal books. In the Han dynasty the fashion for omens and apocrypha (*chenwei* or *chanwei* 讖緯) can be said to have dominated almost fully half the intellectual world.[72]

4.1
In perusing the Han apocryphal books, we find a great deal of knowledge derived from the ancient Chinese medical and mantic arts. Examples are the

---

71 *Bohu tong shuzheng*, j. 8, "Sangang liuji," 1994, 374–375. De Bary and Bloom, *Sources*, 345 with slight modification, and 346 with brackets in original.

72 Omen lore (*chen* or *chan*) used writing or images to communicate mysterious predictions; the apocryphal texts used various types of knowledge to make and disseminate new interpretations of the Confucian classic texts. I focus here on the apocryphal texts. In the past, especially after the 1950s, the study of these *weishu* in Chinese intellectual history was dominated by criticism based on political background, modern scientific knowledge and Western philosophy.

art of calculating good and bad fortune from the *qi* 氣 of the *Book of Changes* trigrams, the method of "watching the vapors" (*wangqi*), divination by the winds and five notes and by examination of every sort of material event. There is also a great deal of cosmological knowledge concerned with calendrical science, astronomy, geography and products of the earth. We should always keep in mind that in the ancient Chinese intellectual world all of this knowledge came from the same cultural background and belonged to the same system of knowledge; it was all derived from experience and the association of ideas, and, on that account, was all regarded as both believable and reasonable. We can say that half of this knowledge was intended to predict good and bad fortune for society and human behavior while the other half was intended to forecast the movements and behavior of nature and the universe.

At that time these various forms of apocryphal knowledge that would later be classified under the headings of astronomy and geography were quite well developed. For example, in astronomy and calendar science, one text already contains an estimated calculation of the orbital cycle of a calendar year when it says that "one heavenly cycle contains 365¼ days (*du*), and one day is 1,932 *li*."[73] Another text also points out that "the earth has four quarters." This is, of course, caused by the fact that the sun's orbit is not perpendicular to the rotation of the earth and so this change comes about when the visual position of the sun is in the winter and summer solstice. When it says that "the earth often moves and people are not aware of it," it even makes us wonder whether the ancient Chinese had not in fact understood the rotation of the earth.[74] A further text even says "Heaven is like a hen's egg. Heaven is large and the Earth is small, and there is water inside and outside, and the entire earth received the life force or vital energy (*qi*) from Heaven and thus formed itself.[75] This geocentric theory that Heaven is round like an egg (*huntianshuo* 渾天說) has also caused us later to marvel at the ancient Chinese people's remarkable intuitive grasp of the cosmos.

In terms of geography and the natural sciences, many passages demonstrate contemporary people's understanding of the world they lived in. Examples include one text connecting the various prefectures—Ji, Yang, Jing, Qing, Xu, Yan, Yu, Yong, Yi, You and Bing—with the realms of the twenty-eight constellations.[76] A similar text contains records about Qi, Chen, Qin, Tang, Wei

---

73 See *Luoshu zhenyaodu* 《洛书甄耀度》, WSJS, 129.

74 See *Shangshu Kaolingyao* 《尚书考灵曜》, WSJC, 94, 139.

75 See *Chunqiu yuanmingbao* 《春秋元命苞》, WSJC, 103.

76 *Chunqiu yuanmingbao, Gu wei shu*, j. 7, WSJC, 185–186. *Gu wei shu* is an anthology of apocryphal texts in 36 *juan* compiled between the late Ming and early Qing by Sun Jue.

and other areas and their associated seasonal time periods, musical notes, distinctive features of the land and popular customs. Numerical descriptions of the lands, mountains and rivers of the world are also recorded in another text in a similar vein. Although in the realm of imagination, these are still attempts to map the resources of the world, and they represent contemporary understandings of the geographical environment. The account of the music of the barbarians of the four corners and the comparison of their implements, written language, musical instruments and daily life with those of China represent contemporary people's knowledge and conjectures about the cultures on their borders.[77]

The two areas of knowledge discussed above all came from the same intellectual milieu and relied on the same background. At the time in the Warring States period when "the art of the Way [was] rent and torn apart by the world," and elite thought and general knowledge separated, it seems as if both these areas of knowledge were pushed to the margins of intellectual history.

This does not mean, however, that such knowledge disappeared. The "Monograph of Arts and Letters" section of the *History of the Former Han Dynasty* contains many references to what was known by the general term of the mantic arts and demonstrates that they remained a large division of knowledge. The first section contains mostly the arts of divination by the stars similar to ancient astronomy; second is the art of making almanacs, related to calendrical science; third come Yin-Yang and punishments and rewards, the art of predicting by the Five Phases and calamities and strange occurrences in nature, including geomancy, divination by musical tones, divination based on cosmic boards and so on; fourth are *Book of Changes* divination by tortoise carapace and milfoil, a very ancient form of prediction; fifth are miscellaneous forms of divination by examination of virtually anything that happens, like ghosts and demons, pig, ox, goat, horse, fowl and dog monsters, ringing in the ears, sneezing, strange dreams and so on; sixth are divination by the shapes or forms of things, including the geography of strange places, choosing where to live, examining the appropriateness of objects and so on.

From all of this, we can see that in the Han period the techniques of the mantic arts were all-inclusive and a very familiar part of everyone's general knowledge. That they continued to persist is evidence that the background of ancient thought was not as pure and elegant as we have generally imagined it to be, and it is not surprising that the study of apocryphal texts grew out of it.

---

77   *Shi han shenwu*《诗含神雾》and *Xiaojing yuanshenqi*《孝经援神契》, *Yueji yaojia* 《乐稽耀嘉》, *Gu wei shu*, j. 23, WSJC, 289, 320.

It is worth noting that although this thought and these techniques all derived originally from ancient China, before the Qin-Han period they remained in a widespread but fragmentary state; at least to this day we have not seen a formal intellectual exposition of all of them from the pre-Qin period. During the Qin-Han period, however, when the Chinese intellectual world gradually developed a fixed form, the original and latent theoretical foundations of this thought and these techniques were also activated. As the ancient Chinese intellectual world developed an integrated authoritative intellectual system, adepts like *wu* priests and *zhu* invocators became aware of the significance of such a system. They then set about consciously to search for publicly accepted, mainstream and systematic theoretical and classic textual support for their own knowledge and techniques.

As the "Biographies of Diviners" (Rizhe liezhuan), chapter 127 of the *Records of the Grand Historian* records, the things that the diviner from the state of Chu, Sima Jizhu, and his disciples discussed already go beyond concrete arts of divination They are rather said to have "discussed the Way of Heaven and Earth, the movements of the sun and moon, and the roots of Yin and Yang and good and bad fortune." When Jia Yi and Song Zhong (d. 219 CE) asked Sima Jizhu to enlighten them, he is reported to have "clarified what he had previously said, distinguished between the beginning and end of Heaven and Earth, and the order of the Sun, Moon and the stars; established a hierarchical order of humanity and rightness and arranged the signs of good and evil. He said a myriad of things and all his words accorded with rational principles (*li*)."[78] The Way in the "Way of Heaven and Earth" and the principles in "accorded with rational principles" were not simply mantic and medical techniques for solving concrete problems. While the theory of the resonance of Heaven and the Human was being validated and accepted by the elite class, they also wanted to seek connections with the authoritative classics and elevate their cultural quality so they could stake out a position in an age when elite scholars monopolized the cultural arena. This was probably one of the reasons for the rise of apocryphal books during the Han period.

4.2

Similar to the tendency of the holders of general knowledge to promote their knowledge into the realm of elite thought, the elite thinkers were also looking for resources in general knowledge. Since the beginning of the Han period, Confucian scholars continually revised their thinking by adopting a great deal of Yellow Emperor Daoist thought to construct their own cosmological system,

---

78   *Shiji*, 127.3 in CTP.

a great deal of Legalist thought to develop their own version of political institutions and legal rules, and a great deal of mantic knowledge to set up their own systematic theory of communication between the cosmos, practical political operations and social life. Here are two examples of all this.

The *History of the Former Han* "Biography of Wei Xiang and Bing Ji," records that during Emperor Xuan's reign, Wei Xiang (?–59 BCE) "several times sent memorials in which he adopted ideas from the "Yi Yin and Yang" (Yi Yin Yang) and from the "Hall of Brightness" and the "Monthly Ritual Proceedings" (Yueling) in the *Book of Rites*."[79] The so-called "Yi Yin and Yang" concerns the transformations of Yin and Yang (based on the *Book of Changes*); the "Bright Hall" concerns the ceremonial and sacrificial system; the "Monthly Ritual Proceedings" concerns the arrangement of many things using calendrical science—all of these texts have nothing to do with ethics and morality, but are close to ways of dealing with practical calamities and changes due to Yin and Yang, prayers to the gods and calendrical calculations of heavenly phenomena.

The *History of the Former Han* "Biography of Yi Feng" also records that Yi Feng "liked to practice divination by Yin and Yang and the twelve tone chromatic scale." During Emperor Xuan's reign, he submitted a memorial telling the emperor that he could employ "the six feelings and the twelve tone chromatic scale" to understand his subordinates. Using the so-called "six feelings and twelve tones" meant correlating the six traditional human feelings—joy, anger, liking, hate, grief, happiness—with the five directions—north, south, east, west and center—and integrating them with the twelve earthly branches. In this way, Yi Feng subsumed all the traditional forms of divination and prognostication—calendrical predictions, "watching the vapors," under the Yin-Yang-Five-Phases system—so that they could function in the political sphere. Yi Feng was originally a Confucian scholar who specialized in the Qi school of commentary on the *Book of Songs* (*Qishi* 齊詩), but he ultimately spurred on the flourishing of the apocryphal texts.[80]

The use of apocryphal texts seems to have been a common practice at the time, and we can see the place they occupied in the popular mind from the following two events. First, the *History of the Former Han* "Biography of Zhai Fangjin" records that during Emperor Cheng's reign (51–7 BCE), Zhai's subordinate Li Xun observed the planet Mars in the center of the sky and believed that a calamity was imminent. He sent a memorial to remind Zhai Fangjin that some government reforms should be made to avoid this impending calamity. This worried Zhai because he also believed in astrology. He heard

79   HS, j. 74, 3139.
80   HS, j. 75, 3167.

that a great official should take responsibility for such an implied catastrophe, and after being reprimanded by Emperor Cheng, he actually "committed suicide on the same day."[81]

Second, the celebrated story of the panting bull occurs in the above mentioned "Biography of Wei Xiang and Bing Ji." When Bing Ji was in charge of current court affairs he showed little interest in most things, but one day, however, when he saw "a bull panting with his tongue hanging out," he paid it very close attention indeed.[82] This implies that someone occupying one the three highest official posts in the land had to be very concerned about the "harmony of Yin and Yang." Whether or not this bull was panting abnormally could be a sign of an improper balance between Yin and Yang, and Bing Jin would have to concern himself with it.[83]

Wei Xiang, Yi Feng and Zhai Fangjin were all Confucian scholars well versed in the classics, but when Confucian doctrines were unable to predict future good and evil fortunes or inform society how to pray and sacrifice to avoid calamities, then they had to incorporate knowledge and techniques from other doctrines. They had to revise their original intellectual system. They could also rely on omens and symbols, "watching the vapors," astrology or miscellaneous divination, or use the theory of Yin-Yang and the Five Phases and employ the trigrams of the *Book of Changes*, the heavenly stems and earthly branches and calendrical science . . . to bring all of these to bear on the practical operations of government.

Knowledge of the mantic and medical arts was originally quite unsystematic. When it entered the upper stratum of society and was required to explain what was already known and what was not yet known as well as present and future events and phenomena, it's practitioners began to incorporate mainstream theories of the cosmos. With the aid of theoretical explanations, experience and creative vision, they rapidly increased the scope of its inclusiveness. As a result, the apocryphal texts developed quite a rich content, most of it related to the knowledge and techniques of *wu* priests, *zhu* invocators, *shi* scribes and *zong* temple masters. All of this knowledge was then absorbed into the philosophical ideas of the various schools, and, on that account, it went beyond concrete, operational techniques to enter into the realm of pure philosophical disputation.

In the Han period, the writers of the apocryphal texts wanted to organize all observable events and phenomena into their system of order and give them

---

81   HS, j. 84, 3421–3424.

82   HS, j. 74, 3147.

83   HS, j. 85, "Du Ye zhuan," 3476.

appropriate and reasonable, or at least credible, explanations. They also strove to broaden the scope of applicability of their ideas and arrange and predict ahead of time situations and events that might possibly occur so as to insure that the authority of their theories would be unchallenged. To do this they had to expand their imaginative and speculative reasoning—to conjure up the unknown from the known, to speculate about future phenomena from those presently existing and to expand from the experiential to the theoretical. They chose *qi* (cosmic energy, vapor, etc.), Yin and Yang and the Five Phases not only because they represented the earliest accepted ideas of ancient China but also because these theories could always offer apparently correct explanations of everything, and they coincided with people's intuition and experience. "[They seem] to have been accepted by most, if not all, of the prominent thinkers of [the] Han [dynasty] as an explanation of the continuation of the world's natural sequences" because they came from the ancient Chinese intellectual world, had a traditionally authoritative nature and their explanations could very effectively justify themselves.[84] No matter whether their explanations represented the imaginative creativity of genius or only involved superficial analogies, they still gave contemporary people great confidence in their ability to understand everything.

4.3

Obtaining cosmic support was undoubtedly one important channel for such mantic knowledge to gain authority and belief, but it was not enough. After the Confucian texts came to occupy the status of official classics, seeking to be analogous to them was another way for mantic knowledge to gain authority and belief.

We know that the idea of regarding the Six Classics as the foundation of knowledge and truth already existed before the Han dynasty.[85] This was because these classic texts were not only the ancient classics of the former kings with a long and glorious pedigree, but also because they really did have very rich contents and rather broad leeway for interpretation.

---

84   See CHC, vol. 1, 1986, 691.

85   Although j. 20, "The Exalted Lineage" (Taizu) of the *Huainanzi* criticizes the classics by stating that "the shortcoming of the *Changes* is superstition; the shortcoming of the *Music* is lewdness; the shortcoming of the *Songs* is foolishness; the shortcoming of the *Documents* is rigidity; the shortcoming of the *Rites* is stubbornness, and the shortcoming of the *Spring and Autumn* is censoriousness," this was only the view of a minority of Huang-Lao scholars; later on there was basically only praise for the Six Classics. See *Huainanzi honglie jijie*, 1989, 674; Major, et al., *Huainanzi*, 20.13, 808.

As noted in the Introduction, Sima Qian's Preface to the *Records of the Grand Historian* lists the contents of the Five Classics as including Heaven and Earth, Yin-Yang, Four Seasons, Five Phases, regulating human relationships, mountains, rivers, streams and valleys as well as grasses, trees, fish and animals and so on. The *Book of Changes* excelled in transformations, the *Book of Rites* excelled in practice, the *Book of Documents* excelled in government, the *Book of Songs* excelled in satire, the *Classic of Music* (lost classic) excelled in harmony, and the *Spring and Autumn Annals* excelled in ruling men. Accordingly, the Six Classics were said to include not only cultural spirit and exemplary individual characters, but also every aspect of the cosmos, politics, nature and society.

This tendency to venerate the classics was even more obvious from the Western Han on. The "Biography of Xiahou Sheng" (HS, j. 75) records that Xiahou Sheng once very confidently said that men of culture must understand the classics because understanding the classics gave one easy access to the higher strata of society. If one did not understand the classics, one was only fit to be a farmer.[86] This demonstrates that in the Han period studying the classics was no longer of merely cultural significance, but was also a form of knowledge with political implications. The relationship between the classics and political power and economic interest had already given them a correct and unchallengeable position of intellectual monopoly and practical use. The *History of the Former Han Dynasty* "Biography of Kuang Heng" records that he submitted a memorial to Emperor Cheng in which he stated that the Six Classics embody the root of Heaven and Earth, the laws of society, that they are the origin of knowledge and "the everlastingly unchanging Way."[87] Writings that were originally about history, literature, divination and ceremonial practices having once obtained such absolute spiritual significance and practical advantages were no longer texts that could be freely examined and interpreted. They had become "classics" that were exalted above all other texts and could only be the object of admiration and belief.

Once there were "classics texts" (*jing*) then there would naturally be "apocryphal texts" (*weishu*) whose compilers hoped to enjoy the authority of the classics. After all, there were a limited number of classics, and, no matter how freely they were interpreted, they were limited by history and their status as canonical texts. Apocrypha, however, could be produced without limit; they could combine popular knowledge, techniques, imagination and experience, and, due to their relationship with the classics, they could share in their authoritative glow. Thus the *Book of Changes*, the *Book of Rites*, the

---

86   HS, j., 75, 3159.
87   HS, j. 81, 3343.

Book of Documents, the *Book of Songs*, and the *Spring and Autumn Annals* all became over-interpreted text and were assigned much sacred and mystical significance. Although the Confucian classics were very important ever since Confucius himself, their meanings were not always clear and these apocryphal texts were necessary for providing concrete foundations and practical examples of their relevance. According to the admittedly incomplete collection of still surviving apocryphal texts in the *Anthology of Ancient Apocrypha* (Gu weishu), there were nineteen *weishu* for the *Book of Documents*, fifteen for the *Spring and Autumn Annals*, eleven for the *Book of Changes*, three for the *Book of Rites*, three for the *Classic of Music*, three for the *Book of Songs*, five for the *Analects*, seven for the *Classic of Filial Piety* and twenty-three for the so-called *Yellow River Diagram* (Hetu 河圖) and the *Luo Writing* (Luoshu 洛書), *Book of Changes* cosmograms. In the Han period these nearly ninety *weishu* had quite a large number readers and followers.[88]

On further analysis we can see that simply having theoretical and intellectual authority was not enough to achieve intellectual hegemony. Another reason for the authority of the Confucian classics was that they were able to obtain a monopoly of interpretation of the state ideology and political, legal and education systems. For the apocryphal texts to gain the same authority as the Confucian classics, the compilers had to establish their significance in the realm of politics. Consequently, the ultimate orientation of the *weishu* was primarily toward court affairs. This passionate interest in politics impelled the *weishu* compilers to search actively through history for past examples they could offer as relevant to contemporary politics; this in turn caused their texts to be replete with stories about the glory and disgrace of historical figures mixed in with mystical legends of successes and failures dictated by destiny or the Mandate of Heaven. At the same time these texts were especially concerned with the contemporary world and employed calamities, strange occurrences in nature and auspicious omens to warn the authorities. They offer quite a few opinions about government policies and present governmental success or failure as intimately connected to the changes in Heaven and Earth. They obviously hoped for an unquestionably rational political order that resonated with the laws of nature. For this reason, they tended to go beyond their authority and recommended plans that were related to the general contemporary political situation. The compilers hoped to employ the rites and ceremonies that held such an important symbolic significance in the minds of the ancient Chinese to rectify the human order. At the same time they hoped by means of

---

88   For the *Hetu* and the *Luoshu*, see Lynn, *Changes*, 66, 72, n. 35, 74, n. 52.

their discussions about order to raise their cultural status and the standing of the knowledge and techniques written up in their texts.

4.4

For three to four hundred years, from the Qin-Han transition to the end of the Han (206 BCE–220 CE), the study of the apocryphal texts in the Chinese intellectual world went from rise to flourish to decline. This study combined the ideas of ancient Chinese cosmology, astronomy, geography, divination techniques, legendary accounts of immortals as well as traditional morality and political theories. In doing so, it demonstrated the tendency toward the systematization of thought during the long Han period and stimulated the birth of a state theology (*guojia shenxue* 國家神學).

We can say in general that the main motive force behind the study of the apocrypha came both from the efforts of the adepts (practitioners) from the lower strata of society to raise their own status in conformity with the authority of the officially recognized classics, and from the efforts of the elite thinkers to absorb knowledge and techniques from popular thought. Ever since the differentiation of elite and general thought, these trends did not always travel separate roads, but experienced various kinds of mutual exchange. Medical arts, the theories of Yin-Yang and the Five Phases as well as astronomical and geographical knowledge were undergoing a process of blending at the same time that Confucian thought was also absorbing ideas from these areas of thought. Elite thought and general knowledge, then, found their common background and foundation in the same ancient Chinese cultural soil and they grew together out of this common environment.

This mixing and growing together, however, led to a collapse of the boundary between thought and knowledge. Confucian scholars after Dong Zhongshu relied on official power to establish firmly the position of orthodox or mainstream thought and, besides the knowledge of the classic texts, they also absorbed various forms of knowledge and techniques from all kinds of thought including the apocryphal texts. By the time the "Memorials on the White Tiger Hall" and the *Discourses in the White Tiger Hall* were compiled, acceptance of the study of omens and apocrypha by Confucian scholars was no longer problematic, and apocrypha were no longer "the other" to the classics. As the study of apocrypha became accepted by the orthodox and mainstream, they also lost their original significance or raison d'être; they had reached the height of their influence and began to decline. Once the Confucian scholars had incorporated their theories of Yin and Yang, the Five Phases and astrological divination into the orthodox mainstream ideology, all that was left of the apocrypha was their original mantic and medical arts. The apocrypha retreated under rationalist scholarly criticism and returned to the arena of popular culture where they had begun.

By contrast, the Confucian classics were established as China's authoritative thought. In the Western Han, emperors Wen and Jing only established academicians or erudites in the *Book of Songs* and the *Gongyang Commentary to the spring and Autumn Annals*, Emperor Wudi "established erudites of the five classics" and Emperor Xuan officially established the five classics and their fourteen erudites. In the beginning of the Han dynasty, these erudites acted only as advisors and could not intervene in politics, but later, during Emperor Wudi's reign, Gongsun Hong was made one of the three chief ministers and awarded the title of Regional Ruler of Pingjin due to his erudition in the *Spring and Autumn Annals*.[89] The students of these erudites went from fifty in Emperor Wudi's time to one hundred in Emperor Zhao's time to two hundred under Emperor Xuan and to three thousand during the reign of Emperor Cheng. Anyone who was an expert on one of the classics would be exempt from corvée labor, and the study of the classics was understandably regarded as the only ladder leading upward to an ideal life; this even more induced the scholar class to regard the classics as the fount of all knowledge. To contemporary scholars, the classics were undoubtedly the pillars of personal character and spiritual values, but they were also a general repository of knowledge and techniques; they could be employed as textbooks for learning language and writing, understanding the names of plants and animals and the ways of proper human conduct in society.

The "Biography of Huan Rong" in the *History of the Later Han Dynasty* records that when Huan was appointed an imperial advisor (*shaofu*) and given carriages and horses by the emperor, he was enormously proud and he declared that all of these honors came to him through his study of the classics. By studying the classics one could achieve worldly position and wealth, but one could also learn the most fundamental humanistic knowledge and gain a most profound understanding of the cosmos. Thus the study of the classics became an absolutely important field of intellectual endeavor. From then on, the science of interpretation of the absolutely authoritative classics also became the origin of knowledge for Chinese elite thought and the evidential proof of all truth. From the classics and their commentaries, one could obtain all knowledge, and in the classics and their commentaries, the truth of that knowledge came to possess complete rationality.

---

89   *Shiji*, j. 121, "Rulin liezhuan," 3118.

CHAPTER 5

Confucianism, Daoism and Buddhism from the End of the Eastern Han to the Early Tang Dynasty, I (ca. Mid-2nd to Mid-7th Centuries)

Prologue: Foreign Influence Enters China

Its particular geographical situation may have limited ancient China's contact with the outside world, but this did not isolate China from the rest of the world. An increasingly interesting topic in recent years has been the question of just when the ancient Chinese started to make contact with the outside world. What was the scope of this contact and what were its results?

Various ancient texts, like the "King's Audience" (Wanghui) chapter of the *Remaining Zhou Documents*, the *Biography of Mu Tianzi* (Mu Tianzi zhuan) and the *Classic of Mountains and Seas*, all contain some anecdotal and fanciful narratives concerning the lands on the borders of ancient China. These stories no doubt represent the limits of contemporary Chinese imaginings about the far off world and cannot be given too much credence.[1] Recently, however, reliable archeological discoveries and serious textual study have made it necessary for us to reevaluate ancient Chinese knowledge of the outside world. Ancient Chinese civilization was rather richer than hitherto supposed and communication was somewhat more developed than we had assumed. Although we cannot fathom the relationships between ancient China and the rest of the world on the basis of hearsay evidence, using the reliable evidence now available it is evident that ancient China was not isolated from the larger world. During the Han dynasty due to a number of factors—the Han struggle against the Xiongnu over the control of the Western Regions, the westward migration of the Tokharians (*Yuezhi*), the rise of the Kushan Empire (*Guishuang Wangchao*), the juxtaposition of the Han and the Roman empires, the development of both land and sea transportation technologies—the Chinese vision

---

1 Volume One, Chapter Three, of Fang Hao's *Zhong-xi jiaotong shi*, 1987 reprint, already points out that there was interaction between China and its border regions in the pre-Qing era; Chapter Four points out that Chinese knowledge was transmitted westward before the Han dynasty, but Chapter Five (44–77) most strongly emphasizes that it was not until 138 BCE when Zhang Qian went on his mission to the Western Regions that "a new situation was created that had great influence on future generations."

© KONINKLIJKE BRILL NV, LEIDEN, 2014 | DOI 10.1163/9789047425076_007

of the world was suddenly expanded. This vision also began to have genuinely significant influences on the Chinese intellectual world. The "Record of the Dayuan" (Dayuan liezhuan, Dayuan is in today's Central Asia) in the *Records of the Grand Historian* and the "Record of the Western Regions" (Xiyu zhuan) in the *History of the Former Han Dynasty* already demonstrate a rather greater understanding of the world west of the Jade Gate and the Yangguan Pass (both in Gansu). By the Eastern Han, Chinese had reached the Seleucid Empire and understood the Roman Empire in the west (Great Qin, *Da Qin* 大秦), knew about the Tiele and the Kyrgyz peoples and had reached Lake Baikal in the northwest; as the golden seal with the inscription "Han King of the Wonu" (Han Wonu *guowang*) discovered in Kyûshû proves, the Chinese certainly had already interacted with the Japanese.[2]

The broadening of the Chinese world inevitably led to cultural intermingling and conflict, and this inevitably led to changes in the Chinese intellectual world. Generally speaking, in an age when the state ideology was maturing and rigidifying, it no longer possessed the internal resources for self-renewal. Even if it did, it would only amount to some internal adjustments that would not influence the overall structure of the intellectual world. At this time, however, the opening out to the world and the collision with different thoughts gave this relatively closed intellectual world some motive forces for change. On the eve of the era we are just about to enter, the most important intellectual resources arriving from outside were from Buddhism that originated in India. In my view, after the Chinese intellectual world had gone through the divisions of the Spring and Autumn and Warring States eras and then developed a systematic ideology during the Han dynasty, it no longer had the internal drive necessary for self-renewal. It was just at this juncture that Buddhism arrived and offered a critical opportunity for the self-adjustment of the Chinese intellectual world.

In great measure, Chinese intellectual history after the Han is simply the history of the transmission of Buddhism and its Sinification, the rise of religious Daoism and its responses to Buddhism, and the continual absorption and blending of Buddhist thought into traditional Chinese thought. During this process of continuous re-discovery of native resources many new ideas and new lines of thought constantly appeared.

---

2 He Changqun, "Handai yihou Zhongguoren duiyu shijie dili zhishi de yanjin," *He Changqun shixue lunzhu xuan*, 1985, 28–29.

1.   Evolution of Autochthonous Chinese Thought and Learning from Han to Jin

The most obvious trend in Chinese intellectual history during the Western Han dynasty was the unification of thought and the merging of the tradition of political power and the tradition of Confucian moral principle as well as knowledge and power.

During the Eastern Han, however, two opposite trends occurred in the Chinese intellectual world. The first was the separation of intellectual doctrines and the marginalization of intellectuals from political power. At this time, the palace eunuchs and the imperial relatives on the maternal side—people who had nothing to do with thought and learning—occupied the center of political power. Han Emperor Ming wrote a text entitled *Comments on Essential Interpretations of Passages by Five Classics Masters* (Wujia yaoshuo zhangju),[3] and also lectured at the state University. Then he actually compared himself in public to Confucius and referred to his minister Huan Yu (?–93) as Confucius' student Zi Xia (ca. 507–? BCE).[4] This anecdote symbolizes well the arrogance of political power toward the Way of Confucian moral tradition.

The second trend was the stifling of thought brought about by uniformity. A few texts became classics, these classics were given standardized interpretations, and all questions came to have ready made answers within the confines of this standardization. This made the political powers that be look down on intellectual endeavors. This was especially so when mastery of this body of thought was a tool on the road to office holding—people simply did not want to explore new worlds of thought, and it was hard for them to doubt the old system of ideas. In the Eastern Han, one Fan Zhun (?–116) submitted a memorial in which he stated that "erudites occupy positions but do not instruct, and Confucian scholars compete in discussing trivial things."[5] No matter how flourishing culture seemed to be on the surface, independent thought and spirit were disappearing. Latent in these two tendencies, however, was a coming transformation of thought and learning.

1.1

When culture contends with political power, its only capital is its possession of "knowledge" and "truth." The intellectual strata, however, lost the ability to contend against power by means of truth in an age when thought had

---

become solidified into an officially recognized political ideology and, through education, had also become standard universally recognized knowledge. At that point, the intellectuals declined from "teachers of rulers" to "servants of emperors." The scholars of this era often had to elevate the spirit of idealism, rely on the concept of the "superior man" (*junzi*) and take the high moral ground to criticize contemporary reality. Through their high sounding discussions they hoped to win back their authority and avoid further marginalization. This was a dangerous enterprise, though. In the latter part of the Western Han, Gai Kuanrao (fl. 1st century BCE) tried to admonish the emperor on the basis of "the Way of the Sages" (*shengdao* 聖道) with the result that the emperor denounced him, and all he could do was to "draw his sword and cut his own throat beneath the northern gate."[6]

Nevertheless the intellectual strata had to maintain this stance because classical knowledge was their only resource and ideals and morality were their hallmarks. They could not themselves become the center of power, but through their discussions, that is, public opinion, they could admonish the holders of power to maintain moral standards. From this we can understand why Wang Mang, usurper of the Han throne (r. 9–23), enjoyed such great prestige and influence at the end of the Western Han. His emergence was praised and approved by virtually all of the scholar official class, and even the quite obviously biased account in the *History of the Former Han Dynasty* could not but aver that Wang Mang was a very learned and modest man just like a Confucian scholar. He respected the wise, honored famous Confucian scholars, sought peace with the Xiongnu, and revered the classical traditions. He made official appointments and reformed the state system on the basis of the *Rites of Zhou* and the "Royal Regulations." He also traveled around performing sacrifices in keeping with the ancient practices, and he followed the ancient formality of granting official positions in the Hall of Brightness. Wang Mang's practices based on classical tradition were obviously impractical and they were strongly opposed by the nobility, but greatly supported by the intellectual class. Wang Mang's ultimate failure, though not the decisive factor, to a great degree actually led to a loss of idealism among the scholar officials.[7]

The tense relationship between thought and power did not really change in the Eastern Han. The ruthless power struggles between the imperial household, the imperial relatives on the maternal side and the palace eunuchs only served to exacerbate the tension. The power holders of the Eastern Han

---

6 HS, j. 77, 3243–3248.

7 See HS, j. 99, "Wang Mang zhuan," 4039–4069. For a fair evaluation of Wang Mang, see CHC, vol. 1, Chapter 3.

generally had a pragmatic attitude toward culture, thought and knowledge. Under political pressure, a segment of the intellectual strata usually had to abandon their morally superior man ideals and enter the civil bureaucracy. There they employed their practical knowledge and technical skills to assert their own value. Another segment of the men of letters, however, even more stubbornly abided by their idealism, criticized the anti-intellectualism of vulgar society and defended classical knowledge. They preserved their status in the intellectual and cultural realms as well as their distance and differences from other social strata. More importantly, this spirit of resistance that was forced upon some Eastern Han men of letters gradually changed the intellectual climate from pragmatism toward idealism.

Fan Ye (398–445), compiler of the *History of the Later Han Dynasty*, once criticized famous Eastern Han scholars for their sensationalism and deliberate search for fame, but this was precisely the position that they had to maintain.[8] As much as vulgar scholar officials continued to be preoccupied with practical knowledge, there were some elite intellectuals who insisted that "upright men" (*zhengren* 正人) were the character model for morally superior *junzi* and continued to maintain the absolutely truthful nature of "upright discourse" (*zhenglun* 正論).[9] In 106 a scholar named Shang Min submitted a memorial expressing his worries about the pursuit of practical gain and handling of government affairs by vulgar officials. He wrote that "vulgar clerks are everywhere numerous while Confucian scholars are very few" and that even if they were Confucian scholars in name they still "do not concentrate on studying the classics, but only compete to gain personal connections."[10] He cited the classics for support, and most interestingly said that "the emperor's ministers are in fact teachers and this means that their moral virtue can serve to instruct the emperor." Here we see the Confucian literati's dissatisfaction with the subservient status of the "emperor's ministers" as well as their attempt to rely on their culturally refined character and moral integrity to realize their hope to

---

8 On the one hand, HHS, j. 82, "Fangshu zhuan shang," 2724–2725 and j. 61, 2032, "Huang Qiong zhuan," quotes Li Gu: "popular opinion all considers that critical scholars simply enjoy a false reputation." We can see that this was not only Fan Ye's view, but the idea already existed in the Eastern Han. On the other hand, though, we see that the famous Eastern Han scholar Fan Pang (137–169) once also said something at his trial that he probably believed was most important. He said that his ideal was to distinguish clearly the superior values of the morally pure group from the inferior values of the morally corrupt groups.

9 See HHS, j. 79 shang, "Rulin liezhuan shang," 2552 and j. 25, "Lu Pi zhuan," 883–885.

10 Yuan Hong (328–376), *Hou Han ji*, j. 15, 2002, 298.

transcend political power. Classical knowledge was the only leverage they had to resist the powers that be.

In the mid-second century CE, this kind of idealism became fashionable and a group of idealistic elite scholars became something like intellectual heroes. They gathered together regularly to discuss politics and various contemporary personalities. It is said that even court officials were afraid of the influence of their discussions and were forced to compromise with them. When this sort of idealism began to intervene in politics and threaten the powerful, however, then they became the object of fierce counter attacks. The persecution of the intellectuals in the "Great Proscription" (*danggu* 黨錮, from 169–184) of the Eastern Han represented a tremendous setback for the spirit of idealism and the general standard of right and wrong. It also led to enormous changes in Chinese intellectual history.

1.2

The final political ideology that developed from the Western to the Eastern Han was a vast overarching system that covered everything. It was as though all knowledge was included in this framework according to which people only had to adjust their lives and supplement their personal knowledge to make everything perfect. Under the umbrella of this complete self-sufficient ideological system, there was little scope for the development of new thought. Even though there were over thirty thousand students attending the officially sponsored schools, genuine thought was steadily declining.[11]

This situation stimulated, however, an intellectual landscape the chief character of which was a search for wide learning and near encyclopedic knowledge. In an age lacking both resources and drive for intellectual change, people quite easily tried to steer their individual thinking in the direction of the accumulation of new knowledge for its intrinsic pleasure in areas that they had never before explored. This was particularly the case when the classics had become compulsory reading and demonstrating ones talent and intellect through interpretation of the classics was increasingly prevalent. Such interpretations stimulated the growth of knowledge in history, language philology, and the natural sciences. The Eastern Han study of the classics transformed thought into a focus on words and phrases or a practical means of advancement; on the other hand, it also formed an intellectual climate that promoted knowledge in those new areas. All of this gave rise to a trend of "studying ancient texts" (*guxue* 古學) and to a tradition of cultivating "Confucian scholars of comprehensive learning" (*tongru* 通儒). Scholars such as Huan Tan

---

11   HHS, j. 79, "Rulin liezhuan," 2547.

(23? BCE–56 CE), Zheng Xing (fl. 1st century), Zheng Zhong (?–83), Du Lin (fl. 1st century), Jia Kui (30–101), Wang Chong (27–97?), and Ma Rong (79–166), whose lives are recorded in the *History of the Later Han Dynasty*, were all regarded as "Confucian scholars of comprehensive learning" who practiced the "study of ancient texts" and were held in very high esteem.[12]

The use of the title "Confucian scholars of comprehensive learning" demonstrates that people were beginning to dislike the limitations of specializing in just one classic text.[13] The esteem given to the "study of ancient texts" not only indicates the rising status of some ancient classical texts, but also symbolizes the increasing importance of the historical knowledge of these ancient classics in intellectual genealogy.[14] The popularity of the term "comprehensive learning" or "erudition" implies an increasing interest in knowledge; without great erudition, it was very difficult for one to become a spiritual leader of the elite.[15] An ethos of intellectualism was then created in which a scholar would "be ashamed if there was even one thing he did not know."[16] This shows that

---

12   For all this, see HHS, j. 28 shang, "Huan Tan zhuan," 955; j. 36, "Zheng Xing zhuan," 1223–1224; j. 49, "Wang Cong zhuan," 1629; j. 60 shang, "Ma Rong zhuan," 1972.

13   HHS, j. 57, "Du Lin zhuan," quotes the *Fengsu tong* that among the Confucian scholars, " 'Confucian scholars of comprehensive learning' (*tongru*) are those who examine the institutions of previous rulers and make the situation clear for their own time, while those who only prater on and are incapable of understanding the past or the present are 'vulgar Confucian scholars.' " HHS, j. 66, "Jia Kui zhuan," also quotes the same source that "those who are concerned with the fundamental system of the state, examine the essential principles and transform them to accord with their own times are the 'Confucian scholars of comprehensive learning.' "

14   HHS, j. 35, 1208, "Zheng Xuan zhuan," states that Fan Sheng, Chen Yuan, Li Yu and Jia Kui all discussed "the study of ancient and modern texts," but it was only with Ma Rong and Zheng Xuan that "the study of ancient texts was truly illuminated."

15   Li Gu and Du Qiao, for example, were both scholars of comprehensive learning. HHH, j. 63, 2073, "Li Gu zhuan," quotes Xie Cheng's lost *Hou Hanshu* saying that Li Gu "read widely in ancient and contemporary writings, was well versed in divination by the winds and the five musical notes, astrology, the River Diagram (cosmogram) and apocryphal books. He searched above and divined below and exhausted the spirits and knew the transformations." "Du Qiao zhuan," in the same HHS j. 63, 2092, quotes Sima Biao's *Xu Hanshu* to the effect that Du Qiao "studied Han Ying's interpretations of the *Book of Songs*, Jing Fang's interpretations of the *Book of Changes* and Ouyang Gao's interpretations of the *Book of Documents*."

16   This phrase comes from Zhang Heng's "Yingjian." See *Zhang Heng shiwenji jiaozhu*, 1986, 283. On 391, Cui Yuan (77–142) said of Zhang Heng "was there anything he did not study or anyone he did not learn from? and "he considered it a shame to be ignorant of even one thing."

the idealist elite leaders were all noted for their erudition and that erudition was extremely important for a person's intellectual status.

As noted in the Introduction, there were two major trends in ancient Chinese intellectual history: valuing inquiry into knowledge (*dao wenxue*) and valuing the cultivation of moral virtue (*zun dexing*). The former primarily relied on erudition and wide learning to cultivate one's own reason while the latter explored the individual's inner moral awareness. The tradition of valuing inquiry into knowledge always had a positive influence on Confucian teaching, Confucius himself having been a very learned man in his time. In the Eastern Han, this trend flourished again and scholars like Xun Shu (83–149), Liang Hong (1st century) and Fa Zhen (100–188) all possessed very extensive knowledge.[17] Many of the Eastern Han's most representative scholars were like Wang Chong who wrote of himself in his *Balanced Inquiries* (Lunheng) that when he was a youth "the books I read became increasingly broad and numerous," and when he became an adult he was even more "immersed in reading ancient texts and pleased to hear different views."[18] Zhang Heng (78–139) also wrote quite clearly that "(the superior man) would be ashamed not to have profound learning,"[19] while Wang Fu (85?–163?)'s *Comments of a Recluse* (Qianfu lun) opens with an essay entitled "In Praise of Learning" (Zanxue) in which he lists the deeds of eleven sages who respected teachers and emphasized learning in order to demonstrate the importance of knowledge in keeping with Confucius' dictum that thinking (*si*) is not as important as learning (*xue*).[20] This general intellectual trend stimulated the development of private learning and popular knowledge and produced a number of works that extensively discussed the five classics and were rich in historical knowledge: *Various Meanings of the Five Classics* (Wujing yiyi) and *Explaining Wen and Analyzing Zi* (Shuo wen jie zi) by Xu Shen (ca. 58–147), the *Rhapsody on the Two Capitals* (Liangdu fu) by Ban Gu (32–92), the *Treatise on Astronomy* (Lingxian, literally, "spiritual statutes") by Zhang Heng and the *Balanced Inquiries* by Wang Chong. Even He Xiu (129–182) also studied various texts on Yin-Yang, mathematics, river diagrams (cosmograms), divination omens and apocrypha while working primarily on the Gongyang School of *Spring and Autumn Annals* study.

This Eastern Han trend of learning was very important in terms of intellectual history because it changed the evaluative standards for right and wrong, true and false from belief to empirical knowledge. In their interpretation and

---

17 See HHS, j. 62, 2049, "Xun Shu zhuan," and j. 83, 2765 & 2774, "Yimin liezhuan."
18 Wang Chong, *Lun Heng jiaoshi*, 1990, 1995, j. 30, 1188.
19 Zhang Heng, "Yingjian," see *Zhang Heng shiwenji jiaozhu*, 1986, 279.
20 Wang Fu, "Zanxue," see Wang Jipei and Peng Zhen, *Qianfu lunjian jiaozheng*, 1985, 1–3.

commentary on the classics, the "study-of-ancient-texts" scholars did not have a devotional attitude toward the philosophy of the sages; they did not seek the "great meaning of the subtle words" (*weiyan dayi*) or their individual understanding. They sought rather for definitive knowledge of the history, real events, personalities and language of the classics. It was precisely on this account that scholars from Yang Xiong (53 BCE–18 CE), Yin Min (?–68), Zheng Xing, Huan Tan and Wang Chong to Kong Xi (?–88) all held in contempt the practice of combining Confucian teachings with the study of omens and apocrypha. They regarded experience, knowledge, logic and reason as the combined standard for evaluating everything. Wide learning and erudition became a much admired form of moral character, and "Confucian scholars of comprehensive learning" like Jia Kui and Ma Rong became intellectuals leaders. Finally the emergence of a scholar like Zheng Xuan (127–200), who brought together the ancient and the contemporary and was proficient in the six classics, represented the culmination of this intellectual trend. This search for wide learning and great erudition unintentionally expanded the scope of Chinese thinking while at the same time greatly increasing the amount of intellectual resources.[21]

1.3
Under political oppression, the ideal moral character and spirit advocated by many Eastern Han scholar officials came into conflict with the vulgar character and practical spirit of the day. In this situation, they passionately defended their own stand and strongly advocated their position. In the end they tended to go to extremes. Some of these scholar officials simply refused to "wallow in the mire" of other low-minded elements of society. They required themselves to live by extremely high moral standards and they used these standards as the foundation of their identity with others of like mind to form a cultural collective. As Yu Yingshi pointed out, the term "comrade" (*tongzhi*) was quite popular in the Eastern Han and signified the "self-awareness of the scholars official class as a collective."[22] Even more worthy of note, as this idealism

---

21   HHS, j. 35, 1207, "Zheng Xuan zhuan," records that "(Ma) Rong had more than 400 disciples; only 50 some of them were accomplished scholars." The "lun" section of the same source says that "Zheng Xuan comprehensively included all the important texts, collected the views of the numerous schools, deleted the false and redundant parts, corrected the mistakes and reinserted the omissions. From then on, scholars basically knew whom to return (to study the classics)." Mou Runsun's essay "Lun Wei Jin yilai chongshang tanbian ji qi yingxiang" already mentions this trend toward erudition; see Mou's *Zhushizhai conggao*, 1987, 307.

22   Yu Yingshi, *Zhongguo zhishi jieceng shilun*, 1980, 1989, 215.

moved toward extreme positions, it developed attitudes close to extreme fastidiousness and fear of contamination. Not only did these men measure and judge everything by unrelenting moral standards, they rejected any form of conformity under any circumstances, to the point of refusing to identify even with political allies or intellectual comrades.

During the Eastern Han, this kind of uncompromising idealism and standard of character identity came to be accepted by some elite scholar officials. Zhu Mu (100–163)'s "On Breaking off Friendships" (Juejiao lun) vehemently criticized popular society's pattern of making friends and forming one's identity on the basis of interests because it would lead to mutual compromise and a lowering of moral standards. He said that one should maintain a self-important, independent and unsociable attitude. Some contemporary scholar officials either refused to accept offices they were recommended for or simply went to live in seclusion in the mountains, and their reputations actually soared. Zhang Zhi (?–ca. 192), Guo Tai (128–169) and Zhao Ye (fl. 1st century) all rejected court recommendations and official promotions and were treated like moral heroes who "possessed the Way." This shows that the state had lost the ability to serve as society's moral guide. All the court could do was to tacitly accept the legitimacy of this disaffected idealist behavior.

In ancient China, however, the sources of this type of idealism came primarily from Daoism rather than Confucianism. At the beginning of the first century CE, Fan Zhun vehemently criticized contemporary culture and learning, expressing his disappointment with Confucian learning and the study of the classics. He believed that in the Western Han because Emperor Wen and Empress Dowager Dou were devotees of Yellow Emperor Daoism, society was stable and peaceful during the reigns of emperors Jing and Wudi. He therefore suggested that the court promote the doctrines of Yellow Emperor Daoism.[23] Somewhat later Zhu Mu interpreted history from the Daoist point of view in his "For Simplicity" (Chong hou lun). Precisely because the promotion of ceremonial rites led to the disappearance of primitive simplicity, he attacked contemporary social customs on the basis of the *Laozi*. He also wrote "On Breaking Off Friendships" to explain and justify his lofty and aloof personal behavior.[24]

This ideal moral character and transcendent spirit stimulated a renewed interest in the thought of Laozi and Zhuangzi among scholar officials. The trend toward erudition and broad learning in the Eastern Han actually led scholars increasingly to go beyond the orthodox classics and provided an opportunity for the marginalized *Laozi* and *Zhuangzi* to make a comeback.

---

23   HHS, j. 32, 1126–1127.
24   HHS, j. 43, "Zhu Mu zhuan," 1464–1467.

The trend toward erudition, after all, went in two main directions. One was to seek within the tradition of explication of the classics for knowledge of history, real events, personalities and language. The other was to explore and discover new intellectual resources beyond traditional classical exegesis. The former was a continuation of the Western Han tradition while the latter represented the establishment of a new Eastern Han tradition. All of the first class intellectuals, including Yang Xiong, Zheng Jun (fl. 1st century), Wang Chong, Zhang Heng, Ma Rong and Zhong Changtong (180–220), exhibited a very obvious interest in Daoism, and this exemplified a change in the intellectual interests of the age.

The trends of employing collective ideals to resist political power and individual transcendence to resist social oppression appear to be opposites but are actually similar, and the latter may be the ultimate destination of the former. The *History of the Later Han Dynasty* quotes Fan Pang (137–169)'s words to praise a kind of ideal intellectual world in which "Sons of Heaven cannot make scholars their ministers and Regional Rulers cannot make scholars their friends" (*tianzi bude chen, zhuhou bude you*).[25] The intellectual stratum that occupied this ideal intellectual world was attempting to use their mastery of culture to reestablish their claim to equal status with imperial power, but this was, of course, an impossibility. Under the universal reach of imperial power, the only road that power would tolerate and even encourage was the road to escape and reclusion. This was the only position for anyone who wanted to maintain his idealism. When this reclusive tendency reached its extreme, however, an even more extreme group of scholar officials turned toward genuine escape and reclusion, and with that the goal sought by these scholar officials changed from social responsibility to the naturalness or spontaneity of life.

The *History of the Later Han Dynasty* "Biographies of Eremites" (Yimin zhuan) states that after the reign of Emperor Zhang (r. 76–88) of the Eastern Han there arose a group of genuine hermits, and Fan Ye cites the words of the *Book of Changes* and the *Xunzi* to explain the legitimacy of this behavior.[26] The widespread popularity of such reclusive behavior was really not due exclusively to the "sublime loftiness" of its practitioners, but also arose because this sort of escape from political power and social responsibility was the only practice the contemporary state ideology and political power would tolerate. This fashion in intellectual history had one striking consequence—alternative ideas and doctrines outside of the Confucian tradition emerged as the "new" knowledge that was of interest to many people.

---

25   HHS, j. 68, "Guo Tai zhuan," 2226.
26   HHS, j. 83, 2757, 2755.

1.4

The year 166 CE (under the Eastern Han Emperor Huan) seems to have been a year full of symbolic implications in which many important things happened. Most significant was of course the calamitous first Great Proscription. At the time, the intellectual elite was increasingly dissatisfied with the social main- stream. They made a great display of the moral character of the "superior man" that ordinary people could not possibly reach and looked down with disdain on vulgar society. Some Imperial University students praised the three scholars Li Ying (110–169), Chen Fan (?–168) and Wang Chang (?–169) as "models for all under Heaven," "having no fear of local strong men" and "the most talented of all under Heaven," implying that the intellectuals were trying to claim equal knowledge and power vis-à-vis the political powers on the basis of their moral character. According to historical records, even the emperor felt himself to be under tremendous pressure. Just then a student who had been severely pun- ished by Li Ying sent up a letter accusing Li Ying and others of forming a faction (*dang* 黨, same word as modern political party). This gave the higher authori- ties the opportunity they needed to counterattack, and with the emperor's support they arrested a large number of "factional partisans" (*dangren*). This counterattack became known as the "Great Proscription."

This first proscription stirred up even greater collective resistance on the part of the intellectuals. A few years later, another group of scholar officials with some famous scholars at the heart of their movement again put forth the so-called "three gentlemen" (*san jun* 三君), "eight talents" (*ba jun* 八俊), "eight moral leaders" (*ba gu* 八顧), "eight able leaders" (*ba ji* 八及) and "eight bene- factors" (*ba chu* 八廚) as their leaders. Subsequently, in 169 (the third year of the *jianning* era of Emperor Ling), the court again cracked down and arrested a large number of intellectual leaders. Yu Fang (?–169), Du Mi (?–169), Li Ying and over a hundred other men died in prison, and even more large-scale sup- pression and persecution was also carried out in the counties and prefectures.

These two repressive attacks within a few years was a traumatic experience for the idealism of the intellectuals and it completely shattered their dreams of contending against the political powers. This convinced a portion of the scholar officials to abandon their mutual praise of the method of forming col- lectives in favor of a search for individual independence and a spiritual world of freedom.

The *History of the Later Han Dynasty* records a situation emblematic of this trend. Just as Fan Pang and the rest were vigorously criticizing the political situation, a scholar named Shentu Pan (fl. 2nd century) saw, however, that their criticism would result in a situation similar to that at the end of the Warring States era when "people with no official position were uninhibited in

the expression of their views" (*chushi hengyi*) and that led to the catastrophic
"burying of the scholars and burning of the books."[27] Shentu then went into
seclusion to seek the life of his own transcendent spirit. Another scholar
named Liu Liang (?–181) wrote a work entitled "On Abolishing Collectives"
(Poqun lun) that opposed the practice of intellectuals grouping themselves
into factions.[28] These ideas so much in opposition to this widespread social
practice revealed a change in the view that collective identification had the
highest survival value. Somewhat later in his *Balanced Discourses* (Zhonglun),
Xu Gan (170–217) criticized the practice of the younger generation of rich and
powerful families organizing into cliques and the practice of influential officials seeking fame among themselves during the reigns of emperors Huan and
Ling. He said that he intended to "close my door and preserve myself, not associate with any groups, and entertain myself with the six classics."[29] This was
an indication that an individualistic orientation was coming to pervade the
intellectual stratum of society.

At this point in 166 the celebrated scholar Ma Rong died. He represented
the Eastern Han intellectual trend of wide learning and erudition and was a
symbol of the continuation of the valuing inquiry into knowledge tradition.
His passing also symbolized the end of an old era and the birth of a new one.[30]
In this same year Xiang Kai (fl. 2nd century) sent up a memorial to the emperor
revealing for the first time that "shrines for the Yellow Emperor, Laozi and the
Buddha had been set up in the imperial palace." From Xiang Kai's memorial
we also learn what general knowledge his contemporaries had about Yellow
Emperor, Laozi and the Buddha. For example, they already knew the story that
Laozi journeyed to the west and became the Buddha, that Buddhists should
not repeatedly sleep under the same mulberry tree and become attached to
it and that the Buddha regarded beautiful women as no more than leather
pouches filled with blood, and so on. They also knew about Gan Ji (fl. 2nd century) transmitting the 170-*juan Book of Great Peace Written in Blue* (Taiping qin-
gling shu, one version of the Taiping Jing, *Scripture of Great Peace*) of religious
Daoism to Gong Chong (fl. 2nd century) of Langya in Shandong.[31] It was also

27   HHS, j. 53, "Shentu Pan zhuan," 1752. The phrase "people with no official position were
     uninhibited in the expression of their views" is from the *Mengzi*, "Teng Wengong xia," in
     Lau, *Mencius*, 114; "are" is changed to "were."
28   HHS, j. 80, "Wen Yuan zhuan," 2653.
29   The "Qianjiao di shi-er," in *Zhonglun*, in *Jian-an qizi ji*, 1989, 292.
30   HHS, j. 60 shang, "Ma Rong zhuan," 1972.
31   HHS, j. 30, "Xiang Kai zhuan," 1077, 1082–1084.

in this year that the emperor officially established a shrine for Laozi in the Longzhuo Palace. Did all of this not suggest that Chinese intellectual history was about to enter a new era?

2.   The Mysterious and Profound: A Turning Point of Intellectual
       History in the Third Century CE

He Xiu died in 182,[32] and ten years later the erudite scholar Cai Yong (132–192) was executed in prison;[33] in 200, the last year of the second century CE, Zheng Xuan, the most celebrated scholar whose erudition had brought together the study of the ancient and modern classics, also passed away. His passing meant the definitive close of an old era and the genuine beginning of a new age.

As noted above, thought and learning had already begun to change at this turn of the century. Scholars were becoming estranged from collective iden-tification and turning toward individual independence and a spiritual world of freedom. At the same time the intellectual trend toward broad learn-ing and erudition represented an attempt to find a space for the expansion of thought beyond the authority of the Confucian classics. It was just these two orientations that caused a change of direction in Chinese thought and knowledge in this era. From Yang Xiong, Huan Tan and Wang Chong on, the long dormant desire of mainstream thinkers to seek out a transcendent spirit and independent thought was activated. In their ever wider search for intel-lectual resources, they gained support from Daoist textual materials, and this led to the birth of what came to be known later as Mysterious Learning or Neo-Daoism (*xuanxue*).

2.1
There was one area in which Confucianism was especially vulnerable to chal-lenge: its overemphasis on this worldly ethics, morality and politics (or govern-ment) and its neglect of a foundational cosmology and metaphysics. Confucians became somewhat embarrassed when people insistently asked about the origin and foundation of thought. In a passage from the *Analects*, "Zi Gong said, 'We can hear our Master's views on culture and its manifestations, but

---

32   HHS, j. 79 xia, "He Xiu zhuan," 2582–2583.
33   HHS, j. 60 xia, "Cai Yong zhuan," 1980.

we cannot hear his views on human nature and the Way of Heaven.' "[34] This clearly reflects the Confucian avoidance of questions about the ultimate foundation of things. It was precisely this avoidance that left Chinese intellectual history with a new topic and actually led to even more serious questioning.

Han dynasty Confucians seldom discussed human nature—the ultimate basis of "human beings" as human beings. From the establishment of the system of rituals and music and the standards of official recommendation and appointment, however, we can see that society operated along the lines of Xunzi's thought. The system of rituals and music was used to restrain human emotions and thought while the system of official recommendation and appointment encouraged high moral character; finally, penal law and government decrees controlled people's behavior in society. This was in essence a realistic strategy of social control. Although in the Han dynasty it seems that there was considerable discussion of the Way of Heaven—the ultimate question of the cosmos—from phenomena like the establishment of shrines to the five (mythical) rulers, the Hall of Brightness and the vogue of studying omens and apocrypha, however, we can see that the general understanding of the Way of Heaven placed particular emphasis on a cosmology that had Yin and Yang and the Five Phases as its framework. This sort of Way of Heaven could be directly reflected in society and government and could also be directly employed in the mantic and medical arts; in short, it too was an extremely realistic form of knowledge. As for the ultimate basis of human nature and the foundation of the profoundly mysterious cosmos, the Confucians did not probe into such questions.

In the Han to Wei period, the modesty of Confucius and the Confucian avoidance of these questions provided precisely the opening needed to undermine their thought. As we know the intellectual resources and classical texts were a shared repository of thought; various thinkers could employ ingenious interpretations of them to come up with new ideas. Passages like the following from the *Analects*—"Confucius said, 'To have taken no unnatural action (*wuwei*) and yet have the empire well governed, Shun was the man!'" and "Confucius said, 'A ruler who governs his state by virtue is like the north polar star, which remains in its place while all the other stars revolve around it.'"—could easily be given Daoist interpretations due most likely to their use of "no unnatural action" and

---

34   *Lunyu*, "Gongye Chang," 5.12 (13 in some texts), SSJZS, 2474. Chan, SB, 28. Chan also writes that "the term *wen-chang* (*wenzhang*, 文章) can also mean literary heritage or simply the ancient Classics." D. C. Lau, *Analects*, 78 takes *wenzhang* to refer to "the Master's accomplishments."

"north polar star."[35] From the Han to the Wei, many people who believed in Daoist thought worked in a similar fashion to find in the Confucian classics the resources they needed to undermine Confucian thought. According to He Shao (?–301)'s "Biography of Xun Can," cited in a note to *juan* 10 of the *Records of the Three Kingdoms* (Sanguo zhi), around the year 227, Xun Can said "We often thought that Zigong said 'we cannot hear the Master's views on human nature and the Way of Heaven,' yet even though the six classics still exist, they are nothing but the useless dross of the sages."[36]

This assertion by Xun Can shows us that his thinking was in many ways quite different from traditional thought. First of all he was seeking the foundations or the origins of thought that past Confucians had either avoided or set aside, and so the unfathomable concepts of the Way and human nature were the central focus of his discussions. Second, he confirmed the priority of "human nature and the Way of Heaven" in his thought. Third, this "human nature and the Way of Heaven" were ineffable and incomparable; they could be experienced but not described and their meaning was "beyond material phenomena or images" (*xiangwai*). From 240 to 249, the *zhengshi* era, He Yan, another scholar fond of Laozi and Zhuangzi, in a note on "human nature and the Way of Heaven" in his *Collected Explanations of the Analects* (Lunyu jijie), emphasized that human nature definitely did not refer to concrete human behavior and character in society, but rather to the ultimate foundations of what makes human beings human. Likewise, the Way of Heaven was not a picture of the concrete sky or the movements of the stars in the heavens; it was rather the profound and subtle Great Way (*dadao*) that brought the universe into existence. At about the same time, Wang Bi also found support for a turn toward enigmatic Daoist thought in the Confucian classics. A passage in the *Analects* states that "Lin Fang asked about the foundation of ceremonies [*li zhi ben* 禮之本]. Confucius said, 'An important question indeed!'" Wang Bi then expounded this to the effect that since his contemporaries had abandoned the roots (essentials) and followed only branches (trifles), Confucius naturally praised Lin Fang for asking after "the foundation" of the rites and ceremonies. This foundation was simply the Way of Heaven.[37] Wang Bi further asserted that

---

35   The *Lunyu* quotations are from "Wei Linggong," 15.4, Chan, SB, 43. Chan points out that this use of *wuwei* is similar to a sentence in *Laozi*, 57, and "Wei zheng," 2.1, Chan, SB, 22.

36   *Sanguo zhi*, j. 10, *Weishu*, "Xun Yu, Xun You, Jia Xu zhuan," note on 319. See also Liu Shao *Renwu zhi*, in which he gives a Daoist interpretation to the "Zhongyong" in keeping with the Warring States Confucian theories of the Five Phases and Daoist theories of spontaneity. See Tang Yongtong "Du Renwu zhi" in *Tang Yongtong xueshu lunwen ji*, 1983, 196–213.

37   *Lunyu*, 3.4 Chan, SB, 25. See "Lunyu shiyi" in *Wang Bi ji jiaoshi*, 1980, 622.

Confucius also discussed the Way, but that the Way of Confucius was not about questions of moral behavior in society or rules of social order, but the foundation that made order and regulation possible, an imperceptible Way that was present in everything. This Way was tantamount to the Daoist idea of non-being (*wu*).[38] In this way of thinking, the Way is the foundation of everything, and the reasonableness of social norms and order all need to be questioned. As a result, the question of ultimate foundations came to the fore again. Tang Yongtong once pointed out that from the end of the Han through the Wei-Jin period, Chinese thought and discussion evolved from "concrete human affairs" to the "abstract and mysterious principle" of Neo-Daoism and that this was "an inevitable tendency in the evolution of learning."[39] Why, then, did this "tendency" come to be "inevitable?" These sorts of seemingly metaphysical issues certainly are very abstract and subtle.

In the mid-third century, this kind of "lofty discussion and empty discourse" grew into an intellectual fashion. Compliments were routinely given using terms like *xuanmiao* and *xuanyuan*, both meaning "profoundly mysterious." These terms were similar to Wang Bi's assertion that the Way of Heaven is profoundly subtle (*shenwei* 深微). The last two lines of *Laozi* chapter 1 describe the Way (Dao) as "Deeper and more profound, The door to all subtleties![40]

When those abstract and profoundly subtle philosophical discussions came to constitute a current of thought, it came to be called the Mysterious Learning or Neo-Daoism. When the most popular subject of discussion for intellectual circles turned from the Confucian classics to Mysterious Learning, the basis of their discussions was Daoist rather than Confucian. In the course of this shift in intellectual history, the end point of Confucian inquiry became the starting point of Daoist inquiry, and the themes developed and elaborated in Neo-Daoism were precisely those that had been neglected in the study of the Confucian classics. The theories of Yin-Yang and the Five Phases in Han cosmology were then replaced by reflections on being (*you*) and non-being (*wu*). Zhang Zhan of the Eastern Jin (317–420) wrote, in a note on the "Heaven's Gifts" chapter of the *Liezi*, that Yin and Yang and the Five Phases are really not the

---

38   "Lunyu shiyi" note on "Zhi yu Dao," in *Wang Bi ji jiaoshi*, 1980, 624.

39   "Du renwu zhi," in *Tang Yongtong xueshu lunwen ji*, 1983, 205.

40   Chan, SB, 139. Compare Waley, *The Way and Its Power*, 1948, 1958, 141: "This 'same mould' we can but call the Mystery, Or rather the 'Darker than any Mystery', The Doorway whence issued all Secret Essences."

foundation of everything. Only the two eternal and transcendent origins, the Way and non-being, can fill that role.[41]

It then turned out that being and non-being and words/speech (*yan* 言) and meaning (*yi* 意) became key terms in intellectual history. In the fourth decade of the third century, men like Xiahou Xuan (209–254), He Yan, Huangfu Mi (215–282), Xi Kang (223–263), Ruan Ji (210–263), Xiang Xiu (ca. 227–272), Wang Bi, Zhong Hui (225–263), and Wang Rong (234–305), appeared one after another in Chinese intellectual history, and their emergence marked the arrival of the age of Neo-Daoism or the Mysterious Learning.

2.2

Since Xun Can, He Yan and Wang Bi realized that Confucianism lacked any consideration of "human nature and the Way of Heaven," they cleverly exploited this deficiency to shift from Confucian to Daoist thought. In yet another source we can see how Wang Bi transformed thinking about being and non-being from Confucianism toward Daoism. A note in the *Records of the Three Kingdoms* "Biography of Zhong Hui," cites a passage from He Shao "Biography of Wang Bi" concerning Wang's audience with the scholar Pei Hui (fl. 3rd century). During their discussions, Pei Hui accepted the ultimate meaning of non-being, but he was worried that it had not been acknowledged by "the Sage." He hoped that Wang Bi could give him an explanation that might alleviate his anxiety. Wang Bi told him that Confucius certainly understood non-being, but he also understood the ineffable nature of non-being, and so he did not discuss it directly. Laozi, on the other hand, accepted the concept of being, and so he habitually talked about non-being from the point of view of being.[42] In this way Daoist thinking about non-being was dressed up in Confucian robes and became a topic that everyone was confident discussing.[43]

According to the *History of the Jin Dynasty* (Jinshu), at that time He Yan and Wang Bi employed Lao-Zhuang thought to discuss being and non-being.[44] What, then, was non-being and being to them? Laozi made non-being the

---

41   Liezi, "Tian rui," in Yang Bojun, *Liezi jishi*, 1979, 1985, 2. English chapter title is from Graham, A. C., *The Book of Lieh-tzu: A New Translation*, 1973 (1960).

42   *Sanguo zhi*, j. 28, 795. Lynn, *Changes*, 11 has a complete translation of Wang Bi's comparison of Confucius and Laozi.

43   A. C. Graham correctly argued that this Chinese discussion of *you* and *wu* was different from discussions of being or existence in modern Western philosophy. See his " 'being' in Western Philosophy compared with *shih/fei* and *yu/wu*," *Asia Major*, New Series, 7, 1–2 (1959), 79–112.

44   *Jinshu*, j. 43, "Wang Yan zhuan," 1236.

origin of the entire universe; for him, it had absolute priority as a first cause and it came before all things and all phenomena in the cosmos. That is to say, only non-being could transcend the individuality and difference of all concrete things and appearances in the world and history and serve as the starting point and cornerstone of everything. In his *Commentaries on Laozi* (Laozi zhu), Wang Bi then expounded this line of thinking.[45] He believed that due to having a "form" (*xing*) or a "name" (*ming*), every material thing or phenomenon that appears in time and space belongs to the realm of being. This being is then relative, transitory and differentiated—it is not at all fundamental or foundational. Only undifferentiated non-being can serve as the foundation that transcends everything else. In his annotations to the *Commentaries on the Appended Phrases* on the *Book of Changes*, Wang Bi states that non-being is simply the Way (Dao). In his "On Non-being and Being" (Wuwei lun), He Yan also states that "the ten thousand things in Heaven and Earth all have non-being as their original substance (root, *ben*)."[46] On this account they believed that non-being should be given priority over everything. Human beings and society as a whole should be modeled on this non-being in order to achieve correct results.[47] A passage in the *Analects* has Confucius telling his disciple Zeng Shen: "There is one single thread binding my way together." Zeng Shen then tells the other disciples: "The way of the Master consists in doing one's best and in using oneself as a measure to gauge others. That is all."[48] Wang Bi, however, interprets the Way of Confucius as the ultimate Way which is simply non-being. In this manner, they employ this simple, ultimate philosophic reasoning in their search for all origins and ultimately shift the discussion in the direction of Daoist thought.

As discussed above, in the period from the end of the Warring States through the Qin-Han era, cosmology was one of the central issues. In the discussions of that time, people paid particular attention to the structure of the myriad phenomena of the cosmos and to their relations of correspondence with human society. They did not search for the abstract origins of the universe, but rather analyzed and speculated about the mutual relations between

---

45   *Wang Bi jijiaoshi*, 1980, 110, 117, 553. For a translation of Wang Bi on the *Laozi*, see Rudolf G. Wagner, *A Chinese Reading of the Daodejing: Wang Bi's Commentary on the Laozi with Critical Text and Translation*, 2003.

46   For He Yan's statement, see *Quan Sanguo wen*, j. 39, *Quan shanggu sandai Qin Han Liuchao wen*, 1274; *Jinshu*, j. 43, "Wang Yan zhuan," 1236.

47   "Zhouyi lüeli," *Wang Bi jijiaoshi*, 1980, 598, 591.

48   *Lunyu*, "Li ren," 4.15. Lau, *Analects*, 74. Waley, *Analects*, 104 translates Zeng Shen as saying "Our Master's Way is simply this: Loyalty, consideration. (*zhong* 忠, *shu* 恕)."

concrete material things and phenomena. Concrete knowledge and even practical techniques were extremely important to them. The enthusiasm for erudition and comprehensive learning was related to this tradition. For example, to understand Heaven required a familiarity with many kinds of knowledge and techniques having to do with heavenly phenomena, stars and planets, calendar science, spirits (gods) and ghosts. People did not necessarily attach great importance to abstract philosophical theories about the Way of Heaven. Between the Wei and the Jin, this intellectual tradition was still being carried on in the south. For example in the Kingdom of Wu, Lu Ji (187–219), Yu Fan (164–233), Wang Fan (228–266) and their contemporaries Yao Xin and Ge Heng were interested in the *Book of Changes* and did meticulous research in astronomy and calendar science.[49]

In the Central Plains, the area of north China with Luoyang as its center, the intellectual climate had, however, already begun to change. Interest in the structure of the cosmos, society and humanity had already given way to interest in their ultimate origins. The tradition of erudition and wide learning had also shifted toward a less elaborate intellectual mood. People were now looking for the sort of ultimate answers that could explain everything; they hoped to understand everything by means of such bold macro-thinking. Just as Wang Bi wrote in his *Brief Commentary on Laozi* (Laozi zhilüe), only by studying the *Laozi* could one hope to reveal the profoundly mysterious origins of everything. From the point of view of Wang Bi and others, the teachings of Confucius, the mantic arts of the apocryphal texts, and the astronomy and calendar science of Yellow Emperor learning simply "expressed their own views of everything, and even if they defended themselves, it only caused more confusion."[50]

In this atmosphere of searching for the simple and the fundamental, the teachings of Laozi and Zhuangzi grew ever more meaningful. According to their understanding, everything—including the configuration of Heaven and Earth, the administration of society and people's attitudes toward life—must depend upon this abstract foundation. After these things came to be seen in a Daoist perspective, all problems began appear simple, clear and concise.

2.3

There was, though, a problem with all this. The ultimate non-being or the Way was beyond the ability of language and extremely difficult to accurately describe, and so at that time "debates on the meaning of words" (*yanyi zhi*

---

49 See Tang Changru, "Du *Baopuzi* tuilun nanbei xuefeng zhi yitong," in his *Wei Jin Nan Bei Chao shi luncong*, 1955, 367–368.

50 *Wang Bi ji jiaoshi*, 1980, 198.

bian 言意之辯) became a popular topic. In his "On the nameless" (Wuming lun), He Yan maintained that the Dao (Way) was different from every real thing and "the Way is fundamentally nameless" (*Dao ben wu ming*)—it cannot be expressed in words.[51]

We know what the *Commentaries on the Appended Phrases* of the *Book of Changes* has to say about "words" and "meaning" or "ideas": "Writing does not exhaust words, and words do not exhaust ideas (*Shu bu jin yan, yan bu jin yi*). If this is so, does this mean that the ideas of the sages (*shengren zhi yi*) cannot be discerned?"[52] No matter how great a tendency the *Commentaries* have to doubt the usefulness of language, they still acknowledged that the "images" (*xiang* 象), "trigrams" (*gua* 卦) and "statements" (*ci* 辭) in the *Changes* are able to express "the ideas of the sages." A note to the "Biography of Xun Yu (163–212)" in the *Records of the Three Kingdoms* quotes the "Biography of Xun Can" by He Shao recording that some people asked an interesting question: If words (*yanci* 言辭) actually can express the profound mysteries of the Way of Heaven and human nature, then way did Confucius say so little about "human nature and the Way of Heaven?" Xun Can proposed an explanation of this. It was because beyond the meaning or ideas (*yi*) that language can express there still exists a further "meaning beyond meaning" (*yi wai zhi yi* 意外之意) that language cannot express.[53] Wang Bi offered an even newer method of demonstration. He first acknowledged that the images and words were able to express meanings, but he arranged images, words and meanings (ideas) in a hierarchical order of value. He argued that the words and images were only symbols, but not meanings (significance or ideas). As soon as one understands the ideas (meanings), he can discard the symbols (images and words). By contrast, though, understanding the language and writing does not mean clearly understanding the meanings (ideas). As he wrote, "once one gets the images, he forgets the words" and "once one gets the ideas he forgets the images."[54] In their comments on "words" and "meaning/ideas," Xu Can, He Yan and Wang Bi thought less and less of words and more and more of meaning/ideas, and this gave rise to the Neo-Daoist trend of contempt for language.[55]

Contempt for language and the quest for a transcendent realm are closely connected; they both encourage a life attitude that privileges the spiritual and looks down on practical concerns. At the same time or shortly after He Yan

51   *Quan Sanguo wen*, j. 39; *Quan shanggu sandai Qin Han Liuchao wen*, 1275.

52   Lynn, *Changes*, "Commentary, Part One," 67.

53   *Sanguo zhi*, j. 10, "Weishu, Xun Yu, Xun Xiu, Jia Xu zhuan," 301–320.

54   *Wang Bi ji jiaoshi*, 1980, 609. Lynn, *Changes*, "Clarifying the images," 31.

55   Ouyang Jian, "Yan jin yi lun," in Ouyang Xun et al., eds. *Yiwen leiju*, j. 19.

and Wang Bi, there were many others who shared the same preferences and quest. Xi Kang's "A Quatrain for my Brother Joining the Army" (Si yan zeng Xiong xiucai ru jun), He Shao's "A Poem for Zhang Hua" (Zeng Zhang Hua shi), and Lu Zhan's "A Poem for Liu Kun" (Zeng Liu Kun shi) and so on all quote Zhuangzi's famous dictum that "once one gets the fish, he forgets the traps" that Wang Bi also used.[56] This idea of "getting the meaning and forgetting the words"—was related to the discussions of non-being and being as well as the life quest for transcendence. Only by being indifferent to the vulgar world and looking inward can one comprehend the profound and mysterious "meaning" or the "meaning beyond meaning"—that is the mysterious Dao.

2.4

Actually recognizing the absolute significance of taking non-being as the root (origin) and emphasizing the priority of meaning/ideas over words/language was really not just mystical thinking.

In the mid-third century, along with the late Eastern Han abandonment of social values and affirmation of individual independence, a tendency to search for transcendence and freedom developed in the lives of the scholar officials, and this stimulated a return of Lao-Zhuang thought. This trend of thought was most widespread in Luoyang and Yexia (in Hebei), the center of the state of Wei.[57] Slightly earlier in time, Kong Rong (153–208) greatly admired the intellectual spirit of Ru-nan (in Henan) that "strongly resisted the Son of Heaven," and "woke up in the night and wailed because social values were in decay." Wang Can acknowledged that the fundamental way to achieve peace in life was to "have few desires" (guayu).[58] A little later, Wang Chang (?–259) gave his sons and nephews names like "silent," "profound," "turbid," "dwelling in quietude," "dwelling in the Way," "mysterious void," and "emptiness of the Way" and so on. He advocated "respecting Confucian teachings and practicing Daoist doctrines,

---

56   The phrase is from Zhuangzi, "External Things," Watson, CT, 302. See Lu Qinli, ed., Xian Qin Han Wei Nanbeichao shi, 1983, 483, 648, 882. Lu Zhan's poem has a preface that quotes the Yijing, "Xici" concerning how "writing does not exhaust words, and words do not exhaust ideas."

57   Tang Changru has a complete introduction to the intellectual world of the late jian-an period (196–220) in his "Wei-Jin xuanxue zhi xingcheng ji qi fazhan." Not only did Daoism make a resurgence, but also the Logicians, Legalism, the Military school, the School of Diplomacy and many others. See Tang Changru, Wei-Jin Nanbeichao shi luncong, 1955, 1978, 313–316.

58   Kong Rong, "Ru ying youlie lun," Jian-an qizi ji, j. 1, 1989, 27 and Wang Can, "An shen lun," in j. 3, 1989, 117, 128.

and so he chose names like mysterious, silent, emptiness, and void."[59] In Wang
Chang's mind Daoism was already equal to Confucianism. Still a bit later, in the
zhengshi era of the state of Wei, Xiaohou Xuan, Xun Can, Xun Rong (fl. 3rd century), Zhong Hui, Wang Bi, Ruan Ji, Xi Kang and Xiang Xiu became prominent
at the same time, and He Yan, who was promoting this trend, was in charge of
official appointments. According to the *History of the Jin Dynasty*, "day by day
empty talk spread throughout the land; everyone joined in and bruited about
their ideas."[60] Scholarly fashion had certainly undergone a great change.

In the discussions of being and non-being, non-being was accorded the
highest status, leading to a great shift in attitudes toward life values. Since non-
being was the root and being was the branch, the spontaneity (*ziran*, naturalness) that corresponded to non-being was ranked ahead of the morality that
corresponded to being. The natural human nature that corresponded to non-
being was also ranked ahead of man's social nature that corresponded to being.
An unsophisticated, simple, honest, natural life attitude of primal innocence
further ranked ahead of the wise, rational, harmonious life attitude fostered by
the rites and music and was accorded an absolute priority in value. In the third
and fourth decades of the third century, this way of thinking gradually grew
into a consensus among a certain group of men of culture in the Luoyang area.
He Yan's "On the nameless" cites Xiahou Xuan to the effect that "Spontaneity
(naturalness)—that is the Way."[61] Wang Bi went even further when he asserted
that "... if you model yourself on Heaven then you will be transformed, and the
Way is the same as Spontaneity (Nature)..."[62] They expounded and discussed
human life on the basis of Heaven, Earth and Nature (*ziran*) and believed that
being spontaneous (natural) was the Way of Heaven; this spontaneity was
simply non-action (*wuwei*, taking no action contrary to nature); non-action
was simply following and obeying Heaven and Earth; and following and obeying Heaven and Earth was simply the correct way to live.[63]

During the Eastern Han and Wei-Jin eras, however, it was really not the
spontaneous Way of Heaven that maintained social order. It was the man-
made Confucian ritual code of behavior (*mingjiao* 名教)—that is the laws, the
political institutions, and social customs and the concepts of justice, rightness
and fairness that guaranteed their application. They were not spontaneous,

59   *Sanguo zhi*, j. 27, "Xu Hu er Wang zhuan," 744–745.
60   *Jinshu*, j. 35, "Pei Wei zhuan," quoting "Chong you lun," 1046.
61   *Quan Sanguo wen*, j. 39, 1275.
62   "Lunyu shiyi," in *Wang Bi ji jiaoshi*, 1980, 626.
63   *Ibid.*, 1980, 71, 77.

but artificial conventions, and consequently there arose in the intellectual world a conflict between spontaneity and the Confucian code of ethics.

It is said that in order to express his high regard for spontaneity and his disregard for the Confucian code of ethics, He Yan asserted that the sages did not have worldly desires—"the sages were without human feelings" (*shengren wuqing*)—and on this account people did not need the external restraints of the Confucian code of ethics to achieve the highest realm of being. Wang Bi noticed, however, that although this idea made the sages appear extremely pure and holy, yet it also made them seem unreasonable and out of keeping with the Way of Heaven and Nature. Furthermore it could also cause spiritual transcendence and spontaneity in life to turn into two completely different things. For these reasons, Wang criticized He Yan by pointing out that the sages also had the same nature and feelings as ordinary people, only ordinary people were held back by their material desires while the likes and dislikes of the sages all emanated from Nature. Deep in their heart/mind people all have a spontaneous nature and feelings, and natural feelings like "filial piety" are then all reasonable. If their feelings originate in reverence for the rites or discrimination in favor of blood relations, they should not be considered reasonable. In an answer to a letter from Xun Rong, Wang also affirmed that every person has a spontaneous inborn nature and no matter how strong some customs become, "they cannot eliminate their spontaneous human nature."[64] Nevertheless, in Wang Bi's thought, so-called humanity and rightness (*renyi*) and Confucian social ethics are still in the final analysis only the products of the social history of later generations. It is only because humanity had become extremely far removed from their natural state that Confucian social ethics and humanity and rightness were constructed to regulate the social order. Because these ideas are man-made social constructions, they remain "the product of the decline of loyalty and honesty and the chief cause of chaos." No matter what, for Wang Bi, humanity still needed the naturalistic Way of Heaven.[65]

The idea of relying on the historical sequence to assess the comparative value of the Confucian code of ethics and Nature/Spontaneity) was derived from pre-Qin Daoism and was very widespread at this time. Mu Bing (fl. 3rd century)'s "Admonitions for sons" (Jiezi shu),[66] Ruan Ji's "Understanding Zhuangzi" (Da Zhuang lun) and "Penetrating Laozi" (Tong Lao lun) all accepted this view.[67] During the *zhengshi* reign period, Xi Kang put things even more clearly.

64   He Shao, "Wang Bi zhuan," appendix to *Wang Bi ji jiaoshi*, 1980, 640.
65   "Laozi zhu," Chapter 38, *Wang Bi ji jiaoshi*, 1980, 94.
66   *Sanguo zhi*, j. 23, "Chang Lin zhuan," a note citing *Weilüe*, "Qing Jie zhuan," 622.
67   Chen Bojun, *Ruan Ji ji jiaozhu*, 1987, 146, 154, 171.

He said that the method of the six classics was control and repression, but human nature wants to be tranquil and relaxed. Repression violates human nature, but tranquility and relaxation allow people to be spontaneous. This way, humanity and rightness were advocated merely to regulate and control society, and the Confucian code of ethics was advocated because society was already teeming with strife.[68] Examining history from this point of view, if we admit that the earlier something occurs in history the more reasonable (rational, legitimate) it is, then the "natural/spontaneous" emanating from Heaven and Earth has to be ranked above the Confucian code of ethics that was constructed later in history. Xiang Xiu who debated with Xi Kang in his "Questions on 'On nurturing life,'" (Nan Yangsheng lun) went even further than Xi on the question of *ziran*. If we say that Xi Kang still scrupulously maintained that *ziran* meant only quietude and non-action, then Xiang Xiu went beyond him to argue that *ziran* should embrace all human feelings and desires: "to be partial to honor and to despise disgrace, to enjoy leisure and despise toil, all of these come from *ziran*." If we say that in Xi Kang's mind *ziran* remained a far off goal, for Xiang Xiu it was already a feeling and desire that people actually had in their heart/minds. Even acquiring power and seeking riches and honors were all natural feelings that were not to be opposed.[69] As a result, the philosophical demonstration that "the Confucian ethical code originally came from Nature" was transformed into the life practice of "transcending the Confucian ethical code and giving free rein to Spontaneity/Nature." Not only did the "Seven Worthies of the Bamboo Grove" like Xi Kang, Ruan Ji, Liu Ling (ca. 221–300) and the others strive to achieve spontaneity, even to the extent of becoming decadent, but after the *zhengshi* era there was also an ethos of seeking to be unconventional and unrestrained in the name of mystery (*xuanmiao*), elegance (*yayuan*) and equanimity or freethinking (*kuangda*).[70]

---

68   "Nan Zhang Liaoshu ziran haoxue lun," *Quan Sanguo wen*, j. 50, *Quan shanggu Sandai Qin Han Liuchao wen*, 1336.

69   "Nan Xi Kang Shuye yangsheng lun," *Quan Jin wen*, j. 72, *Quan shanggu Sandai Qin Han Liuchao wen*, 1876.

70   In Pei Wei's "Chong you lun," there is an excellent explanation of contemporary ideas of *xuanmiao, yayuan*, and *kuangda*. He says that in the minds of contemporary people, *xuanmiao* 玄妙 meant "relying on nihilism to establish one's views;" *yayuan* 雅远 meant "not to take one's duties seriously while in office;" and *kuangda* 曠達 was "to neglect moral integrity in one's daily conduct."

       This passage is almost the same as what is said in Gan Bao's "Jinji zonglun": "they viewed indulgence and corruption as understanding how to get by in daily conduct and ignored integrity and honesty; those who wanted to serve in government considered it valuable to obtain things dishonorably and they despised those who behaved uprightly. Those who were in office regarded ignoring right and wrong as the best policy and

2.5

He Yan was killed and Wang Bi died in 249, and in 263 Xi Kang and Zhong Hui were killed and Ruan Ji died, but the practice of Mysterious Learning or Neo-Daoism that they initiated continued. In the end it caused Chinese intellectual doctrines that had been fixed since the Qin-Han era to turn in a different direction.

A few years later it became conspicuously obvious that the fashion for Mysterious Learning was most exuberant and there was intense competition to be the most unconventional and unrestrained. Works such as the *Records of the Three Kingdoms* with Pei Songzhi (372–451)'s commentaries, the *History of the Jin Dynasty* and the *New Account of Tales of the World* (Shishuo xinyu) all record changes in the scholarly landscape since the Wei-Jin period that fully express the changes in the feelings and the lifestyles of men of culture in that age. Many of them competed in debating Neo-Daoist ideas back and forth. They generally failed to offer any original thoughts, and it would be more appropriate to say that they were just playing at mysterious talk (*xuanyan*). The profound ideas of Wei-Jin Neo-Daoism had nevertheless already become secondary, and many literary scholars simply used them as topics for improving their eloquence or as literary games of self-expression.

These debates may be the subject of literary history, but not necessarily the subject of intellectual history. What we want to discuss is the significance of this kind of thought change for the future development of intellectual history.

The first phenomenon of intellectual history we want to pay attention to is the change in the structure of knowledge and the intellectual practice of Chinese elite scholar officials. Mastery of concrete knowledge began to lose its importance among these literati and was replaced by a simplistic understanding of philosophical ideas. The ethos of erudition and wide learning from the Eastern Han was replaced by a craze for mysterious thought. People became accustomed to or even obsessed with discussing topics that had nothing to do with experience and knowledge—things like the relations between non-being and being, whether or not the ancient sages had normal feelings, thought and language, music and innate character (*benzhi*) and so on. As much as the topics of these discussions may have been potentially pointed at and related to the world of real life, they generally took place on a level separated from life in society. When Tang Changru referred to the "concise and lucid southern learning" of the Wei-Jin period, he was actually referring to the "Henan learning" centered upon Luoyang. No matter how much the Wu area of Jiangnan

---

laughed at those who were conscientious and respectful." In this manner, what had been understood as the meaning of intellectual discourse, social responsibility and personal morality were all undermined. *Jinshu*, j. 35, 1044–1046; *Wenxuan*, j. 49, 692.

(southern Jiangsu, northern Zhejiang and Shanghai) still continued the intellectual tradition of astronomy (astrology), calendar science and divination, after the end of the Wu state (220–280) the powerful Luoyang intellectual style dominated all China. By the Eastern Jin when northern scholar officials were forced to move south, this Luoyang Neo-Daoist trend went with them and even more naturally dominated the entire south.[71]

The second phenomenon in intellectual history worthy of notice is the differentiation of Mysterious Learning itself. This followed two very clear tendencies. One was from non-being to being in which Neo-Daoism split into two different theories, one that most valued non-being and one that privileged being. The other was from the *Laozi* to the *Zhuangzi*, and this change in foundational classic also adumbrated a change in thinking.

If we say that a large number of scholars of *zhengshi*-era Neo-Daoism followed the trend of regarding non-being as the origin (root), then, after the end of the *zhengshi* era in 249, a group of scholars with a different view came on the scene. Take, for example, Pei Wei (267–300) who compiled the two essays "Honoring being" (Chong you) and "Valuing non-being" (Gui wu). Although he carried on the post-*zhengshi* trend of emphasizing the search for origins, he still worried that theories putting "emptiness" (*xu* 虛) and non-being first might provide an excuse for empty talk and lax morals. He hoped, then, to establish being as the ultimate foundation for contemporary social order. He accepted the idea that being grew out of non-being, but he held that the differentiation of being and non-being in later ages was just like the "molting" of some animals. The mysterious and unfathomable non-being could be held in abeyance, and the realistic being, the unity of existence, would naturally become the basic origin of all things. Taking being as the root origin could, consequently, lead to the establishment of "principle" (*li* 理). On the contrary, if the real world already existed in the realm of being, but the intellectual world persisted in its attachment to non-being, there would be no way to deal with the things and events of the actually existing world.[72]

If we say that Pei Wei split non-being and being into two separate entities and held non-being in abeyance while regarding being as the origin (root), then another scholar, Sun Sheng (ca. 302–373), went a step further in criticizing Pei's views. Sun transcended non-being and being by placing them both under "the natural" (*ziran*). He believed that since circumstances had changed, the Way should naturally also follow along. Stubborn attachment to either non-being

---

71   Tang Changru, "Du *Baopuzi* tuilun nanbei xuefeng zhi yitong," in *Wei Jin Nan Bei Chao shi luncong*, 367–371.

72   These ideas are found in the *Jinshu*, j. 35, 1044–1045.

or being was simply prejudice. He criticized them both for "not understanding the way of flexibility and adjustment."[73] This allowed Neo-Daoism not only to break free of its one-directional thinking, but it also allowed the foundational texts of Neo-Daoism slowly to escape from the dominance of the *Laozi* and migrate toward the *Zhuangzi*.

Just at that point in the third century appeared Xiang Xiu and Guo Xiang (252–312)'s outstanding interpretations of Zhuangzi's thought. Guo Xiang's edition of the *Zhuangzi*, the *Annotated Zhuangzi* (Zhuangzi zhu), turned Neo-Daoist thought away from discussions of the ontology of an unfathomable mystery and toward explorations of personal freedom. Xiang Xiu and Guo Xiang lessened the opposition between non-being and being, but heightened the significance of "spontaneity." In a comment to the "Knowledge Wandered North" (Zhi beiyou) chapter, Guo Xiang says that the universe is a kind of natural, spontaneous process: "illuminating why things become themselves, and are not made to be so."[74] The key term that repeatedly appears in their interpretations is not non-being or being, but rather *ziran*: spontaneity, the natural, Nature. When they explain the everlasting nature of the cosmos, they do not emphasize its non-being or being, but go beyond them to regard this everlastingness as a kind of natural spontaneity.[75] This natural spontaneity is the necessary Way of the cosmos, the necessary Way of society and even more the necessary Way of human life.[76] At the same time Guo Xiang's *Annotated Zhuangzi* (Zhuangzi zhu) discusses "independent transformation in the mysterious realm" (*duhua yu xuanming zhi jing*).[77] This so-called "independent transformation" (*duhua*) refers to the universe, society, and human beings residing in a completely natural and spontaneous state of existence without any kind of external interference. For human beings, "independent transformation" points toward an approach to life as a quest for freedom. The highest realm of this "independent transformation" is of course a state of being

---

73   Sun Sheng, "Lao Dan fei daxian lun," *Quan Jin wen*, j. 63, *Quan shanggu sandai Qin Han Liuchao wen*, 1816–1817.

74   zzjs, j. 7, 764.

75   zzjs, j. 1, "Qiwu lun," 50.

76   zzjs, j. 5, "Tian di," note, 404: "Those who practice non-action will naturally become rulers;" j. 5, "Tian dao," note, 464: "Those who always maintain no mind can thus rule all under Heaven without sickness or fatigue;" j. 6, "Qiu shui," note, 591: "Those who deliberately do things without allowing things to develop their own way—in what would their destiny reside."

77   Tang Yongtong wrote that this passage is "very difficult to understand; if you understand it, then you understand the ideas of Xiang Xiu and Guo Xiang. In "Chong you zhi xue yu Xiu-Guo xueshuo," Tang Yongtong, *Lixue, Foxue, Xuan Xue*, 1991, 337.

"free and easy" (*xiaoyao*). At the very beginning of the *Annotated Zhuangzi* there is the following statement: "the chief meaning of the *Zhuangzi*, resides in free and easy wandering, practicing non-action yet achieving one's goal naturally, thus reaching the very smallest and the very largest so as to illuminate the appropriateness of one's nature."[78] Because this extremely transcendent and free realm could be made to correspond directly to human life practices, it very rapidly became the topic of enthusiastic discussion among scholar officials. The *Zhuangzi* also very quickly became a core text of Chinese intellectual discussion, and it grew more and more important in later Chinese intellectual history.

The third significant set of occurrences in intellectual history comprises the playful and literary tendencies of Neo-Daoism. If we look closely, we see that from the Three-Kingdoms Wei to the Eastern Jin, the serious philosophical quests of Neo-Daoism steadily diminished in favor of games of disputation and literary virtuosity. The *History of the Jin Dynasty* "Biography of Yin Hao" cites a letter to Yin Hao (?–356) from Yu Yi (305–345) to the effect that "lofty all day disquisitions on the *Zhuangzi* and the *Laozi* are full of empty talk; although they claim they are discussing the Dao, in reality they are merely idle talk."[79] So-called "idle talk" (*huajing* 華境) refers to empty arguments or pure talk (*qingtan* 清談) devoid of philosophical substance. It was said that Wang Yan (256–311) of the Western Jin faithfully believed in the non-being of Wang Bi and He Yan, but was not opposed to the being of Pei Wei either. That is, he took no genuine stand on what was right and what was wrong.[80] Wan Yan's son-in-law, Pei Xia, once had a debate back and forth using arcane language with Guo Xiang on Neo-Daoist philosophy. He is said to have been a "professional" Neo-Daoist who was "good at talking about the names and principles of things," but did not have any principled position. His audience was also lacking in principles, so that "those who listened to him all sighed in admiration whether they understood or not."[81]

---

78   zzjs, j. 1, "Xiaoyao you," 3.
79   *Jinshu*, j. 77, 2044.
80   *Jinshu*, j. 43, "Wang Yan zhuan," 1236.
81   *Shishuo xinyu*, "Wenxue," *Shishuo xinyu jiaojian*, j. *shang*, 113. On 114 of the same work, the following is said of the celebrated official Wang Dao (276–339) that he "only talked about three principles: music is neither sad nor joyful, nourishing one's life, and exhausting your meaning when you speak, but however he was subtly concerned with life and there was nothing he did not touch upon." It would seem that he made no real contribution to Neo-Daoist philosophy, but he was a good talker who could command people's respect. We can see, then, that by this time "pure talk" (*qingtan*) was no longer concerned with what one was talking about, but with how one talked.

It is interesting to note, however, that just at this time when genuine philosophic interest was waning, this new thought actually became fashionable
and influenced people's daily lives. In that age, the realm of the "mysterious"
(*xuan*), "pure" (*qing*) and "profound (far off, *yuan*) was not only something
scholars sought in their discourse, but also the state they desired in their lives.
"Spontaneity" was not only the subject of literati thought, but also a sign of
their elegant and sophisticated tastes. The *ziran* that various literati wrote
about was both the spontaneous realm of life that they were mentally seeking
and the landscapes and natural scenery that epitomized *ziran* as Nature. Neo-
Daoism was no longer an intellectual doctrine; it was a lifestyle of the upper
level literati. Although Neo-Daoism was habitually present in their discourse
or writings, it was only expressed but not pondered because it was no longer a
problem to be probed. It had become a set of ready-made ideas.

What is most interesting about these developments is that when elite
scholar officials generally accepted Lao-Zhuang thought and Lao-Zhuang
thought became a generally accepted truth, it led to an intellectual climate
that was conducive to the toleration of different forms of thought coming from
outside China. It was precisely with the support of such an intellectual climate
that Buddhism entered the intellectual world of China's elite.

3.   **Purification of Daoist Teachings: The Religionization
      of Daoist Thought, Knowledge and Techniques**

One trend of scholarly opinion concerning the formation of religious Daoism
or the Daoist religion (*daojiao* 道教) holds that the Way of the Five Pecks of
Rice sect (*wudoumi dao* 五斗米道) and the Way of Great Peace sect (*taiping
dao* 太平道) arose toward the end of the Eastern Han and were the harbingers
of religious Daoism. Several events related to religious Daoism also occurred at
this time: sacrifices were offered to Laozi, the *Book of Great Peace Written in Blue*
was published and the compilation of the *Xiang-er Commentary to the Laozi*
(Laozi Xiang-er zhu) and so on were completed. The rise of religious Daoism
was also related to the great social upheaval at the end of the Han.[82] Another
scholarly trend, however, pays more particular attention to the compilation

---

82   See, for example, Qing Xitai, *Zhongguo daojiao sixiang shigang*, 1980, j. 1 and the first vol-
      ume of his *Zhongguo daojiao*; chapter one of Ren Jiyu, *Zhongguo daojiaoshi*, 1990. This
      connection with social upheaval was pointed out long ago. Xu Dishan in his 1920 essay
      "Daojia sixiang yu daojiao," stated that the Way of the Five Pecks of Rice and the Way of
      Great Peace "sects are the direct precursors of today's Daoist Religion." In *Yanjing xuebao*,
      3 (1927), 249–282.

and collection of the classic texts of Daoist Religion, the formation of Daoist monastic discipline, expositions of Daoist thought, compilation of a pantheon of Daoist Gods and Immortals and so on that occurred from the Wei-Jin period on. They take the religious reforms of Kou Qianzhi (365–448) in the north and the religious activities of Ge Hong (283–343? or 364?), Lu Xiujing (406–477) and Tao Hongjing (456–536) in the south as representative of the formation of the Daoist Religion. I would like to bring these two trends of thought together and look at the formation of religious Daoism as "a process of religious reformation (literally: religionization, *zongjiaohua* 宗教化)" that continued without cease from the Han through the Wei-Jin and the North-South Dynasties periods.

According to the "Monograph on Buddhism and Daoism" (Shi Lao zhi) in the *History of the Wei Dynasty* (Weishu), the Supreme Venerable Sovereign (*taishang laojun* 太上老君) once descended to Mt. Song, a traditional sacred mountain in Henan, presented the Daoist text *Precepts of the New Code to Be Chanted [to the Melody] "In the Clouds"* (Yunzhong yinsong xinke zhi jie) to the Northern Wei Daoist master Kou Qianzhi and asked him to "purify and integrate religious Daoism."[83] What was meant here by the term "purify and integrate" seems to have been a kind of reorganization or reformation by combining clarification (making clear, purifying) and integration. The history of the Daoist religion for the four hundred years from the end of the second century to the end of the sixth century can be aptly described by these five words "purify and integrate religious Daoism."

3.1

In the past half a century, Chinese archeology has unearthed many historical relics from the Eastern Han that have written on them phrases similar to later Daoist religious incantations or spells as well as pictures very similar to various kinds of talismanic diagrams of religious Daoism. These writings and diagrams all represent supplications to take advantage of the power of the gods to control evil spirits and to bless and protect one's descendants so they may live peaceful lives. They can be said to be directly derived from the arts of healing and divination of the shamans of high antiquity. The thought and knowledge preserved in these Eastern Han artifacts—from a time before the complete formation of religious Daoism—carried on the tradition of ancient mystical beliefs and led toward the most commonly used knowledge and techniques— like drugs, talismans, spells, seals, and so on—in religious Daoism. These artifacts oblige us to go beyond the accepted thinking about the origins of religious

---

83   *Weishu*, j. 11, 3051.

Daoism and search for them against a broader background of fragmentary and disordered Daoist knowledge and techniques. In doing so we can attempt to work out the process of integration of this knowledge and these techniques— that is, the "religionization" of Daoism.

We have earlier discussed the background of general knowledge and the general intellectual level from the Warring States to the Qin-Han periods. During this rather long period of time, people generally believed that time and space in the cosmos had an absolute and unique center, that the two polarities of Yin and Yang and the Five Phases created a perfect and harmonious order, and that this order was the foundation of everything rational and reasonable. It was also supported by mysterious powers. They also believed that Heaven and Earth, the human and the spirit realms, could mutually communicate and that the knowledge and the mantic techniques involved in this communication was the monopoly of a class of *wu* priests, *zhu* invocators, *shi* scribes and *zong* temple masters. People were most concerned with those questions, like life span, happiness and the state, that were most relevant to their lives. Most of them believed that the knowledge and the technical skills of shamans, diviners, and adepts of the arcane arts were needed to answer these question. For these reasons, various forms of knowledge and mantic techniques for communication between Heaven and Earth, the human and the spirit realms, for extricating people from difficulties, for achieving earthly happiness and even for obtaining eternal life began in high antiquity and continued all the way down through the Qin and Han dynasties. Practices that later religious Daoism was expert in, such as refining gold (alchemy), driving away evil, prayer, divination, nurturing life, selecting auspicious dates and so on, all had extremely ancient provenances.

In the world of the Han dynasty, there were many active shamans, diviners and adepts of the arcane arts. They were in charge or carried out a great variety of official practices. The following is a list of some of them.[84] (1) Communicating with ghosts and spirits, including calling down the spirits, examining ghosts, divining and sacrificing. (2) Reliving calamities by means of various forms of advance prevention or elimination. (3) Driving away or curing illness. (4) Cursing enemies in wartime to gain victory for their own side. (5) Praying for appropriate weather, including calling down or stopping rain and blocking floods. (6) Cursing an enemy so he encounters calamity or praying for oneself to achieve ones goal. (7) Using various methods to pray for childbirth. (8) Arranging funerals, consoling the spirits of the departed in order that the living might obtain happiness and avoid disaster. Besides these

---

84   See Lin Fushi, *Handai de wuzhe*, 1988.

practices, they sometimes also taught nurturing life through breathing exercises and various secret arts of the bedchamber.

These Eastern Han diviners and adepts can be generally divided into three categories. One group explained magic diagrams, prophecies, disasters, strange occurrences and divination. They relied on the study of the classics and the apocrypha. The *Token for the Agreement of the Three According to the Book of Changes* (Zhouyi cantong qi) by Wei Boyang (fl. 2nd century) was published later. A second group, from Gan Ji's compilation of *Book of Great Peace* to Zhang Jue and Zhang Xiu participated in social movements at the end of the Han. They have been regarded as the founders of one branch of religious Daoism. The third group was the Way of the Immortals (*shenxianjia* 神仙家) who emphasized the quest for personal immortality; this tradition extended from Zuo Ci (Zuo Yuanfang, fl. 2nd–3rd centuries) to Ge Xuan (164–244). After this time, from the Wei-Jin through the Six Dynasties period, these three categories of Daoist experts continued their activities and constituted the main force in the formation and integration of the Daoist Religion. Their beliefs, knowledge and mantic techniques inspired later religious Daoism and advanced its core ideas—the search for earthly happiness and immortality.

These people with their knowledge and occult techniques were generally not, however, part of the social mainstream. They were severely criticized by the intellectual elite,[85] and fiercely attacked by the Han dynasty government and officialdom.[86] Because of this, when the Eastern Han Daoist adept Liu Gen went into seclusion in the mountains and many people started to study Daoism with him, the local Prefect Shi Qi issued an edict prohibiting the practice.[87] When Diwu Lun was Governor in Kuaiji Commandery, he also strictly forbade unauthorized and unorthodox sacrifices (sometimes meaning "licentious cult," (*yinsi* 淫祀). Song Jun controlled shamanistic activities in Chenyang (in Hunan) and Jiujiang (in Jiangxi) by setting up schools and forbidding unorthodox sacrifices, while Luan Ba in Yuzhang (Jiangxi) also used rational Daoist arts (*daoshu*) to combat irrational witchcraft (*wushu*).[88] All of this represents the marginalization by the scholarly elite and mainstream society of such knowledge and mantic techniques for communicating with

---

85   For example, Wang Chong, *Lunheng*, j. 25, "Jiechu," in Huang Hui, ed., *Lunheng jiaoshi*, 1990 and 1995, 1046. Wang Fu, *Qianfu lun*, "Wu lie," in Wang Jipei and Peng Duo, *Qianfu lunjian jiaozheng*, 1985, 301.

86   Wang Liqi, *Yantielun jiaozhu*, 1992, j. 6, "Jiu kui," 401 and "San bu zu," 352.

87   HHS, j. 82 *xia*, "Fangshu lie zhuan xia," 2746.

88   HHS, j. 41, "Diwu, Zhong Li, Song, Han liezhuan," 1397 & 1411–1412; j. 57, "Luan Ba zhuan," 1841.

ghosts and spirits and seeking immortality. Consequently, during the reigns of Eastern Han emperors Shun (r. 125–144) and Huan (r. 146–168), when Gong Chong and Xiang Kai twice presented the *Book of Great Peace Written in Blue*, Gong Chong was condemned by the government as being "full of demonic absurdity" and was ignored; Xiang Kai was accused by the Master of Records of using heretic words to confuse the masses, and was put in prison in Luoyang to await punishment.[89]

3.2

Starting in the middle of the second century, due to a widespread plague and other reasons, however, many groups of shamans and magicians appeared using talismans, spells against demons, knocking one's head on the ground and reflecting on one's past errors and such techniques to cure disease. They sprang up primarily in Western Shu (modern Sichuan) and in the eastern part of the country. They first set up Daoist religious organizations (*jiaotuan*). Legend has it that Zhang Ling (34–156? or 178?) set up twenty-four command-eries or parishes for governing and "healing," and Zhang Jue (?–184) installed thirty-six regions or generals (*fang* 方). They tentatively compiled and estab-lished classical texts. Zhang Xiu had his disciples follow the Libationer (*jijiu*) and study the *Laozi* while many early texts of religious Daoism—the *Scripture of Great Peace*, the *Xiang-er Commentary to the Laozi*, *The Kinship of the Three, in Accordance with the <u>Book of Changes</u>* (Can tong qi), and the *Organon of the Twelve Hundred Officials* (Qian-erbai guanyi)—all appeared one after another. Third, they more or less established the rules for their believers. Zhang Jue "ordered the sick to knock their heads on the ground and reflect on their past errors;" Zhang Xiu had the sick "reflect on their past errors" in a quiet room; Zhang Lu ordered the faithful as follows: "those who made small errors should cultivate the Dao and walk a hundred paces" and he "forbade killing in the spring and summer" in accordance with the "Monthly Ritual Proceedings" (Yueling) chapter of the *Book of Rites* and so on.[90] Nevertheless, these as yet rather crude and chaotic religious organizations, ancient texts, rules and activ-ities were looked down upon by most of mainstream society and criticized by most of the intellectual elite.

From the end of the Eastern Han through the Wei-Jin period, internal criti-cism and reflection on religious Daoism grew increasingly severe. It was said that the *Xiang-er Commentary* criticized religious Daoism for its confused state, and that the inner chapters (*neipian*) of Ge Hong's *Master Who Embraces*

---

89   HHS, j. 30, "Xiang Kai zhuan," 1082–1084.
90   *Sanguo zhi*, j. 8, "Zhang Lu zhuan," 264 note citing Lu Huan's *Dianlüe*.

Simplicity (Baopuzi) strongly criticized the Daoist religion from a position inside the faith. Such critiques are emblematic of the believers' desire to raise the cultural quality of religious Daoism. At about the same time or a little later, the *Scripture of the High Lord Grotto Spirit Incantations* (Taishang dongyuan shenzhou jing) also reprimanded the Daoist masters for not carrying out their duties well because since the Eastern Han the people had no faith and so they "do not know there is a Way, do not know there are rules (*fa*), do not know there are classic texts; they only believe in spontaneity."[91] This criticism of "only believing in spontaneity" and emphasis on the Way, the teachings and the classic texts is indicative of an intention to integrate the Daoist religion and move it away from the natural and toward the human world. A little later, at about the beginning of the Liu Song dynasty (420–479) in the North-South Dynasties period, the *Scripture of the Inner Explanations of the Three Heavens* (Santian neijie jing), a southern text, even more fiercely attacked contemporary wizards and magicians, calling their methods of singing and dancing to amuse the gods (spirits) a "heterodox sect" (literally evil Way," *xiedao* 邪道).[92] Attacking a "heterodox sect" was, of course, an attempt to establish their own good "orthodox Way" (*zhengdao* 正道).

It is especially noteworthy that there was internal self-criticism of the organization of Daoist religious groups along military or government lines. Such organizational forms were frequently used by early religious Daoism to administer their believers. The thirty-six regions of the Way of Great Peace used the military title of "General" and the twenty-four commanderies or parishes of the Way of the Five Pecks of Rice used the government bureaucratic term "Libationer." This imitation of government or military organization would usually provoke outbursts of religious sentiment and could lead to suspicion by the government. For example, the *History of the Jin Dynasty*, "Biography of Zhou Zha," records that the supposed octo-centenarian Daoist Li Babai appointed religious officials using contemporary government titles.[93] In a society highly controlled by the government, such behavior could easily be labelled a capital crime and result in execution. Later on Buddhists repeatedly hinted about this in an attempt to alert the officials against Daoism.[94] On this account, from Kou Qianzhi of the Northern Wei on, religious Daoism began to change itself from within, transforming its early semi-administrative, semi-military mode

---

91 *Taishang dongyuan shenzhou jing*, j. 1, *Daozang*, Dongxuan bu (Mystery Grotto) benwen
     lei (Main texts), shi 1, ce 6.

92 *Daozang*, Zhengyi (Orthodox) bu, man 8, ce 28.

93 *Jinshu*, j. 58, 1575.

94 *Guang Hong ming ji*, j. 8 and 9, SBBY edition, 66 & 76.

of organization into one of pure religious practice. The *Scripture of the Recited Precepts of the High Lord* (Laojun yinsong jiejing), supposedly coming from the Highest Lord Lao (Taishang Laojun), but in reality probably compiled by Kou Qianzhi himself, particularly criticizes any directly confrontational actions against the politics, ideology and moral standards of mainstream society.[95]

In the particular social milieu of ancient China, it was impossible for a religion not to submit itself to the mainstream political ideology. After Confucianism became required knowledge for official advancement and the basic criterion of correct conduct was widely accepted by the intellectual stratum and held the center of power in the upper levels of society, all other schools of knowledge and techniques were marginalized. As a consequence, religious Daoism had no choice but to purify and reintegrate itself. This was not only because of pressure from mainstream thought, but also due to its need for legalization and sanctification. There were at least three reasons for this need. First off, although these Daoist religious ideas and techniques that had become customary in daily life had potentially systematic intellectual foundations, they all along lacked a clear and lucid theoretical formulation to make them "reasonable." Second, although these adepts and Daoist masters who functioned as communicators between Heaven and Earth the human and the spirit realms had considerable requisite knowledge, they all along lacked a definite organizational structure to legitimize them. Third and lastly, although the Daoist religious activities were quite effective in secular society and had a rather large popular base, they all along lacked a thorough set of moral and ethical standards or rules that could "sanctify" them. Although people were always hoping for transcendence, happiness and immortality, and so religious Daoism would never lose its base, nevertheless it still needed to think about how to rationalize, legitimize and sanctify itself in order to become a "religion" (*zongjiao*).

We know that any religion has to promise its believers transcendence or emancipation, but to control its followers it also has to have a sanctity and purity that transcends the secular world. This control includes the habit of complying with rules in their moral life, nurturing fervor in their religious feelings and religious commitment in the realm of ideas or doctrine. For these reasons, if religious Daoism was to become a religion that gained widespread acceptance in Chinese society it had first to go through a rather long process of religionization. This process began at the end of the second century and continued for several hundred years.

---

95   *Daozang*, Dongshen bu (Spirit Grotto), jielü lei (Precepts), li 2, ce 18; see Yang Liansheng, "Laojun yinsong jielü jing jiaoshi," in *Yang Liansheng lunwen ji*, 1992, 33–92.

3.3

The first thing we notice in this long process of religionization is that religious Daoism slowly established a set of strict precepts so that the Daoist religion would conform to the accepted moral standards of ancient China. This also served to harmonize their religious practices with the ideology of the intellectual elite while at the same time putting Daoist religious groups in order.

Although the Way of the Five Pecks of Rice and the Way of Great Peace at the end of the Han were later regarded as the "originators" of the Daoist Religion, the rules of their internal organization and their ideas and techniques were actually quite chaotic. This was especially true of their confrontational stance toward mainstream society, a situation that caused a great deal of trouble later on when the Daoist religion attempted to exist openly in society. Those Daoist practices that derived from the tradition of shamans and magicians also caused the religion to come under repeated attack from many quarters, including both Confucianism and Buddhism. As a result, from early on the Daoist religion responded to these attacks with successive periods of reflection and reorganization. The northern Daoist master Kou Qianzhi sharply criticized "the pseudo theories of three Zhangs" (referring to Zhang Ling, Zhan Heng and Zhang Lu), pointing out that they were remnants of the practices of wizards and magicians.

The three practices Kou criticized most were (1) collecting money (taxes) and granting official posts, (2) the encouragement of sexual intercourse techniques called uniting the vital essence (*heqishu* 合氣術) of male and female and (3) the system of inheritance from father to son of the title of Celestial Master (*tianshi* 天師). These practices carried on by the followers of the three Zhangs made it hard for the Daoist religion to escape entanglement in secular interests, forfeited its religious purity and violated the moral and ethical customs of ancient China.

In 415, during the Northern Wei, Kou Qianzhi announced that the Supreme Venerable Sovereign had conferred upon him a twenty-volume text entitled *Commandments of the New Ordinances from the Clouds* (Yunzhong yinsong xinke zhijie). With the support of the Northern Wei Tabgatch emperor Tai Wu Di (Tuoba Tao, r. 424–452), Kou transmitted the god's message, "purified religious Daoism, eliminated the pseudo theories of the three Zhangs, including their taxation of the people and encouragement of uniting the vital essence of male and female." He also advocated that the Daoist religion should be in accord with traditional values and attach most importance to ceremonies while adding Daoist breathing exercises and ingestion of drugs to seek longevity.[96] A short time later the southern Daoist master Lu Xiujing also

---

96   *Weishu*, j. 114, "Shi Lao zhi," 3051.

expressed his reformist intentions in the *Scripture of the Numinous Treasure Profound Fivefold Response* (Dongxuan lingbao wugan wen).[97] In the winter of 453, he also led his disciples into the mountains to perform the purification ritual known as the Mud and Soot Levee (*tutanzhai*), mortifying their flesh to obtain the remission of sins. At the same time Kou and Lu advocated that the Daoist religion stop making offerings of wine and meat to the gods, discontinue the practice of taking money from the faithful and encourage the masses to respect the ethics of compassion (*ci*), filial piety (*xiao*), respect (*jing*) and modest yielding (*rang*).[98]

This process of religionization was a very long one. Some old systems and customs were not easy to transform quickly. Some traditions and methods were carried on as before, but some other practices were abolished. Although it had a very long history and was originally a technique for prolonging life, the practice of "uniting the vital essence" of male and female was strictly prohibited in Kou Qianzhi's time. This specific practice contrary to Chinese ethics and morality was at the very least forced underground and carried on in secret, and believers were consequently restrained by religious discipline.[99]

This self-restraint expressed an acceptance of the ethics and morality of the mainstream society. Right from its inception religious Daoism grew out of the same soil as the ancient Chinese ethics and morality of everyday life. This traditional ethics and morality with its long history and widespread acceptance in Chinese society is everywhere affirmed in the texts of early religious Daoism. The *Scripture of Great Peace*, the *Xiang-er Commentary to the Laozi* and the slightly later work of Ge Hong all affirm that "followers of the Way must first establish their moral virtues and deeds." The *Scripture of Great Peace* has very strict orders concerning respect for traditional ethics and morality; it says that there are spirits in Heaven that investigate one's sins and follow

---

97 *Daozang*, Zhengyi bu (Orthodox), sheng, ce 32.

98 *Lu xiansheng [Xiujing] daomen kelüe*, *Daozang*, Taiping bu (Great Peace), yi 9, ce 24.

99 Some ceremonies and methods required a longer time to change. For example, the purification ritual known as the Mud and Soot Levee, mortifying the flesh in order to move the ghosts and spirits. They had to cover their face with yellow earth, let their hair down and tie it to a pole, tie their hands behind their back to the pole and then knock themselves against the pole. It is said that this practice is related to the confessional tradition of "tying oneself up and knocking one's head on the ground and wailing" as described in the *Taiping jing*. Obviously this practice was of long standing. Even though the Buddhists severely criticized this behavior, the practice still endured for a long time in the south. See Yang Liansheng, "Daojiao zhi zibo yu Fojiao zhi zipu," and "Bu lun," in *Yang Liansheng lunwen ji*, 15–32.

people every day to check up on their behavior.[100] Ge Hong wrote that those who study the Way "must take loyalty, filial piety, humanity and honesty as their basic principles." If one "does not cultivate moral virtue, but only works on the mantic arts, he will not achieve long life."[101] He even said that there are gods to regulate misdeeds in Heaven and Earth who calculate people's good and evil and then decide how long they live.[102] These ideas were supported by the scholar official believers in religious Daoism. During this period of religionization that lasted into the sixth century, the Daoist religion step by step acquired a relatively clear, strict and consistent order. The embodiment of this order was its religious organizational system and its precepts for a religious life.

The Daoist religious system was mainly established to accomplish the standardization of religious activities. Chapter 8 of the *Scripture of the Profound Spiritual Spells of the High Lord* (Taishang dongyuan shenzhou jing) states that Daoist priests must function in secular society as rescuers or redeemers. To perform this function believers in the Daoist religion would need to have authority, but given the chaos and corruption in religious Daoism, they often did not have such authority. It was necessary, then, for them to "purify and integrate" the Daoist religion from within; that is, to establish various rules governing its inner activities. They wanted to establish systems not only to restrain the spirit and activities of the Daoist faithful, but also to regulate the mode of activity of Daoist religious organizations. Books like the *Profound Numinous Treasure Three Grottoes Rules and Precepts for Beginning Camps for Daoist Worship* (Dongxuan lingbao sandong fengdao kejie yingshi) appeared one after the other to set up strict rules for all facets of the Daoist religion including ceremonial activities, building construction, erecting statues (images of saints, masters) and so on. These works established rules for such things as the activities and behavior of Daoist priests and nuns, sitting and rising, lying down and resting, food and clothing and dwelling places. They also established systems for setting up Daoist temples, salvation, setting up statues, writing scriptures, making offerings and worshipping, burning incense, lamp lighting, chanting scriptures, lecturing and explanation, transmitting the Way, invocation, purification ceremonies of fasting, ritual rules, cultivation and understanding the true Way (*faxiang* 法相).[103] All of this gave the Daoist religion a strict set of

---

100   *Taipingjing hejiao*, j. 118, "Tianshen kaoguo jujiao sanhejue di er-er-yi" 672.

101   *Baopuzi nepian jiaoshi*, j. 3, "Duisu," 53–54.

102   These ideas may derive from the *Li gongyi suanjing* and the *Daoshi duo suanjing*. See *Ibid.*, 333.

103   The *Dongxuan lingbao sandong fengdao kejie yingshi*, has Golden Bright Seven Perfected Ones as compilers, but most scholars believe it came from the Liang of the Southern dynasties, in *Daozang*, Taiping bu, yi 3, ce 24.

rules that differentiated it from the popular practices of wizards and magicians and the pseudo theories of three Zhangs.[104] They labelled the former modes of Daoist religious worship "old rules of the Six Heavens" (*liutian gufa* 六天故法) and called their own reformed regulations the "new rules of the Three Heavens" (*santian xinfa* 三天新法).

The gradual completion of these precepts and rules brought about the moralization of the beliefs of the faithful. The Daoist precepts and rules were based on Confucian ethics and morality, but their texts repeatedly referred to Buddhist precepts and rules. According to Chen Yinque's research, after the Later Qin Kingdom was destroyed in 417, the Buddhist *Ten Recitations Vinaya* (Shisong lü), widely popular in the Shaanxi area slowly penetrated southern China, but became less known in the north. This led Kou Qianzhi to set up new precepts and rules for the Daoist religion on the pretext that the High Lord had transmitted the *Precepts of the New Code to Be Chanted [to the Melody] "In the Clouds"* to him. Whether this tradition is reliable or not will require further research, but from early on the *Xiang-er Commentary to the Laozi* and the *Master Who Embraces Simplicity* both contain various passages admonishing people to respect ethics and morality.[105] From this we know that the Daoist religion had precepts and rules very early on; it is only that they were rather crude and chaotic. In the long process of reform, the Daoists used the wording of precepts from Buddhist texts to set up their own system of rules and precepts. For example, the forms of things like the Five Admonishments of the Shengxuan School, the Five Admonishments of the Dongshen School, the Five Admonishments of the Orthodox Unity School an so on were all influenced by Buddhism.[106] In this way during the Wei-Jin and North-South Dynasties periods, many texts full of admonitions and precepts, such as the *Ritual Scriptures of Orthodox Unity Celestial Masters Precepts* (Zhengyi fawen tianshijiao jieke jing), the *Essential Precepts of Master Redpine* (Chi Songzi zhongjie jing) and the *Demon Statutes of Nüqing* (Nüqing guilü) appeared one after another.

These precept texts were all based on traditional Confucian ethics and morality, and they admonished people to practice the moral virtues generally accepted in secular society such as loyalty, filial piety, compassion

---

104   See *Lu Xiansheng daomen kelüe*, and *Santian neijie jing* and *Laojun yinsong jiejing*.

105   For Kou Qianzhi's role in setting up Daoist precepts and rules, see Chen Yinque, "Cui Hao yu Kou Qianzhi," originally in *Lingnan xuebao* 11/1 (1950); reprinted in Chen's *Jinmingguan conggao chubian*, 1979, 121–122.

106   See "Dôkyôkai no kaikan to gokai hachikai," and "Dôkyô ni okeru jukai," in Kusuyama Haruki's *Dôka shisô to Dôkyô*, 1992, 64–82 & 83–113.

and carefulness.[107] At the same time and in imitation of Buddhism, they demanded that their believers scrupulously abide by religious prohibitions and they severely punished killing, stealing, lewdness, lying, drinking and so on. They particularly instituted rules to eliminate those sexual practices associated with the "pseudo theories of three Zhangs" that were consistently being criticized by both Confucians and Buddhists. It is especially noteworthy that during these reformist purifications, as these precepts were regulating the behavior of the Daoist faithful, the Daoist religion was also placing its religious activities within the scope of the Confucian ideology and what was permitted by the political powers of the time. That also brought them into harmony with the ethics of secular society and even led a gradual accommodation with Buddhism. The Daoist religion was at once purifying and sanctifying itself so as to become a rigorous religious community and also adjusting its attitude and position to join with the ideology that was accepted by mainstream society and thought.

3.4

The second thing we notice in this long process of religionization is that the Daoist religion relied on the ancient Chinese framework of Heaven and Earth and the cosmos to re-integrate this ancient symbolic system. In doing so, they established their own complete genealogy of gods and demons to serve as religious Daoism's symbolic system for explaining the human order.

In the early Daoist Religion, besides worshipping Laozi, they also believed in a variety of gods and spirits, and so they lacked a sufficiently comprehensive system of gods and demons. Although from the *Scripture of Great Peace* on, they had tried to set up a symbolic system of worship and had carried out various plans, nevertheless at least up to the fourth century, their ritual system remained diverse and chaotic.[108] If a religion's genealogy of gods and demons

---

107   For example, the *Precepts of the Supreme Venerable Sovereign* (Taishang laojun jiejing) demanded that people "not take money that does not belong to them, save people who are suffering calamities and assist them when in difficulty [and] when talking to the rulers, ask them to benefit the country; when talking to ministers ask them to be loyal to the ruler." *Daozang*, Dongshen bu, jielü lei, li 2, ce 18.

108   It was said that Zhang Ling composed the *Protocols of the 1,200 Officials* (Qian erbai guan yi) as a "liturgical guide that told the Libationer which celestial officials to invoke for assistance in curing various illnesses or remedying other situations." Peter Nickerson, "The Southern Celestial Masters," 271, in Livia Kohn, ed., *Daoism Handbook*, 2000, 256–282. Nevertheless, down to Jin times, after the Way of the Five Pecks of Rice bowed to their Three Masters (Zhang Ling, Zhang Heng and Zhang Lu), they went on to bow to a plethora of other euhemeristic gods. They do not seem to have been well organized and they lacked a theoretical framework.

always remains in a state of disorder and its believers burn incense to any and all gods and strike their heads on the ground before any and all demons, then their beliefs only involve supplication for practical benefit and cannot establish a clear ethic in the hearts of the believers, not to mention rising to the level of spiritual sublimation. In such a situation, the religion might easily devolve into completely unsystematic overlapping sacrifices, worship and consecration of shrines to any gods at will, and that could give rise to antipathy among the mainstream society.

Ancient Chinese governments always wanted to control the world of religious belief; this can be clearly seen from records of the prohibition of unauthorized and unorthodox sacrifices or "licentious cults." When he was in office in Ji-nan, Cao Cao (155–220) issued an order forbidding the populous from casually offering irregular sacrifices.[109] In 224, his successor, Cao Pi (187–226), issued an imperial order announcing that "from today on, anyone who dares to arrange uncanonical sacrifices or mouth the words of shamans and wizards will all be treated as heretical sects."[110] Sun Hao (242–284) in the south also strictly forbade various kinds of uncanonical sacrifices.[111] After the change of dynasty in 265, the new Emperor Wu of the Western Jin reaffirmed the proscriptions of the previous dynasties, and the government repeatedly urged local officials to punish those engaged in religious activities "not in accord with the ritual canon."[112] It was probably due to these conditions that the leaders of the Daoist religion began to realize the importance of purification and integration. From the fourth century on, they began to put their system of sacrifices and prayers to gods and demons in order. From Tao Hongjing's *Declarations of the Perfected* (Zhen-gao), *Diagram for Ranking the True Gods* (Zhenling weiyetu) and *Scripture of Salvation* (Duren jing) to the *Scripture of Divine Incantations* (Taishang dongyuan shenzhou jing) and the *Esoteric Essentials of the Most High* (Wushang biyao), the general outline and the conceptual framework of the Daoist Religion's genealogy of gods and demons became progressively apparent.

We should point out that one of the conceptual frameworks for clarifying and putting in order the Daoist religion's genealogy of gods and demons was the ancient Chinese experience and imaginative visions of the cosmos. For example, the *Book in a Pillow* (Zhenzhong shu) has been called the

---

109   *Songshu*, j. 17, 487.

110   *Sanguo zhi*, j. 2, 84.

111   *Gaoseng zhuan*, j. 1, "Wei Wu Jianye Jianchusi Kang seng Hui," *Tang Yongtong jiaozhu ben*, 1992, 16.

112   *Jinshu*, j. 19, "Lizhi shang," 600–601.

Daoist "Genesis," and is the highest theogony of the Daoist religion. In it are mentioned the Original King of Heaven, the Most High Jade Maiden and the Heavenly Emperor of the East and the Queen Mother of the West who both sprang from a combined transformation of the original and the most high.[113] It also says that the Heavenly Emperor begat the Earthly Emperor and the Earthly Emperor begat the Human Emperor. Behind this theogony are the ancient Chinese speculations concerning the origin of the cosmos as well as the Supreme Ultimate, the two nodes (Yin and Yang) and the three powers of Heaven, Earth and the Human. Then the *Diagram for Ranking the True Gods*, that has been called "the Daoist religion's first complete genealogy of the gods," attached most importance to the Celestial Venerable of Primordial Commencement, the Ruler of the Great Way, the Great Ultimate Monarch of the Golden Palace, the High Lord together with the Master of Records of the Nine Palaces, the Middle Lord of Mt. Mao and the Great Emperor of the Northern Yin realm of Fengdu to compile a genealogy that embraced gods and demons, Heaven and Earth, the spirit realm and the human world. The knowledge and conceptual background that supported the establishment of this genealogy, aside from the ancient Chinese intellectual world's concept of time, were the polar concepts of gods versus demons, birth versus death and good versus evil.

Not only did the process of cosmic time serve as a foundational support for this genealogy of gods and demons, but ancient Chinese ideas about the spatial configuration of the cosmos also offered background support. Several spirits occurring in the Han dynasty apocrypha—such as Lingweiyang, Chipiaonu, Hanshuniu, Yaopobao, Yinhouju and so on, the five emperors correlated with the five directions and the five colors—were also borrowed to compose a diagram of the gods of the five directions of east, south, west, north and center. These diagrams of gods based on cosmic space grew even broader and more organized. In the *Supreme Profound Numinous Treasure Ordination* (Taishang dongxuan lingbao shouduyi), said to have been written by Lu Xiujing, it is recorded that beyond the eight directions there were the thirty-two high emperors in thirty-two heavens above and earthly august lords in the thirty-six heavens below.[114] In the first and earliest chapter of the *Marvelous Scripture of Supreme Rank on the Infinite Salvation of the Numinous Treasure Tradition* (Lingbao Wuliang duren shangpin miaojing), these thirty-six heavens have been further refined into thirty-two heavens—eight heavens each in the east, south, west and north. These thirty-two heavens have been combined together

---

113   Liu Cunren, "Daojiao qianshi erzhang," *Zhonghua wenshi luncong* 51 (8/1993), 215–226.
114   *Daozang*, Dongxuan bu, weiyi lei, hua 2, ce 9.

with the Dipper constellation and the gods of the five directions to comprise the Daoist religion's largest and most complete genealogy of gods and demons.

Ancient Chinese concepts of geography and various myths and legends concerning Chinese geography make up a second type of background knowledge for clarifying and putting in order the Daoist genealogy of gods and demons. Legends concerning the ten continents and three islands probably existed very early in ancient China. Although the *Scripture of Great Peace* says that "below great Heaven, there are eighty-one regions and eleven thousand states," still it would seem that stories about the ten continents and three islands were extraordinarily widespread and popular in the Daoist religion south of the Yangzi.[115] The *Preface to the True Shape of the Five Peaks* (Wuyue zhenxingtu xu), evolved from legends about the Queen Mother of the West, Emperor Han Wudi and Dongfang Shuo (154/160–93 BCE), not only reiterates the stories about the ten continents and three islands, but also adds legends about the five sacred mountains.[116] The *Esoteric Essentials of the Most High*, a Northern Zhou text, even more systematically distributes among the five sacred mountains, the Five Color Demon Emperors and the Five Hells below the Great Emperor of the Northern Yin realm of Fengdu. At the same time, stories about grotto-heavens (*dongtian*) from Han dynasty apocrypha were absorbed, and the real geography of China was mixed up with the rich mystical and mythological geography of all of the various mountains, islands and caverns throughout the country so as to locate and configure the Daoist religion's spatial framework of gods and demons.[117] With this the Daoist religion established bit by bit a mystical realm of the immortals that corresponded to the secular human world, and thus set up a system of gods and demons in the human world.

There is a rather rich element of thought behind the reform and integration of the Daoist religion's genealogy of gods and demons. First was the framework and order of ancient Chinese ideas of Heaven, Earth, time and space in the cosmos. Employing this cosmic framework and order not only gave the Daoist religion's pantheon a clear structure, but also furnished it with a rational

---

115 *Taiping jing hejiao*, j. 137–153, 709; this part has been lost, so I use *Taiping jing chao, ren bu* to fill it in; for the same contents, see j. 93, 389.

116 *Daozang*, Zhengyi bu, sheng, ce 32. See the *Yunji qiqian* (Seven Slips in a Cloudy Bookbag), j. 26 for stories of the ten continents and three islands.

117 For example, j. 1 of the *Zhen-gao* lists the names of the myriad perfected places, including Dongyue (Eastern Mountain), Penglai (Island), Mt. Rong, Mt. Shaoshi, Mt. Min, Mt. Jiuyi, Mt. Hua, Mt. Qian, Mt. Juqu, Nanyue (South Mountain), Beiyue (North Mountain) and so on.

foundation. Second was ancient China's accepted ethics and morality. On the basis of the "good" and "evil" established by this morality, the Daoist religion distributed the hope and despair of life and death to two kinds of people, and this fabulous world of gods and demons symbolized respectively life, goodness and happiness versus death, sin and suffering. The *Xiang-er Commentary to the Laozi* says that "the Way establishes life to reward goodness and death to punish evil."[118] This tells us that the Daoist religion was already using this imagined world of gods and demons to assist the mainstream Confucian doctrine in regulating the practical human order and also to establish clearly its own ethics and morality.

3.5

The third thing we notice in this long process of religionization is that the Daoist religion slowly but surely developed its theological thinking and gave a solid and distinct theoretical formulation to the knowledge and techniques of shamans and adepts that had hitherto only been secretly transmitted. Subsequently it achieved a reasonable form of public transmission at the same time that, with the stimulus of Buddhism, it established and clarified its own systematic canon of classic texts.

From the end of the Han on many ancient classics were continually appropriated and passed on by the Daoist religion, and it also produced many new texts of its own such as the *Scripture of Great Peace, Xiang-er Commentary to the Laozi, Token for the Agreement of the Three According to the Book of Changes* and so on. Daoist religious texts began to be produced in truly large numbers in the Wei-Jin period. This is evidenced in the "Broad Overview" (Xialan) chapter of Ge Hong's *Master Who Embraces Simplicity*, probably the first complete bibliography of Daoist texts produced before the Eastern Jin. It lists more than 250 texts in 1,100 *juan* extant in the middle of the fourth century.[119]

These various Wei-Jin period Daoist religious texts generally fall into three main categories in terms of content and origin. The first was produced from the traditional knowledge and techniques of the medical arts. This category includes the *Pure Maiden Scripture* (Sunü jing), the *Ancestor Peng Scripture* (Pengzu jing, Pengzu being the Chinese Methuselah), the *Lord Rongcheng Scripture* (Rongcheng jing), the *Yellow Court Scripture* (Huangting jing) and works on refining cinnabar to concoct elixirs of immortality. These scriptures come from the systems of knowledge in the medical, bedroom arts

---

118   *Laozi Xiang-er zhu jiaozheng*, 1991, 25.

119   *Baopuzi neipian jiaoshi*, j. 19, 333–336.

and immortals traditions; they provide people with techniques for achieving good health and longevity. The second category came from the knowledge and techniques of the mantic arts and includes the *Text of the Three Sovereigns* (Sanhuang wen), the *Proper Pivot* (Zhengji jing, one of three parts of the *Scripture[s] of the Numinous Treasure* (Lingbao jing) and various talismanic diagrams. These texts include many secretly transmitted magical arts. The third category of texts concerns the philosophy of the Daoist religion and many myths and legends. It includes the *Scripture of Western Ascension* (Xisheng jing), the *Scripture of the Conversion of the Barbarians* (Huahu jing), the *Scripture of the Ten Continents* (Shizhou jing) and so on. These texts are based on the works of the various ancient thinkers and historical records and rely on them to expound upon the Daoist religion's ideas and speculations concerning Heaven, Earth and the cosmos.

At that time, however, these texts were in a rather confused state; Daoist masters in different areas had their own set of texts and different Daoist masters revered different texts. As time passed, then, clarification and reorganization of this confused canon became increasingly pressing. This was simply because the number of Daoist religious texts was continually increasing and they were extraordinarily disordered and in need of screening and classifying. In that state the Daoist religious texts lacked sanctity and canonicity. This did not mean, of course, that the Daoist religion wanted to abandon these texts and revert back to the *Laozi* and the *Zhuangzi* only. The *Laozi* and *Zhuangzi* were after all not theological but philosophical texts and it would be hard to combine them directly with the Daoist religious practices and equally difficult to make them the foundational texts for the religion. Once religious Daoism had actually become a Daoist religion, it could not simply abandon religious knowledge and practices in favor of reverence for Lao-Zhuang thought. The problem facing them was how to canonize and sanctify the many texts that embodied their religious knowledge and techniques. In pursuit of this goal, the texts of the Daoist religion underwent a comparatively large-scale classification and integration during the fourth and fifth centuries. As a result, three sets of classic texts were established. The Canon of the Spirit Grotto (*Dongshen*, also Spirit Divine or Grotto Immortals) had the *Text of the Three Sovereigns* and the *True Shape of the Five Peaks* as foundational texts; the Canon of the Mystery Grotto (*Dongxuan*) had the *Scripture of the Numinous Treasure* (Lingbao jing) as its foundation; the Canon of Supreme Purity (*Shangqing*) had the *Perfect Scripture of Great Profundity* (Dadong zhenjing), the *Yellow Court Scripture* and other writings as its foundation. In 471, during the Liu Song of the Southern dynasties, Lu Xiujing was given an official commission to compile the Catalog of the *Scriptures and Writings of the Three Grottoes* (Sandong jingshu mulu). From then on the canonical texts of the Daoist religion had a general outline that could compare well to the Buddhist canon.[120]

The formation of the canon of the Daoist religion is not really a subject for intellectual history. What we intend to discuss here is that, during this "purification" process, since those many texts that originally belonged to the magical arts of healing and mantic practices, or to the tradition of the immortals, all went from secret to open and public transmission, and from a scattered and chaotic state to an orderly and standard or normative state, even to the extent that they could eminently serve as the classic texts of the Daoist religion, we need, then, to ask three questions:

Did this signify that there was already a rupture in the connection between Daoism as a form of thought (Daojia) and as a religion (Daojiao)?

As the Daoist religion's treatment of classic texts went from the interpretation of the works of earlier Daoist philosophers (Daojia) to reverence for later works—sacred scriptures—of religious Daoism, had it already confirmed that it existed as a religion in secular society?

During the process of canonization and sanctification of the thought, knowledge and techniques of the Daoist religion, did it at the same time undergo a process of secularization and become a part of daily life in China?

3.6

This last question requires some further discussion. There were really two aspects to the process of religionization of religious Daoism. On the one hand was a process of sanctification that included the establishments of precepts and regulations, the reorganization of the genealogy of gods and demons and the systematization and clarification of a canon of classic texts. All of this would seem to have been for the sake of providing the religion with the requisite purity, mystery and theology to justify the faith of the believers. On the other hand was a tendency toward secularization which was intended to establish the value of the religion in everyday secular life. Only this combination of sanctification and secularization can be said to constitute the complete process of religionization from the end of the second century to the end of the sixth century.

The secular tendency in religious Daoism was actually present from its beginning. When Ge Hong and others reaffirmed the significance of religious beliefs and reinterpreted the value of the classic texts, the Daoist reli-

---

120   This bibliography is said to have listed scriptures of religious Daoism, medical texts and talismanic diagrams to the tune of 1,228 *juan*. See *Guang Hong ming ji*, j. 9, 80.

gion had already come to understand the need for secularization. In a passage from *juan* 8, "Resolving Obstructions" (Shizhi) of the *Master Who Embraces Simplicity*, Ge Hong states that the Daoist religion cannot simply believe in Laozi and Zhuangzi because they are far removed from the religion's ideal of the immortals.[121] At this time the Daoist religion made it explicit that its ultimate ideal was not to explore cosmic philosophy but rather to seek happiness in the secular world and everlasting life in the next. Just as *juan* 3, "Rejoinders to Popular Conceptions" (Duisu) of the *Master Who Embraces Simplicity* puts it, the purpose of studying cosmic philosophy is to seek for a way to everlasting life, and what you should really be concerned with are secular life and happiness. Of course we know that people were always most concerned with life and death, and this was the reason they believed in the Daoist religion. That is why all of those seemingly mediocre ideas, concepts and rules and all of those ordinary ceremonies, methods and techniques were constantly being revised as part of the process of religionization of Daoist beliefs.[122] During this simultaneous process of sanctification and secularization a set of core ideas for the Daoist religion emerged. Three areas among these ideas are most relevant to Chinese intellectual history, especially to the history of general thought. They are life, happiness and morality.

First, we all know the Daoist religion's concept of human life. The first *juan* of the most widely popular text of the later Daoist religion, the *Scripture on Salvation* (Duren jing), says that the goal of the religion is "the Way of the immortals and valuing life" (*xiandao guisheng* 仙道貴生). The idea of "valuing life" exerted considerable influence from the Qin-Han period on. The *Scripture of Great Peace* lamented the brevity of human life,[123] the *Xiang-er Commentary* used Laozi's words to interpret the concept of growing old with unfailing eyes and ears,[124] while both Ge Hong's *Master Who Embraces Simplicity* and Tao Hongjing's *Record on Nourishing Inner Nature and Extending Life* (Yangxing yanming lu) even more strongly emphasized that "natural endowment contains a spiritual essence; only human beings will treasure it, and the reason

---

121   *Baopuzi neipian jiaoshi*, 151.

122   For example, the *Laozi Xiang-er zhu* repeatedly criticized "those in the world who falsely discuss shapes and talk about the Way." They worshipped the deities who were described as wearing colorful costumes, having various shapes and sizes instead of following the formless "Way" (17). It even further criticized the worship and prayer rituals of the vulgar shamans (31–32). The Daoist religion's ceremonies and techniques were never abandoned, however, but only repeatedly refined, in all its hundreds of years because they were the chief means for them to realize their function in society.

123   *Taipingjing hejiao*, j. 120–136, 684; j. 110, 532.

124   *Laozi Xiang-er zhu jiaozheng*, 9–10.

why they consider it valuable is because they value life."[125] On this account, the French Sinologue Henri Maspero explicitly labeled the Daoist religion "a religion that seeks eternal life,"[126] and the Japanese scholar Yoshioka Yoshitoyo entitled his contribution to a nineteen-seventies series of books on religion *The Daoist Religion: the Desire for* Eternal Life.[127]

Unlike Buddhism's equal regard for happiness in the next world and serenity in this world, the Daoist religion valued satisfaction in this world and this life. Unlike Buddhism's emphasis on psychological equanimity and spiritual transcendence, the Daoist religion promised its believers practical results and concrete rewards. To obtain these results and rewards, the Daoist religion developed an extremely complex array of physiological and psychological training techniques along with a panoply of ceremonies and ingestion of psychedelic supplements for knowing and making contact with the gods.

Nevertheless, the Daoist religion also enjoined its believers to live according to the requirements of the religion and to stress the following three elements. (1) Believers had to follow the religion's methods of physiological practice to nurture their vital energy, preserve their vital essence (semen) and calm their minds. (2) Believers had to guard their inner moral virtue and their external behavior. As quoted above, if "one does not cultivate moral virtue, but only works on the mantic arts, he will not achieve long life."[128] (3) Believers had to worship and respect the gods and demons of the underworld because they inspect people's thoughts and behavior, calculate their good and evil and lengthen or shorten people's lives. Of these three elements the second one was the most important because human beings can control it. They can nurture their vital energy and treasure their vital essence in order to preserve their spirit, if they obey Heaven and Earth and venerate and serve the gods and demons, but their ultimate anchor is their own moral virtue. Only by following the ethics of the religion could believers make their lives correspond to Heaven and Earth and the gods and demons and thereby obtain their rewards and maintain a tranquil state of spiritual peace. This is why believers had to obey the constraints of the religion in their search for long life. These admonitions were naturally very effective because the believers wanted to obtain the

---

125   *Baopuzi neipian jiaoshi*, j. 3, "Duisu," 46. Yangxing yanminglu, xu, *Daozang*, Dongshen bu, fangfa lei, lin 2, ce 18.

126   Brief quote from Henri Maspero, "Essai sur le Taoïsme aux premiers siècles de l'ère chrétienne, in *Mélanges posthumes sur les religions et l'histoire de la Chine*, vol. 2, *Le taoïsme*, 1950, retranslated from Kawakatsu Yoshio, *Dôkyô*, 1970, 100.

127   Yoshioka Yoshitoyo, "Ense e no negai—Dôkyô," *Seikai no shôkyô*, no. 9.

128   *Baopuzi neipian jiaoshi*, j. 3, "Duisu," 53.

reward of eternal life and they believed they could obtain it if they followed the precepts of the religion.

Second, the Daoist religion's ideas about happiness were probably more meaningful in the minds of the popular masses who followed its doctrines. For the ordinary believer the idea of "becoming an immortal" was probably too extravagant a dream; benefits in this life were certainly more practical. The religion promised its adherents happiness in this life, and, aside from longevity, this happiness consisted of at least the following: peace and security for individual, family and lineage; sufficient food and clothing or even great prosperity; and finally an abundance of offspring. These things are quite ordinary, but they are commonly desired by all of humanity, and they were deep-rooted and long standing traditional ideas in ancient China.

Such a conception of happiness might seem too trivial to mention, but it was the most common of all ancient Chinese ideas. It may have been too petty for the intellectual elite, but general thought was nevertheless built upon a foundation of just such reasonable and fair concepts of daily life. In an age of difficulties, the first thing people need is to survive; with survival assured, it is reasonable for them to seek stability and sufficiency or even riches; with stability and sufficiency assured, they naturally want their bloodline to be carried on by their posterity. Since the religion promises them these things, they necessarily hope for them as a reward for their faith. As soon as people actually become believers in the Daoist religion, the first thing they will think of is their concrete happiness in this life, and as soon as these believers start to abide by the religion's precepts and regulations, then their ideas and attitudes about life will be integrated into the orbit of Daoist religious thought. The religion's mission of rectifying people's hearts and minds will also be rewarded.

Third, the Daoist religion's concept of morality involved the idea that believers had to conform to definite ethical standards in order to obtain the protection of the gods and demons and to win everlasting life. In ancient China these ethical and moral standards included several elements. In individual character, people had to be willing to maintain honest poverty, pure hearts, few desires, proper behavior, modesty and tranquility; in their families and lineages, they had to practice filial piety and affection; in their life in society, they had to be honest and trustworthy, pay attention to ceremonial etiquette, distinguish social ranks and be well regulated in all their behavior.

Ethics and morality in ancient China was primarily an area of Confucian expertise. In regulating the human order, however, the Daoist religion offered another element that was missing in Confucianism. In the words of the *Xiang-er Commentary to the Laozi* quoted above, this was "life to reward goodness and death to punish evil." As early as the Warring States period, Mozi was worried

that if people believed in the Confucian idea of respecting the gods and spirits while keeping them at a distance and practiced the Confucian sacrifices
to the spirits as though the spirits were present, then if Heaven and the
gods and spirits ceased to be effective, people would lose their last vestige of
respect and awe and there would be no way to prevent spiritual decadence.
The Daoist religion, though, made widespread and absolute promises concerning the relationship between life versus death, gods versus demons, and good
versus bad fortune in conjunction with good and evil in people's lives.[129] The
consequences of good and evil social behavior would not only bring rewards
or punishments to the individual person, but also result in benefit or calamity for one's ancestors and one's posterity. That is "calamity and disaster will
be visited on one's self and one's posterity."[130] Many scholars have discussed
the Daoist religion's conception of "inherited evil" (chengfu 承負), that, as the
Commentaries on the Book of Changes has it, "a family that accumulates goodness will be sure to have an excess of blessings, but one that accumulates evil
will be sure to have an excess of disasters."[131] The early Daoist religion did not
actually have the concepts of "previous life" and "after life" of an individual
person, and it only believed that accumulated good or evil could collectively
influence one's ancestors and one's posterity, but this idea of "an excess of
blessings" and "an excess of disasters" actually operated in the same manner as
the Buddhist concepts of karmic retribution. They both express the idea that
good and evil in this life can influence the wellbeing of future generations, and
increase the psychological pressure on people to behave correctly in society
and force them to think about themselves and their posterity in this life and
the life to come.

3.7

At the beginning of the Scripture of the High Lord Grotto Spirit Incantations the
apocalypse (moshi) or last age (jishi) is mentioned. According to the research
of some scholars, the Daoist religion of the Six Dynasties period already had
the concept of a coming apocalypse. Living in a chaotic age, they imagined an
end of the world when Heaven would cave in and the earth break apart as a
major disaster spread throughout the world. This theory of the apocalypse was

---

129   *Laozi Xiang-er zhu jiaozheng*, *zhang* 19, note to *jue ren qi yi*: "Abandon humanity and
        discard rightness," 24.

130   *Ibid.*, *zhang* 30 note to *qi shi hao huan*, 38. Waley's translation is "For such things [use
        of force] are wont to rebound," in his *Way and Its Power*, 180.

131   See Tang Yijie, "Chengfu shuo yu lunhui shuo," in his *Wei Jin Nanbeichao shiqi de dao-
        jiao*, 1988, 333–344. For the translation of this passage from explanations of the hexa-
        gram Kun, see Lynn, *Changes*, 146.

very popular after the Eastern Jin during second decade of the fourth century. The Daoist religion said that society was in chaos and the universe was about to collapse, but the people of the world were still living in ignorant darkness; although they were still alive, they were living like zombies. The religion predicted that a great calamity would soon overtake humankind and a multitude of demons would appear to poison the people. After this cataclysmic upheaval, the evil people would be utterly destroyed and only the good people would survive. Led by the gods and spirits of the Daoist religion, they would escape to a place that the religion would point out for them; only then would they escape the disaster and come to see the sages in the coming world of Great Peace. These good people would be the seeds of the world to come, and so they were called "the elect" (literally, "seed people" *zhongmin* 種民).[132] Those who would be chosen as the "seed people" would naturally be good people among the believers who obeyed all the Daoist precepts. As the "Treatise on Buddhism and Daoism" of the *History of the Wei Dynasty* describes it: "A final calamity will befall the people of the earth. It will then be very difficult to practice our Daoist religion, but we can instruct the men and women to set up alters and worship morning and night as if their family had strict lords whose deeds can be traced back to previous generations. If some of them are able to cultivate themselves, refine cinnabar elixirs and learn the art of longevity, they can be considered true lords and seed people."[133]

Through its process of religionization, the Daoist religion established its position as a genuine religion, and through its process of secularization it established its role as the salvation of humanity. In this salvational role, the Daoist religion of this period clarified its twin goals of seeking transcendent eternal life for the individual and shouldering the burden of responsibility for society. *Juan* 30 of the *Comprehensive Mirror through the Ages of Perfected Immortals and Those Who Embody the Dao* (Lishi zhenxian tidao tongjian) records that, in his dealings with the faithful, the Daoist Master Niu Wenhou (458–539) "followed their natures and guided them with loyalty and filial piety; in his admonitions he showed them the principles of crime and good fortune, and in his prohibitions he relied on practicing the way of talismans and registers." By adopting this attitude of accommodation to the mainstream ideology, the Daoist religion could both clear up its religious rules and rectify the human order. They hoped that under these conditions the religion would finally be able to flourish.[134]

---

132   *Zhen-gao*, j. 14, *Daozang*, Taixuan bu, ding 4 & ding 1, ce 20.
133   *Weishu*, j. 114, 3051–3052.
134   *Lishi zhenxian tidao tongjian*, j. 30, *Daozang*, Dongzhen bu, jizhuan lei, dan 10, ce 5.

The four hundred some years from the second to sixth centuries were the age of transformation of religious Daoism into the Daoist religion. After four centuries of reform and purification, the Daoist religion slowly perfected its mature and fully integrated religious system. What we need to pay attention to here is that these four centuries were also the period in which Buddhism was gradually imported into China and penetrated the Chinese intellectual world. The religionization of Daoism could not escape being influenced by the incoming Buddhist religion. Buddhism stimulated the canonization and sanctification of the Daoist religion, impelling it to establish a religious system, impose strict ethical precepts and regulations and adjust its position in society. Buddhism also activated the Daoist religion's latent nationalism, causing it to affirm the concept of an ethnic state (*minzu guojia*) during the process of its unceasing response to Buddhism and, at the same time, to adjust its position as the indigenous religion of China so as to resist the expansion of Buddhism. We will discuss this aspect of Buddho-Daoist interaction in the next chapter.

Confucianism, Daoism and Buddhism from the Eastern Han to the Tang Dynasty, II

1. The Transmission of Buddhism to China and Its Significance in Intellectual History, I

In general most researchers believe that Buddhism came to China from the Western Regions, that is modern Central Asia and Xinjiang (Serindia). With the exception of a small minority including Liang Qichao, Paul Pelliot (1878–1945), Hu Shi and others, the majority of scholars believe that Buddhism came east into China on the ancient Silk Road.[1] Records of Han Emperor Ming seeking to learn of Buddhist *dharma* (teaching, *fa* 法) from the Tokharians demonstrate that Buddhism came to the Han dynasty from the Western Regions in the middle of the first century CE (around 57–75) along two routes north and south of the Tianshan mountain range passing by Dunhuang and following the Gansu corridor into north China. Recently, however, some scholars studying early writings that mention a sea route between China and India, archeological discoveries of a south-west Silk Road and the distribution of some early Buddhist documents have begun to suspect that besides the north-western land route Buddhism may have also entered China via a southern sea route. This idea is still a matter of debate.

Regardless of this continuing debate, everyone basically agrees that Buddhism arrived in China sometime during the first-century CE reign of Han Emperor Ming,[2] and began to spread widely between the reigns of the Han emperors Huan and Ling (r. 147–189). The entrance of this major element of a foreign civilization was destined to change the entire course of future Chinese intellectual history.

---

1 Liang Qichao, "Fojiao zhi chu shuru," fulu 2, in *Foxue yanjiu shiba pian*, date, 25; Paul Pelliot's "Mouzi kao" is translated in Feng Chengjun, *Xiyu nanhai shidi kaozheng yicong*, 1995 reprint chapter 5, 161.

2 Legend has it that the Tokharian Sramanas (monks) Kasyapa-Matanga and Gobharana (or Dharmaratna) brought Buddhist sûtras on a white horse to Luoyang, the White Horse Temple was built and they started translating sûtras.

1.1

Sometime between 147 and 167, An Shigao (?–168) and Lokaksema (147/167–186) arrived in Luoyang and began the translation of Buddhist sûtras. Following the work of many translators, including Zhu Foshuo (Shuofo, fl. 4th century), Anxuan, Zhiyao, Kang Mengxiang (fl. 4th century), Zhi Qian (fl. 222–252) and Kang Senghui (?–280), in the hundred years up to the beginning of the Western Jin some 265 Buddhist sûtras in 411 *juan* had been translated into Chinese.[3] Among them the most influential in later times were the *Pratyutpannasamâdhi*-sûtra (Banzhou sanmei jing), the *Questions on the Situation in Hell* (Wen diyu shi jing); scriptures containing important stories about the life of the Buddha, such as the *Scripture of the Former Rise of the Crown Prince's Auspicious Omens* (Taizi rui ying ben qi jing); the Mahayana *Perfection of Wisdom Sûtra* (*Prajñapâramitâ-sûtra*, Boruo jing, or *The Heart of Prajñapâramitâ-sûtra*), the Hinayana Chan (Zen) school *Ânâpânasmrti-sûtra* (Anban shouyi jing) and so on.

In discussing the eastern transmission of Buddhism we need to keep in mind that Buddhism did not exert a genuine influence on the knowledge, thought and belief worlds of the Chinese elite strata at the very beginning. Before at least the year 290, the main transmitters, translators and explicators of the Buddhist scriptures were foreigners from the Western Regions. All the way down to the period between the Western and Eastern Jin, native Chinese knowledge and thought still dominated the mainstream intellectual horizon. The Chinese intellectual class still had little interest in or understanding of this foreign religion. In the daily lives of the masses, however, Buddhist stories, rituals and ceremonies and ideas were penetrating people's lives with some worldly images and through some worldly channels.

Many scholars have pointed out that in the first one or two centuries of Buddhist transmission into China, it was regarded in the popular mind as a religion similar to the Daoist religion. For example, *Master Mou's Treatise on the Removal of Doubt* regarded the Buddha as an immortal who possessed great magical powers. He wanted to save all sentient beings and so he pointed out the way to emancipation. This was probably more or less the idea of Buddhism held by contemporary believers, and this sort of impression of Buddhism did not give rise to any changes in the Chinese intellectual world for quite a long time. Nevertheless, Buddhism was after all a foreign religion and its understanding and explanation of and ways of dealing with the universe, society and human life ultimately varied greatly from Chinese views. For Chinese believers

---

3   It is estimated that some 138 *juan* of these translated sûtras still exist today. For the figures in the text, see the chart in chapter 2 of Wang Wenyan's *Fodian hanyi zhi yanjiu*, 1984, 95–97.

Buddhism was, then, both very familiar and very novel and unfamiliar. When it first arrived in China it brought along many ideas that the Chinese people had never heard of before. Things like the illusory nature of the universe, the suffering of existence, *samsâra* or transmigration (*lunhui*) between the three ages (*sanshi*) of past, present and future (or unborn, born and deceased), and all those methods used to search for emancipation and transcendence of the wheel of transmigration. We could make a basic general comparison of some aspects of Buddhist knowledge and ideas with ancient Chinese thought.

(1) According to traditional ancient Chinese thought, everlasting life might be quite wonderful, but, since the world of this life was undoubtedly real, even though it was short it still could bring genuine happiness. Thus from the *Annals of Lü Buwei* to the *Scripture of Great Peace*, from the pictures of Daoist exercises for nurturing life to the great Han physician Hua Tuo's (ca. 140–208) "five animal exercises," they all reveal an idea of cherishing life. For Buddhism on the other hand there was no genuine everlasting; everything was *anitya* or impermanence, and human life was simply an endless round of suffering on the wheel of life and death.

(2) According to traditional ancient Chinese thought, even though after death the vital energy (*qi*) of a person's *hun* soul might still float around everywhere, a person only lived for one lifetime in the real world.[4] This was the traditional Chinese idea as well as the Daoist religion's conception of life. Buddhism, however, told people that one's spirit or soul (*âtman*) was only temporarily lodged in a body, and after the body was destroyed the soul would simply enter into another cycle of birth and death. People had to endure the suffering of an ever-recurring round of birth and death (*samsâra*).

(3) According to traditional ancient Chinese thought, if people wanted to escape into transcendence, they had to ingest elixirs, train their bodies to become celestial immortals and seek eternal longevity. Buddhism, by contrast, taught people that escape and transcendence were extremely complicated problems. First off, because when the body dies the soul remains and has to transmigrate through the three ages of the past, present and future, then a person has to be fully aware of good and evil. Only by believing in the Buddhist teachings with one's whole heart and mind and receiving the Buddha's assistance can one escape from the wheel of *samsâra*. Secondly, because human beings are born with desires and desire is the cause of suffering and the inability to escape the cycle of life and death, people have to come to the awakening (*juewu*, Buddhist enlightenment) that desire is the beginning of suffering, and then render their minds and spirits pure and tranquil. Finally, because the

---

4 *Liji*, "Tangong," ssjzs, 1314.

world is impermanent and life and death are all suffering, people should seek
to transcend life and death and find the Buddhist realm of transcendent existence beyond the human world.

Besides these new concepts, Buddhism also offered Chinese believers a
number of different methods of self-redemption. A completely committed
Buddhist could leave home and become a monk or nun in order to express
to the Buddha his or her desire for emancipation and salvation; this was the
minimum requirement for redemption.[5] There were also many other more
convenient and easier methods besides becoming a monk or nun. For example, according to the categories in the *Biographies of Eminent Monks* (Gaoseng
zhuan), aside from translating Buddhist sûtras, understanding Buddhist
beliefs and scrupulously abiding by Buddhist precepts, other roads to salvation included the following practices.

First were "miracles" (*shenyi* 神異). The appearance of miracles was always
an important way for Buddhism to attract believers. They included things like
observations of the stars, divination, curing illnesses, subduing *nâga*s (ser-
pents/dragons) and subjugating tigers, spells, incantations or mantra, various
miraculous techniques and exaggerated stories; all of these were actually very
effective in supporting Buddhist beliefs.

Next came "practicing *dhyâna*" (*xichan* 習禪, meditation) and "killing one's
body" (*wangshen* 亡身). In general these practices involved controlling, suppressing, disciplining and even sacrificing one's emotions, desires and actions
in order to obtain Buddhism's promised rewards. Practicing *dhyâna* required
following Buddhism's traditional methods of meditation with praying to the
Buddha or chanting the Buddha's name, meditating in darkness and ascetic
practices as their main elements. The "killing one's body" required individual
sacrifice, for example allowing oneself to be eaten by a tiger in order to prevent
the tiger from harming others or giving one's own heart to a gang of robbers in
order to save a child's heart and offer relief to the starving.

Next there was "intoning sûtras" (*songjing* 誦經) and invoking the Buddha
or calling the Buddha name (*nianfo* 念佛). Up to this day, intoning the sûtras is
still one of the most important practices for a Buddhist; at that time it was also
an important form of seeking deliverance. Invoking the Buddha name was
similarly important for deliverance. According to the preface to the *Sûtra of the*

---

5   The strict Buddhist demand to leave home did not abate until after the *Vimalakîrtinirdesa-
     sûtra* became widely known. According to Vimalakîrti, if one's parents do not agree then
     one cannot leave home; one only has to have the correct enlightenment of the Bodhisattva
     Samyak (Samyak-Sambodhi) and "this is leaving home and this is completely sufficient."
     Taishô, j. 14, 541.

Buddha Names (Foming jing), invoking the Buddha name could liberate one from suffering. There were many forms of such recitation intended to demonstrate that the believer was beginning to have a desire to achieve Buddhahood and signaling to the Redeemer his or her hope for salvation.[6]

Finally there was "bringing about happiness or good fortune" (*xingfu* 興福), a very inclusive path to deliverance. To accomplish it, one could build a temple, erect a pagoda, set up a Buddha statue, copy a Buddhist sûtra and so on. The stone grottos, Buddha statues and Buddhist stone pillars existing today are mostly the historical remains of such Buddhist religious ideas. The Buddhist faith continued to spread throughout ancient China from the second to the sixth century. Its profound ideas, miraculous stories, and the various skills and ceremonies brought along by its proselytizers began to interest the Chinese people. Due to its many ceremonies and successful propaganda through music, stories and recitations that the Chinese people had never heard before, Buddhism penetrated more and more deeply into the Chinese belief world.

1.2

Why was the Buddhist faith able to circulate so quickly among the Chinese masses? Aside from the attraction of the Buddhist's miraculous powers similar to the ancient Chinese mantic arts, the Central Plains being governed by alien or *hu* peoples weakened the distinction between Han Chinese and non-Han Chinese peoples. Besides the reasons that others have pointed out, like Buddhism having clear ideas of obvious personal interest, brilliant propaganda methods, as well as strict organization and discipline, I want to discuss this phenomenon of Buddhist belief with reference to some materials concerning its believers that have generally been neglected by other researchers.

In Buddhist materials of the fourth to the sixth century, inscriptions on Buddha statues (*tiji* 題記), inscriptions on sûtras (*tishi* 題識), written vows (*fayuanwen* 發願文) and repentances (*chanwen* 懺文) and so on can be considered generally quite representative of the orientation of the mass of Buddhist believers. From these materials we can see that the faithful believed in Buddhism because of their concern for this life, their personal fate and the future of their families as well as for their fate in the life to come and that of their parents and seven generations of ancestors, and even because of their hopes for all sentient beings and for their country (*guojia*).

In his *Records of Ancient Chinese Buddhist Manuscript Inscriptions* (Chugoku kodai shahon chiiki kiroku), Ikeda On collected a rather large number of

---

6 In the fourth to the sixth centuries, the Buddhist practices of the "Pure Land of Maitreya" and
   the "Pure Land of Guanyin" had already formed.

comments written on manuscripts of Buddhist sûtras. We can summarize some of these from the mid-fourth century to the mid-sixth century to see what the desires of the believers were. The first kind were prayers for good fortune and to avoid disasters for oneself, one's parents and ancestors, and for one's deceased brothers and sisters to be delivered soon from the sea of misery. They all imply receiving happiness and safety for self, family and lineage in exchange for religious belief. The second kind extended these good wishes to all sentient beings regardless of blood relationship, extending compassion and pity from oneself to all others. The third kind brought together the deliverance achieved by religious belief with their hopes and prayers for the secular government and the country. These hopes were frequently expressed by individuals having rather high government positions who supported the state. They expressed their good wishes for themselves and for the state, and also their anxiety about the chaos of war. They even hoped for the appearance of a World of Great Unity (*Datong shijie*) and "wished that the gods would make the emperor and empress compassionate and enlightened, to forever extend their lives and good fortune, so that the nine realms would soon be purified . . . the eight manifestations of the cosmos will finally be regulated and unified.[7]

Not only copying Buddhist sûtras, but the objectives of other religious activities like erecting Buddha statues, building pagodas, making vows and expressing repentance had similar goals. In Wang Chang (1724–1806)'s *Collection of Bronze and Stone Inscriptions* (Jinshi cuibian), *juan* 39, "A General Discussion of Inscriptions on Statues and Stele of the Northern Dynasties" (Beichao zaoxiang zhubei zonglun) there is an analysis of the Buddhist reasons for setting up these statues, stele, shrines, temples and monasteries during the Northern Dynasties. He wrote that Buddhism used the promise of extreme bliss in the Western Paradise of the Pure Land and ascent into the Tushita Heaven to entice the masses, and then it started to become a common practice for uneducated people feverishly to erect statues and pray for happiness. When the believers "cherished life and feared death, worried about chaos and hoped for peace," then they sought out religious guidance and salvation. And when Chinese Buddhists sought religious guidance and salvation, their traditional ideas about accumulating merit for good deeds or suffering calamity for evil conduct made it easy for them to form the idea of combining their native beliefs with the Buddhist ideas of karmic retribution and also easily susceptible to the idea of paying some kind of price in order to obtain religious salvation.

Besides using their money to erect statues, temples and grottos to carry on such spiritual exchange with the divine, people could also practice the methods

---

7   Ikeda On, *Chugoku kodai shahon chiiki kiroku*, 1990, 76–114.

of writing essays of repentance or confession and making vows. The Buddhist practice of repentance (*chanfa* 懺法), originally not just used to repent one's own moral errors, was brought together with the Chinese Daoist religion's practices of "reflecting on one's past mistakes" (*siguo* 思過) and "admitting one's mistakes" (*shouguo* 首過) into the practice of reflecting upon and repenting one's own moral and ethical mistakes. As a result, in the Buddhist faith there were utilitarian implications in the believer raising his or her moral and ethical standards in order to achieve salvation. Buddhism itself also became a vehicle for rectifying the ethical order of Chinese society.

According to the first part of the *Sûtra on the Examination of Good and Evil* (Zhancha shan-e yebao jing), a sûtra said to be forged by Chinese authors, people who commit much evil do not even possess the qualifications to study meditation or cultivate wisdom. They "should first cultivate the method of repentance."[8] If the goal of someone's repentance was to fulfill a wish, then the wish would be very clearly stated in a written vow; that is, the person was simply begging the Buddha and the Bodhisattvas for salvation. The collection *Dunhuang Vows* (Dunhuang yuanwen ji), contains "primarily prayers for the avoidance of calamities." These written vows were the most typical texts written by Buddhist believers. The most interesting of them is the *Eastern Capital Vows* (Dongdu fayuan wen) of Emperor Wu of Liang (r. 502–549). In it he vowed never again to have sensual desires, not even in dreams, or to eat meat, but he asked that the Buddha agree to excuse or remove all of his sins including those of his elder brother, deceased younger brother and his ministers and subjects. If the Buddha would agree, he said that he alone would be willing to bear any suffering, even including the sufferings of hell.[9]

Even though asking for release from distress and praying for blessings are individual religious activities, in Buddhism you could not obtain these results by merely relying on individual behavior. In religious belief achieving salvation or not, originally depends on the individual believer's thoughts and actions, and whether or not these thoughts and actions can receive confirmation is an affair for the individual believer. In China, however, all religious behavior was absorbed into the moral and ethical norms of the Chinese intellectual world where society came before the individual. Individual emancipation and religious salvation was never simply a matter of the individual and his or her religion. It was rather a matter of every individual's thoughts and behavior toward family, lineage, society and state. The power of a religion, then, was to

---

8   *Taishô*, j. 17, 903.
9   Huang Zheng (or Zhi) and Wu Wei, eds., *Dunhuang yuanwen ji*, 1995, 285–286.

acknowledge and consent to this thought and behavior and offer corresponding rewards.

It is important to note here that whether we are dealing with epigraphs or comments on sûtras, Buddhist statues or written vows, we always find that the crucial point is that if a person wants to have a wish fulfilled—receive a promise from the religion—that person must abide by the good and avoid evil, good and evil in the Chinese context generally being a category involving social ethics and morality. In this way Buddhism's promises to its believers were not purely individual; they were involved in the rectification of the social order, the maintenance of social morality and the re-establishment of ethical standards. A saying of Ânanda from the *Ekottara-âgama* (Zengyi Ahan jing)—"To do no evil, to do only good"—became the most commonly used phrase in Chinese Buddhist rituals and in the discourse of the common people.[10]

In the Six Dynasties period, however, the Chinese people's standards for good and evil were already firmly established on the basis of traditional Confucian values and were generally accepted throughout the society. "Evil" generally referred to disloyalty, lack of filial piety, rebellion against the emperor, butchering the common people, licentiousness, avarice and so on. "Goodness" usually meant filial piety, honesty and loyalty, valuing family affection, diligently doing one's duty in society, being hardworking, frugal and self-disciplined and so on. That is to say regarding family feelings and blood relationships as the foundation of interpersonal relationships, valuing humility and harmony in the quality of one's personal behavior and being industrious and economical in one's everyday life. No matter how much the principles of ethical "goodness" and "evil" were regulated by Confucianism, however, it was Buddhism that basically bore the responsibility for supervising the carrying out of these moral principles in daily life. The most powerful tool for this moral supervision was the Buddhist concepts of karma and retribution because the most commonly disseminated idea in Buddhist preaching was that "goodness has a good reward and evil has an evil retribution" (*shan you shanbao, e you ebao* 善有善報, 惡有惡報).

It was for this reason that within the basic thinking about Buddhist redemption of the human world, after the idea of relying on miraculous powers—"someone else's power"—for redemption flourished for a while, it gradually disappeared in favor of the idea of relying on one's own religious belief and moral behavior—"self-redemption." Being concerned only with one's own

---

10   *Fayuan zhulin*, j. 48 quoting *Taishô*, j. 53, 649. The complete quotation is "To do no evil, to do only good, to purify the will, is the doctrine of all Buddhas." Soothill, *Dictionary*: "These four sentences are said to include all the Buddha-teaching."

individual religious behavior became of secondary importance, and religious behavior for the sake of one's family, lineage, society and the state became the mainstream form of public religious activity. In China the idea of transcendent liberation based on an individual's religious belief was soon replaced by the idea of "moral redemption" based on identification with society.

This was quite an important change of direction in Chinese Buddhism. According to original Buddhist thought, there were several things people had to do to achieve Buddhist salvation. They had to leave behind the world of family and society replete with secular desires and by leaving home draw a clear line between secular and monastic life.[11] They also had to live according to the regulations laid down for Buddhists and practice various sacred Buddhist activities that were in clear contrast to secular life. This kind of saintly style of life was a price the believer had to pay, and its significance was to ensure that the Buddha, the Bodhisattvas and the monks would use their supernatural powers to lead the faithful also to achieve transcendent powers. From the very beginning, however, most Chinese Buddhists did not consider a purely individual path to liberation as their mainstream mode of redemption. What most influenced the intellectual world of Chinese Buddhists were the various redemptive activities that Buddhism carried out within secular society, activities that were aimed at society itself. The key to whether or not a Chinese Buddhist believer could achieve redemption came to be the extent to which his or her thoughts and behavior were in accord with social morality and to what extend these thoughts and behavior received acknowledgment from society and protection by the gods and spirits.

The first *juan* of the *Biographies of Eminent Monks* records an extremely symbolic discussion between the monk Kang Senghui and Sun Hao (r. 264–280), the last emperor of the Eastern Wu Kingdom during the Three Kingdoms period. Sun Hao asked the monk an important question. Since the Duke of Zhou and Confucius had already interpreted the nature of good and evil, why should Chinese believe in the message of Buddhism on these subjects? Kang Senghui's answer was extremely significant. He said, "what the Duke of Zhou and Confucius said partly hit upon some of the truth, but Buddhism covers the most subtle and profound details of the truth. If one does evil he will face long suffering in hell, but if one cultivates goodness he will have eternal joy in paradise. I advocate this to illuminate the good and prevent the evil, and is it not indeed important?"[12] This answer contains the following three

---

11　In ancient China it was not really that easy to leave home and become a monk or nun. It is said that Han Chinese were not allowed to do so in the Eastern Han or the Wei dynasties. See *Gaoseng zhuan*, j. 9, "Jin Ye Zhong Zhu Fotu cheng," 352, citing the words of Wang Du.

12　*Gaoseng zhuan*, j. 1, 17.

layers of meaning. First, the reason that Buddhism exists in China is not only because it is a religion seeking individual transcendence and liberation but also because it can regulate thought and behavior in society. Second, the value standards of this regulation of thought and behavior is not in conflict with the values of the Duke of Zhou and Confucius; in fact Buddhism takes their value standards as its own standards. Third, the power to regulate people's thought and behavior is derived from the karmic retribution of the Buddhist gods and spirits. Because of Buddhism's "karmic retribution for good and evil," its religious function moved from concentration on the individual to the society. The difference between the religious redemption of Buddhism and the doctrines of the Duke of Zhou and Confucius, that is, of Chinese tradition, melted away.

1.3

In the second decade of the fourth century, after the Jin court fled south in 317, the fundamental situation of the elite intellectual world, heretofore relatively indifferent to Buddhist religious doctrines, finally underwent a great change. "When [the Jin] crossed the Yangzi [going south], Buddhism flourished greatly."[13] A great number of contemporary officials and literati, including Wang Dao (276–339), Chi Chao (Xi Chao, 336–377), Xie Fu and Dai Kui (326–396) began to take great interest in Buddhism. Of particular note is that it was no longer only a matter of non-Han monks translating scriptures and a small group of lay believers building temples, but now it was mainly Chinese monks and elite literati who were discussing Buddhist ideas.

This was quite an important phenomena. According to the *Biographies of Eminent Monks*, after the Jin moved south across the Yangzi, quite a few monks who lectured on Buddhist doctrines received a warm welcome.[14] According to the *New Account of Tales of the World*, it was not only Yin Hao who exclaimed on reading Buddhist scriptures that they were full of truth, but celebrated scholars highly knowledgeable about philosophy, men like Xie An (320–385), Xu Xun (?–?), Sun Sheng (ca. 302–373), Yin Zhongkan (?–399), Chi Chao (Xi Chao), Sun Chuo (ca. 300–380) Wang Tanzhi (330–375), Wang Xiu (?–?) and

---

13   Quoted in *SSXYJJ*, note to j. *shang*, 143, "Wenxue disi," from *Xu Jin yang qiu*. Huan Xuan, "Nan Wang Zhongling", *Hong ming ji*, j. 12) points out that in the past most people who left home to become monks or nuns were ethnically non-Han, and the government paid them little attention. However, the situation for the intellectual class at the beginning of the Eastern Jin was one of almost historically unprecedented change. At the same time, Neo-Daoist thinking no longer had much creativity or significance for intellectual history. In contrast many new topics of discussion were introduced mostly by Buddhism. At that, the ethnic Han Chinese intellectual elite began to have a high regard for Buddhist thought.

14   *Gaoseng zhuan*, j. 4–5, 156, 159–160, 192.

others were also ardently discussing Buddhist ideas.[15] Precisely because these men were deeply steeped in traditional Chinese knowledge, their discussions of Buddhism went beyond the ordinary concerns about redemption, offerings to the Buddhas, charitable donations and retribution to explore the profound theories of the Buddhist religion. As a result they very soon arrived at quite a few doubts and questions about Buddhism, some of them due to problems of Chinese translations of Buddhist texts.[16]

All these doubts required realistic explanations, and understandable terms were needed to make these explanations, but such understandable terms could only come from the Chinese cultural context. Therefore early translation of Buddhist ideas relied on traditional Chinese terms, especially Daoist terms that seemed to have similar meanings. This gave rise to the practice of *geyi* or "matching the meanings." As Chen Yinque astutely pointed out, the *geyi* method represented the first step in the beginning of the Chinese understanding of Buddhism, and Tang Yongtong's research also shows that it was perhaps used very early on; by this time it was likely already widespread in northern China.[17] The *geyi* method had to be used because the ancient Chinese language simply did not contain terms that corresponded to all those complicated Buddhist concepts. The so-called "names and appearances" (*shishu* 事數 or *mingxiang* 名相) that Chinese writing and language attempted to explain were the many Buddhist concepts that caused Yin Hao and the rest so much consternation, complicated things like the five *skandhas* (*wuyin* 五陰, part of the 81 divisions of the *Prajñâpâramitâ-sûtra*; being enmeshed in suffering); the twelve worlds (in Tiantai Buddhism, *shi-er ru* 十二入); the Four Noble Truths (*sidi* 四諦) or *catvâri-ârya-satyâni*, the primary and fundamental doctrines of Sâkyamuni; *dvâdasanga pratîtyasamutpâda*, the twelve *nidânas* or the twelve links in the chain of existence (*shi-er yinyuan* 十二因緣); the five great *klesa*— (*wugen* 五根) passions, or disturbers: desire, anger, stupidity (or ignorance),

---

15   See *Shishuo xinyu*, chapter 2, "Speech and Conversation" (Yanyu), and chapter 4, "Letters and Scholarship" (Wenxue), in *SSXYJJ*, j. shang. A complete translation is Richard B. Mather, *Shi-shuo Hsin-yü: A New Account of Tales of the World*, 1976, 25–80 & 92–145.

16   For example, according to *juan* of 4 of the *Gaoseng zhuan*, Yin Hao once discussed with the monk Kang Sengyuan "the profound principles of the Buddhist scriptures, but he nevertheless employed the words of secular texts to argue the meaning of nature and feelings." *Shishuo xinyu* also records that Yin Hao read the Buddhist sûtras extremely conscientiously, put bookmarks in them and regularly asked members of the Buddhist community about them. He even wanted to discuss with Zhi Daolin Kumârajîva's abbreviated version (Xiaopin) of the *Perfection of Wisdom Sûtra*. *Gaosheng zhuan*, 151; *SSXYJJ*, 131, 124. From this we know that Yin Hao certainly studied deeply the principles of Buddhist scriptures, but he also had quite a few doubts.

17   Chen Yinque, "Zhi Mindu xueshuo kao," *Chen Yinque xiansheng lunwen ji, xia*, 1977, 1229–1254.

pride, and doubt; the *pañcabala*, (*wuli* 五力) five powers of faith, zeal, memory (or remembering), meditation, and wisdom; the seven characteristics of bodhi or enlightenment (*qijue* 七覺) and so on and so on. Although this method of *geyi* was later criticized and abandoned by genuine theoreticians of Buddhism, still at the time it served both a bridging and an enlightening function and facilitated the emergence of the meanings of Buddhist thought in the Chinese linguistic context.

As more and more Buddhist texts were translated into Chinese, multiple translations of the same text appeared, and different Chinese terms came to be used in different translations of the same Buddhist text. Whether or not these different Chinese terms translated the same or different Sanskrit (or other Indian language) terms was a real problem. Chinese scholars who were beginning to have a deep understanding of Buddhism began to have to make comparisons in order to search out and understand the original text and the original meaning. From this arose the practice of *heben zizhu*, "explanation through collating and comparing texts." This involved comparing the various translated texts side by side to find the correct meanings. Once there were several Chinese translations for the same Buddhist text, then one Sanskrit (or Pali) term would have many different Chinese translations, and at that point scholars began to realize that these different understandings by Chinese translators led to different terms that in fact implied different meanings. What, then, was actually the more correct meaning of the Indian term? When most scholars had no way directly to understand the original language of the Buddhist texts, employing the traditional Chinese method of collating and annotating the translations was undoubtedly one way to try to find the meaning of the original and it stimulated scholars to do so.

The method of collating and comparing texts probably started in the third century during the Three Kingdoms period. For example, the monk Zhi Qian combined three sûtras in the esoteric tradition (*mijiao*)—the *Weimi chi, Tuolinni*, and *Zongchi*—with the title *He Weimi chi Tuolinni Zongchi san-ben*. Somewhat later the monk Zhi Mindu (?–?) collated and proofread the *Vimalakîrti-nirdesa-sûtra* of Zhi Qian, Dharmaraksa (Zhu Fahu, ca. 230–308?) and Zhu Shulan (fl. 266–316).[18] At first this activity was only carried out within the Buddhist community, but very soon Chinese literati joined this quest for the understanding of Buddhism. For example, the scholar scion of a great family of the Eastern Jin, Xie Fu collated the *Sûramgama-sûtra* (Shou-leng-yan jing), originally translated by Lokaksema (Zhi Chan, ca. 147–?), Wu Zhiyue,

---

18   *Chu sanzang ji ji*, j. 8, *Taishô*, j. 55, 58. The esoteric sûtras are also listed separately in the
      Taishô.

Dharmaraksa, Zhu Shulan in the Han dynasty, into a single text.[19] Xie Fu himself annotated the *Scripture of Ânâpâna Mindfulness* (Ânâpânasmrti-sûtra, Anban shou yi jing) and "copied and summarized the corresponding portions of various yoga-sûtras like the *Greater Ânâpâna Scripture* (Da Anban jing) and the *Scripture of Cultivation and Practice* (Xiu xing jing) and brought them together into one text." Scholars had to have a rather good understanding of Buddhist texts and theories in order to do such work.[20] From this collation and annotation and *geyi* type translations, the Chinese intellectual stratum started to find a method to understand Buddhist terms, and, at the same time, through their discussions and disputes, Buddhist doctrines and principles came to have new meanings in the Chinese linguistic context.

On the surface the dissemination of Buddhism in China after the third century of our era looked like "the Buddhist conquest of China." For the intellectual world of the Chinese elite, though, it was equally a case of China also conquering Buddhism because the propagation of Buddhism among them actually continued the Neo-Daoist thinking of Xiang Xiu and Guo Xiang. That is, it carried forward the ancient Chinese intellectual world's mystical thinking (*xuansi*) about the universe and human life.

To understand Buddhism in the Chinese context, specific terms from the ancient Chinese intellectual tradition were first matched with Buddhist terms. Dao (the Way) was used to understand *bodhi* (enlightenment), non-being (*wu*) to indicate *Shûnyatâ* (emptiness), depending on nothing (*wudai* 無待) to indicate *nirvâna*, and so on.[21] In the prefaces to the Buddhist texts included in Sengyou's *Collected Records Concerning the Tripitaka* (Chu sanzang ji ji), *juan* 6–11, Dao occurs ten times while *Wu* (non-being) naturally occurs many more times because it is used for Shûnyatâ and in other combinations such as *wuwei* (non-action) eleven times, *wuxin* (no heart/mind) from *Zhuangzi* four times. We should point out here that one drawback in this *geyi* matching practice was that it often led to a tendency to search for sameness and to neglect differences between Buddhist and Chinese thought. Looking for similarities was a useful approach to understanding, but it could also obliterate differences and decrease the chances of attaining a more complete understanding of Buddhism. It could reduce the enormously rich Buddhist thought to the scope

---

19   *Chu sanzang ji ji*, j. 7, *Taishô*, j. 55, 49.
20   See *Chu sanzang ji ji*, j. 6; for Shi Dao-an and Xi Fu discussions of the Ânâpâna, in *Taishô*, j. 55, 43, 45, and 44 respectively.
21   See Chen Yinque, "Zhi Mindu," in his *Lunwen ji, xia*, 1229–1254, and Qian Zhongshu, *Guanzhui bian*, 1979, vol. 4, 1261–1262. For "depending on nothing," see *Zhuangzi*, "Free and Easy Wandering," where it says that Liezi "had to depend on something (*you suo daizhe ye* 有所待者也) to get around," but it would have been better if he had had nothing to depend on. Watson, CT, 32.

of ancient China's more limited understanding. Still, as the Chinese scholar officials deepened their understanding of Buddhism, everything changed.

1.4

During the Eastern Jin period, the so-called Six Schools of the Prajñā (Wisdom) School appeared.[22] Even though they were not completely the same, their interpretations did not fundamentally surpass those of the collation and comparison practice discussed above.

Let's look first at the concept of "the non-existence of mind" (*xinwushuo*) used to translate the Buddhist idea of the detached or liberated mind (the bodhimind). Buddhist scholars pointed out early that the basic idea of the *Perfection of Wisdom Sûtra* is Shûnyatâ (emptiness, *kong* 空), and this Shûnyatâ means that all phenomena have no *svabhâba* or nature of their own (*zixing* 自性). Having no nature of its own is the only form of existence, and it is impossible to express this form of existence in Heaven and Earth through the medium of language. A realization of this sort of existence can only come from the mind because as soon as one uses language to express it one runs up against various limitations. In order to illuminate this ultimate truth, the *Perfection of Wisdom Sûtra* employs many passages of negation and reversal. Lacking this kind of linguistic experience and background, the Chinese very easily associated Shûnyatâ with non-being (*wu*) and so they first used the *Laozi, Zhuangzi* and Neo-Daoist *wu* to translate Shûnyatâ in Buddhist texts. Secondly, the non-being of Neo-Daoism did indeed have the same sort of original and transcendent nature as Shûnyatâ. Finally, to understand and realize Daoist non-being also required penetrating the barriers of language. For these reasons Zhi Mindu, Zhu Fayun and Daoheng used *xinwu*, non-existence of mind, to interpret the doctrine of Prajñā (wisdom). They employed the doctrines of Neo-Daoism and asserted that the so-called Shûnyatâ was simply "having a detached mind or no mind toward the myriad phenomena" (*wu xin yu wan wu* 無心於萬物).[23] This idea was not really in accord with the Prajñā School's concept of Shûnyatâ, however, nor was it the Buddhist concept of *anâtman* (*wuwo* 無我). It was really more like Laozi and Zhuangzi's Daoist ideas of "clinging to the One" (*shouyi* 守一) and "sitting and forgetting" (*zuowang* 坐忘).

Compared to the idea of *xinwu*, the concept of "primal non-being" (*benwu* 本無) seems to have been rather more complete. "Primal non-being" was originally a proposition put forward by the Neo-Daoists He Yan and Wang Bi. He Yan's "On Non-action" (Wuwei lun) states that "Non-being is the root

---

22   For the "six schools and seven sects, see Tang Yongtong, *Han Wei Liang Jin Nanbeichao Fojiao shi*, 1983, 194.

23   Yuan Kang "Zhao lunshu," Ji Zang, "Zhongguan lunzhu," cited from *Zhongguo Fojiao sixiang ziliao xuanbian*, 1981–1990, j. 1, 77.

(origin) of Heaven and Earth and the myriad phenomena,"[24] and Wang Bi's *Commentaries on Laozi* (Laozi zhu), also says that "all the phenomena under Heaven are born from being (*you*) and the beginning (root) of being is non-being."[25] What He and Wang mean by "Primal non-being" is that everything in the cosmos has its origin in non-being.

The ultimate goal of human life is, then, to return to this original beginning. The basic foundation of this way of thinking is the *Laozi*, but it is also somewhat close to Buddhism. For that reason, *benwu* (primal non-being) was first used to translate *tathatâ* (*zhenru* 真如), "thusness" or "suchness"—one form of the Buddha nature.[26] This way of thinking first confirms that the nature of all cosmic phenomena is illusory, then it demands that one's mind not be harmed by any false phenomena, and finally it urges one to employ a void and silent heart/mind to comprehend an equally void and silent universe and ultimately to become aware of the everlasting state of tranquility.

Take Dao-an (312–385) for example. He seems to have used the *Laozi* quite a bit to interpret Buddhist thought. In his "Preface" to the *Great Scripture of the Twelve Gateways* (Da shi-er men jing xu), he says that if one takes all of the myriad phenomena in the cosmos as having "being" (*you*), then it is hard to avoid obstinacy and obstruction; consequently Buddhism wants to deconstruct this "being" so that human beings will not be obsessed with and attached to the phenomenal world. This is the first step. His "Preface" to the *Skandhadhâtvâyatana-sûtra* (Yin chi ru jing xu) says that human beings must be made to dwell in a state without thought (in the absence of false ideas). This is the second step. His "Preface" (Anban zhu xu) to An Shigao's Commentaries on the *Ânâpânasmrti-sûtra* further says that the way to deal with human desires, feelings, thinking and behavior is "to decrease them and decrease them again, and to forget them and forget them again"—eliminating all desire is the only way to reach the transcendent state of being. That is the third and final step.[27] Here Dao-an not only follows the logic of Laozi but also employs Laozi's language. In his way of thinking and his language, the primal origin of the cosmos and the human world are united and the foundations of this thought and its logical argument are woven together.

Neo-Daoist thinking is even more clearly reflected in the Buddhist use of the idea of "matter as it is" (*jise* 即色). The concept of primal non-being takes a basically negative position toward the phenomena of the universe, but if we

---

24 *Quan Sanguo wen*, j. 39; *Quan Shanggu Sandai Qin Han Liuchao wen*, 1958 & 1985, 1274.

25 *Wang Bi ji jiaoshi*, 1980, 110.

26 See Tang Yongtong, "Zhongguo Foshi lingpian 2: benmo zhensu yu youwu," in *Lixue, Fojiao, Xuanxue*, 1991, 224–225; "Wei Jin xuanxue liubie lun," in *Tang Yongtong xueshu lunwen ji*, 1983, 235–236; *Han Wei Liang Jin Nanbeichao Fojiao shi*, 1983, 170–171.

27 For all of the above, see *Chu sanzang ji ji*, j. 6 & 7; *Taishô*, j. 55, 46, 44, 48.

delve more deeply into this way of thinking we arrive at a rather crucial question. Namely, how are human beings who live in the world of "being" to reach "non-being?" If one refuses to acknowledge the existence of the great world, would that not be a form of self-deception that would make it very difficult to achieve spiritual freedom? Neo-Daoism had also encountered this sort of problem. In the thinking of Xiang Xiu and Guo Xiang, for example, the human realm was not only one of "forgetting Heaven and Earth and abandoning the myriad things," but also "going along with things" and "changing with time." There was no need to be in a double quandary between "being" and "non-being." This idea already implied the logic of "the idea of matter as it is (*jise*) 'matter as we find it' or actual things."[28]

Zhi Dun (Zhi Daolin, 314–366), a chief proponent of "the idea of matter as it is" was perhaps the most important propagator of Buddhism in the upper stratum of Eastern Jin society. According to the *Biographies of Eminent Monks*, he had a profound knowledge of the ideas of the *Zhuangzi*. His explanation of the "Free and Easy Wandering" chapter "made all the Confucian scholars gasp with admiration" and some fragments of his explanation still exist today in the commentary to the "Letters and Scholarship" chapter of the *New Account of Tales of the World*. We learn from this record that Zhi Dun clarified the thinking of Xiang Xiu and Guo Xiang. He did not believe that individual self-satisfaction was "the Great Way." He argued that the sages had an even greater satisfaction that he called the "utmost satisfaction" (or "utmost contentment" *zhizu* 至足). This utmost satisfaction of the sages sought a unified realm where the individual and the cosmos came together in harmony; it was not the mediocre comfort of a little bird, the stubborn pursuit of the great roc, the self-restraint of forgetting food and abstaining from wine, and it was certainly not genuine transcendence.[29]

Zhi Dun argued in his "Roaming in the Supremely Profound State Inherent in Matter As It Is" (Jise youxuan lun) that the phenomenal world or matter (*se, rûpa*, form, matter, the physical form) itself does not possess any original nature; rather, it is all empty (*kong*), and although *se* and *kong* are different, they are ultimately the same: "matter as it is is simply empty" (*se ji wei kong* 色即爲空). The world of consciousness itself (*zhi* 知, *vidyâ, vijñâ*) also cannot obtain perception on its own, and so *zhi* (consciousness) and *ji* 寂 (silence/

---

28 Translation of *jise* is from Chan, sв, 339. Based on Tang Yongtong's research, Chan gives a clear explanation of this concept.
29 See *SSXYJJ*, 120; Liu Xiaobiao (462–521) quoting Xiang Xiu and Guo Xiang "Xiaoyao yi," and Zhi Dun "Xiaoyao lun."

tranquility/rest) are also identical.[30] According to Zhi Dun's thinking, people did not have to insist on making their spirit empty (*kong*) or try to escape the forms of matter (*se*) of the universe, or even strenuously seek to reach a state of being void and silent (*kongji*). They could rather naturally and comfortably achieve the unification of the universe and the individual. He believed that the significance of Prajña (wisdom) was that it allowed people in their transcendence to "make all things equal" (*qiwu* 齊物). When people comprehend Prajña, they should be able to understand the "spontaneity" (*ziran*) of the myriad things in the universe, and from that point they will be able to achieve natural transcendence.

In this manner, Buddhism became clearer by following Daoist interpretations, but Daoism also borrowed from Buddhism and grew more profound. Zhi Dun advanced the Chinese understanding of the Shûnyatâ (emptiness) of the Prajña School of Buddhism from the *Laozi* stage of Wang Bi and He Yan to the *Zhuangzi* stage of Xiang Xiu and Guo Xiang. Once the most profound Neo-Daoist disputations of Xiang Xiu and Guo Xiang were, however, no longer sufficient to further the interpretation of Buddhist thought, people began to transcend Neo-Daoism and move on to a direct understanding of Buddhism. The *New Account of Tales of the World* says that in a discussion of Zhuangzi's "Free and Easy Wandering," "Zhi [Dun] boldly marked out new principles [*xinli* 新理] beyond any proposed by the two above-named commentators [Xiang and Guo], and established a different interpretation [*yiyi* 異義] unlike that of any of the previous worthies,..."[31] Did the commentator's "new principles" and "different interpretation" indicate that the Buddhist understanding of the cosmos and human life was on the verge of transcending Neo-Daoism and beginning to give prominence to itself?

2.   The Transmission of Buddhism to China and Its Significance
       in Intellectual History, II

After the middle of the fourth century, quite a few Buddhist monks were active in both north and south China, Buddhist thought began to enter the mainstream of the Chinese intellectual world, and Buddhist disputations became the central interest of Chinese intellectuals.

---

30   *Shishuo xinyu*, "Wenxue," quoting *Zhi Daolin ji*, "Essay on Subtle Insight" (Miaoguan zhang), *ibid.*, 121. "Jise youxuan lun," quoted in An Cheng, "Zhonglun shuji," in *Zhongguo Fojiao sixiang ziliao xuanbian*, 1981–1990, j. 1, 64.

31   *SSXYJJ*, j. *shang*, 120. Translation is from Mather with one word added, *Shih-shuo hsin-yü*, chapter 4, # 32, 109.

The first monks most worthy of consideration in the hundred years before the first half of the fifth century are Dao-an in Xiangyang (Hubei) and Chang-an (Shaanxi) and Zhi Dun in the south. Dao-an is significant because he re-arranged and re-translated Buddhist texts and changed the interpretation of many foundational texts of various schools, and this led to many different understandings of Buddhist teaching. He also taught quite a few outstanding disciples and established the largest community of monks at that time. Zhi Dun is significant because he blended together the abstruse principles of the Prajña School and Neo-Daoist disputations. Beyond the Buddhist community, he influenced quite a few literati and scholar officials so that the Chinese intellectual world both continued and transcended Neo-Daoism by means of Buddhism. The Chinese intellectuals who were quite interested in Buddhism at that time, men like Chi Chao (Xi Chao), Yin Hao, Sun Chuo, Wang Qia (323–358), Xu Xun and so on, were all most powerful and influential scholar officials.

The other important monks worthy of consideration at this time were Huiyuan (334–416) in the south and Kumârajîva (334–413) in the north. Huiyuan was Dao-an's student. His community was centered at Mount Lu (Jiangxi) and he established wide contacts at the court and among the literati of Jiangnan. He both defended Buddhism's transcendent nature and spurred on it secularization. He brought Buddhism into the Chinese intellectual world with the doctrines of the immortality of the soul (the soul is not annihilated, *shen bumie* 神不滅), theory of the three ages (*sanshi shuo*), theories about transcending the mundane world or renouncing the world to practice Buddhism (*chushi lun* 出世論) and methods of *samâdhi* recollection of the Buddha (*nian Fo sanmei* 念佛三昧). Kumârajîva, a Kuchean from Kashmir, made accurate and elegant translations of Buddhist scriptures and introduced Buddhist doctrines to the Chinese intellectual class. Kumârajîva's students Zhu Daosheng (?–434), Sengzhao (384–414) and others were active among the upper strata of society in both north and south China. They genuinely explained Mahâyâna (Great Vehicle) Buddhist thought to the Chinese intellectuals. This was already the first half of the fifth century, then, and the Chinese intellectual world's understanding of Buddhism was already also far better than in the middle of the fourth century.

2.1

Let us briefly review here the knowledge of Buddhism in Chinese society in the middle of the fourth century. Although more Chinese intellectuals were interested in Buddhism then, their knowledge of it was really not very profound.

We can use Chi Chao (Xi Chao)'s "Essence of the Dharma" (Fengfayao) as a typical work of analysis to show the general level of understanding of Buddhism in upper class society in the mid-fourth century. This essay seems to be a summary of various categories of basic Buddhist thought. It includes knowledge and rules concerning the Buddhist redemption of the world.[32] Compared to the earlier *Master Mou's Treatise on the Removal of Doubt*, this work obviously exhibits a much more accurate and profound understanding of Buddhism and a gradual abandonment of Chinese traditional thought and language in favor of a clear presentation of the original face of Buddhism itself.

The Chinese were still unable, however, to understand thoroughly the most profound and subtle elements of Buddhist doctrines. When discussing some of the most recondite Buddhist theories and concepts, the "Essence of the Dharma" still has to have recourse to Neo-Daoist thinking and vocabulary. For example, the Buddhist idea that the cosmos is originally empty (Shûnyatâ) is interpreted as "forgetting" (*wanghuai*) the phenomenal world. Under the influence of Zhi Dun, Chi Chao (Xi Chao) tried not to separate being and non-being but regarded transcendence as simply "forgetting" about them both. This transformed the Prajña School's concept of Shûnyatâ into a mere search for inner spiritual tranquility.[33]

By the first half of the fifth century, however, a great number of Buddhist scriptures had been translated. Gobharana (Zhu Falan)'s original translation of the *Pañcavimsatisâhasrika Prajñapâramitâ-sûtra* (Fang guang boruo jing) had already been re-translated by Kumârajîva as the *Mohe boruo luomi jing*; besides Zhi Qian's translation of the *Vimalakîrti-nirdesa-sûtra* (Weimojie jing), there was also Kumârajîva's translation as well as Sengzhao and Daosheng (Zhu Daosheng, ca. 360–434)'s commentaries and interpretations; besides Dharmaraksa (Zhu Fahu)'s translation of the *Saddharmapundarika-sûtra* (Fahua jing, commonly known as the *Lotus Sûtra*), there was Kumârajîva's new translation; there were two translations, by Dharmasema (Tan Wuchan, 385–433) and Faxian (ca. 337–424), of the *Nirvâna-sûtra* (Niepan jing); and there were translations of three works, the *Hundredfold Treatise* (Satakashastra ?, Polun), the *Middle Treatise* (Madhyamaka-sâstra, Chonglun), and the *Treatise of the Twelvefold Division* (Dvâdasanikâyashastra ?, Shi-er men lun) [question

---

32 Chi Chao (Xi Chao)'s "Fengfayao" contains quotations from many Buddhist-sûtras, including the *Mahâ-parinirvâna-sûtra*, the *Lalitavistara-sûtra* the *Vimalakîrtinirdesa-sûtra* and so on.

33 *Hong ming ji*, j. 13, SBBY, 111. Other contemporary scholars' knowledge of Buddhism in this work is also on a par with that of Chi Chao, as one can see from Luo Han's "Gengsheng lun" and Sun Chuo's "Yudao lun," in j. 5 and j. 3 respectively.

marks in Tsukumoto and Hurvitz], that provided an even deeper understanding of the Prajña School. By this time, then, both Buddhists and elite literati all had a deeper understanding of Buddhist doctrines, and they felt very dissatisfied when they looked back at the history of Chinese interpretations of Buddhism. Both Sengzhao and Zhu Daosheng criticized the practice of *geyi* "matching the meanings" and the earlier Six Schools. They even found defects in the "nature is empty" (*xing kong*) idea that came closest to the essential meaning of Buddhist Shûnyatâ. Once such a large number of scriptures had been translated and were available as reliable sources, the Chinese understanding of Buddhism could go beyond the general idea of religious salvation and leave behind the domination of Neo-Daoist themes, terminology and thinking.

Several quite significant things occurred about this time. First, fully fledged Buddhism not only began to establish a clear demarcation between itself and traditional Chinese thought but also to clarify the nature of Brahamanic thinking from India. According to the *Biographies of Eminent Monks* "Biography of Daorong (355–434)," during the reign of Yao Xing (r. 394–416), Emperor Gaozu of the Later Qin state, Buddhists and the followers of Brahman engaged in a polemical debate. It is said that at the time Daorong for the Buddhist side read a large number of Brahmanic texts and thereby the Buddhist monks gained a much clearer picture of the Chinese language world's thinking about Indian Buddhism.[34] Second, the upper stratum of Chinese society began publicly to admit that Buddhist doctrines were more profound than traditional Chinese thought. During the Liu Song Dynasty, both Fan Tai (355–428) and Xie Lingyun (385–433) said that the six Confucian classics were primarily aimed at the improvement of society and were useful for governing the state, but if one wanted to discuss profound matters of the mind one had to turn to the Buddhist sûtras.[35] Zong Bing (375–443), author of the *Treatise Clarifying Buddhism* (Hong ming ji), wrote that Buddhism both encompassed and surpassed Confucianism and Daoism.[36] Third, people no longer took for granted their understanding of various Buddhist teachings, such as that all human beings have the Buddha nature, but sought for confirmation in the Buddhist scriptures themselves. For this reason, Daosheng's theory that even "*icchantika* possessed the Buddha nature" was not accepted in China until the translation of the *Mahâparinirvâna-sûtra* (Da po niepan jing).[37] This amounted

---

34   *Gaoseng zhuan*, j. 6, 241–242.

35   *Gaoseng zhuan*, j. 7, Huiyan zhuan," 261.

36   *Hong ming ji*, j. 2, 17.

37   *Icchantika* (*yichanti* 一闡提) were people without the desire for Buddha enlightenment or unbelievers, shameless ones, enemies of the good, full of desires, and those who have cut off their roots of goodness. (Soothill, *Dictionary*)

to admitting that as classic texts the Buddhist sûtras contained self-evident truths. Fourth, Chinese men of culture were no longer satisfied with merely indirectly receiving and applying the available scriptures from abroad, and so the Chinese monk Faxian and his fellow monks made their remarkable pilgrimage to India in search of the dharma and to collect sûtras, and the poet Xie Lingyun studied Sanskrit so as to participate in the translation of the Buddhist sûtras.[38] During this process of reading and explicating the Buddhist scriptures to understand and explore the nature of Buddhism, an indigenous Chinese Buddhist thought was itself also gradually taking shape.

2.2

In the first half of the fifth century, with the translation and dissemination of the various Buddhist sûtras mentioned above, plus Nâgârjuna's commentary on the *Perfection of Wisdom Sûtra*, entitled the *Great Treatise on the Perfection of Wisdom* (Dazhi dulun), and with Sengrui (fl. 401), Sengzhao, and Zhu Daosheng's interpretations of Buddhist doctrines, and Chinese literati like Xie Lingyun and Zong Bing's deeper and more correct understanding of Buddhism, a new landscape in Chinese intellectual history came into view. Behind this new landscape a close re-examination of the Chinese intellectual world was being carried out. The following understandings and formulations of Buddhist subjects during this period are of great importance.

Debates about Shûnyatâ were still most dominant. Even though the traditional Chinese intellectual world had also carried out debates concerning being and non-being, they were imprecise and replete with metaphoric language of uncertain meaning and exaggerated descriptions. This rendered them ineffable and difficult to discuss, rather like the *Laozi*'s "to decrease them and decrease them again" or "[a] dark and even darker [mystery]." In the end it was impossible to infer correctly the full nature of such intangible subjects as emptiness and non-being. Even though the Six Schools of Prajñâpâramitâ studies in the Jin period had already done considerable study of Shûnyatâ, not all schools of Buddhism could reach a profound and accurate understanding of it.[39]

At this time, though, the discussions of Shûnyatâ being carried out among members of the cultivated elite were becoming quite penetrating and complex. Since the widely circulated Prajña School sûtras, especially the *Perfection of Wisdom Sûtra*, all discussed this key term, it doubtless led to a rise in the quality of people's understanding and discussion. Sengzhao's critique of the

---

38   *Gaoseng zhuan*, j. 7, 260.
39   *Ibid.*, j. 2, 71.

Six Schools' interpretation of Shûnyatâ is an ideal example of this. According to him, none of their interpretations were perfect. As noted above, the concept of "the non-existence of mind" was interpreted only to mean "having a detached mind or no mind toward the myriad phenomena," thus transforming Shûnyatâ into a quest for inner spiritual tranquility. The problem was that this only made the myriad phenomena empty in the mind, but did not account for the original emptiness (Shûnyatâ) of all phenomena. Although the idea of matter as it is did point out that the phenomenal world has a transitory "false existence" (*jia you*) and could alleviate people's anxiety about it, the idea still failed to point out that the phenomenal world cannot be produced or exist on its own (it is dependent, and it has no eternality. The theory of original non-being did grasp the origin and directly point out the illusory nature of the phenomenal world, but it remained bogged down in negative thinking, could not transcend negation and affirmation nor embrace both true non-being (*zhen wu*) and false being (*jia you*).[40]

Sengzhao's understanding and interpretation of Shûnyatâ both transcended and included the "false being" of the phenomenal world and the "true non-being" of the mental world. First, although all things that exist and pass away in the phenomenal world have no *svabhâba* or nature of their own, they still emerge in people's consciousness as they move through the course of time. As a result, they also partake of being. Second, due to the illusory nature of time changes, all things in human consciousness that seem to exist and pass away in the phenomenal world are also unreal. They are illusory and so they partake of non-being. Third, the true origin (*benyuan*) transcends everything and is itself absolute existence; it is neither in motion nor is it still; it is neither being nor non-being. On this account, the correct understanding of the absolute and the origin should be that they are "neither being nor non-being" (*bu you bu wu*). The significance of "neither being nor non-being" is that it can prevent people from stimulating their desires due to being, from trying to escape the phenomenal world due to non-being; its purpose is to keep them from clinging to things as though they were real.[41]

---

40   See Sengzhao's "Bu zhenkong lun" and "Wu buqian lun," in *Zhaolun, Taishô*, j. 45, 151–152.
41   Sengzhao quotes the phrase "neither being nor non-being" from the *Zhonglun* in his *Bu zhenkong lun*. Hou Wailu, et al., *Zhongguo sixiang tongshi*, 1957, vol. 3, chapter 10, 445 states that "the development of Sengzhao's Buddhist thought was from Neo-Daoism to Prajña, and from Prajña to an integration of his three treatises." We can generally accept this interpretation.

2.3

Intellectual history is not only concerned with thought; it is also concerned with the understanding and expression of thought. Compared to traditional Chinese discussions of ultimate metaphysical origins, Buddhist reflections were not only more penetrating but also more clearly and precisely expressed.

Firstly, the various Buddhist sûtras and treatises contain very many quite refined and complex similes and metaphors. The 29th *juan* of the *Perfection of Wisdom Sûtra*, "Shizi hou pusa pin 11–3," states that Buddhism employs eight kinds of simile, and Buddhism certainly does have a very rich practice of using similes and metaphors to make complex philosophical ideas apparent to its followers. Besides individual tropes—the moon in the water, clouds in the sky, bubbles on the water, flames in the heat, the sound of shouting, the blind seeing colors, footprints of birds in the sky—used to express Shûnyatâ,[42] Buddhism even more commonly employs a mirror as an image of Shûnyatâ because it could encompass so many of its intricate implications.[43]

Secondly, the terminology of the many Buddhist scriptures is both refined and elaborate. Buddhist terms relating to the concept of Shûnyatâ are far more meticulous and complex than Chinese discussions of non-being. The *Pañcavimsatisâhasrika Prajñapâramitâ-sûtra* has some eighteen kinds of Shûnyatâ, including empty within (*neikong*), externally empty (*waikong*), internal organ and external object are both unreal, or not material (*neiwai kong*), unreality of unreality (*kongkong*), great void, or the Mahâyâna *parinirvâna* (*dakong*) and so on.[44] If we read the Buddhist sûtras and treatises of that time, we can see how the vocabulary of Chinese was increased through them and how Chinese discourse and expression became more meticulous and refined. At the same time we can see how the thought of Chinese speakers and writers grew more complex, orderly and subtle through their analyses of Buddhism.

The Buddhist style of argument and preaching particularly employed positive statements (*biaoquan* 表詮) together with negative statements (*zhequan* 遮詮) and phenomenal truth (*samvrti-satya, sudi* 俗諦 or *shidi* 世諦, common or ordinary statements made as though phenomena were real) together with truth in reality (*paramartha-satya zhendi* 眞諦, the correct dogma of the

---

42 See the *Vimalakîrtinirdesa-sûtra*, j. *shang*, "Fangbian pin 7," j. zhong, "Guan zhongsheng pin 7," and the *Pañcavimsatisâhasrika Prajñapâramitâ-sûtra*, j. 3, "Liao ben pin 14," and so on.

43 There are many examples in the Buddhist sûtras, like the *Prajñapâramitâ-sûtra* and the *Vimalakîrtinirdesa-sûtra*, of the use of a mirror as a simile for Shûnyatâ .

44 *Pañcavimsatisâhasrika Prajñapâramitâ-sûtra*, j. 4, "Wen mo he yan pin di 19," *Taishô*, j. 8, 22–23; also see Kumârajîva translation of the sûtra as *Mohe boruo luomi jing*, j. 4, "Ju yi pin 12, *Taishô*, j. 8, 243.

enlightened) as well as partial revelation that needs to be explicated further to reach the final truth (*buliao yi* 不了義) together with revelation of the entire meaning, or truth (*liao yi* 了義).[45] In their teachings they constantly reminded their audience that they should regard Shûnyatâ as neither a genuine negation nor a true affirmation, neither non-being nor being. Following their teachings, the Chinese understanding and expression of non-being came to encompass many more layers of meaning than in the past. This was especially the case after translations of the *Middle Treatise*, the *Hundredfold Treatise*, and the *Treatise of the Twelvefold Division* became available. The idea of the "mean" (*zhongdao*) that transcends the polarities of realism and nihilism was then applied very well to the understanding of Shûnyatâ. This sort of understanding and expression compared with the Chinese style exposition, expressed Buddhism's subtle inner meanings much more precisely.

Thirdly, Buddhism again emphasized the limitations of language. It pointed out that no language is up to the task of understanding and expressing Shûnyatâ. That is because language causes thought to be caught up again and again in obstinate "distinctions" or "differences" that hinder its ability to inquire directly into the origin of existence. Buddhism of course recognizes language, but it ultimately demands that people transcend language. The command "do not put words on paper" (*bu zhao wenzi* 不著文字) in the *Vimalakîrti-nirdesa-sûtra*, "Dizi pin," and the affirmation that "from your own self you can prove [the Buddhist message]" (*zi nei suo zheng* 自內所證) in the *Avatamsaka-sûtra* (or *Flower Garland Sûtra*) both represent the only paths advocated by Buddhism to comprehend the origin (of existence). Even all of the mysterious and abstruse things said above were only part of a kind of temporary and expedient teaching strategy. The real Shûnyatâ was so much more subtle and profound that it was ultimately unfathomable and ineffable.

2.4

Buddhist discussions of Shûnyatâ as the origin of the cosmos were carried out in the final analysis to provide a foundation for the ultimate meaning of human life. Contemporary Buddhist thinking about human nature and the Buddha nature was extended on the basis of this seemingly metaphysical foundation.

The traditional Chinese intellectual world had also had many discussions concerning the original nature of human beings. There had been fierce debates concerning various ideas, such as original human nature is neither

45   See Lü Cheng, *Zhongguo Foxue yuanliu lüejiang*, 1993, third lecture, 51, concerning the Indian ways of taking account of phenomena, and A. K. Warder, *Indian Buddhism*, 1980, 150, concerning the Indian dual level of discussion. Soothill, *Dictionary* has a detailed discussion of *zhongdao* 中道 or the "mean."

good nor evil, it is good, it is evil and so on. They also divided the origin, degeneration and return (to the origin) of human nature into various levels or categories, such as nature, feelings, goodness and so on. These ideas were all very simple, however, and these concepts of the origin, changes, and regeneration of human nature were either direct statements without analysis, or metaphors cloaked in ambiguous language without clear meaning.[46] There were no detailed studies from the physiological, perceptional, psychological and societal levels concerning how (or from what) human nature was constituted and how it declined or rose to a higher, sublime level. In terms of ideas, the Chinese were used to accepting self-evident conclusions while in practice they were only concerned with ethics and morality with relation to social order. The ultimate goal of the mainstream Chinese intellectual world was not the absolute or the transcendent, but rather the achievement of a consummately satisfactory social life in this world.

The analyses of Buddhism were much more penetrating and sophisticated than traditional Chinese thought. First, they were firmly built upon an intricate and refined analysis of the origin of the universe and were supported by a cosmology that connected everything. Second, they brought together feelings, consciousness, psychology, physiology and social elements based on rigorous experience, logic, and reasoning. Third, they not only had solid foundations and employed meticulous logical thinking, but they were able to offer various strategies and techniques for achieving a perfect state of human nature. The Chinese intellectual elite did not realize these differences until the fourth and fifth centuries. Later, Xie Lingyun regretfully stated that Confucianism and the traditional Chinese intellectual world could "assist the vulgar and save the world" but were unable to probe the "mysteries of nature and mind." In his *Treatise Clarifying Buddhism*, Zong Bing even more frankly admitted that "China's Confucian gentlemen are well versed in rites and rightness, but are in the dark when it comes to knowing the human heart." He compared this stubborn clinging to the Chinese classics without exploring the ultimate profoundly mysterious foundations of human nature to walking along under the clouds unaware that above the clouds there are the sun and the moon.[47] Indeed, when we read the Buddhist sûtras, we find that they begin by clearly establishing the foundations and support for their discussions. Then they employ extremely fine logical thinking to string together smoothly feelings, consciousness, psychology, physical matter and even social life into a minute investigation with a clearly distinct arrangement of ideas.

---

46   See *Wenzi*, j. 6, ESEZ, 847. *Huainanzi honglie jijie*, j. 11, 352. CQFL, j. 10, ESEZ, 791–792.
47   *Hong ming ji*, j. 2, 17.

Buddhist thinking customarily goes forward layer upon layer or concentric ring upon ring. Huiyuan and Kumârajîva actually wrote quite perceptive discussions of the question of the Buddha nature (*Foxing*), but the most typical discussion was given in Daosheng's thought in the first half of the fifth century. He based his discussion on the *Nirvâna-sûtra*, and the reasoning about human life in the *Nirvâna-sûtra* was based on the analysis of the origin of the cosmos given in the *Perfection of Wisdom Sûtra*.[48] We are, then, well advised to start with this sûtra.

The central theme of *Perfection of Wisdom Sûtra* thought is Shûnyatâ: all phenomena have no nature of their own, are just brought together by chance, suddenly born and suddenly perishing. According to Buddhism, the six human sense organs (*sadâyatana, liuru* 六入)—eye, ear, nose, tongue, body, and mind—give rise to various combinations of perceptions and consciousness of colors, sounds, smells, flavors and so on. These are the so-called five aggregates or five *skandhas* (*wuyin* or *wuyun* 五蘊)—"*rûpa*, form or matter; *vedana*, sensation; *samjñâ*, conception or discerning; *samskâra*, the functioning of mind in its likes and dislikes, good and evil, etc.; *vijñâna*, the mental faculties of perception and cognition"—(*se shou xiang xing shi* 色受想行識)—that are transformed into (or give rise to) the phenomenal world in the human mind.

In the same fashion the *Mahâparinirvâna-sûtra* also argues that all phenomenon in the universe have no determinant nature or autonomy. Just as a magician congers up soldiers, chariots, elephants, horses, human settlements, mountains and forests, or like the echoes of water flowing in a ravine, everything is an aggregation of feelings produced by the senses of colors, sounds, smells, flavors, touch and so on. They are all both impermanent (*anitya, wuchang* 無常) and empty (Shûnyatâ).

The human body itself is likewise Shûnyatâ, the mere accumulation of the five aggregates mentioned above. As soon as people regard their bodies as real (substantial), they then possess *âtman* (self, personality, *wo* 我) and fall into suffering (*ku* 苦; *dukkha, douqia* 豆佉). That is to say that this world is, on the one hand, an illusory projection of the mind created by external "dust causes" (*chenyuan* 塵緣) and, on the other hand, a response to the mind's perception and awareness. This world of illusory phenomena gives rise to the illusions, desires and behavior of people in the vulgar world, and from these are produced various forms of suffering and entanglements (bondage and toil) that lead directly to an unavoidable cycle of birth and death. The sins and

---

48   Many scholars have pointed out that the *Nirvâna-sûtra* analysis takes the *Prajñapâramitâ-sûtra* as its foundation, and Daosheng's discourse on the Buddha nature was also based on an analysis of Shûnyatâ. See Daosheng's commentaries on the *Vimalakîrtinirdesa-sûtra* and the *Nirvâna-sûtra* in *Taishô*, j. 38, 347 and j. 37, 548.

the retributive *karma* (*nieye* 孽業) of the *icchantika* (people full of desires) come from all this. Because they have no substantial reality, all of these phenomena that seem to be in the world are in a constant state of origination and annihilation—impermanence. It is only because human beings are stubbornly immersed in this world and cling to unreal things (*abhinivesa, zhi* 執) as though they were real, and also possess *âtman* or self that they are trapped on the cyclic wheel of impermanence.

In the final analysis, though, when has there ever really been existence? The Buddha asked if all phenomena, all right and wrong, all good and evil are within time and space and possess no determinate nature of their own, then can those sins of the *icchantika* actually have determinate natures of their own and cannot be subject to birth and annihilation? And if those sins and the retributive *karma* of the *icchantika* are only impermanent illusions, then why cannot *icchantika* also possess the right of deliverance and become Buddhas? Following this logic, Buddhism arrived at the doctrine that "all sentient beings possess the Buddha nature" and "the dharma of all ignorance or unenlightenment (*avidyâ*) and all life's distresses and delusions possess the Buddha nature."[49]

What, then, is the true Buddha nature? Buddha cannot be established in the experiential world and cannot exist in the phenomenal world. Buddha transcends time, space and the phenomenal world as absolute and eternal. This sort of absolute and eternal is also not some form of existence outside of the phenomenal world either, but is rather an intrinsic essence hidden within the constantly moving constantly changing phenomenal world. The Buddha may be compared to pure gold. Pure gold can be melted down and made into various sorts of utensils, and these utensils can in turn be recast into other implements, but the nature of the pure gold remains the same.

The scriptures ask: what is it to be an *icchantika*? An *icchantika* is someone who in the vulgar world is said not to possess faith (*sraddhâ, xin* 信), goodness (*sâdhu, shan* 善), zeal or advancement (*vīrya, jin* 進), recollection (of the Buddha, *smrti, nian* 念), concentration (in meditation or *samâdhi, ding* 定), and wisdom (*prajñâ, hui* 慧). Those people who establish what faith, goodness, zeal or advancement, recollection, concentration and wisdom are, however, do not necessarily possess the truly transcendent Buddha nature either because they are also involved in refusal, opposition and prejudice. Just like

---

49　Dharma (*fa*) is used here in the sense "all things, or anything small or great, visible or invisible, real or unreal, affairs, truth, principle, method, concrete things, abstract ideas, etc." Soothill, *Dictionary*, quoting M. W.

ignorance or unenlightenment, sins and retributive *karma*, they too dwell in impermanence.

Among these two types of people, however, there are still true transcendence and eternality. No matter how much the external world and the human mind are stuck in impermanence, in their essence they still partake of the everlasting just the same as the Buddha nature does. It is only that they "are unable to see it." They are like people living in poverty who do not know that they have a treasure hidden inside their house, but the truly enlightened never obstinately cling to things; they are able to penetrate the phenomenal world to see clearly the everlasting and the absolute and thus to be everlasting themselves in the midst of this endless process of ceaseless change. They simply transcend time and space and the origin of the universe that is without discrimination or difference. The *Mahâparinirvâna-sûtra* calls this "the highest Void or Shûnyatâ" (*di yi yikong* 第一義空). The true mean is simply Shûnyatâ: the neither born nor dying, neither prolonged nor cut off, neither unitary nor differentiated, neither coming nor going Buddha nature. This is why Daosheng said that the Buddha nature is ultimate and everlasting and his contemporary Huirui said that to experience the Buddha nature is to reach *nirvâna*.[50] This common and everlasting origin that exists in everything and the enlightenment that is able to understand this sort of origin is simply the Buddha nature.

Since this common and everlasting origin that exists in everything and the enlightenment that is able to understand it is simply the Buddha nature, then the difference that determines whether or not a person can achieve Buddhahood is not whether or not that person is an *icchantika*, but whether that person suffers from *moha*, illusion, delusion, doubt or unbelief (*huo* 惑). Sengzhao said that permanence or impermanence, emptiness or non-emptiness, suffering or enjoyment, birth or death are all really just the "functions" and "influences" of the human mind.[51] From this point of view, so-called *nirvâna* is simply to see through all illusions, not to be bound (tied down) by illusory phenomena and so not to suffer any distress (*klesa, fannao*). Human consciousness should realize that any phenomenon possessing an individual or differential nature is an impediment to eternality and transcendence. Only by transcending difference and renouncing attachments can a person enter deeply into the one possible reality and eternality and dwell for ever like the Buddha in a realm that is paradoxically both (or neither) impermanent and

50　　*Chu sanzang ji ji*, j. 5, *Taishô*, j. 55, 41. *Quan Song wen*, j. 62. *Quan Shanggu Sandai Qin Han Liuchao wen*, 1958 & 1985, 2770. Soothill, *Dictionary*: 第一義空 The highest Void, or reality, the Mahâyâna *nirvâna*, though it is also applied to Hînayâna *nirvâna*.
51　　"Da Liu Yimin shu," *Taishô*, j. 38, 156.

(nor) everlasting. This is because the Buddha nature is simply the mean that transcends everything.[52]

In the third decade of the fifth century, basing himself on the *Mahâparinirvâna-sûtra*, Daosheng put forth the proposition that *"icchantika* could all achieve the Buddha nature,"* but his idea met with a great deal of opposition. Consequently, with much indignation he swore in public that "if what I have said be in conflict with the doctrine of the scriptures, then let this body be afflicted with a pox. If there be no conflict with the Marks of Reality, then, when I have cast off this life, may I approach the lion throne [on which the Buddha sits]."[53] After the transmission of the *Mahâparinirvâna-sûtra*, doubts about his idea disappeared. This demonstrates the self-evident authoritative nature of the Buddhist scriptures which, of course, derived from their extremely detailed and elaborate concepts, intricately woven logical thinking and difficult to refute analyses.

2.5

If all sentient beings truly possessed the Buddha nature, then what methods were needed to realize it? This topic was one of the focal points of contemporary Buddhist discussions. Early Buddhism had advocated intoning sûtras, invoking the Buddha's name, keeping the commandments, practicing meditation, bringing about happiness or good fortune (for others) and patience (especially bearing insult and distress without resentment). These were all tangible yet fairly superficial religious practices. Buddhism had always held that one had to travel a long road to pass over (by means of the six *pâramitâs, poluomiduo* 波羅蜜多) from this shore (*ci-an*, the life of endless reincarnations) to the other shore (*bi-an* or *nirvâna*). A true Buddhist believer had to accept these trials and, through difficult cultivation, slowly approach the sacred realm. As far as the fifth century, although Buddhism had already moved the mysterious Buddha nature closer to ordinary human nature, it had still not come to the conclusion that human nature was simply the Buddha nature and, like later Chan Buddhism, swept away the idea that cultivation is necessary to achieve Buddhahood. In Faxian's translation of the *Mahâparinirvâna-sûtra*, he still translated human enlightenment as "developing one's Buddha nature." In the discussion of *nirvâna* in Huirui's "Explaining Doubt" (Yu yi), he also said that one must "cultivate and refine one's true nature."[54] In the "Letters and Scholarship" section of the *New Account of Tales of the World*, Emperor Jianwen

---

52 The passage from the *Mahâparinirvâna-sûtra* are all from j. 21–27, in *Taishô*, j. 12, 488–523.
53 *Gaoseng zhuan*, j. 7, 256; translation is from Tsukamoto, *History*, 459.
54 *Chu sanzang ji ji*, j. 5, *Taishô*, j. 55, 42; also *Quan Songwen*, j. 62, *Quan Shanggu Sandai Qin Han Liuchao wen*, 2771.

is quoted as saying that "... the merit of shaping and refining is still not be despised."[55] This shows that at the time there was still some distance between human nature and the Buddha nature in the minds of Buddhist believers.

This distance was, however, steadily shortening. Let us examine the change in thinking that lead to this. The Shûnyatâ of Prajñâpâramitâ thought was itself a very profound intellectual foundation, but it was also an extremely corrosive form of thought. In its context everything lost any substantial or determinate reality. No matter whether it was the stimuli and desires that caused human depravity or the attempts to resist that depravity, being or non-being, untruth or truth, in Prajñâpâramitâ thinking they all gave rise to obstinate "discriminations." Because of this, when all sins that have been negated and all good works that have been given positive value have become mere illusions, and living within illusion (*moha*) or free from illusion can only be proven from within one's own self (*zi nei suo zheng*), then all of those methods mentioned above, including asceticism or self-mortification (*duskara-caryâ, kuxing* 苦行), will have become unavoidably rendered unnecessary. In the past, Buddhist teaching said that people should practice goodness because goodness would become a cause (*hetu, yin* 因) that would produce an effect (*phala, guo* 果) of blessings. In Prajñâpâramitâ thought, however, concepts like impurity and purity, vulgar and sacred, depravity and transcendence, this shore and the other shore are all species of "discrimination" or "distinction." As long as people continue to harbor in their minds such ideas as going from impurity to purity, vulgar to sacred, depravity to transcendence, and this shore to the other shore, they will still be clinging to things as though they were real, but the Buddhist state of "the highest form of Shûnyatâ" must be one that clings to no "discriminations" or "distinctions." On this account Daosheng proposed the idea of "sudden enlightenment to attain Buddhahood" (*dunwu chengfo* 頓悟成佛).[56]

So-called "sudden enlightenment" referred to a situation in which in one sudden turn of thought a person's consciousness would come to understand absolute truth. There had actually been some discussion of sudden enlightenment in Buddhism before Daosheng. This discussion gave rise to the term "small sudden enlightenment" (*xiao dunwu*). Because it did not solve such problems as the why or *raison d'être*, the where or location, or the expression or manifestation of the Buddha nature, it could not establish itself as a complete and coherent doctrine. By the first half of the fifth century, the Buddha nature had been given established metaphysical principles derived

---

55   *Shi-shuo Hsin-yü*, j. *shang*, 125. Mather, *Shi-shuo Hsin-yü*, 115. The last line might also be translated as "the effort of cultivating and refining should still not be neglected."
56   See Ge Zhaoguang, *Zhongguo Chan sixiangshi—cong 6 shiji dao 9 shiji*, 1995, 103–104.

from the *Perfection of Wisdom Sûtra* and had been widely propagated through the *Nirvâna-sûtra*. The idea of "sudden enlightenment" was therefore given a rather solid foundation.[57] The *Mahâparinirvâna-sûtra* declared that "all sentient beings possess the Buddha nature." Following this train of thought, what did the faithful have to reject or to persist in? Since being bound to things and passions or being liberated from them, being impure or pure, practicing good or sinful behavior, dwelling on this shore or the other shore are, in the phenomenal world, all without substantial existence, then people who always already possess the Buddha nature will realize all this in the instant of enlightenment. There will be no distance between regular human nature and the Buddha nature, and vulgar human nature will be equal to pure Buddha nature. People will transcend the prejudices of love and hate, achieve a kind of spiritual joy and experience a sense of relaxation and freedom, and in this way the road to transcendence and liberation will appear to be a very easy one indeed.

We should mention in passing the influence of this line of thought on Chan Buddhism. Many scholars have pointed out that the two forms of early Chinese Buddhism that had the most influence on later Buddhist history were Prajñâpâramitâ studies and Meditation (*Dhyâna*) studies. The former concerned philosophical analyses and enlightenment while the latter involved cultivation techniques. For a long time there was little fusion of these two schools of thought as they appear to have developed along their separate paths. Because in early Buddhism Chan meditation involved a number of techniques for calming the body and mind, it was simply a way of attaining tranquility and liberation through various forms of harsh physical and mental cultivation. These techniques for self-discipline and self-restraint were not, however, very highly regarded by the cultural elite. They were more interested in the relaxed "sitting in meditation" (*yanzuo* 宴坐) of the *Vimalakîrti-nirdesa-sûtra*. In the Eastern Jin, Xie Fu pointed out in his "Preface to the *Ânâpânasmrti-sûtra*," that there were three paths one could follow to go from wisdom to *dhyâna* (*chan*). The first two both involved various forms of harsh physical and mental training, but they could not lead to true relaxation and freedom. Men of superior character or capacity, Xie Fu argued, do not need to practice strenuous meditation (*zuochan*) because their minds naturally dwell in a state of vacuity, enlightenment and eternal quietude. This natural "empty" state or Shûnyatâ, far removed from being and non-being or right and wrong, is simply human beings' Buddha nature and *nirvâna* (*niepan* 涅槃).

---

57   *Gaoseng zhuan*, j. 7, "Song jingshi longguang si Zhu Daosheng," 257 says that "contemporary people believed that (Dao)sheng argued that *icchantika* possessed the Buddha nature, and there is evidence for this view. Sudden enlightenment without retribution was also a basic belief at that time." 257.

This tendency in Chan studies was already apparent among the cultural elite in the early fifth century. Owing to the coming together of Chan techniques and Prajñâpâramitâ philosophy and the blending of Chan practices with Buddha-nature thinking Chan was no longer a form of cultivation requiring harsh suppression of one's body and mind through an arduous and extraordinarily long process. The seeds of "sudden enlightenment" were already latent in this combination of Chan and Prajñâpâramitâ thought. In time, Chan studies were transformed from a simple series of Buddhist cultivation techniques into a system of thought based on philosophical principles and including methods of cultivation. From a training method for all sentient beings passively to resist external temptations, Chan came to mean the literati's active adjustment to their minds' spontaneous ability to become enlightened.[58] The appearance and development of Chan Buddhism (*Chanzong*) followed from all of this, a subject to be taken up later.

The significance of sudden-enlightenment thinking in Chinese intellectual history needs to be thoroughly evaluated. Many researchers have pointed out that Daosheng's importance to Buddhist studies was comparable to that of Wang Bi in Neo-Confucianism. He turned Buddhist thought from a set of various complicated and archaic ideas toward simplicity and clarity, and, based on a foundation of Prajñâpâramitâ thought, he created a clear form of logical thinking out of the many different arduous and difficult paths to Buddhist liberation. At that, everything became simple and relaxed. Many scholars have also pointed out the connection between this form of thought and later Chan Buddhism.[59] Should they not have also noticed that, due to Daosheng's ideas, Buddhist monastic discipline, methods of cultivation and theoretical analyses, indeed all of Buddhism itself, were on the brink of being disintegrated and deconstructed? If people are able to reach the ultimate realm of absolute transcendence in a mere instant (*ksana, chana*) by means of their own mind or consciousness, then what point is there in the continued existence of Buddhism?

---

58   See Ge Zhaoguang, *Zhongguo Chan sixiangshi—cong 6 shiji dao 9 shiji*, 1995, "Cong fangfa dao sixiang," 79–88.

59   Tang Yongtong, *Han Wei Liang Jin Nanbeichao Fojiao shi*, 1983, 451 & 475. Also see Tang's "Xie Lingyun bianzong lun shu hou" where he emphasizes Zhu Daosheng's pivotal role in the transformation of Buddhism. *Tang Yongtong xueshu lunwen ji*, 1983, 293–294. As Tang says, "ever since Master Zhu Daosheng, people who wanted to surpass the mundane and reach sainthood had no need to seek afar—it was right here and now. As a result, the study of the profound and subtle (Buddhism) took a new turn. Although it was a long period of time from Chan Buddhism to Song Neo-Confucianism, Master Daosheng's new interpretation nevertheless was the crucial key to this transformation."

2.6

According to the "Letters and Scholarship" chapter of the *New Account of Tales of the World*, "once when Yin Hao examined a Buddhist sûtra, he remarked 'The Truth (*li* 理) should be in this.' "[60] After that, in his "Debating the Way to the True Buddha Nature" (Bian zong lun), Xie Lingyun wrote that "We Chinese (Huaren) can easily discern truth (*li*), but are not so ready to accept religious teaching. Therefore we block their path to gradual learning, but open their way to sudden enlightenment. Barbarian people very readily accept religious teaching but have difficulty discerning truth (*li*). Therefore we block their way to sudden enlightenment, but open their path to gradual learning."[61] Yin Hao and Xie Lingyu were the two Chinese scholars from the fourth to the first half of the fifth centuries who were willing to study Buddhism most diligently. They both mention *li*. Just what exactly was this Truth of Buddhism that attracted them?

The *New Account of Tales of the World* records the following quite emblematic passage: "Yu Liang (289–340) once entered a stupa, and seeing there a representation of the reclining Buddha, remarked, 'This man's tired after all the ferrying and bridging of sentient beings to salvation.' At the time it was considered a famous remark."[62] What Yu meant was that the Buddha was overly exhausted from saving the world; he regarded Buddhism as "ferrying and bridging" sentient beings across the sea of bitterness (worldly suffering). That this humorous comment was acclaimed by the upper stratum of Chinese society demonstrates that the Chinese cultural elite did not much accept worldly Buddhist religious practices. They were more interested in Buddhism's profound philosophical thinking and the understanding of human life it produced. In general, the Chinese intellectual elite did not like methods of salvation that reeked too strongly of religion, nor did they like methods of cultivation that relied on "gods" for salvation. By contrast, they welcomed the self-realization of Truth achieve through the efforts of one's own mind or consciousness and the comprehension of the transcendent realm produced thereby. On this account, they could not help being rather cool to the Buddhist "religion," but quite interested in the Truth (*li*) of Buddhism.

---

60   SSXYJJ, j. shang, 116. Mather, *Shi-shuo Hsin-yü*, "Letters and Scholarship" #23, 104. Mather's "Truth" is usually reason or principle in Chinese philosophy. Mather's *a che* (= *a zhe*) for 阿堵 is omitted.

61   *Guang Hong ming ji*, SBBY, j. 20, 169.

62   SSXYJJ, j. shang, "Yanyu di er," 56. Mather, *Shi-shuo Hsin-yü*, "Speech and Conversation," #41, 51. Mather comments that this may be the earliest Chinese literary reference to the *parinirvâna*, final extinction, death of the Buddha scene. According to the *Mahânibbâna-sûtra*, quoted by Mather, "The Tathâgata, bearing his pain, lay between the twin Sâla trees, with his head to the north."

Daosheng once said that among the most profound and subtle Buddhist states there is one that can be comprehended by means of the experience of Shûnyatâ, but ordinary people usually cannot do so. If a person was able to understand and comprehend it, then he would transcend the boundary of thought and language and achieve genuine and complete *prajñâ* (wisdom). Such a person would naturally enter *nirvâna*.[63] What Yin Hao meant by Buddhist *li* was not the religion that relied on rules and commandments to restrain its believers, or on rituals and techniques to demonstrate miraculous powers and promised salvation. It was rather a philosophical theory that penetrated the phenomenal world of concrete experience and directly manifested absolute philosophic principles. What Xie Lingyun meant by the *li* that the Chinese elite found attractive was also a philosophical theory that transcended the rules, ceremonies, methods and techniques of the Buddhist religion. He believed that non-Chinese peoples were unable to understand philosophical theories and could only rely on religious commandments to restrain themselves and on external powers—miraculous forces—to save them. The path from this shore to the other is of course a long and arduous one, but those Chinese scholar officials who were able to understand the Buddhist philosophy could, however, become suddenly enlightened by this *li* and, in the blink of an eye, rise in transcendence to the ultimate Buddhist state. Of course there was a certain amount of ethnic conceit and prejudice toward non-Chinese peoples in this idea, but from this value-ladened discussion, we can also see the interest that the Chinese intellectual elite had in Buddhism. Their sort of interest had a great influence on Chinese Buddhism's direction of development.

3.   Buddhist Conquest of China?

In Chinese intellectual history, the period from the fifth to the seventh centuries has generally been seen as a historical process of disputation, competition and intermingling between Confucianism, Daoism and Buddhism. During this process, each of these three thought tides in the Chinese intellectual world strove to carve out its own niche, and also absorbed some "heretical" ideas. It gradually became fashionable to discuss Buddhist principles and Daoist mysteries together, and a considerable number of people believed in these two doctrines simultaneously. It would seem that some literati had already

---

63   "Jingming jie," and "Dizi pin," in *Zhu Weimojie jing* quoted from *Zhongguo Fojiao sixiang ziliao xuanbian*, 1981–1990, j. 1, 204 & 206.

combined Buddhist and Daoist beliefs and practices and they could even accept Confucian thought and ideas into this syncretic mix.

The intermingling of thought and culture was not necessarily always very straightforward. In the first stage, when foreign knowledge, thought and belief entered China on a superficial level, they did not directly give rise to resistance. Later on, constant provocation and friction with this foreign knowledge, thought and belief stirred up some latent native Chinese thought and brought it into conflict with its foreign counterparts. This seems to be a common occurrence in intellectual history, and the entrance of Buddhism into China was no exception. Under pressure from Buddhism, some Chinese ideas were transformed from unconscious everyday taken-for-granted truths into subjects that required argumentation and demonstration. At that point they entered the purview of intellectual history. These subjects included, for example the legitimacy of secular power during a period of great expansion of religious strength and influence, the question of the value of traditional morality within a new religious belief, the permanence of Chinese civilization under the increasingly powerful impact of surrounding peoples, and so on. Within the scope of intellectual history, I want to summarize the conflicts that arose after the entrance of Buddhism into China by asking three questions: within the particular context of ancient Chinese civilization, (1) could religious communities coexist with the secular state power and also maintain their independence? (2) could religious beliefs take absolute priority over secular social rules of morality and ethical beliefs? (3) could religious ideals eliminate the distinctive character of an ethnic culture (*minzu wenhua*) and acquire universal significance?

3.1

First, could religious organizations coexist with the secular state power and also maintain their independent existence? This would be very difficult in ancient China. The *Book of Songs* (Mao 205) says that "Of all the land under Heaven, there is none that is not the king's land." This idea was already considered an indisputable truth in ancient China at that time, and was also regarded as a self-evident principle among the broad masses. As the symbol of the state, the emperor's Heaven-bequeathed power and authority reigned supreme over everything; this, too, was a self-evident truth in ancient China, and no one would dispute it. This changed when Buddhism came in from an alien land bringing with it the Indian and Central Asian ideas of religious organizations protecting their believers and helping them escape from control by the state.

This posture of competing for equal standing (*fenting kangli*) between religious and secular powers gave rise to a fierce response from the Chinese intellectual world, and first from the Chinese political world. Both the conflict in the mid-fourth century between the officials Yu Bing (296–344) and He Chong (292–346), a Buddhist, and that in the early fifth century between General Huan Xuan (369–404), representing the state, and the official Wang Mi (360–408) demonstrate the prominence given to the consciousness of secular authority—state power—under provocation from Buddhism.[64] There were especially fierce polemics after Huiyuan's celebrated essay, "A Monk Does Not Bow Down to a King" (Shamen bujing wangzhe lun) in which he asserted that at home secular people should respect the laws and the ruler, but Buddhists who have left home to become monks or nuns can "escape the world" and "transform conventions"—that is, they can transcend the control of the secular political powers.[65]

Yu Bing and Huan Xuan made the following three points: (1) the status system of secular society was of very long standing and was therefore an absolutely reasonable, correct and unalterable principle, (2) the emperor as symbol of the state had the same absolute power and authority as Heaven and Earth, and (3) the dignity and authority of the emperor were guarantors of social order; if they were challenged, it would lead to chaos. Originally these ideas did not posses any self-evident rationality, but they had never been challenged in ancient China and no one dared to doubt their foundations. Since these foundational principles could not be doubted, the Buddhist responses seem quite weak to us today. In He Chong's response to Yu Bing, he could only re-emphasize the history of policies that protected Buddhism in China, while Wang Mi's response to Huan Xuan could only say that Buddhism followed "different customs from a different land." It was with such difficulties that they finally managed to introduce some doubt about the history of ceremonial deference to the secular ruler, and yet they then hastily admitted the natural reasonableness of the secular status system. He Chong repeatedly asserted that Buddhism was beneficial for imperial power and moral transformation and that when the monks burned incense and prayed they first had the state uppermost in their minds, while Wang Mi defended Buddhism by arguing that although the *sangha* (community of monks and nuns) did not follow the ceremonies toward the emperor, in their hearts they were still sincerely loyal

---

64   See He Cong, "Zou shamen buying jinjing biao," Yu Bing, "Dai Jin Chengdi shamen buying jinjing zhao," and Huan Xuan, "Yu bazuo lun shamen jingshi shu," in *Hong ming ji*, j. 12, 101–102.

65   See Huiyuan, "Shamen bujing wangzhe lun," *Hong ming ji*, j. 5, 42. Some translations are in De Bary and Bloom, *Sources*, 426–429. At the end of the fourth century, Huan Xuan forced many members of the Buddhist *sangha* to return to secular life. He excepted only those who were learned in the scriptures, followed monastic discipline, live in the monasteries and did not interfere in secular life.

to the throne.[66] Huiyuan could do no more than repeat these arguments that Buddhism was of assistance to secular rule, but the more profound reasons for the conflict between Buddhism and the secular order was never openly and directly expressed.

In his "A Monk Does Not Bow Down to a King," "Letter in Answer to Commander Huan Da Huan" (Da Huan taiwei shu), and other essays, Huiyuan made the following statement four times: "The accumulation of successes or calamities is caused by having a body; if the body did not exist, calamities would cease; you should know that birth and rebirth are due to the transformations of your original endowment; in order to seek the basic principles (truths) of our religion you should not follow these transformations."[67]

This argument finally touches upon the real foundation of the relationship between Buddhism and the secular order. If you accept that the origin of the cosmos and human life is Shûnyatâ (emptiness), then humanity's present existence is without value and the contemporary social order is also meaningless. If you accept that human existence is a form of suffering in a process of causes and effects, then parental love, family, feelings and the ruler's virtue of good government all lack self-evident reasonableness. Why, then, should anyone respect the order and rituals of secular society? In ancient China, however, the reasonableness of the social order had already been validated by history and tradition. Just as Dao-an said: "if we do not rely on the ruler, then it will be difficult to establish our *dharma* (teaching)."[68] In its relations with the secular authorities Buddhism had to give way in the face of superior power,[69] and statements like those of Huiyuan above could only appear in sporadic discussions.

On the government's side, there was still another important point to be made. It is that due to Buddhist religious communities' attraction and control of their believers, Buddhism had already harmed the interests of the secular

---

66 See *Hong ming ji*, j. 12, 101–102 for these arguments.
67 See "Chujia er," "Qiuzong bushun hua san," "Da He zhennan," and "Da Huan taiwei shu," in "Shamen bujing wangzhe lun," *Hong ming ji*, j. 5 & 12, 42, 44, & 106.
68 *Gaoseng zhuan*, j. 5, "Dao-an zhuan," Tang Yongtong edited edition, 1992, 178.
69 Right at the beginning of the fifth century, when Huan Xua and Huiyuan were holding firmly to their different positions in their polemic about whether or not the Buddhist *sangha* had to bow in respect to secular power, in the north the monk Faguo had already changed his position and acknowledged the supremacy of secular power and authority. He is reported to have said that Emperor Daowu of the Northern Wei (371–409) "is the Tathâgata (Buddha) of the present time, and monks should show him every respect ... [and], the ruler is the one who is capable of broadening the Way (*hongdao*) and so I am not worshipping the Son of Heaven but merely paying my respects to the Buddha." *Weishu*, j. 114, "Shi Lao zhi," 3031. In *Lunyu* 15.29, we read "The Master said, 'It is Man who is capable of broadening the Way (*hongdao*). It is not the Way that is capable of broadening Man.'" Lau, *Analects*, 136.

authorities. As these Buddhist communities expanded, they easily began to contend with the secular government in economic matters such as land ownership, labor and taxes. The great size of the Buddhist communities easily created a force that was antagonistic to secular political power. In Huan Xuan's last coercive order, he stated very clearly that due to the rise of Buddhism too many people were escaping from government administration and avoiding the payment of taxes to the state. At this point he had finally brought up the fundamental problem between secular power and Buddhism: Buddhism "was detrimental to governance."[70]

3.2

In a basic sense this was a question of whether or not the symbolic culture of Buddhism could have priority over the government that represented imperial power. From the point of view of its origin and development it was a question of whether or not the Indian tradition in which the Buddhist community attempted to transcend the caste system and establish an ideal religious world could be carried on in China.[71] Because they were wary of allowing their real considerations of practical interests to serve directly as the reasons for their confrontations, in their public disputations the two sides stuck to their own differing positions from first to last and pleaded their separate cases on the basis of ethics and morality.

Now we have to try to answer our second question: could religious beliefs take absolute priority over secular social rules of morality and ethical beliefs?

Naturally, due to the ethnic and religious differences between ancient China and India as well as their different social conditions and political systems, when entering China Indian Buddhism could not avoid China's indigenous ethics and morality. It could particularly not avoid the question of "filial piety"—ancient China's most fundamental ethical value. The Chinese were frequently unable to accept Buddhist ideas, especially the Buddhist concept of Shûnyatâ because they would destroy the ethical order and place the individual's spiritual transcendence above social responsibilities and familial affections. In the

---

70   "Yu liaoshu sha tai seng zhong jiao," *Hong ming ji,* j. 12, 107.
71   On this issue, see Kang Le, "Shamen bujing wangzhe lun—'bu wei bu gongjing ren shuofa'—ji xiangguan wenti." He says that "this should be regarded as a question of religious belief." In the first place, his analysis goes on, "Chinese society did not have the idea that religious authorities could come before secular government power, nor was there a ceremonial class perched at the apex of the social structure. The scholar-official class was at the top of the contemporary Chinese social structure, and the ruler (emperor) was above them all. For these reasons the Indian idea that "the monks do not bow in respect to secular officials (literally, non-Buddhists dressed in white rather than the Buddhist black)" faced a severe test, especially the resistance from Chinese ancestor worship and filial piety. *Xin shixue,* 7/3 (1996), 1–48.

ancient Chinese intellectual world, family and state were self-evident realities, and familial affections based on "filial piety" as their core value were nothing less than natural feelings. The sort of human nature that was established on the basis of these natural feelings was the foundation that maintained the normal order of the family and society. If this foundation was shaken, the entire social order would crumble.

The late second-century *Master Mou's Treatise on the Removal of Doubt* had already raised some ancient Chinese doubts about this aspect of Buddhist thought. People said that because the monks shaved their heads, abandoned wives and children and did not practice the ritual kowtow they violated the *Classic of Filial Piety* dictum that "we receive our bodies, hair and skin from our parents and we dare not harm them;" they did not act in accord with the behavior of filial sons, not to mention violating the code of ritual costumes and official ornaments.[72] From the second to the seventh century, Chinese doubts about these issues never ceased, and the ways of posing the questions and the points of view hardly changed throughout that entire five centuries. Sun Chuo's "Explaining the Confucian Way" (Yudao lun), from the 370s, quoted the questions of his contemporaries that maintained many of the usual ideas: Confucianism is founded on filial piety, but Buddhism incites people to betray family feelings, damage their bodies, abandon their blood relations; in short to "turn their backs on reason and destroy proper feelings.[73] The Daoist-inspired "On the Three Destructions" (Sanpo lun), quoted and refuted in Liu Xie (ca. 465–ca. 522)'s early sixth-century "On Dispelling Confusion" (Miehuo lun) continued to assert that Buddhism "Enters the family and destroys the family, causes fathers and sons to disagree about affairs, and elder and younger brother to hold different views, and abandon their parents."[74] Opponents of Buddhism continued to cite these reasons in the seventh century. They said that they had never seen "a state survive when its officials and people lost all sense of propriety" nor had they seen "a family able to establish itself when its sons and grandsons were not filial." Such behavior belonged to the customs of the barbarians (*yidi*), and Buddhism was attempting to make Chinese people "dress like the barbarians and recite barbarian words.[75]

Buddhism could originally have responded directly to this ancient Chinese idea that kinship feelings represented man's natural nature and possessed absolute significance because in Indian Buddhism the kindness of parents and the nurture of descendants was really not so absolute. When Indian Buddhism demanded that people leave home to become monks or nuns, it was placing

---

72   *Hong ming ji*, j. 1, 8–9.
73   *Hong ming ji*, j. 3, 29.
74   *Ibid.*, j. 8, 67.
75   *Guang Hong ming ji*, j. 14, "Jiu zhen pian," 116.

the value of religious belief above that of secular family feelings. The prince Siddhartha Gautama, later the Buddha, leaving both his home and his state is symbolic of this. For the ancient Chinese, however, this was obviously unthinkable. If a man was not filial to his parents and brought disgrace upon his closest relatives, according to ancient Chinese thinking he could not be truly loyal to his sovereign and the state. By contrast, being filial toward his parents was a man's highest form of good behavior, more important than religious faith and devout religious practice.[76] In a conversation with Confucius, his disciple Youzi said "Is not being filial as a son and respectful to one's elders the root of humanity?"[77] This "filial piety" (*xiao* 孝) did not just constitute the order of family and lineage, but it was extended to include "loyalty" (*zhong* 忠) to the state and was regarded as the foundation of the ancient Chinese social order.

These deep-rooted traditional Chinese ethical principles already had a very long history and made up an entire system of familiar rules and customs. Buddhism only entered China on a big scale in the second and third centuries and could not directly resist these ethical principles the Chinese people considered to be correct and unalterable. Buddhists could only use roundabout methods to defend the sacredness of their religion. *Master Mou's Treatise on the Removal of Doubt* made every effort to explain that Buddhist monks shaving their heads, abandoning their wives and children and not practicing the kowtow ritual were really not unfilial and lacking in propriety. They were, rather, seeking a higher realm of being and a purer, more genuine morality for the age. The behavior of the Buddhist *sangha* was said to be in accord with the ancient Chinese simplicity and honesty of non-action. Under the premise of "filial piety" Sun Chuo's "Explaining the Confucian Way" sought to portray Siddhartha Gautama's leaving home as benefiting his father the king and their state by bestowing upon them greater glory and achievement. Similarly Liu Xie's "On Dispelling Confusion" (Miehuo lun) compared the Buddha to China's legendary Three August Sovereigns (*san huang*) and proposed that the Buddha's "lack of mourning clothes" (*wufu* 無服) was the same as the unsophisticated simplicity of the Three August Sovereigns. He portrayed the Buddha in a Daoist fashion as one who "abandoned the vulgar world and returned to the true Way." There were few people who dared to say, as Zong Bing did, that "what the vulgar Confucian scholars write is concentrated merely on the realm of governance" and that the Buddhist scriptures are superior to the thought of the Confucian and Daoist classics.[78]

---

76   *Shi song lü*, j. 52, *Taishô*, j. 23, 381.
77   *Lunyu*, 1.2, SSJZS, 2457.
78   *Hong ming ji*, j. 2, Zong Bing, *Ming Fo lun*, 17.

In the final analysis, most Buddhists could not directly reject ancient China's traditional secular morality. They could only employ roundabout methods like recognizing the reasonableness of both Chinese morality and Buddhist precepts. They even had to quote the words of the ancient Chinese sages and worthies and employ comparisons and analogies with ancient China's traditional morality to affirm Buddhist beliefs. Consequently, even though the Buddhist faith was acknowledged by the Chinese intellectual world, its reasonableness was established on a foundation of ancient Chinese Confucian ethics and morality.[79]

3.3

The question of whether universal religious ideals could transcend narrow ethnic nationalism deserves further discussion. Why should Buddhism, a religion from India, have to have its reasonableness established on a foundation of ancient Chinese Confucian ethics and morality? From the ethnic nationalist standpoint of the anti-Buddhist Chinese people of that time it was self-evidently legitimate to criticize strongly and even vilify Buddhism. What was the basis of this legitimacy, and how would Buddhism, as an alien religion, deal with the criticisms based upon it? This leads us to a discussion of our third question above. That is, under ancient Chinese conditions, could religious ideals eliminate the distinctive character of an ethnic culture and acquire universal significance?

The fierce and even somewhat excessive nationalist sentiments of that time were aroused and much increased by Buddhism after it entered China in force. In the 570s when Emperor Wu of the Northern Zhou set out to eliminate Buddhism, the Daoist priest Yan Da (515–609) famously answered the emperor's questions by stating that between Daoism and Buddhism, Daoism was the host and Buddhism was the guest, and naturally the host was superior and the guest inferior. Buddhism should be driven back to India.[80] Fu Yi, the most fervent anti-Buddhist in the Tang dynasty, also made some comments that people commonly quoted: "within the gates of official households, they actually receive the evil teachings of bald headed men, in the teaching of Confucian scholars, they even talk about the demonic barbarians and their dissolute language."[81] These extreme statements were not, however, completely fair because the two sides in what contemporaries called the "debate

---

79 The gradual emergence of ideas of "filial Piety" in Chinese Buddhism has long been noted by scholars. For example, see Kenneth K. S. Ch'en, *The Chinese Transformation of Buddhism*, 1973, and Alan Cole, *Mothers and Sons in Chinese Buddhism*, 1998.

80 *Hun yuan sheng ji*, j. 8, *Daozang*, Dongshen bu (Spirit Grotto), pulu lei, yu 8, ce 17.

81 *Guang Hong ming ji*, j. 11, 89 cites Fu Yi's "Shang fei sheng Foseng biao."

on barbarians and Chinese" (*yi xia lun*) were obviously not equal. Centered on Chinese culture, the Chinese scholar officials proclaimed Chinese (Han) culture to be unquestionably superior. As Buddhism entered China, it could only assert the superiority of its religious beliefs with the precondition that it acknowledge the superiority of Chinese culture. It could not help but employ a kind of pluralistic attitude that regarded all things as equal, an internationalism in which all under Heaven are one family and historical examples from present reality or an imaginary ancient China to offset slightly the excessively strident Chinese sense of cultural superiority.

This Chinese sense of cultural superiority had a very long history. Ancient China had a very persistent idea that "all under Heaven" was a square continually extending outward with China at the center, and civilizations were ranked according to this spatial configuration. The closer to the center (closer to China), the higher the rank of a civilization; the farther away, the lower that rank. The ancient Chinese people firmly believed that Hua Xia (China) was the center of civilization, and that the non-Chinese people on four sides were born with a human nature different from that of the Chinese. This sort of human nature influenced social customs, and social customs in turn influenced human nature and could not be changed. After Buddhism entered China, the Chinese regarded it as a religion of the barbarians, and so Buddhism had to face this natural Chinese feeling of superiority. It could not take a strong position and assert the superiority of its own culture, but could only explain that all cultures under Heaven should be equal and therefore it was unreasonable to assert the absolute superiority of Chinese culture.

The Buddhist faithful continued to maintain this roundabout and gentle way of responding to Chinese cultural superiority. In the Eastern Jin, a Buddhist believer from a Chinese aristocratic family, Wang Min, wrote a very representative passage in a preface for the monk Srimitra (Boshi limi duolo). On the one hand, he first acknowledged the universal superiority of the ancient Chinese cultural values of "propriety, music, humanity, and yielding," while on the other hand tactfully emphasizing that non-Chinese peoples could also produce "outstanding individuals" and "preeminent talents" in accord with Chinese cultural traditions.[82] He employed this method of compromise in order to seek

---

82   The *Gaoseng zhuan* (j. 1, 31) records that "in the *Chunqiu* people of the Wu and Chu states are called *zi* (children or junior). The commentators believed that this was putting the Middle Kingdom first and the four barbarian last. Was this not because they were the descendants of the Three Dynasties, practiced different rituals and believed that the barbarians were greedy and lacking in humanity and polite yielding? However, the most outstanding individuals are sometimes born in one time and preeminent talents equal to them are sometimes born in other times. We know that Heaven creates heroic and great men (in any time). Why, then, would it wait for Hua or Rong to do so?"

the stamp of approval of Chinese cultural tradition for the Buddhist elite and scriptures.

After Huan Xuan, from the fifth to the seventh centuries, many Chinese scholar officials probably believed that religions that pay strict attention to discipline or commandments and believe in the mystical or miraculous were mainly designed for barbarian peoples, whereas a civilized state like China that was governed by rites and ceremonies had no need for such barbarian religions.[83] During the Liu Song era, He Chengtian (370–447) wrote that "Hua and Rong (non-Chinese) are naturally different" with the intention of separating Chinese human nature from non-Chinese (barbarian) human nature. In the final analysis, he simply wanted to forbid the spread of Buddhism in China.[84] Since it was being propagated in Chinese territory, Buddhism could not help acknowledging the superiority of Chinese civilization and the correctness of Chinese thought. Buddhists in China could only repeatedly emphasize that Buddhism and its homeland India were just as civilized as China, and so they collected various stories and legends to serve as historical evidence for this claim. For example, Zong Bing simply said that the books of a hundred generations have been lost, so how can you use only today's knowledge to judge that the Buddhist doctrines have no foundations? When Liu Xiang of the Han dynasty compiled his *Biographies of the Immortals* (Shenxian zhuan), Zong Bing asked, were not seventy-four of them also found in the Buddhist sûtras?[85] Zong also answered He Chengtian saying that "there may have been sages and worthies among the Eastern Yi and the Western Qiang (two non-Chinese peoples)." In his rebuttal of the Daoist Gu Huan (fl. 5th century)'s attack on Buddhism in Gu's "On Barbarians and Chinese" (*Yi Xia lun*), Xie Zhenzhi (fl. 460) also wrote that "under the rule of the three unified powers (*sancai* 三才, Heaven, Earth, Man), how can you separate Yi from Xia (non-Chinese from Chinese)?" At that he actually touched upon the universal nature of "humanity" (the human race) and "truth."[86]

---

83 Huan Xuan, "Nan Wang Zhongling," *Hong ming ji*, j. 12, 103.
84 *Hong ming ji*, j. 3, 27 contains He Chengtian's "Da Zong jushi shu."
85 "Ming Fo lun," *Hong ming ji*, j. 2, 20.
86 Zong Bing, "Da He Hengyang shu zhi er," *Hong ming ji*, j. 3, 27; Xie Zhenzhi, "Yu Gu daoshi shu xi *Yi Xia lun*," *Hong ming ji*, j. 6, 55. Many ancient Chinese do not seem to have accepted the idea that religious truth could transcend the universality of their ethnic nationality (*minzu*). This was especially so after the Daoist religion joined the polemic of barbarian versus Chinese. From then on, that argument changed from one about cultural superiority versus universal religious truth to disputations about the qualifications and history of Buddhism and the Daoist Religion. The Daoist-Buddhist polemics of the entire Six Dynasties, Sui and Tang eras brought to the fore the conflict between nationalist sentiments and the claims of religious universalism.

Not everyone, however, was willing to accept this universality of human nature and truth. In the second half of the fifth century, Shen Yue (441–513) attempted to argue in his "On the Equal Sacredness of the Two Teachings" (Jun sheng lun) that truth was eternal and universal in nature and should then transcend historical time and geographical space. Just because Buddhism came from the Western Regions and not from ancient China, Shen argued, it should not be regarded as lacking in value. Shen's arguments were refuted, however, by the Daoist Tao Hongjing.[87] During the Northern Zhou, Dao-an argued in his "On Rectifying the Two Teachings" (Zheng erjiao lun) that sages were not necessarily only born in China; India could also produce sages.[88] Although these Buddhist arguments made sense, not many people accepted them. Interestingly enough, even Emperor Wu of the Northern Zhou who was himself a Xianbei (Särbi), also believed that Buddhism was a foreign doctrine that was not needed in China. In an imperial edict of 578 he strongly defended Chinese cultural exclusivism. He argued that the Buddha was born in the Western Regions, and although his doctrines had been transmitted to China, on close examination they were unsuitable for China. In the Han, Wei, and Jin eras, Buddhism was only slightly known. It was not until the period of division when "the five barbarians created chaos in China" (wuhu luanhua) that Buddhism began to flourish. We are not barbarians and we certainly do not need to worship the Buddha. Therefore we should eliminate Buddhism.[89]

3.4

Chinese traditions placed an enormous pressure on Buddhism after it entered China. The first pressure was the coercive power of the secular regimes. The second was the pre-existing ways of understanding and interpretation common to the Chinese cultural area. Finally, there was the authority of the historical tradition to carry on Chinese culture. Buddhism could not change this cultural environment and its ways of thought, and so over a long period of time Chinese Buddhism itself was also transformed.

Buddhism did not originally need a long historical pedigree to validate its reasonableness. When this alien religion encountered the Chinese historical tradition of "reverence for antiquity," however, it leaned many times toward advocating a kind of attitude that "follows the present" to offset the formidable pressure of Chinese history and traditional customs. In China where everything had to be verified by history or have existed in the ancient past before

---

87   *Guang Hong ming ji*, j. 5, 43.
88   *Ibid.*, 68.
89   *Ibid.*, 82.

people would believe in it, having a long or a short history was related to, even determinative of, what was believed to be the high or low truth value of any ideas. As a result it was quite important for any doctrine to be supported by ancient texts and the authority of tradition. Chinese opponents of Buddhism repeatedly used Buddhism's supposed lack of a long history to attack the alien religion, and so Buddhism had no option but to employ its own form of historicism.[90] Buddhists were really not very good at this, but they searched out evidence of the historical beginning of Buddhism in ancient Chinese legends and historical records. They argued, for example, that the *Spring and Autumn Annals* recorded exceptional astronomical phenomena in the year of Gautama Buddha's birth, or that the Han Emperor Ming's dream of a golden man historicized the Buddha's birth. Such things were considered to be evidence that Buddhism had entered China very early on.[91] In its dialogue with Chinese tradition, Buddhism had unwittingly adopted Chinese habits of thought.

Buddhism also did not originally need to seek the foundation of its religious truth from the perspective of its geographical location, but from the Chinese point of view China was the center of the universe, and the significance of this spatial centrality was intimately related to the significant central position of its cultural values. The significance of Great China (Daxia Zhonghua 大夏中華) was not only that the Han Chinese people lived in the exact center of Heaven and Earth; it also implied that their culture was the only cultural system with universal values. To overcome this difficulty, Buddhism had to apply Chinese methods of disputation. Buddhists argued that not all alien people were demons and not all Chinese people were superior gentlemen; although the Buddha was born in the west, he could still become a Chinese Sage; Chinese history also had its share of terrible rulers, like Emperor Jie of the Xia and the First Emperor of the Qin; people did not become sages and worthies simply by being born in China.

These arguments should have been sufficient, but some Buddhists still slipped into the Chinese mode of thinking and brought the difference of centrality or marginality in geographic location together with the superior or inferior value of cultures. For example, Daoxuan (596–667) simply had to prove that China did not really occupy the center of Heaven and Earth, and besides "where there is Dao there is honor and it is not limited to the Chinese

---

90   For example, Gu Huan (5th–6th centuries) said the Daoist canons came from the Western Zhou, but the Buddhist scriptures only existed in the Eastern Han: "(Daoism) is more than 800 years old and has crossed tens of generations," Daoism should therefore take precedence over Buddhism. *Nanqi shu*, "Gao yi zhuan," j. 54, 933.

91   See *Guang Hong ming ji.*, j. 11, 90 for Falin (fl. 618)'s refutation of Fu Yi and j. 12, 105 for Shi Minggai's "Jin zou juepo Fu Yi bangfo huiseng shi batiao."

or the non-Chinese." He also very earnestly declared that since the Chinese people were limited to the area called Spiritual Continent (Shenzhou 神州, Zou Yan's name for China), they thought China was the center of the universe. By contrast, he said, the Buddha actually lived in the area called Jambudvîpa (*Yanfuzhou* 阎浮洲 or *Yanfuti* 閻浮提 "one of the seven continents" or "the central division of the world"). From the Buddha's (and Daoxuan's) point of view, China was on the margin and the true center of the world was in fact Tian Zhu 天竺, the Indian subcontinent. As he wrote, "Tian Zhu (India) is in the center of the earth. If you walk to the extreme north in the summer, you will cast no shadow. It is, indeed, the most important country between Heaven and Earth."[92]

The grounds that Buddhism relied on to maintain its independence in secular society and its search for spiritual transcendence came from its important teachings about human life. The first important Buddhist message about human life that we should consider is, of course, its doctrine of the immortality of the soul (*shen bumie*, "the soul is not annihilated"). According to Buddhist doctrine, when a person's physical body dies his or her intelligent spirit (*shenshi* 神識) or soul does not perish but is passed on like a flame from one piece firewood to another even though the original piece is burned up. This doctrine is meant to explain how humanity experiences continued transmigration (*samsâra*) through the six ways or conditions of sentient existence (*gati, liudao* 六道), but the soul is never extinguished and karmic retribution is accumulated from generation to generation. The significance for believing in Buddhism is to go beyond life and death and to reach the stage of *avaivartika* or *avinivartanîya* (*butuizhuan* 不退轉) in which they are never retreating but always making progress toward nirvana and out of the cycle of rebirth. During the era of the North-South Dynasties, there were heated debates about topics like "the soul is destroyed" versus "the immortality of the soul" and "not receiving retribution" versus "receiving retribution." He Chengtian, Zong Bing and Yan Yanzhi (384–456) of the Song, Fan Zhen (ca. 450–515), Cao Siwen (?–?), Xiao Chen (478–529), Emperor Wu of the Liang and others during the Liang all engaged in quite a few of these disputations. These discussions of the meaning of human life were generally rather superficial with those who argued that the spirit was destroyed regarding the soul as attached to the physical body while those who advocated the immortality of the soul regarded it as something mysterious and transcendent. The two sides became tangled up in symbolic tropes and historical texts, and used sharpness and a knife blade, fire and

---

92   For Jambudvîpa, see Soothill, *Dictionary*, under *Yanfuti* 閻浮提. *Guang Hong ming ji*, j. 6, "Bian huo pian di er zhi er," 48–49 and j. 11, "Bian huo pian di er zhi qi," 92.

firewood, the dreaming body and the soul as metaphors for form (body, *xing* 形) and spirit (*shen* 神).

The key point to these arguments was actually something else more practical. If the Buddhist doctrine concerning human life replaced that of ancient China, then the ancient Chinese traditional value system of seeking to establish one's virtue, meritorious deeds and writings (*lide, ligong, liyan*) would collapse. Furthermore things like kinship feelings, family ethics and social responsibilities that served as foundational criteria for Chinese values would also lose their significance. Why? Because human existence would become a meaningless mistake, morality, accomplishments and writings would all be as ephemeral and meaningless as clouds and smoke. There would also be no absolute distinction between moral nobility or wickedness and rational correctness or absurdity. Since they are all part of humanity's continued transmigration through the six ways or conditions of sentient existence, their results would really amount to the trivial difference between walking fifty paces or a hundred. Humanity's highest realm of being, then, would be found in transcending secular society and escaping both life and death. In this way, Buddhism would act as a powerful corrosive that would dissolve the basic Chinese way of being human and all the standards of the ancient Chinese philosophy of life and correct human behavior.

These polemics did not go on much deeper, and their goals soon became very concrete and practical. According to the participants themselves, those in favor of the doctrine of the annihilation of the soul only wanted to prevent "Buddhism from ruining government and monks poisoning popular customs," while those defending the immortality of the soul only did so because "The being or nonbeing of the Buddha depends upon the existence or elimination of the sacred doctrine"[93] The ultimate goals of these polemics had already moved to the conflicts between Buddhism and Chinese society, and they became mixed up with various elements of political necessity and economic interest. The difference between the two sides changed from a philosophic debate on the soul's annihilation or immortality to one about punishing evil and rewarding good in society. It would seem that the believers in the annihilation of the soul did not have to fear any karmic retribution, but the believers in the soul's immortality had to accept their karmic fate. The topic of debate no longer concerned the ancient Chinese philosophic principles of humanity's ultimate foundation, but entered rather the realm of ethics and social order. Especially when Emperor Wu of the Liang used his political power to engage directly in these discussions, they were no longer centered on a pure theory and their

---

93   Xiao Chen, "Nan shenmielun," *Hong ming ji,* j. 9, 76.

CHAPTER 6

conclusions no longer depended on firm grounds of justification or the correctness of a particular way of thinking. When those who conscientiously abided by Chinese tradition began to realize that this Buddhist doctrine did not undermine the foundations of traditional Chinese thought and that the existing Buddhist doctrines were only about providing grounds for believing in "karmic retribution" or "transmigration through the three worlds of being," the disputation very quickly moved to center on one very practical aspect: the straightforward question of the reincarnation of the soul.

Some things that really should have been discussed were not. India had quite a well developed cosmology and body of astronomical and geographical knowledge. Such knowledge formed the background of Buddhism and supported Buddhist thought, and this Indian conception of the universe and their descriptions of geography and astronomical phenomena were very different from those of ancient China. For example, the *mahâbhûta* (*sida* 四大)—four basic elements of which all things are made, or the four realms of earth, water, fire, and air; the *catur-dvîpa* (*sizhou* 四洲)—the four inhabited continents of every universe situated on the four sides of Mt. Sumeru; the cyclic destruction and rebirth of the cosmos after every eon or *kalpa* (*jie* 劫) and so on were all very different from the ancient Chinese concepts of history, Yin-Yang, Five Phases, nine continents, etc. Nevertheless, these differences never presented much of a challenge to the traditional Chinese views of these issues. This was because from the very beginning this Indian astronomical and geographical knowledge seems to have been incorporated into the Chinese context. For example, when the Liu Song monk Shi Huiyan answered He Chengtian's questions about what calendar system was in use in the Buddha land, he immediately transformed Indian astronomy and calendrical calculations into the Chinese format. It seems that only Sengyou (445–518), in his "Record of the World" (Shijie ji) collected discussions of the universe from Buddhist scriptures such as the *Dirghâgama-sûtra* (a collection of scriptures), the *Mahâ-vaipulya-buddhâvatamsaka-sûtra* (another name for the *Flower Garland Sutra*), the *Aggañña Sutta* (the 27th Sutta of *Digha Nikaya* collection of scriptures) and so on in an attempt to establish a Buddhist view of the cosmos that was different from the Chinese view and could support Buddhist thought. In his preface to this work, Sengyou fiercely challenged the Chinese intellectual world by stating that Chinese society reverenced Confucius and the Duke of Zhou and followed the Confucian classics, but only speculated about the cosmos; on the surface they worshipped Heaven, but in reality they did not understand Heaven at all.

This Indian cosmological, astronomical and geographical knowledge and thought received a rather indifferent response in China. The ancient Chinese believed in their own astronomy with its long history, its correspondence with what they could see and its ordered regularity; they also believed in the geography of the Great Earth that was described in their own ancient texts, clearly divided, well-ordered and corresponding to their psychology; and finally they believed in the cosmic order implied by this body of knowledge.[94] Based upon this astronomical and geographical knowledge, the Chinese intellectual world continued to believe that "Heaven does not change and neither does the Way."

3.5

From the first White Horse Temple in Luoyang to the Jianchu Temple in Jiankang (Nanjing), the Eternal Peace Temple in the north and the Dinglin Temple in the south, the area served by the Buddhist religion continued to expand after the fifth century. The canon of Buddhist scriptures was steadily completed, the organizational rules for the *sangha* were fixed and their ceremonial rules were also finalized.[95] In the three following centuries Buddhism was widely propagated throughout China while, at the same time, it also blended in with the worlds of Chinese daily life and thought. Let me give a few examples.

First off, it is easy to see that not only were many types of Buddhist sûtras translated into Chinese but those texts that corresponded with Chinese values were particularly chosen for translation. Later on, apocryphal Buddhist texts began to be fabricated. If we look at the increasingly popular *Sûtra of Golden Light* (Suvarnaprabhâsottamarâja-sûtram) and the *Benevolent King Sûtra* (Renwang boruo jing; "Benevolent king" referring either to the Buddha or to other Indian kings), and see that they advocate that the king and officials protect the *dharma* while Buddhism protects the state, we can understand the process by which the Buddhist religion in China gradually submitted to the state and accepted the mainstream ideology. By this time Buddhism had already closed the deep gap that once existed between its doctrines and the ethics of ancient Chinese society. In the admonitions in the supposed Chinese Buddhist apocrypha *Fanwang (Brahmajâla)-sûtra* and in the *Kindness of Parents Sûtra* (Fumu enzhong jing) and the apocryphal *Lake of Blood Sûtra* (Xuepen jing)

---

94   In the preface to the second edition of his *Buddhist Conquest of China*, 1972, xi, Erik Zürcher also noted this. He writes that "around 400 AD we find the beginning of what might be called 'Chinese Buddhist sub-culture', notably in the field of cosmology, cosmography, and ideas concerning the physical world. It marked the beginning of a remarkable dichotomy in Chinese proto-science:...This process of cultural transplantation, in which a large complex of foreign ideas was borrowed *in isolation*, without in any degree influencing the 'official' world-view (as e.g. represented in the early Chinese encyclopedias), reached its highest point in Tang times."

95   *Gaoseng zhuan*, j. 1, 13, *"Tankejiluo zhuan* (Biography of Dharmakâla, fl. 250)," says that Chinese monastic discipline and commandments started here."

of unknown provenance, the gap between Buddhist and Chinese ethics had already virtually disappeared.[96]

Secondly, and not so easily noticed, in the realm of what in ancient China were regarded as daily life techniques like the arts of healing, divination, horoscopes and so on, Buddhism had already blended in with Chinese traditions. This not only imperceptibly transformed the Chinese world of conceptual knowledge but also continued the transformation of Buddhism itself. For example, Indian astronomical and calendrical knowledge came into China with Buddhism and was quite in harmony with traditional Chinese astrological divination by the stars and calendar-making. We can clearly discern this phenomenon if we compare the sections on astronomy and calendrical science in the "Bibliography" (Jingji zhi) of the Tang dynasty *History of the Sui Dynasty* with the material copied out in the *Treatise on Astrology of the Kaiyuan Era* (Kaiyuan zhanjing) compiled by Gautama Siddha (fl. early 8th century).

Indian medical knowledge and techniques also came into China with Buddhism. They were already recorded in the *Prescriptions of Nâgârjuna* (Longshu pusa yaofang) and the *Prescriptions of the Brahmans* (Poluomen zhuxian yaofang) before the seventh century and in books on mantic and medical arts written by Buddhist monks. From these works, we can see that Chinese traditional mantic and medical arts were blended into similar Indian knowledge and absorbed the Brahmanic and Buddhist massage and meditation techniques while Buddhism accepted Chinese mantic and medical practices such as ingesting drugs, Daoist breathing exercises, arts of the bedchamber and so on. After Buddhist theurgy entered China it's techniques also started to combine with Chinese supernatural arts and grew into popular methods for saving people from various difficulties. Buddhist and Chinese incantations and curses were mixed together, and even the Chinese use of talismanic charms was absorbed by Buddhism.

A third thing that has been remarked upon but not very thoroughly studied is the production of various suspicious or apocryphal texts between the fifth and seventh centuries that demonstrates both the blending in of Buddhist thought in China and contemporary Chinese interpretations of Buddhist doctrines. The above mentioned *Kindness of Parents Sûtra* and its discussions of "filial piety" is an example of these texts as are the *Trapusa-Bhallika-sûtra* (Trapusa and Bhallika were merchants said to be the first two disciples of the Buddha) and the *Sûtra on the Examination of Good and* Evil. According to the research of French scholars, the latter works "reflected the popular

---

96   See De Bary and Bloom, *Sources*, 1999, 429–432 for some admonitions from the
        Fanwang-sûtra.

face of Buddhism in the late fifth and early sixth centuries and presented a general summary of the contemporary mixture of monastic Buddhism and popular Buddhist practices." The appearance of such works also clearly demonstrated Buddhist reception and transformation of traditional Chinese knowledge and techniques.[97] Even more importantly are those suspicious or truly apocryphal texts such as the *Diamond Sutra* ("Vajra Cutter Perfection of Wisdom sûtra" or Vajracchedikâ Prajñâpâramitā-sûtra), the *Awakening of Faith in the Mahâyâna* (Mahâyâna Sraddhotpâda-sâstra), about which controversies still persist, and the slightly later *Sûrangama-sûtra* (Da Fo dingshou lengyan jing). It is just these sûtras that more broadly manifest the transformation of basic doctrines of Indian Buddhism in the Chinese context and the new understandings and interpretations of Buddhism by Chinese believers in terms of their own cultural background. Just as Ono Genmyo wrote, in the Tang and Sui dynasties these suspicious or apocryphal texts were very popular and "although these suspicious or apocryphal texts are not true Buddhist classics—mixing up different kinds of thought, and even appropriating things deliberately fabricated by lay believers—nevertheless from a dispassionate and objective scholarly position, we can say that they still constitute very useful research materials rich in implications and significance.[98]

3.6

Buddhism gradually became universal as the sixth century began, and the Chinese understanding of it grew much deeper. Various different understandings and interpretations emerged, each one favoring a particular Buddhist scripture. With different texts there were different interpretations, different background sources and trains of thought. All this gave rise to several different orientations, some of which formed schools of thought, and some of which grew into Buddhist communities that followed definite traditions passed down from particular masters to groups of disciples.

In the north the Dasabhûmikâ School masters used the *Dasabhûmikâ-sûtra*, the "Ten Stages" chapter (*Shidipin* 十地品) in the *Flower Garland Sûtra* as their central text. They concentrated on Vasubandhu (fl. 4th century)'s commentaries and discussed things like the idea that the "triple world is but one mind" and the "eight *parijñâna*, or forms of consciousness."[99] The Samgraha School

---

97 Guo Li-ying, "Zhongguo Fojiao zhong de zhanbu youxi he qingjing—Hanwen weijing *Zhangchajing* yanjiu," a Chinese translation in *Faguo Hanxue* 2 (1997), 193–223.
98 See *Fojiao jingdian zonglun*, part two, chapter five, "Luwai jingdian kao," in *Bussho kaisetsu daijiten (Foshu jieshuo da cidian)*, vol. 11, 1981, 448.
99 The "triple world" is in a verse in the *Flower Garland Sutra*: "outside mind there is no other thing; mind, Buddha, and all the living, these three are not different." Soothill, *Dictionary*, 71.

masters in the south used Asanga's *Mahâyâna Compendium* (Mahâyâna-samgraha, She dacheng lun) as their central text. During the Chen dynasty of the Southern Dynasties, Paramârtha (499–569) wrote a commentary on this text, and, during the Sui dynasty, Tan Qian (542–607) came to the capital Chang-an where he lectured and also wrote a commentary on the Indian Yogâcâra School's consciousness only theories. Different styles of Buddhist thought grew up in the north and the south. Besides these, there was also a group of Buddhists whose central texts were the *Hundredfold Treatise*, the *Middle Treatise*, and the *Treatise of the Twelvefold Division* and who were later called the Mâdhyamika or Middle School. There was also the Tiantai School that was based on the *Lotus Sûtra*. Finally, two major schools of Buddhism arose, one based on the *Flower Garland Sutra* and the other based on the *Lankâvatâra-sûtra*; they later formed the Huayan School and the Chan School. All of this clearly demonstrates that Chinese Buddhism had begun to depart from its Indian origins and go its own way.

The path of Chinese Buddhism was, however, always conditioned and restricted by Chinese politics, government, society and ideas. As an example, in 574 Emperor Wu of the Northern Zhou ordered the abolition of both Buddhism and the Daoist religion and set up a Temple of the Comprehensive Way (Tong Dao guan 通道觀) in Chang-an. There he assembled one hundred and twenty literati with backgrounds in Confucian, Daoist and Buddhist thought. This Temple of the Comprehensive Way lasted until the end of the dynasty and was the one and only cultural organization in Chinese history that combined the "three teachings" into one institution. The name of this institution, Comprehensive Way (Tong Dao), aptly symbolized the gradual tendency toward the fusion of the thought of Buddhism, Confucianism and the Daoist religion under absolute imperial rule from the fifth to the seventh centuries.

In 1957 Eric Zürcher gave his history of early Buddhism in China the title *The Buddhist Conquest of China*, but in 1973, Kenneth K. S. Chen entitled his textbook on the relations between Buddhism and Chinese society the *Chinese Transformation of Buddhism*. My view is more in line with the latter interpretation of events. The course of Chinese intellectual history from the fifth to the seventh centuries does not seem to have confirmed the Buddhist conquest of China, but rather to have witnessed a transformation of Buddhist thought under the influence of Chinese culture. Buddhism underwent a quiet shift in the three aspects of the relations between (1) the Buddhist community and secular power, (2) Buddhist commandments and monastic discipline and social morality and ethics, and (3) the essential spirit of Buddhism and ethnic Han Chinese nationalism. As noted above, to survive in the area of Chinese culture with its long historical tradition of civilization, Buddhism could not help but adjust to Chinese ways. In seventh-century China, then, Buddhism was already quite well blended in with the Chinese intellectual world, and Buddhist thought had also become considerably Sinicized.

4.   Basic Outline of the Mainstream World of Knowledge and Thought
        in the Seventh Century

It is a formidable task to describe the overall intellectual situation of an entire age, especially one that experienced as dramatic a series of changes as occurred in seventh-century China. There is, however, one way to do this, and that is by examining contemporary books or library catalogues, encyclopedic *leishu* materials arranged according to subject and commentaries on the classic texts. From these we can map out the general contours of the contemporary intellectual world. Most ancient Chinese knowledge and thought was recorded in texts that were mainly stored in government collections or libraries, and their holdings were recorded in various catalogues. By perusing these catalogues, we can judge the general scope of contemporary knowledge and reading as well as gain a sense of contemporary intellectual interests. Ancient Chinese *leishu* encyclopedias collected together as many texts as contemporary people could locate and arranged them according to various subject categories so the collection was similar to a modern encyclopedia. This *leishu* format was, then, a direct presentation of literary materials that allow us to glimpse contemporary attitudes toward the intellectual categories laid out in front of us. The categories exactly constituted the intellectual order of the era. Owing to their interpretations of the classic texts, the annotations and commentaries undoubtedly represent the contemporary understanding of most authoritative knowledge and thought. In ancient China most educated people received their first instruction in these classic texts; their first knowledge was derived from them. The commentaries on the classics read from childhood on provided an abundance of knowledge and thought while at the same time relying on the authority of the classic texts imperceptibly to set the reasonable boundaries of that knowledge and thought.

The compilation of the *Collection of Literature Arranged by Categories* (Yiwen leiju) was completed in 624; the manuscript of *The Exact Meaning of the Five Classics* (Wujing zhengyi) was finalized in 642; the *History of the Sui Dynasty* "Bibliographical Treatise" (Suishu, Jingji zhi) was completed in 656. All of these large-scale *leishu* and collected commentaries were produced in the middle of the seventh century. The appearance of these literary materials was the result of the tendencies toward intellectual fusion, thorough understanding and summing-up that characterized that age; they are also materials for the description of the intellectual world of the time.

4.1

If we regard the "Monograph of Arts and Letters" bibliographic section of the *History of the Former Han Dynasty* as an evaluation of the basic texts of Chinese thought between the Eastern and Western Han, and the "Bibliographical Treatise" (Jingji zhi) of *History of the Sui Dynasty* as an evaluation of such basic texts at the beginning of the Tang dynasty, we can discern three things about the Chinese intellectual world: its growth, harmonization and change.[100] First, the *History of the Former Han Dynasty* "Monograph of Arts and Letters" records 13,269 *juan*, while the *History of the Sui Dynasty* "Bibliographical Treatise" records 36,708 *juan* or 2.8 times as many. The quantity of textual production in the Chinese intellectual world had certainly increased a great deal in the previous five hundred years. Second, from the various categories of knowledge recorded in these bibliographies, we can see that Chinese knowledge and thought had undergone a considerable change. Having become a large country, the records naturally demonstrate that the search for historical foundations and the classical texts of previous generations had become a tradition itself. Furthermore, although the knowledge of mantic and medical arts had flourished and grown even more developed for a while, conceptually speaking these ideas were being constantly marginalized and were held in a state of dormancy by the mainstream cultural elite. By contrast knowledge of literature and history—what today is known as "humanistic knowledge" or "the humanities"—increasingly moved to center stage and became the mainstream thought of the Chinese intellectual world. Third, the fact that the quantity of Buddhist and Daoist texts was now quite large demonstrates that in the intervening centuries Buddhism and the Daoist religion had already grown so fast that they formed two of the three legs of the great tripod of traditional Chinese thought and knowledge, thus effectively transforming the structure of ancient Chinese thought. Finally, from the works and authors recorded in the *History of the Sui Dynasty* "Bibliographical Treatise", we can see the traces of mutual penetration and influence in many areas of thought and knowledge. To give a couple of examples: (1) in mainstream classical studies after the Sui-Tang reunification, northern traditional approaches and new changes in southern studies mutually influenced and alternated with each other, and (2) in the medical and mantic knowledge and techniques employed in practical everyday life,

---

100   See Zhu Yiming, "Xiancun liangbu zuigu de tushu mulu," *Wenshi zhishi* 7 (1982), 53–57, on the changes that took place from the *Hanshu* to the *Suishu* bibliographies.

Buddhism brought with it a great deal of Indian knowledge and techniques that blended quite easily into the world of Chinese knowledge.

4.2

Using the form and categorization of the *leishu* to discuss the outline of the mainstream intellectual world in the seventh century, we will primarily rely on the *Collection of Literature Arranged by Categories*.[101]

Because I am writing intellectual history here, I have to be concerned with the integration and standardization (or regularization) of knowledge and thought, their order of presentation as derived from the principles of *leishu* categorization as well as how much literary material that can be used as intellectual resources is actually provided in the works collected and catalogued. Compiled in 624 under Emperor Gaozu of the Tang, the *Collection of Literature Arranged by Categories* assembled together all of the currently available texts and arranged them under a number of intellectual categories, establishing a huge library of knowledge up to the seventh century. The knowledge presented in this library was divided into the categories of Heaven (including seasons of the year), Earth (including prefects, counties, mountains and rivers), the human realm (including rites, music, official positions, penal law, habitations, clothing, boats and carriages, foodstuffs, etc.), Buddhism, Daoism and the ten thousand things (of the material world). We can see from this list of categories that the thought embodied in the *Collection of Literature Arranged by Categories* simply reflected a series of narratives and understandings of the world.

The narratives and understandings in the *Collection of Literature Arranged by Categories* begin with the categories of Heaven and Earth, symbols of time and space. Heaven was placed in the premier position. All of the included texts, such as the *Book of Changes, Book of Documents, Book of Rites, Analects, Laozi, Zhuangzi,* the *Book of Master Shen,* the *Book of Master Wen, Erya, Chunqiu yuanming bao, The Armillary Sphere* (Huntian yi), *Basic Questions of the Yellow Emperor's Inner Canon* (Huangdi suwen), transform the astronomical phenomena in the sky above their heads as symbols of morality, philosophy, space and time. In the intellectual world of the seventh century, Heaven constituted the basic foundation of their mutual existence. Then in the *Book of Changes,*

---

101   The *Yiwen leiju*, compiled by Ouyang Xun, et al. in 100 *juan* is "divided into 47 sections and many subsections. Criticised by the *Siku* editors as 'of uneven quality and unsuitable categories.' Nevertheless, the *Yiwen leiju* covers all subjects and contains many quotations from works long since lost. It also cites its sources. Endymion Wilkinson, *Chinese History: A Manual,* 2000, 603.

the *Book of Shennong* (Shennong shu), the *Basic Questions of the Yellow Emperor's Inner Canon* (Huangdi suwen) and many other literary sources, the Earth was changed into a symbol corresponding to Heaven, and together they constituted the universe in which humanity lived. Then heavenly phenomena and the changes of geographical space constituted the temporal order of the human world, and the seasons of the year appeared between Heaven and Earth. Spring, summer, autumn and winter as well as various kinds of festivals of the year successively divided this human world under Heaven into many different periods of time. The four seasons, twelve months and twenty-four solar divisions not only corresponded to the Five Phases, the five directions, Five Virtues (or Powers) and various other seasonal natural phenomena indicating various elements of political significance and symbolizing movement and change in the human order, but they also gave definite regulation to human life. The various rituals, ceremonies and sacrifices of the festival days intensified the meaning of the human order. In this way, Heaven, Earth and the seasons were manifest in a framework of space and time and functioned to dominate all human and cosmic order as well as bestow a foundation of rationality on that order.

After the symbolic position of Heaven and Earth as the ultimate foundation of everything in space and time was established and confirmed, next are narrated the important ancient Chinese concepts of "emperors and kings" (*diwang*) and "receiving the Mandate" (literally omens of receiving the Mandate of Heaven, *fuming* 符命). Emperors (and Kings) were the masters of the human world. They received the wishes of Heaven from above and governed the lives of the people below. Whether or not the emperors (and kings) were actually reasonable (i.e., worthy to rule) was, however dependent on and restrained by the will of Heaven (receiving the Mandate of Heaven). This meant that the power of the rulers of ancient China was, in theory, limited to some extent by Heaven, and this fact could lend a certain legitimacy to the occasional "revolution" (flaying off the Mandate, *geming*) or change of dynasty. The emperors had command over the human realm, and so "human beings" come next in the order of *Collection of Literature Arranged by Categories* categories. Besides the three *juan* on human physiology, figures and bearing, there are also eighteen *juan* on human morality, ethics, behavior, character, feelings and various styles of human social life. The importance attached to these regulations of human life in society together with discussions of the system of rituals and music and the administrative control system in relation to the human social order all reveal seventh-century conceptions of human society. For example, social order took priority over individual freedom, social values were of higher importance than individual accomplishments, the evaluations of other people took priority over one's own feelings. This had not only been the case for a long time in ancient Chinese society, but it is also very clear from the order of arrangement of categories in the *Collection of Literature Arranged by Categories*.

That the *Collection of Literature Arranged by Categories* placed Buddhist and Daoist knowledge relatively near the end and only allotted two *juan* each for these categories would seem to show that in seventh-century world of knowledge, thought and belief these two religions could not be ignored, but that they were nevertheless devalued in the mainstream ideology. At the very end the *Collection of Literature Arranged by Categories* records books on different kinds of concrete knowledge of the natural world. Although ancient Chinese tradition had the idea of "acquiring of a wide knowledge of the names of birds and beasts, plants and trees" and a good deal of understanding and tolerance of this form of knowledge, in the seventh-century *leishu*, however, we can see that this knowledge was increasingly considered inessential and vulgar.[102] That the *Collection of Literature Arranged by Categories* placed this knowledge last shows us that its importance had declined in the minds of scholar officials. In terms of later Chinese history, this disdain for and abandonment of concrete knowledge and techniques dealing with the natural world must have influenced the advance of technical knowledge in ancient China.

Right around the turn of the seventh century various forms of knowledge and thought seem to have been undergoing a process of summarization, harmonization, coordination and integration. There was, as we have discussed, the one-hundred *juan* official *Collection of Literature Arranged by Categories*. Before that, at the end of the sixth century during the reign of Emperor Wu of the Northern Zhou, followers of the Daoist religion had already compiled their own comprehensive one-hundred *juan* encyclopedia entitled *Esoteric Essentials of the Most High* (Wushang biyao). Somewhat later than the *Collection of Literature Arranged by Categories*, in 666 during the Tang dynasty, the Buddhists also compiled quite a large encyclopedia entitled the *Dharma Park and Jewel Orchard* (Fayuan zhulin) also in one hundred *juan*. If we compare these two religious encyclopedias, we can see that the thought trends in the *Collection of Literature Arranged by Categories* did not reflect only the official ideology. The Buddhist and Daoist encyclopedias also come very close to or even rely on the same ways of thought. For example, both the *Esoteric*

---

102   The quotation is from *Lunyu* 17.9, Lau, *Analects*, 145. We should also note that the these particular entries in the *Yiwen leiju* primarily describe things that exist in nature; they very rarely record the discovery of techniques or human manufacturing; the essays also use literary language for stylistic ornamentation and rarely record theoretical and technological knowledge.

Essentials of the Most High and the *Dharma Park and Jewel Orchard* employ religious terminology to place Heaven before everything in the universe and give prominence to Heaven and Earth as the ultimate foundation of all rationality. After Heaven the *Esoteric Essentials* lists "human beings" and "emperors and kings," demonstrating that the order of values in this autochthonous Chinese religion was basically identical to that of the state ideology. After giving strong prominence to its religious ideas, such as "reverential worship" (*zhibai* 致拜) and "fields of blessedness" (*futian* 福田, any sphere of kindness, charity, or virtue) and so on, the *Dharma Park and Jewel Orchard* also turns very quickly from the *Cakravartî-râja* (sovereign ruler or king) of Buddhist legends to the "rulers and ministers" who hold power in the secular world. From this we can detect that Buddhism in the Chinese context had also adopted a value system and classificatory thinking that was quite similar to those of the official ideology.[103]

After experiencing a changing and turbulent era, the people of the seventh century suddenly discovered that the world was continually expanding before their eyes; unfamiliar knowledge was growing rapidly and the connections between diverse forms of knowledge was increasingly confused. When the Tang dynasty reunited north and south, then, people were particularly desirous of a clear-cut and definite order of knowledge and thought. The compilation of *leishu* encyclopedias was simply an attempt to tidy up and clarify this changing world of knowledge. Their compilers divided the diverse and confused world of knowledge, according to their own value systems, into various categories that gave all knowledge a clear and well-defined sequential order. They also attempted to piece together all the available writings into a number of categories, weaving them together into a vast textual network that they could easily consult whenever necessary. On the one hand these "encyclopedic" *leishu* represent this intellectual climate, and on the other hand they exhibit the order, scope and boundaries of the world of knowledge and thought of that age.[104] To discuss the boundaries of knowledge and thought at that time, I need to further examine the commentaries to the classics.

---

103   *Wushang biyao*, j. 1, mulu, *Daozang*, taiping bu, shu 1, ce 25, 1–3; *Fayuan zhulin, juan* 1, Taishô, *juan* 53, 269. There are other Buddhist and Daoist *leishu*, but we have concentrated on these two because they each have 100 *juan* and were produced in the late sixth and early seventh centuries.

104   Many important later *leishu*—such as the *Writings for Elementary Instruction* (Chuxue ji), *Bo's Encyclopedia in Six Parts* (Boshi liutie) and the *Imperially Reviewed Encyclopedia of the Taiping Era* (Taiping yulan)—followed this classificatory trend.

4.3

As we noted above, from the Han Dynasty on the Confucian classics had become authoritative texts. These texts together with their many annotations and explanatory and interpretive commentaries were believed to encompass almost all human knowledge and thought. They not only dealt with the human spirit and character but were also concerned with the cosmos, politics, government, nature and society. The status of the classics remained the same even in ages when Neo-Daoism and Indian Buddhism were very popular. For cultured people, studies and explanatory commentaries on the classic texts were not only their intellectual baptism but constituted their study of knowledge, especially knowledge related to political power and economic interests. This gave the classics a monopoly position in the world of knowledge and the status of works of practical use. The classics were not only ranked high above all other texts, but even their annotations and commentaries became primary sources of knowledge and thought in China.

Several hundred years of north-south disunity along with the vast number of commentaries to the classics left the knowledge and thought of the people of the seventh century rather chaotic and confused. The different choices of annotated texts of the classics and the differences in intellectual styles in north and south left people at a loss as to which one to follow. In a unified empire they felt they needed a unified system of explanations of the classics. This would be beneficial for the clarification of knowledge and thought, for correct education and for the selection and appointment of the best officials. Education, especially early education, was after all the foundation for establishing the intellectual orientation of every educated person. Selection, especially the selection of officials that carried practical benefits, was the most forceful incentive to encourage the orientation of knowledge and ideas.

The work of comprehensive summing up and reconciling the intellectual tendencies of north and south had already begun at the end of the sixth century. The *History of the Sui Dynasty* "Biographies of Confucian Scholars" (Rulin zhuan) records that after the Sui dynasty pacified all under Heaven, the rulers greatly encouraged the study of Confucianism. They recruited many Confucian scholars to come to the capital at Chang-an, discuss the classics and submit their results to the court. Such study and lecturing on the classics also took place among private individuals outside the court. The most famous scholar of his time, Liu Zhuo (544–610), is said to have compiled the *Commentaries on the Five Classics* (Wujing shuyi) while Liu Xuan (ca. 546–ca. 613) also compiled comprehensive summaries of various classics and their commentaries.[105]

---

105   *Suishu*, j. 75, "Rulin zhuan," 1720.

At that time the two Liu had already started to include and reconcile northern and southern scholarship. By the early Tang this kind of fusion and harmonization became the orientation of the official ideology. According to the "Biography of Chu Liang (560–674) in the *Old Tang History* (Jiu Tangshu), after Emperor Taizong (r. 626–649) pacified all under Heaven he became "mindful of Confucianism." He called many celebrated scholars, such as Du Ruhui (585–630), Fang Xuanling (579–648), Yu Zhining (588–665), Lu Deming (ca. 550–ca. 630) and Kong Yingda (574–648), to court to discuss Confucianism, the foundation of the state ideology.[106] The *New Tang History* (Xin Tangshu) "Preface to Biographies of Confucian Scholars" (Ruxue zhuan xu), also records that in 646 Emperor Taizong established twenty-one historical figures as the transmitters of Confucianism and decreed that people could "use their texts, practice their Way," and should "praise and elevate them, and from this day on they shall have the honor of being worshipped in the Confucian Temple."[107] From this list we can see that the opposition of ancient and new text classical studies that had existed since the Han had now been eliminated. What southerners like Wang Bi for the *Book of Changes*, Kong Anguo (ca. 156–ca. 74 BCE) for the *Book of Documents* and Du Yu (222–285) for the *Zuo Commentary* (to the *Spring and Autumn Annals*) advocated together with what northerners like Zheng Xuan for both the *Book of Changes* and the *Book of Documents* and Fu Qian (fl. 2nd century) for the *Zuo Commentary* promoted were all equally chosen as worthy to be placed in the imperial Confucian temple. Emperor Taizong used his political power to demand an interpretative system for the classics that was richly inclusive, and Kong Yingda's *The Exact Meaning of the Five Classics* fully embodied his wishes.

Kong Yingda's work integrated the interpretations of various schools from the Han dynasty on in an extremely comprehensive work. Various divergent interpretations faded after the appearance of this official work. In the intellectual atmosphere of the time, however, the southern academic tradition seems to have become more prominent than the northern tradition and emerged as the mainstream in the amalgamation of the two traditions. Lu Deming, whose interpretations were incorporated into the *Exact Meaning of the Five Classics*, was a southerner and his *Textual Explanations of Classics and Canons* (Jingdian shiwen) reflected southern scholarship. Although the chief editorial compiler of the *Exact Meaning of the Five Classics*, Kong Yingda, was a northerner and his early classical training was more in the northern tradition, *The Exact Meaning of the Five Classics* was completely inclined toward southern scholarship.

106   JTS, j. 72, "Chu Liang zhuan," 2582.
107   XTS, j. 198, "Ruxue *shang*," 5636.

Zuo Commentary (to the *Spring* and *Autumn Annals*) commentaries basically followed those of Du Yu and the *Book of Documents* commentaries were primarily those of Kong Anguo that were popular in the south. All of this demonstrates that the compilers of *The Exact Meaning of the Five Classics* represented not the individual compiler's views, but more importantly, the will of the state.[108] Collective interpretations had already replaced individual understandings, and individual academic approaches had already given way to the political orientations of the state. In this way, these works were actually transmitting the official state ideology. Of particular interest for intellectual history is that the preface to the *Exact Meaning of the Five Classics* not only eliminated the new text-ancient text controversy, but also, and most importantly, transmitted the official message of the court, that is, the court's criticism of Six Dynasties interpretations of the classics that tended to be individualistic and strove to go beyond traditional textual interpretations.

We are all familiar with a phrase commonly used in the history of interpretations of the classics: "comments should not violate annotations" (*shu bu po zhu* 疏不破注). It means that later interpretive comments should not overstep the scope and boundaries of the original textual annotations; even less should they violate or refute the interpretations of the earlier scholars. These comments on the meanings by Kong Yingda and his criticisms of commentators from the Jin and Liu Song on repeatedly remind scholars of this point. Styles of scholarship diverged during the North-South Dynasties, and northern and southern forms of knowledge and thought appeared. The differences between traditional knowledge and new thought left people without a definite standard while it was difficult to establish a basic framework for education. It was, then, necessary to employ this syncretic form of north-south annotation on the classic texts to ameliorate disputes between academic styles and eliminate scholarly divergences in different regions. It was also necessary to employ the rule that "comments should not violate annotations" to provide a general boundary for knowledge and thought. The seventh-century *The Exact Meaning of the Five Classics* employed selected annotated texts to expand the scope of classical knowledge and maintained a protective stand to defend the purity of thought of the classic texts. Its symbolic implication was to confirm and maintain the traditional authority of the classics since the Han and Wei as well as the widened scope of knowledge they had already developed. Within the body of this accepted world of knowledge, individuals had the freedom to comprehend and explicate thought, but the core of classical knowledge and thought were fixed and the boundaries were prescribed.

---

108   JTS, j. 75, 2642, "Zhang Xuansu zhuan," cites Zhang Xuansu comments on Kong Yingda.

4.4

The *Collection of Literature Arranged by Categories* was completed in 624, the final draft of *The Exact Meaning of the Five Classics* was ready in 642 and the *History of the Sui dynasty* was finished in 656, but these were only a few of the works representing the large-scale integration of knowledge and thought at the time. My use of these texts for analysis should not imply that they were the only texts of this kind available. Indeed there was a great deal of large-scale official compilation going on in the middle of the seventh century. Not only were there compilations of bibliographical works, *leishu* encyclopedias and commentaries on the classics, there were also many histories such as the various official histories of the North-South Dynasties, private works like the *History of the North and South* (Nanbei shi) and theoretical works like Liu Zhiji's *Generalities of Historiography* (Shitong). The important legal work, *The Tang Code with Commentary* (Tanglü shuyi) was also completed in 652.[109] These extremely large compilations present an extensive outline of the knowledge and thought of the syncretic and normative seventh century.

I have always had a nagging question, though, about the formation of this world of knowledge and thought in the seventh century. After they had produced so much accepted knowledge and thought, would they feel any need for new knowledge and thought? Would they still need such new knowledge and thought to disturb their serenity and sense of satisfaction? These are questions to be answered in volume two of this study.

---

109   Complete translation: Wallace Johnson, *The Tang Code: vol. I, General Principles*, 1979
        and *The Tang Code: vol. II, Specific Articles*, 1997.

Bibliography

Traditional Sources

Baopuzi neipian jiaoshi《抱朴子内篇校釋》, Wang Ming 王明, Beijing: Zhonghua (all Zhonghua shuju citations are to Beijing unless otherwise listed), 1985.

Bohu tong shuzheng《白虎通疏證》, Chen Li 陳立, Zhonghua, 1994.

Chu Ci buzhu《楚辭補注》, Hong Xingzu 洪興祖, Zhonghua, 1983.

Chunqiu Fanlu《春秋繁露》, Dong Zhongshu 董仲舒, ESEZ edition.

Dadai Liji jiegu《大戴禮記解詁》, Wang Pinzhen 王聘珍, Zhonghua, 1983.

Daozang《道藏》, Beijing: Wenwu, Shanghai shudian, and Tianjin guji chubanshe photocopy, 1988.

Er Cheng ji《二程集》, Cheng Yi and Cheng Hao 程頤, 程灝, Zhonghua, 1981.

Ershier zi《二十二子》, Shanghai guji photocopy based on Qing Guangxu Zhejiang shuju edition, 1985.

Ershiwu shi《二十五史》, Zhonghua shuju punctuated edition 中華書局標點本.

Fayen《法言》, Yang Xiong 揚雄, ESEZ edition.

Gaoseng zhuan《高僧傳》, annotated edition by Tang Yongtong 湯用彤, Zhonghua, 1992.

Gongsun Longzi xuanjie《公孫龍子懸解》, Wang Guan 王琯, Zhonghua, 1992.

Guanzi《管子》, EZES edition.

Guodian Chumu zhujian《郭店楚墓竹簡》, Beijing: Wenwu, 1998.

Guoyu《國語》, Shanghai guji punctuated edition, 1988.

Guwen Shangshu shuzheng《古文尚書疏證》, Yan Ruoqu 閻若璩, Shanghai guji, 1987.

Hanfeizi《韓非子》, ESEZ edition.

Hanshu《漢書》, Ban Gu 班固, Zhonghua, 1962.

He Guanzi《鶡冠子》, annotated by Lu Dian 陸鈿注, *Daozang* edition《道藏》本.

Hongming ji《弘明集》 and *Guang Hong ming ji*《廣弘明集》, Sengyou 僧祐 ed., SBBY, Zhonghua, 1936.

Hou Han ji《後漢紀》, Yuan Hong 袁宏, Zhonghua, 2002.

Hou Hanshu《後漢書》, Fan Ye 范曄, Zhonghua, 1965.

Huainan honglie jijie《淮南鴻烈集解》, Liu Wendian 劉文典, Zhonghua, 1989.

Jiali yijie《家禮儀節》, Qiu Jun 邱濬, ed., Jinan: Qilu shushe, 1997 reprint.

Jian-an qizi ji《建安七子集》, Zhonghua, 1989.

Jingxue lishi《經學歷史》, Pi Xirui 皮錫瑞, Zhou Yutong annotated edition 周予同注釋本, Zhonghua reprint, 1981.

Jinshu《晉書》, Fang Xuanling 房玄齡, Zhonghua, 1974.

Jiu Tangshu《舊唐書》, Liu Xu 劉昫 et al., Zhonghua, 1975.

Laozi jiaben ji juanhou guyishu《老子甲本及卷後古佚書》, Beijing: Wenwu, 1974.

Laozi yiben juanqian guyishu shiwen《老子乙本卷前古佚書釋文》, Beijing: Wenwu, 1974.

Laozi Xiang-er zhu jiaozheng,《老子想爾注校證》, Rao Zongyi 饒宗頤, Shanghai guji, 1991.

Liezi jishi《列子集釋》, Yang Bojun 楊伯峻, Zhonghua, 1979, 1985.

Lunheng jiaoshi《論衡校釋》, Huang Hui 黃暉, Zhonghua, 1990, 1995.

Mingru xue-an《明儒學案》, Huang Zongxi 黃宗羲, Zhonghua, 1985.

Mozi xiangu (jiangu)《墨子間詁》, Sun Yirang 孫詒讓, Zhonghua, 1986.

Qianfulun jian jiaozheng《潛夫論箋校正》, Wang Jipei and Peng Duo 汪繼培, 彭鐸, Zhonghua, 1985.

Quan shanggu sandai Qin Han Liuchao wen《全上古三代秦漢六朝文》, edited by Yan Kejun 嚴可均編, Zhonghua photocopy, 1958, 1985.

Renwu zhi《人物志》, Liu Shao 劉邵, Shanghai guji, 1990.

Ruan Ji ji jiaozhu《阮籍集校注》, Chen Bojun 陳伯君, Zhonghua, 1987.

Sanguo zhi《三國志》, Chen Shou 陳壽, Zhonghua, 1969.

Shanghai bowuguan, *Shanghai bowuguan cang Zhanguo Chu zhushu* (2)《上海博物館藏戰國楚竹書（二）》, Shanghai guji, 2002.

Shangjun shu《商君書》, ESEZ edition.

Shanhaijing jiaozhu《山海經校注》, Yuan Ke 袁珂, Shanghai guji, 1980.

Shenzi《慎子》, ZZJC edition, vol. 5, Zhonghua, 1978.

Shenzi《申子》, Shanghai guji photocopy, 1990.

Shiji《史記》, Sima Qian 司馬遷, Zhonghua, 1959.

Shirzi《尸子》, ESEZ edition.

Shisanjing zhushu《十三經注疏》, Zhonghua photocopy, 1980.

Shishuo xinyu jiaojian《世說新語校箋》, Xu Zhen-e 徐震鍔, Zhonghua, 1984.

Siku quanshu zongmu《四庫全書總目》, Zhonghua photocopy, 1965, 1981.

Song Gaoseng zhuan《宋高僧傳》, punctuated edition by Fan Xiangyong 范祥雍, Zhonghua, 1987.

Song-Yuan xue-an《宋元學案》, Huang Zongxi 黃宗羲, Shanghai: Shijie shuju, 1936.

Taishô shinshû daizôkyo (Dazheng xinxiu dazangjing)《大正新修大藏經》, Taibei: Xinwenfeng photocopy based on 1924–1932 original edition by Society for the Publication of the Taisho Edition of the Tripitaka.

Taipingjing hejiao《太平經合校》, Wang Ming 王明, Zhonghua, 1960.

Wang Bi ji jiaoshi《王弼集校釋》, Lou Yulie 樓宇烈, Zhonghua, 1980.

Weishu jicheng《緯書集成》, Shanghai guji photocopy, 1995.

Wenxin diaolong《文心雕龍》, Liu Xie 劉勰, Jinan: Qilu shushe, 1984.

Wenxuan《文選》, Xiao Tong 蕭統, ed., Zhonghua photocopy, 1977.

Wenzi yaoquan《文子要銓》, Xu Huijun and Li Dingsheng 徐慧君, 李定生, Shanghai: Fudan daxue, 1988.

Xian Qin Han Wei Nanbeichao shi《先秦漢魏南北朝詩》, Lu Qinli 逯欽立, Zhonghua, 1983.

Xin Tangshu《新唐書》, Ouyang Xiu and Song Qi 歐陽修, 宋祁 et al., Zhonghua, 1975.

Xinyu jiaozhu《新語校注》, 王利器, Zhonghua, 1986.

Xu Zizhi Tongjian Changbian《續資治通鑑長編》, Li Tao 李燾, Zhonghua, 1979.

Xunzi jijie《荀子集解》, Wang Xianqian 王先謙, ZZJC, Zhonghua, 1957.

Xuxiu siku quanshu zongmu tiyao (gaoben)《續修四庫全書總目提要（稿本）》, Jinan: Qilu shushe photocopy, 1997.

Yantielun jiaozhu《鹽鐵論校注》, Wang Liqi 王利器, Zhonghua, 1992.

Yi Luo yuanyuan lu《伊洛淵源錄》, Zhu Xi 朱熹, CSJC edition, Zhonghua 1985 photocopy.

Yinqueshan Hanjian shiwen《银雀山漢簡釋文》, Wu Jiulong 吳九龍, Beijing: Wenwu, 1985.

Yiwen leiju《藝文類聚》, Ouyang Xun 歐陽詢, et al., eds., 2 vols., Zhonghua, 1965; reprinted by Shanghai guji, 4 vols., 1982.

Yizhoushu huijiao jizhu《逸周書滙校集注》, Shanghai guji, 1995.

Zhang Heng shiwenji jiaozhu《張衡詩文集校注》, Zhang Zhenze 張震澤, Shanghai guji, 1986.

Zhanguoce《戰國策》, Shanghai guji, 1978.

Zhongguo Fojiao sixiang ziliao xuanbian《中國佛教思想資料選編》, Zhonghua, 1981–1990.

Zhuangzi jishi《莊子集釋》, Guo Qingfan 郭慶藩, Zhonghua, 1978.

Zhuzi jiali《朱子家禮》, Zhu Xi 朱熹, SKQS edition.

Zhuzi yulei《朱子語類》, Zhu Xi 朱熹, Zhonghua, 1988.

Zizhi Tongjian《資治通鑑》, Sima Guang 司馬光, with commentary by Hu Sanxing 胡三省, Zhonghua, 1956.

Modern Sources

Allen, Sarah, *The Shape of the Turtle: Myth, Art, and Cosmos in Early China*, Albany, NY: SUNY Press, 1991.

Ames, Roger, *The Art of Rulership: A Study of Ancient Chinese Political Thought*, Albany, NY: SUNY Press, 1994.

Baumer, Franklin L., *Modern European Thought: Continuity and Change in Ideas, 1600–1950*, New York: Macmillan, 1977.

Black, Alison Harley, *Man and Nature in the Philosophical Thought of Wang Fu-chih*, Seattle: University of Washington Press, 1989.

Bodde, Derk, "The State and Empire of the Qin," in the CHC, vol. 1, 1986, 69–72.

Boltz, William G., "Shuo wen chie tzu 說文解字," in Michael Loewe, ed., ECT, 429–442.

Bussho kaisetsu daijiten (Foshu jieshuo da cidian)《佛書解說大辭典》, Ono Genmyô et al., 小野玄妙等, Tôkyô: Daitô, 1981.

Cai Shangsi 蔡尙思, *Zhongguo sixiangshi yanjiufa*《中國思想史研究法》, Shanghai: Commercial Press, 1939.

Cai Yuanpei 蔡元培, *Cai Yuanpei quanji*《蔡元培全集》edited by GAO Pingshu 高平叔編, Zhonghua, 1989.

Cass Lishi Yanjiusuo 中國社會科學院歷史研究所, ed., *Bashi nian lai shixue shumu, 1900–1980*《八十年來史學書目 (1900–1980)》, Beijing: CASS, 1984.

Chen, Wing-tsit, *A Source Book in Chinese Philosophy*, Princeton, NJ: Princeton University Press, 1963, paperback, 1969.

Chang Naide 常乃德, *Zhongguo sixiang xiaoshi*《中國思想小史》, Shanghai: Zhonghua, 1930.

Chen Dongyuan 陳東原, *Zhongguo funü shenghuoshi*《中國婦女生活史》, Shanghai: Commercial Press, 1928.

Chen Guofu 陳國符, *Daozang yuanliu kao*《道藏源流考》, Zhonghua, 1963, 1985.

Chen Guying 陳鼓應, "Laozi jiaoding wen"〈老子校定文〉in Chen Guying's *Laozi zhushi ji pingjie*《老子注釋及評介》, Zhonghua, 1985, 442–473.

Chen Guying 陳鼓應, *Laozi zhushi ji pingjie*《老子注釋及評介》, Zhonghua, 1985.

Chen Hanping 陳漢平, *Xi Zhou ceming zhidu yanjiu*《西周冊命制度研究》, Shanghai: Xuelin, 1986.

Chen Lai 陳來, "Zhuzi 'Jiali' zhenwei kaoyi"〈朱子 '家禮' 真僞考議〉, *Beijing daxue xuebao*《北京大學學報》3 (1989), 115–122.

Chen Mengjia 陳夢家, *Yinxu buci zhongshu*《殷虛卜辭綜述》, Beijing: Kexue , 1956. Zhonghua reprint, 1981.

Chen Shengyong 陳剩勇, "Dongnan diqu Xia wenhua de mengsheng yu jueqi"〈東南地區夏文化的萌生與崛起〉, *Dongnan wenhua*《東南文化》1 (1991), 14.

Chen Yinque (Yinke) 陳寅恪, *Chen Yinque xiansheng lunwen ji xia* (zengding ban), vol. 2,《陳寅恪先生論文集》下, 增訂版, Taibei: Jiusi revised and enlarged edition, 1977.

———, "Zhi Mindu xueshuo kao,"〈支愍度學說考〉, *Chen Yinque xiansheng lunwen ji, xia*《陳寅恪先生論文集, 下》, 1977, 1229–1254.

———, "Cui Hao yu Kou Qianzhi"〈崔浩與寇謙之〉, *Lingnan xuebao*《嶺南學報》11/1 (1950); reprinted in 陳寅恪, *Jinmingguan conggao chubian*《金明館叢稿初編》, Shanghai guji, 1979, 121–122.

———, *Jinmingguan conggao chubian*《金明館叢稿初編》, Shanghai guji, 1979.

———, *Jinmingguan conggao erbian*《金明館叢稿二編》, Shanghai guji, 1980.

————, *Chen Yinque xiansheng biannian shiji (zengding ben)* 《陳寅恪先生編年事輯》(增訂本), Shanghai guji revised and enlarged edition, 1997.

Chen Yuxian 陳毓賢, *Hong Ye zhuan* 《洪業傳》, Taibei: Lianjing, 1992.

Chen Zhongfan 陳鍾凡, *Liang Song sixiang shuping* 《兩宋思想述評》, Changsha: Commercial Press, 1938.

————, *Chen Zhongfan lunwenji* 陳鍾凡論文集, Shanghai guji, 1993.

Ch'en, Kenneth K. S. (陳觀勝) *Chinese Transformation of Buddhism*, Princeton, NJ: Princeton University Press, 1973.

Cleary, Thomas, tr., *Wen-tzu: Understanding the Mysteries, Further Teachings of Lao-tzu*, Berkeley, CA: Shambhala, 1991.

Cohen, Paul A., *Between Tradition and Modernity: Wang T'ao and Reform in Late Ch'ing China*, Cambridge, MA: Council on East Asian Studies, Harvard University, 1974 (reprinted in 1987).

————, *Discovering History in China: American Historical Writing on the Recent Chinese Past*, New York: Columbia University Press, 1984.

Cole, Alan, *Mothers and Sons in Chinese Buddhism*, Stanford, CA: Stanford University Press, 1998.

Collingwood, R. G., *An Autobiography*, London: Oxford University Press, 1939.

————, *The Idea of History*, London: Oxford University Press Paperback, 1956 [1946].

Comaroff, John and Jean Comaroff, *Ethnography and the Historical Imagination*, Boulder, San Francisco, and Oxford: Westview Press, 1992.

Cook, Scott, *The Bamboo Texts of the Guodian: a Study and Complete Translation*, Vol. 1 and 2, Ithaca, NY: Cornell East Asia Series, 2012.

Creel, Herrlee G., *Shen Pu-hai: A Chinese Political Philosopher of the Fourth Century B.C.*, Chicago: University of Chicago Press, 1974.

Crump, J. I., trans., *Intrigues: Studies of the Chan-kuo ts'e,* translated by J. I. Crump, Ann Arbor: University of Michigan Press, 1964.

De Bary, Theodore and Irene Bloom, eds., *Sources of the Chinese Tradition from Earliest Times to 1600*, 2nd Edition, Vol. 1, New York: Columbia University Press, 1999.

Dubs, Homer H. with Jen T'ai and P'an Lo-chi, *The History of the Former Han Dynasty: A Critical Translation, with Annotations*, Baltimore: Waverly Press, 1938.

Duyvendak, J. J. L., trans., *The Book of Lord Shang: A Classic of the Chinese School of Law*, Translated From the Chinese with Notes by J. J. L. Duyvendak, Chicago: University of Chicago Press, 1928.

Ebrey, Patricia B., *Chu Hsi's Family Rituals*, translated with annotation and introduction, Princeton, NJ: Princeton University Press, 1991.

————, *Confucianism and Family Rituals in Imperial China*, Princeton, NJ: Princeton University Press, 1991.

Eliade, Mircea, *A History of Religious Ideas 2: from Gautama Buddha to the Triumph of Christianity*, translated from the French by Willard R. Trask, Chicago: University of Chicago Press, 1982.

Fairbank, John K., ed., *Chinese Thought and Institutions*, Chicago: University of Chicago Press, 1957.

Fan Shoukang 范壽康, *Zhongguo zhexueshi tonglun*《中國哲學史通論》, Shanghai: Kaiming shudian, 1937, 1941.

Feng Youlan 馮友蘭, *Zhongguo zhexueshi xinbian* 中國哲學史新編, Beijing: Renmin, 1985.

———, *Zhongguo zhexueshi* 中國哲學史, Shanghai: Commercial Press, 1930; Zhonghua, 1984.

Fischer, Pau, trans. & ed., *Shizi: China's First Syncretist* (by Jiao Shi), New York: Columbia University Press, 2012.

Forke, Alfred, *The World Conception of the Chinese: Their Astronomical, Cosmological and Physico-philosophical Speculations*, London: Probsthain's Oriental Series, 1925.

Frazer, Sir James George, *The Golden Bough: A Study in Magic and Religion (1890–1915)*, New York: Macmillan Press, 1922. Abridged paperback edition published by M. Papermac, 1987.

Fu Sinian 傅斯年, *Fu Sinian xuanji*《傅斯年選集》, Taibei: Wenxing shudian, 1967.

Gale, Esson M., *Discourses on Salt and Iron*, Leiden: E.J. Brill., 1931. Translation of chapters 1–19 of the *Yantielun* by Huan Kuan.

Ge Zhaoguang 葛兆光 *Zhongguo Chan sixiangshi—cong 6 shiji dao 9 shiji* (revised edition)《中國禪思想史——從6世紀到9世紀》(修訂版), Beijing daxue, 1995; Shanghai guji, 2008.

———, "Gudai Zhongguo haiyou duoshao aomi?"〈古代中國還有多少奧祕〉, *Dushu* 讀書 11 (1995) 3–11. Also available in English as "How Many More Mysteries Are There in Ancient China?, in *Contemporary Chinese Thought*, Vol. 34/2, Armonk NY: M. E. Sharpe, 2002–3, 75–91.

———, "Lun wan Qing foxue fuxing"〈論晚清佛學復興〉*Xueren* 學人 10 (1996), 89–120.

———, "Sixiang de ling yizhong xingshi de lishi"〈思想的另一種形式的歷史〉, *Dushu* 讀書 9 (1992), 36–43.

———, "Zhiyu sixiangshi de shiye zhong,"〈置於思想史的視野中〉*Dushu* 讀書 10 (1994), 58–64.

———, "Zhongmiao zhi men—Beiji, Taiyi, Dao, Taiji"〈眾妙之門—北極, 太一, 道, 太極〉, *Zhongguo wenhua* 中國文化 3 (1990), 46–65.

Gernet, Jacques, *Daily Life in China on the Eve of the Mongol Invasion, 1250–1276*, Stanford, CA: Stanford University Press, 1959.

Graham, A. C., " 'Being' in Western Philosophy compared with *shih/fei* and *yu/wu*," *Asia Major*, New Series, 7, 1–2 (1959), 79–112.

———, *Later Mohists Logic, Ethics and Science*, Hong Kong: Chinese University of Hong Kong Press, 1978.

———, *The Book of Lieh-tzu: A New Translation*, London: John Murray, 1960, reprinted in 1973.

Granet, Marcel, *Danses et légendes de la Chine ancienne*, Paris: Presses Universitaires de France, 1959 (1926).

Gu Jiegang 顧頡剛, "Wuxing zhongshishuo xia de zhengzhi he lishi"〈五行终始說下的政治和歷史〉, *Qinghua xuebao* 清華學報 3 (1984), 71–268.

———, et al. ed., *Gushi bian* 古史辨, 7 vols. 1926–41, Shanghai guji reprint, 1982.

———, *Gushibian zixu*《古史辨自序》, Shijiazhuang: Hebei jiaoyu, 1982 reprint.

Guo Baojun 郭寶鈞等, et al., "1954 nian chun Luoyang xijiao fajue baogao"〈1954年春洛陽西郊發掘報告〉, *Kaogu xuebao*《考古學報》2 (1956), 1–33.

———, *Zhongguo qingtongqi shidai*《中國青銅器時代》, Hong Kong: Sanlian shudian, 1978.

Guo Li-ying (Kuo Li-ying) 郭麗英, "Zhongguo Fojiao zhong de zhanbu youxi he qingjing—Hanwen weijing *Zhangchajing* yanjiu"〈中國佛教中的占卜遊戲和清净——漢文僞經占察經研究〉a Chinese translation in *Faguo Hanxue*《法國漢學》2 (1997), 193–223.

Guo Moruo 郭沫若, *Qingtong shidai*《青銅時代》, Beijing: Kexue, 1957.

———, *Yinqi cuibian*《殷契粹編》, Beijing: Kexue, 1965.

Hall, David L. and Roger T. Ames, *Thinking Through Confucius,* Albany, NY: SUNY Press, 1987.

Han Zhongmin 韓仲民, "Changsha Mawangdui Hanmu boshu gaishu"〈長沙馬王堆漢墓帛書概述〉*Wenwu*《文物》9 (1974).

Hansen, Chad, *Language and Logic in Ancient China*, Ann Arbor: University of Michigan Press, 1983.

Hawkes, David, *Ch'u Tz'u: The Songs of the South: an Ancient Chinese Anthology*, Boston: Beacon Press, 1962 [1959].

Hayashi Minao 林巳奈夫, *Chugoku kogyo no kenkyu*《中國古玉の研究》, Tôkyô: Yoshikawa Kobunkan, 1991.

He Changqun 賀昌群, "Handai yihou Zhongguoren duiyu shijie dili zhishi de yanjin"〈漢代以後中國人對於世界地理知識的演進〉(1936), *He Changqun shixue lunzhu xuan*《賀昌群史學論著選》, Beijing: CASS, 1985, 28–29.

———, *He Changqun shixue lunzhu xuan*《賀昌群史學論著選》, Beijing: CASS, 1985.

He Jiejun, Zhang Weiming, eds., 何介鈞、張維明編《馬王堆漢墓》*Mawangdui Hanmu*, Beijing: Wenwu, 1982.

Henderson, John B., *The Development and Decline of Chinese Cosmology*, Columbia University Press, 1984.

Hong Ye 洪業（Hong Weilian 洪煨蓮）*Hong Ye lunxue ji*《洪業論學集》, Zhonghua, 1981.

Hou Wailu et al., 侯外盧等, *Song Ming lixueshi*《宋明理學史》, Beijing: Renmin, 1987, 1997.

———, 候外盧等, *Zhongguo sixiang tongshi*《中國思想通史》, Beijing: Renmin, 1957.

Hu Houxuan 胡厚宣, "Chonglun 'Yu yi ren' de wenti"〈重論"余一人"的問題〉, *Gu wenzi yanjiu lunwenji*《古文字研究論文集》6 (1981), 15–33.

———, "Jiaguwen sifang fengming kaozheng"《甲骨文四方風名考證》, *Jiaguxue Shangshi luncong chuji*,《甲骨學商史論叢初集》, Jinan: Qilu daxue guoxue yanjiusuo lithographic copy, 1944.

Hu Shi, 胡適,《中國哲學史大綱》, Shanghai: Commercial Press, 1919.

———, *Hu Shi lunxue jinzhu*《胡適論學近著》, Shanghai: Commercial Press, 1935.

Hu, Shih (Hu Shi), review of Feng Yu-lan, *A History of Chinese Philosophy. Volume I, The Period of The Philosophers (From the Beginnings to Circa 100 B.C.)* and *Volume II, The Period of Classical Learning (From the Second Century B.C. to the Twentieth Century A.D.)*, translated by Derk Bodde, in *American Historical Review*, 60/4 (July 1955), 898–900.

Hu Shi, 胡適, *Zhongguo zhonggu sixiangshi changbian*《中國中古思想史長編》, in Jiang Yihua et al., eds., 姜義華等編, *Hu Shi xueshu wenji*《胡適學術文集》, Zhonghua, 1991.

———, "Qixue de zhengtong,"〈齊學的正統〉in 胡適, *Zhongguo zhonggu sixiangshi changbian*《中國中古思想史長編》, in *Hu Shi xueshu wenji*《胡適學術文集》, Zhonghua, 1991.

———, *Hu Shi wenji*《胡適文集》, Beijing daxue, 1998.

———, *Hu Shi koushu zizhuan* 胡適口述自傳, translated [from *Reminiscences of Dr. Hu Shih*] by Tang Degang 唐德剛, Beijing: Huawen, 1989.

Huang Zhi 黃徵, Wu Wei 吳偉, eds., *Dunhuang yuanwen ji*《敦煌願文集》, Changsha: Yuelu shushe, 1995.

Hulsewé, A. F. P., *Remnants of Ch'in Law: An Annotated Translation of the Ch'in Legal and Administrative Rules of the 3rd Century BC.*, (Sinica Leidensia, No 17), Leiden: E.J. Brill, 1985.

Ikeda On 池田温, *Chugoku kodai shahon chiiki kiroku*《中國古代寫本識語集錄》, Tôkyô: Daizô Shuban Kabushiki Kaisha, 1990.

International Encyclopedia of Social Science, New York: MacMillan Company and Free Press, 1972.

Itô Michiharu 伊藤道治, "Ôken to Saishi"〈王權與祭祀〉, *Huaxia wenming yu chuanshi cangshu—Zhongguo guoji Hanxuejia yantaohui lunwenji*,《華夏文明與傳世藏書—中國國際漢學家研討會論文集》, Beijing: CASS, 1995, 327–332.

Jahanbegloo, Ramin, *Conversations with Isaiah Berlin*, London: Peter Halban, 1992.

James, William, *The Varieties of Religious Experience* (1902), Cambridge, MA: Harvard University Press, 1985.

Jaspers, Karl, *The Origin and Goal of History* (1st English ed.), translated by Michael Bullock, London: Routledge and Keegan Paul, 1953.

Ji Wenfu 嵇文甫, *Wan Ming sixiangshi lun*《晚明思想史論》, Chongqing: Commercial Press, 1944.

Jin Guzhi 金谷治, "Han chu daojia de paibie"〈漢初道家的派別〉, in *Riben xuezhe yanjiu Zhongguoshi lunzhu xuanze*《日本學者研究中國史論著選擇》, vol. 7, Zhonghua, 1993, 28–50.

Johnson, Wallace, *The Tang Code: Vol. I, General Principles*, Princeton, NJ: Princeton University Press, 1979.

———, *The Tang Code: Vol. II, Specific Articles*, Princeton, NJ: Princeton University Press, 1997.

Johnston, Ian, *The Mozi: A Complete Translation*, Hong Kong: Chinese University of Hong Kong Press, 2010.

Kalinowski, Marc, "The *Xingde* 刑德 Texts from Mawangdui," *Early China*, 23–24 (1998–99), 125–202.

Kang Le 康樂, "Shamen bujing wangzhe lun—'bu wei bu gongjing ren shuofa'—ji xiangguan wenti"〈沙門不敬王者論——"不爲不恭敬人說法" 及相關問題〉 *Xin shixue* 新史學 7/3 (1996), 1–48.

Karlgren, Bernhard, *Grammata Serica Recensa*, Stockholm: Museum of Far Eastern Antiquities, 1964.

———, *The Book of Documents*, Stockholm: Museum of Far Eastern Antiquities, Bulletin, 1950. Translation of the *Shangshu/Shujing*.

———, *The Book of Odes*, Stockholm: Museum of Far Eastern Antiquities, Bulletin 22, 1950. Translation of the *Shijing*.

Kawakatsu Yoshio 川勝義雄, *Dôkyô*《道教》, Tôkyô: Hebonsha, 1978, 1992, 2000.

Knoblock, John and Jeffrey Riegel, *The Annals of Lü Buwei: A Complete Translation and Study*, Stanford, CA: Stanford University Press, 2000.

Knoblock, John, *Xunzi: A Translation and Study of the Complete Works*, 3 vols., Stanford, CA: Stanford University Press, 1988, 1990, 1994.

Kohn, Livia, ed., *Daoism Handbook*, Brill, 2000.

Kusuyama Haruki 楠山春樹, *Dôka shisô to Dôkyô*《道家思想と道教》, Tôkyô: Hirakawa, 1992.

Lao Gan 勞榦 "Liubo ji boju de yanbian"〈六博及博局的演變〉, *Lishi yuyan yanjiusuo jikan*《歷史語言研究所集刊》35 (1964), 15–30.

Lau, D. C., *Mencius*, Hammondsworth, Middlesex, UK: Penguin Books, 1970.

———, *Confucius The Analects*, Hammondsworth, Middlesex, UK: Penguin Books, 1979.

Le Goff, Jacques, and Roger Chartier, and Jacques Revel, eds, *La Nouvelle Histoire*, Paris: Retz, 1978.

Levenson, Joseph R., *Confucian China and its Modern Fate: a Trilogy*, Berkeley, CA: University of California Press, 1968.

Levi-Strauss, Claude, *Structural Anthropology (Anthropologie structurale)*, translated by Claire Jacobson and Brooke Grundfest Schoepf, New York: Basic Books, 1963.

———, *The Savage Mind (La Pensée sauvage)*, London: Weidenfield and Nicolson, 1962.

Lévy-Bruhl, Lucien, *How Natives Think (Les fonctions mentales dans les sociétés inférieures)*, translation by Lilian A. Clare, New York: Arno Press, 1979.

———, *Primitive Mentality (La mentalité primitive)*, translation by Lilian A. Clare, New York: AMS Press, 1978.

Li, Feng, "'Feudalism' and Western Zhou China: A Criticism," *Harvard Journal of Asiatic Studies*, vol. 63, No. 1 (Jun., 2003), pp. 115–144.

———, *Bureaucracy and the State in Early China: Governing the Western Zhou*, Cambridge, UK: Cambridge University Press, 2008.

———, *Landscape and Power in Early China: The Crisis and Fall of the Western Zhou, 1045–771 BC*, Cambridge, UK: Cambridge University Press, 2006.

Li Hongqi 李弘祺, "Shilun sixiangshi de lishi yanjiu"〈試論思想史的歷史研究〉, in Wei Zhengtong ed., 韋政通編, *Zhongguo sixiangshi fangfa lunwen xuanji*《中國思想史方法論文選集》, Taibei: Dalin, 1981, 134–161.

Li Huang 李璜 ed., "Granet yu shehuixue fangfa"〈葛蘭言與社會學方法〉, *Faguo Hanxue lunji*《法國漢學論集》, Hong Kong: Zhuhai shuyuan, 1975, 133–155.

Li Ling 李零, *Changsha Zidanku Chu boshu yanjiu*《長沙子彈庫楚帛書研究》, Zhonghua, 1983.

———, *Zhongguo fangshu kao*《中國方術考》, Beijing: Renmin Zhongguo, 1993.

———, *Zhongguo fangshu xukao*《中國方術續考》, Beijing: Dongfang, 2000.

Li Xueqin 李學勤, "Ganzhi jinian he shi-er shengxiao qiyuan xinzheng"〈干支紀年和十二生肖起源新證〉, *Wenwu tiandi*《文物天地》3 (1984), 41–43.

———, "Lun Hanshan Lingjiatan yugui yuban"〈論含山凌家灘玉龜玉版〉, *Zhongguo wenhua*《中國文化》6 (1992), 144–149.

———, "Shangdai de sifeng yu sishi"〈商代的四風與四時〉, in *Li Xueqin ji*《李學勤集》, Heilongjiang: Heilongjiang Jiayou, 1989, 104–110.

———, *Jianbo yiji yu xueshushi*《簡帛佚籍與學術史》, Taibei: Shibao wenhua, 1995.

———, *Li Xueqin ji*《李學勤集》, Heilongjiang jiayou, 1989.

———, *Zouchu yigu shidai*《走出疑古時代》, Liaoning daxue, 1998.

Li Zehou 李澤厚, *Zhongguo gudai sixiangshi lun*《中國古代思想史論》, Beijing: Renmin, 1985.

Liang Qichao 梁啓超, "Yin-yang wuxingshuo zhi laili"〈陰陽五行說之來歷〉, *Dongfang zazhi*《東方雜誌》20/10 (1923), 70–79.

———, *Zhongguo lishi yanjiufa*《中國歷史研究法》, Shanghai: Commercial Press, 1922; Hebei jiaoyu reprint, 2001.

———, *Intellectual Trends in the Ch'ing Period* (Qingchao xueshu gailun), translated with introduction and notes by Immanuel C. Y. Hsü, Cambridge, MA: Harvard University Press, 1959.

———, *Foxue yanjiu shiba pian*《佛學研究十八篇》, Zhonghua reprint, 1989.

Lin Fushi, 林富士 *Handai de wuzhe*《漢代的巫者》, Taibei: Daoxiang, 1988.

Lin Qingzhang 林慶彰, *Qing chu de qunjing bianweixue*《清初的群經辨偽學》, Taibei: Wenjin, 1990.

Liu Cunren 柳存仁, "Daojiao qianshi erzhang,"〈道教前史二章〉, *Zhonghua wenshi luncong* 中華文史論叢 51 (8/1993), 215–226.

Liu Xiang 劉翔 "Guanyu 'you', 'wu' de quanshi"〈關於"有"、"無"的詮釋〉, *Zhongguo wenhua yu Zhongguo zhexue*《中國文化與中國哲學》, 1989, 67–86.

Liu Xiang 劉翔 & Chen Kang 陳抗, et al., eds., *Shang Zhou guwenzi duben*《商周古文字讀本》, Beijing: Yuwen, 1989.

Liu Yizheng 柳詒徵, "Huozang kao"《火葬考》 in *Shixue zazhi* 史學雜誌,《火葬考》1/3 (1929), 1–5.

Liu Zijian 劉子健, *Liang Songshi yanjiu huibian*《兩宋史研究匯編》, Taibei: Lianjing, 1987.

Loewe, Michael and Edward L. Shaughnessy, *The Cambridge History of Ancient China from the Origins of Civilization to 222 B.C.*, Cambridge, UK: Cambridge University Press, 1999.

Loewe, Michael, "The Former Han Dynasty," in the CHC, vol. 1, 1986, 152–179.

———, ed., *Early Chinese Texts: A Bibliographical Guide*, Society for the Study of Early China and the Institute of East Asian Studies, University of California, Berkeley, 1993.

Lovejoy, Arthur O., *Essays in the History of Ideas*, Baltimore: Johns Hopkins Press, 1948 [1965 printing].

———, *The Great Chain of Being: A Study of the History of an Idea*, Cambridge, MA: Harvard University Press, 1964.

Lü Cheng, 呂澂, *Zhongguo Foxue yuanliu lüejiang*《中國佛學源流略講》, Zhonghua, 1979.

Lu Guolong 盧國龍, *Zhongguo zhong xuanxue*《中國重玄學》, Beijing: Renmin, 1993.

Lynn, Richard John, ed. & tr., *The Classic of Changes: A New Translation of the I Ching as Interpreted by Wang Bi*, New York: Columbia University Press, 1994.

Ma Heng 馬衡, *Fanjiangzhai jinshi conggao*《凡將齋金石叢稿》, Zhonghua, 1977.

Machida Saburo 町田三郎, *Ryoshi Shunshyu*《呂氏春秋》, Tôkyô: Kodansha, 1987.

Mair, Victor H., translated, *Wandering on the Way: Early Taoist Tales and Parables of Chuang Tzu*, New York: Bantam Books, 1994.

Major, John S., Sarah A. Queen, Andrew Seth Meyer, and Harold D. Roth, trans. and eds., *The Huainanzi: A Guide to the Theory and Practice of Government in Early China*, New York: Columbia University Press, 2010.

Mather, Richard B. Mather, *Shi-shuo Hsin-yü: A New Account of Tales of the World by Liu I-ch'ing with commentary by Liu Chün*, Minneapolis: University of Minnesota Press, 1976.

Morgan, Lewis Henry, *Ancient Society: or, Researches in the Lines of Human Progress from Savagery, through Barbarism to Civilization*, with a new introduction by Robin Fox. New Brunswick, NJ: Transaction Publishers, 2000 [1877].

Mou Runsun 牟潤孫, *Zhushizhai conggao*《注史齋叢稿》, Zhonghua, 1987.

Needham, Joseph, *Science and Civilization in China*, volume 2, *History of Scientific Thought*, Cambridge, UK: Cambridge University Press, 1962.

Nickerson, Peter, "The Southern Celestial Masters," 271, in Livia Kohn, ed., *Daoism Handbook*, 2000, 256–282.

Nylan, Michael and Thomas Wilson, *Lives of Confucius: Civilization's Greatest Sage Through the Ages*, New York: Crown Archetype, 2010.

Nylan, Michael, *The Five "Confucian" Classics*, New Haven: Yale University Press, 2001.

Pang Dexin 龐德新, *Cong huaben ji nihuaben suo jian zhi Songdai liangjing shimin shenghuo*《從話本及擬話本所見之宋代兩京市民生活》, Hong Kong: Longmen, 1974.

Pang Pu 龐樸, "Wuxing manshuo"〈五行漫說〉, *Wenshi*《文史》39 (1994).

Peerenboom, R. P., *Law and Morality in Ancient China: the Silk Manuscripts of Huang-Lao*, Albany, NY: SUNY Press, 1993.

Pu Muzhou 蒲慕洲, "Shuihudi Qinjian "rishu" de shijie"〈睡虎地秦簡日書的世界〉, *Lishi yuyan yanjiusuo jikan*《歷史語言研究所集刊》62/4 (1993), 623–675.

Qian Mu 錢穆, *Guoxue gailun*《國學概論》, Taibei: Commercial Press, 1979.

———, *Qing ruxue an xu*《清儒學案序》, in *Zhongguo xueshu sixiangshi luncong*《中國學術思想史論叢》vol. 8, Taibei: Dongda, 1980.

Qian Zhongshu 錢鍾書, *Guanzhui bian*《管錐編》, Zhonghua, 1979.

———, *Limited views: Essays on Ideas and Letters (Guanzhui bian)*, by Qian Zhongshu, selected and translated by Ronald Egan, Cambridge, MA: Harvard University Asia Center, 1998.

Qing Xitai 卿希泰, *Zhongguo daojiao sixiang shigang* vol. 1《中國道教思想史綱》第一卷, Sichuan renmin, 1980.

—— ed., *Zhongguo daojiao*《中國道教》, Shanghai: Zhishi, 1994.

Queen, Sarah A., *From Chronicle to Canon: the Hermeneutics of the Spring and Autumn, According to Tung Chung-Shu*, Cambridge, UK & New York: Cambridge University Press, 1996.

Rao Zongyi 饒宗頤, "Weiyou wenzi yiqian biaoshi fangwei yu shuli guanxi de yuban" 〈未有文字以前表示方位與數理關係的玉版〉, *Wenwu yanjiu*《文物研究》6 (1990), 48–52.

Ren Jiyu 任繼愈, *Zhongguo zhexueshi* 中國哲學史, 4 vols., Beijing: Renmin, 1966.

—— ed., *Zhongguo daojiaoshi*《中國道教史》, Shanghai: Renmin, 1990.

Rickett, W. Allyn, tr., *Guanzi*, Princeton, NJ: Princeton University Press, 1998.

Sahara Yasuo 佐原康夫, "Kandai shidô kasho ko"〈漢代祠堂畫像考〉, *Tôhô gakuhô*《東方學報》63 (1991), 1–60.

Schwartz, Benjamin I., "The Intellectual History of China: Preliminary Reflections," in John K. Fairbank, ed., *Chinese Thought and Institutions*, 1957, 15–30.

———, *The World of Thought in Ancient China*, Cambridge, MA: Belknap Press of Harvard University Press, 1985.

Shih, Vincent Yu-chung, *Literary Mind and the Carving Of Dragons*, Hong Kong: Chinese University Press, 1983 [1959].

Shu Jingnan 束景南, "Zhu Xi 'Jiali' zhenwei bian"〈朱熹 '家禮' 真偽辯〉, *Zhuzi xuekan*《朱子學刊》5 (1993), 112–120.

Song Zhenhao 宋鎮豪, "Jiaguwen churi ruri kao"〈甲骨文出日入日考〉, *Chutu wenxian yanjiu*《出土文献研究》, Beijing: Wenwu, 1985, 33–40.

———, *Xia-Shang shehui shenghuoshi*《夏商社會生活史》, Beijing: CASS, 1996.

Soothill, William Edward and Lewis Hodous, *A Dictionary of Chinese Buddhist Terms*, London: Kegan Paul, 1937. Also available online.

Spengler, Oswald, *The Decline of the West*, authorized translation with notes by Charles Francis Atkinson, New York: A. A. Knopf, 1939.

Tang Changru 唐長孺, "Du *Baopuzi* tuilun nanbei xuefeng zhi yitong"〈讀抱朴子推論南北學風之異同〉, in *Wei Jin Nanbeichao shi luncong*《魏晉南北朝史論叢》, Hong Kong: Sanlian, 1955, 1978, 367–371.

———, *Wei Jin Nanbeichao shi luncong*《魏晉南北朝史論叢》, Hong Kong: Sanlian, 1955, 1978.

Tang, Degang (唐德剛), *Reminiscences of Dr. Hu Shih*, Microfilming Corporation of America, 1975.

Tang Lan 唐蘭, "Shi shi, zong ji zhu"〈釋示、宗及主〉*Kaogu shekan*《考古社刊》6 (1937), 328–332.

Tang Yijie 湯一介, "Chengfu shuo yu lunhui shuo"〈承負說與輪迴說〉in 湯一介, *Wei Jin Nanbeichao shiqi de daojiao*《魏晉南北朝時期的道教》, 1988, 333–344.

———, *Wei Jin Nanbeichao shiqi de daojiao*《魏晉南北朝時期的道教》, Shaanxi shifan daxue, 1988.

Tang Yongtong 湯用彤, *Sui-Tang Fojiao shigao* 《隋唐佛教史稿》, Zhonghua, 1982.

———, "Du Renwu zhi"〈讀人物志〉in *Tang Yongtong xueshu lunwen ji* 湯用彤學術論文集, Zhonghua, 1983, 196–213.

———, *Tang Yongtong xueshu lunwen ji*《湯用彤學術論文集》, Zhonghua, 1983.

———, *Han Wei Liang Jin Nanbeichao Fojiao shi*《漢魏兩晉南北朝佛教史》, 重印本, Zhonghua reprint, 1983.

———, *Lixue, Foxue, Xuanxue*《理學、佛學、玄學》, Beijing daxue, 1991.

Tang Zhijun et al., 湯志鈞等, *Xi Han jingxue yu zhengzhi*《西漢經學與政治》, Shanghai guji, 1994.

Tjan, Tjoe Som, *Po-hu t'ung: The Comprehensive Discussions in the White Tiger Hall*, Leiden: E. J. Brill, 1949 & 1952.

Toynbee, Arnold J., *A Study of History*, 12 vols., London: Oxford University Press, 1934–61.

Tsukamoto, Zenryû, *A History of Early Chinese Buddhism* (Chûgoku Bukkyô tsûshi), translated by Leon Hurvitz, 2 vols., Tôkyô: Kodansha, 1985.

Twitchett, Dennis and Michael Loewe, eds., *Cambridge History of China, Vol.1, The Ch'in and Han Empires*, Cambridge University Press, 1986.

Wagner, Rudolf G., *A Chinese Reading of the Daodejing: Wang Bi's Commentary on the Laozi with Critical Text and Translation*, Albany, NY: SUNY Press, 2003.

Waley, Arthur, tr. *The Analects of Confucius*, New York: Vintage Books, 1938.

———, *The Way and Its Power: A Study of the Tao Te Ching and Its Place in Chinese Thought*, New York: Macmillan, 1948, Grove Evergreen, 1958.

———, *The Book of Songs*, New York: Grove Press, 1960 [1937].

Wang Fansen 王汎森, "Shenme keyi chengwei lishi de zhengju?"〈甚麼可以成爲歷史的證據？〉*Xin shixue* 新史學 8/2 (1997), 93–131.

———, "Zhongguo jindai sixiang wenhuashi yanjiu de ruogan sikao"〈中國近代思想文化史研究的若干思考〉, *Xin shixue* 新史學 14/4 (2003), 177–191.

Wang Guowei 王國維, *Guantang jilin*《觀堂集林》, Zhonghua, 1959, 1994.

———, *Wang Guantang xiansheng quanji* 王觀堂先生全集, volume 13: Taibei: Wen hua, 1968.

Wang Wenyan 王文顏, *Fodian hanyi zhi yanjiu*《佛典漢譯之研究》, Taibei: Tianhua, 1984.

Warder, A. K., *Indian Buddhism*, Delhi: Motilal Banarsidass, 1980.

Watson, Burton, *Han Fei Tzu: Basic Writings*, New York: Columbia University Press, 1964.

———, tr., *Records of the Grand Historian of China*, 2 vols., New York: Columbia University Press, 1961.

———, tr., *The Complete Works of Chuang Tzu*, New York: Columbia University Press, (1968), 1971.

Wei Zhengtong 韋政通 ed., *Zhongguo sixiangshi fangfa lunwen xuanji*《中國思想史方法論文選集》, Taibei: Dalin, 1981.

Wenwu 文物, "Fajue jianbao"〈發掘簡報〉, *Wenwu*《文物》11 (1977), 24–26.

———, "Shandong Zouxian Gaolicun Han Huaxiang shimu"〈山東鄒縣高李村漢畫像石墓〉, *Wenwu*《文物》6 (1994), 25–27.

Wilkinson, Endymion, ed., *Chinese History: A Manual, Revised and Enlarged*, Harvard-Yenching Institute Monograph Series, 52, Cambridge, MA: Harvard University Asian Center, 2000.

Wu Jiulong 吳九龍, "Tiandi bafeng wuxing kezhu wuyin zhi ju"〈天地八風五行客主五音之居〉, *Yinqueshan Hanjian shiwen*《銀雀山漢簡釋文》, 1985, 243.

Xie Wuliang 謝無量, *Zhongguo zhexueshi*《中國哲學史》, Shanghai: Zhonghua, 1916.

Xu Bingchang 徐炳昶, *Zhongguo gushi de chuanshuo shidai*《中國古史的傳說時代》, Beijing: Kexue, 1960.

Xu Dishan 許地山, "Daojia sixiang yu daojiao"《道家思想與道教》, in *Yanjing xuebao*《燕京學報》3 (1927), 249–282.

Xu Fuguan 徐復觀, *Lüshi chunqiu ji qi dui Handai xueshu ji zhengzhi de yingxiang*《呂氏春秋及其對漢代學術及政治的影響》in Xu Fuguan 徐復觀 *Liang Han sixiangshi*《兩漢思想史》, Taibei: Xuesheng shuju, 1976.

Yan Buke 閻步克, *Shidafu zhengzhi yansheng shigao*《士大夫政治演生史稿》, Beijing daxue, 1996.

Yang Jianfang 楊建芳, "Yu cong zhi yanjiu"〈玉琮之研究〉, *Kaogu yu wenwu*《考古與文物》2 (1990), 56–57.

Yang Kuan 楊寬, *Zhanguo shi*《戰國史》, Shanghai: Renmin, 1957.

Yang Liansheng 楊聯升, "Laojun yinsong jielü jing jiaoshi"〈老君音誦誡律經校釋〉, *Yang Liansheng lunwen ji*《楊聯升論文集》, Beijing: CASS, 1992, 33–92.

———, *Yang Liansheng lunwen ji*《楊聯升論文集》, Beijing: CASS, 1992.

Yang Shuda 楊樹達, *Jiaguwen zhong sifang fengming yu shenming*《甲骨文中四方風名與神名》, in *Jiweiju jiawen shuo*《積微居甲文說》, Beijing: CASS, 1954.

Yang Ximei 楊希枚, "Zhongguo gudai shenmi shuzi lungao"〈中國古代神秘數字論稿〉, *Zhongyang yanjiuyuan minzu yanjiusuo jikan*《中央研究院民族研究所集刊》33 (1972), 89–118.

Yang Zhigang 楊志剛, "Zhuzi jiali: minjian tongyong li"〈朱子家禮：民間通用禮〉, *Chuantong wenhua yu xiandaihua*《傳統文化與現代化》4 (1994, Zhonghua), 40–46.

Yao Xiaosui 姚孝遂 and Xiao Ding, 肖丁, *Xiaotun nandi jiagu kaoshi*《小屯南地甲骨考釋》, Zhonghua, 1985.

Yoshioka Yoshitoyo 吉崗義豐, *Seikai no shôkyô*, no. 9《世界の宗教》第9种, "Ense e no negai—Dôkyô,"《永生への願い──道教》, Tôkyô: Tankosha, 1970.

Yu Weichao 俞偉超 and Gao Ming 高明, "Zhoudai yongding zhidu yanjiu"〈周代用鼎制度研究〉, *Beijing daxue xuebao*《北京大學學報》1 (1978), 84–98.

———, "Hanshan Lingjiatan yuqi he kaoguxue zhong yanjiu jingshen lingyu de wenti"〈含山凌家灘玉器和考古學中研究精神領域的問題〉, *Wenwu yanjiu*《文物研究》5 (1989), 57–63.

Yu Yingshi (Yü Ying-shih) 余英時, *Lishi yu sixiang*《歷史與思想》, Taibei: Lianjing, 1976, 1992.

———, "Qingdai sixiangshi de yige xin jieshi"〈清代思想史的一個新解釋〉 in his *Lishi yu sixiang*《歷史與思想》, 1976, 124–125.

———, *Zhongguo zhishi jieceng shilun*《中國知識階層史論》, Taibei: Lianjing, 1980, 1989.

———, "Han Foreign Relations," in CHC, vol. 1, 1986, 377–462.

———, *Shi yu Zhongguo wenhua*《士與中國文化》, Shanghai: Renmin, 1987.

———, "Handai xunli yu wenhua chuanbo"〈漢代循吏與文化傳播〉 in Yu Yingshi 余英時, *Zhongguo sixiang chuantong de xiandai quanshi*《中國思想傳統的現代詮釋》, Taibei: Lianjing, 1987, 167–258.

———, *Zhongguo sixiang chuantong de xiandai quanshi*《中國思想傳統的現代詮釋》, Taibei: Lianjing, 1987 & 1992.

———, "Xueshu sixiangshi de chuangjian ji liubian"〈學術思想史的創建及流變〉 in *Gujin lunheng* 古今論衡 3 (1999), 68–69.

Zhang Dachun 張大春, *Zhang Dachun ji*《張大春集》, Taibei: Qianwei, 1993.

Zhang Guangzhi 張光直, *Zhongguo qingtong shidai*《中國青銅時代》, Hong Kong: Sanlian, 1983.

———, *Zhongguo qingtong shidai erji*《中國青銅時代二集》, Hong Kong: Sanlian, 1990.

———, "Shuo Yindai de yaxing," (說殷代的亞形) in *Zhongguo qingtong shidai, erji*, Hong Kong: Sanlian, 1990, 82–94.

Zhong Tai 鍾泰, *Zhongguo zhexueshi*《中國哲學史》, Shanghai: Commercial Press, 1929, 1934.

Zhou Shirong 周世榮, "Hunan chutu Handai tongjing wenzi yanjiu"〈湖南出土漢代銅鏡文字研究〉, *Gu wenzi yanjiu*《古文字研究》14 (1986), 69–185.

Zhu Yiming 諸億明, "Xiancun liangbu zuigu de tushu mulu"〈現存兩部最古的圖書目錄〉, *Wenshi zhishi*《文史知識》7 (1982), 53–57.

Zhuo Zhenxi 禚振西, "Shaanxi huxian de liangzuo Hanmu"〈陝西户縣的兩座漢墓〉, *Kaogu yu wenwu*《考古與文物》1 (1980) , 44–48.

Zürcher, Erik, *The Buddhist Conquest of China—the Spread and Adaptation of Buddhism in Early Medieval China*, 2 vols., Leiden: Brill, 1959, 1972, 2007 (online).

Index

on *Laozi*   282, 283

opposes He Yan on sages   287

Wang Can (Han) "have few desires" (*guayu* 寡欲)   285

Wang Chong (27–97?)   12

as *tongru*   270

Balanced Inquiries   175

contempt for apocrypha   272

interested in Daoism   274, 277

on Zou Yan   175n9

self-characterization   271

Wang Dao (276–339)   292n81, 326

Wang Fansen   58

Wang Fu (85?–163?) praises learning   271

Wang Fuzhi (1619–1692)   8, 51

Wang Guowei   92

Wang Mang usurpation (r. 9–25 CE)   250

great prestige of   267 in HS   267

Wang Min non-Chinese also outstanding 358, 358n82

Wang Rong (234–305) and Neo-Daoism 281

war, arts of (*bingfa* 兵法)   66

warding off calamities   163

Watanabe Hidekata   48

Way of Ancient Kings   132

Way of Eight Proscriptions (*babu zhongdao* 八不中道)   12

Way of Great Peace   293, 298, 300

Way of Mankind (*rendao*)   95

Way of the Five Pecks of Rice (*wudoumi dao* 五斗米道)   293, 298, 300, 304n108

Way of the Immortals (*shenxianjia* 神仙家) 296, 311

Sage Kings   18, 48, 72, 139, 142, 144, 200, 243, 249

Way of   17

Way of the Sages (*shengdao* 聖道)   143, 267

Way/Will of Heaven (*tiandao/tianyi* 天道/意) 3, 19, 22, 26, 36, 112, 113, 122, 128, 131, 140, 141, 157–8, 159, 160, 167, 170, 174, 176, 178, 167, 174, 195, 196, 201, 215, 224, 226–7, 229, 231, 235, 243, 247, 256, 278–80, 281, 283, 284, 286–7

and human feelings   112

and social hierarchy   112

and Yin, Yang, Five Phases   278

calamities from   248

foundation of everything   178

Wei Xiang (?–59 BCE)   257, 258

wen 文 as "good form"   146–7

Western learning (*xixue* 西學)   19, 38

Western missionaries   27

and Chinese cosmology in

Western Paradise of Pure Land   322

Western Regions (Xiyu 西域 Central Asia and Xinjiang)   118n80, 264, 265, 317, 318, 360

Western Zhou thought   91–9

background in ceremonies, symbols and numerology   106–19

wheel of transmigration/*saṃsâra*   319

wheel of impermanence   343

wisdom (*prajñâ*, *hui* 慧)   343

Wonu (Japanese), Han King of the   265

World/Society of Great Unity   71, 188, 322

worlds, the twelve (Tiantai, *shi-er ru* 十二入) 327

writing/Chinese script (*wenzi* 文字) and intellectual history   99–106

and mystical diagrams (*tufu* 圖符)   101

and understanding of the world   101

category formation   102–04

Chinese characters (*hanzi* 漢字)   99

Chinese v. Western classification system   103

importance of character *shi* 示 to manifest or reveal   105–6

language of ritual sacrifices   105

li 理 to cut jade, demark fields, reason, principle   104, 104n52

logic and order v. symbols and metaphors   105

oracle bone syntax   104–5

pictographic script and concrete thinking 100–01

statistical analysis of radicals   102

syntax and thought   104–6

you 有 to have   104

written vows (*fayuanwen* 發願文)   321

wu priests, *zhu* invocators, *shi* diviners/scribes and *zong* temple masters   69, 82, 90, 98, 107, 115, 244, 247, 256, 258, 295

and numerical classification   115